MW01620691

AN HONOR
★ ★ ★ ★
TO SERVE

This volume was produced with financial assistance for the Commonwealth of Pennsylvania Department of Community and Economic Development.

O'ER THE RAMPARTS WE WATCH
UNITED STATES
ARMY AIR FORCES

AN HONOR
★ ★ ★ ★
TO SERVE

General Editors
Richard David Wissolik, Ph.D.
John DePaul, Fellow of the Center
David J. Wilmes, Fellow of the Center
Gary E.J. Smith, Fellow of the Center
Eric Greisinger, Fellow of the Center

Editors
Barbara Wissolik, Fellow of the Center
Erica Wissolik, Fellow of the Center
Mark Gruber, O.S.B., Ph.D., Fellow of the Center
Frank Chappell
Emily Rohosky
Gretelyn Nypaver

Contributing Editors
Marjorie Wertz
Joseph Adams, O.S.B.
John J. DiBattista

World War II Veteran History Series 2

Publications of the Saint Vincent College Center for Northern Appalachian Studies Latrobe, Pennsylvania, 2007

Publications of the Saint Vincent College Center for Northern Appalachian Studies
Richard David Wissolik, Ph.D., Director, Fellow of the Center
rwissolik@stvincent.edu

Saint Vincent College
300 Fraser Purchase Road
Latrobe, PA 15650
724-805-2316
rwissolik@stvincent.edu
http://www.stvincent.edu/napp

An Honor to Serve

Series: World War II Veteran Histories 2

General Editors
Richard David Wissolik, Ph.D.
John DePaul, Fellow of the Center
David J. Wilmes, Fellow of the Center
Gary E.J. Smith, Fellow of the Center
Eric Greisinger, Fellow of the Center

Editors
Mark Gruber, O.S.B., Ph.D.
Frank Chappell
Emily Rohosky
Gretelyn Nypaver
Barbara Wissolik
Erica Wissolik

Contributing Editors
Marjorie Wertz
Joseph Adams, O.S.B.
John J. DiBattista

Design Agency
J.S. Downs and Associates

Chief Designer
Michael Cerce, Fellow of the Center with
Richard David Wissolik, Ph.D., Fellow of the Center

Chief Illustrator
Michael Wilkey

Printer: Sheridan Books, Ann Arbor, MI

ISBN-13: 978-1-885851-20-8
ISBN-10: 1-885851-20-0

This Book is Dedicated to the Men and Women Below
Who Have Enhanced the Academic and Life Experiences of Saint Vincent
College Students Enrolled In "Faces of Battle"

"How many times have they heard the old, long-drawn-out, faint field command pass down the long length of vast parade grounds, fading, as the guidons moved out front. So slowly it faded, leaving behind it a whole generation of men who would walk into history looking backwards, with their backs to the sun, peering forever over their shoulders behind them, at their own lengthening shadows trailing across the earth. None of them would ever really get over it." - James Jones

Harry Bee, *63rd Infantry*
† **Richard Buchanan**, M.D., *704th TD*
John DiBattista, *25th Cavalry*
John DePaul, *USN, Korea*
† **Mario DiPaul**, *63rd Infantry*
Sam Folby, *1st Infantry*
James Herrington, *101st Airborne*
Joseph Kay, *63rd Infantry*
† **John "Jack" McDaniel**, *86th Infantry*
† **Richard Radock**, *80th Infantry*
† **Charles Fisher**, *Eighth AF (Evadee)*
Tom Cable, *Fifteenth AF*
† **Thomas J. Evans**, *704th TD*
Jim "Red" Foley, *4th Marine*
Joseph Folino, *691st TD*
Jim Garrity, *Fifteenth AF*
Cathy Greisinger, *US Army Nurse Corps*
Justin Grieco, *USMC, Iraq*
Edwin P. Hogan, *Civil War Historian*
William Hudson, *Vietnam*
† **Stefan Jodlowski**, *Polish Underground*
Chester Lapa, *63rd/90th Infantry*
† **Joe LaValle**, *17th Field Artillery, POW*
Paul Luther, *28th Infantry*
John Martino, *81st Chemical Mortar Bn.*
Nick Matro, *Twentieth AF*
Harry McCracken, *99th Infantry*
Jack McCracken, *Eighth Air Force, POW*
David McNaughton, *28th Infantry, Iraq*
Robert Mendler, *Holocaust Survivor*
Peter Messer, *17th Airborne*
† **Robert Nelson**, *Eighth AF, POW*
Fielder Newton, *Eighth AF*
Orlando Pietropaoli, *629th Engineers*
† **Antonio "Tony" Priolette**, *24th Infantry*
Thomas Reid, *Vietnam*
Ross Saunders, *66th Infantry*
Leroy Schaller, *28th Infantry, POW*
John Slaney, *Royal Air Force, POW*
Elmer Slezak, *USN, WWII, Korea*
Henry "Hank" Stairs, *66th Infantry*
Lew Steck, *2nd Marine*
Jim Takitch, *United States Navy*
Pete Talarovich, *26th Infantry*
† **Harvey Waugaman**, *87th Infantry*
Gladys Waugaman, *US Army Nurse Corps*
Paul Yeckel, *Vietnam*
Robert Yowan, *Eighth AF*

With Special Remembrance -

† **Professor Roy E. Mills**, Saint Vincent College History Department,
82nd Airborne, Korean War, Silver Star Medal, Bronze Star Medal,
Purple Heart Medal
*" The General" Created and Team-Taught Faces of Battle With
Professor Richard Wissolik For Twenty-Eight Years*

U·S·ARMY

Table of Contents

About the Editors and Artists

DICK WISSOLIK, PH.D., is a Professor of English at Saint Vincent College. He is a Fellow of the Center for Medieval and Renaissance Studies at California State University, Long Beach, a Fellow of the Center, and a recipient of the General Arthur St. Clair Award for Historical Preservation. He is also a co-founder, director, and general editor of the Saint Vincent College Center for Northern Appalachian Studies. During his years at Saint Vincent College, Dick founded the Saint Vincent Community Camerata, producing and performing in many of its concerts. He also produced a number of stage shows, including Gilbert and Sullivan's *HMS Pinafore*, and he sang the roles of Balthasar and Habakuk in the medieval music drama *Play of Daniel*. Under his direction the Center has produced *Listen to Our Words: The Oral Histories of the Jewish Community of Southwestern Pennsylvania; Out of the Kitchen: Oral Histories of Women in World War II; The Long Road: Oran to Pilsen; A Place in the Sky: A Spoken and Pictorial History of the Arnold Palmer Regional Airport; Ice Cream Joe: The Valley Dairy Story and America's Love Affair with Ice Cream; They Say There Was A War; The Flag is Passing By; Typhoon Pilot; Reluctant Valor, and This American Courthouse: 100 Years of Service to the People of Westmoreland County, Pennsylvania.* He has published several articles on the Bayeux Tapestry and the Norman Conquest in *Medium Aevum*, *The American Benedictine Review*, *Annuale Mediaevale*; and a critical essay on Old English heroic poetry for *The Dictionary of Literary Biography*. His other publications include *The Bayeux Tapestry: A Critical, Annotated Bibliography; Bob Dylan: Anerican Poet* and Singer and *Bob Dylan's Words: A Critical Dictionary and Commentary*. At Saint Vincent College, Dick teaches courses in Myth, African Studies, Satire, Epic, Medieval Studies, Short Fiction, and Shakespeare to Verdi. He continues to teach Faces of Battle: War and Peace in Literature and the Arts, a course he created and team-taught with the late Professor Roy E. Mills. Before coming to Saint Vincent, Dick directed programs for Catholic Relief Services in East Africa where he developed self-help school lunch programs, nutrition programs, oversaw shipments of US Title III commodities and other goods through the Port of Mombasa for distribution in Kenya, Uganda, and parts of Central Africa. While in East Africa, Dick traveled extensively in Kenya, Tanzania, Somalia, Uganda and Southern Sudan, mostly by road and small aircraft. He worked closely with members of Oxfam, Care, Freedom From Hunger, Misereor, the World Health Organization and other international agencies in creating and developing self-help development projects and refugee programs. Dick also served on the Board of Directors of the then John F. Kennedy Memorial Home for Crippled Children in Nyabondo, Kenya. In 1972 he returned to Africa with nine Saint Vincent and Seton Hill students on a study program where the students saw first-hand the successes there of missionaries belonging to all denominations.

JOHN DEPAUL is a graduate of Carnegie Mellon University, Class of 1959. Upon graduation, John began a forty-one year career in the advertising agency business; first in the Pittsburgh office of Batten, Barton, Durstine & Osborne, then as a partner with Dudreck, DePaul, Ficco & Morgan until his retirement in 2000. He is a veteran of the Korean War, with service in the U.S. Navy from 1951-1955. His writing credits include articles for *U.S. Trade* magazine, *The Pittsburgh Business Times* and various advertising journals. Foreign credits include articles in *Millimetri*, a regional magazine published in the Molise region of Italy, and *Il Sole 24 Ore,* the Italian equivalent of the *Wall Street Journal.* John has been very active in economic development efforts to build trade relations with Italy and France, and to bring European investment to southwestern Pennsylvania. He was appointed to the Western Pennsylvania District Export Council by Secretaries of Commerce in both the George H.W. Bush and Clinton administrations. John was a founding director of the Italy-America Chamber of Commerce of Pittsburgh and served as its first president. He was also one of the early members of the French-American Chamber of Commerce of Pittsburgh. Both chambers were active in organizing trade missions, which brought together small-to-medium size European enterprises with their American counterparts in the Pittsburgh area. The most important of these activities was the World-Wide Energy Conference held in Pittsburgh in 1992, which was organized by the French and Italian chambers in conjunction with the United Nations Energy Commission headquartered in Geneva. In recognition of his volunteer work in trade relations, John holds numerous citations and awards from regional governmental bodies in Italy, France and Spain. In addition, he was honored by the Columbus 500 Committee of Western Pennsylvania in 1992 for distinguished service on the occasion of the 500th anniversary of the discovery of America. In 2007, he received the National Italian-American Sports Hall of Fame's Dominick Roppa Award, given annually to an amateur athlete who achieves excellence in his or her professional career. John is a Fellow of the St. Vincent College Center for Northern Appalachian Studies. He has served as a general editor for the Center's most recent publication, *They Say There* Was *a War,* and was a contributor to the previous book, *The Long Road.* John also serves as a consultant for the advertising and marketing of the Center's publications. As a veteran of the Korean War, he continues to share his experiences in the College English Department's Faces of Battle Class.

DAVID WILMES, a 1996 graduate of Saint Vincent College and a Fellow of the Center. As interviewer, author, editor, and general editor, his publication credits with the Center include *Reluctant Valor, The Flag is Passing By, Listen to Our Words, Mission Number Three: Missing in Action, The Men of the 704th, The Long Road, Waiting for Jacob, A Place in the Sky, They Say There was a War, and Ice Cream Joe: The Valley Dairy Story.* On behalf of the Center, David has conducted seminars on the oral history process to the Westmoreland County Historical Society, the Westmoreland County Community College, Saint Vincent College, East Stroudsburg University, the Pennsylvania Historical and Museum Commission, Veterans of Foreign Wars groups, the Pennsylvania Humanities Council, and the Veterans History Project of the Library of Congress. His work has been especially recognized by community groups who have invited him to deliver Memorial Day addresses at their celebrations. He has created and presented numerous programs to public libraries, historical societies, high schools and veterans' groups. David is largely responsible for taking the Center's work of interviewing and publishing the spoken histories of American veterans out of the Northern Appalachian region and extending it across the nation. David is a member Phi Alpha Theta, the National Honor Society in History, and is currently finishing his M.A. thesis on the Battle of Bushy Run at East Stroudsburg University in Pennsylvania. He resides in New Jersey with his wife Cathleen.

GARY E. J. SMITH is a Fellow of the Center and 1992 graduate of Saint Vincent College with a B.A. in History. He is a pioneer member of the Center, having conducted the first of the Center's military oral histories in his senior year. He has also been a guest lecturer in SVC's Faces of Battle history course. Gary conducted research, interviews and editing on the following Center publications: *Out of the Kitchen: Women in the Armed Services and the Home Front* (1994); *Reluctant Valor: The Oral History of Captain Thomas J. Evans* (1995); *Typhoon Pilot: John Samuel Slaney, Royal Air Force* (1995); *A Mile In Their Shoes: The Oral Histories of Three Veterans of the Vietnam War* (1995); *Men of the 704th: A Pictorial and Spoken History of the 704th Tank Destroyer Battalion in World War II* (1998); *The Long Road: From Oran to Pilsen* (1999); and *They Say There Was a War* (2005). During his academic career Gary published several original poems in the Saint Vincent College English Department's literary magazine *Generation* and the college yearbook *The Tower.* Gary has been conducting genealogical research since 1977. He served on active duty with the US Air Force's Strategic Air Command, at both overseas and stateside assignments, from 1981-1985. He later served in the Pennsylvania Army National Guard's 1st Battalion, 110th Infantry Regiment as an infantry scout squad leader and a heavy anti-armor infantry section leader. He also completed a tour of duty as an infantry skills instructor at the PA Army National Guard Military Academy at Fort Indiantown Gap. He is a former Westmoreland County (PA) 911 dispatcher and is currently employed by the Commonwealth of Pennsylvania.

Eric Greisinger is a Saint Vincent College graduate and a Fellow of the Center. He has been lecturing on special topics in history for twelve years to civic groups, high schools, colleges and the National Park Service. For more than a decade, he has been a volunteer guide and interpreter of the events of the American Civil War at Antietam, Gettysburg and Harper's Ferry. Eric is also the founding member and commander of the 36th Division World War II Living History Group and spent fifteen years as a Civil War Living Historian with various Pennsylvania-based groups. Eric holds an M.A. and a B.A. in history and has worked for the past eight years on regional oral history projects in the Appalachian region. He is the author of *A World Away but Close to Home*, a book detailing the experiences of World War II veterans from the Somerset, Pennsylvania area. Eric has written several articles for military magazines, and serves as interviewer, editor, and general editor for the Center. Aside from his dedication to the study of history Eric is an avid artist whose works can be found at his website at www.arrival-art.com. As an adjunct to his lifelong interest in military history, Eric has developed a personal collection of military memorabilia any museum would be proud to display.

Barbara Wissolik is a Fellow of the Center and a pioneer in its creation in 1991. She is graduate of Saint Vincent College in Liberal Arts with concentrations in Psychology and Sociology. She has worked with personnel at the Pennsylvania State Correctional Institution/Institute of Forensic Psychology conducting intake and screening interviews primarily as they pertained to drug and alcohol addiction and anger/stress management. Barbara has been an interviewer and editor since 1991 on all of the Center's books including: *Listen to Our Words: The Oral Histories of the Jewish Community of Westmoreland County Pennsylvania; The Long Road: From Oran To Pilsen; A Place in the Sky: The History of the Arnold Palmer Regional Airport; Ice Cream Joe: The Valley Dairy Story and America's Love Affair with Ice Cream; Out of the Kitchen: The Oral Histories of Women in World War II; They Say There*

Was a War. Barbara also conducted twenty-seven interviews of monks of the Saint Vincent Archabbey for one of its future publications. She enjoys gardening and is a Red Cross volunteer. She also did volunteer work with the Carmelite nuns in Latrobe. In the late 1970s she worked as a dental assistant.

Erica Wissolik is a Fellow of the Center for Northern Appalachian Studies, and a Saint Vincent College graduate with a major in Political Science. She also has a Master's degree in Public and International Affairs from the University of Pittsburgh. Erica is a pioneer of the Center, having worked since 1991 on several of its publications. Erica is part of the government relations staff at IEEE-USA, the Washington office of the Institute of Electrical and Electronics Engineers, Inc. She is responsible for overall management of government activities, and specifically works with the IEEE-USA Intellectual Property Policy Committee focusing on the issues — patent reform, fast-moving technology, technology transfer, and U.S. competitiveness — that affect the IP rights and careers of IEEE's U.S. membership. She is also responsible for managing the IEEE-USA's Government Fellows and Washington Internships for Students of Engineering (WISE) programs. Prior to joining IEEE-USA, Erica spent six years in living in Austin working for the Texas Legislature's Sunset Advisory Commission as a policy analyst. As an analyst and project manager, she conducted statutory reviews of several state agencies, including agencies that regulated health and human services, the funeral industry, educators, and parks and wildlife facilities. Her work resulted in substantive changes to the statutory authority and responsibilities of the agencies. Erica was also the Sunset liaison to the U.S. State Department's International Visitor Program, helping to inform foreign professionals about the concepts behind the Sunset review process. Before working in Texas, Erica worked for the Congressional Research Service (CRS), Library of Congress as an Information Specialist and a Program Coordinator for the Special Congressional Task for the Development of Parliamentary Institutions in Eastern Europe, which was administered by CRS. As an undergraduate, Erica studied at Oxford. She travels extensively in Europe and the United States. Erica also worked with Get Hip Records, a Pittsburgh-based independent record label, helping Rock & Rollers file trademark and copyright applications. If offered another life, Erica would make her living as a combat/documentary photographer. In this life, she photographs her friends and travels; examples of her work may be viewed at: http://www.flickr.com/photos/ericawissolik/. Erica was born in Nairobi, Kenya and grew up in Pittsburgh, PA, retaining very little ability to speak KiSwahili.

Father Mark Gruber, OSB, Ph.D, is a Fellow of the Center. He graduated from Saint Vincent College in 1978 with a BS in Philosophy, and from the Saint Vincent Seminary with a MDiv in 1982. Father Mark entered Saint Vincent Archabbey as a novice in 1978, was simply professed as a Benedictine monk in 1979, solemnly professed in 1982, and ordained a priest in 1983. He received a Masters in Anthropology and a Ph.D. in Anthropological Sciences (Physical Anthropology, Archaeology, Cultural Anthropology and Linguistics) from SUNY, Stony Brook, in 1990, having lived a year in Egypt doing ethnographic fieldwork among the Desert Fathers there for his dissertation. His anthropological studies in religion of the Middle East have helped establish him as a nationally circulated spokesman regarding the culture of Islam. Father Mark is a full-time Professor of Anthropology at Saint Vincent College, a member of the Board of Directors of Walsh University, North Canton, Ohio, and a nationally circulated retreat master for educators, clergy, religious and laity. In addition to several volumes published through Saint Vincent Spirituality Publications, he has published *Journey Back to Eden: My Life and Times Among the Desert Fathers* (Orbis Books), *Sacrifice in the Desert* (American University Press - a study of a minority religious community, the Copts, in Egypt), and a study of the Copts in *The New Encyclopedia of Africa* (Charles Scribner's Sons). His articles, studies, and papers appear in numerous journals and as chapters in professional anthropological and religious publications. He has provided introductory materials to several of the Center's publications.

Michael Wilkey lived and worked in Nairobi, Kenya before *Uhuru*. He is a Fellow of the Center. His teaching position at the Prince of Wales School was 'Africanised' shortly after Independence in 1964. He stayed on and worked at a variety of jobs until he was obliged to leave the country. He went to Uganda but once again political changes there forced former 'colonials' to leave the country. He moved to Nassau in the Bahamas and saw British colonial rule come to an end there too. He eventually made a new life in Western Canada teaching in various schools, colleges and finally at the University of Victoria in British Columbia. Michael has written many columns and feature articles in internationally published magazines on subjects as varied as automobiles, aviation, travel, wildlife conservation and of course Africa. He published two non-fiction books in Canada, *Pillars of Faith* the history of the oldest Anglican Church on Vancouver Island and *They Never Gave Up* a fully self-illustrated book about early aviation in North America. It was nominated for the Canadian Red Cedar Award 1999 and the

American Public Library Association voted it in the top five books for new adult readers in 1999. Currently at his publisher is *Going Straight Up* a fully self-illustrated history of helicopters. He has also just completed a collection of short stories about his life in Africa titled *The Lions of Kamboyo* and is presently working on an extensive historical novel *Ivory Candlesticks* about colonial times in Kenya. He has also illustrated several books for Orca Publishers in Canada and drawings for Saint Vincent College Center for Northern Appalachian Studies' *They Say There Was a War*. He has a Bachelor of Arts in Education from Sheffield University in the UK and a Masters degree in Educational Administration and Curriculum Development from Gonzaga Jesuit University in Spokane, Washington USA.

Mike Cerce is a Fellow of the Center and a graduate of Indiana University of Pennsylvania with B.A. in Marketing. He is also avid motorcycle enthusiast and traveler. He has been with J.S. Downs and Associates for the past thirteen years as a designer, senior designer and currently is employed as the Art Director. He has worked with Dick Wissolik and the Center for Northern Appalachian Studies on a variety of projects over the past ten years. He contributed designs for *The Long Road* and *Mission Number Three: Missing in Action,* and designed the Center's *Waiting for Jacob, Men of the 704, A Place in the Sky, Ice Cream Joe: Valley Dairy Story, They Say There Was A War* and *This American Courthouse: 100 Years of Service to the People of Westmoreland County, Pennsylvania.* Currently, Mike and his wife Jen reside in Greensburg along with their dog, Shane.

Emily Rohosky is a senior history major at Saint Vincent College. Raised in Mount Pleasant, Pennsylvania, she was home-schooled from eighth to twelfth grade. She has been working for the Center for two years. She spent the Summer 2007 studying at Beijing Normal University and researching her thesis on the Taiping Rebellion in Nanjing. In her spare time, she trains in the Korean martial art of Tang Soo Do, in which she holds a third-degree black belt.

Grettelyn Nypaver is a Sophomore Creative Writing major at St. Vincent College. She is active in campus theatre and musical productions. When she isn't transcribing oral histories and organizing the rough material into coherent narratives, she uses her spare time enjoys singing, fencing, acting, reading, and writing poetry. When she graduates, Grettelyn hopes to become a professional writer of poems, short stories and the occasional novel.

Frank Chappell published his first book of poetry *An Atheist Who Prays*, in 2004 and is currently a Senior Anthropology and Sociology double major at Saint Vincent College. He has been a member of the United States Air Force Reserve since 2003, serving duty at the 911th Airlift Wing in Coraopolis, Pennsylvania. Frank's Anthropology major has taken him to various locations to study Primatology on Ometepe Island, Nicaragua, Paleoanthropology in South Africa, and Buddhism in Kandal Province, Cambodia, where he was ordained a Theravada Buddhist monk during his period of ethnographic research. His editorial work for the Center for Northern Appalachian Studies, combined with his work in the Anthropology Department editing upcoming scholarly articles by Mark Gruber O.S.B., Ph.D. have been preparing him for the pursuit of a Ph.D. in Cultural Anthropology

"In the strength of great hope
we must shoulder our common load."
BUY VICTORY BONDS
VICTORY
LOAN
AN OFFICIAL U.S. TREASURY POSTER

"East Wind, Rain."

—John DePaul
Fellow SVC-CNAS
Jeannette, PA
Winter 2006

As the watershed year of 1941 moved into winter, the mood in America was one of hope, tempered with fear. With the Great Depression finally showing signs of abating at home, a still-neutral nation nervously looked over its shoulder across two oceans at a world lurching toward global war.

Across the Atlantic, Nazi Germany had subdued France and much of continental Europe; had pummeled British urban centers with almost nightly air raids for months; and, after launching a fearsome Blitzkrieg against the Soviet Union in June, had advanced to the suburbs of Moscow.

In the Pacific, an unchecked Japan continued its inexorable march toward Nipponese dominance of the Far East and implementation of its dream of a Greater East Asia Co-prosperity Sphere. This was in direct conflict with American economic and political aims in the western Pacific, resulting in the imposition of severe economic sanctions on Japan by the United States in October of 1940.

In this atmosphere of uncertainty, America's preparation for war in 1940 was sporadic and hotly contested by isolationists in government, the press and society in general. To the provincial mind-set of isolationists, protection provided by the vast expanses of the Atlantic and Pacific Oceans over the first two centuries of the nation's existence promised continued safety from attack by the likes of Germany and Japan.

Americans were reluctant warriors during the first half of the Twentieth Century, particularly in regard to those conflicts considered "none of our business." In 1914, America showed no interest in becoming involved in a rapidly spreading European war that broke out in August, based on the assassination of the heir presumptive to the Austro-Hungarian throne and a series of tangled alliances. Not until German U-boats began a campaign of unrestricted attacks on American merchant shipping did the United States react with a declaration of war in 1917, nearly three years after the shooting in Europe had begun.

It took a similar catalyst to generate American military action in December 1941, more than two years after the start of hostilities in Europe. Just as American public opinion had changed with the U-Boat menace in World War I, the Japanese attack on Pearl Harbor, while America was still officially a neutral nation, had the same result in 1941.

The military, largely disbanded and greatly reduced in striking power from its zenith in 1918, had diminished capability for defense in 1941. As a first step in rebuilding the military, the first Selective Service Act for peacetime conscription was passed by Congress in September 1940, giving the president the power to draft one-hundred-thousand men between the ages of twenty-one and thirty into the armed services for a period of service restricted to twelve months. This was the initial mechanism by which most of the men and women whose personal recollections of service appear in this book found themselves in the Army, Navy and Marine Corps.

While America slowly and haltingly began to rebuild its military capability, Japan became more bellicose. Diplomacy between the two nations went from bad to worse during 1941 as their relationship took on a more pronounced tone of belligerency.

To counter growing Japanese aggression in China and Southeast Asia, the United States Pacific Fleet's base of operations was transferred from the West Coast to Hawaii in April 1940, an act which provoked Japanese planning for an attack to destroy, or at least greatly curtail, American naval power in the Pacific.

Contrary to then Secretary of War Henry Stimson's astonishing quote that "gentlemen do not read each others mail," military code-breakers were actively engaged in tracking Japanese diplomatic traffic during the late 1930s. As the threat to American military bases in Hawaii and the Philippines increased, code-breakers began monitoring Japanese military traffic in earnest in 1940.

By mid-1941, cryptologists were able to determine that attacks against British and American military installations were not only possible, but probable. The question was where and when such an attack might take place. America's slide toward military involvement began to accelerate.

On 26 November 1941, the Japanese Combined Fleet's Carrier Striking Force, the *Kido Butai*, left its major anchorage at remote Tankan Bay in the Kurile Islands; destination unknown. On 29 November, an intercept of a "Winds" message from Tokyo to its embassies worldwide warned that if diplomatic efforts over the next few days failed, one of the following messages–disguised as a weather report–would be broadcast from Tokyo via shortwave radio, alerting all embassies of a possible attack on one of three adversaries:

Westerly wind, fine–Diplomatic breach with England
North wind, cloudy–Diplomatic breach with Russia
East wind, rain–Diplomatic breach with the United States

In advance of a military attack virtually certain to follow the announcement, embassies in targeted countries and their allies would be instructed to destroy cryptographic equipment, codes and documents via broadcast of the applicable "Winds" execute order, either by voice transmission or Morse code on Tokyo radio.

As the powerful *Kido Butai* continued its voyage undetected across the stormy north Pacific, it received the message "Climb Mount Niitaka" on 2 December. This was the order to launch an attack on the Pacific Fleet on 8 December Tokyo time, which was 7 December, Hawaii time. Since Mount Niitaka was the highest peak in Japan, the significance of the phrase used in the context of an attack by Japanese forces was one of accomplishment of a great feat. No evidence exists that this order was intercepted and decoded, but cryptologists generally believed that if the Japanese Navy launched an attack against United States forces, it would probably be against bases in the Philippine Islands.

Intelligence personnel manning the United States Navy's shortwave monitoring station at Cheltenham, Maryland, claimed that an "East wind, rain" message, signaling an impending attack on United States forces, was intercepted on 4 December. But in subsequent investigations, no definitive evidence has ever been produced to support that claim. Controversy over the "East wind, rain" execute message has raged on ever since.

There were the usual conspiracy theorists, who asserted that the "Winds" execute message was either hidden or purposely disregarded by the administration to allow the attack to take place, thereby plunging the United States into an unwanted war. Other intelligence officers tracking Japanese diplomatic and military communications maintained that at the very least an unusual set of unfortunate circumstances borne of ineptitude and bureaucratic ego prevented important intelligence from getting to the commanders on the ground in time to prepare for the attack. Others held that the "Winds" execute orders were either never transmitted or, if they were, were not what they appeared to be.

Whatever the case in regard to the handling of intelligence, whether or not "East wind, rain" was actually transmitted and no matter who was to blame, on the morning of 7 December 1941, United States military installations in Hawaii were severely damaged with great loss of life in a surprise attack by Japanese aircraft from the *Kido Butai.* The Pacific Fleet, in particular, suffered heavy losses with twenty-one ships, including battleships and cruisers, sunk or heavily damaged. A total of 2,403 servicemen and sixty-eight civilians died that day in Hawaii.

As the initial shock of the attacks wore off, a wave of patriotism swept the nation. Young men eager for adventure and defense of home and hearth rushed to volunteer for military service. Patriotic songs in the vein of "Let's Remember Pearl Harbor," "Praise the Lord and Pass the Ammunition" and "Comin' In on a Wing and a Prayer" fanned the flames of allegiance and quickly became popular hits.

Eventually, the Selective Service Act drafted more than eleven million Americans into the Armed Forces from December 1941 through December 1946, based on United States Census Bureau records. In addition, more than six million volunteered for service, half of whom served in the Navy. Given that the population of the United States was recorded at 132 million in the 1940 census, citizens in the military represented 12% of the nation's total population during the War. Relative to Pennsylvania, the Commonwealth's Historical and Museum Commission claims that nearly one in seven of those Americans who served in the military during World War II—more than 14%—were Pennsylvanians.

Interesting statistics, to be sure, but the numbers alone tell us nothing about these young men. Some were descendants of families with generations of history as Americans. But many others were a mix of new Americans, sons of immigrants, with surnames that bespoke their heritage as descendants of Poles, Slavs, Hispanics, Scandinavians, Irish and Chinese. Great numbers of Americans of Italian, German and Japanese descent fought against the totalitarian governments then ruling their ethnic homelands. Native-Americans and African-Americans served with distinction as well, in a military truly representative of its citizenry.

Women also became an important component of the military, with more than

350,000 in service during the War according to the United States Department of Veteran's Affairs. Women served as nurses in the Army Nurse Corps and in the Navy Nurse Corps. They also served in a wide variety of capacities in the WACs (Women's Army Corps); the WAVES (Women Accepted for Volunteer Emergency Service); the USMCWR (Marine Corps Women's Reserve); the SPARS (Coast Guard Women's Reserve); and the WASPS (Women Air Force Service Pilots). Readers will find several oral histories of female veterans of World War II in this volume, detailing their contributions to the war effort.

As Japanese conquests in the Western Pacific continued without respite during the first five months of 1942, the exercise of finding scapegoats for the attacks was set aside—at least by the general public—in favor of winning the War. As the Christmas season of 1941 drew near, it was unlike any other I have experienced since. Christmas trees and lights and toys and food were still abundant in those eighteen days after Pearl Harbor, but the tone of material celebration was muted; a portent of what future celebrations would be like over the next three holiday seasons. In December 1941, "with peace on earth, good will to men" became a sentiment of immediate and heartfelt desire.

While soldiers, sailors, airmen and Marines endured great suffering and sacrifice, everyday life at home was complicated by shortages of gasoline, food, shoes, appliances and many other items, all controlled through a consumer goods rationing program administered by the Office of Price Administration. Americans learned to do without, in ways not seen since 1945, even during major military actions fought in Korea and Vietnam.

Readers will find the veterans' narratives in this book both disturbing and entertaining, but never dull. These personal experiences are presented here as unexpurgated recollections indicative of what America was at the time—a raw, brash and energetic new superpower on the world scene.

Now More Than Ever

— Rev. Mark Gruber, Ph.D., O.S.B.
Saint Vincent College
Fellow SVC-CNAS
Latrobe, Pennsylvania, February 2007

STORIES OF WWII have dominated western media, its cinema, theatre, novels and television; its arts, photography, music and song; its social science, historiography and politics for more than sixty years. No other narrative themes approach their evocative powers and cosmological compulsion. From Holocaust Studies to military strategies; from the psychology of despots to the pathology of institutionalized cruelty; from the physics of the Manhattan Project to the economics of the Military Industrial Complex; from the sociology of the Nuremburg Parades to the jurisprudence of the Nuremburg Trials; from the analysis of martial rhetoric to the deconstruction of nationalistic propaganda, no corridor of history has been so thoroughly traveled and scrutinized. The thoughtful reader may rightly inquire: do Americans really need another book of war stories?

The short answer is: now more than ever.

The tellers of stories are the bearers of alternative worlds and exotic landscapes. The more alternative and exotic they are, the more compelling. But if they go too far the hearer is more likely to feel doubtful, and worse, the credibility of the speaker is more likely to seem compromised. For the great majority of the years following WWII, the veteran had to balance his recollections of soldiering against the limited perspectives of noncombatant Americans. One only has to see the transformed faces of aged veterans come home to visit their former battle buddies to realize how orphaned they may otherwise feel among the citizenry for whom they fought.

At Saint Vincent College, in weekly dinners in the Metten or Eichstaat dining rooms—affectionately called "The Meadhall" by the participants—and in the course *Faces of Battle: War in Literature and the Arts*, many of the veterans of the War assemble in order to meet in the warm residual fellowship of Hell's afterglow to tell their accounts to mesmerized collegians.

Many of these accounts and others gleaned from veterans from the local Northern Appalachian countryside (and from other areas in the United States) comprise this book. A community of honesty, authenticity, mutual support and commiseration has taken shape. Stories forgotten, lost, buried and suppressed have re-emerged. A subtle phenomenon we have observed in the unfolding of this historical and communal pedagogy more than justifies the publication of this text: the older the veteran lives, the more disarming and unapologetic his story becomes.

When a soldier is still enlisted he must tell the tale of his unit, his branch of the service, his hometown and his commander-in-chief. When he is discharged he must legitimate his time, investment, his comrade's sacrifice and his nation's faith. As the years pass he must try to conform his private accounts to the national ethos of war and peace and the situational morality of changing generations. The present book answers a gnawing question that a more reflective readership should rather be asking: will survivors of man's most awful War ever be old enough to freely tell their personal stories in a setting that respects both the specific desperate times from which they arise and the timeless though tragic truths they embody?

The short answer is: now more than ever.

An aging soul sometimes emerges from the chrysalis of the years unfettered by the social obligations and narrative sanctions that once may have burdened him. As a child is blissfully free to blurt out outrageous observations in familial settings, senior veterans are free at last to emit the stories that may confound their public audiences. Too old to arrest for war crimes; too cynical to confute; too near to judgment for human intimidation; too weathered to care anymore about prestige or shame they want now more than ever to tell the truth from their hearts.

Maybe there is an element of confession to be heard behind the frank and unadorned recollections below. Maybe the veterans, the men and women recorded here, are calling out their memories down the canyon walls of our collective readership with a faint but human hope that before long a word of divine absolution will echo back. Their unmasking of WWII exposes all war for what it is. May the readers also see in the stories provided here the unveiling of a grand humanity that terrible War could not forever obscure and great age at last poignantly reveals.

A book-signing at a Barnes and Noble store, November 2006 for the Center's *They Say There Was A War*. The veterans pictured are regular participants in Dr. Richard Wissolik's course Faces of Battle. Their interaction with Saint Vincent students and at educational and public programs in the region changes the lives of the young and bridges the gap between generations.

Our Modern-day Epic

Albert C. Labriola, Ph.D.
Duquesne University
Winter 2006

WHETHER EXAMINING ACCOUNTS of warfare from classical antiquity, from Anglo-Saxon England, or from other early eras, the reader will note that the literature of warfare involves epics, tragic dramas, or narrative poetry. In such literature, however, the focus is almost always on the heroism of kings or noblemen. Framed to highlight traits such as bravery, anger, pride, revenge and determination, this literature presents indelible portraits of characters who exercise power and authority, who may be deemed heroic and whose proficiency in warfare is often matched by the intensity of their amorous interests. Indeed, "love and war" are the twin topics often interrelated in the literature of warfare. This linkage of love and warfare often distinguishes much of what was written in classical antiquity and the Middle Ages. Chaucer's knight in The *Canterbury Tales*, for instance, is a martial hero, but the young Squire who serves him, a knight-in-training, is a lover. We can infer thereby that the knight is both a warrior and a lover, each endeavor requiring particular sets of skills that were inculcated in the Middle Ages. Even into 17th Century England, the era when the royalists in the English Civil War were called cavaliers, the warrior-lover composed lyrical poems to his beloved, for he was as skilled with the pen as he was with the sword. Called courtiers, these warrior-lovers dominate literature of "love and war" in the Renaissance.

In all of the foregoing examples, royalty and noblemen were at the center of attention. Their traits of character, their extraordinary skills at literary composition and heroism, their conscientious dilemmas, their aspirations and their triumphant homecomings are recounted and celebrated in literature. Because of their standing in society, their lives were deemed both influential and important even to the degree that these figures entered into legendary history.

Overlooked, however, is the so-called populist army, the common warriors who often fought on their feet at close quarters with the enemy. Unlike their noble counterparts who were astride horses, these foot soldiers and archers engaged in the brutality of war, inflicting traumatic injuries on their adversaries and incurring wounds, often mortal. Rarely if ever is their saga recounted, though they are the very warriors through whom battles are won or lost and because of whom their commanders achieved at times legendary status. There is no better example than Shakespeare's *Henry V*, a play that centers upon the warrior-king, who is also a wooer and a lover. At the battle of Agincourt in 1415, he enacted a remarkable *tour de force*, overcoming seemingly insuperable odds to achieve a major victory against the French. Outnumbered, decimated by illness and beleaguered by a pursuing French force, the yeoman archers of the populist army led by Henry were headed to Calais in order to board vessels and return home. A French blocking force, however, forced the battle. Henry's speeches at Agincourt are cited as having instilled courage and determination in his populist army, but, in fact, the archers and the foot soldiers enacted the successful tactics that defeated the French cavalry. One fusillade after another of arrows from English long bows descended into the onrushing cavalry to cause disarray and confusion. With halberds, axlike weapons also with a beak and a spike, the English foot soldiers dragged the top-heavy French armored cavalrymen from their mounts and axed or punctured them thereafter. The stuff of heroism and of legendary history rests not with the king or the commanders but with the men in the field who engage the enemy on the front line.

An Honor to Serve redresses the imbalance about which I have been speaking. And it does so by reference to the men and women who served in World War II. Each interviewee provides his or her recollection, akin to a memoir. These oral histories individually recounted are compiled into a single volume. Collectively, the narratives converge to produce a work of epic proportions, but not in the traditional sense. Not focused on men and women of renown, these oral histories cite the achievements of men and women on land and sea and in the air. Many of them were enlisted personnel, some were prisoners of war, still others after sustaining injuries journeyed back home from the European or Pacific theaters in order to recuperate. In their personal accounts, we have a saga of fighting men and women of World War II, the very personnel, for instance, who composed General George S. Patton, Jr.'s fabled Third Army, which raced in armored columns across France and into Germany. Though Patton garnered the glory, the enlisted men and women won the War. Standing down at night in the mud, these foot soldiers bonded with one another in a camaraderie often never before experienced in their lives and never encountered afterwards. Their bonding is the catalyst for reunions, for the perpetuation of friendship, and for indelible memories imprinted with the dramatic immediacy of warfare. Their heroism enacted on a seemingly small scale embodies gallantry in action not often publicly acknowledged, for the medals and ribbons tend to festoon the uniforms of commanders. But in their hearts, these foot soldiers can say with conviction: We were there, we fought, we prevailed.

Entering this book and proceeding from one memoir to another, the reader inevitably is inspired to continue, for the oral histories are multivalent, complementary and suspenseful. A page-turner, this book incites its readers to assimilate the experiences of World War II warriors, who unfold a comprehensive and composite history definitely authentic and surely second to none. Indeed, their saga is our modern-day epic.

So, You Want to Be an Oral Historian?

— Gary E.J. Smith
Fellow SVC-CNAS
Latrobe, PA
January 2007

ORAL HISTORY IS a calling, and one not to be entered into lightly. It is not as simple as sitting down and asking, "What did you do in the War?" To properly prepare for the task, you must determine the veteran's service branch, unit and military specialty, and then research the theater of war, any campaign or battle, and the ship, plane, or weapon with which the veteran might have been involved. Being conversant in the general aspects of the veteran's experience will go a long way toward putting him (or her) at ease during the interview; your knowledge of a topic can jog the memories of interviewees, thus helping them bring forward long-forgotten details.

We at the Saint Vincent College Center for Northern Appalachian Studies use the United States Army War College's Military History Institute World War II-Era Service Survey Questionnaire, which we have further developed to incorporate questions specific to each branch of the military. The questionnaire, in its original format, was "Army" biased. We simply cloned a separate questionnaire for each of the other branches of the service, making changes where necessary. Of course, the questionnaire is but a starting point; each veteran's experience is different and our interviewers need to be nimble enough, and well-versed enough, to keep up with any possible departures from the general to the specific.

I've done a lot of interviews, and I still get a case of the butterflies before each new session. Each oral history is a roller-coaster ride. There are shocks, thrills, agonies, smiles and tears, and it is not for the faint of heart. To begin with, these men and women are heroes. It's an awe-inspiring experience to meet them, spend an afternoon with them and hear their stories. There is often a small shock, a disconnect if you will, between how I first envisioned the veteran and what I see when I meet one for the first time. For example, this volume contains an interview I conducted with an Army nurse. During her first interview session, all I could think of was, "My God, we sent this waif-like grandmother off to war!" Later, this caused me to reflect not only upon the resilience of women in combat situations, but upon the necessity of placing them in harm's way in the first place.

The most difficult aspect of conducting oral histories is looking into the veteran's eyes while he remembers some far away place from a long time ago. Sometimes, it happens without warning. A completely innocuous question about life in basic training usually evokes an instant answer. Once, when I asked such a question, the veteran stopped in mid-sentence, his face clouded over, and tears welled up in his eyes. Why? A few minutes later he explained that he remembered some silly incident in basic training involving him and his best buddy, and that memory instantly triggered another, that of the same buddy broken and bleeding in the snow outside the town of Bastogne. For decades the sight remained with him together with the soul-searching guilt of "Why him and not me?"

When something like that happens, and it happens often, I give the veteran time to collect himself, then I press on with the interview. Because I have also been in uniform, I think, "There but for the grace of God . . . ." I feel like a heel for having made a combat veteran cry; I imagine his once-peaceful nights now visited by the khaki-clad ghosts of battles past. I suppose my *angst* is penance for having wanted so badly to learn about the War, about these brave men and women. Others have assured me that these emotional episodes can be cathartic for the veteran; that's easy to say when you're not the one looking into their eyes. I can't help but wonder, did Cornelius Ryan, Martin Caidin or Russ Weigley ever lose sleep over an interview?

Sometimes, the most thrilling part of the history reveals itself during the editing process, when the real "fun" begins. Our interviewers consult historical sources, looking for support and corroboration. Once in a while, some new facet of history comes into view, as if we'd turned a diamond and seen it from a different angle. It is in these rare cases that we are able to add to the body of previous historical works. Two cases in point are included in this volume. Bob Davis' and Peter Muse's stories both shed light on rather obscure arenas of the War. Davis was a ship's officer aboard a radar-equipped landing control craft at Normandy, while Muse was a radar counter-measures operator aboard a B–17. Let the reader be assured that small steps forward in history represent a giant thrill for the researcher.

I'd like to close this brief note by paying respect to two members of my family.

First, to my paternal grandfather, Malcolm Graham Smith (1910–2004), who served with the Atlantic Fleet during WWII. Drafted at age thirty-four, leaving two young sons and a wife behind, he entered basic training in March 1944. Following basic and Naval Fire Fighter's School in the Panama Canal Zone, he joined the *PC–1195* in June 1944. *PC–1195* was a 174-foot steel-hulled sub chaser armed with one 3–inch deck gun, a single 40mm AA gun and depth charges. Her area of operations was the Caribbean Sea, patrolling between Guantanamo Bay, Cuba and the Panama Canal, escorting convoys and conducting antisubmarine operations. Graham, as he preferred to be called, was a Seaman, Second Class and, later, became a Storekeeper, Second Class. Graham was awarded the American Theater Campaign Medal, the World War II Victory Medal and the World War II Honorable Service pin. Like the vast majority of WWII veterans, he never fired a shot in anger and never saw an enemy ship.

My maternal grandfather, Joseph Edward Valasko (1914–1994), enlisted in the Pennsylvania Army National Guard and served as a Private in Company F, 2nd Battalion, 103rd Medical Regiment from January 1934 until his honorable discharge in January 1937. In accordance with the Selective Service System's 1940 requirements, he registered for the draft. His draft number was twenty-one, but since he was employed as a coal miner, a vital war related industry, he was exempt from being drafted into the armed forces. Joe spent thirty-nine years in the coal mines, from 1930, when he had to quit school to help support his family, until his retirement in 1969. I learned more from this man than I did from any formal school.

To my grandfathers and all other veterans: Thank you. Well done, carry on.

They Are Extraordinary

— *Cathy Greisinger, RN*
Army Nurse Corps
339th Army Medical Reserve Unit (1965–1968)
Fellow SVC-CNAS
Pittsburgh, PA
February 2007

For the past three years, I have been privileged to join the veterans who participate in Dr. Richard Wissolik's Saint Vincent College *Faces of Battle* course. I have also had the pleasure of being a guest at various luncheons and gatherings of Veterans of the Battle of the Bulge, Chapter 14, Southwestern Pennsylvania.

Last year, before the first *Faces of Battle* meeting, a student in the class turned to me and said, "Look at all these grandfatherly types."

"Wait until you hear what they did and what they went through."

Though I have listened to these "grandfathers'" stories time and again, I am still awed not only by their accomplishment, but also by the truly awful conditions—lack of food and water, the wet, the cold, the noise, confusion and the constant fear—in which they carried out their duties during the War.

I am particularly struck by those that were wounded, those that had to endure the painful journey from battlefield or ship, to aid stations and field hospitals where they were cared for under sometimes primitive conditions with very little medical supplies. Then there are those who were prisoners of war. They endured additional hardships, not the least of which was the abject fear of never returning home, of never being free again.

Yet, out of the grim horror that was World War II came many advances in medicine and trauma care. One of the most significant improvements was the rapid movement of the wounded by aerial transportation. That method decreased mortality and morbidity in all subsequent conflicts. Other advances included the recognition of Post Traumatic Stress Syndrome and the discovery and the widespread use of antibiotics. These techniques and tools are used effectively in today's civilian medicine, thus extending the impact of the War into our own time and beyond, and certainly during the time that I cared for the wounded returning from Vietnam.

It is a testament to the physical and mental resilience of those who fought in the War that they are still active and busy among us, though in diminishing numbers. It is truly amazing what the human body can endure. All of these men have some physical and psychological side effects from their time in battle. It is unbelievable that they did what they were asked to do and survived to come home and back to the lives they had left interrupted. That makes them, in their quiet way, extraordinary.

I was born during WW II and I remember some of the shortages and the big party we had when my uncles came home from the War. They were my heroes then, but they are gone. The gentlemen I have met in *Faces of Battle* are my heroes now, and I thank them.

YOU ARE NEEDED NOW
JOIN THE
ARMY NURSE CORPS
APPLY AT YOUR RED CROSS RECRUITING STATION
1324(7)

"The Wounded Never Complained."

Marjorie Smart Butterfield

United States Army Nurse Corps
United States Third Army
59th Field Hospital
Born in Allison Park, Pennsylvania, 11 May 1920
† 26 October 2006

"The 59th Field Hospital was assigned to Patton's Third Army. When we were stationed in a building in Nancy, France, General Patton's headquarters was just down the street from our hospital. The Germans shelled his headquarters every night. For the first few nights we went into the bomb shelters, but after so many times of nothing happening, we just stayed in bed and hoped the Germans didn't hit us! I never met Patton, but I saw a lot of him. I couldn't miss him with his shiny helmet and ivory-handled revolvers. The troops all liked him because he was a winner."

FRANK SMART, MY Dad, was an architect in Pittsburgh. He was in the infantry during World War I, but he didn't serve overseas. My mother was Ruth Leggate. I went to Perry High School for college prep courses. I played volleyball and took swimming. I graduated in 1938.

I went to Sewickley Valley Nursing School, in Sewickley, Pennsylvania for three years. We took classroom and practical training at Sewickley Hospital. We also trained for three months at a psychiatric hospital and also at Children's Hospital in Pittsburgh. I graduated from nursing school in 1941.

I was listening to the radio in my room at the nurses' home when they announced the surprise attack at Pearl Harbor. I signed up in the Pittsburgh recruiting office in September 1942 and told them I was ready to go anytime. I felt it was my patriotic duty to look after our soldiers.

The first camp I went to was Camp Pickett, Virginia, where we learned to march and salute. I was at six other camps in the eighteen months before I went overseas. I went in as a Second Lieutenant and was discharged as a First Lieutenant. They told me that if I stayed in for two more months, I'd automatically be promoted to captain.

I said, "No, thanks."

I went to desert training[1] in Yuma, Arizona, a general hospital in Clinton, Iowa, to Fort Leonard Wood in Missouri, then to Camp Carson, Colorado, and finally to New York Port of Embarkation in February or March 1944. I think it took about twelve days to cross the Atlantic, because of the zigzagging to dodge the German submarines. We were twelve nurses jammed into a stateroom designed for two people.

We arrived in Liverpool, England. There were a lot of soldiers everywhere. We were taken in a truck and every so often the truck stopped and dropped us two at a time at pretty houses with gardens. Another nurse and I stayed with a very nice family—a lady, her four-year-old son and her mother. We fashioned bedding out of downed barrage balloons. We met in the center of town for training.

I was assigned to the 59th Field Hospital. We went to Weymouth for a month and then went over to OMAHA Beach in July 1944 in a small ship. Barrage balloons floated above each ship in the convoy. When we hit shore, they dropped the front ramp and we waded to the beach. Walking up the bluffs above the beach, I imagined how hard it must have been for the soldiers on D-Day. They must have been sitting ducks for the Germans on that hill.[2]

Our hospital was divided into three platoons. Each could be sent on a different assignment. When we first arrived, I had to dig a foxhole. We hadn't been trained to do that, so I had to learn as I went. One of us would have a shovel and the other would have a pick. Fortunately, our enlisted men came to our rescue and helped us dig the foxholes.

The 59th was a mobile unit with tents. We set up about two miles behind the front lines.[3] Very often artillery shells passed right over our heads. We only treated the seriously-wounded casualties. We sent the others back to a general hospital. I took care of the postoperative cases, gave them intravenous and other medications. The ambulances brought us as many as sixteen casualties at a time. Once they were well enough, they'd be shipped farther back and by then we'd have fresh casualties.

We had two surgical teams; each operated twelve hours on and twelve hours off when casualties were heavy. We'd stay in one place until all the patients were evacuated. Then, if the front line had moved ahead, which it did quite a bit, we'd move forward. Sometimes we had to leave someone behind to care for the stragglers. Nobody liked to be left behind, so we had to take turns on that detail. Sometimes they'd find a building that we could use, so we didn't have to sleep in tents.

Once, a single German plane flew over and dropped a bomb that exploded not far from me. We had just arrived and were setting up, so we didn't have our red cross on the tents yet. The German pilot obviously didn't know we were a hospital. We weren't supposed to bomb each other's medical units. All us nurses stuck our heads out, looking at what was going on, while all the enlisted men dove under trucks. We quickly learned not to be so curious!

The 59th Field Hospital was assigned to Patton's Third Army. When we were stationed in a building in Nancy, France, General Patton's headquarters was just down the street from our hospital. The Germans shelled his headquarters every night. For the first few nights we went into the bomb shelters but after so many times of nothing happening, we just stayed in and hoped the Germans wouldn't hit us! I never met Patton, but I saw a lot of him. I couldn't miss him because of his shiny helmet and ivory-handled revolvers. The troops all liked him because he was a winner.

We were sent to Belgium during the Battle of the Bulge. The first set of trucks they sent for us was attacked and destroyed, so we had to wait for another set of trucks to come. We eventually set up in a convent in Belgium. Frostbite among the troops was so terrible we had to amputate fingers and toes.

When we had time, we'd get together and sing songs. One of our surgeons recited poetry. We'd play bridge once in a while. Occasionally we'd get a USO show. I was in a USO show once. It was in an auditorium set up for some of the infantry guys. One of the nurses was the magician's assistant. I was on a game called "Blind Date" where three fellows I couldn't see tried to win a date with me. I had thought it would be a small group, but, my goodness, there were hundreds and hundreds of soldiers there. The prizewinner got to ride home in the ambulance with me. The interesting thing about that was, when we moved up to Belgium during the Battle of the Bulge, we hadn't had anything to eat on the trip. We were so hungry. My friend and I went for a walk, looking for some food. We smelled some food cooking, so we followed our noses and walked into this kitchen where some guys were making dinner. One of the guys yelled out, "There's my blind date!"

It was the fellow that I'd picked out in that game show. So they gave us a lot of food.

As the War was winding down, we were sent to the Gusen concentration camp[4] on the Danube near Linz, Austria, to look after the inmates. It was terrible. They were living skeletons. We didn't have enough supplies to take care of them all. They had lice, tuberculosis and other diseases. That was a terrible experience for me. Gusen was a sister-camp of Mauthausen. I was at Gusen for two months.

Then we went to Czechoslovakia as the Army of Occupation. We lived in a hotel and worked in a regular hospital. After I'd been there for a few months, I had enough points to be able to go home. They sent around a questionnaire asking whether we would prefer to stay where we were, go to the Pacific, or go home. Well, of course I wrote, "Go home." I was transferred to a camp outside Paris. The dockworkers in New York had gone on strike,[5] so I sat in that camp for about six weeks waiting to get a ride back home. It wasn't too bad, because I could always get a three-day pass into Paris. I'd go to Paris for three days, then come back to camp for three, then go into Paris for three more. I enjoyed that because I had free hotel rooms and meals in Paris.

After I got a physical exam, I returned to the States. My mother and dad and sister met me at the railroad station in Pittsburgh. It was wonderful to see them. I hadn't seen them in two years.

I had been so cold during the War; sometimes the places we stayed had no heat. I promised myself I'd never be cold again. After the War I went to Florida and got a job in a city hospital. I stayed there for a year and a half, then came back to Pittsburgh. I got married in 1948 to Henry Dreier and had a daughter, Carol. We got divorced after a few years. I remarried a couple of years later to Jim Butterfield. We lived very happily in the North Hills of Pittsburgh. I worked in various hospitals and then became a school nurse.

After the War I tried to suppress my awful memories of Gusen, the concentration camp in Austria. I never talked about it when I returned home. One evening about forty years later I heard a man on television say the Holocaust never happened, that it was all false propaganda. I became very angry and knew that it was time to speak up. In the next day's newspaper I read about a man from the Holocaust Center in Pittsburgh who asked anybody who had any information about concentration camps to get in touch with him. I called right away and have been involved with their programs ever since.

During the War, we had a lot of brave soldiers and I was glad that I could take care of them. I'd do it all over again. I think they felt safer with women there. The wounded never complained. Throughout the War, my faith in God kept me strong and kept me from being afraid.

American troops liberate the Mauthausen concentration camp. *Shoah Education Project*

"I Still Make Beds the Navy Way."

Violet Byrer

United States Navy WAVES
Born in Butler, Pennsylvania, 19 August 1924
Valencia, Pennsylvania

"In our neighborhood, there were a number of fellows that were killed in service. I felt so bad for the families, so when I was telling my friends from the neighborhood that I was thinking of joining the service, nobody said a negative thing about it."

DAD AND MOTHER CAME from Yugoslavia and never wanted to go back again. Dad thought America was the country of freedom and that I should do what I could for my country.

We were patriotic to the core. Everyone in the family did something during the War. Before I went to the service I was in business college and then I worked for a little bit after finishing there. We had a restaurant, where my sister worked until the War broke out. After the War started, she thought that they needed bus drivers in the city of Pittsburgh because all the men were going to the service, so she went and worked as a driver. My older brother joined the Air Force, which also made me think about joining up. He made a career out of it.

In our neighborhood, there were a number of fellows that were killed during the War. I felt bad for their families, so when I told my friends that I was thinking of joining the service, nobody said a negative thing about it. In fact, my mother was all for it. She was a very progressive woman anyway. She said it would teach me a little bit about life, especially discipline.

At first, I didn't know which branch to go into. The only exercise I really liked was swimming, something we did often in the Allegheny River. I thought the Navy they might have me swimming somewhere, so I joined the WAVES.[6]

I left from Pittsburgh on a train with a group of other women. It was winter and freezing and we were all huddled together as we waited on the platform to get on the train. We really had no idea what was going on. The train took us to Hunter College in New York where we did our basic training.[7]

We had four women per room in our barracks that had been a college dorm before the War. Each of our rooms had double-decker beds. Our drill instructors were women noncommissioned officers. I had never marched in my life and I didn't even know how to walk a straight line. At home I never was really supposed to do very much because I was the little one in the family, so I didn't know anything much about responsibility or chores. The Navy taught me how to do a lot of things. I still make beds the Navy way.

We had required uniforms. In the summertime we wore blue and white seersucker dressers. We didn't have to wear our caps on the job if we didn't want to, but if we went out we had to be in full uniform, including caps. We also had to have proper shoes and purses. Our dress uniforms were skirts, white blouses and blue jackets

From Hunter College I went to the University of Iowa at Cedar Falls. I was sent there to learn the Addressograph, a machine that put addresses on brass labels. They used those to imprint everything.

At Cedar Falls it was more like being in a sorority than on a job or in school. We started around eight in the morning and we finished at three in the afternoon. The rest of the time was our own. We could do whatever we wanted. I used my time to take courses in shorthand and typing.

From Cedar Falls I was shipped to Yorktown, Virginia, where I spent almost all of my service time. Navy women, unless they were nurses, were not permitted to go to overseas.

Yorktown at that time was a mine-warfare school. It was a small-duty garrison. There were about twenty-eight Marines and twenty-eight Waves, exactly the same number of men and women on staff. On top of that, there were several hundred sailors taking courses on mines. It was very small compared to some places during the War.

The Marines were the guards at the base. They were just killing time until they got discharged. It was light-duty for them. Yorktown was where I met my husband Ben, who had just come back from the Pacific awaiting discharge.[8]

We had women officers all along the way. I couldn't get along with one of them at Yorktown. She had me at the Captain's Mast[9] more than I want to talk about. I never really knew what I had done, but evidently, whatever I was doing, it wasn't what she thought was right.

Life at Yorktown had a routine. In a typical day, if I felt like it, I got up in the morning and went to breakfast. The Navy galley had wonderful food and I guess I gained a little bit of weight when I was in. That was the first time I ever had canned figs. They had tray after tray of sausage and bacon for breakfast.

Then I'd come back and go to work until midday. We had some time off at lunchtime. Sometimes we'd go to the parade grounds to listen to an orchestra some sailors had formed. Then it would be back to work to finish out the day. In the evening we had our own time to read, sit around, swim in the river, play volleyball or go bowling. I set up pins for Ben when we bowled!

Since there wasn't a bridge over the river we rode the ferry, back and forth, back and forth. The fare was only ten cents and we could stay on as long as we wanted. I liked feeling those fresh breezes and watching the moon come up and go down.

I was stationed at Yorktown about a year. From there I was transferred to Norfolk, Virginia. Ben rode the bus with me. On the way we saw people standing by the side of the road, crying and holding up signs. It was Victory Over Japan Day, V-J Day, 15 August 1945. That was wonderful because it really gave us spirit; we had won! The War was over!

I was sad too because I was leaving the base that I loved so much and I was leaving Ben and all the rest of the people with whom I had made friends. When I got to Norfolk I didn't do much because it was near the end of my time in the Navy. They'd call me once in a while to come into the office and maybe do some typing or take some dictation. I was only there a month. We had the option of staying in, but Ben was already discharged from the service and we were planning to get married. We were married one month before I was released.

I was transferred to Havre de Grace, Maryland and was discharged in March 1946. We went down on a small transport ship. It rocked back and forth and one of the women got seasick. Her head was always in the sink! I didn't feel so good myself. That was the first time I got to ride in a real ship!

I always regretted the fact that I didn't stay in the service. I really should have stayed in because Ben and I were married for thirteen years before we had a child. I could have had all those years in.

Soldiers' Life
Make the
REGULAR
ARMY
your
CAREER
Tom Woodburn

"We Were Fighting Nature As Much As the Enemy!"

John H. Campbell

31st Infantry Division
"Dixie Division"
Alabama, Florida, Louisiana National Guard
Motto: *"It Shall Be Done'*
167th Infantry Regiment, Cannon Company
18 February 1922

"I was on that ship for about seventy-four days. The boilers leaked fresh water into the hull. Eventually, the water was pumped out into the ocean so we ran out of fresh water. We had no refrigeration. The food got spoiled and we had to throw it overboard. It was then that the sharks came by. One was twelve or fifteen-feet long. We took a meat hook, put it on the cable, put a piece of meat on the hook and then cast it into the water. The shark came up and he got hooked, but there was no barb on the meat hook, so he got away. Then we went toward the back of the ship where we hung a piece of meat at the surface. The shark came up and we shot him with our rifles."

I WAS DRAFTED ON 3 October 1942. I left for the service two weeks later. I went on a street car down to the Pennsylvania Station and then over to Fort Meade, Maryland. I stayed there for a few days until we left for basic training at Camp Shelby. Then I went to infantry training. We conducted maneuvers down in southern Mississippi for two weeks, went back to camp, and then went to maneuvers in Louisiana for two months in July and August 1943.

We didn't see any beds during that time. We moved out in the woods, slept on the ground and ate a few bugs. Two men shared a tent barely big enough to cover them. We had to watch for coral snakes in our tents. After we lived for two months in the wild, they put us on a Pullman to Louisiana where I learned to live like an animal in a cage.

We were on the train for about four days, moving from Louisiana up to Camp Pickett, Virginia. At Camp Pickett, I got a driver's license and I started driving a Jeep.[10] From Camp Pickett we went to the Chesapeake Bay for amphibious training. We had to waterproof the Jeep and make sure we could drive it in the surf. After that, they sent us to West Virginia for mountain maneuvers. I was driving the Jeep and we were moving along the road and there was a mountain and they told my company, "There's your bivouac area up there; start climbing."

Fortunately, I was driving the Jeep and didn't have to march up the hill. There were four of us in the Jeep, two in the back seat, myself and the first sergeant. So, we start up this hill in the Jeep. It was so steep that the front wheels started coming off of the ground. I backed down, put two men on front of the Jeep and then put it in low range and low gear and went up the hill.

We had "blackout drives" and all I could see in front of me were little tail lights. I followed those. It was quite an experience. After maneuvers they sent us to Newport News where we got on a Merchant Marine[11] transport ship, the USS *Cape Kanzo*, converted in New York at the Navy Yard to haul soldiers. The engineer rode on the ship from New York down to Newport News. He said the ship wasn't seaworthy, but we didn't have a choice but to ride it through. We got on, about twelve-hundred men; it wasn't a big ship, maybe three-hundred-feet long and not very wide. This was 1943 and I guess anything that floated was good enough for us.

We went from Newport News into the Caribbean and through the Panama Canal. The only time we had fresh water for a shower was when we were in the Panama Canal, but it was just salt water on the ocean. In the open Pacific we had no escort and we were not in a convoy.

The Pacific is the most beautiful ocean in the world, blue as the sky. We saw flying fish jumping out of the water into the air and back into the water. And there were days when a porpoise would be right on the front of the ship, playing, riding the bow waves for hours at a time.

I was on that ship for about seventy-four days. The boilers leaked fresh water into the hull. Eventually, the water was pumped out into the ocean so we ran out of fresh water. We had no refrigeration. The food got spoiled and we had to throw it overboard. It was then that the sharks came by. One was twelve or fifteen-feet long. We took a meat hook, put it on the cable, put a piece of meat on the hook and then cast it into the water. The shark came up and he got hooked, but there was no barb on the meat hook, so he got away. Then we went toward the back of the ship where we hung a piece of meat at the surface. The shark came up and we shot him with our rifles.

The hold was always hot, so we came up on deck with our field equipment and slept there. Our latrine was a couple boards placed over the side of the deck because we didn't have any power to pump water and flush the ship's latrines.

Finally, they signaled an empty Liberty ship that was going back to the States. It was sitting up about twenty-feet higher than our ship and its sides were big and rusty. Our ship signaled for water. They took life rafts to act as bumpers and lashed the two ships together. It didn't work. The ropes snapped like shoe strings. The ocean was smooth, but there were swells in it and their ship would go up twenty feet and we'd go down and then our ship would come up. We had big, cast cargo hinges on the side of our ship that were getting knocked off. I thought we were going down to see Davy Jones [12]

We were all on the opposite side of the ship with our life belts on, but fortunately, before we got sunk, they pulled away from us. We never did get enough water. Three-hundred miles out from New Caledonia, they sent a seagoing tug and dragged us there. They made repairs to the boilers and we got fresh water. Then we continued on to New Guinea.

We disembarked in April 1944 at Oro Bay, near Buna.[13] There was no dock, so we went over with full field equipment climbed down cargo nets into DUKWs ("Ducks") and they took us in. I got Dengue fever[14] there that lasted about seven days. All my joints and bones ached. I was in the hospital for a week.

The supply line for food while we were on the islands was really good. They'd send us down to the quartermaster to unload crates of fruit, vegetables and canned ham from the DUKWS after they got loaded from the supply ships. Sometimes the crates got "broken." We'd take the stuff that spilled out back to our camp. We collected so much stuff we didn't go to the mess hall to eat!

Our captain said "Anyone who has any of that stuff, we're going to take it and put it in the kitchen because we want you guys to eat right."

That night we dug a hole and hid the food.

We made do. In the bay area, there was a crater where a bomb had exploded. There was water in the bottom of it, like a spring. We fixed it up with a pump from a fifty-five-gallon drum above us. That's how we took showers. Once I had a wisdom tooth that needed to be filled. There was no electric power, so this guy used a drill that he ran by hand.

In Oro Bay, we could get a free "trip-tick" to get a Jeep so we could drive out of camp and not get hassled by the MPs. The guy who got the "trip-tick" was responsible for the Jeep. Lieutenant Broach was in charge of the motor pool. As a point of order, officers weren't supposed to drive vehicles. If one wanted to go somewhere, he'd get one of us to do it. I had a "trip tick," and one day I parked the Jeep on the company street and went to my tent to get something. When I came back, the Jeep was gone!

I asked, "What happened to the Jeep?"

Someone said "Broach took it back to the motor pool."

I walked down to the motor pool. There was Broach with his foot on the Jeep. Without saying a word I got in the Jeep, started it up and drove off!

Later, the motor pool sergeant said, "Campbell, the lieutenant wants to see you in his tent."

I went up. The lieutenant put me in the gun crew as a punishment for leaving my vehicle unattended.

We stayed there for a couple months, moving to Maffin Bay in July 1944. We had listening posts out away from the perimeter. Each company had its own little area. The problem with this was that each area was split out so far that they didn't have an overall perimeter and the Japanese would infiltrate between them.

On 11 September, we left. On the fifteenth, we invaded Morotai, a small island three-hundred miles south of the Philippines.[15] I was on an LST, a pretty big ship that had big barges on the side. The LSTs usually made amphibious landings, but this time we couldn't get in close because of a reef. We had to cut the barges loose and put them in front of the ship. The dozers were able to get to the shore and push sand into the barges to make a ramp for our trucks to run on.

Planes had dive-bombed and strafed the whole area. From the way it was bombarded, I didn't think there could be anyone left alive. But, in the jungle, there were lots of Japanese.

They used us like donkeys to carry rations. Not only that, we had a case of rations in a backpack and we were wading in deep muck and vegetation. When we took our shoes off, our feet would be wrinkled and wet. We had to endure that for days before we came back to camp.

We moved into the jungle and into a banana grove. It started to rain and we couldn't move the trucks through the muck. We didn't sleep in the hammocks we brought because sleeping high off the ground made us good targets. So we slept on the ground behind a log or behind a piece of shrubbery. Every shadow looked like a Jap to us. Nobody moved around at night.

The disease over there was bad. Some guys would contract scrub typhus. They'd get temperatures as high as 106 degrees. It fried their brains; those guys were like zombies after they had that. We were fighting nature as much as the enemy.

Four days later, we moved into Mapia.[16] When we first went in, there was nothing but jungle. Within ten days, we were flying C–47s off landing pads and posting MPs at new roads to direct traffic. Apparently the Japanese had evacuated the place earlier.

I developed red lesions that came up like mosquito bites on my wrists and ankles and they didn't recede; they just stayed there. Then they turned gray. The lesions moved up my arms, up my legs and up over my buttocks.

We didn't have any quinine to prevent malaria, so we took a substitute called Atabrine. It turned us yellow. I was yellow from the antimalaria drug, gray from the old skin lesions and red from the new ones.

Finally, I was sent to a field hospital in Hollandia, New Guinea. One day there were ships as far as I could see. A day later they were gone. We knew at that time that there was going to be an invasion of the Philippines

At this time, the Philippines were still in Japanese hands. They were moving our division from New Guinea to aid in the invasion. After about a month, my outfit moved into the Philippines. If I had been with them, I'd have gone too, but I was fortunate because I had this tropical skin disease.

At the field hospital, a lot of us were suffering from tropical ulcers. The nurses took the scabs off my ulcers, from the knees down, cleaned out the pus, put on penicillin, then bandaged me. I healed. It's amazing what the body can do, but I still have scars on my legs.

It's funny, the Atabrine kept me from getting malaria out there, but about four years after I was discharged, I did get malaria at home!

"From Now on It Would Be Mutilation."

Joseph R. Chapman

80th Infantry Division
"Blue Ridge Division"
Mottoes: *"The 80th Only Moves Forward," "Vis Montium"*
319th Infantry Regiment
"Patton's Trouble Shooters"
Company A
Born in Freeport, Pennsylvania, 28 October 1921

"It wouldn't be long before we came to realize we weren't on a picnic. This was for real and we'd lose a lot of men, guys like Raymond Martinez from Texas. When we left the States, he had a six-month-old daughter. A sniper got him between the eyes just beneath the lip of his helmet. I'd lose a lot of friends, guys that were like my family. From now on it would be mutilation."

After the Normandy hedgerows, the enemy artillery, the skirmishes, the battles at Le Mans, four days at St. Lô and being captured by the Germans, it was only by the grace of God that I survived the War. This is my true story.

When I got out of high school in 1939, I was like every other guy. Things were still pretty tough in those closing days of the Depression. In no time, along came Pearl Harbor and that put the country into the war business, both fighting and production. I got a job down at the Allegheny Ludlum Steel Mill. I worked there for about two years, until I was drafted.

In July 1942, I went to Kittanning in Armstrong County, Pennsylvania, for my physical. From there we went to Pittsburgh for more tests. They let us take care of personal business. After two weeks had passed, I left the mill and got ready to go.

In the early evening of 5 October, my sister, my mother and I climbed into my old car and drove to the train station in Kittanning. The Kittanning High School Band was already there playing. I kissed the family goodbye and boarded the train. We stopped a couple times along the way to pick up more guys. We arrived at Fort Meade, Maryland about six-thirty in the morning.

The first thing they did was give us breakfast in an immense building with rows and rows of tables. I wondered who was paying for all of that. It didn't take long for me to figure out that I was. We all did. It was our tax money at work.

After breakfast, we got another physical. After that, we got our dress uniforms. Then they sent us to a place that pressed the uniforms. That cost us twenty cents.

Then they gave us wrapping paper with which to wrap our civilian clothes for mailing home. Postage was free for servicemen then and all through the War.

After three days at Meade, we took a train west. We had no idea where in the world we were going, but there were lots of coaches and lots of men. When we went back through Pittsburgh a lot of guys wanted to get off and go home. We rode all night to Indianapolis, Indiana, then made a turn south. We ended up in Nashville, Tennessee. From Nashville we went down to Tullahoma, almost on the border of Alabama, to the camp named after Confederate General Nathan Bedford Forrest where they were reactivating the 80th Infantry Division. I had never seen so many people in one place. I ended up in Company A of the 319th Infantry Regiment of the 80th Infantry Division.

A cadre of noncommissioned officers from Fort Jackson, South Carolina, ran the place. They got impatient with anybody who didn't know his right foot from his left, and their were a lot who didn't. I couldn't understand that. I thought everyone knew the difference.

The sergeant said to one guy, "Don't you know your right hand from your left hand?"

He said, "No. I don't know which one is which."

The sergeant said, "Well, you go over there and pick up that stone and you carry it under your arm and every time I say 'right,' you go toward the stone. If I say 'left' you go away from it."

We went through the business of learning to be a squad and then a platoon and then a whole company. There were three rifle platoons and a weapons' platoon in a company. The guys in the weapons' platoon had two light machine guns and three 60mm mortars. The rest of us were issued regular M1s or Browning Automatic Rifles and all the equipment we'd need.

In June, July and August we were in the mountains for the Tennessee Maneuvers.[17] Our "enemy" was the 83rd Division . It was hot and everything was by the book. Our canteen held one quart of water and it had to last all day. I didn't know of anybody that keeled over from the lack of water, but it was awful hot. We carried all our equipment. Pretty soon we knew when we were dehydrating because our sweaty clothes would start to dry out.

If we got around a town where people had a hose connection on the outside of the house we'd get some water there. I never did that. I was a little timid about doing some of the underhanded things the other guys did. In time I got a little hardened to that sort of thing.

After maneuvers I got a fifteen-day furlough and came home to get married. As soon as we all got back to Tennessee, we shipped out for Camp Phillips, Kansas.[18] That was a complete change. We were all used to hilly country, but Kansas was like a table top and the wind never quit blowing. It blew the barracks' doors open all the time and carried in dust that got into our rifles. That added to our cleaning chores.

On the other side of the camp was the 817th Tank Destroyer Battalion. There must have been at least twenty guys from Freeport in that group. Whenever I got the chance I went over there and met up with them. I got caught up on a little news from home that way.

After Kansas we went to Camp Laguna in Yuma, Arizona, for desert maneuvers and to the Mohave Desert in southern California for extended maneuvers. At the time, the war in the Pacific was going pretty well and they figured the Japanese were in no position to come flying over the country. They broke up a lot of anti-aircraft units and sent the men into the infantry. Well, these men had been serving for two years or more and they weren't used to what we were used to. Apparently, they didn't march any farther and back than the barracks or the mess hall. Either that, or they rode in trucks.

The first days these guys got with us the 319th was doing flanking movements in the lower portion of Death Valley. The 104th Division out of Oregon was to take a mountain pass and we were to stop them. We made a 126-mile march in five-and-a-half days. We left Monday morning and got there about noon on Saturday.[19]

Our artillery got to ride on trucks. When they passed us they yelled, "We feel sorry for you!"

We hoped their trucks would break down. Believe me, if they stopped we were going to pull some of those guys off!

The poor coast artillery guys were a mess in no time. One guy's foot was just one big blister. They just couldn't understand how in the world we could be doing this.

We told them, "We're getting ready for the other side of the Pond. You better be in good shape when we get there."

We had to go through infiltration courses where there were machine guns set up in a semicircle on wooden frames. The guns rested on the frames that kept them level. There were double-apron barbed-wire fences stretched across the place. Since the wire was slack, it was easy for us to get snagged. They sprayed the ground with a fire hose, and that created a foot of mud. Here and there they had marked off places with chalk where they had set up smoke explosions to simulate artillery bursts. Observers watched us from two towers. When they were ready for us to go they blew a whistle.

We crawled through on our bellies, pulling ourselves along on our elbows, with our rifles cradled in our arms. If we got dirt in the barrels, we had to go through the whole process again. They were trying to teach us to protect our rifles because they meant our lives in combat.

We also had to wear our combat packs when we crawled through. On the back of the pack was our shovel. It never failed to get stuck in the muck and hold us up. All the time the machine guns fired live rounds just over our heads. We could see tracer rounds pass four-feet above us.

After we finished the maneuvers, we went to Fort Dix. On 1 May 1944 we boarded the *Queen Mary* and headed for Scotland. There were thousands of us on that ship. I slept on the deck because there was no room inside. We got to Scotland in five days, marched off the ship and got into railroad cars that took us to a staging area in England. We didn't know a thing; everything was so hush-hush.[20]

They sent our Division over to France from Southampton.[21] They needed us fast because infantry units were getting shot up so badly. The ship we were loaded onto was a British freighter with a crew from India. When we got to Normandy we were in the middle of all the Navy ships that were were still firing support because all the artillery hadn't yet been unloaded. My platoon, the 3rd, was the first to go down the cargo nets. I was loaded down with a lot of ammunition, my belt, my sidearm and a Browning Automatic Rifle (BAR) that weighed twenty-one pounds. In addition, they expected the Germans were going to retaliate with gas. In case of that we were wearing our wool shirt, pants, field jacket and impregnated fatigues over top of that in case they used mustard gas.

I had the gun slung over my back over the pack and when I started down the side. It was a very high ship. It was rocking back and forth. I had to reach up inside to hold on. Halfway down I thought, *'I don't know if I'm going to make this or not. If I slip off it's a long way down there.'*

But I got down and settled. The next thing I heard was the Captain yelling down, "Hey Chapman! Move up to the ramp and make room for the rest; we're going to send some more down."

I had a notion to yell back up, "You want to get me killed first?"

We all got loaded in the landing craft. We were packed in so tight we couldn't sit, kneel, nor fall down. I don't know how many hours we were in that thing. Some guys got seasick because every time a battleship fired a barrage the landing craft rocked back and forth. It was sheer misery, but we had to wait until all the landing craft were ready. Those Navy ships never stopped firing. What a roar! Finally we got going at a pretty good speed.

We landed on UTAH Beach[22] where the Cherbourg Peninsula starts to jut out into the English Channel. That's where the 4th Division had landed on D-Day. In the days since the initial landings the engineers had gotten in there and cleaned out an awful lot of the obstacles.[23] By the time we got up to the top of the hill, it was dark. There was a guide there who took us to a bivouac area. We just dropped down in the field and went to sleep. Big guns boomed all night long, but we were so tired we slept right through the noise.

At daylight, I found out we were near the old German headquarters at Ste. Mère-Église.[24] The engineers had set up a water depot and while I was filling my canteen from a Lister bag someone yelled, "Hey, Chapman!"

It was Frank Check, another fellow from South Buffalo Township. I saw Frank all the time at home. He married a girl that lived in the house next door from us. What a place to see people you know, in the middle of a battle zone.

It wouldn't be long before we came to realize we weren't on a picnic. This was for real and we'd lose a lot of men, fellows like Raymond Martinez from Texas. When we left the States, he had a six-month-old daughter. A sniper got him between the eyes just beneath the lip of his helmet. I lost a lot of friends, guys that were like my family. From now on it would be mutilation.

We moved across France and ended up at Le Mans.[25] There was so much destruction! The retreating Germans were demolishing what they could. They had taken the warning signs out of their minefields and our infantry got caught in them. There were heavy casualties. Replacements arrived in the morning and by evening they would be dead. It didn't pay to make new friends.

In July we joined Patton's Third Army and moved on toward Orleans, south of Paris. Once that was liberated, we went on to the Moselle River.[26] We moved to the high ground and slowly got chopped to pieces. I don't remember whether we had fifty-two or fifty-six men by the time I was captured, but there were one- hundred-eighty-seven in the company when we first got there. They had whittled us down to nothing.

We were up pretty high and from our position we ran patrols to Pont-à-Mousson where there was a big bridge over the Moselle that the Germans didn't want us to have, but one that we wanted. One day Company B was ordered to run a patrol down through the wooded section below us. Near it was a farm and some freshly-cut grain fields. They were just stubble low to the ground. There was a wagon road down along the edge of the woods and the rest was all open ground for quite a distance. We were supposed to sweep the woods of any Germans that might still be there. We knew they'd been there earlier in the day. What few guys we had joined up with Company A and went to sweep the woods.

I was the BAR man so with the two scouts I was out in front. The scouts and the BAR team were always first. The riflemen and the bazooka and the machine guns and whatnot were in the back.

We started down. Sergeant Janosic, the squad leader said to me, "Joe, I don't like this."

I said, "I don't like it either! It's a perfect place for an ambush."

It was all open country to the tree line and if the Germans were in there we were exposed and they could just chop us up. We were halfway down the road when they did just that. Everybody hit the ground, but there was no cover. They just picked guys off one at a time, like sitting ducks. I returned fire that silenced them for a minute, but then they started hunting for me. Every place I moved, everything I tried to do, they were right on me. There was a wagon road, an access road, that went into the field off to the side and I crawled down there. By that time the scouts were gone and I wasn't getting any supporting fire. I was laying in one of the wagon ruts low enough so that the Germans fired that machine gun right over me.

They had me pinned down. 'This is it!' I thought.

I was sure I was going to die. I was face down and I had the gun with me and I could hear their hobnail boots as they came toward me.

There were about six of them and one officer. They kicked me over on my back and when I opened my eyes that officer had his machine pistol pointed right between my eyes. He said to me, *Kamerad?*

I thought, *'Yeah. Comrade.'*

They got me up off the ground and unhooked my cartridge belt, took my pack off and stripped me down. The rest of their group was going through the field, checking to see if there were any wounded or anything like that.

"I Don't like it either! It's a perfect place for an ambush."

I'd caught a piece of shrapnel from a mortar shell across my right knee cap during the fight. My leg had been bleeding and burning like you wouldn't believe. I wondered if I'd be able to walk and what would happen if I couldn't.

It seemed they were going to take me prisoner, but I didn't understand why. Why take one guy prisoner? I know they didn't want information out of me. There was nobody else left. The tail-end of the column had gotten away but the rest, the ones I was with were all dead.

So the Germans took me along and I was afraid that if I hobbled they'd think, 'Well, we're not taking this guy along. He's got a bad leg, just shoot him, get rid of him.'

But by the time we got going it was dark and we stopped for the night.

There was a young soldier with them about my age. He could speak some English. It seemed that a lot of the younger Germans could.

He said to me, "Oh, you'll have a good life in Germany."

I thought, *'Hah! That's not where I want to spend the rest of my life!'*

He went over and got my canteen out of my carrier and brought it over to me and said, "Here. You better take this with you."

Boy, I was glad I did because that's the only water I had for a long time afterwards.

They marched me with my hands over my head. After a while they handed me over to an older man. He stayed behind me with his rifle the whole way. When we passed the bridge, I could see it was wired with explosives. We got to a farmhouse and when we went in it was pretty much like we'd seen in the movies. There was no furniture, just was a table in the middle of the room. On it was a lighted candle in a wine bottle and spread-out maps. Two officers were looking at the maps. They never even looked up to see who walked in the room.

The older guard went over, opened a door and pushed me into a darkened room. There was a mattress on the floor and when I dropped on that mattress I just went out; I was dead tired. The next thing I knew somebody was kicking the sole of my shoe. It was the same guard.

He yelled at me, *Raus, raus!*

I got up and I came out into the room and there was one officer there; the other one apparently had gone. The guard went over and picked up a field ration of cheese and gave it to me. It tasted good because I hadn't had anything to eat for a while. Pretty soon two guys came in that were apparently like MPs; they wore a little plate around their necks on a chain and had submachine guns.[27]

They motioned me outside.

'Okay, now they're probably going to shoot me, I thought.

I started down the road in the direction they motioned me to go. They were behind me laughing and carrying on. Then artillery rounds started coming in. I was half-afraid to run into the brush or some place for cover but they took off and so did I. From where they were they kept an eye on me.

I said to myself, *'Well, the battle for the bridge is on. If those Germans get pushed back here and they see me, then one of them will shoot me for sure.'*

Finally things got a little quiet and we walked on.

We went through a small village. I saw the name " Ste. Jean" on one of the buildings. Eventually, we came to the city of Nancy. There was a park just as we came into the city. It was well-maintained, had a beautiful lawn and flower gardens. In the middle was a big stone building. One of my guards made me sit on a bench while the other went into the building. There was another fellow sitting way down on the other end of a bench with a guard watching him. Eventually, they took him into the building. I went in a little later. There wasn't much inside. Just a table with an officer and a private sitting behind it.

When I came in, I paid my respects to the officer, as we were trained to do. He responded with, *Heil Hitler!*

Then the private spoke to me in perfect English, "May I have your dog tags, please?"

I gave them to him. He wrote my name down and all that other stuff that was on the tags and he gave them back to me. He said, "What was your outfit?"

I responded with my name, rank and serial number.

The officer sitting there never said anything. The private said, "Well, our report is that you were taken on the high ground so you would be with the 319th Infantry, from Company A, B, or C. Company A was James Romo, Company B was Sam Woods, Company C was Mike Gold. All of them captains."

They knew more than I did.

He said, "All right, go out that door there."

There some other fellows out there waiting and as I was leaving the private said to me, "You know, I'm American. I graduated from the University of Chicago in 1938."

I thought, *'How did you ever get in a mess like this?'*

Over time I met other Americans in the German Army. They'd gone to Germany to visit their grandparents or something and the War came along and they just couldn't get home and they were drafted. It was strange when a German would come up and say, "I'm an American. How are things in the States?"

Once we were all collected and they had taken the information from our tags they were ready to march us. There were twelve of us in total, one staff sergeant and the rest privates. We got out to the street, lined up four abreast, three ranks deep ready to go and the staff sergeant said, "Let's cut it off sharply here. Let's let the Germans know that they haven't got us down."

We started out down the street and we could hear the old German hobnail boots pounding on the pavement. They had a slower cadence than we had and they were having to move along pretty well to keep up. They were older fellows, most likely veterans of North Africa and Italy. As we went along the streets, the locals held up their fingers in a "V" for "Victory" sign. They weren't afraid of the Germans, because the countryside was crawling with American troops by then.

After a time we came to the compound which had once been a school for boys. It had a cyclone fence around the tops of the building so prisoners could be held there.

We went inside. There were quite a number of us there. They brought some rations and that was my first time to have a slice of black bread. It was very sour, very bitter and very heavy. But I was hungry enough to eat anything.

We spent the night there in one of the classrooms. We got up the next morning and they took some of us to a railroad siding. We were put to work loading ammunition into box cars. That was against the Geneva Convention. Prisoners of war weren't supposed to help the enemy in the war effort.

Once that job was done, we went back to the building. Later that same day they got fifty of us and lined us up on the blacktop road. The group, two officers, a couple noncoms, two medics and the rest like me, started a march down the road. The Germans let the medics keep their medical bags.

Around six or seven in the evening a flight of P–51 Mustangs strafed us. Nobody got hit. One of our officers said, "Now when they come back—*if* they come back—we're going to line up in the middle of the road and we're going to spell P-O-W. The guards can do what they want to do; if they want to run away, why, that's their business, so . . ."

Sure enough, those planes came flying over in our direction again. The medics had given us gauze so we unrolled that and we all stood in the middle of the road with our arms up spelling "P-O-W." The first plane came down to strafe. We all just stood there. That was really scary, I'll tell you! He came down and he took one look what we spelled out and he just passed over us and swung around. The second plane and third did the same. When they flew over for the last time, they just rocked their wings in recognition. Talk about nervous! Those .50–caliber machine guns, they do an awful piece of work.

After they left, everybody just said, "Oh, man!"

The next morning some fellows from recon outfits that had gotten captured and a few others that had never walked any distance could hardly stand up. Their business was to ride every place they went. Their muscles were all knotted up, and they were hobbled up. The rest of us infantry dogs were all a walking outfit, but those poor guys were in real torture. I really felt sorry for them. Eventually a truck came along and the German in charge put up his hands and stopped the truck. All those guys that couldn't walk were loaded on the back of the truck.

We walked the rest of the day and started to feel weak. We hadn't had anything to eat the whole time. At one place, St. Avold, a lady came out of an office and had a long conversation with one of the German officers. After that we got back on the road and walked until four or five-o'-clock in the afternoon until we came to a farm that had a big barn and an apple orchard. We were going to spend the night there, so the Germans let us gather up some apples.

The next morning we gathered up some more apples to take with us. We had apples for breakfast. I stuffed four or five in my shirt. Throughout the day we'd eat an apple if we got hungry. I had no water. For some reason, a German had taken away my canteen.

Late in the evening we came to the town of Limburg. We were passing all kinds of farm lands and villages all along the way but we didn't stop. When we got to Limburg, they stopped us. It was one of the collection points for prisoners. While we were there, the air raid sirens went off. The guards pushed us into some trenches. The planes just passed over. I guess that wasn't the day to bomb Limburg, thank heaven.

There was a big hospital there and I could smell it! There were an awful lot of wounded American boys in there. As soon as the Germans found out we had medics with us they put them to work in the hospital.

Eventually they took us to get something to eat. They had a big cauldron out in the yard and it was bubbling away with cabbage and potatoes. The cooks gave everybody a can and a wooden spoon. They ladled this stuff out. We were happy because we were finally getting something warm to eat. Then a cook came out with a long paddle and plunged it in the cauldron. He brought that paddle up as he was mixing. Along with it came a horse's head! That's what they used to make broth. Some of the guys got sick when they saw that, but I chewed on a potato and a bit of cabbage and tried to get myself some nourishment.

They had a big circle of pipe that had a spigot every six, seven feet. The water that came out was just a trickle. Everybody tried to get a drink. Guys got into fights and started pushing each other around. It was really miserable going. I didn't get any water the first day. I didn't want to wade into some guy that weighed two-hundred pounds!

The next morning, we had some kind of breakfast. It was black bread and maybe a boiled potato. I got some water then. When they turned the thing on, I was quick enough to get my can up to the spigot and I got enough that I got a drink.

Eventually, I started to worry about things at home and my future. I'd been in the field and in a weakened condition. All I could think was when will Mary know that I'm still alive? All she'd get was a telegram that I was missing in action. Well, that could mean anything. I was worried about my mother and two sisters also. My mother had already lost my father when I was two.

We spent some time in Limburg. One day they loaded us in boxcars. We were packed in those cars so tightly we couldn't sit down. I was one of the first ones pushed in. I got back in a corner. I thought I could squat down, but it wasn't possible. When the car was full, they locked the doors.

After a while we were hooked onto a train and started to move. We pulled off on the siding once while another train, a faster train, went past. It seemed in no time at all after that we heard fighter planes flying over. They hit the engine first. There was an explosion and that stopped the train. We could hear the guards; they'd been riding on the car on the back end of the thing, running around and yelling. Then the planes started to hit the ammunition cars and they were exploding. We were terrified. Some rounds came through the roof of our car and killed two guys and wounded five.

After it was over the Germans opened the doors and they all had their guns ready in case we decided to run. We got out of the car into the open. Thankfully, the thing hadn't been set on fire. Some of the cars had. We got the wounded guys out quick. One was hit in the shoulder with a .50–caliber round. His arm was just hanging by a thread. We took him and the other four over to a field to be collected.

When they brought the two dead bodies out, somebody called attention and we all saluted. I think the Germans were a little taken aback by that. They carried those two bodies over and put them in the field as well. After that we walked up the railroad track, past what was left of the wreckage. We walked a pretty good piece until we got to another field where we were collected. I can't remember what time of day it was but we seemed to be there a long time. Finally, a train came that had passenger cars on it and they loaded us in the passenger cars. We spent the night on that thing and the next day we came to Moosberg, the location of *Stalag VII-A*.[28]

They unloaded us. The first thing they did was register us and take our pictures. Then we got a shower. That felt good! They took our clothes and put them on hangars, then ran them through disinfection to kill lice. We didn't have lice at that point, at least.

After that we got a shot for typhus fever right between the ribs. That was the first time I ever had anything like that happen and I thought, *'Maybe this is the end. Maybe that's poison; I might fall over here.'*

Afterwards, we got our clothes and put them back on. After that we went to our barracks. There were guys who had already been there awhile and as soon as we got in they hit us with questions. What outfit were you with? Where were you captured? How fast is the front moving?

While we were at that camp, we worked in Munich repairing the damage our bombers made. They got us up early in the morning, like four-thirty or something like that, loaded us into boxcars and hauled us into Munich.

Munich was probably twenty-five, thirty miles away and when we got there they'd break us up into work-gangs of five or six. We worked on a house one time that had been knocked down and the man who owned it had a band. All of their *Lederhosen* and tunics and so on were all in a room in this house in a big cupboard and he wanted to get them out. Well we had to move a lot of lumber and stuff like that and finally we opened that thing up and there they were. They were beautiful. Let's face it. Germany did have some wonderful and beautiful music. There were those hats with the plumes on them. And we got a kick out of that. We thought that was really nice that we had maybe done something good for somebody.

Another day we were put to work in the downtown section where there had been quite a bit of destruction. There was a little variety store there. While I was cleaning up the rubble, I found a nice little notebook and a couple good pencils. I started to keep a diary with those.

I never knew what time or day it was. I didn't have a watch and we didn't have a calendar. We had a general idea of what month it was by asking somebody, "When did you get captured?"

Finally we found out that we didn't have to work on Sunday. That helped us keep track a little bit.

In the barracks the bunks were three high. Over the years they had gotten all wobbly and they only had five bed slats: one for head, shoulders, body, butt and legs and feet. They were just long enough to grip onto the side rail a quarter of an inch or so. Our mattress was just a burlap sack and it was filled with wood shavings and that kind of stuff. It was always a tricky operation to get in because if the guy on the tops lets go he drops and hits the guy below and the poor fellow on the floor down on the bottom gets "crushed." Things like that added to the misery. We always said if you took that mattress and put it on the floor, it would do close order drill because it was so full of bugs.

One morning the technical sergeant in charge of the barracks came in and said, "Now I've got a list of forty men here that's going to go on the work detail. Now, when I call your name, I want you to gather up all your belongings."

My name was among them and there was a fellow by the name of Joe Darnell that I'd gotten well-acquainted with. Joe was with the 36th Division[29] and he had made the southern invasion to France from Italy and had been captured. He'd been overseas awhile, all through It aly and he'd seen a lot more combat than me. We met another fellow named Paul Dane. The three of us hung together.

They took those of us they had selected and they loaded us on the train. It was late October or the first part of November and by then it was getting quite cold. Before we left, we lined up and the Germans threw each of us an overcoat as we moved along. I got one a little longer than a Mackinaw. I don't know what army it belonged to but it had some fancy buttons on it. It was too small for me so I had to tear the lining out to get it on over my field jacket.

There were forty of us when we got off the train near a little town near Austria, Landshut, not quite as far as Vienna. We were in a position where we could see both the Austrian Alps and the Swiss Alps.

I thought, *'Boy, I wish I could get away from here and get over there and get to Switzerland, that would be all right!'*

Nobody tried that I knew of; it was too far.

We were taken out to the edge of town to what had been a bakery in peacetime. It was a three-storey building, all brick masonry. The first floor had been converted into a machine shop. There they were making or working on carburetors for the German Air Force. That meant we were going to be living in a target.

They took us upstairs where there were rows of bunks and some tables on the end. That was to be our home without stockades. Everybody grabbed a bunk. This time they were only two-high and they were well-constructed. They had solid bottoms but they still had the old mattress that could've done close order drill from the bugs inside of it.

Every day they marched us out of town about a mile to dig trenches. We didn't have manufactured shovels; they had the shovel portion of it, but the handles were made out of saplings. That didn't make digging too easy, because the handles always bent. Of course, we had been well-trained in the business of looking busy, but really doing nothing.

We had one fellow with us from a German family and neighborhood in South Dakota. He was fluent in German and became our interpreter.

They had a couple of Germans that would come out from town occasionally on their bicycles to see what progress we were making on the trenches. Most of the guards we had by then were old men or veterans who had been wounded. One fellow had been on the Russian Front. They amputated part of his foot because it was frozen. When he got out in the cold weather, he was just in absolute torture. He'd get out on the blacktop road that went past where we worked and he'd just pound his feet on there just as hard as he could trying to get rid of the pain. He had a pretty good-sized nose so we called him "Eagle Beak." We had names for all of them all, believe me! I was a little afraid of him.

I always thought, *'Well, if he gets upset, he's liable to shoot one of us!'*

Soon we found out that we were digging footers for air raid shelters. They brought out the concrete slabs on horse-drawn wagons because all their gas was gone. The boss of the job, a civilian, was the most high-strung guy I ever saw in my life. He'd curse and swear at us, shaking his fists. I don't know whether he wanted the guards to threaten us or not, but he'd yell all the time. One day he didn't show up so we asked what happened to him and one of the guards said, "He got drafted into the army."

At one point they brought out a couple of men that were bricklayers, Max and Schlissel. Max was almost blind and wore glasses that looked like the bottoms of Coca-Cola bottles. He'd pick things up and hold them right to his glasses to see for sure what he had.

It was freezing and they were pouring mixed concrete, which is a bad thing to do. They'd hand-mix it, throw it in and then hand-mix another batch and throw it in because they didn't have a machine to do it; they just had a trough. It took a long time to do and one batch would freeze while they made another. Finally, we got one shelter finished and they got the arches up and cemented everything together. By that time it was Christmas. The old folks were riding around the countryside in horse buggies and they were all dressed up in their fancy Christmas clothes.

A day or two before Christmas three P–51s came in and hit the electric plant and there went all the electricity. The townspeople got upset. We were the only Americans around so we got the blame. When we got back into town that day, some of the people were out to get us with sticks and stones. Before that, we were kind of what you might call celebrities. People wanted to see what an American looked like. Not that day though.

Then a few days later there was another attack and the railroad tracks were damaged, so they took us off shelter building and sent us to fix the tracks. We had big tongs to lift the ties with. They had long handles and four of us would pick up one tie and carry it to a certain spot. We'd stand there a minute, pick it back up and carry it to the other side of the tracks. We did that with the same tie all afternoon and the Germans never caught on.

There were some Russian prisoners kept near us but they never got out of the compounds like we did. The Germans and the Russians hated each other. One day they brought some Russians out to work on the rails. They did absolutely nothing. I think they were daring the German guards to do something.

At lunch time, the Russians were sitting near us and they got a fire going and were eating meat! The Russians thought we were all right, so they gave each of us a piece of meat. It was kind of gray-colored, but it was good. It was the first meat we'd had in a long time. We asked what it was. One Russian told us there had been an old dog running around and they smashed it in the head, skinned it out and cooked it up. Anyway, I enjoyed it; after all, it was nutrition!

Finally, the War really came to the town. The British bombed at night and the Americans bombed during the day. We made many runs to the air-raid shelters. The British didn't seem to care too much about whether they were hitting their target or even getting near it. They just unloaded and went home. Well, we weren't more than thirty miles from Hitler's private castle, and so you can imagine what it was like. We'd have to get up every night during the coldest winter in forty years.

Whenever the air-raid siren blew, we went out to be counted. We never went anywhere without first being counted. Just to agitate them, one guy moved down the line after he got counted. The numbers never some out right. Then the guards would count again, and someone else would move. Then they'd count again and argue over whether or not they had the right figures. They'd count again and again and again and then they'd again argue whether they had the right numbers or not. Little things like that agitated them. We were paying them back just a little.

As the War progressed, we abandoned the railroad job and moved on to digging sand and gravel out of a hillside. They had quite a sizeable amount of gravel there, which was what they were using for the footers on the air raid shelter. One day this young German soldier drove in with a team of horses and a wagon to get a load of sand and some gravel. We were about to shovel the stuff up on there when he said, "Where are you guys from?"

We said, "What do you mean, where are we from?"

He said, "I came over here to see some of my people and I got stuck and I've been in this War ever since."

It was another case where we met an American in the German Army. He'd been around a long time and seen a lot of action in Poland. I think he'd been wounded so they gave him a job driving a team of horses.

That was the only day I was out at the gravel site. From there, we moved over to the center of town. There was a hill there and on the top of it, like every place near there, was a big mansion. I don't have any idea who lived there or anything about it, but it was very large, all stone. Around it was a very large wall built up about six feet tall that had pointed stonework on top of it. It had probably been there for a century. It was moss-covered and down inside that walled off area was a big forest. We were supposed to cut down some of those trees and we saw trees in there that had initials cut in them from the 1600 and 1700s. Imagine that, a heart with initials in it from 1648.

I'm not a forester, but some of the guys that were in the group with us knew some stuff and one of them said, "Those are beech trees." I never saw trees that big; I couldn't reach around them.

They brought out some cross cut saws for us to use. The only trouble is, a cross cut saw is about four-feet long and we could only cut in about a foot because those trees were so big! One of the guys had an axe and he was going to try and chop it when the air raid siren blew. We had to get out. We went up a road that ran along the wall down the hill to an air-raid shelter built into the hill. The shelter had big doors on it and right past it was a German garrison.

We were on the road when one fighter plane came down to see what progress they were making repairing that railroad. The tracks went east to west across the country and it branched out and went up north to Bismarck and the places up on the coast. So this was a very strategic place. The fighter flew over, swung around and came back. When he turned around to come back, they fired on him from that garrison with anti-aircraft. Well, he just took off; if he got hit, it didn't bring him down.

We said, "Uh-oh, he went home to get his brothers."

And they came about an hour later. I never saw so many bombers. They came in low, about ten-thousand feet, in groups of ten or twelve. We went along toward the shelter and they started to unload. They worked that town over, block by block, tearing everything apart. There were big grain silos, six of them on one edge of town. They hit them with incendiaries. They must have been full of grain because they burned for days.

Joe Darnell and I got up against the wall. Paul Dane was up ahead. Other guys were scattered all around. The shelter was so packed a lot of people couldn't even get inside. There was an Austrian guard who laughed every time a salvo of bombs came down. Joe and I hugged the wall. The Austrian thought he was a real hero.

All of a sudden, everything went black and my mouth was full of dirt. They had just laid a row of bombs right down the road. When the wall started to crumble, I threw my arms over my head. Joe and I crouched down. The Austrian got between us. His left leg was sticking out and a piece of bomb casing tore it clean off. The only thing left holding it on was a piece of muscle. He yelled and screamed.

Joe and I got out of the rubble. Paul Dane yelled, "I've been hit! I've been hit!"

We ran over to him and grabbed him up by each arm. Paul was not a very big man and hard to carry. We took off up the road between five-hundred-pound bombs. After we got up the road, they exploded. They had delayed-action fuses.

With Paul between us, we jumped into the nearest crater. Three German soldiers were in it. We got Paul's shirt off and pulled down his undershirt. He had a hole in his back above his lung, under his shoulder blade. It was big enough to stick a finger in.

When the bombing was all over and were getting collected, we found out that one of the guys that was with us, Francis Fatler from some place in Ohio, had been on the edge of the woods when a bomb shattered a tree. Half the tree fell on Francis and crushed him to death.

One of the guards took Paul to a hospital. They just dressed his wound. The Germans said the shrapnel was so hot when it went in it cauterized the wound, so there was no danger of infection. Paul walked around with that shrapnel in his body until 1979, the year he died.

When we started back across town to our quarters, the people started throwing sticks, rocks, anything at us. They were screaming and spitting at us. I suppose we couldn't blame them. The bombers had dropped a lot of incendiaries. Those things fell in packs and they pitched all over the place setting fires. Water wouldn't put the fires out. It would just make the fires burn more. Talk about havoc! That town really got torn apart. There was nothing left. Finally, one of the old guards let us go and we ran for our lives.

After we got into our building, they brought Paul from the hospital. He was in a lot of pain, but we had no morphine or other pain killers. The only thing Joe and I could do for him was to soak a handkerchief in cold water and put it on his shoulder.

Not too long after the bombing, a lot of fighters started to come over. We'd go out to work, but the planes would take shots at any group they saw.

We used to think about trying to get away to get to the American lines. Then we heard artillery rumble. We wondered if American troops would ever recognize us if they did come. We were dirty, filthy with ragged beards and what clothes we had on couldn't be recognized. By April we got rid of the overcoats and we just had the dirty old field jacket on and no hat, no cap, no helmet, nothing on top. My shirt was full of old, white hog lice. I took my shirt off and ran my thumbnail right down the grease on the back of it. Those white lice came off along with the grease. Just filth, that's all it was. Just filth. We never got washed up; we never had any hot water. We washed our faces the best we could, but we were still crud from head to foot.

One day they told us to stay in. An officer came into our quarters and talked to the man who was the commander of our group of guards. They had a long conversation and that evening, they said to us, "Get your stuff all together; we're going to take you out of here."

We didn't have much, but what we had, we took. I had my notes that I kept in my shoe.

We went outside at dusk and there was a big convoy of German equipment out there, all horse-drawn. We walked up the road a couple miles until we came to what had been an inn. They had the tables and everything out in the front yard, but the place was abandoned. It started to rain a little bit so we crawled under the tables to keep from getting wet. While we were there an officer came in. He was all decked out in great regalia; he must've been a colonel at least.

Our interpreter said, "Now, when it gets daylight, we're supposed to go up the road a couple miles. There's a couple of big tents up there and that's where we're going to be housed. They're going to wait there until the troops come and this officer will surrender to the Americans."

About five-thirty the next morning the artillery of the 80th Division moved into the area What the bombers hadn't done to the town, the artillery did. They fired what must have been about a forty-five minute concentration. I didn't go back to take a look, but I bet you that you could have stood on a ten-foot ladder and looked over that town. They just blew it down to powder.

We walked up the road in the morning and we found these big tents and we met guys from every place. There were some British troops who were taken in the early stages of the War and were taken to Poland where they worked as labor in the coal mines for three years. The Germans moved them out because the Russians were coming. The guards shot the ones that fell behind.

In the afternoon, a column of Sherman tanks came down the road and they stopped and wanted to know who we were. We told them we were prisoners of war.

Someone said "There's British, Americans and Canadians."

I said, "They were supposed to get some trucks to come and haul us out of here."

They said, "Okay, we'll go on about our business."

The tanks moved down and pulled off the road. The British guys went down to them and asked one of the tankers, "May I try that gun?"

The tank commander said, "It's all right with me."

One got up there behind that .50–caliber job and asked, "How do I use it? What do I do?"

The tanker said, "You just press your thumb on the trigger there."

The Germans begged for their lives and everything but that guy killed them anyway. He said, "We've been waiting for revenge and we got it today."

That's war. I think of things like that and that's part of what helps to drive you crazy.

We waited for those trucks but nobody showed up. So Paul and I and our friend Joe decided that we'd walk up the road and maybe find some troops somewhere. There was no use hanging around. There was no food, anyway.

The three of us started up the road. After a couple miles, a truck pulled out of a field and I saw the 80th Division marking on the back bumper.

I yelled, "Hey, 80th Division! Stop the truck!"

The driver stopped. He yelled, "What are you doing?"

I said, "We're prisoners of war. The 80th Division is my old outfit. I was with Company A, the 319th Infantry Regiment. We're trying to get to Regensburg where they're collecting the prisoners."

He said, "Hop on the back end. I'm going to a water depot up the road a few miles."

There were some MPs at the depot. The one in charge put us into a 4x4 and we headed for Regensburg, about twenty-five miles away, to an airfield they were flying guys out of. At Regensburg we went into a building. Some guys took our names and checked our dog tags. They asked some questions about where we had been in Germany and so on. Then one of them said, "Okay, get with a group of twenty-five because we're flying out of here in C–47s. You'll be given a group number."

We had to wait a day or two, but in the meantime they fed us. We couldn't eat much because our stomachs had shrunk. We were down to skin and bones. They put us on baby food until we got to the States.

Before we left, they put is in a big cage. We stripped down, closed our eyes, held our hands over our noses and mouths. Medics with pump guns full of DDT came in and gave us the works. We had to bend over and spread. After they dusted our old clothes and we put them back on, even the underwear we had worn for months.

Finally, we boarded a plane. We had to sit on seats that were made to take guys wearing parachutes, so our feet couldn't touch the floor. It was uncomfortable, but we were getting out of there. We flew over countryside that looked burned. Most of the buildings were rubble. We landed in Le Havre, France.

When we got off of the plane there were two or three chaplains and a couple of other officers to greet us. They loaded us up in a bus and they hauled us over to the water depot where they had portable showers.

There was a big, older African-American fellow sitting there handing out little ditty bags.

He said, "Now, anything you want to keep, your wallet, your dog tags, everything like that you want to keep, put it in here and take that with you. Everything else you got goes on the burn pile!"

Then they gave us like a half a cake of GI soap which was about 75 or 80% lye. Then they gave us another cake of face soap to finish off with. We could stay in there as long as we wanted to. The water was just lukewarm because we had to get acclimated. Boy, oh, boy was that nice. Rub that old lather on and chase those bugs away! Each guy had his own little cubicle. They gave us towels and cloth slippers. We were there for a half hour.

When we came out we went to a tent and it was just like the day we started back at Fort Meade, Maryland. "Here is your underwear. Here are your socks. What size shirt do you wear? Here's your . . . Here's this, that and the other thing."

We were completely outfitted in brand new clothes and they gave us razors and all the toilet articles and everything we needed. We hadn't had a toothbrush for months, so you know what condition our teeth were in. After they outfitted us, we got a nice tent and a cot and pillow and a good mattress and a couple of nice wool blankets.

"Get established. When you know where you're going to be, we're going to get you something to eat," they told us.

They gave us baby food!

We had nothing to do and we weren't required to do anything. We weren't in good enough shape physically to do anything, anyway.

Finally, they came around after about two or three days and they said, "All right, anybody here from Pennsylvania, New Jersey, or New York State?"

I told them I was from Pennsylvania. Paul Dane told them he was from New York. Joe Darnell was from Chicago, from Illinois. So they took Paul and me to be shipped out and we had to say a good-bye to Joe. We'd been together all that time and we were leaving without him. He had to wait to go on a ship that was going later to Virginia or Massachusetts.

We went down to the shore where they were landing Army of Occupation troops. We went out to the SS *Brazil* on the same landing craft. The *Brazil* had been a luxury liner. There were about 150 of us on board. Someone got on the public address system and told us to go to quarters. We were supposed to hear a special message from Winston Churchill telling us the War was finally over. After he spoke, nobody said anything.

After about five minutes somebody said, "Well I guess it's all over."

Then we started to get acquainted by asking each other questions.

"Where did you get captured?"

"What did you do?"

"What was your outfit?"

The Battle of the Bulge happened while we were POWs. We didn't know anything about it. Some of the guys on the ship were with the 106th Division, the one the Germans came straight through, told us about it.[30]

A full bird colonel from the Air Force came to the door and he just stopped dead in his tracks and said, "Oh, my God!"

He just stood there for a minute. Until then I didn't know we were so hideous-looking.

He told us, "Nobody will bother you; you're in quarantine. Now we're loading a lot of wounded, but we're also taking the Fifteenth Air Force back to the States; they're going to get regrouped to go against the Japanese. You will be fed at a separate time and nobody will be allowed to be around you."

I went in the toilet room and looked at myself in the mirrors. My cheeks were hollow; my eyes were deep-set. I was a skeleton.

Then they took us over to Southampton, England, where they loaded on wounded, mostly amputees. They put them in the state rooms.

It took us two weeks to come across the Atlantic. We were the last convoy to cross. We went as fast as the slowest vessel, which was about five knots. When those guys from the Air Force were out on the decks, the MPs would move them back up half a deck to keep them away from us when we came on deck. It wasn't that they were scared of us; it was just that nobody wanted to get scurvy or whatever we had.

They yelled at us, "How many of you guys are infantry?"

Well, about everybody put their hands up.

"Oh, my God," they said.

They must have thought the infantry was the worst place in the world after that. It was!

When we got to New York Harbor, it was too late to come in through the submarine net so we stayed out for the night, but the Statue of Liberty was lit up. I don't think anybody slept that night. We were all out looking over the railing. We could see some cars moving.

Some of the guys said, "Boy, maybe they lifted the gas rationing. Look! There are cars running on the roads there."

There were lights in some of the buildings that I guess had been blacked out all during the War. The next morning they brought the ship in. The Army band was playing and reporters crowded around. We were all on deck waving. We got off the ship and after a lot of picture-taking, we loaded up on buses and took off for Fort Hamilton in Brooklyn, where we were put into the hospital.

After about five days, we got accustomed to what day of the week it was, what the date was and things like that. When we were ready to leave, we had to critique our experience.

At last, the chaplain came in and said, "Well, boys I have some good news. We're going to send you home for sixty days for a little rest."

I called my family from New York. They met me in Pittsburgh. I was home for sixty days and then we went back to spend ten days in a recreation area in Asheville, North Carolina. Paul Dane was there, so we met up again. I was allowed to bring my wife. We had ten wonderful days of swimming and sightseeing, dancing at the ballrooms and all that stuff. By that time we could eat regular food, so we enjoyed ourselves.

After our time was up, I sent my Mary home and I went on to Camp Rucker in Alabama where I was supposed to be a rifle instructor, something I didn't want to be. I had enough of rifles! When I arrived, I went into a casual company and then I went to Company E of the 144th Infantry Regiment, a training regiment. A first sergeant named Wilson, a big guy, had a young soldier take me to the barracks. Later on, I went to see the company commander, who wondered why I hadn't been discharged because of all I had been through. I told him that I had to wait for my records to catch up with me.

When they got ready to close that camp down, I got a two-week furlough and then went back to Fort Benning where I was assigned to Infantry School, to a demonstration unit. It was a waste of time demonstrating whatever to Ninety-Day Wonders—would-be officers—while they listened to lectures. It was a waste of time. Most of the time we did whatever we wanted—write letters, get on a bus and ride into the main post, go to the movies, go here or there, just so long as we got back in time for bed check. It was a waste of time I thought.

One day my name was called. I got on a bus and rode ninety miles to Rucker, Alabama, where they told me I'd be discharged the next day. We went through the formalities on the discharge papers to be sure that everything would be exactly right and if there was anything I wanted to add. I wanted it to be marked that I was a prisoner of war.

I was discharged on 4 November 1945 and I got home in time for Thanksgiving. I didn't think I'd ever get out of that bloomin' outfit, but I did. I got home and got to work. I didn't want to go back to the mill; that was hard, dirty work. I thought maybe I'd try something else for a while so I went to Pittsburgh Plate Glass. I worked there crating for a couple of years. I thought about going to school, but the quotas were filled and there was a long waiting period. In the meantime, someone retired from the local post office. They advertised for people to take the Civil Service Exam.

I said to Mary, "I'll try that."

So I took the Civil Service test and passed. In 1949, I started out as a mail carrier and a truck driver, delivering parcels posts and things like that. I retired in 1981. I went from military service to civil service. I stayed in government service for thirty-six years.

"I Don't Know How I Lived Through It."

Robert "Bob" Davis

United States Navy
Landing Control Craft USS *LCC–80* - UTAH Beach
Born in Greensburg, Pennsylvania, 25 March 1921

"On the second day of the invasion, we were losing Rhino Ferries. These were large, empty gasoline tanks that were welded together to make big platforms. They had a couple of engines on them. They were used to transport more men and supplies onto the beach. One of them was hit and we couldn't figure out how the batteries inland were able to fire so accurately. There'd been a woman on the beach who had been there since we landed. When she disappeared, I asked one of the soldiers on the beach what had happened to her. He said, 'As soon as we figured out what she was doing, I took care of her.' The woman had been using a walkie-talkie to direct German fire at our boats. I never asked him how he 'took care of her,' but I knew."

I WAS THE OLDEST of four children. I have two sisters and my brother was ten years younger than I. We lived in a two-car garage when I was four-years-old. That's all my dad could afford. Everyone kept chicken coops in their back yards. But Mother and Dad never talked about being poor.

My father was William Davis. He had to quit school in fourth grade to help support his parents and brothers and sisters. He was a fruit and vegetable peddler with a team of two horses. When he married my mother Sarah in 1920 he sold the horses and started a little corner grocery store in the Arlington section of Jeannette. My mother was from Pittsburgh, then moved to Jeannette. She was the most wonderful mother in the world. She helped my dad in the store, just talking to customers.

It was a small store; he had one refrigerated counter for meats and two or three for produce. There were only three different kinds of soap powder and beans came in one-hundred-pound bags. In 1929, when the Crash came, Dad allowed everyone to buy on credit. If a customer was an electrician, carpenter or a plumber Dad allowed them to charge their groceries. Whenever dad needed work done in the store, he'd call one of them in to do it, then deduct it from their bill. He gave hundreds of families credit so they could survive the first years of the Depression. All Dad wanted to do was keep his head above water, because of the conditions that existed at the time. He was a good man.

I went to grade school near the Elliot Company[31] in Arlington when I was six years old. I was a skinny kid and I ran a lot. When I was in third grade, a man grabbed me by the shoulder as I was leaving the school.

He pulled me aside and said, "Davis, I like the way you run. My name is Bill Greig. I'm a marathon runner. I think I'm going to make a track star out of you."

He pointed his finger an inch from my nose and said, "Don't ever smoke and don't ever drink coffee."

Now, I'm eighty-five-years old and I never smoked or drank coffee. I was disciplined my whole lifetime. I took care of my body and I was number one in the State of Pennsylvania when I graduated from high school. I was breaking track records in my sophomore and junior years. That helped me get into the University of Pittsburgh on an athletic scholarship.

I graduated from Jeannette High School in 1939. Mathematics classes were my favorites. I took two years of Latin and two years of French. I wasn't an "A" student, but I wasn't a "C" student either. I had a job during my freshman year at the University of Pittsburgh, from seven to ten o'clock every night, sweeping the steps of the Cathedral of Learning from the 36th floor to the basement. I made fifty-cents an hour. That dollar-and-a-half bought me three meals the next day. The hamburgers at White Tower were two for a quarter, so I lived pretty well. My second year I washed windows in the Commons Rooms in the Cathedral of Learning. In my junior year I ran a hand-operated elevator. In my senior year I worked as a garbage man. I worked two-and-a-half hours and got paid for three.

I almost failed out of college in my first semester. What got me through was taking Engineering Mathematics. It was a four-credit course and I got a "B" in it. I had to get acclimated very quickly to being away from home. It was a survival kind of thing. I was good enough in track to be invited to Madison Square Garden, Van Cortland Park in New York and the Penn Relays.

I was almost done with my first semester in my junior year. The war in Europe was going on and I paid attention to it. I found the time to go to Buhl Planetarium to get a head start on some of the things I was going to get into in the Navy, like celestial navigation and using a sextant. There were recruitment centers going up all over the place. I volunteered right away.

When I enlisted in the Navy, they said that they needed me to stay in school until I finished, and then I could go to officer's candidate school. I graduated in January 1943. When I graduated, I told them they could do with me whatever they wanted. Five days after graduation I was on a train to Chicago for boot camp.

Four months later I reported to the Amphibious Base at Little Creek in Norfolk, Virginia. Six or eight of us were sent to MIT for three weeks of elementary training in navigation and how to use radar, which had just been developed.

Two weeks before we left, one of my commanders said, "Davis, get your ten men and get over here. You've never had gun practice."

I'd never shot a gun in my life. The instructor told me where to stand and I shot at the target six times and I missed it every time!

A man came over, patted me on the shoulder and said, "That's it, Davis. Next!"

But there was just no time for me to take any more practice. We were rushed into service because we were all needed. None of us complained.

I went to Europe in December 1943 as an ensign. It was seven-and-one-half months before the Normandy Invasion (OPERATION Overlord). The safest way to get to England was to go up the Firth of Clyde, to Scotland. We got off in Glasgow and took a night train south to England. The English people were so friendly and co-operative. The mood of the people was one of realism. When the Germans bombed in the night, we'd all go into the underground shelter until it was over. In the morning, we'd see homes with large holes blown out of the walls. Women with scrub brushes would be cleaning sidewalks and men would be repairing holes with plywood and paint. Soon it was hard to tell that there had been a bombing the night before.

I was assigned to the USS *LCC–80*, a "Landing Craft, Control." It was fifty-six-feet long and had a crew of two officers and ten enlisted men. I was the navigator and was in charge of the radar operator technician. Being responsible for other men was an emotional thing for me in the beginning. It was new and different. But I came to realize that I had to look at it as just a job. Even though we were all told dozens of times, over and over, about what was going to happen, no one can really describe the combat experience until one goes through it.

We knew about three days before the invasion where we were going. They kept that information pretty close until the last minute. We were all in our boats in Southampton Harbor, ready to go across the English Channel and hit the beaches on 5 June 1944. Then the invasion was postponed for twenty-four-hours. So we had ship upon ship upon ship next to each other in the harbor. If the Germans had sent planes over, they could have destroyed a lot of divisions.

The afternoon of 5 June, the boats had to get in line like they were marching in a parade. We were in this formation all night, crossing the Channel. We were the lead LCC at UTAH Beach. Not too far away to our east was the lead LCC at OMAHA Beach. As the assault craft formed up, some of them followed us and the rest followed the other ship to OMAHA.

There were spikes set in concrete through which the Germans had stretched cables about a foot under the water in front of the beaches. About two hours before sunrise, the shafts and screws on our ship got caught on one of those cables. We were dead in the water, but the troops had to keep moving toward the beach. The first wave was able to make it the rest of the way on their own. There was a destroyer heading straight for us preparing to blow us out of the water because no one was supposed to stop. We broke silence with the signal lamp and told them we had a problem and were trying to get free. We sent two guys over the side with hack saws and they freed us. So we were about forty-five-minutes late getting into the rhythm of the invasion.[32]

On the second day of the invasion we were losing Rhino Ferries. These were large, empty gasoline tanks that were welded together to make big platforms. They had a couple of engines on them. They were used to transport more men and supplies onto the beach. One of them was hit and we couldn't figure out how the batteries inland were able to fire so accurately. There'd been a woman on the beach who had been there ever since we landed. When she disappeared, I asked one of the soldiers on the beach

Ensign Bob Davis, England, *1944*.

Bob Davis' USS LCC 80, the boat he took to UTAH Beach on D-Day, *6 June 1944*

what had happened to her.

He said, "As soon as we figured out what she was doing, I took care of her."

The woman had been using a walkie-talkie to direct German fire at our boats. I never asked him how he "took care of her," but I knew.

At UTAH, no enemy planes ever got through to the beach. Our Air Force took good care of them. There were some gun emplacements in the hillsides that were firing down on OMAHA Beach. We had a difficult time with those, until the Army got in behind them and smoked them out. We would lead the landing craft until we got forty or fifty yards off the beach. Our ship had a shallow draft of twelve or fourteen inches. We continually guided the landing craft back and forth from the ships to the beach. As soon as a troop ship was unloaded, they had to hurry back to England to pick up another unit. We did that for seventeen straight days.

When our job was done, we returned to Plymouth, England and got cleaned up. Then we got on a freighter back to the United States. I returned to Little Creek following a thirty-day leave and the commander told me there were orders coming down to send us through the Panama Canal and into the Pacific. About a week later those plans were put on hold. I went to work at the Naval Photo Intelligence Center in Washington, D.C.

I was in the States for eight or nine months. Shortly before I was discharged I was promoted to lieutenant, junior grade. I didn't get my full honorable discharge for several years, though. My monthly pay as an ensign was around $200. Those were good wages. It went up to $230 when I made lieutenant, jg. None of us ever carried a lot of money around. I sent probably half my paycheck home each month.

On VJ-Day I went to synagogue to pray. I continue to do so every year. After the War I went to work with my father at the store in Greensburg. Later we expanded to three large supermarkets. I belong to the American Legion and the VFW.

Veterans Administration doctors decided that I received nerve damage in my ears from the seventeen days of bombing and shelling I went through in Normandy. But I count my blessings because there were too many men who never made it home. To this day, I don't know how I lived through it. I consider my survival to be a blessing and an obligation to walk humbly and act justly. I was in the same clothes for seventeen days, I ate K-rations, I fell in the water, I got banged around and I never knew what day it was. None of that made any difference, because we all had an important job to do.

The Tanker

John J. DiBattista[33]
United States Third Army
4th Armored Division
"Olympic"
25th Cavalry Reconnaissance Squadron (Mechanized)
Combat Command B
Born in Greensburg, Pennsylvania, 4 January 1925
York, Pennsylvania

[Mr. DiBattista's story, "Cowboys and Germans," appears in the Center for Northern Appalachian Studies The Long Road: From Oran to Pilsen, published in 1999. The following are anecdotes he submitted to the Center especially for An Honor to Serve.]

Iggy

Ignatz Klics (we called him "Iggy") was born in Europe. Iggy's father got his family out of Nazi Germany and brought them to the United States. For some reason his father returned to Germany with the intention of returning to America, but the Nazis arrested him and he was never heard from again.

The War was a personal thing to Private Ignatz Klics. Iggy also fully understood the German psyche as it related to responding to authority. He spoke fluent German and had the innate talent to transform his manner, gestures, posture and he assumed a haughtiness that made the German civil populace tremble and German soldiers snap to attention. I personally witnessed a German farmer who had a large contingent of Hungarian slave laborers lose control of his bladder during a confrontation with Klics.

One day in April 1945, just after President Roosevelt's death, the 4th Armored Division was the easternmost unit of the entire Western Allies drive into Germany. We were approaching the outskirts of Chemnitz (we later turned over this huge, hard-fought-for chunk of territory to the Soviets for their Zone of Occupation).[34] We had been ordered to halt our offensive by SHAEF(Supreme Headquarters Allied Expeditionary Force).

Iggy and I were standing in the street of a town we had just taken. Opposite us, across the street, was a crowd of townspeople, five-deep, with their backs to a building. Iggy was watching them intently.

He turned to me and asked, "Do you notice anything unusual about that crowd of Krauts?"

"No," I answered.

"Look at the last row of people. About in the center there are three men. Take a good look at them."

I did as he asked and noticed three men who looked to be in their twenties or thirties, their overcoats buttoned to the chins, prominently standing out among the crowd of mostly elderly and children.

"They're soldiers," Iggy said, "civilian clothes or not!"

Iggy paused and then went into his transformation.

"Let's go," he said.

He started his "strut" across the street, his right wrist bent and cocked on his hip. His face was expressionless except for the fire in his eyes. As he approached the first row of people they instantly parted to make way. He halted in front of the first young man.

Du bist soldat? Iggy firmly asked the first man.

The first man snapped to attention, clicked his heels in the process and shouted, *Jawohl, Herr Oberst!* (The first man thought Iggy was a colonel, the way Iggy approached him).

Iggy tore open the collar of the first man, revealing the uniform of a German soldier. Iggy repeated the scene with the other suspects.

Their response was the same. *Jawohl, Herr Oberst!*

One of the suspects was wearing an Iron Cross. Iggy reminded them that soldiers hiding their identities by wearing civilian clothes didn't qualify for protection under the Geneva Convention. I witnessed Iggy "do his thing" many times in combat and in occupation duty after the War. I never ceased to be awed by the instant "Jekyll and Hyde" metamorphosis of the enigmatic Ignatz Klics.

The Mad Russian

My buddy John Marko and I rode together with 3rd Platoon, B Troop, 25th Cavalry Reconnaissance Squadron, Mechanized, a unit of "Tiger" Jack Wood's 4th Armored Division. John was the son of immigrant parents from the Ukraine. He fluently spoke the language of his parents, something that was common with first generation Americans of that era. When we liberated slave laborers, John always took care of the Ukrainians by opening the food storage lockers of their captors and encouraging them to fill their starving bellies. Oh, what magnificent celebrations when we "liberated" the Schnapps. John Marko was to those unfortunate people, their Bolivar,[35] their Garibaldi.[36]

John and I were on the high sea aboard the nine-thousand-ton *India Victory* during the week of Thanksgiving 1945, bucking the weather of the North Atlantic, hanging on for dear life to anything we could. The skipper broke a record for such a ship Le Havre to Boston in eight days and so many hours.

We sat out the first night home in the harbor looking at the lights of Boston. There was a longshoreman strike and no one to unload us. Needless to say, the situation fomented an ugly mood with the combat vets on board. The next day a couple of longshoremen bucked the picket line and got us off. We proceeded to the other side of the pier where a train was waiting to take us to Camp Myles Standish.

Right after getting to our seats, we noticed a train next to us loaded with German POWs waiting to board the *India Victory* for return to the *Vaterland.* They were wearing the khaki uniform of the Afrika Korps. They were also smiling and waving at us, something that infuriated Marko.

John jumped out of his seat and shouted, "I'll show those Kraut sonsofbitches! I'll take those goddammed smiles off of their goddammed faces!"

John vaulted off of the train and marched up and down between the trains shouting and waving his arms, "Berlin *KAPUT*! Nuremberg *KAPUT*! Munich *KAPUT*! Hamburg *KAPUT*!"

When John was done ranting, there wasn't a German smile left. John had just executed his last mission, successfully, against the German *Wehrmacht.*

About seven or eight months later, I was honored when John asked me to be best man at his wedding. He said it would be the first traditional Ukranian wedding to be performed since before the War. It was an uproarious three-day party. It reminded me of the Ukranian slave laborers celebrating their liberation. However the marriage celebrants of Tonawanda and Buffalo, New York left out one honor. They didn't kiss John's feet as the liberated slaves did.

Gilpin

During early spring of 1944 the planners for the invasion of northern Europe discovered they failed to make plans to insure replacements for the casualties incurred while gaining a beachhead on French soil. Where would they get the replacements? They decided to strip the divisions that were training in the States of their privates and privates first class. I was a member of Company C, 18th Tank Battalion, 8th Armored Division. There were at least ten privates and privates first class in a medium tank platoon. Not all of the potential corporals and technicians, fifth grade (gunners and drivers) had yet been promoted. In my tank crew of five, three of us didn't "make the cut." Our gunner had yet to be promoted to corporal. Out of twenty-four enlisted men in a tank platoon, about half were to leave.

Our first stop was Fort Meade, Maryland. During this move I became acquainted with a Private Gilpin. Gilpin was a tall and lanky guy. He said he was from Illinois but he spoke with an accent that we characterized in those days as "hillbilly." Our barracks were about seventy-five yards from the edge of the post bordered by Route 175. Lining the other side of 175 was a string of bars. We called the area "Boomtown." The bars were Spartan in looks and furnishings. They looked like barns with storefronts. Gilpin and I decided to go to Boomtown and have few beers. After a couple of beers in some of the saloons, we were walking along the road and decided to go into one of the bars to use the restroom. We walked in and realized the total population of this crowded joint ("joint" in the true sense of the word) were exclusively Airborne guys. Luckily, before we left Camp Polk we had to remove our 8th Armored insignia from our shirts. The Airborne hated Armor. Gilpin was carrying a long neck quart of beer. Our walk to the back of the building was uneventful. There may have been halfhearted taunt or two for the "straight legs." We entered an empty toilet. It was as plain as it could get—no urinals and just a wall with a cascade of water from a perforated pipe with a ditch in the concrete floor. Gilpin was to my left. While we stood relieving ourselves, a drunken paratrooper came in and took his place to Gilpin's left. He glances to his right and sees the imprint of the distinctive triangle design of an armored patch.

He says, "Oh! One of those armored sonsofbitches, eh?"

Gilpin didn't say a word. The quart of beer was in his left hand. He didn't even look at the guy. He executed a vicious backhand swing and smashed the bottle in the paratrooper's face. I'd never see a body go down like that until I got into combat.

I said, "Gil, the next paratrooper comes in here, we'll be dead meat."

"Take it easy, John. We'll walk out slowly as if nothing happened."

We left the restroom and started to walk toward the front door. It seemed we'd never reach it. Surely, with all of those guys drinking beer, one of them would have to go to the latrine.

We got outside, and as soon as we got by the front windows, Gilpin said, "Now run!"

We ran like hell back to the barracks. The next day we shipped out to the staging area at Camp Kilmer.

On the Way to Bastogne, December 1944

After a grueling, nineteen-hour, 130-mile road march, our platoon stayed overnight in Neufchâteau, Belgium. At around 5:30 in the morning, we were awakened and informed that our platoon would be the point. We rotated that duty on a daily basis. Every third day we would be on point. That meant that our Peep was to lead the entire Combat Command B. Sergeant Hal Mayforth[37] had the map and he was to guide the command. I was the radio-operator and machine-gunner. Private Sims was our driver.

We started down a secondary road while it was still dark and in a heavy snowstorm. Combat Command A used the Arlon-Bastogne Highway. Just after daylight, we started passing woods on the left that came up to the road. The boughs of the trees and the road were covered in a heavy snow that seemed to muffle the sounds of our vehicles. The tension increased with each mile as we anticipated running into the enemy.

Suddenly, from the woods, we heard, "Hey, GI!"

Sergeant Mayforth halted the column. He asked Sims and me if we had said anything.

We replied in the negative, but confirmed that we had also heard the voice.

Then, we saw snow being shaken of some bushes, followed by a man with his hands raised and shouting, "Don't shoot! We're 101."

Then, eight more men stepped out. They were in terrible condition, with heavy beards and soaking wet from the heavy snow, so wet the overcoats they were wearing looked black. They weren't wearing helmets. We had heard about Skorzeny's[38] commando group, so we asked them some American pop-culture questions to convince ourselves that these were American soldiers. They told us they were members of the 326th Engineers of the 101st Airborne that had been cut off from their units during the fighting around Bastogne. We sent them to the rear and proceeded on our way.

The scenario was repeated a few miles down the road where men suddenly appeared from the woods shouting, "One-oh-one, one-oh-one!"

As we approached the village of Burnon, we started to receive artillery and tank fire. Our platoon leader got wounded and we evacuated him. The War was over for him. We never saw him again.

Trying to slow our advance, the Germans had blown the bridge in Burnon, so we halted and, while we waited for the engineers to come up and build another one, we went into a house to get warm. The house was on high ground overlooking the valley and river. On the opposite side of the river was a German tank facing downhill on the forward slope. Having been trained as a tanker, I couldn't believe the stupidity of the tank's commander. In training, they taught us to "hull defilade." That meant to deploy one the reverse slope with only the top of the turret and gun exposed. The tank fired trying to hit the house we were in, but because he was facing downhill, the crew couldn't elevate the tank's gun enough to be effective. All the shells landed in the backyard.

The lady of the house impressed me. She went on with her baking, completely ignoring (or at least I thought so) the explosions a few yards from her home. The tank must have been immobilized, otherwise the commander would have backed up the hill to get more elevation for his cannon. Anyway, our tanks came along and took care of the matter.

At nightfall, we got orders to go into Burnon where we took shelter in houses while the engineers continued work on the bridge. The houses were filled with soldiers, but no one wanted the upper floors because of enemy artillery. We were desperate for shelter so we broke all the rules and climbed up into the hayloft of a barn. The Germans were sporadically firing something of a heavy caliber from the time we arrived. The shell seemed to go directly over the barn and hit about one-hundred-yards down the road.

We spread our blankets on the hay and were about to bed-down when a tank crewman came up the ladder and told us we had been ordered to move out again. Cursing, we picked up our stuff and started our climb back down the ladder. I was the last one to go. Halfway down, I heard the big shell coming, but this time it sounded a little different. This time it wasn't going to go over us. It hit the roof of the barn and exploded in the hayloft. I found myself sprawled on the cobblestones outside. I picked myself up and stumbled into a house where my section was. For a few minutes, I couldn't talk. My buddies examined me with a flashlight, looking for wounds. Finally, I came around.

Mayforth ordered Sims to go out and see what happened. Sims came back and reported that the roof of the barn was gone, as well as the hayloft.

Soon, we mounted up and sat in our vehicles waiting for the order to move out. It was after midnight when 1st Platoon took over the point. It was extremely cold that night. We moved out, crossed the new bridge and headed toward Chaumont, a mile or two from Burnon. At dawn, a company of 8th Tank Battalion tanks and a company of the 10th Armored Infantry Battalion, 4th Armored Division, attacked the town.

In Chaumont, the Germans had, in addition to their own, captured tanks of the 7th Armored Division still bearing American markings. Needless to say, that made things a little confusing. The fighting was fierce and the town changed hands three times.

It was our job to defend the flanks. About seventy-five meters on the east side of the road was a forest defended by the German 5th Parachute Division. We tried to dig in, but our small entrenching tools couldn't penetrate the frozen ground. We got mattocks and full-size shovels from our armored vehicles and managed to break through the crust with them. After that, we could finish digging foxholes with our entrenching shovels.

In the middle of digging, we started to get mortar fire. High-explosive projectiles are at their greatest efficiency on frozen ground. Some of us were desperate, hugging the ground, waiting to get a turn on a mattock. A boy twenty-feet away from me (I say "boy" because we were convinced he was underage) was breaking through the crust with one. My turn to use it was next. A mortar round hit between us. Incredibly, he was wounded while I didn't get a scratch! The Germans were using small-caliber mortars and that might have been the reason why.

Second Platoon, to our right, was ordered to charge the woods. It was a strange order for a cavalry unit, because we weren't supposed to seize and hold ground. They were repulsed twice. Our troop commander, Captain Fred Sklar, got angry with them and drawing his pistol, he led the platoon to their third try. Sklar was wounded in the attempt and died later in a German POW camp.

Combat Command B's drive continued on to Grandru, and from there we went to the Arlon-Bastogne Highway where we dug in along the road with the 10th Infantry. Our mission was to keep the supply line open so that the 101st's wounded could be evacuated. After that we crossed the road and went into Marvie on 4 January 1945, my twentieth birthday.

In Marvie, we stayed in a large red-brick home. There were four 81mm mortars around the house. Whenever our men fired them, the Germans would immediately counter with their 88s. So as soon as we heard the 88s we headed for the cellar. On one occasion, the Germans finished their usual barrage, waited a minute or so, and, just as we were emerging from the cellar, fired another barrage. After the first salvo, a voice inside me said *'Do **not** go upstairs yet!'*

It also felt like some force was holding me back. It was very real to me. When the second salvo hit, the man ahead of me stumbled down and said, "John, I'm hit!"

He laid down on some hay. When I took off his upper clothing, blood spurted from his back. I stopped the bleeding with a compress, applied sulfa powder and tied down the compress. It seemed a minor wound and I envied him for being out the War. He didn't come back until it was over.

On 7 January, Patton relieved us and sent us to Luxembourg for rest and replacements. We were to prepare for the drive to the Rhine River.

Our 4th Armored Division's time in the Battle of the Bulge had been brief, but it accomplished the mission of breaking the encirclement of the 101st Airborne.

[Hal Mayforth, John DiBattista's sergeant in the 25th Cavalry, sent a number of items to Mr. DiBattista that the Editors thought appropriate to include here. Mr. Mayforth's story appears in the Center's They Say There Was A War.]

A Note to John DiBattista, 17 June 2007

I RECENTLY FOUND SOME WWII items that my Mother had saved. Here's a letter that I wrote to her. You remember the 1944 "Franksgiving" dinner, because you were one seated on one of those coffins.

Mayforth's Letter

Dear Mother and Dad:

I've just returned from the vicinity of the kitchen truck where I had dinner. With due observance of "Franksgiving" the truck was brought up from rear echelon and we were accordingly afforded the GI traditional, over-flowing mess kit. Everyone in the troop is presently so stuffed with turkey, cranberries, potatoes, carrots, peas, apple sauce and pineapples that the Third Army will be unable to clock off its daily five kilometers if everyone is in a corresponding state.

The festivity that surrounded this Franksgiving day dinner was confined solely to the quality and quantity of the food and nothing more. Certainly the environment was unbecoming and incongruous with a feast.

Our platoon was the last one to go through the "chow line" and, as we approached the barnyard where the truck was situated, the remainder of the troop had already scattered and were grouped wherever they might eat more comfortably.

Some were squatted on the leeward side of a steaming manure pile seeking shelter from the rain. Others snuggled against the sides of farm buildings, but with water from the eaves dripping on both them and their food, that wasn't much of a haven. Finally, there were a select few who not ever enjoying a meal unless seated, planted their posteriors on four wooden coffins that encased four civilians shot by Nazis prior to our arrival.

War being as unconventional as it is, we usually ignored what formerly might have been considered a sacrilege. However, I passed a chance remark to one of the men seated on a coffin that with hardly more effort he could do himself "one better" by sitting on a dead Kraut's chest, there being two inert ones about ten yards behind him. This isn't at all appropriate for an inscription, but this is fresh in my mind and I knew you would like to hear how we spent the holiday. Much love, Hal.

The Road to Chaumont, December 1944

B Troop of the 25th Cavalry was attached to Combat Command B that included the 8th Tank Battalion, 10th Armored Infantry Battalion, the 22nd Field Artillery Battalion, Battery A of the 289th Anti-Aircraft Special Battalion, Company B of the 24th Armored Engineer Battalion, and a platoon of engineers from the 995th Engineer Battalion.

Combat Command B made the 161-mile trip from the Saar Basin to Belgium in eighteen hours. I was quite certain the only person who knew our destination was our commander, General Dager, who guided the route. Rumors were rampant. At one point, as we traveled northwest, we were ordered to remove our canvas covers and proceed with headlights on. It was then that our favorite rumor took shape. We were headed back to Normandy to train troops for combat! Our trek, however, ended in darkness on the evening of 19 December.

We had gone through the town of Neufchâteau, Belgium, and bivouacked at a farmhouse on the outskirts adjacent to the road leading to Bastogne. One of the first indications we had of the severity of our situation was when all men on guard duty that night were ordered to carry carbines with grenade launchers capable of firing anti-tank rounds. In all of our combat experience we had never been given such an order.

At first light on the morning of 20 December we witnessed an ominous sight. Down the Bastogne road came a seemingly endless parade of refugees approaching Neufchâteau along the Bastogne Highway with their prized possessions piled aboard perambulators, wheel-barrows and the occasional horse-drawn wagons. We had never seen such a thing before and realized that what lay ahead of us was of considerable magnitude.

A, B, and C Troops of the 25th Cavalry were line soldiers, and each was to lead the Combat Command to which it was assigned. Within each Troop were three platoons. For the sake of fairness, platoons were rotated on a daily basis so that every third day a different platoon would ride "point." On 20 December it was 3rd Platoon's time to head the column. I was the platoon sergeant riding in the first armored car (M–8), while John DiBattista was the radio/gunner in the point Peep (Jeep). We left Neufchâteau lat that afternoon proceeded eight miles to the town of Burnon, where we bivouacked in a farm house, barn, and several outbuildings.

Next morning around two-o'clock we started to take artillery fire, and by three Combat Command B reassembled and we moved out toward Bastogne with 1st Platoon now in the lead. Jim Bennett, who had just received his field commission, was platoon leader. It was another first for us. We were operating in total darkness and in fog. When we approached Lambay Cenet, several miles away, all hell broke loose.

Third Platoon was third in line, so we were conscious only of enemy small-arms fire from the edge of the woods on our right. The bolt on John DiBattista's machine-gun had frozen. In the heat of battle, he stood up and urinated on it. How he managed to be his "plumbing" going under such duress I'll never know. Later, when the action subsided, I asked him how he had acquired that field expediency. He replied that he learned it at the replacement depot when he first landed on the continent.

The lead Peep had been fired upon by a Jagdpanzer ('tank destroyer'), a Mk III chassis mounting a fixed 75mm gun. The Germans missed, and one of light tanks from the 8th Tank Battalion came up to neutralize them. Jim Bennett jumped on to tank's rear deck to point out the enemy's position. It was then that the Jagdpanzer scored a direct hit on the tank, killing all four crew members and Lieutenant Bennett.

B Troop remained in the area, guarding the road. German paratroopers were in the woods, and we positioned ourselves on the right of the highway directly adjacent to them. And we didn't dig foxholes; we dug slit trenches. Because we were reconnaissance troops, we weren't used to static defense. Yet, we were ordered to position ourselves in the way that we did. If the Germans decided to counter-attack they could easily have annihilated us without ever leaving the cover of the woods.

On Christmas Day, our Captain Sklar sent a patrol from 2nd Platoon to reconnoiter the Krauts in the woods. They were soon repulsed and came back. This infuriated Sklar. Someone heard him say, "I'll show you how to do this!"

Sklar whipped out his .45 and led the patrol back into the woods. Sklar never came back out.

The enlisted men's reaction to Sklar's disappearance was one of exuberance. They hailed it as if it were a Christmas present. It was a far cry from the usual expression of grief over a lost comrade. Sklar was very unpopular. He always remained aloof, never recognized merit, and continually harped on deficiencies. He had an uncontrollable temper and frequently ranted out of control, so much so that he leaned toward the psychotic. Rather than generating respect, he groomed loathing.

After Sklar disappeared, the morale of the troop improved dramatically. Our new commander, Lieutenant James E. Carberry, prudently moved the troop's location to the other side of the road, away from the enemy infested woods.

We still dug slit trenches, however, and in a haphazard way. If the enemy attacked, we would've exposed our upper torsos as we stood to fire our small arms. There was also a good chance that we would've shot as many of our own men as we would the Germans. We were thankful that the enemy wasn't aware of our vulnerability, and that they never did attack us.

About a week after our first tanks rolled into Bastogne, the entire 4th Armored went back to the vicinity of Luxembourg where we were billeted in the surrounding hamlets. There we received an order to remove all 4th Armored identification from our clothing and vehicles. The order had us baffled.

As we settled into our billets, a small convoy of radio-equipped vehicles headed north. By their radio transmissions they were to convey the impression to the enemy that the entire Division was headed in that direction. We remained as a reserve if the Germans attempted another large-scale offense.

After a month in that position, we got ready to penetrate in to Germany.

John DiBattista's buddies. Left to right: Cornell, Dickson (a mechanic), Bates, DiBattista. Seated is John Marko, the Mad Russian.

Hal Mayforth, Dick Wissolik, John DiBattista. Mayforth was DiBattista's platoon sergeant in the 4th Armored Division's 25th Cavalry Recon. Mr. Mayforth's story appears in the Center's *They Say There Was a War.*

“We Killed and Killed and Killed.”

Harold E. Dougherty

United States Fifth Army
36th Infantry Division
Texas National Guard
“Texas Division,”
“Lone Star Division”
133rd Field Artillery, Battery C
Born in Penn Hills, Pennsylvania, 25 October 1921

“It was in France that Sergeant Luis Chavez got killed. Luis replaced Jack Singleton after Jack lost his legs at Salerno. Luis was killed by a mine. The explosion blew him straight up into the air. It was such a terrible explosion that we had to collect his body parts in a bushel-basket. A couple hours later and farther down the road, we found one of his arms. His death was such a shock to us. One minute he was laughing, and the next his body was in pieces.”

MY DAD CONTRACTED POLIO and it struck him so badly that one leg grew shorter than the other. When they started taking guys for World War I, they cleaned out his neighborhood. There were no young guys left except him. They wouldn’t take him because of that leg. He begged them to give him any kind of job, ambulance driver, whatever they had, but to no avail.

I was living in Wilkinsburg when the announcement about Pearl Harbor came over the radio. My mother, like any mother, didn’t want any of her sons to enlist. All three of us boys ended up in the military. My older brother was in an anti-aircraft outfit in Europe and my younger brother was in the Naval Armed Guard in the Pacific. We all came back unharmed but humbled by the tragedy of war. What sticks with me is how my younger brother begged to get out of the Navy; he wanted to go to the Army like his brothers. He couldn’t do it. He was told that they needed men in the Navy.

The time came for me to go into military service. That was in October 1942. I took basic training at Fort Bragg, North Carolina.

I was picked one day during training to lead a group of soldiers down a hillside. I was supposed to show them how to do it in the proper manner. So I did one of those John Wayne yells and then started down. To stop our advance, they had strung a wire across the pathway. I didn’t know it was there, and it caught me across the ankles and threw me down the hillside. That was my introduction how not to lead soldiers into battle.

I had some experiences in training whereby I ran into authority and discipline, and I learned very quickly, after a few episodes, to learn to be quiet and listen. One time, late at night, I was in the latrine and everybody else was in bed. For one reason or another, the intercom system was on in both our barracks and in the officer of the day's office. Someone in the barracks room said an uncomplimentary remark about the officer in the barracks and he heard it. Right away he came up and accused me. I said I was innocent, but he had to blame someone. He decided to make us all pay. He turned the lights on in the barracks and had everybody fall out with full pack. Once we were outside, he marched us up to the parade field; it was raining cats and dogs at that time, and we marched back and forth, back and forth, for a couple hours until he stopped us. Then he asked if anybody had anything to say. I was very new to the Army so I spoke up. I said I thought it was unfair to punish a whole group of people for the sayings of one person.

He said, "I'll see you tomorrow morning."

The next morning I went down to his office and he disciplined me. He sent me out into the field where there was a parking lot full of trucks, and I washed trucks all day in the rain.

Another time, we were having a weapons class, learning how to care for and tear down weapons and put them back together in a certain amount of time. A call came over the intercom calling for fellows for KP duty.

The officer who was teaching us said, "You, you, you, you," to four random soldiers.

The class went on and we got another call from the kitchen, "Those four didn't show up. Send four more."

The officer said again, "You, you, you, you."

This time he picked me.

I hadn't learned my lesson yet. I spoke up and said, "I wasn't picked the first time. Why was I this time?"

I wanted to learn about the guns rather than go to KP.

He said, "I'll see you in the morning."

That was my next level of education on how to keep quiet. He had me scrubbing floors, digging holes, all kinds of things. I learned after that to keep my mouth shut and to never volunteer for anything.

In North Carolina we were training at a spot called "Pneumonia Hill." It was a very cold winter and I ended up with pleurisy. To treat me, they taped the middle of my chest all the way around to the middle of my back.

When the time came for them to take the tape off I said, "I'll take it off."

"No," they said, "We take it off!"

And they did. They pulled the tape, and they took some of my skin with it.

Once I finished my basic training at Fort Bragg, I went by train to Camp Edwards, Massachusetts, the embarkation point for the 36th Infantry Division. I became a replacement in the division, assigned to the 133rd Field Artillery Battalion. Our job was to support the infantry with 105mm Howitzers.

We shipped out from Camp Edwards for North Africa by way of New York Harbor.[39] The weather was hot, but the Army made us wear our wools in order to fool German Intelligence into thinking we were going somewhere else. On the way over, one fellow died of an illness and they preserved him in a freezer until we landed. Soldiers weren't supposed to be buried at sea, so they preserved him until we hit land.

We also had a fellow go overboard. He was a guy some people didn't like. They just didn't accept him because he was a little different in the way he spoke and acted. He was a loner. One morning he didn't show up for roll call. They searched for him all over the ship, but he was gone. I don't know to this day whether he went overboard because of a choppy sea, or whether some people made sure he went overboard.

In Africa the Army kept us in reserve. Only our officers went up to observe the battlefield. The fighting was winding down and we weren't really needed, but they did train us for the next step, the invasion of Italy.

One night, after bedding down, I felt a little uneasy. I lit a candle inside the tent and saw hundreds of bugs running all over my body. Someone explained that though the bugs were annoying, they were harmless, so I disregarded them and went back to sleep.

We could use our free time the way we wanted. One evening, around dusk, we were sitting around playing cards, listening to music, writing letters and so on. Our captain came in and ordered the first sergeant to get us all in line with full packs. We did as we were told, and then we started to march. We marched for hours through torrential rain and mud. Finally, after hours of marching, we came to an open field, and the captain ordered us to pitch tents. Once everything was in order, they told us to bed down. It was all mud, but we bedded down anyway. We weren't settled in very long when the captain ordered us to start marching again. We had to take everything that was soaked in water and covered in mud and pack it back up. That meant our loads were twice as heavy. We marched until daybreak.

When we got back to our starting point, the captain came out and said, "You know, I've noticed since we've been in Africa, that you people never talk about the Germans. You'd swear there was no war going on. You're probably very angry at me for doing what happened last night, but don't blame me. I had nothing to do with it. You're here on account of the Germans; the Germans brought you here. I didn't bring you here. You better get toughened up to it. Blame the Germans for all this."

I remember my buddy; how he complained! I took it in a good stride. I laughed all the time.

Finally, we shipped out for the invasion of Italy.[40] We were the first American division to set foot on the European mainland. It was also my first taste of combat.

When we were preparing to go ashore, I noticed my life preserver wasn't working and told the sergeant that I didn't want to carry it.

"The rules are every man going off this ship's going to have a life preserver on him," he said.

"But it's not working."

"That's what the rule says: every man going off this ship has a life preserver on."

So, I wore that life preserver, but it wouldn't have done anything for me.

The hard part of the landing was coming off the ship and getting on the landing craft. The ship rocked back and forth, and the landing craft bobbed up and down. When I came down that rope ladder and stuck my feet out to get on the landing craft, I had to be very careful. If guys didn't time it just right, they'd drop down between the ships. We were so heavy wearing all our equipment that our chances of coming to the surface alive were quite slim. After we loaded, the craft headed toward Salerno Beach.

The landing craft next to us took a direct artillery hit. When that happened, I started to wonder about my chances. All those guys lost their lives before they even saw the enemy. All their training was for naught. Thoughts ran through our minds. 'What's going on in front?' 'What's going on alongside?' We were never sure of what our emotions were going to be. We were unprepared for death, seeing so many people die beside us. On the shore, we were bottlenecked. On top of that was mass confusion.

It wasn't until our equipment caught up with us and we got organized that we took our first loss. Our sergeant, Jack Singleton, was so intent on making sure we got our foxholes dug, that he wasn't paying attention to his own. We started to get enemy artillery. He jumped to his unfinished hole, but he couldn't get his whole body in. His legs were exposed, and he lost both of them. Luckily, he wasn't killed. They got him to a hospital ship and then back home to Texas. We heard from him a couple months later. He told us he was being fitted for new legs, and then a couple months after that he wrote and said he was learning how to dance.

We landed at five-thirty in the morning. We were exhausted because we didn't sleep the night before. After digging our foxholes, we got in them and slept. The Germans shelled us all night that first night but I never knew it.

At daybreak, I got up out of my hole and looked out and thought, *'Geez, I'm in a different place!'*

The shelling had changed the landscape overnight.

I yelled, "Anybody out there?"

One of the guys said, "Where have you been?"

"I've been in the hole all night, but I don't recognize this place."

"You mean you slept through all that shelling last night?"

"I sure did!"

During our fight at Salerno we made our first kill. We heard a German tank on the road, so we positioned our gun, dropped the barrel straight down and aimed through it. The tank turned a corner, but before it could get off a shot, we fired and knocked it out. That was a glorious day!

As we moved up into Italy, we took under our wing a teenaged boy who had lost his mother and father. He stayed with us all through the War, until we were ready to ship back home.

The weather in Italy was terrible, nothing but rain and mud, mud, mud. Our feet never dried out, and the mud affected our movement, especially when we tried to climb slopes. We took a lot of casualties because of trenchfoot. When I started to get it, I told them right away, and they sent me to the hospital. They kept my feet exposed all the time; nothing was supposed to touch them. They were very itchy, but I wasn't allowed to scratch them. Once, I moved my a foot just a little to rub it against the sheet. The doctor caught me, and he chewed me out. They caught my trench foot in time, but I saw a lot of fellow soldiers who had to have their feet amputated. When they took off their boots, the flesh came off with them. A bunch of them were Japanese-American soldiers, the 442nd, the Nisei.[41] They were terrific fighters, but they stayed on the line longer than they should have. In fact, they helped save a group from the 36th who were surrounded.[42]

I was put in a hospital a later time with bronchitis. It was during the battle for Monte Cassino[43] when I was released and on my way back to my outfit. It was around that time that I started to be affected by the suffering of civilians. I was coming up a street while the Americans were bombing the top of the hill. Some of the bombs were off target, and they caused massive casualties among the people. I saw a woman by the side of the road trying to put a child's brain back into her head. A couple days later, someone put up a sign where the child had been killed.

The sign read, "This is an example of American precision bombing."

The suffering of that poor woman was unimaginable. I'll never forget that scene, never!

Not long after that, on a Sunday morning, we were staying near a farm house, and we had a command car parked behind the house next to our position. The woman of the house was inside cooking spaghetti, and she had her son come out to offer us some. The Germans fired a shell that killed the boy, ignited our command car and blew off the driver's head. His head rolled underneath the car. One minute it was a happy occasion, and the next minute two people were dead and we're carrying a woman's dead son into her house. It was strange, but a similar thing happened when we got into France. A French couple had gone out into their front yard, and we were in back of their house where our chaplain was holding Sunday service. Germans on the next hill fired some artillery, obviously at us, but it landed in the front yard, killing the couple. Unfortunately, sometimes our actions got innocent people killed.

Our division really took a hit during the fight for the Rapido River, below Monte Cassino. During the fight one of our high-ranking officers was so drunk he wasn't able to fulfill his duties. The men took exception to that. Sometime later, when he was supposed to be in his tent, one of our soldiers rolled in a grenade and blew up the tent. It turned out that the officer wasn't in the tent at the time. Pretty soon the Army got the idea that they had better remove him from command because his life was in danger. He was sent back to the States.

On our way to Rome a buddy of mine and I saw a couple retreating Germans in a field and we went out to get them. I went after the one and my buddy went after the other. My buddy wounded his guy, but I had a problem with the one I was after. He was at the back of a house, and I was at the front. We came around the corner at exactly the same time, faced one another pulled triggers. Both guns misfired, and we were both shocked! We darted back to our original positions. I reworked my gun.

I imagine he did the same. We turned again to face each other, and again our guns misfired! The second time, the German ran into a nearby cornfield. I took aim, and this time my carbine worked. I missed, and I was thankful that I did. I still wonder if he made it back to Germany to tell the story of the two misfires!

The German artillery had areas zeroed in. As soon as they saw anything crossing a grid, they'd open up. On Christmas Eve, we were on the side of hill; it was cold, it was miserable, and they were bringing replacements into our outfit. One of them looked like he was just out of high school. The Germans heard us moving around and started showering us with shells. We veterans knew where to take cover because our holes were ready. The young replacement didn't know what to do. Everyone yelled for him to get down, but he never made it. He had been at the front for ten minutes, and already they were carrying his dead body back down the hill. We never even got to know his name. He was one of those guys who hadn't started to shave. They were bringing them in all the time, and they just seemed to get younger and younger.

One day they pulled us back to Salerno to get ready for the invasion of southern France.[44] On the way we passed the tank we had knocked out, the one that was our first kill. It was still sitting at the side of the road, rusting away. It was a nice feeling to see that again!

Our landing in Southern France was a lot less brutal than the one at Salerno. We were mechanized, and we moved fast. We caught up to the German Nineteenth Army at Montelimar.[45] For once, we were on high ground. Usually, it was the other way around. They were stretched out for sixteen miles and moving slow because they had horse-drawn equipment. Dead soldiers, dead horses, and knocked-out vehicles blocked the road in places. We opened up all along that section of road, and our planes came in to strafe them. We killed and killed and killed. When the battle ended, we enlisted civilians with ox carts to take away the dead. We buried the Germans and their horses in long trenches. Some were so bloated from the heat that they burst. The stink was so terrific that we gagged.

Another time we circled a group of Germans in a forest. We had them cold, but we really weren't up for a fight in the woods, so we sent two guys in with white flags and asked the Germans to surrender. Their officer in charge said he couldn't do that, so we started shelling. We just blew that place apart. As long as there were cries and screams we kept shelling. Finally, there was silence. We had killed that whole group because one officer wouldn't give up and surrender when it was hopeless. We moved on without checking the devastation. We left behind a job for the burial people.

When I earned my Silver Star, I was in a four-man forward-observer party. With me was a lieutenant and two sergeants. One of the sergeants was named Parker Johnson, but we called him "Pop" because he was in his thirties. To us, he was an old man. I was carrying the radio, and I transmitted messages from the lieutenant to the fire control center. Then fire control contacted artillery who fired on enemy targets based on my information. The Germans were laying down a heavy barrage of artillery as we approached a walled city we were to assault. The city had a cemetery on one side.

Eventually the order came for us to fall back; the infantry wanted us to regroup and go in with a more coordinated attack. Also, they wanted to soften the town up more with artillery before the next attack. With all the noise going on, Pop and I didn't hear the command to fall back, so we were alone in No-Man's Land. I had no gun, because my gun was with the sergeant who had fallen back. So there I was with just a radio and nothing else to defend myself with. Pop had a handgun and just a few rounds. He suggested we save two bullets, one for him, one for me. In other words, we were to commit suicide rather than be captured. I told him he could just save one, for himself. Fortunately we didn't ever get to that point. Instead, I started calling fire missions into fire control. I picked out a target and asked for smoke rounds. When the smoke round hit, I determined how much more distance I needed to hit what I wanted to hit. Once they came close enough to the target I called for high-explosive shells. That's what I did, and the artillery took effect. The Germans hadn't counterattacked before the barrage. Instead, they stayed behind the walls and the artillery kept them pinned down. In the meantime, they returned fire. At one point, I called in a command to fire twenty rounds of high explosives on them and the Germans fired just a second or so after I called it in. Pop thought our shells were landing on us. That wasn't out of the question in a situation like that, but my measurements were correct. It was just that the fire and counterfire were so timed and intense he couldn't tell the difference.

There was a lull in the battle. It was getting dark, and our chance of survival was nil. We had to get out of there. We headed back with me still carrying the radio, but it was muddy and I was weighed down by the radio and I kept slipping. Pop was way ahead of me. A sniper in the cemetery was shooting at us, and every time he'd shoot we'd hit the ground, get our breath back and get up and run again. Luckily, the road we were running beside was elevated so he kept shooting across it, and we were able to take cover when prone.

The sniper in the cemetery earlier shot a medic that had been moving through the same place as Pop and me. It was surprising how powerful that bullet was; it had gone right through the medic's torso, from right shoulder to left hip. I'll never get that picture out of my mind of two medics carrying that wounded medic back. Medics didn't carry weapons and weren't to be fired on. That got to me because I always liked to go by the rules, but there are no rules in war.

There were many times that my life was on the line, but fortunately it wasn't my time to go. I was with the forward observer party and we were in a valley. We had just gotten into a house, and I was standing in the back doorway tuning in the radio, trying to get fire on a German tank. The tank's gunner fired first and hit the house. Many inside became casualties. I was just blown into the back yard. I'd been in the right place at the right time.

One time I was squatting over a hole I had dug, attending to my toilet needs, my bare backside in plain view. A sniper took a shot at me. I jumped up, pulling at my trousers, stumbling, running, wetting on myself. My comrades thought it was funny. I couldn't understand how the sniper could miss a six-foot-four target with a bare backside. He must have been laughing as well. Thankfully, he missed.

Sometimes pure instinct saved me. Once we were approaching an open field the

Germans had just evacuated, and it was filled with foxholes dug by them. The Germans started to shell us as we moved through the field. As soon as that started, we scrambled for cover. The soldier next to me jumped in a foxhole, and I jumped in on top of him. He couldn't handle the situation for some reason and cracked. Whether it was claustrophobia, or whether he thought I was a German, I never did find out. He lost it entirely, screaming out of his head, thrashing in the hole, doing everything to try to get out, but I wouldn't let him out because the artillery was bursting all around us. Finally, when the artillery stopped, I let him out and he started running around all wild. The medics had to take him back to the hospital. When he returned a couple months later he was okay, but it was a very frightening situation to be in when it happened. I felt so bad because I thought I had caused his crackup by jumping in on top of him, but all I was trying to do was save myself. It was just instinct.

In combat, I saw a lot of things. We all did, and we saw it for three hundred and sixty-six days. There were times when we didn't fire a shot, and there were other days that were just the opposite.

Whenever we liberated French towns, intense emotions broke out among the locals. While the Germans were out one end of a town, and we were coming in the other end, the loyal French people would take into custody the people who had fraternized. There were telephones poles all along the streets and on each we saw hanged men. With the women, they'd take them and cut their hair off, bare them to the waist and paint swastikas on their breasts. It was amazing how quickly the people's emotions changed. One minute they were so happy about being liberated, celebrating with us, and the next minute they were hanging and otherwise punishing collaborators.

One thing we hated was the "Screaming Meemies." We called them that because of the noise they made. Their shrapnel wasn't bad, but the concussion was. One time I was out in the front yard of a house when a Screaming Meemie hit it, went inside and exploded. A bunch of guys who survived came running out with blood streaming out of their noses and ears from the concussion.

We saw a lot of tough situations that were hard to handle. At a place in France, we came upon ten dead American POWS who'd been shot by the Germans. Farther along, there were two German soldiers lying dead in the middle of the road. Normally, we'd have stopped, picked them up and set them on the side of the road but, being so upset at seeing their buddies killed, the fellows driving the trucks just ran over the bodies until they disappeared into the mud.

It was in France that Sergeant Luis Chavez got killed. Luis replaced Jack Singleton after Jack lost his legs at Salerno. Luis was killed by a mine. The explosion blew him straight up into the air. It was such a terrible explosion that we had to collect his body parts in a bushel-basket. A couple hours later and farther down the road, we found one of his arms. His death was such a shock to us. One minute he was laughing, and the next his body was in pieces.

A lot of the fellows liked to take souvenirs home with them. They'd go into houses right after the Germans pulled out even though we had been instructed not to, especially because of booby traps. There had been cases of fellows losing their hands because of booby traps.

After our final push through Germany into Austria, the War ended. From Austria we were sent back into France where we heard the terrible news that they were going to send us to the Pacific. But the Atomic bomb ended that notion. The Italian boy who had been with us all the way to the end had to leave us. Some of the guys tried to hide him in the ship, but he was discovered and sent back. We had to leave him but we all felt that in the couple years he'd been with us, he'd become capable enough to look out for himself.

I didn't have enough points to leave for the States with the first group, so I was placed in the 63rd Division until it was my time to go back home. They offered me the rank of first sergeant, but I refused the promotion because I would've had to stay longer overseas, and I wanted to go home. I left the Army as a technician, fifth grade.

When I got out of the service I went to Robert Morris Business School on the GI Bill. While I was attending school I married Elva. We raised two daughters and have five grandchildren, one great-grandchild and are expecting more. Elva and I have been married fifty-seven years, and we are thankful for a life of blessings.

I graduated from Robert Morris and eventually went to work with People's Natural Gas. I worked there until retirement.

Jack Thompson, my granddaughter Melissa's husband, nominated me for induction into the Hall of Valor, Soldiers and Sailors National Military Museum and Memorial, in the Oakland section of Pittsburgh. I was accepted and inducted 6 March 2005.

I lay in bed and flashes of the War pop into my head. I think what comes back most to me is the suffering, especially among the civilians. It's been over sixty years, but still I see those civilians in my mind.

September 1944. Harold Dougherty poses with buddies and members of the FFI (Free French or French Forces of the Interior). LR: "Huck," Julien (FFI), Dougherty, Lowell. Kneeling LR: Ernest (FFI), Bill (?).

The 105mm gun crew ready for action. Harold Dougherty second from right.

Harold Dougherty with Sergeant Roberty Lynch.

Harold Dougherty (right) with Charles Fellona.

Harold Dougherty (far left) and buddies prepare to receive their medals for valor.

Harold Dougherty receives his Silver Star Medal.

Harold Dougherty on the day he was inducted into the Hall of Valor, Soldiers and Sailors Memorial, Oakland (Pittsburgh), Pennsylvania.

“Don’t Cry, Honey. He’s Home Now.”

Joan Baxter Dunlap
United States Navy WAVES
Born in Beaver, Pennsylvania, 8 January 1925
New Brighton, Pennsylvania

“Another time, Norma and I were riding on a bus and it was awful crowded. Again, we were going into town. There were two gentlemen who got up and gave us a seat and we thanked them and sat down. Well, these two Marines had been standing there talking and carrying on and making smart remarks before we even sat down. After we sat down, they kept it up. The people around us were getting annoyed, but we couldn’t do anything about it. They both had been drinking. Finally the one Marine said, ‘Why don’t you two get up and give the seats to somebody that deserves them?’ That’s the kind of harassment women in the service sometimes had to put up with, but no one knows much about that.”

I worked at Babcock & Wilcox Tube Company in the East Works office after I graduated from high school. I’d leave to go to another office, and some of the men would come in and sit down with grease on their pants. I’d come back and end up sitting on the grease. It seemed I was always sitting in grease. That happened so many times that it finally got to me. Another experience that pushed me toward the service was the time I bought a nice, expensive pair of shoes. To get to our plant I had to go through the muddy mill yard and I always got mud on those shoes. Every time I came home I let them dry, then brushed them. They finally fell apart. I found out why. The pickling plant nearby had spilled acid in the mill yard and it ate through my shoes. That was the final straw. In 1944, I quit and joined the Navy. I was supposed to leave in October, but there were a couple postponements and I didn’t leave until December.

When we got to boot camp in the Bronx, in New York, it was the coldest part of the winter. It was really cold! We weren’t allowed to put our hands in our pockets when we marched because we had to swing our arms, and we only had cotton gloves to warm them. There were a lot of girls that got frostbite because of it. We wore Havelocks that covered our hats, and sometimes rain and snow would freeze on them. We had only two minutes in the mess hall to finish our meals and didn’t have time to take anything off. So we unsnapped the neck part of our Havelock and pushed it back. Then we’d lean over and start eating. Then the hat thawed and water dripped onto our food. We had a lot of fun with that!

When we’d go outside for formation, we’d have to stand at attention until the whole building emptied, and then we’d all march together. We sometimes sang to keep warm, but if the flag wasn’t up, we weren’t allowed to sing, so we just stayed cold and marched to mess or classes or wherever we were going.

During boot camp each recruit had an admiral in her bed every night! At least, that's what we called our blankets! When we were given orders for fire drills we were told to grab our admirals and get out of the barracks as fast as possible.

We did our boot camp at a college, so the barracks didn't seem like a barracks to us. It was really nice and comfortable because it had been a dorm. We had to keep it clean, and they checked everything with white gloves during inspection. There was a girl in our cubicle who wasn't too clean. She gave us a few problems. Some of the girls got together and scrubbed her down and cured her of being so untidy. After that we didn't have any more trouble with her.

One day during boot camp we were lined up to get our shots and since my name was Baxter I was first in line. After we waited for a while, two nurses came in and set up their needles, making us even more nervous. Each nurse grabbed a needle and stood on each side of me. One of them said to the other, "Which way does this go in, straight or at a slant?"

That scared me stiff, but I wondered later if she had said that on purpose to see how we'd react.

On Navy Day a bunch of us went to the special events. We saw Admiral King's flagship docked and the sailors on board waved to us and wanted to know if we wanted to come aboard. We went, and they took us on a tour of the ship and asked if we wanted to see the galley and have a sandwich and something to drink. While we were eating our peanut butter and jelly sandwiches, they said we had to sign the log. As we were signing the log, Admiral King[46] came aboard. He was very nice to us but the sailors looked pretty tense. Later we wondered if they were allowed to invite us aboard. We never received any mail from those sailors so maybe the Admiral took the log we had signed away from them.

After graduation from boot camp, I was sent to IBM School in downtown New York City. We got a leave there, and we were just like kids turned loose. We rode the ferry and we climbed the Statue of Liberty. After we got back on duty, we got notice to meet at a certain building. One of the girls was put in front of everyone and stripped of her insignias. They just ripped things off her uniform and really degraded her. That really taught us a lesson. We felt sorry for her, but we learned we'd better obey, unless we wanted that to happen to us.

After IBM School I was sent to Washington, D.C. I had joined the Navy to see the world, and what did I see? I saw D.C. I'd already been to D.C. because my uncle was an officer there and we'd go there quite a bit to visit him. I wasn't a happy sailor. But when I got there, the cherry blossoms were out. The cold snow and ice and hail in the Bronx compared to cherry blossoms in D.C. made me change my mind about the assignment there.

I was stationed at California Hall, Arlington Farms, Virginia, near Arlington Cemetery. In that hall we had fifty WAVES to a unit on each floor with twenty-five bunks down each side, two of us to a cubicle. We had top and bottom bunks, one dresser, one desk and chair and two cupboards that we had keep neat and clean. At the end of the hall there was a lounge where we got together to play games, talk and enjoy the fellowship of the service.

I was asked to go to the Navy Department building and help rewrite the *Blue Jacket Manual* because it needed an update. I never saw an IBM machine again after that, even though that's what I had trained for. We worked on the *Bluejacket's Manual* revision for a good while. They told us we had to work overtime because they needed it right away. We had two WAVES, two sailors, two civil service girls and seven lieutenants working on that one book. They told us at the time they couldn't pay us. They said, "But we'll give you time off; the time you work overtime, we'll give you that much off."

We worked overtime every night and finally got it finished!

While we were stationed at Arlington Farms there was no cafeteria for us. Instead we were put on subsistence allowance. We didn't know how long we'd be on that and I had vowed never to send home for money. At that point, my money was getting down really thin. To save money we were only spending a nickel for a pint of milk for breakfast, and we'd skip lunch. At night we'd walk from Arlington Farms, Virginia into D.C. to the Pepsi-Cola Canteen[47] and have a nickel hamburger for supper and drink all the Pepsi we could drink to fill us up. That was our only real meal of the day.

Usually we didn't walk into town on Saturday because we'd get even hungrier from the walk, but one Sunday afternoon we took a walk near the White House.

We passed a USO and I said, "Oh, we'll go in there, and maybe we'll get something to eat."

So we went in there and there were great big trays covered with cupcakes, cookies, anything we could've imagined. We dove into that and a Marine started smart-mouthing us about eating so much.

He said "You act like you hadn't eaten for a week!"

I said, "No, just two days."

We stayed because the music was really good, and we might dance. Around dinner time, we could smell the cooking. We tried to remember the last time any of us had a real meal. We couldn't believe it had been so long. Soon an announcement came over the loudspeaker, "Will the women please leave?"

So we grabbed more cupcakes and left. We never thought too much of the USO after that.

That wasn't the first negative run-in we had with Marines either. My friend Macy and I were coming out of the movies one day and two Marines came up behind us. They said, "Oh, come on girls let's go back into town."

We said, "No, we have to get back to the barracks."

They started carrying on and saying smart things and we were getting kind of upset.

Then they started pulling us back toward town, and I said, "No, we're not going back toward town, we have to get back to the barracks."

They said, "No, you don't!"

A sailor must have been watching all of this.

He hollered, "Hi, girls! I thought I'd missed you!"

He came up and grabbed our arms and away we went. We were never so tickled to see someone.

Another time, Norma and I were riding on a bus and it was awful crowded. Again, we were going into town. There were two gentlemen who got up and gave us a seat and we thanked them and sat down. Well, these two Marines had been standing there talking and carrying on and making smart remarks before we even sat down. After we sat down, they kept it up. The people around us were getting annoyed, but we couldn't do anything about it. They both had been drinking. Finally the one Marine said, "Why don't you two get up and give the seats to somebody that deserves them?"

That's the kind of harassment women in the service sometimes had to put up with, but no one knows much about that.

After I finished working on the *Bluejacket's Manual* I was sent to a Building X on Capitol Hill which was clear at the end of the streetcar line. My barracks changed from Arlington Farms to the Continental Hotel. The night I transferred they put the lights on for the first time in the city. It was like Times Square on New Year's Eve with all the people out in the streets. Everyone was just so thrilled. I could hardly get through with all my bags in tow.

While at Building X I had a really bad cold and one day the lieutenant said, "I want you to go home. Go back and get some APC pills. I can't stand to see you sniffling while you're typing."

So, I left and I got back on the streetcar and headed for Capitol Hill. I started down the path toward the hotel and I saw a big commotion over by the Capitol. I went over to see what was going on. It was General Wainwright,[48] who had come to Washington for his Medal of Honor ceremony. I stood there watching him walk up the steps. He looked so thin and I just felt so bad. My eyes got teary, not from sadness, but from my cold. I felt arms around me. I looked down, and there was a little old lady standing there.

She said, "Don't cry, honey, he's home now. He's up there."

I thanked her, but I didn't tell her I had a cold and wasn't really crying. Still, it was sad to see the condition the General was in.

I saw a few other celebrities while in the service. At a reception at the USO I met Mrs. Truman, her daughter Margaret and the Countess of Halifax. The Countess had a mink stole on that we girls thought was out of this world. We were more impressed with that mink stole than we were with her.

When Eisenhower came home, I was at the parade. There was a bunch of us standing on the curb there, and he was standing up in a convertible. We waved to him and as he turned to return the wave, I snapped a picture. That was the only picture missing after I got the roll developed. Somebody stole my picture of Eisenhower.

I was at Roosevelt's funeral also. It was quite a sad day when we heard about him dying. We just looked at each other and the tears started because we thought a lot of him. He was such a good president.

I was married near the end of my service and our wedding was something else! I liked the cake most of all. The chief in the mess hall knew me from when I had three months mess-hall duty. Because of that, he baked us a wedding cake with real butter!

During World War II, you didn't hear of butter; it was all rationed. It was such a special treat. My dad flew down to give me away and we had a Navy wedding in the Navy chapel by a Navy chaplain with a Navy organist. The only Army person there was my cousin. After that Bill, my husband, took me back to D.C. and I was discharged.

I had my time in and, since I was married to a discharged veteran, I had enough points to get out. I kept my promise to my husband and left the service. I loved being in the service though and I think if I hadn't made that promise to him I would've stayed in longer.

On the Same Team
Enlist in the WAVES
APPLY TO YOUR NEAREST
NAVY RECRUITING STATION OR OFFICE OF NAVAL OFFICER PROCUREMENT

"What's War All About?"

Daniel Anthony Ezzi

United States Seventh Fleet
Battleship USS *California* (BB–44)
"The Ghost Ship"
Gunner, 5-inch Cannon
Born in Boonton, New Jersey, 7 August 1921

"During the Battle of Lingayen Gulf a Kamikaze hit our bridge, and there was a big fire ball. Guys were running around, burning and screaming. I ran up to one guy who was on fire. I had just started patting the flames when his arm fell off. His burns were so bad, he died soon after. We found out later that the Kamikaze was a twin-engine bomber that had a five-hundred-pound bomb. The bomb didn't go off, but the plane's gas tank exploded. They found the bomb later and rolled it off the side of the ship. The blast killed forty-four crew and wounded another 155."

I WAS A FOREMAN at Picatinny Arsenal[49] in the loading division. We were playing football when the attack on Pearl Harbor happened. Someone came onto the field and said the Japs bombed Pearl Harbor. A silence fell over the field and from that moment on we all knew we were going to war and that everything would be different. I wanted to join up, but I was in an essential industry so they deferred me.

After the War started everybody said to me, "What's wrong with you? How come you're not in the service?"

Finally, I went to my bosses and I said, "I want to go down to the Draft Board."

At the Draft Board in Picatinny, Mrs. Morizetti said, "Are you crazy? You're gonna kill your mother and your father!"

I said, "Listen, I can't walk the streets. What good am I if I don't join up? I got a good job with Picatinny, but I gotta go."

So they changed my status and I ended up in Newark. After going through the physical there, they asked me what branch of the service I wanted.

I said to the recruiter, "I got three brothers in the Army. I got nothing against the Army, but my heart is set on the Navy."

The guy looked at me and then stamped, "NAVY" on my papers. I was on cloud nine.

I came home and I said to my mother, "I got in the Navy!"

She said, "I hope you're satisfied!"

We were a close-knit family. My brothers, Lou, Benny and Gabe all went into the service before me. I guess my mother wanted to hold onto her last son, but I felt I had to go.

Before I was assigned to the *California*, I came home on leave and married Josephine. We had a reception with a band. The Italian community pitched in with food.

It didn't feel like a war was going on.

The night I arrived in Puget Sound where the *California*[50] was docked they were showing a movie on the aft deck. We could see the audience from the landing craft they took us in on. When we got on board, we bumped our heads on bulkheads and pipes. We weren't used to walking around this big, old ship in the dark. They didn't assign us to our quarters that night so we had to sleep on the floor of the mess hall. The next day they started putting us into divisions. I got into the 6th Division. I had no training on 5-inch guns, but I was strong, so I guess they figured I'd be good at carrying around those heavy shells. They showed me how to load the gun and ram the gun, but the officer in charge of the gun, he pulled the trigger. The shells would be loaded into the gun by a conveyor. But we also had to learn how to load the gun by hand. We got training on both manual and automatic loading. There was also a powder man. He put the powder into the gun after the shell was loaded.

During training, the officer in charge of our gun said to me, "Ezzi, you think you can lift these bullets?"

"Sir," I said, "These ain't bullets, they're projectiles."

He laughed because I knew the proper terminology. We were a close-knit gun crew. All together, there were four of us in the gun cabinet. The projectiles would come up on the hoist and they were already timed. They set them to go off after so many seconds. We were used a lot for anti-aircraft defense. We also did shore bombardment. We had a seaplane on the *California* that would go out and radio back to us the range and where to fire. Sometimes we'd start shelling at the waterline and walk the shells inland. We'd fire for hours and being in that gun cabinet it got hot! Even with the cotton in our ears our heads rang. I got a perforated eardrum from our gun. I was loading and the cotton fell out and I didn't have another piece to put in my ear, and then the gun went off.

We'd be in that gun cabinet until they ordered a cease fire. With the heat and the noise, it was rough in there. And during an air attack, when we heard our 20mm guns going off, we knew those Jap planes were getting close. That was scary because we couldn't see what was going on outside.

It wasn't too bad being aboard the *California.* Our captain was the greatest; he should live forever! He was our second captain. The first captain, he was terrible. We were going to pull a mutiny on him because he wouldn't feed us! But our second captain, he couldn't do enough for us.

He used to say, "Anything you fellas want, you'll get."

He'd stand in that chow line, and he'd stop you and he'd say, "Can you eat more than that?"

"Yes, sir!"

He'd tell the mess cooks, "These guys can't fight on an empty belly. You give them what they want as long as they finish what they take."

After that, the cooks were slopping it on our trays! And the food was fantastic. We got ice cream too! We were treated well.

For example, prior to the invasion of the Philippines, we were loading supplies on

"They're not bullets, Sir. They're projectiles."

board the *California.* This cargo ship was alongside and we worked all night long, and the captain worked with us.

He said, "Anything you guys want, you name it and you'll have it."

So one wise guy pipes up, "Well, we want the band to come out and play for us."

It was midnight, and the ship's band came out! I about died! They had to play music all night for us, until six in the morning! And they were as mad as hell at us!

While we were loading this food, some of us took a few cans of fruit cocktail and hid them in our lockers. I had a couple gallons of the stuff. But they did an inspection because they found out some of these cans were missing. The guys were throwing theirs over the side so they wouldn't get caught.

But I got caught with mine. They brought me before the captain and he asked why I took it.

I said, "Well, we haven't seen canned fruit in our chow line since I can't remember when."

"Is that right? Forget it!" he said. "I'd have done the same damn thing."

The next day they had fruit cocktail in the chow line, as much as we wanted!

We got the good food, and we really didn't feel the motion of the ship like we would on a destroyer, except during typhoon weather. Then we could feel the swells in the ocean. The bow would go completely under the water! Once we rode swells for three days, but I never got seasick and I don't think anyone got swept overboard. We wouldn't have been able to find them, anyway. Our sleeping quarters were decent. Our bunks hung from the wall by chains and they were stacked four or five high. When we got up in the morning or for our watch, we just pushed up the bunk and locked it against the bulkhead.

We had mailboxes, and a sea plane would come by to pick up and deliver mail. Most of what we wrote was censored. When my parents wrote me they'd say that they couldn't read my letters because they were full of holes where the censors cut stuff out.

We had Sunday Mass. The services were always filled because the guys never knew what was going to happen to them tomorrow or the next day.

There was a lot of gambling; guys shooting craps, playing cards. On payday, everybody would throw their money away trying to get rich. As long as no one was abusing the situation, the officers didn't care. Gambling was something I never cared for. I just wanted to serve my time and get out. And God was with me, to make that trip for me, because I came home.

Our first action was during our invasion of the Philippines in 1944. I was on the 5-inch gun. The Jap planes were making their first Kamikaze attacks of the War. They flew low over the water between the ships so we couldn't shoot at them for fear of hitting our own ships. But we waited until they got past our bow and when they turned around, that's when we could get them. They never made it in between the ships the second time. We were ready for them. The Japs were smart. They always had one plane out of range watching the action, and reporting on what was going on so they could tell the next wave coming in how to attack us. They were nasty. We were told their pilots were all dressed in black and had a going-away party because they knew they weren't coming back.

During the Battle of Lingayen Gulf a Kamikaze hit our bridge, and there was a big fire ball.[51] Guys were running around, burning and screaming. I ran up to one guy who was on fire. I had just started patting the flames when his arm fell off. His burns were so bad, he died soon after. We found out later that the Kamikaze was a twin-engine bomber that had a five-hundred-pound bomb. The bomb didn't go off, but the plane's gas tank exploded. They found the bomb later and rolled it off the side of the ship. The blast killed forty-four crew and wounded another 155.

One of my buddies, after the fires died down, found this Jap pilot's pistol lying on the deck in all the debris and wreckage. This officer came up to him and tried to take it from him, pulling rank, you know. Our captain found out and ordered that officer to give it back to this buddy of mine.

I always felt tense after those Kamikaze attacks. When the general-quarters bell sounded, we had to get to our battle station. It made us feel jumpy. Sometimes the bell sounded and we were in the shower! I had to run out naked except for a towel and try and get dressed as I made my way to the 5-inch gun! I had to have my shirt buttoned up tight. I couldn't have loose clothing in case of fire. That was regulation. Another tense situation was a submarine alert. The destroyers would be out there throwing depth charges out. The explosions would send these huge geysers of water up. The guys would all cheer when they saw that.

When the War ended we went into Tokyo. The Japanese people thought we were barbarians. People ran like the devil from us, but once they got used to us, they couldn't do enough for us. They wanted to take us to their house. They wanted to feed us. It was strange after being at war with them.

Prior to coming home, we had to paint our ship. Each division had their own section of the ship to do. Our ship was camouflaged with different shaded stripes of gray and black. Before we came home, we had to paint that whole ship battleship gray. One day I was hung out over the side scraping paint, and I lost my grip on the scaffold and did a back-flip into the water. I went down so deep, I thought I'd never come to the surface. I fell around chow time, and all this hot water from the kitchen was shooting out of the side of the ship. I got scalded and covered in a mess of food and garbage from the dishwashing machine. They threw me a line, hoisted me up and took me to sick bay. I was burned all over. They gave me some ointment for my skin.

We also had brig duty. I hated that. One time, I had to guard a guy and they gave me a .45 pistol. Shit! I never handled a .45. This guy kept carrying on, hollering and such.

I said to him, "Listen, buddy. I don't know nothing about this .45, but don't get smart with me because I'm going to have to shoot you."

I got discharged from the Navy in Sampson, New York, and from there I came home. It was hard to get adjusted after coming home. I had a few nightmares, but I got used to those after a while. But being back home was like a dream.

I said to myself, *'Jiminy Crickets! Here I am. I'm home. Did I really go through all*

Cover of the *USS California's* 1945 newsletter *The Cub* that was put together by crew members at the end of the war. The twenty-eight page, mimeographed newsletter contains diary entries, personal accounts, rosters, memorials and cartoons on various subjects. *Courtesy: Daniel Ezzi.*

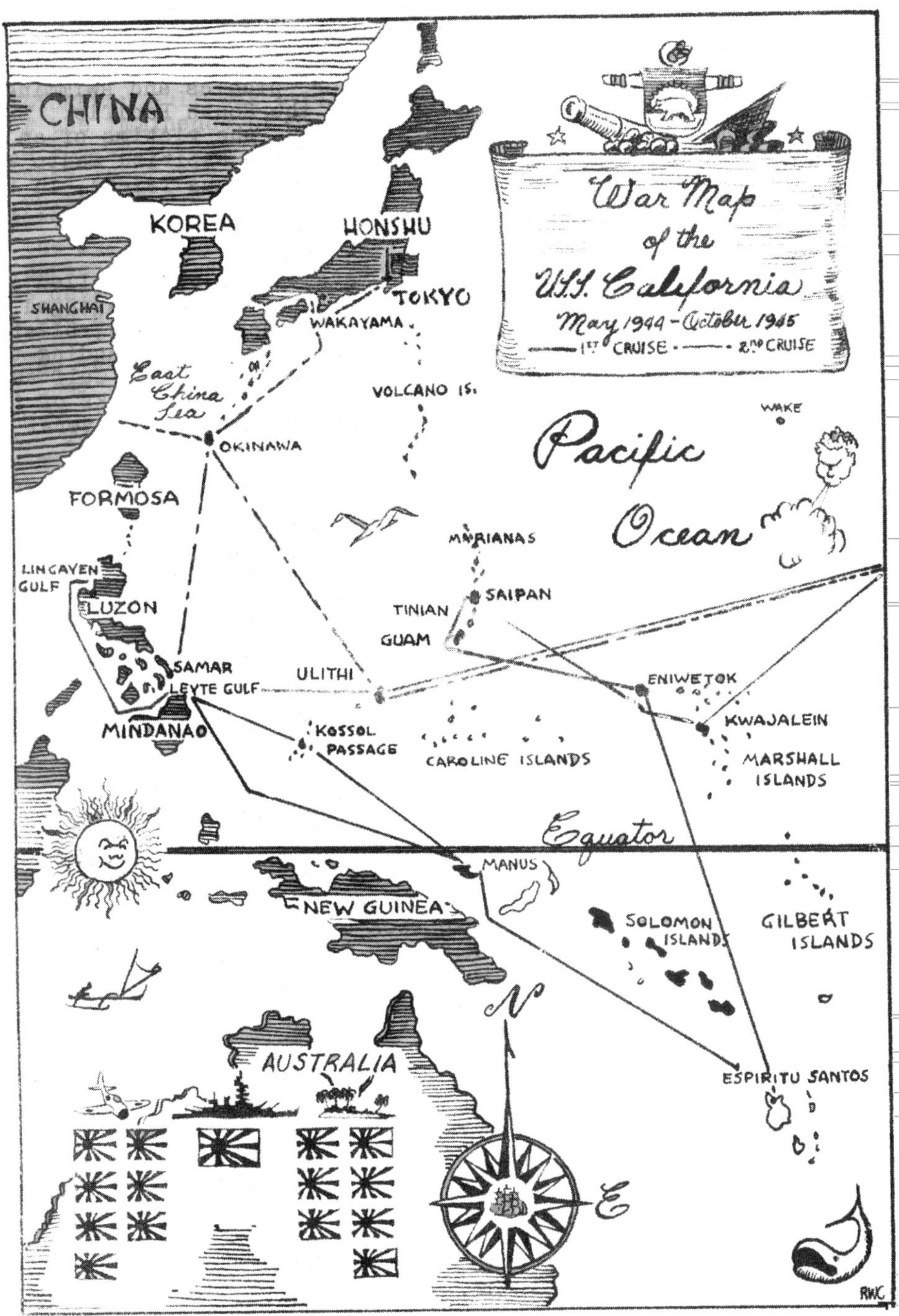

The *USS California's* war map from the ship's newspaper *The Cub.*

Some pages from the *USS California's The Cub.*

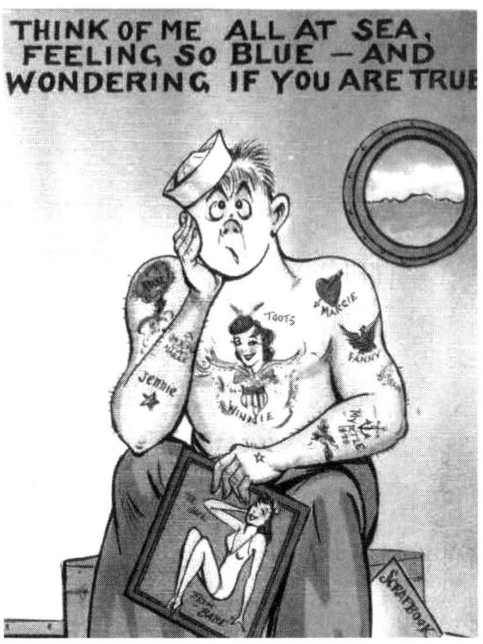

His Majesty Neptunus Rex and Court

STANDING, L. TO R, THE CHAPLAIN, DENTIST, UNDERTAKER, SCRIBE, DAVY JONES, PRINCESS, HIS MAJESTY, QUEEN AMPHRITRITE, LADY IN WAITING, THE JUDGE, NAVIGATOR, DOCTOR, PROSECUTOR. SEATED, L. TO R., ROYAL TWIN, CHIEF BEAR, ROYAL TWIN.

CUNNINGHAM 9

that?'

It was hard to believe that I went through the War and everything I saw. I never liked to talk too much about it. I just wanted to get it out of my system. I didn't want to remember some of the stuff.

After the War I went back to work at the arsenal, but they started to shut a lot down because the War was over. To keep me on they wanted me to do the pick and shovel work outside the grounds, but I wouldn't do that. So I quit and went to work at a pocketbook factory as a foreman. I had twenty people under me. I remained there until I got into the flooring business. I worked hard all my life, and it paid off.

In World War II we were one-hundred-percent together. Sometimes I can't believe what we did, and then I see the war we're in now and I wonder what it's all about. I just can't take that. I don't want to see anyone get killed anymore. I don't want to see that. What's war all about? Do you know what it's about?

The 6th Division, *USS California*. Daniel Ezzi is second from the right, last row. *Courtesy: Daniel Ezzi*

"A Guy Could Really Get Hurt in This Job!"

James P. Garrity

Fifteenth Air Force
98th Bomb Group
343rd Squadron
Born in Youngwood, Pennsylvania, 3 February 1922

"A piece of shrapnel severed my oxygen hose, but I didn't know it. We were at twenty-thousand feet and I felt myself getting woozy. I thought maybe it was just because I was scared or something. I drifted in and out of consciousness. I caught a glimpse of bombs dropping from other planes, so I flipped the switch for ours to drop, and that was all I remembered."

I WAS THE THIRD CHILD born to James M. and Sarah A. Garrity. My older siblings are Margaret and Sarah, and my younger siblings are John, Charles, and Mary Helen. We were raised during the Great Depression years, and jobs were scarce.

I was sixteen when I graduated from high school in 1938 and went to work for the American Glass Company. I worked for United States Steel-Homestead Works in Pittsburgh, and then Westinghouse Electric in Derry, Pennsylvania before enlisting in the Aviation Cadet Program in 1942. In early March 1943, I reported to the Classification Center in Nashville. After being chosen for pilot training, I went to pre-flight school at Maxwell Field, Alabama, and from there to Carlstrom Field in Arcadia, Florida for primary flight training.

My first seven hours in pilot training were a total loss. I got sick and upchucked all over the side of the plane. I fell about six or seven hours behind the other students, but managed to get through a flight in my eighth hour and I felt that I had conquered it. I soloed after eleven hours, and I thought I was doing OK, but that I still wasn't up to snuff with the other trainees. I washed out. The Air Force was fairly unforgiving—Navy flight school washouts fell back one class, but were allowed to start over—but the Air Force only gave us one chance.

Not only did washing-out threaten to end my flying career, but it practically canceled any hope I had of receiving a commission. But it went deeper than that. Washing out was a terrific blow to my pride. I had always done well in school, and I had also been at least an average athlete. I guess I hadn't yet reached an age where I would start to run into really tough problems, but I had never failed in anything I tried to do. I felt plenty blue and discouraged about it all. I called my wife to break the news.

Well, maybe I called to get a little sympathy. She sounded sorry that I'd failed to realize one of my most earnest ambitions, but she was also relieved to know that I wouldn't be flying any longer. She thought flying was very dangerous. In fact, she still does.

After three days of "massaging the sack"—days made even more heartbreaking by the fact that I could look out the window and see my buddies continue with their flight training—the Cadet Commander called me into his office and told me that I was to leave the following morning for navigation school at Selman Field, Louisiana.

I was a little surprised at those orders, and a little doubtful about whether I really wanted to take any more flight training. I'd get a commission if I graduated from navigation school, but that was about the only part of the deal that appealed to me. The next morning I got on a train bound for Selman. Along the way the wheels seemed to chant, *'Wash out, wash out, wash out, wash out!'*

All kinds of thoughts ran through my head on the ride to Louisiana, but the fear that the new training would lead to another disappointment was at the front of my mind.

When we took the classification tests, we were told that geometry and trigonometry were mandatory prerequisites to navigation training. What a joke that was! I'd had all of one semester of algebra in high school, and that was in 1934–1935. I figured it'd be a matter of time before I became a casualty of Air Force standards.

They assigned me to a flight of forty-eight cadets. As I built new friendships with my classmates, the keen disappointment of failing pilot training slowly waned. But the fear of washing out of navigation school remained. Half of the men in the flight were college grads, and most of the rest had two years of college. Only one other cadet beside me had no college training. A quota of cadets was routinely eliminated from each class, so I knew I'd be up against some pretty stiff competition.

The first couple weeks went by without a serious setback, but I wouldn't let myself be lulled into a false sense of security just because I was getting good grades. I knew the coming days would get tougher as training progressed. As the weeks rolled by, I became more and more interested in navigation, and I adopted the attitude, *'If I make it, OK; if I don't, OK, too.'*

But the more I delved into the various problems of aerial navigation, the more I wanted to succeed. I studied hard—very hard. Every Saturday we had a four-hour exam. Every third Saturday, we were treated to a six-hour exam! We also flew on regularly scheduled practice missions. I was kept so busy that I had very little time to worry about washing out. Before I knew it, training was over. I became a navigator!

I felt elated over the fact that I had successfully completed this course when some college graduates had been eliminated because of low grades. It gave me a great deal of personal satisfaction. But I felt even better on the morning of our graduation exercises. My wife was in the audience at the post theater for the ceremonies. The formal part of the program was completed and then they announced the names of the top twenty-five students of the class. They read my name as ranking eleventh in the class of 385.

As my wife pinned my wings on my blouse, she smiled and said, "Still sorry you washed out of Pilot Training?"

I laughed and said, "Pilot Training? Never heard of it."

Normally, graduates got an eight-or ten-day leave to go home and visit family and friends. There was some tension after graduation because some of the Navigation School graduates were being picked at random to get minimal training on B–25s and B–26s so that they could function as combination navigator/copilots. They were pulling names out of a hat, and I didn't want to be called. I wanted my ten-day leave to spend with my wife. We had gotten married in August 1943, and hadn't been married even a year. Thankfully, my name wasn't picked and I got my ten-day leave to come home.

After the leave, I reported to Westover Field, Massachusetts, where combat crews were formed. From there, our crew reported to Charleston Army Air Base. From March to June, we went through operational training, just flying training missions to get used to working with each other. While we were in Charleston, something happened that affected all the rest of my time in combat.

One of the B–24 instructor pilots volunteered for combat duty, and was assigned to our crew. He was a captain with two-thousand hours of B–24 time. His name was James Stewart, like the actor. Even to this day when I go to Bomb Group reunions, I never fail to get everyone's attention by casually mentioning that I was Jimmy Stewart's navigator. I then tell them he wasn't *the* Jimmy Stewart.

Stewart was an outstanding pilot. He always knew what to do. But even with all his experience, he still had to go through the same training as if he were a rookie pilot with our crew.

After we got through the operational training we went by train up to Mitchel Field,[52] on Long Island, close to Homestead, New York. Captain Stewart was the ranking officer among crews that were going into combat, so he was made "train commander." We had our full run of the train!

At Mitchel Field we got our brand new B–24. The B–24 had a ceiling close to thirty-thousand feet. The B–17 could go a little higher, but it wasn't as fast and couldn't carry as heavy a bomb load as the B–24. The B–24 was unique in that it carried on sustained operations in every theater of the War. There's still a friendly rivalry between the B–24 and B–17 guys. I heard it summed up pretty well by a pilot who flew both of them. He said you could teach your grandmother to fly a B–17, but it took a real pilot to fly a B–24.

We flew the plane to Grenier Field, New Hampshire. From New Hampshire we flew up to Newfoundland, and from Newfoundland to the Azores Islands, off the coast of Africa. It was a very uneventful trip, but I was a little terrified wondering how I was going to find a tiny set of islands out in the middle of the Atlantic. But everything worked out. We got there two minutes before I said we would, but we were "dead on" the islands. We landed and parked in a hard stand. A four-engine transport landed and the pilots got out. To our surprise the pilots were women! We expected some big guys to have been the pilots. The ladies were part of the Women's Auxiliary Ferry Service.

From the Azores, we flew to Marrakech in Morocco. Then from Marrakech we flew to Tunis, and from Tunis we headed to Italy. We landed at Gioia. From Gioia, we went by truck, a six-by-six, down to Lecce on the heel of the Italian boot where the 98th Bomb Group was stationed. We didn't know it at the time, but the 98th already had a pretty full set of missions under its belt. The 98th was one of the groups that participated in the low-level raid over the Ploesti oil fields. We first flew a few indoctrination flights so we'd get to know some of the territory right around our base. We were the southernmost group based in Italy. This was good in one way, but not in another. Because we were based in southern Italy, our missions usually lasted an hour or two longer than those of the groups up north.

My first mission was over the San Michel railroad bridge in northern Italy on 3 August 1944. Overall, we had thirty-five times over the target. The Air Force credited people that went through what we did with fifty missions, and it's in my record somewhere that I flew fifty missions. The first few missions, when we didn't get any hits in our plane, no one got shot down, and nobody got hurt, we didn't think it was that bad. But once we got some holes in the plane and we saw what shrapnel could do, it got us to worrying. When we saw a plane disappear in a ball of fire and knew ten men were gone, we felt a little guilty about fussing over a little wound. When those of us who survived a mission got back to base, we had nice warm beds to crawl into. That's why I have a lot of admiration for the infantry guys who were out there in the mud and snow twenty-four hours-a-day, seven-days-a-week.

Our Flak suits were really heavy, but they worked. They were just a couple of plates layered over other plates, like an apron, and they really weighed us down. We didn't mind the weight, especially if the suit saved our lives. Some guys refused to wear them, though, but would instead spread them on the floor of the plane and stand on them.

Immediately prior to the invasion of southern France, we were scheduled to complete our first, and only, night mission. Beforehand, we flew to practice formation, practice bombing, or to practice night formation. We had instructions not to bomb after a certain time of day because that's when the boats with Allied forces were going to be landing. One of the planes taking off from another squadron blew up on takeoff. There was a lot of debris on the runway and that delayed our taking off. I could hear them on the intercom talking about how they had to delay the takeoff for the rest of the group because it sounded like they were picking up body parts off the runway.

My most memorable mission, my twenty-second, was over the Aviso Viaduct in the northern Italian Alps. That was 13 September 1944. They had anti-aircraft guns in the mountains, and it seemed like they were firing down at us. We took thirty Flak holes on that mission, three of them in the nose.

A piece of shrapnel severed my oxygen hose, but I didn't know it. We were at twenty-thousand feet and I felt myself getting woozy. I thought maybe it was just because I was scared or something. I drifted in and out of consciousness. I caught a glimpse of bombs dropping from other planes, so I flipped the switch for ours to drop, and that was all I remembered. They told me later what had happened.

It must have been eight or ten minutes after "bombs away" before they started the crew check. They start with the tail gunner:—Tail gunner? Okay. Waist gunner? Okay. When they came to me they got no response.

The bombardier said, "Garrity's passed out; I don't know if he's hit."

We didn't have CPR way back then, so he just thumped on my chest and lifted my belt up. Thankfully, there were transportable oxygen bottles we carried on the plane, and he put one of those on me.

He told me afterward, "Your face was blue, and I didn't know what to do. They said there were fighters in the area so I had to get back in the turret!"

Once we got back, the flight surgeon said "Once you're without oxygen for five minutes, you're dead. That's just enough time to say your prayers!"

After that mission I got to thinking, *'You know, a guy could really get hurt in this job!'* I carried a silver dollar with me on all my missions, plus a nickel and a couple pennies. I also wore my wife's high-school ring on my little finger. For luck, I guess. No. It was more than simple luck. We all felt a closeness to have a personal item from a loved one on our person. My wife, Mary Lou, and I were expecting an addition to our family in January of 1945. We were hoping to get my mission completed and then getting sent home in time for the birth of our first child. It wasn't to be, though. I finished my missions on 16 December 1944. Our baby, James P. Garrity, Jr., was born on 13 January 1945. Our ship arrived back in the United States on 10 February, and I was home on leave by the twelfth. What a joyous homecoming!

The missions were anywhere from five to ten hours. There were a lot of missions where we wouldn't even see any fighters. On one return mission we were skimming right on top of the clouds. I was looking out one of the windows when, all of a sudden, an Me–109 appeared not more than thirty yards away. The pilot looked toward our plane and saluted. I saluted back. And down through the clouds he went. He might've been out of ammunition. On two straight missions we had to crash land with a flat tire. Another time, a German jet, an Me–262 came in just off to our left. Then he must have kicked in his afterburners and took off.

On our thirty-second mission, 22 November 1944, we went to the Ferrara railroad bridge in northern Italy. Captain Stewart was hit by shrapnel that almost severed his arm, and we got more than fifty holes in the plane. To get Stewart medical attention we landed at the closest Allied field, near Ancona. We had radioed ahead and the ambulance was waiting. When we landed, we left the engines running. We got Stewart down the flight deck, out through the bomb bay, and onto a stretcher. Two medics picked up the stretcher and headed alongside the plane to the front. Stewart raised his one good arm, grabbed one of the medics by his shirt and pulled him down. The stretcher went down as well and Stewart got jarred a bit, but he saved the medic's life. He would've backed right into one of the rotating propellers.

Things were not always so hectic. When our crew completed twenty-five missions, we were sent to a rest area for rest and relaxation. Our rest camp was a luxury hotel on the Isle of Capri, located in the Bay of Naples. I don't have the vocabulary to describe the beauty of Capri. We were there for ten days in October 1944. The older men and the younger boys would gather on the steps of the church in the evening and sing. The men would start the singing and the boys would join in, and the audience was encouraged to join the singing. This is one memory that has not been diminished by the passage of time. I always told myself that I would revisit Capri once the War was over.

There were times when missions did not go as planned. Such a mission was my number thirty-three. The target was the Moosbierbaum oil refinery--northwest of Vienna--and defended by ninety-three anti-aircraft guns. Our secondary target was Wiener-Neustadt (four-hundred guns). Nearby Vienna had 1,100 guns. The mission plan was to head toward Moosbierbaum, feint toward Wiener-Neustadt, then resume course to bomb the Moosbierbaum oil refinery. After the bombs were delivered, each squadron was to break right and return to base.

Here is how the mission played out. Our squadron was the lead squadron. Our plane was flying in the number-three position. One plane from our squadron turned back due to mechanical problems, leaving us with a five-plane box. On our feint toward Wiener-Neustadt, the lead plane kept right on going. Since we were headed toward the secondary target, it seemed ok. But no bombs were dropped and we were headed toward Vienna and flew a 360-degree turn over the heart of Vienna and then headed for Moosbierbaum and dropped our bombs. Number one and number-two planes were hit. Number one landed on an island in the Adriatic. Number two was hit and couldn't maintain altitude. After coming off the target as briefed, we headed for home, slowing down to escort number two until we could get over friendly territory. They were throwing out stuff to lighten their plane. When they thought they were over friendly territory, they bailed out. At a 98th Bomb Group reunion years later, I talked with Charles Wossilek, the bombardier on number two. They actually bailed out over German-held territory, evaded capture for four days, and eventually were captured and wound up in a prison camp.

After the other three squadrons dropped their bombs, they peeled off the target to the left and had a shorter route to home base. Our longer return route and the fact that we slowed down to match the crippled plane's speed got us back home a good ninety minutes after the other squadrons from our group. Needless to say, we got a royal welcome.

As I look back on our missions, they were very similar to each other, but in the same breath I could say that each had something unique about it. I was always interested in bomb-strike photos. We know from the photos that not every bomb hit its target. We could see that bombs hit fields and backyards, and I couldn't help but wonder if there had been children playing in the area. It's sometimes said that Air Force duties were impersonal, but we really had a lot to think about if we were so inclined.

No one ever really started to ask about what we did in the War until lately. The feeling was—and it was widely publicized and accepted—that when the veterans came back, they wouldn't want to talk about what they did in the War. So, at the time, people never asked.

I never talked much about World War II, so I'm making sure my grandchildren know this story. When my grandson Doug Boyle was little, he saw a box with some of my military stuff in it. I showed him a few things, and he'd ask me to tell him about a mission or two. Now, my wife, Mary Lou, my children, Jim, Larry, Suzanne, and Betsy, my grandchildren, Laura, Christine, Doug, Carolyn, and Elise, and my great-grandchildren, Lizzy, Katie, A.J., Amanda, and Caleb will know some of what I did while I was serving in the Air Force during World War II.

German Me-262 jet fighter, a formidable weapon that entered the War too late.

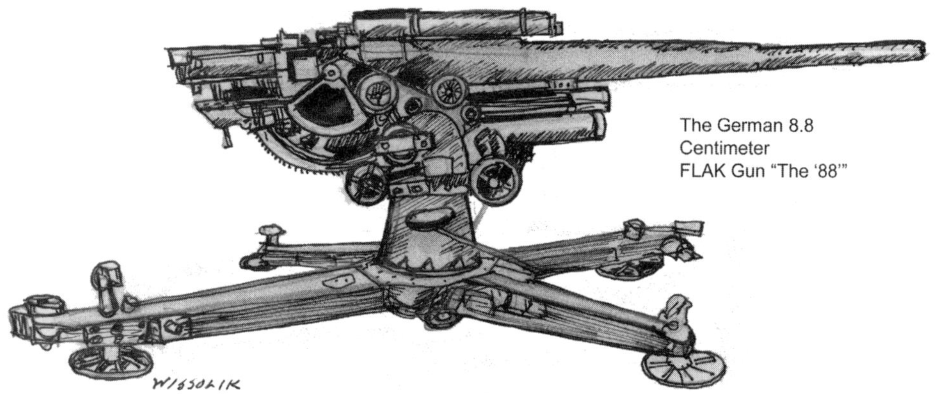

The German 8.8 Centimeter FLAK Gun "The '88'"

Jim Garrity inspects FLAK damage on his B-24.

Cowboy or Hot Dog? A Lockheed P-38 "Lightning" buzzes Jim Garrity's 98th Bomb Group Headquarters.

Innsbruck marshalling yards under bombardment by the 98th Bomb Group. *Courtesy: James Garrity.*

B-24s of the 98th Bomb Group coming off the raid through heavy flak over the Ploesti oil refineries.
Courtesy: James Garrity.

James Garrity with "Kathryn Anne." at an airfield in Italy.Sergeant Gerald Viola painted "Kathryn Anne" on the right front fuselage of this B-24 (Serial # 42-78600). The painting is combination of a typical Varga-type pinup and the pilot's girlfriend. On the left front fuselage he painted "Dopey," one of the Disney Seven Dwarfs. The plane was interned in Switzerland, *8 April 1945.*

"We Were in a Hurry to Get Those People Out of There."

Louis Gazza

672nd Amphibian Tractor Battalion
Company B
37th Infantry Division (Attached)
Born in Waterman, Indiana County, Pennsylvania, 22 April 1924
Belle Vernon, Pennsylvania

"There was a Japanese ship out in Manila harbor. It had been hit and damaged by aircraft some time before. There was a Japanese hiding on the ship. One day he swam to shore and the Filipinos got to him. They beat him to death with shovels."

MY FATHER, ROBERT Gazza, was a coal miner in Graceton, a small town near the city of Indiana, Pennsylvania. He worked in the mines all his life, until he retired. My mother was Palmera Beneri Gazza. I had five sisters and three brothers. We didn't get a car until after the War. Very few people had cars at that time. My dad walked to the mine every day. I remember walking to school in snow up to my knees, but I was small then and my knees weren't too high above the ground. We ended up in Homer City, which is where I went to high school. I liked geography and history, took Latin and graduated in 1942.

Before the service I worked for a construction company near Saltsburg. They were cutting a railroad right-of-way in that area and were drilling with a wagon drill. It was on wheels and would drill down through the rock, then they'd blow the rock with dynamite. I was a helper and the pay wasn't very much.

There was a service station near our home, and I was down there one Sunday afternoon when I heard over the radio that Pearl Harbor had been bombed. It was a low blow that the Japs would pull something like that while they had a fellow in Washington negotiating. It gave everyone more of a reason to want to fight them. Everybody was for the War. Everybody felt that we should retaliate. It was something that we felt we had to do. A lot of people volunteered. Even kids sixteen-years old were trying to get in; that's how eager they were.

I was drafted on 23 April 1943. I went from Homer City to Altoona, then to Camp Hood, Texas for training. There was a fellow from Blairsville, one from Wall and a couple of guys from Pittsburgh in my group. Then there were several from this area that I got to know once we got to Camp Hood. I enjoyed the Army life when I got into it. I liked the physical training.

Basic training consisted of thirteen weeks of calisthenics, marching, drill and a lot of what they called "forced marches." We had to run a mile with full field pack and a twelve-pound submachine gun. We had to carry a person so many feet. At the end of that training, we marched sixty miles from South Camp Hood in three days and with a full field pack. Then we had a hard-boiled egg for breakfast. We were in the tank destroyers, and I didn't know why we had to go through such strenuous training, because once we got into the vehicles we never walked anywhere. We had no radio training, but we did learn first aid. We shot the .30-caliber M1 rifle and the Thompson submachine gun. When we finally went overseas, I carried a carbine. It was a nice little carbine, but I never had to use it.

It was hot down in Texas. We put Lister bags, canvas bags filled with drinking water on tripods. In summer, the heat made the water too hot to drink. We were there during the winter, too. They got a little bit of snow down there, but it was the first time they had seen snow for years. It was funny seeing some of those people reacting to the snow.

After basic, we didn't have to go out on all the marches; we went out in our tank destroyers and had target practice. The difference between a tank and a tank destroyer was a tank destroyer had an open turret and was faster since it was less heavily armored. We went on map exercises. They sent us out at night with a compass, dropped us off at a certain place, and we had to find our way back to the camp. We also had instruction in detecting and deactivating mines. I was promoted to corporal when we were still in Texas. I had been a gunner on the tank destroyers, then I became an AMTRAC[53] commander. I was a corporal until the end of the War.

In April 1944, we were sent to Fort Ord, California and converted from tank destroyers to AMTRACs. I was assigned to Company B, 672nd Amphibian Tractor Battalion. My company commander was Captain Bullard, and the battalion commander was Colonel Gibbs.[54]

There wasn't that much difference between the tank destroyer and AMTRACs. AMTRACs had very light armor and pontoons on the sides. The cleats on the tracks were made like cups, so they could scoop into the water. Primarily, they drove the same way as a tank. The only difference is, when we'd come in from the beach we had to be careful, especially if there were big waves. Whenever we hit the beach, we'd have to shift gears quickly, otherwise the surf would flip the tractor out of control. It had two .50-caliber machine guns that had shields around them. I think the engine was made in England. It was a big, round aircraft engine, right in the back. We never had any breakdowns with engine trouble.[55]

There was a driver, assistant driver and tractor commander. It could carry about thirty troops. The cargo compartment must have been about six-feet deep, and it had a ramp in the back. We'd flip a lever and the ramp would drop down. We'd have to wind it up manually. An AMTRAC was longer than a tank, but not as wide. In a company, there'd be about fifteen AMTRACs and there were three companies in a battalion. Headquarters company did the maintenance on the tractors. But every time we took them out in the salt water we had to grease the joints and fittings and tighten up any loose cleats.

We got quite a surprise whenever we practiced coming out of an LST. To load into the LST we backed into the cargo compartment so we would be facing the right way when we left the ship. When we came down the LST's ramp, the front of the AMTRAC went under the water. The driver and assistant driver were completely under water. It bobbed right back up, but that sure was a surprise. And they'd move pretty slowly; I'd say five-miles-an-hour was top speed. They made a lot of racket, too. We'd go out maybe four or five-thousand yards into the ocean and just sit out there and bob up and down. Boy, I'd get seasick! AMTRAC training in California lasted for about five months.

We left San Francisco in early Fall of 1944. We traveled to Bougainville on the USS *Monterey*, which was a cargo ship.[56] When I first got on, I was sicker than a dog! Some guys got seasick as soon as they got on the boat at San Francisco; they never saw the Golden Gate Bridge! At nighttime, we'd be out on deck and the ship would roll over to one side so far that we wouldn't be able to see the stars. Then it would tip back the other way.

We stayed on Bougainville for at least three months. We were attached to the 37th Infantry Division. Most of the fighting was over by the time we got there.[57] There  were still some Japanese crawling around, but we never got into any fighting. We had sentries out on guard duty; everybody did that. Every once in a while we'd hear some shooting. It rained almost every day on Bougainville. In fact, we went around in skivvies, just shorts and shoes. It was sloppy all over the place.

One time, we were playing baseball on Bougainville, and I slid into second base. I didn't think anything of it when it happened. I was a pitcher, so I continued pitching. But the next day we were out on a march, and I felt something snap in my leg. I walked back to the hospital, and the doctor told me I had a fractured leg. The only way I could feel it was if I was laying down on the bed. That caused some pressure and I'd feel it. I was in the hospital for six weeks, and they put a cast on my leg from my foot right up to my hip. It was so hot, I'd have to get a bayonet slipped down inside the cast so I could get that itchy feeling out of there. Then I found out my outfit was leaving. I didn't want to be left behind.

I said, "I want to get the heck out of here."

So some of the guys came to the hospital and helped me take the cast off. I didn't have any physical therapy like they have today. I needed a lot of help from the other  GIs climbing the cargo net to get onto the ship.[58]

We were on that LST for a month from December 1944 to January 1945. We got to know the crew so well, we started trading clothing; we couldn't tell a soldier from a sailor after a while. The sailors had a certain job to do. We were just passengers and, with nothing to do, it was a dull, dull life. It had a flat bottom, so it didn't roll back and forth like the other ship. We only ate twice a day on the ship, breakfast and supper. Even though we ate C-rations aboard ship, I didn't mind; it was something to eat. We hid a bunch of canned fruit cocktail inside the pontoons on the AMTRACs, so we had fruit cocktail whenever we wanted it. Most of the time we sat on the deck all day.

On 9 January 1945 we made the landing in Lingayen Gulf in the northern part of the Philippines. We took part of the 37th Infantry Division in. We didn't meet very much resistance because the Navy had pounded the heck out of that beach. We never encountered any opposition. We weren't there to do any shooting; we were there just to transport troops.

I had guard duty at night. I'd be out there, maybe two or three hundred feet ahead of my company with a machine gun, waiting, just in case. It was rough, especially at night, because I never knew what was out there in the dark. But I never had to shoot at anybody. We stayed with the 37th all the way to Manila. If they came upon a river, we'd ferry them across. There wasn't too much opposition until they hit Manila. Once the 37th captured Manila[59], we put our tents right near the ocean. There was a Japanese ship out in Manila harbor. It had been hit and damaged by aircraft some time before. There was a Japanese hiding on the ship. One day he swam to shore and the Filipinos got to him. They beat him to death with shovels.

One day, we were told we were going out on a raid, which was the Los Baños prison rescue.[60] There were some rumors that the Japanese were going to try to get rid of the prisoners, and that's why it was so urgent for us to get them out of there. It was unusual for our tractors to go overland; they were primarily used for beach landings.

We left camp sometime after midnight and arrived at the staging area at about four o'clock in the morning. Then, it took at least a couple of hours to get across the lake.[61] I can't remember how big the lake was, but at 5mph, it took a while to cross it. As soon as we hit the beach on the far side of the lake, the 11th Airborne paratroopers jumped in. It was pretty well-timed. About two or three hundred paratroopers jumped in and quickly overcame the Japanese; took them completely by surprise. There were also some Filipino Scouts and some special forces from the United States already waiting there at the camp. When the paratroopers jumped, they joined in on the fight. The only casualties on the raid were two Filipino Scouts that were killed.[62]

We could see the camp from where we were parked, and we could hear the shooting. The whole raid took maybe an hour or so. It wasn't very much longer because the paratroopers wanted the prisoners to hurry. We didn't know how soon the Japanese could get to us. The Jap garrison was about ten miles away, and it would take some time for them to come down. But if they had vehicles it wouldn't take long at all. We were in a hurry to get those people out of there. Fortunately, we never did see any Japs.[63]

We had medics assigned to us. Most of the prisoners were in bad shape. They were malnourished and some of them couldn't walk very well. There were some small children. The children seemed like they could get around pretty well, but the older people couldn't maneuver that well. Any prisoners who were able walked back to the staging area with the paratroopers. The prisoners couldn't believe they were finally free. They also couldn't understand how our AMTRACs were able to go in the water. They all wanted to hug us. We loaded them into our AMTRACs and took them back across the lake. It took a couple of hours to get them back to the staging area where we dropped them off. From there, they were transported by truck to Manila.[64]

The Los Baños rescue didn't get too much publicity because that same day, 23 February 1945, the Marines hoisted the flag up at Iwo Jima. We really didn't get much recognition on that raid until Colin Powell said that it was the most successful raid in World War II.[65]

After the raid we trained for the invasion of Japan. We were all concerned about invading Japan because we all felt that it wasn't going to be an easy job. We had moved from Manila to another place on the beach when we heard they dropped the Bomb. We were all very happy. These people who criticized Truman for dropping the Bomb, well, they don't realize what war was like. The majority of people then felt it was justified. Everybody I knew thought it was justified. But some people still don't think it was the right thing to do.

We stayed with the 37th Division until the War was finally over. We didn't have enough points, since we were only over there a short time, but we got to come home with them. They'd been over there for a while. Their skin was yellow from taking the anti-malaria pills. It was August 1945. It took us about a week to get back to the States. We spent several months in California before we came back by train to Fort Campbell, Kentucky, which is where I was discharged in January 1946.

After the War, I went back to work for the Endike Construction Company. Then I put my application in for the Pennsylvania State Police, which was the best thing I ever did. There wasn't a lot of work in the area, except in the coal mines, so I decided to give it a try. I went to the State Police Academy in Hershey. It was a big wooden frame building with a stable and corral. I was there for three months, then I had three months of training in the field.

My wife's name is Dena Vannucci. We were married in Belle Vernon on 12 August 1950. I was on the job with the State Police then. We have two daughters, Janie and Janet.

After I retired from the State Police, I did some carpentry work and got into the antique business, refinishing furniture. We were having unit reunions every five years, but now it's every two years. The first one we had was at Seven Springs in 1975, and sixty couples showed up. But every year the numbers get smaller. At the last reunion in Mercer in 2004, there were fourteen couples. One guy was in a wheelchair and two were using canes. I'm lucky I can still get around pretty well. We've had reunions in Boston, Baltimore, Chicago and Williamsburg, Virginia.

I enjoyed my time in the service. It taught me how to get along with different people. It could have been a lot worse.

Louis Gazza (left) and a buddy.

"The War Lingered in My Memory."

Percy Hiatt

32nd Infantry Division
128th Infantry Regiment
3rd Battalion
Company M
(Company L)
Born in Emporia, Kansas, 30 October 1923

"My squad decided to run down the river. If we stayed close to the river bank, maybe we'd get out of there. It wasn't but one or two miles to the ocean where there'd be a lot more American troops. We ran down this river bed and there was a tree that had blown over or fell over in the river and as I rounded it there was a Jap standing there with his bayonet and I ran right on top of that bayonet! If he had had that bayonet down lower I'd have gotten stuck through the gut. It was just a scalp wound but it scared him as bad as it scared me and my number-two gunner was right behind me and he shot him. They grabbed me and picked me up. I thought my whole head was gone. Blood was running down my face."

MY ANCESTOR, GEORGE Hiatt, came over on the second voyage of William Penn to Pennsylvania. He settled in Pennsylvania, Maryland and New Jersey. My parents were Percy and Irma Hiatt. They lived in Emporia, Kansas, which is also where I was born. Emporia is in the Flint Hills region of Kansas. That's mainly pasture land, farmland and cattle country.

Before the Depression I think we were better than average in terms of wealth. My father owned a portion of the only laundry and dry-cleaning establishment in Emporia. In those days everyone wore wool clothing, so that meant everything had to be dry cleaned. Then everyone started wearing cotton and nylons and washing machines came along, too, and the laundry business went downhill. He got out of that and went into the trucking business and then into farming.

Emporia was a county seat; all brick streets in town. Emporia was also on the mainline of the Santa Fe Railroad. It was a big division point for the Santa Fe, so there were a lot of railroaders coming into town. But it was a nice town, and no one locked doors. Of course we had the county fairs in Emporia. We had a county high school and grade school. Everybody in the county came to that school. No buses, no lunch programs. The children who lived out on the farms and ranches either lived in apartments or group homes, or maybe the mother stayed with them during the school year and then they moved back out onto the farms and ranches in the summertime.

Kansas, of course, has always been considered one of the best educated states in the United States because of its public schools. I personally liked history when I was in school. I've been a history buff ever since.

I had two brothers and two sisters. Both brothers were in the service before the War. My oldest brother, Roy, was in the Army Air Force, and my brother Vernon was a gunner in the Navy. He was killed off of Guadalcanal. He served on the USS *New Orleans*; a heavy cruiser. A torpedo blew off the whole front of the ship. Vernon is still in Iron Bottom Sound in the South Pacific. Roy served mainly in the United States and down in the Caribbean patrolling for submarines when the tankers came out of Venezuela.

When Pearl Harbor was attacked, I was waiting in my car for my date, a nurse at the hospital. The news came over the car radio. I knew about Pearl Harbor because Vernon was stationed there. Vernon sent a telegram to my parents within a week to let them know he was okay. I met Vernon in California in January of 1942. He came up from the Port of Los Angeles where I was stationed in Camp Roberts. We spent a few days together. That was the last time I saw him.

Where I grew up, I wasn't too far from Fort Leavenworth and Fort Riley. When we were small kids, I remember my dad taking all of us, five kids and my mother, up to Fort Riley and there was a cavalry post there with horses. I suppose it was Army Day and they had open house and the cavalry troops put on a demonstration charging with their horses, and they had cannons behind the horse teams. It was pretty impressive to a little kid like me. When it came time for me to go into the service, I picked the Army, probably because of that early exposure, and also because my brothers were in the Air Force and Navy. I wanted something different.

We had been farming a pretty good-sized ground of wheat and corn. When my brothers went into the service, it left only my dad and I and an occasional hired man doing all this work. It was just too much, and I was kind of sick and tired of it really. I was ready to go and do something else. So, after I enlisted my dad had to reduce the farming operation.

I had to ask permission from my parents to go into the Army because I was underage. I don't remember any discussion about it except "I'd like to go" and they signed the papers. That was it. When I went in my Dad rode me to town, dropped me off at the bus station, shook my hand, and that was the end of it. There was nothing extraordinary at all about me leaving home.

I got to Fort Leavenworth on 22 December and they swore me in on 2 January. They didn't swear me in right away because of the large number of draftees that were also arriving. They couldn't handle everyone at once. After a week they sent me to Camp Roberts, California, for basic training. At Camp Roberts we were issued a lot of older equipment, even World War I helmets. We didn't do any jungle training. Even after we got to Australia, we didn't do jungle training even though there was plenty enough jungle in the northern part of the country.

In January-February 1942, there were a lot of alerts and invasion scares on the West Coast. We actually went to take up battle positions around the camp. There was that much fear. It was kind of scary to be on top of a hill all alone and thinking the whole Japanese nation was going to come up after me.

After the accelerated eight-week course at Camp Roberts, they sent me to Fort Ord where I joined the 32nd Infantry Division's 128th Regiment, 3rd Battalion, Company M. The 32nd was a National Guard outfit but I had a regular Army serial number, and that got me paid ahead of everyone else, even the first sergeant. That made a lot of people mad.

They took us from Fort Ord to San Francisco on city buses; big old, awkward things. They weren't designed to be running up a highway, but that's what they had to use because there wasn't anything else. They took us down to the dock in San Francisco into this warehouse. We walked in columns and we came to what I took to be a big building. When I looked up the side of it, I noticed it was a ship. They hadn't totally converted the ship over to troop transport. There was still some carpeting on the floor, some of the staterooms were still there, and the mess hall was made of temporary, stand-up tables only.

The ocean was rough as we left the coast. They assigned me to the top deck for eight hours a day to watch for airplanes. I sat in a canvas reclining chair, and I spent most of my time laying on this thing looking up into the sky. I got some sunshine, while everyone down in the holds was getting sick! I had a pretty good trip. The food was lousy, but to be on the ocean (I had never seen the ocean before) was quite something.

The whole Division was in this convoy and we were escorted by a destroyer or two and a cruiser, but they were pretty far off. There were also some cargo vessels with us. In the rough weather they looked like submarines half the time. I think we were originally scheduled to go into northern Australia, but the Battle of the Coral Sea had taken place, so they sent us instead to southern Australia. We debarked at Port Adelaide and went to an Australian Army camp. The Australian Army cooked for us quite a while. There was nothing but sheep pastures, and we trained in them. We ate mutton, slept where the sheep were, and our uniforms smelled like mutton! It was cold, damp and rainy all the time. They had wood stoves but they had little wood for them.

We got along well with the Australians when we were in battle. But there were some incidents. When we were in Brisbane, they brought back the 1st or 3rd Australian Division from North Africa and they parked most of them in the Brisbane area and of course it was full of American GIs. There were a lot of clashes. In fact, there was one big riot in Brisbane that caused a lot of problems. I wasn't in town when that took place, but I know we were restricted from going into Brisbane for a few weeks. The Australians said "We were over paid, over sexed and over here."

The pay thing was the big thing. The Australians drew practically nothing; about three dollars a month or something like that. It was a miserable pay. Of course, we weren't paid a whole lot more than that. When I went into the service, the maximum I drew as a private was eleven-dollars a month. It was actually twenty-one dollars a month, but I had to pay for my insurance, and in the States, I had to pay for my laundry. So the maximum cash I got over the table was eleven-dollars a month. Back then, that wasn't all that bad. Cigarettes were five-cents a pack, and beer was five-cents a cup. If we were careful, eleven dollars could last a month, unless we gambled!

After we got to Port Adelaide, they moved the whole Division up the Australian continent and established Camp Cable outside Brisbane. Some went by ship, but many of us went by train and by truck transport. A bunch of us were designated drivers. A lot of equipment had to be shipped, too. It was stacked up all over the countryside, and we had to move it down to the port. We were down there for several weeks getting all this stuff loaded onto the ships. Finally, we loaded some of our equipment on a train and went by rail to Brisbane. Each state in Australia at that time had different rail gauges. When we came to a state line, we had to unload everything, move it across a loading platform onto the new state's railroad, and move on. We went from South Australia to Victoria up to Queensland. I think we changed four times. It took us ten to fifteen days, and it wasn't very far really as the crow flies! All the locomotives were small and they couldn't pull very much. On the southern half of Australia, there are some pretty good mountains and they had trouble hauling these loads. I remember, on the way, they did a lot of timbering up there; huge trees, monstrous trees! They had oxen pulling those trees out of the forest and putting them onto rail cars.

After we got to Camp Cable, we set up tent areas and mess halls and did a lot of physical training. We got up to where we were doing hundred-mile hikes in full-field equipment plus weapons. We carried a forty-pound pack and a forty-pound piece of machinery from the .30-caliber machine gun. So we were loaded down with eighty pounds of equipment and we were supposed to walk a hundred miles! We started out with the water-cooled .30-caliber, but they were just too heavy to hump into combat. Then we went to the light .30-caliber, air-cooled machine gun. We just had to have a lot more barrels for it because we burned them out real quick. We had to carry around a supply of water for the water-cooled version. It was a good gun, and we could fire a lot of ammunition once we got it set up, but it was awkward to tote around.

New Guinea was a surprise move for us. There was no preparation time at all. We got on a train and we went to Townsville, Australia. They used any type of airplane they could get their hands on to get us there because the Japanese were just outside of Port Moresby in New Guinea. My regiment, the 128th and the 126th had the distinction of being the first troops to be flown to a combat area. I flew in a B–17. They threw some planks across the bomb bays, and we put all the packs and machine guns and ammunition on there. I think there were quite a few of us trying to get on that thing and we were scattered all over the plane. They tried to take off, but they couldn't get off the ground. They had to stop, go back, and then make everybody move as far forward as they could. I stood with my stomach against the pilot's seat! It was quite a thrill knowing we didn't get off the ground the first time, but now, as we tried the second time, I could see where we were going! It was pretty scary, but they got it off the ground and we flew over to Port Moresby. I think we flew about three-hundred miles before they dumped us off. They had all the airbases named by the miles they were from Port Moresby. I think this one was seven miles, so they called it "Seven-Mile Strip." It was kind of in a gully in some hills!

The Japanese bombed us all the time so we had dump trucks parked up on the hillside loaded with dirt and after the bombing raid was over, these trucks came barreling down the hillside and dumped the dirt in the bomb craters. They didn't keep them down around the airstrip because they'd get bombed too.

My first impression of New Guinea was hot! Hot! We thought Australia was hot, but New Guinea was something else. Of course, this was the last part of September into the first part of October 1942 and of course that's their summer down there. Plus, there were no facilities for us at all. We were sleeping in pup tents and slit trenches because of the bombing and the threat of the Japanese who weren't far from us.

The 126th Regiment went up with the Australians immediately. My regiment went up this river to the right side of the 126th. We went up into the foothills quite a way and saw some dead Japanese, but we didn't get into any combat at that time. They pulled us out of there and we went back down to the airstrip and they loaded us onto DC–3s that had no windows, and they flew us over the Owen Stanley Range to the north coast of Papua New Guinea. There was no airstrip there at all, and we landed in a field of Kunai grass, ten to twelve feet high and sharp as a razor. They just taxied the plane, and we had to jump off. The ground was soft and the pilot didn't want the plane to get stuck. We threw our equipment out first, and then we jumped out, taking care to dodge the tail. This was a little south of Buna, and we started walking through the jungle.

They made no provisions to feed us. They dropped rations to us but they'd hit the ground, break open and spoil. Then they tried parachutes. That didn't work either. Then they finally got smart and dropped us rice in Army socks. So we got a sock full of rice! We scrounged for food in the jungle. We ate palm nuts, bananas and cockatoos, but the birds were hard to hit with our M1 rifles. We didn't have any shotguns. The trees in the jungle were one-hundred-feet high and cockatoos were always on the top branch. We had to lay on our backs and fire straight up in the air into these trees. When anyone shot like this, their shoulder was on the ground. A couple men got broken collarbones because the rifles had a pretty good kick. If we hit a bird, there was nothing left of them. We wanted to actually miss it because the concussion of the bullet passing by a bird knocked it silly. We did some fishing with grenades too; strange fish, really strange fish. That was part of the coral reef extending into New Guinea. We threw a grenade in one time and got a big old fish out of there with teeth like a boar hog! There was a strange color to him and we didn't know if he was good enough to eat so we asked some old native man and he said, "Yeah, good."

So we ate it.

My very first combat experience was an attack across a Japanese-held airstrip at a place called Simemi Creek, a deep stream that ran through the south side of the airstrip. The Japanese were in pillboxes on the other side. The Japanese had built a bridge across the creek, and anytime we tried to cross the bridge, they zeroed in on us with everything they had. We fought there for I don't know how long. We finally brought up an Australian artillery piece. I don't know how they ever got it up there. They called it a 24-pounder. I think it was about equal to a 105mm and they gave us support. I got across that bridge three times and got chased back three times! We couldn't envelop them, and we couldn't get enough people across at one time to do anything. It was quite a struggle. This whole area was a mixture of tall grass, jungle, and tide-controlled streams and swamps. We could be engaged in any or all in one day's fighting.

Our first night was in a swamp consisting of water six to ten-inches deep with tree roots and fallen limbs under the water. Since this swamp was controlled by the tide, the water got deeper, and a couple times we had to stay up in the trees. Just outside the swamp was an open, wooded area with trees twenty-feet tall. The next day we tried to get across, but the Japanese had a perfect field of fire. It was nearly impossible for us to advance. The Air Force had been dropping bombs with parachutes attached to them. They hung from the branches like large fruit. We had to fight under them. Talk about puckered rectums! One round hitting these bombs in the right place, and that would have been it.[66]

This whole fight about used us up, and then they pulled us out of there and took us to the beach. We fought there in a coconut plantation that was owned by the Palmolive Soap Company. It was dry there, but there were a lot more Japanese. It couldn't get much worse. The ocean was on one side of us and the Japanese had torpedo boats with machine guns on them firing at us at night.

We were going to make an attack that afternoon, and they pulled us back because the Air Force was going to do some bombing for us. We pulled back about one-hundred yards from our normal position. They brought up Thanksgiving dinner for my platoon. It consisted of one can, which is about one-foot square, of Australian hardtack biscuits, and they were as hard as rocks. The date on the outside of the can was "1912!" We also got some jam and some beef. That was our Thanksgiving Day dinner.

We ate in a relatively safe area. There was some rifle fire and machine gun fire, but it was rather high and it didn't bother us. But when the Air Force came in, they came from our rear instead of across our front. They dropped a short stick of bombs on top of us. I was sitting at the base of a big tree and a bomb went off on the other side. I got bounced around a bit from the concussion, but I wasn't injured. But we lost several men from the rifle companies. It was demoralizing. To be honest, I fired more rounds at American planes than I did at Japanese planes! That's just the way it went. It finally got to the point where we didn't want air support any more. After that incident, we never asked for it again because it was just too dangerous. They couldn't drop a bomb where they were supposed to.

I had been strafed by our own Air Force prior to this. We had been walking south of Buna for quite a few days and they couldn't supply us by air anymore. We got to be in pretty bad shape. We came to a cape that stuck out in the ocean. There were a couple of little luggers, little twenty-ton boat. They picked us up and eventually took us to Oro Bay off Buna. They put two squads of us on this boat and they gave each man a can of pork and beans. We hadn't had any food for several days, so as soon as we ate those beans, they went straight through us! We were sitting on the rail of this small vessel "getting rid of the beans." We hadn't got very far out when this plane came over low. It made a pass over us, and we didn't think anything of it since it was one of ours, then it came back and strafed us! It killed the captain of the vessel that was one of a pair of brothers in the Pacific. They killed him and this reporter named Byron

Darnton[67] from the *New York Times*. I had a BAR at that time and I fired a few rounds at the plane, but it was so damn fast I didn't get anywhere near him.

After we got to the beach area and into the plantation, we saw that it was heavily fortified by the Japanese with pillboxes made of oil drums filled with sand and covered with coconut logs and very well camouflaged. The Japanese had trenches running out from these pillboxes. When we fired artillery or mortars at these trenches, the Japanese ran into the bunkers and pillboxes. After the fire lifted, they'd go back out into the trenches on the sides.

They'd tell us, "Okay, we're going to jump off at two o'clock and we're going to go up here and try to take what's in front of us."

They never told us what was in front of us. There'd be lot of fire coming at us, but we couldn't see from where. When the time came, our mortar platoon and some artillery would fire. They had a certain quota they could fire and when their quota of ammunition for that day was used up that was it (sometimes they didn't even have any for that day). Sometimes we'd call our mortar platoon and say, "We need some fire!"

They'd say, "We don't have it."

Then we'd give what support we could to the rifle companies we were always attached to.

There were also times when we restricted the amount of ammunition that went through our machine guns. We'd like to have fired more, but we didn't dare run completely out. The only way to get more was we'd use some old native man. He'd sling some between two poles and carry it up, but he wouldn't come too close to us, so we had to walk back and get it. It was the same way with machine gun barrels and food. These native carriers did help, but only as long as they didn't get too close to rifle fire or the front.

When the rifle companies moved out, we'd tag along behind them until they got stopped and couldn't go any farther. Then we'd set up our machine guns, and they'd point out targets to us. I was the number-two gunner on the .30- caliber. I fed the ammunition in. I also used a BAR. It was a good weapon. Sand affected it a little bit, but not too much. It had a distinctive sound to it and the Japs learned what it was. I didn't want to stay in one position for too long because the sound drew fire.

The Japanese were equipped with artillery, but mostly mortars. They had these little so-called "knee mortars." The ammunition wasn't that powerful, but they had a lot of them and they could move them around quickly because they were only about two feet in length and weighed about ten pounds.[68] They could drop a round into your hip pocket.

These advances and assaults against bunkers and trenches would go on until dark, and then we dug in and spent the night. There'd be dead and wounded on both sides. We had one medic per platoon, and we had no litter bearers. We fought all day and had seriously wounded people to take care of. If they weren't too wounded, they could walk back by themselves, and if not, we tried to get them back some way. Some we just didn't move; we just stayed with them until they died. This went on day after day after day; the same thing, seven days a week. Time and time again, we'd fight over the same fifty yards. We'd make fifty yards, couldn't hold it, or the rifle company couldn't go any farther. Then we'd move back fifty yards and retire to the same old hole and try again the next day.

The Australians eventually brought up Bren Gun Carriers.[69] We were going to move in behind them in the attack. I think there were seven of them. I remember it was so hot that day and we were excited because for the first time we had armor supporting us. They moved out and I don't think they got twenty-five yards. The Japanese just threw grenades into them. They were open on the top. We tried to recover the wounded and the dead but were driven off by enemy fire. We waited until dark. That whole attack lasted about fifteen minutes, and then it was over with.

A dead body in New Guinea lasted about three days. Then there'd be nothing left but clothing and bones, or just a pile of maggots. The stench of death was terrible. I can still smell it. Usually, all we did was stick a rifle in the ground with a bayonet and put the dead man's helmet on it and just left the body there. I don't know what happened to them. In the three years I was in the Pacific, I never saw a cemetery, and only once did I see dead bodies being taken off of a truck. Otherwise, I never saw a cemetery in the three years I was in the Pacific. I never saw anyone pick up bodies. I hoped that they did something with the bodies, but I very much doubt it. We always picked up one dog tag, and left the other with the body. Whenever we got to company headquarters, and that might not have been for months, we gave the dog tags to the first sergeant. That was the end of it.

When I was in combat I couldn't let certain things bother me. I always said to myself, "This is what we're going to do today."

I didn't think of the ramifications of combat, I just went ahead and did it, and I always said that I had to have a laugh a day! Sometimes what I laughed about, and my men laughed about, one would think strange. We didn't think it strange at that time but we were a little weird! This type of thing kept us going. I had a fellow by the name of Shute. He's a cattle rancher today up in Western Nebraska. Shute always said, "By God, if I get wounded I'm gonna go and you're never gonna see me again! I'm gonna go right straight back to the United States!"

Well, Shute came by one morning and he held up his hand, blood was running down it, and he said "I'm going! You sonsofbitches are never gonna see me again! I'm going to the States!"

About thirty minutes later he was back with the tip of his finger shot off. That's all there was to it!

We got a big laugh out of him about that, "Yeah, you're not gonna get back to the States!"

He did, eventually. And there was another one with an Australian. This Australian soldier came by us and he must've had three or four bullet wounds in his right arm and right shoulder. He walked by me and he held up his bayonet scabbard that had been hanging at his side. It had a bullet hole right through it.

He said, "Pretty god damned close, wasn't it, Yank?"

Here he was, blood all over the other side of him and he was looking at that bayonet scabbard that had a bullet hole right through it! The Australians were something else!

Nights were awful in Buna. We didn't move at night. We didn't send out any patrols. The Japanese tried it occasionally with disastrous results. It was scary, and what was really scary in this coconut plantation was the coconuts fell off the trees on their own. Also, big tree limbs would fall off. This plantation was planted in rows. If we wanted to be safe, we wouldn't stay under a tree, but it was difficult because the trees nearly overlapped.

They also had these monstrous crabs that were bigger than a dinner plate, and they ate coconut sprouts. They'd thrash around at night. I shot at a lot of coconut crabs at night! I threw a lot of grenades at them I'm sure! I thought they were Japs. In the jungle, we had very little starlight or moonlight through the trees, so it was pitch black. I remember one night, another fellow and I were out in front of the lines at a listening post to see what was going on. I stood the first watch, and he was on the second watch. We were in the same hole together and he kept poking me and saying, "Hiatt, there's something out there, there's something out there!"

I said, "Keep your eye on it, Joe."

He did this three or four times and I finally got mad and said, "Then shoot the sonofabitch!"

So he did! We were out in front of an L-shaped line, we were on the south side, the Australians were on the east side and the Japs were over on the north side. He fired, and some of the rounds went into the Australian line. That pissed them off so they fired back, and then the Japanese got involved in it and there was one hell of a war that went on that night all because this guy shot a small tree kangaroo! I don't know how many thousands of rounds were fired that night just because he shot that damned kangaroo! Everybody was awake that night; no one slept! If we thought there was something moving in front of us, we'd call back for parachute flares. They'd light up everything and we'd go blind for awhile. We really didn't like using them.

When we stopped for the night, if we were in a different area, we tried to memorize everything that was in front of us before it got dark. We looked at trees, at tree stumps, rocks, or whatever. Even though we got to know damn well where they were, those trees, stumps and rocks got to moving at night in our imaginations.

The Japs did a lot of yelling at us. I was surprised at how many spoke English. They'd say things like, "Who's sleeping with your wife at home?" or "You're going to die!" or "We're going to kill you tomorrow!" or just curse words.

We didn't usually yell back; we'd throw grenades at them. That would start the war again, too. Some battalions had those big radios and could pick up Tokyo Rose.[70] She played pretty good music. She called the 32nd Division, "The Butchers of Buna." She was always referring to us and what was going to happen to us. That lasted all during the War, so she managed to keep pretty good track of us.

We were on one-third rations for over two months, nearly three months actually. We all lost weight and were sick with malaria. Just fighting and moving around wasted us away. Everybody's teeth went to hell because of poor diet. Men went barefoot.

The uniforms rotted. We ran around with our butts hanging out most of the time because the pants rotted out. Before we left Australia, they took all of our uniforms, our "fatigues" or "work uniforms" and took them to an Australian dye shop where they dyed them green. That dye wasn't a good dye and it got into our skin. It also sealed the clothing so that it couldn't breathe. It was a mess. A lot of people had sores on them from the dye getting into their systems. In fact, the first pair of shoes I got were Australian Army shoes with hobnails on the bottom of them and they were made with such stiff leather, there was no way I could bend the toe of the shoe. I walked flat footed all the time. It was pitiful, but I was better off because I had a pair of shoes that actually fit me. There was a fellow from Nebraska and he had real small feet and he barely got into the service because of his height. He went barefoot a lot. We finally got in contact with a shoe store in Brisbane, Australia and bought shoes for him. They were a long time getting to him, but that's where he got his shoes for the rest of the War.

When General Eichelberger came up to the front line, he was aghast at the shape we were in. He pulled us off the line for three days and made us clean up and shave; we hadn't shaved in a long time. Naturally, we didn't shave when we had someone shooting at us all the time!

One day I walked past Eichelberger's headquarters. He saw me. I didn't know who he was at the time, except that he was a three-star general. He gave me a package of Raleigh cigarettes! I had never smoked a Raleigh cigarette. They were a pretty sad tobacco. I never smoked one since. I guess he felt sorry for me.

The Japanese fought to the death at Buna. One way or the other, they knew they were going to die. They were trapped, they couldn't get replacements, and they couldn't get any food. There was quite a bit of cannibalism that took place among them. They had to fight or die, and a lot of them committed suicide. We burned a lot of them out. We didn't have any flamethrowers on Buna but we did use five-gallon cans of gasoline that we'd pour into a bunker, and then throw in a grenade.

We had some good officers and bad ones. We always had a shortage of company officers. If we did get one, he didn't last long for some reason or another. One officer they had to haul off and one got killed, and some just went back and stayed away from us. They called them "90-Day Wonders" because they had three months training, then they sent them over to us. They knew absolutely nothing. They'd give the wrong information to us or wrong commands and if we obeyed them, most of the time we were in trouble. My company captain, I never once saw him in combat in three years! I saw the battalion commander more, and I became good friends with him. He'd get a lot of things done at the front. There was one lieutenant we had at Buna. We were on one-third rations; I think there were several times we'd go three or four days without any ration at all. They happened to drop a case of peaches. He divided them up. I wasn't there when he did this, but this lieutenant divided them up and when I came back, it was late in the afternoon and my men told me he didn't divide them up properly. He kept more for himself.

I said, "Well, I'll take care of it in the morning."

They killed him that night. Over two or three cans of peaches. I think I could have resolved it the next morning, but they shot him. That was the only case of an officer getting killed by his own men that I know about. I'm sure it happened to other units too. Another thing, being that we were a National Guard outfit, there were a lot of relatives serving together. In my company, there were four sets of brothers serving. The first sergeant had a brother there, the supply sergeant had a brother, and the platoon sergeant had a brother. A lot had cousins they had grown up with and gone to the same high school or grade school. If one or the other was in a position of authority, it was hard for them to order a brother or cousin into harm's way. What happened is that replacements like me ended up doing the hard stuff. Eventually, a lot of these National Guard people transferred out to Division HQ or Regimental HQ, and I went from PFC to staff sergeant all in one day and I was only nineteen! I had two men under me that were thirty-eight, but they eventually got out of the service.

The fighting got stalled on Buna and there was a big reorganization of the 32nd. General Eichelberger[71] took over as the commander relieving our division commander, General Harding. There was a big shake up of regimental commanders, even down to the company level. There were a lot of staff officers of Eichelberger's running around trying to see how to win the War. I think he really got on all these guys to get up there and see what was going on. One day, this General MacNider came up to the coconut plantation area. He had quite an armed guard with him, which we thought was rather strange because everybody was armed. Anyway, he strolled up there like he was going to win the War single-handedly. I think it surprised him when he found out he was at the front. There were no lines on the ground or anything like that to indicate where the front was.

We told him, "You better get down because you're going to get shot!"

Somebody no more than said that and he got shot in the arm! It took him by surprise, I'm sure, and scared the hell out of all the armed people that were around him. It knocked him down. I think there were three in the hospital at one time because of Eichelberger sending these guys up to the front. MacNider was one, there was another general, and I think a full-bird colonel in the hospital.

The problem was one can't attack pillboxes with rifles alone; that was the thing. In that whole division we had one 105 mm artillery piece. The Australians were on our left flank and they had one at one time and I think they got a couple more, but they were using them mainly for themselves. We had 81mm mortars, that were the worst weapon in the world to fight underneath. They'd scare us to death, but they wouldn't knock pillboxes down. Until we got some tanks up there, probably a month or two later, we didn't make much head way. They were Australian-manned but they were American Stuart[72] tanks. They had a 37mm gun on them. That was good enough; they could get up to the damned pillboxes with them at least. The Japanese didn't have any tanks on Buna. We saw some later on, but they were real light tanks and they didn't amount to much. In the Philippines, we saw some heavier tanks, but they were no match for our tanks or our artillery.

It was around the last of December or the first of January 1943 when I got wounded. I was moving forward through some fairly heavy timber and brush. It was dry ground for a change and I felt something squash in my boot. I stopped to look and it was blood. It was merely a spent round, and it penetrated a little bit just below my ankle bone and a little forward of it. It broke some bones. There was so much going on I never heard the shot, and I didn't even know I was hit. During combat we're flopping around, we're running into things, things are running into us and the adrenaline was up. We'd stub our feet on everything because we're not looking where we're running, we're looking forward all the time. It took place without me even knowing I was hit. It hurt like hell, but I walked to the aid station. I walked, I suppose you could call it that, another five or six miles to the hospital they had put up at the end of the air strip. There were several of us walking wounded, and there was a Jeep that came by that had a trailer, and the driver stopped and picked us up. As we got over onto the airstrip, the Japanese were bombing the hell out of it. This guy got excited with the Jeep and he tried to evade the bombs, I guess, but he tipped the trailer and threw us all out! We probably would have been better off walking. The Japs kept up the bombing. We could see the stars and the trees through shrapnel holes in the hospital tent roof. It wasn't a very safe place.

Then they sent me back to Australia. I didn't really want to go. After what we'd been through for the past three months, I wanted to stay with my organization. One of the worst thoughts wounded guys had was that they would get transferred to another outfit after they recovered.

I was in the hospital for about four months. It was also while I was there that I had malaria and jungle sores and ulcers. I never got dengue fever, thank God! The only place I ever saw dengue fever in our division was on Goodenough Island. Thank God we weren't there very long. That was after Buna. It was a grassy island, there wasn't too much timber on it really and we were just in a staging area there prior to our next landing on Saidor.

The hospital care was great; I couldn't ask for more. The first big hospital I went to had American, female nurses! We got good treatment there, but they wanted me to get back to a bigger hospital to do work on me. The second one was in an Australian agricultural college. There were no American nurses in that hospital. They were all Australian Sisters. They weren't nuns, but they wore some sort of habit.[73] We did have American GIs and medics in there.

I had quite a few operations on my ankle, then they finally got me in the 4th General Hospital in Melbourne, Australia, where they put in a metal plate about the size of a quarter to hold the bone s together. They were going to send me back to the States, and MacArthur put an edict out that everybody who was recuperating would return to duty, so I stayed.

During this time in the hospital, most of us were sick from malaria. We ran temperatures all the time, so we didn't go anywhere. We went for five, six, seven months without pay because we had been at the front, and when we did get paid we got paid in Australian money. Where were we going to spend it? Not many of us were going to town, so we just gambled! They were friendly games, although there was a lot of money that changed hands. I played a lot of poker, shot a lot of dice, and I don't remember anybody having any problems.

While I was in the hospital, there was a 1st Marine Division sergeant that was the first one to earn the Medal of Honor on Guadalcanal.[74] There's a street named for him at Camp Pendleton in California.[75] He and I shared the same room and they had him there to fatten him up and clean him up a little bit. They were about ready to discharge me from the hospital and we were bemoaning the fact that we were capable of going downtown and they wouldn't let us.

Some old Navy chief came in to see this Marine and said, "What are you doing around here, you're going to be awarded the Medal of Honor, you can get anything you want!"

He asked the doctor if we could have a staff car to take us downtown and he said, "Well, sure!"

We had a staff car and we'd go downtown every night and get drunk! The driver would haul us back!

After the battle for Buna ended, they brought the whole Division back to Camp Cable in Australia. It wasn't much longer before we got replacements. I rejoined my company and then we went to Goodenough Island and made the landing at Saidor. The Japanese had three airstrips there and we secured them for the Australian Air Force and our own Air Force. We ran into some patrols. The Japanese 18th Army was inland, moving north all the time; we just kind of kept track of them. The Japanese weren't interested in doing any combat with us. They were just trying to escape north. The Australians were after them, too. They were behind them while we were on the side or flank. There wasn't much combat, but the Japs bombed our ammunition depot and there was a big Fourth of July celebration with all that ammunition exploding!

For some unknown reason, our Navy brought in a small refrigerator ship, and it was full of boxed steaks.

The ship's captain said, "My orders are to discharge it here."

So they discharged the meat, but we had no kitchens. We built fires out of boxes and anything we could get our hands on and cooked some of the steaks and seasoned them with salt from our ration kits. We couldn't eat them all, and a lot of them spoiled.

We made some practice beach landings around Saidor form LCIs, which were Landing Craft, Infantry. There's a picture of me in *LIFE* coming off one of the LCIs. It's in the 27 March 1944 edition. I'm coming off, facing the vessel on the right hand column, and I'm the third man in the picture. I have a BAR slung over my shoulder. I think the reason why I was carrying a BAR that day was because my BAR man had malaria and was feeling bad. We swapped weapons, so I carried his. The caption in the picture has it wrong. It says we were landing in Sicily!

After Saidor and before we made our next landing up on Aitape, we helped the Australian Army in the Markham Valley.[76] We went up and plugged the end of that valley for awhile while the Australians were pushing the Japs up to us. It was a steep-walled valley and we sat at the end of that and let the Japs come to us. I think we were there for about ten days. It was a slaughter, a complete slaughter. The Japs were starving, most of them didn't have ammunition, but they just kept coming. We had quite a few people who couldn't take that. In our platoon, I had some men that went off the deep edge, and we had to evacuate them. Not that they went wild or anything, but I guess you could say that. One of them started collecting ears, one started collecting gold teeth. This type of brutality took place on both sides, though I don't think we ever tied anyone up and bayoneted them like they did to our people. We certainly didn't take many prisoners. Usually, when we came across wounded enemy, somebody shot them. Even if they were dead, somebody put a round into them.

I was involved in taking one prisoner, but I never got him back to battalion headquarters. I was taking him back with a buddy. The Jap was wearing nothing but a loin cloth. As we walked him by battalion aid station the chief doctor, a major of Polish descent, came out of the operating tent and shot him dead. They raised hell with me for not getting the prisoner back, but what was I supposed to do? The major shot him, not me! I guessed the major had enough of patching up our wounded and he just flipped. That was probably the only enemy soldier he killed during World War II! That prisoner had been knocked unconscious, and that was the only reason we got him. He was lucky, well, not all that lucky after he ran into the major.

Around the time we were in the Markham Valley, the 1st Marine Division was going to make a landing on New Britain. We were in a support role in case they needed us. The Army was always sending us here and there and everyplace. The Sixth Army Headquarters didn't like my regiment for some reason or another. We were a bunch of rabble-rousers! They gave us a lot of nasty jobs like that one in the valley. We were more "independent" than the Army liked us to be. I guess we were pretty cocky if one can be that way in the jungle in the Pacific. If there was any booze around anywhere, we got a hold of it, and the results of drinking led to altercations with other units.

Next we made a landing on Aitape in New Guinea. There wasn't much going on at the beach landing itself. But probably two or three weeks later they moved us to the Driniumor River, which is a little south of where we made the initial landing. We went up the Driniumor River, a big, wide, stream bed, but with very little water in it, and lots of rocks. It was a meandering stream right at the foothills of some fairly good-sized mountains. We set up a defensive position on the banks of the Driniumor.

The rifle companies ran patrols up over there and they'd keep coming back saying, "God, there's a lot of Japs over there."

I don't think they were believed, but I knew these rifle company people; our lives depended on them for most of the War and I knew what they were saying was true. They just kept saying that and we kept digging deeper on the bank and building some pretty good pillboxes with dirt and logs or anything we could get our hands on. One day, the Japanese came across that river and there were a lot of them! It was early morning. There were just battalions of them moving right towards us; they weren't in any hurry. It was a field day for a machine gunner! Our field of fire was completely bare, only rocks in the river. We ran out of ammunition, and had no alternative but to shag ass out of there! We didn't take our machine gun. We pulled the back plates off and that made it inoperable. The Japs were in among us. They broke through our lines and were in back of us and on the side of us. There probably was some hand-to-hand combat there, but we were long gone.

My squad ran down the river. If we stayed close to the river bank, we thought we could get out of there. It wasn't but one or two miles to the ocean where there were a lot more American troops. We ran down the river bed, and there was a tree that had blown over or fell over in the river. As I rounded the tree, there was a Jap standing there with a bayonet on his rifle, and I ran right on top of that bayonet! If he had had that bayonet down lower, I'd have gotten stuck through the gut. It was just a scalp wound, but it scared him as bad as it scared me. My number-two gunner was right behind me, and he shot him. They grabbed me and picked me up. I thought my whole head was gone. Blood was running down my face. We got down to the beach and there was an aid station there and they put two stitches in my head. That was it!

We reformed the next day and went back up supported by the 112th Cavalry. We were quite a ways up the river the next day and a lot of Japanese were still all over the place running around like flocks of geese. They tried to get the hell away from us, but we had to watch everywhere because they were scattered. We ended up in the mountains in a native village. That was the end of that battle. The battle report said we killed around 9,300 up there. That was the last big action by the 18th Japanese Army. That just about finished them.

The environment and the weather on Saidor and Aitape were pretty much the same as at Buna. The big difference was the Japs didn't have the prepared positions they had at Buna. That made it somewhat better, and as time went by, we were being supplied better with ammunition, especially. We had all the ammunition we wanted and we kept getting more artillery support. They brought in a lot of separate artillery units; big guns, 155 mms. Many times we'd run into something and we'd pull back and the artillery would just make kindling out of them. Air support? We didn't want it. By the time we got to Leyte, they brought up the damnedest amount of artillery.

After Aitape, we went up to Hollandia, in Dutch New Guinea. They assembled all kinds of troops there for the eventual landing in the Philippines. It was a God awful place. It was red volcanic dust and we'd step in it and dust would fly up around us. Anything we ate was red, our clothing was red and our skin was red. We stayed there for about a week. They took us out of there and we went across the bay to Hollandia, which was on a huge bay. There was a massive amount of shipping. They took two rifle companies and my squad, and we ran some patrols into the jungle trying to keep track of what was left of the Japanese Army. We ran patrols about seven days out and we'd come back seven days. There were leeches; I never saw so many leeches in my life! We had to stop and light up a cigarette and burn the bastards off of us. It was a terrible place over there except for one native village down on the coastline. These people were pretty black and smelly! But all these nice coconut groves were on the beach, and thatched huts and women ran around bare-chested.

They got high all the time, the natives did! They ate the betel nut, which is a red nut. They had a gourd tied around their waist, most of the men did, and this gourd was full of lime, what we'd call household lime. They'd eat this betel nut, they'd chew on it and the blood-red juice ran out of their mouths and down their chins. They'd take a stick and run it down into that gourd of lime and put that in their mouths and it made them "dingy." They got intoxicated on it! These guys were there with sharpened teeth and bloody stuff running out of their mouths, but they were happy! We didn't have any trouble with them.

We spent a couple of days there. Every time we'd make a trip out into the bush, we'd come back and bathe in the surf. We tried every time we got a chance to have a saltwater bath and use the sand to kind of scrub up and get the crap off of us. I think it helped these bites we were getting all the time from mosquitoes and leeches.

We saw some Japanese on these patrols, but we only needed to find out their location. We were on a reconnaissance patrol, and we only saw them at a distance. They were in bad shape and leaving dead behind them all the time. They had some cannibalism there, too.

We took a bunch of natives up a river. All those rivers over there are big coming down those mountains. We escorted an engineering outfit up there. They were going to build a bridge across this river. We tried to get up stream where it was a little bit narrower, because it was a mile wide down to the coastline. We had natives carrying all this cable and ropes for the engineers. The natives had wives with them. One of them was pregnant, and she had a baby while we were walking! She stopped along side of the trail, had the baby and then slung him in a pouch on her back and caught up! We got up far enough where these engineers were supposed to build this bridge and the river was flooding and there was about seven feet of water where they were supposed to work, so we gave up on that and came on back down.

We'd walk across these little creeks or swamps on foot bridges made of small logs only a couple inches thick. We'd get some weight on them and those logs would give so we'd be wading through the water. We knew damn well that there were crocodiles in there. Sometimes, we'd want to become Jesus and walk on water! The first time we went across pretty fast. It was scary! Once there was a big old crocodile that came out of a tide-controlled swamp by the ocean. There was an antiaircraft outfit there that had the four 20mm cannons on a mount and they started shooting it! This old crocodile got out in the ocean and pretty soon everybody was shooting at that damn crocodile! Finally they sunk him, I guess. Several thousand dollars worth of ammunition! All in that one croc!

Hollandia was the first place I saw black American troops. They were quartermaster and ordinance troops discharging cargo. This was the first time we'd seen any service units. A lot of people didn't like the blacks. There were quite a few incidents where white troops tried to harm these blacks and a few where they did harm them. It wasn't a good thing, but there were always a lot of southerners in the Army. Believe it or not, the Civil War hadn't quite ended for a lot of them. It wasn't pleasant, but it happened. They called them "niggers" at the time, or Negroes, but mainly "niggers."

One of the things that didn't help the blacks was of the two organizations that mutinied during World War II, both happened to be black organizations, and this didn't sit right with combat troops. Both of these mutinies took place in the United States.[77]

On Leyte, I was sitting on Mile Post 14 on Highway 1 or Highway 2, I forget which one. We all watched as hell broke loose as the Japs dropped parachute troops on them.[78] The next morning, when it got daylight, I had a black GI sitting beside me.

I asked him, "Where the hell did you come from?"

He said, "I'm from a truck outfit and things got scary back there so I left!"

I asked him what he did; what his job was.

He said, "I drive one of those big mother-fers that bend in the middle."

He was a semi-truck driver. So I had the first integrated unit in the Army! We kept him around for a few days until someone came down and said we ought to send him back. He kind of liked it out there; we weren't doing a lot at that time. We were sitting along this highway but we had to send him back. We'd keep anyone we could get our hands on because we were always short of people.

After we finished the patrolling around Hollandia, we then went to Morotai. The 31st Division went through there first, so the fighting was pretty much over with by the time we got there. We stayed there a few days. We were scheduled to go to Leyte and we got new equipment and new uniforms and everything. As we got farther north in the Pacific, the War changed. It became more sophisticated, and we had a lot more troops, a lot more equipment, not that the fighting became any easier, but these support organizations made it a lot easier to get the ammunition to us and to take the wounded away.

We got into Leyte harbor and Jap planes were all over the place. We were going slowly into the harbor. Japanese planes were on top of us and all these escort vessels with us were firing at them. The vessel we were on fired, too. At this point we went over the sides of the ship down into the landing craft. We hung over the sides on the cables on these landing craft, and this ship we were on dodged around trying to evade all these aircraft and this one plane came down, straight down. It wasn't going to hit anybody; he was scaring everybody though. All of these ships shot at this airplane and when it got down to the surface of the ocean, the ships were firing at us! It was a madhouse! It wasn't much longer after that, the ship we were on hit a sandbar or a reef or something. It came to a stop and we didn't, we were swinging like pendulums! So we were real happy to get to shore where it was a lot safer!

When we got to shore on Leyte we went on up Highway 1 or Highway 2 and relieved the 24th Division. They had taken a pretty good licking up on Breakneck Ridge. We never did carry any extra uniforms into combat, but for some reason, they had brought up some of their duffel bags, their barracks bags, and the Japs got a hold of a bunch of the uniforms. It was chaotic at Breakneck Ridge for about ten days. At a distance we didn't know who the hell was who.

We were about a mile and half from a river but the water was bad. There was a water hole that had good water, but every time we tried to get water out of it, so did the Japs. We fought them once a day to get water out of this hole. There finally were so many dead around it that we had to give it up.

We got sent a replacement officer when we were in Leyte. Some of my men were on one side of this ridge, and I was on another. The Japanese were on the top of the ridge.

My men called me on the phone and they said, "We got somebody here for you."

I said, "Send him on over, and tell the guy to really move."

My men were coming back and forth all the time, and they had to run like hell across that ridge because the Japanese would shoot at them. But they didn't tell this officer to do that. He just wandered across and that was the end of him. I never even knew his name.

We fought around the town of Limon. On the other side of the town was a Jap artillery organization, and their guns were horse-drawn. There were hundreds of dead horses in there. They couldn't move those damn guns without those horses, and here ours were dragged by tractors or trucks and we could put those anywhere we wanted to. We could sure load a truck a lot easier on a ship than a kicking horse. The Japanese just hadn't modernized enough. Our company headquarters ended up right in the middle of those dead horses. I'd rather have been up on the front. The bellies of those horses were exploding from gas. The smell made me sick to death.

We got through Limon and up over a mountainside. We stopped at a banana plantation. I was with Company L, and I thought those guys were the bravest people on the face of the Earth. All at once, the Company L boys came running toward me.

I thought, *'God, it must be the whole Japanese Army after them!'*

When they went by me, I said, "What's coming?!"

They said, "Snake! Snake!"

It was one of those great big boa constrictors of some kind. Of course, this banana plantation was full of rats so that's why he was in there. Those Company L boys fought Japs all day long, but by golly, they weren't going to fight that damned snake! They wounded him and he was thrashing around kind of bad.

About a day later, I got the word I had enough points to go home. They said, "Get rid of your equipment. Give it to your new squad leader and come on back to Division rear."

Division rear was at Talcoban and by that time, we were probably thirty miles from there. There was one other man that was going with me and we took off back up through No-Man's-Land until we got to the highway. We saw some Japs on the way, but we slipped around and got on the road. The first truck we saw, we flagged it down and jumped up in the back of it. It was full of dead GIs so we rode the fenders down to the other side of Limon. The Japs had a roadblock down there. They had cut the road and we messed around there for a few hours and finally said the hell with this and we went out around it. We got back over to the bay and there was another roadblock. They were fighting there and by that time, there were probably about ten of us who'd been picked up along the way. We appropriated a DUKW and went out into the ocean, and around what was taking place there toward Talcoban. Then we got on a 1st Cavalry truck and they took us down to the Division rear and that was Christmas Day, 1944.

They processed us and we got onto a Liberty Ship or a Victory Ship in the first few days of January. There were maybe four-hundred of us on there. We joined a convoy and sat in the harbor for about a day. Then the convoy started leaving the area at dusk. As we cleared the harbor mouth, there was an outrigger canoe that came by and we tried to get the gun crew to shoot it because we thought it was the enemy. The Filipinos never poked around in the dark. But they wouldn't do it.

We joined a convoy that had all kinds of ships in it, supply ships mainly, but right next to us was an Australian troop ship. It was a big, converted liner that didn't have anybody on it. And all the rest of the ships we could see were just empty cargo vessels. We did have some destroyers and destroyer escorts with us. The second day, the Japanese started bombing us. They only bombed our ship! They missed us the first go-around.

The second go-around, they came by and dropped a bomb that just missed the bow of the vessel. It raised us out of the water a little bit and water came up over the deck. The next day around noon I was up toward the bow again. I sat on the railing and I had a life preserver on my arm. A Kamikaze came down and hit us right square in the ship and that damn thing went down like a rock. It blew me off! I went sailing off on my back. Thank God the ship was loaded with some ballast so it was only a fifteen-foot fall into the water, but it felt like hitting cement, nonetheless. I was off the vessel and it went right on by me and went down. There were vessels behind me that went by and some of them did throw off two-by-fours and some lumber, but the stuff didn't come anywhere near me. Of course, being the first one off the vessel, I was the furthest one back. I was in the water maybe two hours when a destroyer escort came by, threw me a life ring and pulled me up the side of the ship. I went from there to Hollandia on this destroyer escort.

When all this happened, I wondered whether I should go home or stay. The rest of the Division was on its way to Luzon and the Villa Verde Trail. They stayed there until the end of the War. Actually, my battalion accepted the surrender from General Yamashita[79] on Luzon.

From Dutch New Guinea I went to Melbourne, Australia, with a bunch of war brides and women Russian sailors. Where the hell they ever came from I don't know! But believe it or not, they were big old broads, and they tried to buy all of Australia and carry it on the vessel with them!

I was classified as a "survivor" by Navy regulations and I had a state room with two other guys all the way back home to San Francisco. What "survivor" meant was that I was picked up out of the ocean. The Navy gave special treatment to "survivors." There was a small library just down the hall from our stateroom. I'd go there, get a book, and then lay on the deck in the sun and read. It was a nice trip home! We went top speed all the time and zigzagged every twenty minutes until we got close to Hawaii, then we went straight.

In San Francisco we thought we'd be met by a band and pretty girls and all that kind of stuff, being that we were conquering heroes coming home, but there wasn't any of that. They unloaded us onto a ferry and took us over to Angel Island and processed us. We stayed there for a few days and ate pretty good food for a change and drank a lot of beer. They served it all in paper cups. They didn't want us to get hurt by getting drunk and throwing things.

They had Italian POWs there. The first time we went into the mess hall, all the Italian POWs were ahead of us. That changed; we didn't let that happen anymore. They went to the end of the line. There were some Jap POWs below our barracks and somebody had all the sidewalks lined with rocks painted white. I suppose the Italian POWs had painted them white. For recreation, every time the Jap POWs came out of the building, we'd through a rock down on them! It was a tin roof building and it made a lot of noise! So we had a little fun down there.

Then they took us again by ferry to Oakland and we got on a train and we went back to Fort Leavenworth, Kansas and were processed again. They kicked us loose on a twenty-one-day leave home. We partied in a hotel in Kansas City for a couple of days and finally I called my parents and said I was going to be coming home. I left there in the morning on a train and got back home in the afternoon. I planned on being home sober, but when I got on the train, there were all kinds of civilians who wanted to celebrate with me. They were happy I was going home.

When I got off the train, I was pretty well loaded and here was my mother and my dad and my sister. I was twenty-one, I had gray hair, I was drunk, and all I could say was, "Take me home!"

So they did! The neighbors flocked in and brought food. I always liked how in Kansas, around the rivers, there were wild gooseberries, and I loved gooseberry pie! Well, there were people who brought in gooseberry pies and I couldn't even get around to eating them all there were so many. I had a friend who was sheriff of the county and he had a supply of whiskey. Of course Kansas was dry, but he had a supply he picked up from bootleggers, so he gave me the key to this building that had a semi-load of booze stacked in it! He said I could use it! I only took one bottle, though. I sat around home and went to town several times but there was no one around at all. Everyone I knew was still in the service.

After my leave was over, I reported to Hot Springs, Arkansas. The Army had taken over all those big hotels in Hot Springs and they were doing a psychological study. I wasn't particularly interested in what they were doing. I talked to a lot of doctors, and one of my company buddies was there. He was in supply. We had a pretty good time there, and they had some gambling rooms in Hot Springs. I stayed there for two or three weeks, and then they transferred me to Fort Warren in Cheyenne, Wyoming. I got there 1 April 1945 in a blizzard, and I was freezing to death! I went out to the post and it was cold! I went into the orderly room and they assigned me a room up on the second floor of the barracks. It was too cold up there so I told them I was going to call a cab and go back downtown and get a room in a warm hotel and when it warmed up, I'd see them. They said, "Okay!"

I moved downtown until it warmed up a little bit, then they put me in charge of guarding German POWs at night, only at night. The post was scared to death of those Germans, but we couldn't have driven them off with a stick. They were perfectly happy there. They were having a good time. They were living good and they were doing jobs for us. The Army assigned me five light Stuart tanks and the only ones I could get to repair them were the Germans! They did all my repair work for me and they also worked in the quartermaster depots. If I needed butter or sugar or anything like that, they brought it to me.

Black troops were on the post training for quartermaster posts. The post was run by white troops, but the trainees were all black. They switched me over to the training command, and I taught mines and booby traps to these black troops. We set up little bridges across Crow Creek. It ran through the post. To give them a thrill, I'd let them step on pressure releases and I'd blow up a quarter pound charge in the creek.

Then they sent me up to North Dakota and Minnesota where we trained the State Guard. These weren't National Guard, they were State Guard, and they were really young kids and old men. I did that for about a month. There was a big airplane hanger there and I was giving bayonet training to a bunch of guys during a hail storm. I gave up on it! Then I went back to Cheyenne and did some more training. There were only about three of us that had any combat experience on the post and they really didn't know how to treat us. They kind of stood away from us. They were leery of us.

I worked for this Colonel Black, a retiree, who lived at the end of the parade ground and he had me give a speech at a parade about fighting in the Pacific.

The general called me over and he said, "You need some fortification to stand up there!"

He handed me a water glass full of whiskey. I don't remember much about my speech after that!

They discharged me in Denver. Then I went home to find a job. My dad had reduced the farming operation down to practically nothing, and he wasn't too well. I plowed for a few days and that was about all. I looked around and everybody was being discharged from the service and there weren't any jobs. I didn't particularly want to go to college on the GI Bill.

I went back up to Leavenworth and asked to be sworn back in the service and they said, "No, you've got malaria and we don't want you."

I said, "Okay."

That same day I went from Leavenworth over to Fort Riley and there was a WAC captain over there and she said, "Sure I'll swear you in here and you can go on a ninety-day vacation. You don't have to report for ninety days."

I called my wife-to-be and said, "Will you marry me?"

June and I got married and had a three-month honeymoon! Then I reported to Fort Sam Houston, but they didn't have any jobs for me down there.

They said, "Do you want to become a cook or a baker?"

I didn't want to become a cook or baker so I ended up for a short time over in Arkansas training people that had been in Army prisons. They figured they could rehabilitate them. We gave them basic training again, and I worked one cycle over there. I asked for a transfer, and they sent me to Japan! I landed at the replacement depot outside of Yokohoma. My wife came over to Japan in September 1946, as I remember. I worked with a general in railroad repair, and I supervised forty-five-thousand Japanese employees. We were given a Japanese house and the Japanese government paid for it and we were authorized four maids. We swapped one maid for a cook. He had been a chef on a vessel and he'd been trained in Europe. Tremendous food! We also had four guards on the property and we had four boiler men and we had one gardener.

The Japanese people I worked with had been in the Japanese Army. A lot of them worked in the liaison office right next to my office. I had about twelve of them working in there. Most of them had served in Manchuria. They really hadn't seen much of the War other than with the Chinese. I got along very well with them. I never had an argument with all of these employees that I had. I couldn't ask for better people. I had one fellow work for me who I called Chuck. He was taller than I was. He went to the Olympics in Berlin in 1936. He was a javelin thrower and from a very wealthy family. A lot of the Japanese were like that. I had one fellow, I can't remember his last name, but I called him "Curly Head." He had curly hair! Strange for a Japanese! He was a Kamikaze pilot who never took off! My wife and I communicated with the people we worked with over there after we came back to the States. Most of them have died. We had one maid, her name was Ryubi. We sent her to sewing school and bought her a sewing machine and she became a seamstress for my wife. She still corresponds with my wife.

I finished my first tour in Japan in 1952 and then they sent me to Germany. I was in Frankfurt for about four years in a traffic-regulating group. Then we came home and they assigned me to the transportation school of Fort Eustis where I taught traffic management for nearly five years. I was about two years from retirement, and they shipped me to Korea and I was there with a military advisory group. I was there six, seven, eight months.

Then my son died. We had twins that were born in Virginia and they had heart problems. We took them to Walter Reed. Our daughter's condition they were able to correct, but never the boy's. They just said treat him like a normal kid. And we did and we had him for four years.

After that I called the chief of transportation office and asked to be stationed in Colorado. They said, "Go find a home."

So I went to Fitzimmons Army Hospital and they gave me a job there until I retired from the Army.

After the War I still suffered from malaria until about 1948 or 1949. That was about the last time I had it, and that's while I was in Japan. I also discovered tiny slivers of shrapnel were coming out of me. During the War, I must have been getting a lot of these tiny splinters or slivers of shrapnel in me. I never recall getting hit with any of this but the stuff must have been in the air after a shell burst. These pieces would work their way out of my body over time. I'd have a pimple and then it'd bust out. The last one I had was on my hip. It was a little sliver of metal, a half-inch long; like a needle but smaller than a needle.

Psychologically, the War had a profound effect. From the time I left Hollandia in New Guinea until I got home I had a lot of time that I don't remember. There were some vacant spots, but that disappeared. I know when we were first married I had malaria every month. I could tell the day of the month by a malaria attack, and I don't know how my wife put up with me for the first year that we were married. I was somewhat of a mess, but I think being married to the right person helped and I still say it sixty-one years later; she's still the right person. If I stayed busy, I felt that was the key to getting over it. But the War lingered in my memory.

My post-war service in Japan changed my opinion of the Japanese. They were just serving their country, like I was doing. I went back over there in 1960 and saw the people I worked with. We had a big reunion. While I was there I spoke to this civic group in Morioka. Every town in Japan, much like the United States, had army units taken from those towns. One was called the Morioka Division after this town. We fought them in New Guinea and we killed them all. These people knew that. They knew I was with the 32nd Division and they never, ever let on that this bothered them, if it indeed bothered them at all. Death in Asia is a lot different than death in the United States.

Since World War II we've been called "saviors" and "heroes." We certainly didn't think that way of ourselves during the War. I didn't know anybody that thought they were a hero or anything like a hero and I certainly didn't think that way of myself. But one thing World War II taught me was how good men could be under adverse conditions and at Buna we had some of the worst conditions. I'm also proud to have served with the 32nd Infantry Division. It was the first US Army unit on the offensive during World War II. We went through a lot of campaigns and a lot of battles. It was a rough three years!

[A few weeks after his interview, Mr. Hiatt generously prepared a video for use by the Center and the Saint Vincent College class Faces of Battle. The video includes anecdotes in addition to what he presented on audio tape. This additional material follows].

When Nature Calls in the Jungle

WE WERE ON SUCH short rations all the time that bowel movements were not normal in anyway shape or form. We'd go a week or ten days without having a normal movement and when we did have the urge to go, all that came out was maybe a tablespoon of white material like heavy grease, like Crisco. Most of the time unit sanitation was not a big problem because we weren't having any BM's to dirty up the areas. We'd dig a cat-hole and bury what we had. In a normal unit one would have a lot of people digging holes all the time! I am sure it was just due to the lack of food and also because we were using up every bit of that food in our bodies so there was nothing left over to get rid of.

Malaria: "I'm Sorry... You're Not Sick Yet."

I DON'T THINK THERE was a man in my squad wasn't sick with malaria while we were at Buna. I remember reading in a book that there was a medical officer who took the temperature of every man in one unit, a company-sized unit, and every man in there was running a temperature of some kind of varying degrees. It became a policy in December 1942 that (I don't know whose edict this was from) a man could not be sent to the battalion aid station unless his temperature was 105 or more! At a 105, most people aren't functioning right! That's what we were expected to deal with.

Percy Hiatt after the fighting on Buna in New Guinea.

Percy Hiatt (center) with his fellow gunner.

If someone said, "I'm really hot!," the medic man would stick a thermometer in his mouth and if it didn't come up 105 he would have to say, "I'm sorry but if you walk all the way back to the battalion, they're gonna kick your butt out of there because you're not sick yet."

The aid man did have a supply of APCs. That was a standard pain killer that the Army allowed him to carry. It was aspirin, paregoric and codeine. That did a pretty good job on the aches and pains of malaria, but beyond that it didn't do too much for severe pain. One could take three or four or five of them at one time and get kind of squirrly; a guy would be walking around a little light-headed. But that did help drive away the pain of malaria and with malaria, we'd just ache from head to foot, and that's the awful truth! Everything aches! It was a thing that the Army, evidently, hadn't even thought about over there because there was no issuing of repellents and there were no units set up at that time to drain the swamps or water areas where these mosquitoes could breed. This was the first battle the Army was in during the war in the Pacific. We, including our whole Army and including General MacArthur, didn't know what the hell was going to happen and they did not make provisions for these situations.

The Ape People

The next thing was jungle rot. I don't know the technical name but I think it was a parasite of some kind that usually got into the fleshy part of the leg. If the infected area went unattended, one could stick a little finger down into the hole it created in the leg where the flesh was just eaten away. It didn't stink like putrefied flesh, but a lot of people had it and it hurt! We were all issued in our First Aid packs sulpha powder and sulpha pills.[80] We'd pack those jungle rot wounds with sulpha powder and put a bandage around them and hoped that they would heal. Later on, after I got wounded and ended up in the hospital, I saw a lot of people in the hospital who had jungle rot and they were treating them with what I thought looked like blue vitriol. The only thing I knew about blue vitriol is that I used to sell it to irrigators who built cement ditches. Moss would grow in these ditches and this stuff would kill the moss. I may be wrong on the blue vitriol but it turned their bodies a reddish blue. Some of them had this jungle rot on their rear ends and they would get bathed in this blue stuff. Consequently, their butts turned a reddish blue and we called them "Ape People" because of their red rear ends![81]

Water: "It Tasted Like Hell!"

There are lots of films about the war in Europe where guys are carrying water cans around to people. I never saw water cans in combat around Buna other than the ones for our machine guns. They really didn't furnish us with water. We had to dig wells or we had to drink out of streams or collect rain water in our ponchos and in our helmets. Fortunately, a lot of the Company M men who were in the National Guard had gone to the University of Wisconsin in Platteville and studied mining. So we had guys who knew how to dig a well and crib it up with sticks. Sometimes, if we were long enough in one position, they'd take a hardtack can from the Australians, perforate it, set it down in the sand and let the water would seep into this one-cubic-foot can and we could get our drinking water. Of course a lot of units did not have this expertise, so we became the water men for part of the battalion.

When we saw a stream in the jungle, or even along the coast coming out of the jungle, it was brown; the color of a dark tea. I suppose that was from all the dead leaves that were filtered down through it. Also, we never knew what was up stream from us, whether there were dead Japs or even dead Americans or Australians in the streams. If we did have to use stream water we had to have Halezon tablets[82] with us. We could put one Halezon tablet to a canteen of water and let it dissolve, shake it up and it would kill most everything. It tasted like hell! I mean it would gag a goat trying to drink that stuff, but we drank. Those people who did not take this precaution of using Halezon tablets ended up with severe cases of dysentery. That will put a person flat on their backs. Some of them actually died with this damn dysentery.

Old Ammunition: Short Rounds and Misfires

THE 32ND DIVISION was brought into federal service in 1939 and went to the Louisiana maneuvers. They carried ammunition supplies with them all the time. I am sure we ended up with that same old ammunition over in New Guinea, for a while anyway, that they'd toted all over the world, practically. Some of it, probably, was World War I ammunition, especially the .30 caliber. We had a lot of misfires; we had trouble with the ammunition coming out of the webbing belts for the machine guns. They were just rusted or corroded in so that the bolt from the machine gun wouldn't extract them. That was a problem with the machine-gun platoon and, of course, we used a lot of that same ammunition for our rifle clips. The mortar platoon of the company (they had 81 mm mortars) had a heck of time trying to adjust their firing with ammunition that was old. The worst thing a mortar platoon could do, or want, was have a short round. Then they over compensated by firing so far out that sometimes they couldn't even find the first round to zero in! When they used smoke, they couldn't even see it.

General Wooten and the Pillbox

AT BUNA, MY BATTALION fought primarily on Cape Endaiadere and Duropa Point; those two pieces of land stuck out into the water just before we entered Buna. I suppose the area of these two pieces of land was a square mile; maybe a little bit more, but it wasn't very big. The mortar platoons and even the machine-gun platoons had to be careful not to fire too far because they might hit one of our units who were God-knows-where because we did not have too much contact with each other. In Cape

Endaiadere and Duropa Point, the Japanese had about fifty big pillboxes and probably one-hundred firing pits and an equal number of trenches. The pillboxes were very well built. They were made of sand-filled oil drums faced with coconut logs, topped with coconut logs and three-feet of dirt. They had firing slits, two doors and benches inside where the Japanese troops could go in and rest, cook or do whatever they had to do inside. They also used them as toilets, as I found out later on.

As we progressed across these two pieces of real estate, there were a lot of dead people inside and outside these fortifications. My estimation is that up until the time I was wounded and evacuated there must have been probably over three-thousand dead Japanese in those two little places and they had been there since October, November and December 1942. It was real smelly. I could smell it a long way off; our clothes were impregnated with this odor. I couldn't open my mouth to breath; I just couldn't do it. I breathed through my nose. It'd gag a maggot. It was a terrible place to be in.

The Australians were with us and we were backing them up. They did have some tanks there and also an Australian brigadier general named Wooten. I think he was a civilian soldier; he was a fat, jolly man. On the day that I saw him he had on starched clothing, shorts, knee-high socks and shined shoes. He came up to see if he could go into one of these pillboxes and see what they actually looked like. Well, they weren't about to let a brigadier general go into a pillbox first by himself! They grabbed me and a guy named John Crank, a little, short, curly-haired, good-looking guy from down in the southwest corner of Missouri. He was a lead miner in civilian life. They sent he and I into this pillbox that was twenty-feet long, eight-feet wide. It had a low roof and I couldn't stand up straight. We had to go in and make sure everything inside was dead. We just started at the door firing. Dead or alive we didn't care. We put some rounds in everybody. Well, this general standing outside thought we ran into a bunch of live Japs! He got as excited as hell and was hollering around for more people to come up! This old general thought that we were quite brave to go into this place and kill all those people in there! There might have been a wounded one in there, but most of them were already dead. He was so pleased with us that he gave me a pair of his woolen, knee socks! I don't think I had a pair new socks for a couple of months and here he pulled out of his pack this pair of nice, brown, desert-colored knee socks and gave them to me!

"He Woke Up Screaming and Went Berserk."

It was hot! All the time, day and night! I don't care what time of the day it was, It was hot! The days were in the nineties and the nights in the eighties. It rained two or three times a day. We never got dry, our equipment never got dry. Everything moldered if we weren't careful. Most of our clothing rotted and fell off; our shoes rotted and fell off. We were in mud and water all the time. Even though we were over on a beach area on Cape Endaiadere, which was mainly sandy, water would stand in most spots. All these people had malaria, were running temperatures, were sick and then to have the rain come by, they felt cold. This rain water really felt cold. This aggravated their symptoms and made them sicker each time.

Before we left the United States we were issued wool sweaters; that was standard Army issue. Some people continued to carry them and in some ways they were pretty smart because when they got malaria, and got the chills, even though that sweater might be wringing wet it felt warm when they put it next their bodies. So guys who still had these sweaters passed them around when someone was really feeling the chills.

I had this one man who had a wool sweater. He had a malaria attack and he laid down and he put this sweater over his face to keep the sun out of his eyes. He went to sleep, and thank God he slept for a while because he was going to feel better when he woke up. Or so we thought. Blowflies were all over the place, there were swarms of blowflies laying eggs on dead bodies which turned into maggots. Evidently, the blowflies had laid some eggs on this guy's sweater and while he was sleeping they hatched out and he had some maggots on his face. He woke up screaming and went berserk! He knew that he had maggots up his nose and in his ears. Well, maggots don't bother anything except dead flesh, but we couldn't convince him of that. We sent him back to the aid station and they told him the same thing. They poured alcohol in his ears and probed up his nose and didn't find anything. This man went insane just because of some goddamn blowfly maggots!

"Are You Short a Man?"

THERE WAS A MAN named Utterberg, a Jewish boy from Hollywood. We were bombed pretty severely one day. The Japanese used some pretty good-sized bombs that day. Normally they used a two-hundred, 250-pound bomb, or some smaller than that. But this day they must have dropped something bigger, probably in the range of five-hundred pounds.

After this air raid was over, the first sergeant of Company K hollered over to me and said, "Are you short a man?"

I looked around and Utterberg wasn't there. We found him sitting on the edge of a bomb crater; his feet were over the edge down in the crater. He had no clothing on, he had very little skin left on the front on him, and he was blind. God knows what happened but evidently this bomb blast just must have skinned him. It was an awful sight! I hated to see him go in more than one way. He was a good ammunition packer for me, he did what he was told and also he didn't smoke, I did. Utterberg liked me so he gave me his cigarette rations. I really missed him when he left because I had no more extra rations.

Harold's Club in Reno, Nevada sent us, (and why they did this I have no idea, I don't know where the association came in) carton after carton of cigarettes throughout the War. They also sent us used decks of cards and dice. We were always tickled to death when Harold's Club supplies finally caught up with us. And they were usually a pretty good brand of cigarette. Most of the time we got Raleighs, Pall Malls and a bunch of off-brand stuff. We very seldom saw Camels or Luck Strikes. We appreciated Harold's Club for doing that for us.

Building a Road in a Swamp

They pulled our company off the line for a few days and our cannon company as well and took us over to Dobadura which they were developing into an airstrip and the hospital was over there as well. They were trying to get a road built through the swamp. The engineers were over there too and they gave us axes and cross-cut saws, a two-man saw, and we were to cut down ever damn tree we could get our hands on and build this corduroy road. This swamp was two or three-feet deep and we had to build this thing up through the water and above the water several feet so truck traffic could go through. The only nice-sized trees available to make this road were coconut trees and, also, a rubber plantation happened to be there. We sawed down somebody's rubber trees. I don't know who owned them! They were a nice, straight tree and so were the coconut trees, some of them had bends in them. But we learned as soon as we got an ax and swung at a coconut tree we'd better stand back because it was just like hitting steel! An ax hardly cut into them at all. Coconut trees are made up of fibers that run the whole length of the tree. That's why they can stand all that wind. But we could cut them with a cross-cut saw into lengths and put them across this corduroy road. I rode on it later on after I was wounded. So I got some benefit out of it.

"The Only Japanese We Wanted to See Were Dead Ones."

When they evacuated me out of the hospital at Dobadura back to Port Morseby, the plane could have pulled right up to the hospital. The hospital was on the edge of the airstrip. But it didn't do that. The airplane we were loaded on was at the end of the airstrip probably half-a-mile away. Walking wounded walked down there in 110 degrees, no trees. I rode several planes over in the Pacific and none of them ever had a door on them and never had a window on them. I suppose they kicked them out or took them off to let some air in because it was hot in those old planes. It was just like inside an oven. So we got down there, got on the plane, they fired it up and tried to move it but the damn thing sank down into the mud. We had to get off, not only the walking wounded but the ones on stretchers too. They had to unload them and they brought down a couple of Jeeps and tied up ropes to this old plane and tried to pull it out. They couldn't get it out. So then they revved the motors on the plane up as high as they could and it kind of leap-frogged ahead a little and finally got it onto some solid ground. We reloaded everybody up again and this time they put a Japanese prisoner on there with us accompanied by two MPs. The feelings were not good. Most of the people did not like this at all. The only Japanese we wanted to see were dead ones.

We took off and we got up in the air pretty well going over the Owen Stanley Mountains. We had to gain altitude quick because this mountain range was right beside us.

I noticed a lot of the men were talking among themselves about this Jap. Some of the walking wounded said to the MPs, "Throw that sonofabitch out and if you don't throw him out, we'll throw you out!"

So the MPs threw this guy out! This was war. A terrible thing! But I had no sympathy for that Japanese at that time. I would now, but not then. That was one of the few things I saw that happened in the War that really shouldn't have happened.

The Supply Problem

They built a big supply point at Oro Bay which was down the coast from Buna quite a ways but sadly there was no road from Oro Bay to where we were. They were unloading all that ammunition, food and supplies down there but they couldn't get it up to us by land other than a single-file trail that the native carriers used. They could carry fifty pounds max but there weren't enough native carriers to haul enough ammunition to keep two divisions in supply. So they brought up these steel barges and they had some small horses pulling them up. They couldn't move them in the day time and at night there were some Japanese PT boats operating off shore. They would sneak them in. They would run these barges into the beach and the following day we unloaded their cargo. We got into the water maybe waist high. Several times while we unloaded these supplies, Japanese PT boats came by and fired on us. One time it happened, I wasn't quite sure it was the Japanese. By the silhouette of the boat we thought it looked like a Navy PT boat! This was the type of supply situation we had. We were tickled to death to go out and unload this stuff because sometimes it was food but mostly it was ammunition or medical supplies.

"I Would Have Liked to Have Shot the Sonofabitch Instead of Paying Him."

This is kind of a pet peeve of mine but we didn't see much of the Red Cross during World War II. I saw them once and this wasn't at Buna, this was up in Saidor. After everything had quieted down up there they pulled us off the line and low and behold here was the Red Cross set up in a coconut grove. They had a big tent and they had tables set out in the coconut grove They had socks, handkerchiefs, shorts, chewing gum and shaving equipment. The normal things one would expect the American Red Cross would be distributing to troops free of charge. They weren't, they were selling them. I bought some handkerchiefs, some socks, some shorts and I bought some chewing gum from a Red Cross representative in a Red Cross uniform. I would have liked to have shot the sonofabitch instead of paying him. But I didn't. After I got home to Emporia in 1945, an Army intelligence agent came down and interviewed me for two days. I told them about it and at that time I remembered the Red Cross representative's name. I don't now, I've forgotten. I hope he's in Hell, but anyway I told them the story and they couldn't believe it. But that actually happened. Things aren't nice in wartime and that was one of them. I have never given to the Red Cross since then.

When I was stationed in Japan, the Korean War broke out and there were hundreds of thousands of Korean refugees and orphaned children and abandoned children. The American Red Cross came to my wife in Morioka and asked her is she could supervise making layettes for the Korean orphans using the Japanese Red Cross organization which was in town. They promised my wife that if they would do this, they would give these Japanese ladies for the efforts in making all these layettes an American Red Cross pin for each of them. This was a tremendous incentive for these ladies to do this; just to be able to get this American Red Cross pin. So they sent to them these pre-cut-out layettes that all they had to do was sew together. They sewed together thousands and thousands of these things and sent them to Korea and the project ended.

My wife said to this Red Cross gal in Tokyo, "Where are the pins?"

They said, "Oh no! We're not going to give these damn Japanese any American Red Cross pins!"

Well, that's what they promised. Anyway, it got to General MacArthur's headquarters and they finally did get their pins. The American Red Cross was not the organization at that time that we thought they should be.

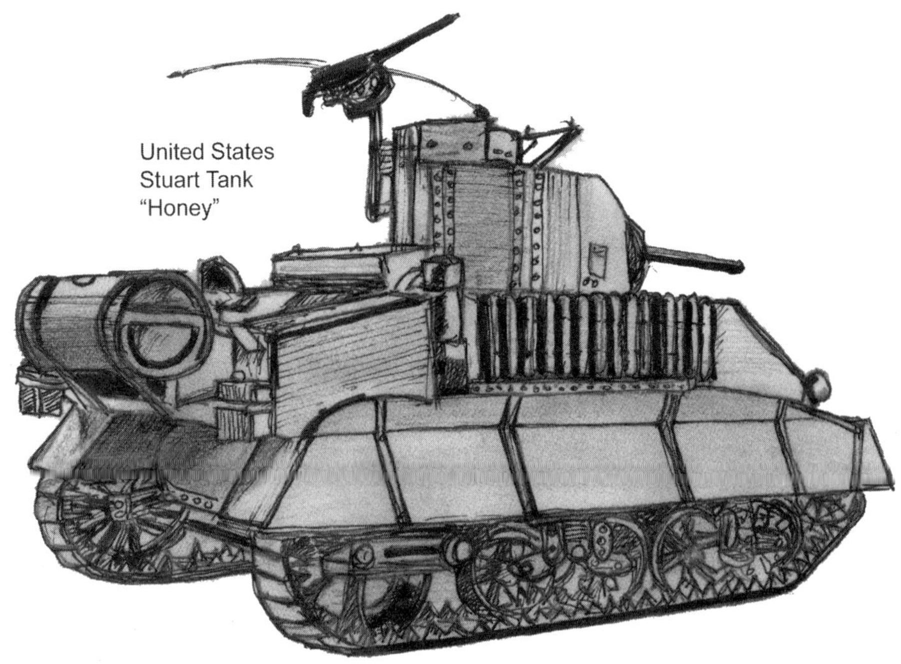

"When Those Big Guns Went Off, the Whole Ship Shook."

James Weston Humphreys

United States Navy
Battleship USS *Massachusetts* (BB–59)
Destroyer Escort USS *Fowler* (DE–222)
Born in Derry, Pennsylvania, 12 November 1921

"I stayed aboard the Fowler from her commissioning until the end of the War. We were in Boston when the war in Europe ended. From Boston, we went to Florida. We went to sea to ride out a hurricane, and that was a rough ride. We joked that we'd go over two waves and under one! Our 'critical' roll was seventy-one degrees; if we had rolled over that far, we might not be able to roll back. During that hurricane, we rolled seventy degrees. Everything came out of the bins. Potatoes and canned goods were everyplace. The cooks couldn't keep water in the steam kettles to make coffee. I didn't take my clothes off that night, and I slept with my life belt on."

I WAS BORN AT 317 North Chestnut Street in Derry, Pennsylvania. My father was Davis Humphreys. He didn't have a middle name, but he carried a middle initial of "E," because his pay checks kept getting mixed up with another Humphreys that also worked for the railroad. My father was a foreman in the maintenance shops. He was born and raised in Ebensburg. He started on the railroad at Old Allegheny[83] on the North Side, then they moved him to Derry in 1921. He worked for the railroad his whole life. He had an eighth-grade education, which was a little more than most had at that time. He was seventy-seven when he died.

My mother was Twila Adora Brown. Her family originated in Lewisville, Indiana County, Pennsylvania. Her father was killed on the railroad. He was an engineer and his boiler blew up at a place known as Denny's Curve. During World War I, my mother worked on the railroad as a telephone operator. She went to Blairsville Academy.

I have two brothers, John, who passed away, and Bob, who lives in Maryland. He's six years younger than I am, and John was five years older than I. John's death had a lot to do with what had happened to him during the War. He was in the combat engineers. He was a German prisoner of war for eleven months. He was in bad shape after the War. He'd gotten captured in Italy. He was a sergeant and his outfit was on a night patrol. He leaned up against a tank that he thought had been destroyed, and a German came out of it, tapped him on the shoulder and took him prisoner.

Growing up in Derry, if I got into any trouble, my parents knew about it before I got home. We were Ridge Runners[84] for the most part. We played baseball in the middle of the street, since there were hardly any cars. We used to sled ride down the hill up near the Catholic church. We only got two or three rides a night, since it took forty-five minutes to walk back up the hill. We'd ice skate on Ethel Springs Lake. One winter the ice on the lake was twenty-two-inches thick.

It was very bad for us during the Depression. The railroad was the main business in Derry, and Depression hit at about the same time the mines were beginning to run out of coal, so a lot of the mines closed. Dad had thirty years of service on the railroad, and when the Depression hit, he got bumped from foreman back to a machinist. Then in the middle of the Depression, he got sick and was off for almost a year. He was the next one in line to be laid off. Some of the guys I ran around with, their dads lost their homes, everything. When things started to pick up, they got other jobs and never went back to the railroad.

I graduated from Derry Boro High School in 1939. I enjoyed mathematics, history and English. I sure didn't like Latin! I played tackle and guard on the football team. My junior year we were pretty good. We only lost one game. My senior year was a whole other story. Most of the kids on the team were new. I think we won two games that year.

After high school I worked for V.W. Smith. He ran a country store in Derry across from the post office. He sold canned goods, fresh meat, shoes, yard goods, sweepers, electric irons. I clerked in the store and made deliveries in a little Ford pickup truck. I think I made twenty-one dollars per month. That was for a six-day week and a twelve-or-fourteen-hour day. I worked there for five or six months.

We knew back as far as 1937 that we were going to get into a war. Then in 1939, even as a kid, I didn't see how we could stay out of it. I was working on the railroad when I saw I was probably going to get drafted, so I enlisted in the Navy in June of 1942. I had gone down to visit my brother John at Fort Belvoir, and that helped convince me I didn't want any part of the Army!

I said goodbye to my parents and got on the train in Derry. I went to Pittsburgh and raised my right hand, got sworn in, and then boarded a Pullman car. We rode all night and all day the next day. They ran us almost up into Maine and then brought us back down into Newport, Rhode Island. At that time, Newport was a small town with a Navy base about a mile or so outside of town housing fifty-thousand sailors. They all went into town on the weekends and just milled around. The locals posted signs in their yards, "No Dogs Or Sailors Allowed."

At Newport, they spent hours teaching us how to tie the various knots. I think it was just to keep us busy. We ran "The Grinder" every morning before breakfast; that was the obstacle course. It seemed like it was three-miles long. I spent part of the Fall up there, and it was cold! I slept in a hammock, and I put newspapers under me to help keep in my body heat. After basic training, I stayed at Newport for Electrical School because I had been an electrician's apprentice on the railroad. I was up there for about sixteen weeks.

I came out of Electrical School as an Electrician's Mate, Third Class. The electrical work I did in the Navy was completely different from what I had done on the railroad. In the Navy, I worked on sound-powered phones and the regular telephone systems, and the Selsun motor, which communicated the captain's wishes from the bridge to the engine room. They called it the "engine order telegraph." I also trained on the desalination system. There were four sensors on the line that measured the salt content of the water. The boilers required water with less than two grains of salt per gallon. What we drank contained at least five or six grains of salt per gallon. The boilers got the best water. They'd have been damaged if they'd have been given the same amount of salt we were drinking. When I first started drinking it, I could taste the salt. But after I got used to it, I could hardly taste it at all.

After training, I went up to Maine and picked up the USS *Massachusetts.* When I first went on board, I thought I'd never find my way around. It was huge! When I got below the armored deck, I couldn't get to the next compartment over. I'd have to go up a level to go down; it was compartmentalized. The armored deck was sixteen-inches thick. There were three voids on the outside of the hull, two on the inside and a sixteen-inch armor plate in between. They claimed we could take five torpedoes in the same spot and still fight the ship. The crew complement was around three-thousand men.[85]

I was turned over to Chief Petty Officer Muir, who was the chief of the "E" Division. He was responsible for my on-the-job training. He placed me with a first or a second class electrician to learn the job. After they thought I knew what I was doing, they turned me loose on my own. Once I had to crawl back into the shaft alleys to change the repeaters on the Selsun system. Things didn't break down that often. Usually it was rough handling that caused the problems. On another instance, they sent two of us down into the bowels of the ship to clean the paint off of the decks and bulkheads. The paint had to be removed because of the threat of fire during a battle. The other guy was overcome by the fumes and I got sick. They had to drag him out of there.

There was a lot of "hurry up and wait." It's really, really boring from day to day. We had a few movies, and we played penny-ante poker every so often. Religious services were held on deck under the main guns. We listened to Tokyo Rose all the time. She sank us three times when I was in the Pacific! I didn't stand any watches on the *Massachusetts*, and had nothing to do unless something needed repaired. The captain was a nice guy. I screwed up his call signals one morning, and he sent for me.

All he said was, "You learned something, son."

That was it! He could have taken my stripes away just as easy. Most of the officers on the battleship thought they were gods. The chiefs were pretty laid-back.

I really don't know what happened off Casablanca![86] I was wearing sound-powered phones at my battle station, but no one ever really told us what was going on. That was the hard part, not knowing what was going on. My battle station on the *Massachusetts* was the aft gyro, which was the backup compass. The only thing below me was the keel! I was on the same level as the shaft alleys. Whenever they'd fire the main guns, I never knew if we were the hitter or the hittee. When those big guns went off, the whole ship shook. We were laying about twenty miles offshore throwing shells onto the beach in support of the North Africa landings. We were hit three times by enemy fire. They hit the butcher shop, the Marine compartment and they hit the flag. There was very little damage and no casualties.[87] We were only there for a couple of days, and then we returned to Maine to refit.

We were off Cape Hatteras, going to the South Pacific, when we hit a hurricane. It was bad enough that the three destroyers that were escorting us were taking water down their stacks. We had our number-one turret flooded out. The bow apron was torn away, and the leather around the main guns was torn off, which allowed water into the turret. The main electrical cables that drove the turret went to ground. That wasn't my Division, but I was down there with every electrician on the ship helping to rewire the turret. We picked up three or four spools of new cable in Panama. We started pulling the wire in as soon as we cleared the Canal, and it took about two weeks to get that turret back in service.

It was hot going through the Canal. We had to stand at quarters as we went through, and my face got sunburned. We stopped at Gatun Lake to get degaussed. The ship would take on a static charge, and to counteract any magnetic mines, they'd wrap cables around the hull of the ship to demagnetize it. They started degaussing at around six in the evening and by the next noon, we were under way again. The *Massachusetts* had a 109-foot beam and the Canal is 110-feet wide. A couple of anti-aircraft gun blisters that stuck out a little too far scraped against the sides. They had to be patched back together.

From the Canal we went to Noumea, New Caledonia, which lays about nine-hundred miles east of Australia.[88] I got to go ashore at Noumea every eighteen days, unless we were at sea. They had trenches dug around the town. We stayed around there for two or three months, until the Japanese cleared out, and we were involved in the Munda campaign. Then we moved up to the New Hebrides. We worked with the British carrier HMS *Illustrious* in our battle group. We worked with the USS *Enterprise*, too. "Bull" Halsey[89] was our fleet commander. As far as I can remember, we never fired a gun while I was aboard in the Pacific.

In the New Hebrides, I caught the USS *North Carolina*, which was on her way back to Pearl Harbor for repairs. She had damaged a screw on a reef. At Pearl, they put a bunch of us on a truck and took us to a pineapple grove where we spent the night. Next day, after breakfast, they trucked us over to the old USS *Pennsylvania*. Talk about a piece of junk? She had four turrets of three 14-inch guns. She could fire any one gun on any turret at any time. She couldn't fire two guns from the same turret at the same time. The *Pennsylvania* took us to San Francisco where I got a thirty-day leave.[90]

From 'Frisco, I caught a train to Florida. It was a steam engine with wooden coaches. I had to sleep sitting up. Smoke came in one window and went out the other. We stopped in Houston, Texas and then they dropped us off in the middle of nowhere in the Florida panhandle for an eight-hour layover. From there, they took us to Miami where they put us twelve-to-a-room in a hotel. We had to march down Biscayne Boulevard every day to breakfast. After being in the Pacific, I had to wear my peacoat some mornings. I damn near froze to death. They gave us indoctrination training for destroyer escorts. When the hull was ready for us in Philadelphia, they shipped us up there and we put the *Fowler* in commission.

I was a plank-owner[91] on the *DE–222*, the USS *Fowler*.[92] By this time I was an

Electrician's Mate, Second Class, and I made sure the whole electrical system was working. We did have to rewire a panel that had gotten wet. It had been exposed on the weather deck and shorted out. My battle station was damage control in the number-two engine room. Actually, if they'd have put a 5-inch shell at the waterline, they'd have sunk the ship. Our outer hull was only about 5/8-inch thick.

It seems I went from the sublime to the ridiculous. On the *Massachusetts*, we had nine 16-inch guns, twenty 5-inch/38s and a couple hundred anti-aircraft guns. The *Fowler* had three open-turret 3-inch guns, which were loaded by hand. Nothing was automated on them. Our biggest weapons were our depth charges. We were a submarine chaser. We had two racks of depth charges, six K-guns, three on each side, and a battery of hedgehogs. The hedgehog could throw many different patterns of smaller depth charges. We had a crew of about two-hundred men and the ship could do twenty knots.[93]

We were a week from Gibraltar with our first convoy when the Normandy invasion took place.[94] We did not know what had happened until we got to Bizerte. Sometimes we had convoy duty with French corvettes. The *Fowler* chased several submarines in the Atlantic, and we got credit for one kill off Gibraltar. We got that one with depth charges.[95] I never saw a German aircraft.

Once, a sub sneaked into the middle of our convoy and shot two of our Liberty ships with acoustic torpedoes. We weren't even at general quarters when it happened. We stayed alongside and escorted the Liberty ships while the rest of the convoy continued to Gibraltar.[96] All told, we escorted about six convoys across the Atlantic and into the Mediterranean.[97]

One night we got the daylights scared out of us. We were on convoy duty in the middle of the Atlantic, and we went in close to tell one of the freighters that he was showing lights. Under three-hundred yards yards, the radar went blank; it didn't show anything. The freighter ended up turning our lights out: he rammed us. He almost took our bow off. We managed to get it braced and got going again. The Old Man, the Commodore who was running the convoy, wanted to know if we could still fight our ship.

"Oh, yes," our captain said, "we can fight. There's not that much damage."

The Commodore came aboard, took one look at the damage and said, "You can't fight this ship."

The captain was relieved of his command after that convoy.

We were tied alongside a partially-sunken hull in Bizerte where some black market activity was going on. I wanted to go over and see what they had. I was standing at the rail, and one of the officers walked up to me.

"What are you doing, Humphreys?"

"I'm just looking."

"C'mon," he said, and then jumped over the rail. That's the kind of officer we had aboard the little ship. An officer on the battleship would never have done that. We were a much closer-knit crew on the *Fowler*.

Even though we got fed regularly, we were always hungry. One time I cooked pork chops under the Statue of Liberty. We were supposed to go to Philly, but they sent us to New York instead. We got there in the early evening, but it was too foggy to get into the port. The ship's food storage locker was right next to the gyro room on the *Fowler*. Whenever the cook came down to get stuff to make the next day's meals, he'd leave the food locker open. Well, we'd have to help ourselves to what was inside there. So I got some pork chops, I got my hot plate, which I wasn't supposed to have, and dogged myself into the aft gyro room. I fried the pork chops thinking nobody would know I was down there. Well, they were smelling pork chops all over the ship! I'd forgotten about the ventilation system. So everybody was looking for the guy who was cooking the pork chops.

I stayed aboard the *Fowler* from her commissioning until the end of the War. We were in Boston when the war in Europe ended. From Boston, we went to Florida. We went to sea to ride out a hurricane, and that was a rough ride. We joked that we'd go over two waves and under one! Our "critical" roll was seventy-one degrees; if we had rolled over that far, we might not be able to roll back. During that hurricane, we rolled seventy degrees. Everything came out of the bins. Potatoes and canned goods were everyplace. The cooks couldn't keep water in the steam kettles to make coffee. I didn't take my clothes off that night. I slept with my life belt on.

I was sure I'd be going to the Pacific, so I came home on leave and got married to Phylis. If Harry Truman hadn't dropped the Bomb, I'd have gone back to the Pacific. I was a First Class by then, and if the War had lasted another six months, I'd have made Chief. But, I had my points and was discharged in August of 1945.

I came home, joined the VFW and went to work for the railroad. We have a *Fowler* reunion every year.[98]

The service gave me confidence. When I got out of the Navy, I knew where I was in the world.

http://www.navsource.org/archives/06/222.htm

“We Had Our Baptism of Fire, and We Survived.”

James J. Jochen

United States Army
89th Infantry Division
“Rolling W,” “Midwest Division”
Motto: “Get It Done”
355th Infantry Regiment, Company K
Master Sergeant, Texas National Guard (1950)
36th Infantry Division, 136th Tank Battalion, Company C
Born in Schulenberg, Texas, 10 October 1925
College Station, Texas

“I looked up and saw Colonel Harris, the regimental commander, calmly striding down the road toward the front of the column to see what the delay was. Harris was about six-feet, six-inches tall, and from my position in the ditch looked like a Texas pine tree. Before the colonel got out of sight, my friend, John Searle, hustled his mortar up to a position where he could engage the enemy gun. John's first round was close, and the Germans chose to vacate their position. John had to expose himself to the enemy before he could fire his mortar. Either he fired before they could sight their gun on him, or they didn't see him at all. At any rate, John got a citation for his bravery.”

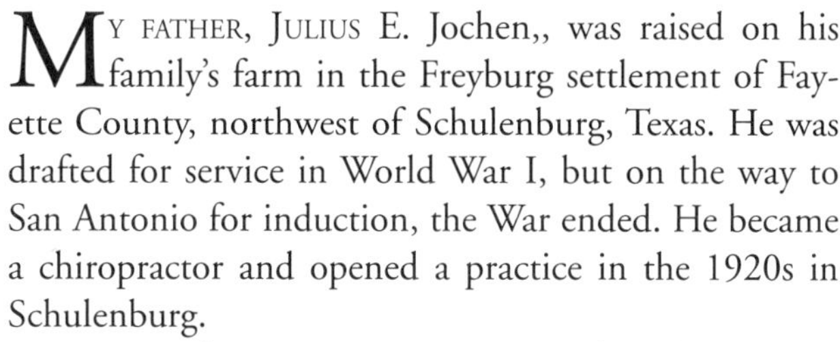

My father, Julius E. Jochen,, was raised on his family's farm in the Freyburg settlement of Fayette County, northwest of Schulenburg, Texas. He was drafted for service in World War I, but on the way to San Antonio for induction, the War ended. He became a chiropractor and opened a practice in the 1920s in Schulenburg.

My mother, Eva Parma, was raised on her family's farm in the Ammansville settlement northeast of Schulenburg. She married my father in October 1924. Before her wedding, my mother worked in a dry goods store as a sales person and seamstress.

After Mass on 7 December 1941 my father, my brother and I headed for the woods to hunt squirrel. Since it was December, I hoped that weather wouldn't ruin the outing that I had been looking forward to for several days. Thankfully, the weather favored us, so we stayed in the woods until late afternoon and didn't get home until it was dark. Once inside the house, we found my mother and sister intently listening to the radio. They informed us that the Japanese had attacked Pearl Harbor.

As a senior in high school, I was relatively ignorant of much of what was going on in world affairs, especially as regards the strained relations between the United States and Japan. I knew that Japan and China had been at war for years, and that a war was going on in Europe. Newsreels at the movies showed stories occasionally, and newspapers, magazines and radio covered it in sketchy and general terms, but all of that was far away and we teenagers didn't see what possible effect the events there could have on our tiny, personal worlds.

At school the next morning, we gathered in the auditorium to listen as President Roosevelt delivered his "Day of Infamy" speech and a declaration of war against Japan. Soon after, Germany and Italy entered the War on the side of Japan. It took several days for our seventeen-year-old minds to realize what was happening.

Actually, Americans began to feel the effects of war before Pearl Harbor. In 1940 the United States Government instituted a military draft, and all males between eighteen and forty-five had to register and receive a draft number. Those of us in high school who could type moved the school typewriters to the community hall and helped with the paperwork required for the "sign-up." That took several days of that week of school!

After Pearl Harbor, people on the east and west coasts reported seeing enemy submarines searching for military and merchant ships. At school, they showed us instructional films on how to deal with incendiary fires and how to administer First Aid. The whole country, even the young, went into a wartime posture.[99]

It became hard to find things that we usually took for granted. For instance, clothing made of silk virtually disappeared from the marketplace because the government needed silk for parachutes and other military goods. Even cotton goods were hard to get or very expensive because most of the cotton cloth went to make military uniforms. Importing was out of the question because cargo space on merchant ships was at a premium. I heard people say that the Great Depression helped prepare us for all the scarcity.

We got used to our mothers saying, "Use it up, wear it out, make it do, or do without!"

If someone bought a car before the War, they were lucky. Buying a good, serviceable car after the War started was nearly impossible. Fortunately, two of my uncles were in auto sales. Since my father was a chiropractor and made house calls in our town and also nearby towns, he was entitled to extra gas rations. Our family car was a 1935 Ford sedan, but Dad needed a car that would last the duration of the War. Uncle John discovered a well-cared-for 1940 Ford sedan. Family connections paid off! That 1940 Ford lasted until 1950 when new car production got back to normal.

In May 1942, I graduated from Schulenburg High School. I was just under seventeen. At seventeen I could have enlisted in some branch of the service with my parents' consent, but they wouldn't have been too keen on the idea. Anyway, they felt that I'd be rejected because of my asthma. College in the Fall appeared to be a default option.

In the meantime, my uncle, Emil Pratka, who operated a feed and produce business, gave me a job at an hourly wage of thirty cents. I worked twelve to fourteen hours a day supplying boxes to the onion graders and carrying the boxes to the appropriate sacker. The onion harvest lasted about six weeks, and during that time I progressed to the position of grader on the conveyer and got a five-cent raise!

Life was good!

One of my classmate's father, the president of the First National Bank in Schulenburg, was concerned that he was going to lose at least one of his two employees to the Draft. He was aware that I'd studied accounting in high school, and that I could type. He also felt that I'd be rejected by the military because of asthma, so he offered me a permanent job at the bank. This was toward the end of the onion season, and since none of us wanted to disrupt Uncle Emil's business, we agreed that I'd start at the bank when the season ended. My life appeared to be charted. Or so I thought.

Soon, I decided that college was where I wanted to be, and in December 1942 I was accepted by the Southwest Texas Teacher's College at San Marcos (now Southwest Texas State University), and planned to enroll in January 1943. I left my job at the bank. My military obligation was still ahead of me, so I applied for Air Force pilot training with my friend and classmate, James Gebert. We passed all the exams except our physicals. James had bad eyes, and I failed because of my asthma. I also didn't meet the weight requirement.

At any rate, I was six weeks from my eighteenth birthday, so I registered for the draft. Since it might be as long as one year before I got called up, I looked for work to fill in the time. The Frost National Bank of San Antonio, like many firms, had lost a number of employees to the military and because of my experience in the banking business they hired me on the spot at a monthly salary of seventy-five dollars.

Then it happened. On the early morning of 1 December 1943, I actually looked forward to the day's schedule. I was to report to the United States Post Office in downtown San Antonio and be taken to an induction center for a physical. All bets were that I'd be rejected because of chronic asthma. Rejection would place me back in college for the January semester where I'd spend the next several years finishing a degree. By then, the War would be over, and everything would be back to normal.

Life would be good.

By late evening of the same day, I had to rethink all of my plans. Apparently, my asthma didn't show up in the physical. No one asked me if I suffered from it, and we had been instructed to remain silent unless someone asked us a direct question. Anyway, I passed the physical, was sworn in, and then got orders to report for duty in thirty days. I called my parents to update them with the "good" news, but it was more a job of convincing than updating. They just couldn't believe it.

Around two o'clock in the morning of 2 January 1944, I said goodbye to my parents and boarded a train for San Antonio. At around eight the same morning, Army trucks arrived to take us to Fort Sam Houston.

At the post, some "old soldiers" (they had a total of two-weeks service) cheered us with, "You'll be sorry!"

After a roll call, we went to the quartermaster building for our uniforms and other

GI items, plus the usual GI haircut. That meant total loss of hair.

"We do that so you won't need a comb," the barber said. "Besides, one less personal-care item helps the war effort."

After the haircut, we went to a barracks where we got our beds and instructions on how to prepare our civilian clothing and personal effects for shipment home. We also learned how to make a bed the Army way. We practiced doing that for several hours until we satisfied the instructor.

I was surprised by the quality and variety of food in the mess hall, and always looked forward the to meals. Some inductees learned a hard lesson at the first meal.

We were told, "Take all you want, but want all you take."

Several returned trays with food left on them, and they immediately got assigned to KP (Kitchen Police) cleaning trays. After that, they "took all they wanted, but wanted all they took!" Fortunately, I had been briefed by a friend who preceded me into the service on the military dining tradition of "waste not, want not."

We spent the next two weeks getting immunized, viewing training films, receiving instruction in basic military lore, working in the kitchen, doing guard duty at night (basically fire watch) and becoming militarized. We learned how to wear our uniforms, how to salute, how to march in formation, and how to change direction or halt as one.

Though we were confined to post, we were allowed to visit the PX (Post Exchange) and the movie theater. We were encouraged to write home. Guard duty relieved one of KP duty, and since I disliked kitchen work, I always volunteered for one of the guard shifts. Guard duty began at five o'clock in the afternoon and ended at five o'clock in the morning. Each guard did a two-hour shift watching out for fire or forbidden activity.

"Police call" began at quarter-past-five in the morning when they turned the lights on. We got up, washed, made beds, swept and mopped the floors, emptied the cans we used for ashtrays, and then we went outside, formed a line, and moved forward picking up each cigarette butt, scrap of paper, stick of wood, or anything else that wasn't a part of the natural environment. If the person in charge following behind found anything we missed, he made us repeat the process until the area was perfectly clean.

Our time at Sam Houston was an interim period before we began basic training. Many of us felt Fort Sam Houston was the place where the Army wanted to check our character and mettle to see who was worth the effort to send to basic training. A few recruits with special skills were soon removed and sent to schools where they could enhance their skills and thus become more valuable to the military.

Finally, the waiting came to an end. In mid-January came THE roll call. For security reasons they didn't tell us when or where we were going. Two-hundred-fifty of us were told to be ready to move out in thirty minutes. We loaded onto a troop train that had originated on the west coast. We still had no inkling of where we were heading. It was a true adventure for the "country boys" who had never been away from their hometowns.

We stopped several times, sometimes for hours, to let more critical trains pass. From the road signs, we knew we were headed east. We slept in our seats as best we could. We had sandwiches and water, and there was coffee for those who wanted it. Breakfast was a cold-egg sandwich. Gone were the days of sumptuous meals at Sam Houston.

Finally, at noon of the third day of traveling, we pulled into Camp Wheeler, Georgia, near Macon, the state Capitol. Military buses carried us to the 9th Training Battalion area where they broke us down into platoons of fifty men each. I was placed in 2nd Platoon, Company C, 9th Battalion. Lieutenant Ward and two assistants, Corporals Floyd and Meadows commanded the platoon. The ages of the men in my platoon ranged from eighteen to forty, and it was like that throughout the whole battalion. Our seventeen weeks of training were about to begin.

During the seventeen weeks, fifteen battalions trained simultaneously, each in a different week of the cycle, depending on when recruits arrived. Troops who finished their training cycle were processed for dispersal, but were first given a furlough home. Dispersal points varied. Most of the troops went to different divisions throughout the United States to fill rosters and undergo advanced combat training. Some went directly overseas as replacements, while others went to specialist schools like communications, food service, medics. Those who had several years of college, and especially if they had been in Reserve Officer Training Corps programs, might be sent to Officer Candidate School. A select few who had adjusted in an extraordinary way to military discipline might be held back to serve as instructors.

At Camp Wheeler we got our combat kits—M1 rifle, bayonet, gas mask, cartridge belt, canteen, mess kit, First Aid kit, entrenching tool, steel helmet, half of a small tent called a "shelter half" (we shared our half with a buddy's), rope, short pole, wooden pegs (all used for raising the tent or "shelter half"). Calisthenics were the order of the day. We marched, and marched, and marched. We practiced erecting our tents. We scrubbed the barracks. We policed the area.

According to the military, "Idle hands were the playthings of the Devil."

The only time we were idle was during ten-minute smoke breaks. At the end of the day, the battalion formed up, and the commanders reported the status of their groups. After the bugler sounded "Retreat," we retired to our barracks.

Our barracks were two-storey buildings; each building held a full platoon, and the non-coms had small, private rooms at one end. The platoons were organized into four squads of twelve men each, plus two platoon guides. Two squads occupied each floor of the building, one squad on each side of each floor. One trainee from each platoon was made "squad leader." He had no special authority except to be a sort of "mother hen" to the other eleven men. I became an "acting squad leader," and I wore an armband with corporal's stripes on it. The armband announced to everyone that I was "acting squad leader." The greatest benefit accorded an acting squad leader was that he was eliminated from the duty roster and was never assigned KP. As acting squad leader, I did get assigned to guard duty, but did not walk the tours; instead, I was in charge of the guards who did. I was expected to see that all squad members did all their chores in timely fashion, kept their beds and personal areas tidy, knew the serial number of their rifles, kept the rifles clean and were ready to go at "go time" for any activity. In other words, I made sure the men did everything they were supposed to do, and did nothing they were not supposed to do. Though I was the youngest in my squad, the men accepted me as their "leader," and we never had any problems.

During off-duty hours, we visited the PX and the Service Club. The PX was the Army's version of Wal-Mart. It also sold a less potent version of beer than "civilian beer," and almost anyone in uniform, of age or not, could purchase it. No one asked for ID. I had never acquired the taste for beer, so it made no difference to me. Almost anything else was available for purchase at the PX, and the prices were reasonable.

The Service Club was a social center of sorts where we could "hang out," write letters, shoot pool, play dominos, or read books and newspapers. Monthly, on a Saturday night, there was dancing, and young ladies from Macon and nearby towns came out to spend the evening. The Service Club also sponsored USO shows. For these, we'd gather outside where we'd sit on the ground and watch the show taking place on a raised stage. There was more entertainment going on, really, than we had free time to take advantage of. The Army took a lot of trouble keeping morale high.

After a couple of weeks of training, it came time to evaluate our conditioning. We left the barracks one morning and set off in full packs toward a trail that had been cut into the woods.

As soon as we were off the parade ground someone shouted, "Double time!"

We broke into a trot about twice the speed of normal marching. After some couple-hundred yards, I started breathing pretty hard.

Then we heard, "Quick time!"

We slowed down to a regular march pace.

Then came, "Double time!"

And it was back to the trot. I got really winded, and I started panting. The alternate walking and trotting went on for several miles. I was at the end of my rope when we finished and broke for a rest. Several of the older fellows had to get medical attention for cramped leg muscles. There were two or three athletic types who still had enough breath to jeer at us. When we stopped for the break, all I could do was fall to my hands and knees, head to the ground, gasping for air.

Lieutenant Ward sidled over and asked, "Are you going to recover?"

I didn't even look up. I just nodded. The lieutenant chuckled and moved on to the next victim.

In weapons training we spent days disassembling and reassembling our rifles until we could do it blindfolded. Then we learned firing postures—standing, sitting, kneeling and prone. We learned to squeeze, not jerk, the trigger. We learned how to adjust the sight for distance. We did this without firing a shot. Finally, we were ready for the firing range. Some of the trainees had never been close to a gun of any kind, and there was more than a little anxiety among them. Hunters like me looked forward to the range.

At the range that we put into practice all we had learned in weapons training. Squeezing the trigger the way we had been taught produced good results. We first fired three rounds at a range of one-hundred yards to check the rifle's accuracy, and then adjusted the sights according to whether the round hit high, low, right or left. After that, we fired confirmation rounds. Our goal, of course, was to get the rifles sighted so that they'd place shots in the area of the bull's eye.

Pit crews, protected from stray rounds by a dirt embankment nearly twenty-feet thick and eight-feet high, lowered targets (which were about ten-feet above ground level) after each shot, glued a paper patch over the entry point, raised the targets for the next shot, and then pointed out the entry points with a long pole that had a round, black piece of metal on the end. After the rifles were "zeroed in," we fired from the different firing positions, extending the range out to five-hundred yards. Each of us fired until he achieved a qualifying score. A few got rated as "Expert." Most, like me, became "Marksmen." We got medals denoting our status. We also trained with the M1 carbine, the the Browning Automatic Rifle (BAR), the Browning M1919 .30-caliber machine gun, and the 60mm mortar. Weapons training took about six weeks, and the intent was to make us familiar with a variety of weapons in case we had to use any one of them (aside from our rifles) in combat.

We all learned map-reading. Normally, in combat, the platoon leader, the platoon sergeant, or the squad leader had a map appropriate to a particular mission, but it was always possible that one or the other would become a casualty, and someone else in the unit would be responsible for interpreting the map. Military maps were different from ordinary road maps, and covered only four or five miles of the immediate area where a given unit might be operating, and they contained every terrain feature—main highways, secondary roads, trails, bridges, railways, buildings, churches, rivers, smaller streams, sloughs, wooded areas, as well as elevation lines spaced for every ten-feet of elevation change. We learned to tell whether the slope of a hill was gentle or steep, where the land was flat, or where there might be a gully or ravine. A favorite exercise the instructors used was to give an acting squad leader a map with several check points and an objective that was typically a mile or two away. The squad then went on "patrol." An instructor waited at each checkpoint to verify that the squad had found its way. Before it left, the squad was told to expect the presence of an enemy any place along the way, and to observe all strategies and techniques of movement. On night "patrols" we learned to cover any source of light with things like blankets or tent materials. In the dead of night, a match being struck looks like a small explosion and can be seen from a distance of a half mile.

Training in First Aid was something the Army really stressed. Even though combat units had medics, they couldn't be expected to be everywhere at once. Each of us was issued a small First Aid kit in a pouch that we attached to our cartridge belt so we would be able assist a wounded man until a medic arrived. The rule of thumb was, "Use your buddy's kit first, not your own."

Troop control under combat conditions was another important phase of training. Though we had radios down to platoon level, they were prone to damage because they depended on vacuum tubes, not transistors. Knowing that, we learned a system of hand signals for maneuvering and deploying. Night movements were particularly difficult because of the necessity for silence and the absence of light. Since the cardinal sin for infantry troops was "bunching up," they taught us to stay just barely within sight of the man ahead who would be close enough to pass on any hand signal.

After fifteen weeks, we were ready for the final test, a two-week "camping trip" on the far corner of the military reservation where we were supposed to bring to bear all that we had learned. Our instructors set up the kinds of combat situations we were likely to experience. Sometimes we were the Americans, and other times the "enemy." Blank ammunition made the games more realistic, but we hated it. Blanks dirtied the barrels of our rifles and made them very difficult to clean.

During our "camping trip" the instructors paid special attention to our ability to stay personally clean enough to stay healthy. A sick soldier was a drag on his comrades.

The instructors set up several drills involving live ammunition. The ammunition was totally in their hands for safety's sake. In one of the drills, we had to cross an area fifty-yards long cradling our rifles in our arms and crawling under barbed wire on our bellies while machine gunners fired live rounds three-feet over our heads. The machine guns were set in rigid positions, so there was no danger unless a trainee panicked and lifted his body. One member of my squad wasn't as mature as he might have been at his age, and he did require a bit of extra attention. I made sure that he was within reach as we made our way under the wire. I still wonder if he survived the War. At any rate, there were no casualties that day, and we all breathed a bit easier when the last group finished.

Hand-grenade training also caused us some anxiety. At first we practiced with dummy grenades, and then live grenades. When we started with the live grenades, there was always a concern that someone would drop the grenade after pulling the pin. For safety, two people were placed in oversized foxholes, one to do the throwing and the other to watch the thrower. The thrower threw a grenade out and over an embankment where it exploded harmlessly. The instructors explained to us that if a thrower dropped a grenade in the foxhole, both occupants were to scramble out, shout an alarm, and crawl away. Of course, the thrower would have some explaining to do, be given extra duty, and undergo lots more practice in throwing dummy grenades. We had no dropped grenades that day.

In another exercise, we formed the platoon into attack mode, and then moved out from our initial position toward a ridge suspected to be defended by the "enemy." When we reached the ridge, we hit the dirt just short of the crest and waited for artillery to fall about one-hundred yards to the other side of the ridge. In a real combat situation, the barrage was supposed to cause problems for any enemy that might be there. The shells, fired a couple miles behind us, were live. Again, the gunners had positioned and sighted their guns, had been firing the same mission each week, and so they knew exactly where their shells were going to impact. The only imponderable was the possibility that a shell might have been imperfect in its manufacture. A shell that fell "long" was OK. One that fell "short" would spell disaster. The platoon talked about such a possibility the night before the exercise.

The next day we moved out "on the attack." The ridge was about a half-mile away. On the approach, the instructors moved with us and had us perform a number of maneuvers enroute. At the ridge we flattened out just as we were told to do and waited for the barrage. Soon, we heard the whine of the shells as they passed overhead and exploded on the far side of the ridge. There were no short rounds, and we moved on to rout the enemy. We were congratulated on our spectacular "victory." The "attack" on the ridge was our final exercise of the seventeen-week cycle. Or so we thought.

We finished the "Battle of the Ridge" in the morning and went back to the bivouac area to rest. Late that afternoon we were informed that the "enemy" had blown all bridges on our return route and getting back would take longer than thought. In fact, they told us we'd probably have to walk all night with full packs. In real combat infantry often moved from one engagement to another in trucks. That *never* happened in training. The only transportation we had was our two legs, but all of our marches were never more than ten miles. On this our last day of training, however, we were to march twenty-five miles in eight to ten hours with a few minutes' break each hour. The added "good news" was that anyone unable to complete the march would be required to repeat the seventeen-week training cycle with the next group of recruits. This was a great incentive for us to put forth maximum effort.

After a light meal and a short rest to let the food settle, we set out just before sundown. We marched "route step." That meant that we kept formation but marched without trying to keep in step. We were allowed to talk, as long as we didn't get boisterous. We could take a swallow of water from our quart-sized canteens occasionally, but could smoke only during the breaks. It was early June and warm, and around two o'clock in the morning everyone's water supply ran out. God smiled. When we stopped for a break, someone saw an abandoned shack just off the road. In the front yard was a well. We lowered the bucket and brought up some water. It looked and tasted fine, and there was a rush to quench thirst on the spot and to fill canteens. We spread word up the line for the rest of the men to watch for the shack and the well. When we got back to camp, we were called into "march formation" so that we'd look like veterans to the new recruits. We were really proud of ourselves having just completed one of the most rigorous training courses in the Army's book. Lieutenant Ward told us that we had actually marched thirty-two miles instead of the proposed twenty-five. One of the instructors had taken a wrong turn. His mistake added the additional seven miles. Most of us slept through the day. A few got up for an evening snack at the mess hall.

Lieutenant Ward and Sergeant Weaver had received orders for overseas duty. Corporal Floyd left the previous week. The invasion of Normandy had taken place, and the Army was in need of experienced replacements. The three were excellent leaders, and I wish I knew whether they survived the War. It wouldn't be long before we'd find ourselves at Fort Meade, Maryland, a staging area for replacements.

After a furlough home, I set out for Fort Meade. My asthma was gone, and I had gained thirty-five pounds, all of them muscle in the right places. When I was first inducted, I felt exhilarated because I looked at the military life as a great adventure. There was no exhilaration when I left home after my furlough, but there was plenty of trepidation. This time I had an inkling of what might happen to me. The seventeen-weeks of training had done that. The thought entered my mind that I might be looking back at my hometown and all it stood for the last time.

The trip to Meade took three days. None of us were aware that Congress had just passed a bill requiring the Army to keep back all younger soldiers who hadn't reached

the age of nineteen. That included me. The other underage soldiers and I compared birthdays, most of which were in October or November. We came to the conclusion that we'd spend the rest of 1944 in the United States. It was comforting to know that we have six more months to learn more about staying alive. Who knew? Maybe the War would be over by that time.

I left on a troop train with others of my age for Camp Butner, near Raleigh, North Carolina. Trucks waited for us at the station. It was then that we learned we'd be joining the 89th Infantry Division. I went to the 355th Regiment, Company K, Captain J.E. Brown, commanding, Lieutenant John Adams, platoon leader.

I reported to Staff Sergeant Ross Harlow, leader of the machine-gun section. He introduced me to Sergeant Tony Smazenka, Private First Class Joe Liszka, Private First Class Peter Strickland, and Private Don Koth. Together, we rounded out the crew of number-one gun. That evening Tony took us all to the local beer garden to introduce us to the "old timers" who had arrived earlier. I never fancied beer. In fact, I had never drunk a beer in my life, but it was evident that if I wanted to become a member in good standing with the machine-gun crew, my view of the beverage had to change. Fortunately, I had several good coaches, and change became evident after I had viewed the empty bottoms of several bottles. The beer garden's popularity thrived!

Much of our training at Butner was review, and we picked up details that we missed the first time around. We learned how to deploy our gun in support of troops who were in offensive or defensive positions, and we practiced house-to-house combat. What was different was that we grew to be more like a family, that we somehow belonged where we were. Officers and non-coms seemed more tolerant of their men, even cordial. That sense would be important when we finally faced combat. In the back of everyone's mind was that nagging idea *'maybe old Joe will have to save my life some day.'*

We always had Saturdays and Sundays off after a Saturday-morning inspection. Several of us went to Raleigh one Saturday for a swim in the public pool, and there we met some ladies. The meeting was a fortunate one. They were student nurses from one of the Raleigh training hospitals. After the swim, we all had dinner, and the ladies invited us to their dormitory where we played cards, shot pool, played ping-pong and met a lot of other student nurses. We had struck gold! To the younger chaps at Butner we were heroes, especially after we introduced them to the nurses.

While rumors floated about when the 89th would depart for Europe, I was taken out of the machine-gun crew and became a company clerk. The logistics of moving a unit from a camp onto a ship for transfer to another country required a mountain of paperwork in triplicate. Apparently, I was the only one in Company K, except for a few who were already in supply and personnel, who could type. My new place of business contained a chair, a typewriter and lots of government forms. Since the weather was cold and I'd be inside all day, I was thankful for the transfer. God had smiled one again.

Life was good!

I clerked all through the month of November, and then got a ten-day leave at home in early December. We were all on strict orders to stay silent about things at camp or anything about possible troop movement, but it was hard to pretend that all was normal. The furlough ended, and this time on my way back to camp I knew for sure what was in the cards. The only unknown was how bad was it really going to be? The only consoling thought I could muster was, *'I sure wasn't going to be alone.'*

I got back to camp just before Christmas. On 28 December we moved out of Camp Butner on troop trains to Camp Myles Standish, near Boston. It took twenty-five trains to complete the job. We spent several days while a convoy assembled. The 89th boarded five of the ships, and the rest carried cargo and supplies. In Europe, the Battle of the Bulge had been on since 16 December, and our imaginations went into overdrive. What were we headed for? The temperature hovered around zero, and snow and ice covered everything. The clock ticked, and the curtain was rising on the next act. God and the Army wait for no man.

The 355th Infantry loaded onto the SS *Uruguay*, an ancient merchant ship converted to a troop carrier. There were 4,500 of us, and the quarters were even more cramped than anything we had previously experienced. Metal and canvas bunks were stacked five, sometimes six, high, and there wasn't much space between them. Somehow we crammed all our gear into tiny areas and still managed to wedge ourselves into spaces large enough to sleep in. No one stayed in the hold longer than necessary. During daylight hours, most fled to the open decks to walk about or do calisthenics to stay in condition, but the bad January weather and high seas tossed the ship around making it impossible to keep balance without some sort of support. There was plenty of food, but also a lot of seasickness. Don Koth never left his bunk because of seasickness. There was no hot water for showers, just cold sea water. At night, we weren't permitted on deck because the ship's captain feared that someone would carelessly light a cigarette, and that would have been akin to painting a bull's eye on the ship's bow. There was always the possibility of a lurking German U-Boat.

After ten days we entered the English Channel and anchored near Le Havre, France. We unloaded at night to avoid enemy attack and went to shore on small boats. Unbelievably, the Red Cross was there with doughnuts and coffee. We crammed one hundred each into trucks that had huge, open-air trailers and headed for our destination. The trip was brutal. We sped along at forty-miles-an-hour through the twenty-below temperature and falling snow. The wind tore at our souls. We spent the better part of five hours in this rolling deep freeze. At our destination, Camp Lucky Strike, everyone was about frozen, and it wasn't easy to walk.

Camp Lucky Strike had recently been selected as a place where new troops could reorganize. "Recently selected" meant that there were no tents, no streets, no walkways. There was nothing but a broad, open area, frozen with snow, and utterly empty. Our duffel bags were still on the way, so we didn't have blankets or sleeping bags. We built fires from the wood of trees the bulldozers had excavated, but we were discouraged from doing even that. Though we were a long way from the front line, there were still worries that enemy planes would spot the fires.

The Army did provide twelve-man tents, and the next day we set about pitching them. With fifteen-thousand troops feverishly working it wasn't long before a "city" appeared. It was almost magical. They brought cots, and the engineers "found" several truckloads of lumber that we used for walkways. There were no cooks yet, so we heated C and K rations on small, wood fires inside the tents.

Just after truck after truck of our equipment began to arrive, the temperature took a freakish turn upward, and our field of snow and ice turned into a sea of mud. When we ventured off of the wooden walkways, we'd sink up to our knees. The mud was like quicksand. Each step was extreme exertion. Wrestling crates off the trucks was a nightmare job. It took several days to get the job done. If that wasn't enough, we had to remove Cosmoline from practically everything. Finally, we got our kitchen going, and we dug a latrine. Of course, instead of tableware, we had to use our mess kits and canteens, but we got into the routine.

At Camp Lucky Strike we took our first casualties. Two men from another regiment were killed by land mines that our engineers must have missed. We made an anxious search of our occupied area for more mines but found none. In several nearby areas, however, the engineers recovered more than one thousand of them.

At last the order came to move out. We went by truck about fifty miles into France to a railhead to await a train to take us three hundred more miles to Mersch, Luxembourg.[100] Our accommodations on the train weren't the "luxurious" kind we experienced in the States. They loaded us on 40x8 cars, or cars that were meant for forty men or eight mules. The trip was stop-and-go for several days, mainly because there were no restrooms in the cars. When the train stopped for the last time, we got off and boarded trucks for the remainder of the trip to Mersch, where my company settled into the nearby village of Rodenberg.

Since I knew a little German, Sergeant Smazenka sent me to the village to see if I could barter cigarettes and candy for some real food. I came back with some sausage links and loaves of bread. After that, I was the platoon's "Chief Forager."

We were quite near to where the business of war was going on, so we dug a shallow slit trench next to where we slept, just in case. Eventually, we learned that we had been assigned to Patton's Third Army and that we were to relieve the 5th Infantry Division near the Mosel River.

At Mersch, the engineers set up a huge shower facility under a tent near a small stream. The water was heated by a large, wood-burning heater. Company by company, we all took showers. We hadn't had a real shower for a month. Someone said the Army arranged the facility so that the enemy wouldn't smell us coming. We also got fresh socks and uniforms. Some even fit.

After a couple days, we crossed into Germany at Echternach, a border town on the Sauer River. Destruction was everywhere. We spent the evening checking our weapons. I wiped every cartridge in my carbine's clip. There wouldn't be time for any sort of malfunction. We had been made aware that our first encounter with the enemy would happen the next day.

Just about the time we were getting ready for a few hours sleep, trucks arrived to take us a few more miles closer to our objective. The distant "crump" of artillery brought reality a little closer. It was some time after midnight when we detrucked and marched toward the town of Ernst on the Mosel River. Our orders were to "take and clear" the town and the surrounding area.

During a night march, we occasionally halted and called for our artillery to drop a few rounds on suspicious wooded areas or buildings along the road. That was a better choice than sending out patrols to make sure we weren't walking into an ambush. Dawn broke as we approached the outskirts of Ernst.

We heard a sound new to us, a sound like paper ripping. The sound came from German "burp guns," firing at another of our units[101] that was running into opposition. When we got close enough to see the town, we saw white bed sheets hanging from windows as signals that the town was surrendering. What they were really telling us was that there were no German troops left in town so we wouldn't call in artillery. When we entered the town, however, we started to take sniper and machine-gun fire from a village a couple hundred yards downstream on the opposite side of the river.

At that point the river was probably two-hundred yards wide. Even at that distance, the enemy fire posed a serious hindrance to us clearing out Ernst and the surrounding area. We worked out a plan to discourage whoever was doing the shooting. Captain Brown and the platoon leaders decided to have one machine gun team and some riflemen set up a fire base near the waterfront to distract the enemy. On our side of the river, directly across from the village where the enemy was, were several small outbuildings. Between Ernst and the outbuildings was a grape arbor. The plan was to send another machine-gun team through the arbor to the outbuildings, and place effective fire on the village.

It all seemed practical to me until our machine gun team was the one chosen to hustle down through the grape arbor. I became troubled by a few questions: *'How much cover is there in a grape arbor in the winter? How far did he say it was to the buildings? How much protection is there behind an outhouse? Who knows where some Germans are in the buildings waiting to lay an ambush?'*

There wasn't time to hash out answers. Suddenly we were on our way, dodging among the buildings in Ernst to reach the edge of town and the grape arbor. Once there I found an answer to my first question. There wasn't any cover in a grape arbor in the winter!

We waited until the first team started to fire and then, carrying our gun, tripod, ammunition and all the rest, we ran through the arbor as fast as we could. With the noise of the fire fight across the river and behind us, we felt the distraction part of the plan was working. About halfway across the grape arbor there was a place where the vines were especially thick. I stopped and crouched behind them, trying to catch my breath. Almost immediately bullets snapped over my head, and I got spattered with pieces of grapevine. Refreshed, I resumed my run, this time much faster that before. To ensure that no one with plans for us was waiting inside the buildings, the first pair of our crew to reach them fired their personal weapons into them. It turned out there was nothing in them but bags filled with various types of fertilizer, and they were excellent protection. That was a good thing because we started to get attention from across the river. The roofs of the buildings were not steeply angled. Joe Liszka climbed up onto the nearest one and set up the gun on the peak. Sergeant Smazenka, who was searching for targets through binoculars, directed Joe to place fire on the window of a house where he though he saw an automatic weapon. It wasn't long before the Germans realized we were the nearer targets, and they directed their fire at us.

Joe shouted down to Smazenka, "Hey, Tony! Those sonsofbitches are trying to shoot me!"

"Damn it, Joe! If you aimed a little better, they wouldn't be able to!"

Captain Brown in the meantime placed in position a platoon of 81mm mortars. The mortar guys had a good supply of white phosphorus projectiles with them. They dumped them across the river and set the whole village on fire. Gradually, enemy fire lessened. Finally, our artillery started dumping shells on the burning village. As the enemy troops left for safer places, Joe and his gun encouraged them on their way. After everything got quiet, we made our way back to Ernst and rejoined the rest of the company.

After more than sixty years, no matter what happened in the rest of the War, my most vivid memory is of that first combat.

When everything quieted down, we made our way back to the town and rejoined the rest of the company. We had our baptism of fire, and we survived. We learned that a couple of the riflemen had been wounded in the process of clearing some of the wooded areas where diehards were hiding. Sadly, we also learned that Herman Casey had been killed when the jeep in which he was riding came under fire. In both cases the diehards did pay the price.

Later we learned that all the activities of the 89th division for the past several days had been part of a larger plan to make the enemy think that the 89th was going to attempt a crossing of the Mosel. During the diversion, the 5th division, farther up the river, did sneak across with little difficulty and was already enlarging their bridgehead.

While cleaning up Ernst, someone discovered a pen of rabbits. The rabbits, rather than be taken prisoners, committed "suicide." The house we occupied had a generously furnished kitchen, and Smazenka and a couple of helpers converted the suicidal hares into a delicious stew. Lieutenant Adams, while eating his stew, commended Smazenka for observing the rule of conservation. The rabbit stew was truly a manifestation of the Army's "waste not, want not."

For the next several weeks, activities settled almost into a routine. Armored units thrust forward with very direct methods. They deployed as widely as available roadways and other terrain permitted, and as they moved forward, they simply annihilated opposition or anything that presented itself as a target, sparing nothing that looked suspicious. Enemy troops usually hid when the armor advanced, and it was our job as infantry to follow and clear out any pockets of resistance. Sometimes we moved by truck, sometimes we walked, sometimes six or eight of us rode on the backs of the tanks, sometimes the "die hards" were intimidated enough to surrender. Other times they tried to disable the tanks and paid the consequences. Alternatively, they might feel God was on their side, and take some kind of action to try to disable the tanks or the accompanying infantry, in which case they suffered the consequences. I have no recollection of any tank or tank destroyer suffering any damage while working with our groups. Now and then we came into the view of enemy aircraft, and usually they made one or two strafing runs at us without inflicting much, if any, damage.

Sometimes in the midst of the organized confusion of war something happens that in retrospect seems ridiculously humorous. One night, while we were forming a convoy to relieve another unit, someone heard conversation in German coming from vehicles in the rear. Cautiously, we investigated and discovered several vehicles that were filled with enemy troops. Their plan had been to simply follow along as part of the convoy. We took appropriate positions and demanded their surrender. They were more than happy to oblige. They were familiar with the roads in the area and felt that they could peel off along the way and head for safer territory. We explained that the safest territory for them was to their rear and offered to show them the way to our prisoners' collection point. After disarming them and providing an armed escort, they disengaged from the convoy.

Our process of hit, run and cleanup continued until we reached the city of Worms on the bank of the Rhine River. The entire battalion was assigned to attack and secure the city. We made our approach during the night. Even in the dark we could tell that our bombers had been at work during the previous months and weeks. As daylight broke, we climbed aboard tanks and prepared for battle. Worms was nothing but rubble that afforded hiding places for the enemy, but there was no resistance. The first sign of life was a Jeep. On it was a newsreel cameraman taking pictures of our approach.

We learned that the enemy had fled during the night, blowing up a Rhine bridge in the process. Reconnaissance by one of the other divisions had provided information to the news camera crew, but somehow the word never got back to headquarters. There was some rifle fire nearby, and a squad of infantry went with a tank to investigate, but when we got to the spot, all was quiet. We spotted a tiny building several hundred yards distant. Smazenka looked through his binoculars and saw some smoke rising from it. I suggested that it was an outhouse in which someone was having a smoke while attending nature's call. The sergeant did not consider my remark to be relevant. He apparently assumed that we, as well as the entire war effort, were in danger. Smazenka alerted the tank commander who sent in a round of high explosive that eliminated the danger. We were saved. We approached the remains of the building, and discovered that I had been right about it being an outhouse, but there was no evidence of it having been occupied.

Later, we gathered to wait for trucks to take us to the rear for some rest. We were scattered up and down the roadside, passing the time. I took the opportunity to sit under a tree and disassemble my carbine to give it a good cleaning. I was in the process of doing this when I heard an anti-aircraft wagon begin firing its four .50-caliber machine guns. I moved around to the other side of the tree opposite from the sound. Sure enough, an enemy plane buzzed over, strafing the road. Then it turned around and strafed again. Nobody got hurt since we all took cover when the firing started, but the only thing I could think of was, *'That so-and-so has probably blown dirt all over my clean carbine.'*

And he had!

On another occasion our convoy was heading down a tree-lined road toward Pressburg when we came to an abrupt halt. Fortunately, the lead vehicles spotted an antitank crew defending the road on the town's outskirts. We backed up out of sight of the gunners. Nevertheless, they fired their antitank gun to where they assumed we might be, but they fired into the tree tops so that the overhead explosions would send not only shrapnel but fragments of tree branches down into our convoy. We quickly left the trucks to seek protection and then tried to decide how best to neutralize the gun. The distance was too great for our machine gun or rifles. I lay as flat as possible in a ditch. I looked up and saw Colonel Harris, the regimental commander, calmly striding down the road toward the front of the column to see what the delay was. Harris was about six-feet, six-inches tall, and from my position in the ditch looked like a Texas pine tree.

Before the colonel got out of sight, my friend, John Searle, hustled his mortar up to a position where he could engage the enemy gun. John's first round was close enough that the Germans abandoned their position. John had to expose himself to the enemy before he could fire his mortar. Either he fired before they could sight their gun on him, or they didn't see him at all. At any rate, John got a citation for his bravery.

In March 1945, Patton issued orders to three divisions— the 5th, 87th and 89th—to prepare a crossing of the Rhine at three points in the vicinity of Frankfurt. It was the worst place for a crossing. There was practically no landing area on the other side. The river bank was a twelve-hundred-foot bluff, and ran for miles up and down the river. Moreover, because of the spring thaw, the river was swollen to a width of three-hundred yards and the current was dangerously swift. We were to make the assault in paddle boats, the only kind available on short notice. The divisions made the crossing, but with serious losses. My regiment was in reserve, so we were spared. The other two regiments of the 89th made the assault after midnight of the designated morning. The enemy was waiting for them with lots of firepower, and the regiments suffered several hundred casualties. The paddle boats made slow progress and were easy targets. A number of the boats were sunk and their occupants, loaded down with equipment, were drowned. In the end we prevailed. Patton could then announce to the media that his troops had crossed the Rhine north of Frankfurt in the vicinity of the famous Lorelei Rock.[102] After that, our troops moved eastward against scattered resistance. That afternoon my regiment followed across the river in now available Navy landing craft. We passed through the assault troops and continued the attack. More than fifty years later, in 1992, I learned that one of my high school classmates, Billy Lux, had been a member of the 87th Division that had crossed the river the same day only a few miles north of us.

On Easter Sunday there was a brief pause in the action and we attended a religious service that was hastily assembled. That afternoon, the word came to prepare to move. The 4th Armored Division had made a successful thrust many miles eastward, and there was immediate need for infantry to back them up to protect their rear from a counterattack. We loaded into trucks and set out just as darkness fell. It was raining, cold and miserable. On convoy operations in "questionable" areas the canvas tops of the trucks were taken off so troops could bail out of the vehicles as quickly as possible if they came under fire. Sometime after midnight we ran into a roadblock made of tree trunks and stopped. The tanks simply blew it apart, and we proceeded on high alert because experience had taught us that enemy troops often permitted strong forces to pass through their defenses and then returned to defend against less formidable traffic. I got up from my seat and kneeled on it, keeping one leg over the sideboards, ready to go over the side. Suddenly, the truck lurched. I felt something hit me, and then felt nothing. I was knocked out cold. I didn't know it, but my war was over.

I came to next day and found myself in a medical tent strapped to a stretcher. A nurse noticed I was awake and spoke to me to make sure I was able to respond.

"What happened?" I asked.

"You have some head injuries and a compound fracture of your left leg between your knee and ankle. You're going to be all right."

She gave me a shot of morphine, and I went back to sleep. The next time I awoke it was night. Captain Lucius Curry, the battalion personnel officer, was standing over me. Curry's job as personnel officer was to write letters of explanation to families of those killed in action or who had been suffered serious wounds.

"What happened to me?" I asked him.

"I'm not really sure, but I will let your folks at home know that you have been wounded but that you'll come out of this OK."

Fifty years later, after meeting with John Searle, who was on the truck with me that Easter night in 1945, I learned what had happened. When our truck had passed through the partially demolished road block, it sideswiped a portion of it. I was between the truck and the roadblock, and I was knocked back onto the truck bed. A medic was in the truck with us, and he stopped my bleeding, used my carbine as a splint and gave me a shot of morphine to lessen possible shock and keep me unconscious. When the convoy stopped to refuel, they transferred me to a medical Jeep, and transported me back to the medical facility.

Later that evening, the medical staff gave me a spinal anesthetic, set the bone, and put my leg in a cast. The next day I went by military ambulance to an evacuation facility from which I'd be flown to Oxford, England, to be examined and to get a permanent cast.

After fifteen days, I joined a group bound for the States. We boarded a ship and almost a week later docked at Charleston, South Carolina, where I was transferred to a receiving hospital. Within a week, I left on a hospital train to Hoff General Hospital near Santa Barbara, California. It was late May 1945. The hospital was also close enough to Hollywood that we had quite a few celebrities visit and entertain the patients.

After I mended, they gave me a thirty-day convalescent furlough home. I hitched a ride on a military transport plane from a nearby airbase to Amarillo, Texas. From there I went home by bus. My leg was still in a cast, and I had to use crutches. I showed up just in time for a meal. My family was surprised to see me, and the reunion was a happy one. I discovered that I could drive the family car even though my leg was in a cast and the car had a standard transmission. I went fishing with my brother or friends, visited nearby relatives, listened to the radio and just rested and read.

Toward the end of my furlough I wired the hospital requesting a thirty-day extension, which they granted. There was no pressing reason for me to be in the hospital taking up valuable space which someone else might need.

The war in Europe had ended about the time I arrived back in the States, and the war in the Pacific ended while I was at home on leave. The government ended all rationing, and life took on a completely different look.

Finally, my leave ended and I returned to the hospital. They kept me under observation, but told me that my time was my own, as long as they knew where I was. In November, they removed the cast, but I still had to use crutches. By Christmas time I was transferred to Fort Sam Houston, having shed the crutches in favor of a cane, and I was able to spend the holidays at home. Some of my classmates had returned by this time, and I learned that we hadn't lost a single one in the War.

I was separated from the Army on 29 January 1946. My great adventure ended where it began. I had come full circle.

On 25 May 1947, I married Gloria Maroul. In 1950, the time when the United States got involved in the Korean War, I decided to use my spare time in a useful way and joined the National Guard in Columbus, Texas (not far from our home). My job was instructing new recruits. The Columbus unit was the 36th Infantry Division, 136th Tank Battalion, Company C. In a short time, I rose to the rank of master sergeant, the highest of the enlisted ranks. Eventually, after taking the required Army correspondence courses, I was promoted to warrant officer by the Texas National Guard, but the promotion had to be approved by the National Guard Bureau and the Department of the Army. As it turned out, my commission was denied because several asthma attacks I had experienced while hospitalized during the War appeared on my records. I simply reenlisted as a master sergeant.

Eventually, several employees of the Shell Oil Company gas processing plant in Sheridan, Texas, who were also veterans and with whom I shared memories of the War at weekly National Guard meetings, told me of a vacancy that would soon be opening at the plant. After an interview Shell hired me, ending my employment with the Guard. I started with Shell on 17 November 1952 and retired in 1981. Right after I retired, I took a job with the Michigan-Wisconsin Pipeline Company as supervisor of all their United States gas processing plants. I retired for good in May 1985.

Gloria and I raised three sons and two daughters who have given us nine grandchildren and one great-granddaughter (so far).

Life has been good!

"To This Day, It Seems Like Another World."

Eugene F. Jones

75th Infantry Division
290th Infantry Regiment, Company C
"Diaper Division," "Bulge Busters"
Born in Latrobe, Pennsylvania, 10 September 1925

"Eventually, we jumped off and made contact around four-thirty in the afternoon I could see movement ahead of us. I fell to the ground and started shooting. I got behind a tree and a German jumped up and was shooting at me and me at him. The other guys were lying on the ground shooting too, but we were not making any headway. For some stupid reason, I got up. I had a clip in my rifle and one in my hand. I start moving forward shooting. The clip 'pinged' out and I threw the other one in as quickly as I could. Looking back, I noticed that the guys started following me! I finally wised up and hit the ground again! I thought, 'What the hell am I doing?'"

The War started when I was a sophomore in high school. One Sunday I was doing homework, drawing a human body, skeleton, circulatory system, the whole thing. I can still see it; I'm at the dining room table, doing my biology project when news came on the radio of Pearl Harbor. My brothers were outside playing ball, so I ran down the street and told them "Hey, the Japs bombed Pearl Harbor!"

They didn't believe me, so I said "Yeah, I just heard it on the radio!"

It's funny how I was drawing the human body one minute, then all that started. Anyhow, I used to follow the Navy and the war in the Pacific. I used to cut out all the ships that were sunk and aircraft carriers and put them in a scrapbook.

In the first semester of my senior year, January 1944, I was called up to be inducted into the service. I went to Greensburg and was drafted there. I was one of about thirty seniors in my senior year to get pulled out and drafted because of the war effort. Then we went by train to Fort Meade, Maryland and officially got inducted into the service. When I got down to Fort Meade, I realized there were more fellows like me, high-school seniors. I took a test in high school to qualify to go to college in the service. I passed the test for the Army, Navy and Air Force. When we got down to Maryland they said, "Forget about that; if you're going anywhere, you're going infantry."

My twin brothers were already in the Eighth Air Force. They had volunteered to be pilots, but one, Phillip, ended up as a gunner and the other, Charles, a ground crewman. They separated them because they were brothers, one went East and the other West. They didn't want them in the same outfit where they could both get killed. My mother said she wrote a letter to Roosevelt because she wanted them to be together when they got overseas. Finally, they did put them together over there.

They wrote home while I was still in school, and they said, "Gene, don't go into the Air Force, we got screwed."

So that's why I volunteered for the Army Engineering Program, so I could attend college and all that jazz, but that didn't work. I got infantry.

I had sixteen weeks of infantry training at Camp Wheeler, Georgia. I came in the door of my house in July on furlough, and my mother was crying. She just got a telegram from the War Department; my brother Phillip, who was the tail gunner on a B–17 bomber, was shot down 20 June over Berlin. We didn't hear any more from the Army about my brother until I reported to the 69th Infantry Division at Camp Shelby, Mississippi. I was there for about a month or so when I got a letter from Mum saying, "Phillip's a prisoner of war in Germany."

Camp Shelby was a hell of a place. It was summertime and all swamp. We'd take an azimuth and head into the swamp without deviating. Oftentimes, we did this at night, midnight, when the swamp was completely dark. I thought about how water moccasins could float on the water! We didn't really stay in the camp at all, we just went there to get more supplies, then go back out to train again. The general of the 69th Division was Bolte,[103] and we were "Boltie's Bivouacking Bastards." There was a GI obstacle course that we had to run in full combat gear. A captain, a graduate of West Point, took a liking to me and he bet on me. I was pretty good in track in high school, and I almost cracked the camp record.

After a month I got transferred to Camp Breckinridge, Kentucky. I was glad to get out of Shelby. It took us three days to go to Sharpsburg, Kentucky by Chattanooga Railroad. At Breckinridge, I was assigned to the 75th Division, the youngest Army division in age at that time. They called us the "Diaper Division" because we were all eighteen and nineteen-year-old soldiers, right out of high school. I was in Kentucky for about a month, went home for a furlough, returned to Kentucky, and then the whole division boarded a train to New York.

On 22 October 1944, the Division crammed into the luxury liner SS *Brazil* and sailed for Europe. We landed in Wales ten days later. In December, we sailed across the English Channel and landed in Le Havre. The place was shot to hell because of the invasion on 6 June.[104]

They stationed us in Northern France, but they couldn't figure out what to do with us. We just went out into a big open field with pup tents and started unloading ammunition to keep us busy. Finally, we crossed the French border and went to Hasselt, Belgium. We saw "Buzz-Bombs" going over our heads.

The Battle of the Bulge had started on 16 December. We didn't get to the front until 20 December, four days after the Battle of the Bulge started. Until this time, the 75th was a reserve division used to reinforce other units; we thought we'd be the Army of Occupation, and now we were moving together as one force.[105] After the Malmédy Massacre on 17 December, we got orders to take no prisoners. They weren't written orders, only verbal.

On 20 December, we were instructed to move to Liège, Belgium. When we got to Liège, our objective was to cross the Meuse River and move east. However, we saw tanks and artillery moving west across the bridge. When they got across the bridge, the tanks and the artillery turned and blew up the bridge. We knew something was going on and they finally told us the Germans broke through the Allied lines. They didn't tell us there was a breakthrough before we saw it for ourselves. We knew were going to have to combat them.

We went on farther past Liège and to a small town where we lodged for the night because we were not close enough to engage the enemy. The next day we got out, unloaded our big duffle bags and took only our field packs, ammunition, rations and raincoats. We got in the trucks and started moving farther east. Then one night we were laying on the ground setting up all our artillery. The Germans had been shelling for a good while; the ground was ugly and there were puffs of smoke from tank cannons. So some idiot yelled, "Hey German paratroopers are coming down in the smoke!"

Everybody started shooting.

Someone yelled, "What the hell's going on? Stop that stuff!"

After that, we got in trucks again and moved up farther. We could see and hear in the distance more shells going off. We got closer and closer and about five miles away from the actual noise, they stopped the trucks, and we all got out and cut the engines. There was gasoline in barrels that we used to make a fire to keep us warm. Then, the truck drivers took off; they were glad to get out of there anyway.

On Christmas Eve we started marching toward the sound of the War. The snow covered our tracks, and everything looked black and white. I didn't know where the enemy was. They sent our company, Company C, out to find them. There were four Sherman tanks, a couple of heavy machine guns and mortars. In the afternoon, we were in a clearing, near the woods getting ready to jump off. I was in the first platoon. The third platoon between us and the second platoon, and the tanks were in the back. You'd think they'd put the tanks in front, but they stayed back and launched shells into the woods! I can't say I blame them, they didn't want to make contact with the German Tiger tanks because they'd blow a Sherman apart. For that reason, we nicknamed the Shermans "Coffins."

Eventually, we jumped off and made contact around four-thirty in the afternoon. I could see movement ahead of us. I fell to the ground and started shooting. I got behind a tree and a German jumped up and was shooting at me and me at him. The other guys were lying on the ground shooting too, but we were not making any headway. For some stupid reason, I got up. I had a clip in my rifle and one in my hand. I started moving forward, shooting. The clip 'pinged' out and I threw the other one in as quickly as I could. Looking back, I noticed that the guys started following me! I finally wised up and hit the ground again!

I thought, *'What the hell am I doing?!'*

We had just wiped out a machine gun nest when, suddenly, I saw someone jump into it. He wasn't wearing a helmet, and that's one reason why I didn't shoot. I couldn't tell if the person was an American, a German, or even a civilian.

I hollered to the sergeant who was nearby, "Hey, Sarge, somebody jumped into the machine gun nest we just wiped out! I don't know if he was American or German!"

The sergeant sent my buddy Russ, a five-foot-four guy from Boston, over to see. I told Russ not to shoot because I wasn't sure who might be in the hole, but Russ was so nervous he couldn't wait. He started shooting into the hole! Finally, we got up there and it turned out to be a German soldier after all. I turned then to my squad (I don't know why because I wasn't in charge) and began taking over.

"You guys," I said "you, you, look behind us for German snipers in the trees. We're going this way."

We started moving again. All we knew was what was in front of us. Later I heard that 3rd Platoon, which was in the middle of the formation, was pinned down and cleaned out by German machine guns. I also found out that we had advanced our platoon, 1st Platoon, too far out; we were getting so far ahead that we were in the flank. They ordered us to stop, so we held up.

At that time of year it got dark around five o'clock in the afternoon, and that's when the Germans started shooting at us. They'd open up with machine guns, and all we'd see was the flash from their guns. I'd shoot at a flash and roll. They'd fire at the place I'd been in. The next time, I rolled the other way. I kept doing that, but the machine gun kept shooting.

I said to myself, *'Why can't I knock him out? What's is going on?'*

I crawled closer, my adrenaline going. I could've sworn I saw the end of a tank. I thought I was shooting someone in a machine-gun nest, but it was the machine gun from a tank that kept firing back!

I turned around and yelled to the guys behind me, "I think that's a tank!"

But they were all gone! I was up there all by myself! I hightailed it back and ran into three guys from my squad.

"Where did you guys go?"

"We had orders to pull back."

"Why didn't you tell me that?!"

At this point, they were all confused, and they didn't know which way to go, so I said, "I remember how we got here. You guys do what I tell you."

We came to a point in the woods where there was a road, and the Germans were shooting their machine guns down the road.

I said "You know what to do boys? I'm going to cross after the next burst, and you just wait for another burst then go across the trench, because they can't shoot them continuously."

So we got across.

We finally got back to where we jumped off and these guys turn around and said to my lieutenant "Did you see what Jones did out there?"

The lieutenant said, "You all did well."

How could he have known? He wasn't even with us!

We found out later that the Christmas Eve attack was the last thrust the Germans tried in the north to break through to the west, and that it was the 2nd Panzer Division[106] that was pushing us.

We dug in shallow trenches for the night; we couldn't dig foxholes because the ground was frozen. I saw a guy coming up from the right side of our camp trying to cross. We had a password, but not everybody knew it, that is how mixed up things were there.

I yelled "Halt!"

He didn't respond, so I said it again. He didn't know the password, but he said that he was from the 17th Airborne Division. I didn't know that there was a 17th Airborne, but I found out that there was, and that they were coming up from southern France to help to stop the Germans at the Bulge.

As I was talking to him, he said "I just fired my rifle up here."

I said "What?! You came up here from southern France and you never fired your rifle until you got here? I must have fired sixty rounds of ammunition the first time I got here!"

We had to be on guard because that night a lot of Germans were sneaking down to our command post. They were still trying to push us and there was a crossroads coming into our camp that they were using. One German came down on a motorcycle and our guy on the machine gun shot him right off his seat. Everything settled again for a while after that. Around midnight we took the machine guns off of our tanks so we could use them ourselves. The plan was that we were going to march out of the trap we were in. We all started moving out, walking through snow, toward a farmhouse up the road. All of a sudden, a German 88 opened up! They saw us coming. There was a fence by me, and I hit that fence, somersaulted and kept on going across a field! The whole platoon did the same. The Germans were still shooting with 88s and machine guns. Half the platoon hit the dirt behind me. I kept going toward the woods, where I told the guys to pass word up to the lieutenant that half the platoon had hit the dirt in the field. We didn't know where the Germans were, or where we were. We were there about an hour or so then we started sneaking out going the way we came. We were being really quiet, like a bunch of Indians, and we thought we kept moving where our platoon was heading.

I found out later that, while I was getting my baptism of fire, my first cousin, John Vince, had been killed on Christmas Eve. His ship had been torpedoed in the English Channel. His best friend, John Martino, who was in a ship just behind my cousin's, witnessed the event.

The next morning, Christmas Day, we ended up in some little town where we had tankers, artillery guys, infantry guys, paratroopers, the rest of our platoon, Company E, but no command. The whole front was full of it really; everything was so mixed up. We were trying to find something to do for Christmas, so we went to all these stores looking for wine, but couldn't find any.

Finally, some Major took over and got us all lined up and said "We're going to move out and run this way."

We started moving out and there was some shelling. We were on a bank on the side of the road. I crawled up the bank and looked over and saw the German tanks. They were trying to pick us off as we were trying to sneak out of town. We managed to get away from them and back to our outfit.

Some guy said to us when we got there, "Hell, we heard you guys were wiped out."

I said "Hell no. Here we are!"

When we got back to our battalion, we set up a defensive line. Our company was the lead company of the battalion when we marched; our platoon was the lead platoon. In front of me were a colonel and a major in charge of the battalion. My sergeant sent me out as a scout, something I wasn't trained to do. I was going down the road with the whole battalion, more or less, behind me. Sometimes the Germans let the scout pass, so that they can get at the rest of the group.

I said to myself, *'The only thing I got going for me is if the Germans let me pass, they'll get the captain.'*

There was a barn on my right, and the door started to move. I didn't know if it was the wind or what. I stopped the whole battalion because they were going toward the barn. Nothing happened, so I thought it was just the wind.

I got back on the roadway and said "Come on!"

We got to where we were supposed to be, but I didn't want that scout job anymore, and I told the lieutenant that. I think I shocked him. We finally set up a defensive position. That was late December.

The sergeant said to me, "Okay Jones, you go back down the hill to the command post and bring up some replacement troops for our squad."

So I went down and picked up these three guys; they were just a couple of cooks. They had no infantry training whatsoever.

I told them "You guys follow me, and do what I tell you."

The followed, but they were scared to death, I was scared, too, but at least I had some experience. We came to a clearing at a crossroad. The Germans started lobbing shells at us.

I told them what to do. "All right you guys," I said. "After the next shell lands, you just take off and go across instead of all going at once because they can't shoot continuously."

I got all three of them back as quickly as I could.

At times we had to go back to the command post for ammunition. One night, I went back to get some. While I was there, the Germans started shelling. There was a big crater there, and we jumped in. Some medic yelled, "Jesus, they're throwing gas shells!"

We had no gas masks. We had thrown them away, but kept the cases to hold cigarettes, candy and other stuff. We weren't about to lug gas masks in combat.

Someone yelled, "What the hell are we going to do with this gas attack?!"

Another guy yelled back, "All you can do is piss in your handkerchief, put it over your nose and mouth and try to filter out some of the gas."

Most of us who could, did just that.

Ten minutes later, the medic yells, "Oh, false alarm!"

Honest to God, I couldn't believe it! I could have killed that medic!

We finally got back to our platoon and the Lieutenant says "Where were you guys?"

We told him the whole story.

One night during the Bulge (the Sergeant always picked on me, or the officers always called on me when they wanted something, like ammunition, or chow, or whatever) the Sergeant said, "Okay, Gene, get someone to go with you to find a rifle position in between us and the Germans. The engineers are going to plant some mines"

We went out and the engineers followed, putting the mines behind us. We were walking back, and the Germans could have picked us off anytime. Three days later, the Sergeant said, "Jones you got to go back out there and pick up those mines because we are going to counterattack!"

Where were we supposed to walk? Those engineers had to remember where they placed the mines!

One night the Germans were shelling us again. We were positioned in two-man foxholes; one guy slept, one guy kept watch. I had my head up, while my buddy slept. Shells kept coming in, but I could swear it was our own artillery. I knew the different sounds ours and the enemy's shells made. One shell kept getting louder and louder, but it didn't go over my head. I got my head out at about ground level, and I looked over at my buddy. I reached over to pull him down. Just as I did, that shell burst off to my left. I felt an instantaneous, burning sensation on my left shoulder.

I looked at my buddy. Blood was coming out of his mouth. I hollered for the medic. He said, "They're still shelling."

I pulled my buddy out of the hole and then crawled down the barrage. I met the medic halfway and yelled, "Get the hell back here!"

The medic looked at my buddy. There wasn't a mark on him, but he was still bleeding from the mouth. The medic said, "Keep him face down so he won't drown in his own blood."

We made a stretcher out of two poles and a raincoat, and four of us started carrying him back to the Aide Station. We came to a roadway where one of our tanks was.

I told the tanker "Call on your radio, tell them to send a Jeep up. We have a wounded man, and we're bringing him back. We can walk halfway or whatever, as long as we get him back."

The Jeep never made it. We walked him all the way back.

A medic came over and said, "He's dead."

"He's not dead!" I said. "Put your hand on him, you can see he's still breathing, feel the warm air."

He shined a flashlight on him.

I said again, "He's not dead; he's still breathing."

I took my jacket off and showed him what kind of wound I had on my shoulder, and there was nothing there! I had blood all over my shoulder, but it was his blood. I couldn't figure out why there was a burning sensation, but no mark. In a couple of days, I found out that he died because they couldn't give him any blood plasma. They told me the plasma had frozen. He bled to death. He had been sleeping with his mouth open, and a piece of shrapnel must have gone in.

One night, I was in a foxhole and the ground had thawed a little bit, so there was water in there. I was sleeping and I woke up and my feet were in the water, over my ankles. I didn't feel a thing. I brought my feet up and started pounding them on the side of the foxhole to get the circulation back. I had no change of socks, and I couldn't take my boots off. I finally got the circulation back.

On 3 January 1945, we counterattacked from the South, reinforcing the 84th and 106th Infantry Divisions along with the 3rd Armored Division in the North where they jumped off. My feet were hurting, and I couldn't keep up with the guys. As I moved ahead, I saw wounded GIs, some carrying their buddies and others walking alone. By that I had lost contact with my outfit because I was too slow and couldn't keep up. I heard a tank coming, and I didn't know if it was a German tank or an American tank. So I jumped on the side of the road in a ditch. This tank kept coming and he stopped. He saw me go in the ditch.

He jumped out and said "Hey, Buddy! Where in the hell is my division?"

I said "I'm looking for my own. I don't know where the hell yours is!"

He scared the hell out of me when he stopped. I kept going, and I finally caught up with my company. They stopped for the night and they were in foxholes on the outside of this little town. I jumped in the first foxhole I saw, and I yelled, *Sieg Heil!*

The guy who was in the foxhole nearly jumped out of his skin!

At one point, we got sent back by twos to this farmhouse to get a change of socks, get dried off and get something to eat and all that jazz. I went back, took my shoes off, took my socks off, put my feet up and I couldn't get my shoes back on. My feet started to swell.

I said to the sergeant "Hey! You've to call a medic because I can't put my shoes back on."

He said "We'll send you back to the Battalion Aid Station to get your feet checked."

I said "What do you mean you'll send me back there? I need a doctor to look at it!"

But there was no doctor where I was. I got into a Jeep. I kept my rifle. I wouldn't give it up. One the way back, the Germans were lobbing in 88s, but we got through that safely.

All the guys in the Jeep were guys like me; guys with problems with their feet, and they had us in a barn. There were about twenty guys, and the doctor started checking our feet.

As he went from man to man, he'd say "Cold feet."[107]

When he got to me, he said, "Come here you guys, this is the only guy that has a problem. You've got to go back to the hospital."

I wouldn't go on a stretcher. I said, "No! These guys here have arms off and legs off, I can sit on the floor of the ambulance."

All I had on my feet by now were rubber galoshes. I sat in the ambulance all the way back; it seemed like we drove all night. We ended up back in Liège at the Army hospital. I helped unload the wounded from the ambulance. Some guys were really hurting. The doctor said "What the hell is the matter with you?"

I said "My feet."

He said "Take those damn galoshes off!"

I did and my feet were swollen up twice the size they were before. They were black and blue and he told me to get the hell onto a stretcher. I was really scared. I got on the stretcher and they took me inside on a bed. A buzz-bomb hit nearby, and all the plaster came down out of the ceiling.

The next day they moved me to Paris. All night long at the hospital in Paris they kept taking guys into the operating room. They were guys like me, with trenchfoot. They were cutting off toes, feet, anything with gangrene. I wondered when it would be my turn, but they didn't take me.

The next day and the day after, they had me on a hospital train to Cherbourg, France. Then they moved me to England for treatment. I ended up in Salisbury, at an Army hospital. My skin from the ankles down was white, and I had a black spot on one toe. I didn't know if it was gangrene or not, and it seemed like they couldn't tell either.

They kept putting needles in me to see if I felt them, but I couldn't. They didn't know what they were going to do with my feet. Finally, they gave me exercise to do: out of the bed, a little walk. Then the circulation started to come back. Two or three layers of skin all peeled off along with the black spot. I was lucky it wasn't gangrene! I was in there for about a month. The doctor had diagnosed me with frostbite, trench-foot—moderately severe. I was then on "limited assignment."

One day they came out with Purple Hearts, and they passed my bed up, because I didn't get a wound that bled.[108] From February to April 1945, I was assigned to an Army Postal Unit in Antwerp after I got out of the hospital. At the time, Antwerp was getting hit with buzz-bombs by the Germans, and the day before we got there, one killed a lot of civilians. They said there were bloody streets in Antwerp. One night, we were near the railway station at Antwerp and a V–1 hit the railway station! Guys were screaming and I thought here I was on my new assignment and I'm still in a combat zone!

A GI came to our post office and he had orders from some general to go to Aachen, Germany. We were to take him in our postal truck to visit a cemetery because he was looking for somebody. Aachen is a hell of a long ride from Antwerp. So my Captain he said "Jones, you had infantry training?"

I said "Yeah."

"You ride shotgun on the mail truck to protect the mail."

So I went along as "shotgun."

This kid, I don't know what he was looking for, but we went to that cemetery. I got out and started looking for my buddy to see if they buried him up there, but they probably didn't. This kid found what he was looking for, and we had to drive him all the way back. It was a hell of a long ride in the mail truck, and we had the mail with us too! We ran across some German civilians waving at us from windows. We waved back. They had been "liberated" since 21 October 1944.

Every month they reexamined my feet. The war in Europe was over on 8 May

1945, and they reexamined me at about that time. They marked me "1-A" and planned to send me back to the infantry. Orders were cut and they sent me to a "repo-depo"[109] in Le Havre to get on a boat for Texas. I was to get more training, to get ready for Operation OLYMPIC, the planned invasion of Japan.

When we dropped the first Atomic Bomb, everybody at the repo-depo went crazy. We were restricted to the area, but we were climbing over the fence trying to get something to drink! Then the second bomb dropped three days later and I was sitting there wondering if maybe would use me for the Army of Occupation. I was on pins and needles waiting for my day of departure. Finally, we headed for the States, through the Azores and across the Atlantic. There was no hurry. At the Azores, a storm kicked up, and everyone got seasick except me and this other guy. We just sat and kept eating our breakfast—powdered eggs. We landed in New York Harbor on 1 September 1945, the day before Japan signed the surrender papers. There were whistles blowing, and when we got off they gave us donuts and milk.

I didn't get discharged immediately after I arrived in the States, there was a point system, and I missed being discharged by one point, so I had to stay in. After the War, that duffel bag I dropped off in Belgium before we got into combat came to my house in 1946 with all the personal stuff still in it!

I got discharged in May 1946. I signed up for the Active Reserves and stayed in that for three years. I was out of the Reserves in 1949 and missed the Korean War by one year! I got a letter from West Point in 1946, too.

I was in the transportation office, and the colonel there said, "Hey GI, did someone put your name in for eighteen months for OCS to come out a lieutenant?"

Someone did. It was my captain from basic training, the one who bet that I'd win the obstacle course, but I was in no mood to do that. Instead, I took my GI Bill and went to Saint Vincent College. I had played football in high school, and the coach at Saint Vincent wanted me for football. I played in 1947 and 1948, until I messed up my shoulder. In 1949–1950, I played semi-professional football for the Latrobe Zimbos. In 1956, I got a job at Westinghouse and enrolled again at Saint Vincent. I took the history of Western Civilization there in night school one year. Then I took three courses of metallurgy from Penn State University at the Greensburg High School Extension. I worked at Westinghouse for thirty-four years.

I got a job with Westinghouse where I had a "classified" clearance because we were producing material for the nuclear submarines. I worked with mechanical instruments. This was before we had computers. My computer was in my head. I knew all the formulas of all these parts' shapes and sizes.

In 2005, after sixty years, I began to collect disability for my trenchfoot. Originally, I tried getting it several times after I was discharged, but the VA said they lost my medical records and couldn't prove that I was in that Army hospital in England. By coincidence, a doctor I had gone to high school with, Walter Hazlett, Jr., happened to be there in the Army hospital, and he wrote a letter to the VA, telling them that he had been in the hospital with me, and that I had been treated for trenchfoot. Not too long after that, they found my records!

When I was younger, I couldn't talk about the War. I didn't tell my parents. I didn't tell my wife or my kids. I don't often think about it, either. Like a lot of GIs, I kept a closed mouth. I only started talking about ten years ago to my kids and grandchildren. Years ago, around Christmas time, it was snowing. I looked outside and it all came back. I could picture myself back there. To this day, it's hard to picture me doing any of the things I talked about. I mean I did it, I know I did it, but to this day it seems like another world. When I was there, I didn't think about home. I only thought about what was right in front of me. I tried to beat the enemy and survive. If I had though about anything else, I'd have hesitated, and I'd have died.

In 1946, I cut a piece by a guy named John Ackerson out of the *Stars and Stripes* magazine. I've carried it in my wallet all these years. It's called "My Comrades," and it goes like this:

> *Well, Dick, it snows along the withered hills; the ice pools tinkle under Roger's feet. We climb. The wind is keen, but summer fills our hearts, for we are close; your young minds meet my own, that harks back to the fields o f France I traversed when a boy, like you, beside this veteran, with tales of glints that dance upon the bayonets of lads who died . . . And Roger's gone, Dick's gone, in bold affray, while I, who once more ventured, have come home to walk alone, yet not alone; a day like this recalls my comrades; now we roam white hills and hear the far-off guns, whose ire is mellowed by our cheery evening fire.*

THE STARS AND STRIPES

Man Spricht Deutsch

Ici On Parle Français

1 Fr. New York—PARIS—London 1 Fr. Tuesday, Dec. 19, 1944

Crucial Battle On in West

Air Fights Drive Off Luftwaffe

Frauleins in the Front Lines

'All Now at Stake,' Nazi Troops Told; First Strikes Back

B29s Rock War Plants At Hankow and Nagoya

2 Slovak Forts Fall to Soviets

The Battle Area

Portion of a front page of *The Stars and Sripes Magazine*, 19 December 1944, three days into the Battle of the Bulge. The newspaper was printed in several editions over several Wartime fronts. Courtesy: *Richard Wissolik, private collection.*

Eugene Jones (second from right) and friends in April or May 1945, just before Jones left Belgium.

Eugene Jones (standing, center) with buddies outside the Army Post Office in Antwerp, Belgium.

"That's What They Called Me, 'Sergeant Joe.'"

Carl L. Josefoski, Sr.

United States First and Third Armies
1st Infantry Division
"Big Red One"
18th Infantry Regiment, Company L, 2nd Platoon
(1st Coast Artillery, Panama, 1934–1936 - Honorably Discharged
With the Rank of Corporal)
Born in Natrona Heights, Pennsylvania, 5 December 1915

"Another sergeant came up, and as the rest went back he and I took cover behind the transformer building. While we were there, a German tank came up. The sergeant got up on the tank, but let himself wide open. A round blew his testicles apart. He fell off the tank, and a medic ran up and pulled him to some cover. I worked my way back, and we got on a half-track and went into the woods where the fire was coming from. As soon as we went into those woods, we saw in a ravine Germans that had been shooting at us. I opened up, but the machine gun jammed. We could've killed them all, but they escaped, all of them."

THEY CALLED ME "Sergeant Joe." Every platoon was supposed to have either a second lieutenant or first lieutenant, but we didn't have either. We always had a sergeant for our platoon leader. We never had more than six or seven men in a squad at one time and as far as new guys were concerned, didn't get to know them, nor did we want to because, when they got killed, we felt so bad. These new guys were eighteen, nineteen, twenty, and I was a twenty-nine-year-old married man. To them I was like a father. My job was to keep them alive. Well, those kids couldn't do anything without Sergeant Joe. That's what they called me, "Sergeant Joe."

I was already in and out of the service before World War II. I had served with the 1st Coast Artillery Corps in Panama from 1934 to 1936 so I knew what the Army was about when I got drafted for World War II.

I had been discharged in 1936 as a corporal. That was a big deal in those days, a nineteen, twenty-year-old guy that made corporal when many of the guys in my squad were World War I vets. Most of them didn't have any rank because they were drinkers, but they had made their home in the service. So, by the time I got out I had them beat in rank. I made forty-two dollars a month plus five dollars as a First Class Gunner. That was during the Depression, too, so I was pretty well off.

I came home after being discharged, but I was in no hurry to go to work; things were pretty slack anyway. I came home with some money which I gave my parents because things were bad. My mother was very thankful for that money.

The beer gardens used up some money, too. What money I did have went fast. It was the same old thing, "Carl has money, Carl's buying the drinks."

I had a buddy, Joe, that came out of the service the same time I did. He was in the Hawaiian Islands when I was serving in Panama. There were no jobs around at home so he said, "Carl, let's go back to the service. You were in Panama. I was in Hawaii. What do you say we go to the Philippines?"

I was on the verge of doing that, nothing else looked good, and they weren't hiring anybody down at the mill. In the meantime, I met my future wife, so I hesitated to join again, even though I tried to talk my brother and friends into joining.

One day a neighbor came running down to the house and said, "Carl, they're hiring down the mill!"

So I went to the mill and got a job. I said to Joe that he could get a job at the mill as well. He went to the service instead and did end up in the Philippines. He died on the Bataan Death March.[110]

I was at the mill when World War II broke out and finally got called in the draft in January 1944. When I was drafted, I already had a wife and two children at home, Sonny and Marsha. There were no celebrations when we left, just a lot of crying. The last memory of my children as I left was looking back out of the car and seeing them standing on the side of the street crying.

I went to Fort McClellan, Alabama for seventeen weeks of basic training. I got cadre duty, but got pulled off that when I got a hernia. After fifteen days, I got sent to Fort Meade and about a week later shipped out from Portsmouth, Virginia on a Liberty ship.

We landed in Africa and went into a training camp there for a while, but we didn't train; we were just staying there while they gathered soldiers from different parts of the United States to serve as replacements. When we had enough guys we went to Naples, Italy, to the repple-depple there. That was in the winter, around December 1944. By then things were slowing down in Italy but the Battle of the Bulge had started up in Belgium, and they needed men badly. They shipped me out to Marseilles in southern France. From there I got on a train and ended up in the 1st Division. I got into Northern Europe just after the Battle of the Bulge ended and entered the Rhineland. There we battled from town to town, village to village, farm to farm, house to house.

We crossed the Rhine and then drove on into central Europe. I got a Bronze Star when we crossed the Rhine River, but who put me in for it I have no idea. I had just been made sergeant, and I was in charge of a squad when we paddled across. It reminded me of George Washington crossing the Delaware River. We got a lot of opposition there and found out that a lot of it was from Hitler *Jugend*, Hitler Youth, just teenagers.

I said, "This is a stupid way to go on fighting."

It was to be a company size attack but the battalion commander, a lieutenant colonel, was there when we pushed off.

I said to him "We're going in these little boats and we're supposed to get across in

"I was wounded 20 March,
in a small firefight we were in."
Michael Wilkey 2006

this rough water?"

He said, "Yeah."

I smelled the booze on him; he was drunk.

I said to myself, *'You stupid bastard. You don't know what the hell you're doing.'*

We were supposed to land at a certain point, but we landed down the river quite a distance because the water was rough from all the melting ice. We had to work our way back up to try to meet the other guys who paddled across. On our way up to where we needed to be a flare shot up in the sky. A lot of guys were still exposed on the river and a machine opened up from a house. I had an M1 with antitank grenade launcher on it. We were close enough so I could use it and I knocked that machine gun out, together with whoever was firing it. One of my men, May, got killed and another man, Kelly, was wounded, in the *dupa* (backside). That same lieutenant colonel that ordered us across later awarded me my purple heart.

I was wounded in 1945 in a small fight we were in. The Germans were trying to drive us back across the Rhine River but we held our ground. I was a sharpshooter and I was doing a lot of careful aiming and shooting. As I took aim, a German sharpshooter that was just as good as I fired first and hit my rifle. I got splattered with slivers of shrapnel. If I put a flashlight on my cheek, I could see the slivers of steel still in there.

My buddy, Lou Nova, from Massachusetts, was also wounded by that shot. When the bullet hit my rifle, it ricocheted and hit him in the cheek and knocked one of his teeth out. He never came back to the company until after the War.

In that battle we took eight German prisoners and Lou and I were to take them back with us on our way to the aid station. We were both in bandages and I had to take a Luger off one of the prisoners to guard them with since my rifle was busted. Before going to the aid station I was going to turn them over to the MPs back in the reserve area but in the meantime a first lieutenant from Graves Registration stopped me and said, "I'll take those prisoners off your hands."

I handed them over and moved on, but I didn't get very far when I noticed that he had a BAR in his Jeep. He wasn't supposed to do any shooting because was a noncombatant. I know he shot those eight prisoners because they never got back to the holding area near the aid station.

It was already late when I started back to my unit so I stopped off at a German house for a rest. They were very nice to me and gave me a cup of warm milk. When I left, I thanked them in German.

I tried to find my company again but I didn't know how many kilometers they were ahead. It was dark as hell, but the first thing I knew, a Jeep pulled behind me. An MP asked, "What are you doing, soldier?"

"I'm trying to locate my company. I was wounded."

I gave him my outfit, and they put me in the Jeep and took me to my unit. On the way, I thought about my squad leader, Sergeant Anderson, and how he got killed and about some of the things that happened after we crossed the Rhine.

We were on the outskirts of Cologne in a wooded section. We were marching in battle formation, and the Germans opened up on us. We had ten yards between each man and when they opened up we hit the ground. When I hit the ground, I saw Anderson. He was standing beside a brick electrical transformer building. Anderson was standing on the corner of that building. I got up to him and I said, "What the hell we going to do?"

No sooner were the words out of my mouth, when something zipped past my head. I was facing Anderson, when his right eye popped out of the socket. The round that killed him could just as easily have killed me. I just hit the ground. I hollered to the men to crawl back.

Another sergeant came up and as the rest went back he and I took cover behind the transformer building. While we were there, a German tank came up. The sergeant got up on the tank, but let himself wide open. A round blew his testicles apart. He fell off the tank, and a medic ran up and pulled him to some cover. I worked my way back, and we got on a half-track and went into the woods where the fire was coming from. As soon as we went into those woods, we saw in a ravine Germans that had been shooting at us. I opened up, but the machine gun jammed. We could've killed them all, but they escaped, all of them.

Most of our tough fighting was in woods and small towns. The only larger city we fought in was Bonn. In Bonn I had a .30–06 with a scope. They knew my record from basic as a sharpshooter so I was made a sniper there. I had to camouflage myself and everything. From where I was I could see into the town ahead. I could see the church steeple from there and I could see a German walking around in it. We had been getting artillery and he must have been the spotter because after I got rid of him we took no fire.

I had a very close call once when we were on the edge of a town in a defensive position and I was in my foxhole. Usually, it was a one-man hole, but sometimes it would be a two-man hole. Well, this time it was a one-man hole and I was sitting in it on branches I had cut down off a pine tree. I always made sure I had a log or something in front of me. It gave me some protection, and it made a rest for my rifle. I dozed off a little and when I opened my eyes I saw a huge German, maybe 250-pounds, standing over me and holding a submachine gun. For some reason, he looked down for an instant. I pulled the trigger and hit him between the eyes. I didn't bother aiming.

He fell down on the little log I had in front of me, and I tugged his body over it a little more to give me more protection. Then I took his burp gun, and when the Germans got to moving, I opened up with it. That was stupid as hell, because that gun had a distinctive sound and the guys in some of the other holes thought there was a German firing, and they started firing at me!

Apparently, those Germans were escaping from some other town and didn't know we had taken the place where we had defenses set up. The German I shot probably was surprised to find an American in the hole when he came up to it.

We lost men quickly in battle. One time we were in an attack, after our company commander, Captain Paulson, had left and we had a new captain. I never did find out his name. He was a tall, skinny guy who had never seen any action. He must have been one of those reserve officers. During the fight he was running with me into a town when they opened up. We thought the whole German Army was in that town, but in

"I went downstairs, and here was a German General!"

the end it was nothing but young kids, Hitler *Jugend.* I happened to look back and I could tell he had been shot because of the way he hit the ground. I never found out, but I think he got killed.

The city of Tale in the Harz Mountains is where I captured a German General. It was a rich town with big mansions. We were moving from house to house. Upstairs in one of them we found a couple of German officers and some civilians having dinner. While we dealt with them, I happened to look out a window and saw a German. I went down and said to him, Hande hoch!

He put his hands up, and I saw a nice watch. I said, "Give me that!"

He wouldn't, so I motioned with the rifle that I was going to hit him. He gave it to me. The guy was a general! So, in total, we captured a General and two other officers.

A little after that, we hooked up with a Sherman tank. Down the road came a German truck and another vehicle all-covered in dirt. They had no idea we were there and we shot the hell out of them.

After we had captured a bunch of Germans one started running away, and a Sherman tank opened up on him with a machine gun and killed him. Unfortunately, they also killed an American lieutenant that was farther down the street. The lieutenant was a case of "friendly fire," and that wasn't unusual, especially at night.

That's the worst time there is. We always operated in squads and we never knew who was on our right, or who the hell's on our left and that was true, especially at nighttime. Somebody would be moving around and we wouldn't know whether they were friendly or not. We'd fire anyway.

Besides that, everyone is nervous to begin with. I know on one occasion we had a kid from Texas with us and he was on the verge of a nervous breakdown. I went up and told one of the officers, "Get that man to report to the medics. Give him the pass to go to Paris or something. He's going to kill somebody." He'd fire at anything that moved. He didn't know whether it was an American soldier or what it was; he'd just shoot.

Civilians got killed, too. We hit one town and while we were in this town going from house to house a woman was killed.

The houses were twenty yards or so apart and we were moving from one to the other. Pretty soon a German tank came down the road. As soon as it passed me, I shot an antitank grenade from my rifle and I hit that tank from the back. The tank went dead and two Germans, one after the other, came out of the tank. The BAR man opened up and he killed them both. As soon as that happened two girls came running out crying from the other house. I don't know whether a ricochet off of that tank hit that house or what but the mother of the two girls had been killed.

Eventually, as we moved deeper into Germany, Germans started coming in larger and larger groups to surrender. Together, the 1st Infantry Division and the 4th Armored Division that were with us, took over some 118,000 German prisoners in the city of Tale alone.

By mid-April we were in Czechoslovakia and that's when we heard we'd meet the Russians.

By then we were with Patton's Third Army. We had transferred over from the First Army. We were about sixty-some kilometers away from Berlin when the transfer came. That's what the rumor was anyway.

The orders came not to drive northeast, but to drive southeast. Patton's Third Army was in the southern section. We ended up being about thirteen to fifteen kilometers away from Pilsen, where they make the beer. That's where I met two Russians. They were scrounging around like a raiding party and they didn't seem to be attached to any sort of unit. I picked up some Russian words from them.

I speak Polish and when we got into a town and there were Polish PW's there, who were brought in to work at German factories, farms and different places, I approached them and talked to them in Polish. I'd ask, "What's in the next town? Are there any Panzers, are there any Germans? Are there very many soldiers there?"

And they'd say, "No, no soldiers," or they'd say, "Yeah, there are some soldiers."

That's the way I got information as to what we could expect in the next town. The women were more talkative than the men, and the kids were, too. One time an older person said in Polish, "Don't tell them anything! Don't talk! Don't tell them anything!"

I swore in Polish and said, "Shut your mouth!"

I told the scared ones, "Germany is *Kaput*!"

I'd also ask them, "Are there any deer? Any kind of animals that we can shoot?"

All we were getting was C-rations and K-rations. We got sick and tired of those after awhile. We'd scrounge around towns for food. We'd find German rye which was just like the Russian rye. That's what I was always looking for because I was raised on rye bread. Then in the smokehouses there were hams hanging. We were pretty good at finding food. We looted, too.

One time there was a dead German and he had a nice ruby ring on his finger. I stooped down and I was trying to get it off of him but we were still fighting. Maybe less than an hour later we had the section secured and I went back for that ring and goddamn it, the finger was chopped off and the ring was gone. That kind of thing happened though.

Everybody looted. Once we got into town, we looted, mostly for jewelry. I had rings and necklaces and different things like that in my pack. During a fight I threw my pack off and lost all my stuff.

When we'd go into the towns, I'd always say *Sieg Heil* to the citizens and they'd do it back. They always said they weren't Nazis, but they'd return that salute. I used to get a real kick out of doing that. The medic he got mad at me one time when I did that and he said, "Why are you like that, Sergeant? You shouldn't be doing things like that."

We were in Czechoslovakia for a long time because Czechoslovakia fell into German hands in 1939, and there were German people settled there by the War's end. We had orders to stop them from entering back into Germany because there would have been a food problem with all those refugees. That's what we were told as to why we were there.

Once in a while some tried to escape and we'd fire a mortar to try and scare them back. I don't think we ever hit any of them. We were just trying to scare them. They were afraid of the Russians.

The War ended on 8 May 1945, and I spent June, July, August and September in Germany before I got shipped home. We were not too far from Nuremberg. The 1st Infantry Division was picked for duty at the Nuremberg Trials. Our MPs were doing all the police work there. But by the time that all started I was shipped home.

I got my shipping orders sometime in October. I had the most points because not only did I receive the Bronze Star Medal, I received a Purple Heart. I got points for each one of those items and points for every month in service and for my two children. That gave me a total of about eighty-six points. I was the first one out of the whole company that got shipped home.

When I came back, I landed in Norfolk. Then I got on a train to Indiantown Gap, Pennsylvania, and that's where I got discharged.

They gave me my papers in the afternoon about four-o'-clock and by the time I got to Harrisburg it was already evening. I landed in Pittsburgh about ten-thirty or eleven-o'-clock, and by then there were no buses running to Natrona Heights.

I was standing at the bus station and a woman came up to me and she said, "Are you waiting for a bus?"

"Yes, I am."

"Where do you want to go?"

"I have to go to Natrona Heights," I answered.

"Oh, I'm from Natrona! I'm waiting for my husband."

He worked for the government in the Pittsburgh area and her dad ran the baker shop in Natrona Heights. He pulled up, and I jumped in with my luggage. They dropped me off on the corner. I was finally home.

Nobody was expecting me. My kids, Sonny and Marsha, were sleeping and my wife was up sitting on a couch. The kids woke up and Sonny came running. He jumped into my arms. I opened up my bag and I handed him a German Luger, binoculars and a German parade SS bayonet. It was beautiful.

I decided to take a little vacation, and about the second week the mill called me and said, "We know you're home! How come you're not coming to work?"

So I said, "Okay. I'll be down."

I went back to work, had another child and eventually retired.

Carl Josefoski (center) with friends in Panama before the War.

A twelve-inch Barbett cannon used in Panama by the United States Army, mid-1930s. *Courtesy: Carl Josefoski.*

Arnold and I

Thomas A. Katana

87th Infantry Division
"The Golden Acorn"
Motto: "*Stalwart and Strong*"
347th Infantry Regiment, 1st Battalion
Born in Latrobe, Pennsylvania, 18 September 1922

"I used the rifle to pick myself up, turned to start back and man; all of a sudden I was flying through the air! I thought, 'What in the hell am I doing way up here?' After I hit the ground, the toe of one of my boots was next to my face. My femur was completely smashed, and my left leg was lying across my chest. I thought they had blown my leg off!"

My brother Ted was called up in the summer of 1942, about two months before I was. When I got my notice I went to the draft board in the old Mellon Bank building in Latrobe, PA, and they told me I had to report to Greensburg instead. In the meantime I had an appendicitis attack and ended up in Latrobe Hospital. The folks there notified the draft board and I was placed on hold until late December 1942. Then I was called up again and they asked me if I felt well enough to go into the service. I said I was, and before I knew it I was in. The day that we all went for our swearing in, we were supposed to be allowed to pick the branch of service we wanted.

Since my brother was already in the Air Force, I said, "I'd like to be in the Air Force."

That didn't work. They put me in the Army.

In early January of 1943 they had a big parade for us. We walked down Main Street, the whole gang of us from Latrobe, and the Boy Scouts held up a big flag and people threw money.

After the parade, we went to Fort Meade. It was early morning there when we arrived. We went into the warehouses, and they gave us all duffel bags; then we stripped down to our skivvies and walked along while they looked at us. As we went along, they asked us our shirt size and so on and then gave us complete outfits, all of our clothes and shoes.

Afterwards, a corporal took us to our barracks. There, they told us to put on our uniforms for inspection. After that, we went into the medical center. They had us walk through two curtains and the next thing I knew this fella hit me with a needle in the right arm. There was a big guy in front of me and when they hit him, down he went! I didn't mind the shot, though. They gave me one in my right arm and one in my left, and as I walked through they asked me my name, where I lived, what my hobbies were, and so on. They wanted all the names of family members as well. They asked me if I did anything special.

I told them that I worked at Westinghouse, in the electronics section and that my preference was going to the Air Force. Standing behind me was a guy who became a good friend, Frank Ammon, from Philadelphia. He said, "Gee, I'd like to go to the Air Force, too."

But then a sergeant came up to me and said, "Would you like to be a clerk here at the fort? Some of our clerks are going to leave because they want to go to the branch of the service that they'd like."

I said, "Gee, I'd like that, too."

And Frank said, "Gee, so would I."

We had only been there two days when we heard that a group was going to go to Mississippi. When I looked down the listing, I saw that Mississippi had all the air bases, so I said to this corporal, really nicely, "I'd like to go to the Air Force."

I don't know why, but I felt this corporal and I didn't hit it off too well. He said, "Hey, okay, so you want to leave?"

Frank said, "I'm going to go with Tom."

I thought we were headed to the Air Force base in Biloxi, but when we got off the train I saw a sign that said "Camp McCain."

There were barracks, if you could call them that. They looked like they were made out of tar paper. An MP came up and said, "Katana and Ammon—312th Combat Engineers."

I said, "No, no. I think were supposed to go to the Air Force."

"Not if your name is Katana. You're going to the 312th Combat Engineers, Company B, Pal. Get in the truck."

Later on, they called me in because someone had seen in my records that I had worked at Westinghouse.

"You'll be in the rigging business," they said. "We're going to teach you to be a rigger."

Eventually, the commanding officer of the 87th Division[111] decided he wanted to see how good we were, so he ordered us to go and build a bridge. We built one over the Columbia River, and we did a heck of a nice job! We were really proud of that bridge. But in the Army, if you were ordered to build a bridge, you could also be ordered to tear it down.

The soldiers wanted to leave it where it was, but the officers said, "Hey, you put it in, it's Government Issue, tear it down."

The locals loved that bridge, though. There had been a bridge there at one time, but it had washed away years before, and these people had to travel many, many miles around to get into the city. I don't know how it happened, but it came about that the mayors came down from the different towns and convinced the commanding officer to let them keep the bridge. I understand it's still standing.

After that, we went on maneuvers in the mountains near Nashville, Tennessee, where we were told to go out and "blow" a bridge. There were two teams of us; my team went down and we put up a sign, "The Bridge is Blown," so when the trucks came down on either side, they couldn't cross it; they had to cross the stream. There

"There were two teams. Arnold had one, and I had the other."

were three of us guarding the bridge: one on one side, two on the other, and then on relief we'd switch and watch the other side.

While this was going on this black fella, a very nice gentleman, came down and saw the trucks going through the creek.

He asked, "What's the matter? These trucks, how come they're going through the creek?"

I said, "Well, we're simulating that this bridge is blown. The Army can't go across, but you can."

He didn't hesitate. He took his mule and his buggy and off he goes through the creek!

One of the other guys ran across and said, "What's the matter with you guys? He can cross the bridge!"

When the black fellow came back, I stopped him and told him again, "You're allowed to cross the bridge."

Just then one of our trucks crossed the creek. The black fella looked at me, and then he took that cart back through the creek. We were there for about four days, and every day he'd drive that cart through the creek. I had given up.

I said, "If he's happy, I'm happy."

One time his whole family came down and crossed the creek; I guessed they were going to church or something.

One Friday we were told, "You guys are now relieved; pull the signs and go back to camp. You can go in to get your leave and go into town. You get a break."

It was Thanksgiving and we went into town to the USO, where we got to meet girls and go to dances and we could get chow and drinks, but no alcohol. I had an Elks' card, and that got me into the local Elks Club. They treated me really well, too. I always had a good dinner and beer, and I always enjoyed myself. Well, this particular Thanksgiving evening, the Elks was closed, so I went to the USO. Another soldier and I were sitting there and one of the USO ladies came up and said, "Would you like to go to a Thanksgiving dinner? You can go to this family's home-as a guest-and he will pick you up in his car."

The gentleman was standing there and he came over and said, "Would you soldiers like to come have dinner with my family?"

I was tickled to death. He was a young guy, only in his thirties. It was a really nice affair.

After maneuvers, we headed to Fort Jackson in Columbia, South Carolina. While we were there, the war in Africa was going on, and they told us that they'd like volunteers out of the infantry regiments to fill in as replacements for those that were wounded or killed in the desert. I heard a lot of guys volunteered; a lot of sergeants, a lot of GIs.

But I said, "No way."

I was still trying to get into the Air Force, but every time I applied, they said, "No chance."

At that time I was in weapons training: the .50–caliber, the .30–caliber, mortars, the bazookas, the small arms and the M1, a fantastic rifle.

My captain called me in one day and said, "Katana, you're a drill sergeant. They need drill sergeants over in the infantry and since you were a regular, a drill sergeant and a weapons sergeant, your name was brought up. They need those three types."

I told him I didn't want to go, but I had no choice. It was either that or the brig, and I definitely didn't want to go to the brig.

In the meantime, I got pass to go home. I was in a train going from Mississippi to Pennsylvania and something kept hitting me on the back of my head. I looked down and picked up a little piece of paper. On it was the name "Marie Corbett Campbell."

There were a few girls on the train, but one of them was sitting with a big guy.

I thought, *'That couldn't be she.'*

So I turned back around and bang! I got hit again. I looked, and the girl with the big guy beside her waved. When she got up to get a drink of water, I got up, too, and we started talking to each other. Not too long after that Marie Corbett Campbell and I got married.

At Fort Jackson I met Arnold Van Quickenburg from Mechanicsburg, Ohio. Arnold and I were really close; he pulled all kinds of duty for me while we were at Fort Jackson so I could go home to see my wife.

In September, Arnold and I got our orders, and I told my wife that she had better head back home. We were together just a few months when she got on a bus and headed back to Ohio. In the meantime, we were getting prepared, learning how to load equipment. By the end of September we had everything packed up on a truck, and we headed for the debarkation point at Camp Kilmer, New Jersey. When we were getting ready to board the ship, an officer came over and told me I was in charge of our rail car. "You get off the train first and make sure nobody makes a run for it. In New York, you're going to be right on the docks, and the gangplanks will be there. You must make sure that you count your guys as they're going up the gangplank."

I agreed with that, figuring that maybe some guys didn't want to go and would make a run for it.

Our ship, the *Queen Elizabeth*, was huge! Including the crew and us, there were around eighteen-thousand men aboard that ship. And it was so fast! Most ships would take anywhere from seven to ten days for a crossing like ours; I think it took us four.

When we got out to sea, it was bright and sunny but the water was rough. So many guys were sick! They were lying over the side of the ship, but I didn't get sick. One of the crew I met, a British sailor, gave me some bread and said, "Eat this bread and stay away from greasy food."

That was tough because most of the British food was very greasy! I was a gunner on that ship. They took all the weapons sergeants and put them at .50-calibers; then they shot up a puff of smoke and we'd fire at a target for practice.

Once across the ocean we docked on the Clyde River, in Glasgow, Scotland.[112] I saw the castle, but I never got to the town. I was assigned to wait for weapons; in the meantime, most of my battalion was loading aboard a train to go to Cheshire, England. I had gotten on the train, too, but a lieutenant said to me, "You better wait; take your duffel bag and your weapon and wait until all of our trucks come. You're supposed to mount those .50-calibers on the trucks and clean them off."

I think there were four trucks, and eight of us were cleaning these weapons. I was in the lead truck. We didn't know where we were going. Everybody else had taken off, and we were just waiting there. Of course, every regiment was going to a different area.

I asked the first sergeant where we were going, but he didn't know. Then along comes this British Jeep. An officer got out, shook our hands, told us his name and ordered us to follow him to get to our billets. We took off. I mean, we went flying down that highway, and those roads weren't very wide! I'm looking as we're going, and I saw tanks, artillery, ammo dumps.

I thought, *'If we hit something, we're all going to get blown up.'*

We stopped at night and slept in the truck; they didn't want to run any lights at night because the Germans were still bombing targets in England. And we saw lot of explosions going off, courtesy of the *Luftwaffe.*

When we got to Cheshire, we went into the billet, which was a two-bunk barracks. It was an old mansion—beautiful, circular stairways, beautiful hall, everything you could imagine. One day I was out on a hike, drilling, when I was called back and told to report to headquarters along with all the other sergeants. We went down to Headquarters Company, all of us from Company C.

A lieutenant colonel said, "You're going to get a new captain, Captain Wilkins."

Captain Wilkins was a Texan and he was Gung-Ho. He walked to the first sergeant, who snapped to attention and saluted. He looked at the first sergeant, and I didn't know what he said, but the first sergeant's face turned red. So, he started down the line.

When he got to Arnold he said, "Don't you know how to dress?" and gave him a talking-to, and then he stepped to me, looked at my feet and said, "Don't you know how to clean your shoes?"

"Yessir, I do."

There was no argument with him. He was the boss. All the sergeants got a little bit of hell. None of us were really dressed, some weren't even wearing a tie, and that really got him mad. But nobody warned us that we were going to see a new captain.

After we were relieved, we stood outside and talked a little bit, wondering what a pain in the butt this guy was going to be. Then we started back to the billet, and as soon as we walked in the door all the guys crowded up, "Boy, we leaving? . . . We're going into France right now!"

They were all Gung-Ho, talking of going to France.

I told them, "No, we've got a new captain, a real sonofabitch."

Just then, this little corporal, Bruno Jarosz, hollered, "Attention!"

Little did we know that Captain Wilkins was standing right behind us, picking up every word! Instead of hollering attention right away, though, Bruno had been trying to alert us first, trying to tell us we shouldn't be bitching about the new guy.

So we turn around, and right behind us is the captain.

I thought, *'Ohh, there goes the rank. I'm out of here.'*

He never said a word, just looked both of us in the eye, turned around and walked out.

Everybody said, "Uh-oh, something's going to happen to this outfit."

It couldn't have been five minutes and then a runner came up, a guy named Petrosky, from Latrobe. He had been a student at Saint Vincent College.

He said, "You're supposed to report to the first sergeant."

So Arnold and I go down to the first sergeant, and he said, "What the hell did you guys do?"

We told him we thought that this new captain was really lousy, booting us around, looking for everything that was wrong.

He said, "Well, the two of you are supposed to pull extra duty."

"What's our duty?"

"You're going to patrol at night, from six to ten; anybody that's caught out after ten o'clock reports to me, and I'll report to the officer."

About three or four days later, Captain Wilkins came into the barracks. It was ten o'clock, we were just done, and he said, "Sergeant, I'd like to see who's in their bunks at ten o'clock. I hear you had a very good report."

Arnold and I were in charge of the guys. There were twenty guys on each floor. I was in charge of the downstairs and Arnold had the upstairs. It was a little after ten. I opened the doors, and we went in. The captain walked up one side of the room and down the other, trying to see if all the boots were there. Everything was in order. He asked whose floor it was, and I said it was mine. As we were leaving, I heard this little noise in the back, but I ignored it, and we went upstairs. We went into the room, and there were all the guys in their bunks. Well, little did he know that the guys from downstairs were going up the stairway in the back of the kitchen and climbing into bed upstairs.

I was hoping, "Please don't go down there and go through that room again!"

But the captain just said, "You guys are doing all right. Looks pretty good."

There was a pub that we went to called the Bleeding Fox. In England at that time, when it was ten o'clock, they'd holler, "Time!" and pull down this window on the bar, and that was it. If our drinks were on the other side, they were gone. Well, one night Arnold and I were standing with our backs to the bar, talking to the other guys, when they hollered, "Time!"

When I reached over and grabbed my beer, I heard someone behind me say, "You took my beer!"

Then some guy pushed another guy, and he bumped me, and I dropped my beer.

I said, "Hey, you knocked my beer out of my hand!"

His collar was open, and I could see a cross.

I thought, *'Oh, my God, it's a chaplain.'*

He said, "Well, I owe you one."

The place was closing, but I figured we'd be back another night. But I never saw him again. Not in that pub, anyway.

After our training in Cheshire they finally told us we were heading for France. Our battalion went in really quickly. In November we went down to Plymouth and boarded an English ship. It was manned by guys from India, and they ran around trying to get our money. One guy told me a story about how one of the Indians wanted to sell a three-cent Baker's chocolate bar—which sold for three pennies in the United States—for a dollar. And I understood that after so many attempts, the guys threw him overboard. I was at the other end of the ship so I never saw it happen, but that's the story I heard.

When we got into the harbor at Cherbourg[113], we had to get into landing craft, which were manned by Navy guys. They'd roll back and forth and we really had to hold on! I was fortunate; I went down and held the net until we loaded it up. We were supposed to take the landing craft and circle until this group formed up on our battalion, and then head into the beach.

We had a light colonel with us, and he was giving everybody orders, "When this thing drops its ramp, no matter who falls, keep going."

I'm thinking, "This is December. That beach ought to be cleared. What the hell's he talking about?"

Thank God we didn't have to hit the invasion part. They dropped that ramp and this colonel's all Gung-Ho, ready to lead us out, and he slipped on the wet ramp and went flying in the air. I was so happy that he hit that water! When the guys missed the ramp, they stepped on him, and he just kept going down. I came down the other side, I didn't even get wet, I was just lucky. And when he came up, he's hollering for somebody to get him dry clothes. Nobody was going to give him any!

So we got in, and we went into this billet, a warehouse that the German officers had used as their headquarters. As we were waiting for our equipment, a major came up and said he was looking for the weapons' sergeant. I told him that was I. He said he needed a machine gunner. Well, Gene Garrison was a machine gunner. And this major said, "I want you and the driver."

I think Norm Panther came with us as well; it was his Jeep. The town had been destroyed. There was just one road, and somehow they'd made space for one Jeep to go through. We were going to circle the city to see if there were any snipers left, which there weren't. We rode around that whole town,[114] but there was nothing, no problems.

The following afternoon we were told to move out to an apple orchard. When we pulled in, tents were already up for us. From there we were going to move to the front. There was a guy by the name of Herman in our unit; we called him "Herman the German." He was a really nice kid. He had come over from Germany as a young man around fourteen and volunteered to join our Army so he could go back and free his mother country. He hated Hitler.

One night a fella from Company B was sitting on a stool or a box, cleaning his weapon. He left a round in the chamber, and accidentally pulled the trigger. The round hit Herman in the head and it came out through the jaw. Herman died instantly. He was the first accidental casualty in our division.

Herman's head was a mess; I got sick as a dog looking at him. The lieutenant wouldn't even look. The captain didn't want to know about it. We covered Herman with a blanket. The guy that had been lying next to Herman was shocked; he didn't know what to say. He couldn't talk. They took him away for a bit and when they brought him back he was completely out of it. His nerves were gone. He was crying, "Why? Who did it?"

Some guys wanted to go back and beat up the guy that shot Herman. I understand they were going to court martial him, but we were going into combat, so maybe he didn't make it; I don't know what happened to him.

Shortly after that incident we boarded a train and headed for Walsheim and my first combat.[115] We got to the place at night, and there were German artillery flashes in the sky. In the morning, two teams went out on our first patrol. We were all rookies; we didn't know what the heck was going on. There were supposed to be ten men on the right and ten men on the left, with a scout in front, seeing how we're doing for the first time. We started down the road. Arnold and I each had a team, and everybody else was either in reserve or waiting back. We came up on this farmhouse, and the two scouts ran in and got captured. There was a shot. We all stopped. I was on the upper side, and Bruno Jurosz was the scout. He was from Chicago and, boy, he was a good shot. When the Germans came out, he fired and hit the first German, and then everybody started shooting. The Germans thought the guys were coming up the road, and they were coming out to shoot at them. We were above them and ahead of them, and we opened fire. It was no contest; really, they didn't know what hit them. It was too early in the morning, and they must have thought nobody else was around. We made a heck of a mess of them. Only two got away.

We were ordered to fall back, and while we were doing that I got nicked in the wrist. It just stung so badly!

I stumbled and I thought, *'Man, I'm outta here!'*

I started complaining. Gilbert, the medic, came up and asked what was wrong.

"Geez, I think I lost my wrist."

"Not a chance, Tom!"

I wanted to leave! I was scared. I'd seen what had happened. But Gilbert just put a little bandage on it and said, "You're okay."

And then I heard Lieutenant Lister say we were falling back. So we retreated back up the hill, toward Walsheim. That night we were in a woods digging in and we took one heck of an artillery barrage. Gene Balick, from Milwaukee, was dragging a log over so we could hide behind it; that way the shrapnel would hit the log instead of us. I saw him go down. I wasn't too far away from him so I went over to him to see what had happened. He had his heavy topcoat on and it looked like he had a cigar hole burnt in the back of it. I rolled him over. I was trying to talk to him. Then I saw that inside, he was a mess. He was dead right off the bat.

Gilbert came over then and dug in with me. We were all covered up so that tree bursts wouldn't get through. Well, after we'd beaten the Germans that day, I knew something was up. Late that night, they sneaked up on us.

We had Guy Wick, from Charleston, West Virginia, and Armand Verdun, from Phoenix, Arizona, out there, and John Burnes was on point. If the Germans came,

"I'm Outta Here. I got nicked in the wrist!"

he was supposed to fire a flare so that we had a target to shoot at. Well, when they got in, a guy named Zubick stood up between them and shot a German or two. The flares never did go off, and, boy, there were a lot of bullets flying around! I lay in that hole and fired, just hoping to hit a German. We were afraid to throw hand grenades because we might throw one in a friend's foxhole. Then suddenly the fire stopped. We waited a while and then fell back.

The next morning we all came out of our foxholes and found the lieutenant and Bill Petrosky still dug in together, and the lieutenant had this grenade that he couldn't throw. He'd lost the pin. So he stuck the grenade in his pocket, with his hand over it so it wouldn't go off—if he let the handle go, it was gone and we were gone.

They got out of the hole and the lieutenant said, "Fellas, I have a live grenade in my pocket. I lost the pin!"

So we're all looking, too excited to really find it.

He said, "How am I going to get it out of there?"

One of the guys took his bayonet and he cut that officer's pocket out and said, "Now you can pull it out."

It was his brand-new Army officer's coat, too, a nice heavy one.

Then the lieutenant asked, "Where in the heck am I going to throw it?"

We didn't care! So he tossed it and where did it go? Right into the first sergeant's foxhole! It exploded, and the sergeant's papers, his ammo, anything that was in that hole flew in the air. Heck of a noise.

The lieutenant said, "Boy I'm glad to get rid of that!"

The first sergeant was all upset. He kept saying, "All my paperwork, everybody's casualty list . . . ! What the heck did you have to throw it in there for?"

But of course, we were all just glad the lieutenant got rid of it.

We went up just by Bastogne, heading for Tillet,[116] which was a crossroads town in Belgium; we were supposed to secure the area and keep the Germans from driving on to Antwerp.[117] The Battle of the Bulge was going on at the time, and the saddest thing that happened was the massacre of American troops in Malmédy.[118] We heard about it no more than a day later. I was really upset. A lot of guys were, and they took out a German if they had a clear shot. We didn't know, though. We shot and hoped to hit; we never went to look.

We went to a small village near Tillet and billeted there. Arnold and I spent the night in a loft above a barn. What a good rest that was! The following morning we headed up the road toward Tillet. There was supposed to have been reconnaissance, but we didn't have any. What really got me, though, was that our mortar squads threw away our mortars! But at any rate, our scout found a set of German tank traps in the snow.

I thought, *'Man, the Bazooka team is going to go in, and we're going to kill a tank.'*

From the field to the farm house it was about a hundred yards. They decided we'd set out in three groups: Arnold and I went out; he was on the right, I was on the left, and Kelly went up the middle. The Bazooka team was with Kelly. We took our teams and headed up through the woods. We had no contact, no enemy fire, and we wondered where the Germans were. When we got to this open field, we saw the farmhouse; we could see that the tank tracks in the snow went around the right side of the house. They decided to fire a Bazooka round at it. They missed the house, but the missile went over in the back, and there was one heck of an explosion. We didn't know what it was. It was amazing-there was no infantry fire, no soldiers. But then, after the first round went off and they were loading the second, one tank came around to the right of the house and another came around to the left. They had trapped us. They had set up one set of tank tracks to lure us in, and then they started firing.

My group set up a .30-caliber machine gun. The rounds just pinged off that tank. We were trying to make him blind, hoping to hit his bogie and knock a track loose. Then they started firing into the trees. Kelly got hit in the face. I saw him go down; he was blinded. Gilbert went after him, tried to get him back, but he was going in circles, he couldn't see, he was hollering. Then he ran out in the open and they cut him down, just machine-gunned him to death.

We attacked with seventeen men that afternoon; boy, what poor leadership that was! We should've waited for reserves; we should've waited for another company to come up and support us. We had no artillery and no mortar; that was another mistake. But who do you blame for a soldier's dumb mistakes? It's dumbness that causes wars in the first place.

We were ordered to fall back and regroup. As we headed back down, I see this tank coming up the road. I tap on the side of it, and this black fella opens the hatch. I could see the roof of the farmhouse, and I asked him to fire a round at it. Well, he said he was told to fall back also, and that he was so low on gas that he was afraid if he'd get into a fight, he wouldn't have enough to get out of it again.

Lieutenant Lister came over then, and I said to him, "Why don't you give him an order to shoot and knock the roof of that house down?"

But Lister said, "No, Wilkins ordered us to fall back."

So we fell back over the hill. When we got back, Captain Wilkins came to me and he said, "How about you take three guys and a medic and go back up and see who's wounded and where they are."

I wasn't too happy about it, but we went. There was Gilbert, our medic, and Gene Garrison, and Crooks, who lived in Bethlehem, PA, and one other guy. We took off and went up the left again, but through the woods, of course. I removed the dog tags from Kelly and Holmes, but that was it. There was nothing else we could do for them.

I had thrown a few hand grenades at first just for noise, and I had one left. We saw this little pile of German mortar shells.

I was going to set the grenade in there but I thought, *'If I pull that pin, and that bundle lets go, we won't have a chance.'*

And I had a strange feeling in the back of my neck, too. My hair stood up, and I figured somebody had me under the gun sight.

So I had the grenade in my hand, and I thought, *'Should I throw it?'*

The guys weren't too happy with the whole idea. Could we get away in time, they wondered, with that stuff flying all over us? So we just went back, reported the dead and gave Captain Wilkins the dog tags of the guys that were killed.

No sooner did we get back there than the Germans started firing mortar round after mortar round, banging off everything. Just then, the major comes driving up in his Jeep with his driver. I ran to this foxhole and saw Arnold dive in, then Elmer Zeichner, then I'm on top of them trying to work my way to the bottom! There was all this lead flying around. We came out after the barrage stopped. We found the Jeep driver dead. Shrapnel just tore out his throat. The major had gotten under a tank, though, so he was fine.

He said to the captain, "You've got to go back again."

I was upset; we had no mortar fire, we had no artillery fire. We were relying on tanks.

I said to the captain, "I'm tired. We've been up two times already. I'm beat!"

And the major said to me and Wilkins, "You can't refuse! You have to go."

So I said, "I'll take the left again."

But they said, "No, you're going to get in back of the tank."

Arnold and I went up again, right and left, behind the tank. Gene Garrison got on the tank behind the .50-caliber.

I thought, *'I'm going to hug this thing. I'm going to eat all kind of carbon monoxide, but I'm going to be real close to this tank!'*

We started up the field, our tanks firing into the woods, and out came two German tanks. When our tanks turned for protection, there we stood, Arnold and I, out in the open.

They just cut Arnold down. The second round I got hit in the chest and went down on my knees. I felt like somebody had punched me.

So I'm kneeling there and Crooks is beside me, telling me to shoot. "How come you're not shooting?"

I was bleeding from the mouth. I laid down and thank goodness it was cold, because I was able to take some snow and wipe my face. Boy, did my chest hurt! Crooks kept saying to me, "Shoot! Shoot, Sergeant, shoot!"

I don't know how long we kept going; I just shot and hoped to hit, shot and hoped to hit. I could put a clip in, but I could hardly hold onto my rifle. Then the guys said, "Hey Tom, we're falling back."

"Go ahead," I said, "I'm too slow. You guys start back."

I used the rifle to pick myself up, turned to start back and man; all of a sudden I was flying through the air! I thought, *'What in the hell am I doing way up here?'*

After I hit the ground, the toe of one of my boots was right next to my face. My femur was completely smashed, and my left leg was lying across my chest. I thought they had blown my leg off! I had gone through over an hour of a firefight, I had gone up three times. I knew I had to use a tourniquet or I'd bleed to death, so I took my bandoleer and wrapped it around my leg.

As I was tightening it, I kept thinking, *'Will I remember in twenty minutes to release it for blood to flow?'*

Pretty soon Gilbert crawled up beside me. "I'm going to pull you. Can you help yourself? I'm going to pull you over to this little ditch."

God love Gilbert! He grabbed me by the coat collar and pulled me into this ditch; then he said, "I'm going back for help."

I said, "Gilbert, can you do anything . . . ?"

"I can give you a shot of morphine."

"I don't want morphine yet, I don't want to pass out. If you're leaving, I'll be by myself. I'll bleed to death."

I took my rifle. I figured they weren't going to bayonet me to death, either. I was going to shoot them first. As I was lying there, Panther and Blanchard came up and told me, "We're going to pick you up."

They tried to hunch down so they wouldn't get hit; shells were still going off, rifle fire, machine gun fire. They tried to keep low and drag me with them, and I said, "Nah, leave me alone, go ahead back."

Gilbert came up and said, "We're going to get you out of here, Tom. We're going to go back and find a stretcher."

No sooner he said that, than they bought up a stretcher. He took my M1. That felt strange, because it was the first time my weapon had been out of my hands. Then they put me on a stretcher. They were almost on their knees, crawling me back, bouncing me along.

When we got back to the Jeep, I said, "Now's the time to give me that shot of morphine."

So they gave me the shot and put me over the front of the Jeep, where it was warm. By then it was around 4:30 in the afternoon and getting dark.

We pulled into the aid station and I told them I had to go really bad. The sulfur had loosened my bowels. But after what I went through, I thought maybe sometimes a guy defecates and then passes away. But then I told myself to get that out of my mind, that I was going to make it. When I got in the aid station, they re-bandaged my leg so they could send me back to the general hospital for further operations. When they went to move me, there were shells banging everywhere.

As I'm lying there, a chaplain came over and said, "I see you're a Catholic. I'm going to give you the Last Rites of the Church. Do you have anything to say?"

"Father, I'm glad you're a Catholic."

And then I looked at him and said, "I think I know you from somewhere. Maybe in the States?"

He said, "No."

I couldn't remember where. And then I said, "Were you ever in England, Father?"

He looked at me and he said, "I remember you! I'm the guy that owes you a beer."

I said, "Yeah, that's it, Father! I can't drink right now, but you owe me one."

Then he told me he was going to give me the Last Rites of the Church and asked if I had anything else to say.

I said, "Every chance I had, I went to church."

Maybe not to church, really, but any Mass or service in the field, any religion at all. I didn't care. If I had a chance to go listen to a preacher I did. Some guys said their prayers before they went into battle, some carried their rosaries. They all prayed.

So he gave me the Last Rites of the Church.

But I said, "Father, I'm not going to leave this earth yet. No. I'm not ready."

"That's a good way to feel," he said.

"Father, I've got a terrible bump on my neck."

He looked and said, "Oh, my God, Sarge, there's a hunk of steel sticking out of your neck!"

"Can you take it out, Father?"

"No, no! I'm going to tell the medics right away."

The medics said I had to be moved, so they took me to the general hospital in Reims, France. The first two guys I saw as they pulled me out of the ambulance were these two German POWs and I was mad at all Germans, including them. I didn't want to hit them, though, because I was afraid they'd drop me. They took me inside and put me in this huge room. I was kept in there I don't know how many days and then the doctors finally told me that they were sending me back to England for further recuperation.

As I lay there a Red Cross woman or a nurse came in and asked, "Can I do anything for you? Maybe I can write home and tell your parents you're all right?"

I thought that was great. So she wrote two letters, one to my wife and one to my parents, telling them I was wounded in action.

I was in and out of consciousness for about three days. I was getting penicillin in my right arm, in my left arm, in my right arm, in my left . . . Every four hours they'd give me a shot of penicillin. Thank God for penicillin; it really saved a lot of lives. But oh, were my arms sore! I was complaining, so finally the nurse said to me, "Well, can I give it to you in the hip."

I said, "Yeah."

She rolled me over and gave me a jab and I said, "Oh, my God. Next one, give it to me in the arm!"

There's no pain like that needle in the butt!

I laid there for I don't know how long before they decided they'd move me back to England. I was supposed to be on a train, but they put me in an ambulance that took me to an airport. I was told I wasn't supposed to fly. They put a red tag on top of my pajamas, and they had me in a body cast. First they wrapped me in plastic, making me look like a mummy. The only thing that stuck out was my arm and the wound and, of course, the private area was open, but the left leg was straight in this body cast, except for my toes and my heel. They put a rod across between my knees so they could pick me up like a turtle.

In the meantime, I had to go to the toilet badly. I saw this little girl; she might've been a nun. She had on a dress like nuns wear, anyhow. I told her I had to go.

She said, "Okay."

Then she came over with a shaving-mug and a razor!

I'm trying to tell her, "No, no, no . . . !"

But she just pulls out this razor and starts shaving me. She talked to me in French, too; I don't know what the heck she said.

Well, when a woman gets a razor and starts shaving your neck, you don't say too much.

But as soon as she's getting ready to do the other side, I saw this guy walk by and I told him, "I need to go. Bad!"

He laughed and told the nurse, or whatever she was, in French. She didn't hesitate. She reached under the bed, pulled out the bedpan, picked me up, slammed me on it, laughed like hell and walked away. I was so pleased to see her go!

Then the ward guy came over, looked at me and said, "What are you doing here? You're not supposed to fly."

I said, "How the hell do I know? They don't tell you anything."

He told me I was supposed to go on a ship (I think it was called the USS *Hope*, which was anchored in the English Channel) and that I was going to be in a convalescent ward until I was ready to go back home to the States.

I said to the guy, "I don't care what you do, but if you want to fly me . . . "

"No," he said, "you've got chest wounds, so you can't fly."

On the way to the ship, my ambulance drivers decided that they wanted to go through Paris and see the Eiffel Tower. So they're driving through Paris—they have to be 150 miles away from where I'm going—saying, "Oh, look, there's the Eiffel Tower; there's the Arch of Triumph . . ."

And they're asking me, "How you doing back there? You need coffee? You need any cold drinks?"

When we finally got to Cherbourg, they picked me up and carried me aboard the ship. All I had to my name was a knitty hat and my prayer book and inside my prayer book I had hidden invasion money. On some of the invasion money (which I still have) are the names of some of the fellas that were in my outfit, most of whom were killed. But once I was aboard and they were getting ready to operate on me, I said to the doctor, "Don't take my knitty hat or my prayer book!"

And he said, "No way."

I never took my hat off.

One time this sailor went running down through the wards grabbing stuff off the soldiers—cigarettes, candy, anything he could eat or smoke, he took. He grabbed my knitty hat, but thank God he didn't steal my prayer book, the little GI book they gave me when I left Latrobe. We were all hollering, but there were no walking wounded. Everyone was bedfast. If I had had a gun, the bastard would have been dead. He was as low as anyone could get. I never heard that the Navy did anything about it. That scumbag probably took the cigarettes and candy to the Black Market.

In Plymouth, England I was in one of those Quonset huts in the 94th General Hospital. The guy that was lying next to me had little American-made radio.

He said to me once, "I'm going to leave here and when I leave, you can have my radio."

Well, that was the nicest gift a guy ever gave me. I don't remember his name.

I was in the 94th General from late January until April. Finally they told me I was going to be moved. They took me into the operating room and they wrapped me up again, like a mummy, all this plastic and plaster around me.

Then they said, "Now we're going to take you aboard the *Queen Mary.*"

They carried me down and when I saw the big white cross on the side of the ship, I thought, *'Thank God!'*

They laid me down in an upper bunk near a porthole, and I watched them bring the other guys in. Most of them were blind or burned. Once I told one of the blind guys that he ought to see what a good-looking girl his nurse was. I'll never forget it. I tried to apologize, but he said I didn't have to; he already figured out that she was pretty.

When our ship landed in New York and I saw that Statue of Liberty, what a glorious feeling that was! They took me to Holland General Hospital in New York and put me in a ward beside a guy with half a face, hardly any nose, a missing ear . . . They had all kinds of salves and cream all over his face. There were guys with terrible burns in that ward.

This poor guy said to me, "I'll take care of you."

Hell, he was laid up himself. I said, "Nah, you better take care of yourself."

"One thing, I don't want my girlfriend to see me," he said, "I don't want my parents to see me."

He was a mess; he'd talk to you out the corner of his mouth. He was such a wonderful guy, though, and so young to be scarred like that.

Once they carried me into a private room so I could talk to these psychologists; they said, "You got to forget about what you went through. And your experiences, and do you have any regrets, blah, blah, blah."

Then they told me that they were going to take me to Walter Reed for treatment on my leg. But the doctor said, "I think you're coming along pretty well though; would you sooner go to convalescent?"

I figured if I was going to Walter Reed they might cut my leg off. So I said, "No, if I can go to a convalescent doctor, I'd prefer convalescent."

So they took me to the general hospital in Camp Pickett, Virginia. The doctors there told me, "It's not healing like it should. We're going to drill through your leg, drive a steel pin in two places and somehow pull your femur so it's attached."

Of course, today I can't turn it to the left at all. But it's still my leg, and it's good to have.

I lay in that hospital until July, and my parents and my wife came to see me, and my brother, who had just got in from the Navy, came too. When Mum first saw me, she didn't believe that I still had my leg. She thought it had been blown off; she had to reach over and touch it to see if it was really there. She didn't believe a word the doctors said. Next door to me was my cousin Johnny Maddox, another graduate out of Saint Vincent College. He found out I was in the next ward, and he came over to visit.

Then, in July the doctors said, "Tom, you haven't walked in seven months; we're going to get you up."

I couldn't wait. I said, "Oh, thank God!"

"We're going to pull those pins out of your legs," they told me, "one out of here and one out of here, and we're going to let you sit for a couple days, until that all heals."

It didn't feel too good when they took the pins out of me. And then they said, "We checked your chest. We took the steel out of your ribs and they've healed, but we didn't take out the three hunks of steel below your heart that are embedded in your lung, so don't get hit in the chest."

They're still in there, too-three pieces of steel as big as my thumb. I can't go through airport security; I get dingdonged when they scan me.

Around 10 July they got me up. I said, "Don't worry about a thing. I've gained strength; I feel good, I'm eating good, just let me sit at the side of the bed."

Then I tried to stand up, but I couldn't do it. I just went down. I couldn't believe it! Here I am, twenty-three years old, and I'm falling down! I tried to catch the bed, but the bed wasn't there. The nurses grabbed me while my cousin, John, stood there saying, "Come on, Tom, do it again!"

They made me sit a while, and then they all helped me walk to the end of the bed. And I did, back and forth. They told me, "Don't get out of bed unless a nurse is with you."

I got out anyway that night, but I figured I should've listened! All the blood was out of my feet, I guess.

They asked me then if I'd like to go home on a thirty-day leave

"Oh," I said, "I'd love to."

They made me a brace out of iron that opened up and had a ring so I could sit on it. There was leather over my knee, leather over my calf, and then through the heels of my shoe they drilled a hole straight through. Springs were bolted to this steel that went through the leather; this way, I kept that leg straight, and when I got up I could ride the ring. Whoever invented it was a smart man.

So I came home and visited the families. I went back down to the Corbett farm and had a wonderful stay there. I also visited a lot of my friends who were also home from the service. On the day of the Japanese surrender, we decided that we were going to meet in Washington, D.C. and celebrate. We were going to rent a room and stay in Washington for one night before I had to report back into the hospital the next day. When I got off the train in Washington and saw all the people celebrating that the War was over, I was really happy. One guy came up to me and offered me a drink.

I was no real drinker, but I said, "Oh, what the heck, I'll take a sip."

He gave me the bottle and said, "Do you want anything else? I'll buy your hat."

I said, "Well, how much will you give me?"

"Five bucks."

So I gave him my hat! Five bucks! Holy heck, I only got $128 a month! Someone bought my tie, too. I sold that and my shirt and even my shaver! Someone wanted my old Gillette blades!

So I said, "Give me five bucks."

I must've made forty, fifty dollars that day and got about ten bottles of liquor. While all this was going on, the MPs came up and said, "All you wounded, you're going to the hospital right now."

They said to me, "Let's see your papers."

I said, "I can't go to the hospital, I'm way down in Virginia."

"We're going to take you back. Our orders are to take you back to the hospital."

"I don't have to be in until tomorrow. Can I go to this hotel?"

"No," they said. "It's too rough. The town is going crazy."

Orders are orders; there was no question, so I told them they could take me back. I had all these bottles rattling in my bag, so as we pulled up in front of the ward, I said, "Thanks fellas, here's a bottle."

So I gave them a bottle of booze and went into the ward. The guys were all excited, shouting, "The war's over, Sarge, the war's over! Did you bring us anything?"

Now I knew what bad shape they were in; many had lost arms and legs, but I said, "Yeah, I sure did! Here. Take a drink and pass it down."

Then I went next door to see John. I said to him, "John, I got all this booze, so I'm giving some to these guys. You can keep a little pint and I'll keep a pint, and we'll save one for Baron."

But when I went back to my ward again, the guys were whooping it up, singing songs and throwing water; their legs were pinned, and still they were hollering and trying to get out of bed.

I was sitting out on the porch, looking through the screen door, and I thought, *'Oh, my God, what did I do? I might be going to jail.'*

Then the nurse walked in (she was a cute little heavyset thing) and started hollering at the guys: "Where did you get this?"

I thought, *'Oh, please don't mention my name!*

Three of the guys got the fire hose. They were in bad shape-one was missing an arm and another had no bone in one of his shoulders; I don't even know how they got out of bed.

Then the one guy said, "Turn it on!"

And I thought, *'Oh, no, Geez . . . !'*

But they turned it on and hit her in the pants, and she went flying. They couldn't hold the hose, either, so it went everywhere. Pretty soon the whole place was soaked. Medics came running.

I said to John, "Let's get the hell out of here!"

We went next door. I got into a bed. Next morning when I went down to report to the officer of the day, he said, "Boy, did they have a lot of problems in your ward!"

I said, "Really? I didn't know!"

God love those guys! I was so glad later on that I did it, too. John even said, "That was the nicest gesture I think you ever did. A lot of those guys didn't make it."

I stayed in that hospital until September when they said, "Tom, how you doing?"

I said, "Well, I'm walking."

"Can you walk without that brace?"

"Yeah," I said, "but I have to use a cane or crutches."

I was using crutches more than a cane, but I didn't tell them that. I wanted out of there.

They said, "Well, we'll discharge and put you on total disability. But you have to promise that if something goes wrong you'll go to the veteran's hospital in Aspinwall."

I was glad to be able to go home, but I cried when I left that ward. All the guys did. I was with them for so long, they became my brothers. They were such wonderful heroes, much better than me, and such good guys. The chaplain came in and we all said a prayer. Imagine that: the day I left the service, we all said a prayer. I was lucky to get out of there.

There was an officer outside going to Washington, D.C. and he asked if I wanted to ride with him in his limo. I said, "Heck, yeah!"

He took me right into the station, and he took care of the limo charge, too. I got off at Latrobe where my parents and wife met me. I was so glad to get home! After I had been home for a bit, my dad asked me, "You going to go back to work?"

I said, "I'd like to go back to Westinghouse and see if I can get my job back."

So I went up and they asked me, "You ready to come back to work?"

"Yeah, I want to come back and make some money. I can't walk too well yet, though."

They told me maybe I could be a clerk.

I said, "Yeah. I'll do that. But I can't come back right away."

"That's okay," they said, "your job's waiting for you when you come back."

I think I took a month off, then I went back, but I still didn't feel too good. Westinghouse had their own clinic there, so I went to see them, and they told me, "No, you can't come back yet."

I finally went back to work about the middle of December. It was a nice job, too; I liked it. But then, the next month, Westinghouse went on strike.

I thought, 'Oh, here I am, trying to make some money . . . !

Of course I ended up in the 52/20 Club, as well, that gave all the GIs twenty dollars a week for fifty-two weeks. It was really nice. I joined the American Legion, too, as well as the Purple Heart Association and Veterans of the Battle of the Bulge.

And so, I was finally a civilian again. After all I had been through, I was damn happy about it, too, settling back into the old routine in my old hometown.

Marie and I have been married sixty-one years, and we have three kids, Tom, Pam and Lisa and thirteen grandchildren. Tom is a retired Lieutenant Colonel.

May God bless all my buddies.

"It Was an Honor to Serve My Country."

Charlotte Frederick Lally

United States Army Nurse Corps
280th Station Hospital
Born in Ambridge, Pennsylvania, 25 February 1921
Sewickley, Pennsylvania

"... in France I was in a ward of paratroopers who were not allowed out of bed because of trenchfoot and frostbite. They had exercises to do, so I directed the exercises. When the food cart came up, we'd fill a tray with food and give it to the first guy, and he'd pass it clear down to the last guy on each side; it went fast. Every third day they got their beds changed; the ward boys did all that. One patient would hop to the next bed while his bed was being made. The paratroopers were healthy except for frostbite and trenchfoot, and we had a lot of fun with them then, because they were young. They were nineteen, twenty, and they wrote a lot of poetry."

WE HAD A MAID. We were wealthy, and we played the market, buying stock on margin. Then the Depression came along and everything crashed. People bought groceries on the tab; they didn't pay until payday. That was all forgotten. The stores both went bankrupt. After living royally, suddenly all was lost, and, like everybody else, we went without. It was awful, terrible. The rich people killed themselves, but the poor people didn't. They struggled and got through. I had a great mother who did everything. My stepfather was okay, but she was the backbone of our family. We didn't buy anything new. We had enough food, we had a home, but we had nothing extravagant. Nothing. Three years of that and then things started to pick up.

My father's name was Selage, and he died when I was two weeks old. My mother, Rose, four years later married Robert Frederick, and he adopted us. I had one older brother, Alex and one younger stepsister, Ella. My stepfather had a good job in the mill. We had two grocery stores: my mother had one in Beaver Falls, and he had one in Monaca Heights. We lived in Rochester, so he'd take her up and drop her off with my little sister. My brother and I were in school.

I went to high school at Rochester and graduated in 1939. I did science, math, history and English. Back then there were the commercial and academic tracks. Commercial was the getting ready to be a secretary, typing and shorthand, and the academic was the sciences and so forth. Students who were planning medical careers took the academic courses. I played basketball and was a cheerleader. I danced my legs off back then, too. I took French in high school. When I was in the service in France people would say to me, "Freddie, come up and talk to this man."

I'd always wanted to be a nurse. It was the best way to get an education at a cheap price. Three hundred dollars covered three years—a hundred dollars a year. And my mother was able to do that. By that time it was the end of the Depression, so it worked out. I went into nurse's training at Allegheny General Hospital, in Pittsburgh, in September 1939. We lived in the nurses' home and everything was provided for us. We had great training and we worked hard night and day. But we were young and we were able to do it.

We studied everything pertaining to medicine, a lot of science, anatomy and physiology. We did class work in the morning, and then we went on ward duty in the afternoon. Then it was lights out at ten o'clock. So we had to hurry up and get homework done. There wasn't much free time. We went home once a month. At AGH we did have parties—dances—you know, we could invite a friend from home. Everything was nice at AGH; it was a brand-new hospital then.

There wasn't a better nursing school anywhere, we thought. It was strict and we had to exceed all the time. We had to be topnotch, and we were. Two of us got the best grades on the state boards. Our head nurse was proud of us. They were very strict. We wore black stockings, black shoes and blue uniforms with white aprons. We looked really bad. Of course the girls at Presbyterian Hospital wore white shoes and white stockings, and they bragged about that.

It was a terrible shock when Pearl Harbor happened. I never thought that we'd be going into the War. Then everyone got enthusiastic. There were a lot of recruiting signs, "Join the Army," "Uncle Sam Wants You."

I graduated in September 1942. I worked on a private room floor, the ninth floor, at AGH for a few months and then I signed up for the Army. That was the thing to do. It was really an honor to go in the Army. Everybody admired you for it. Of course, when you're twenty-two, it's an adventure, right? Everybody was patriotic. My mother put a blue star in the window, which meant one of her children was in the service. My brother had been in, too, but he had a shoulder problem, and he got a medical discharge. Right after I volunteered, there was a freeze on nurses leaving, because they needed nurses here. I waited about three months for my orders.[119]

I had signed up at the Red Cross in Pittsburgh. When my orders came, they read, "Proceed on or about certain date to Camp Pickett, Virginia."

And that was my first taste of the Army. Camp Pickett had a big hospital. I worked in the medical department—not the surgical, medical. I got there in August 1943. We had close order drill in the mornings. We had a lot of regulations. At Camp Pickett it was very strict, I thought. It was very regimented. There was a lot of apple-polishing. Some of our nurses who wanted to move up did a lot of that, and they became captains. I was a first lieutenant. There was a lot of protocol. And we weren't allowed to date the enlisted men.

One of our nurses became what we called "Section Eight." This gal was taking drugs. She'd get into the medicine cabinet and take drugs. Once, she crushed a glass in her hand, just like that. She was whacko. Then there were two or three who got pregnant, and they had to be sent home.

Around October we went to Camp Livingston, Louisiana, which was our staging area. We had gas-mask drills, we had to swing over a creek on a rope, we had to climb a wall. We had so much fun. Then in December we went to Camp Kilmer, New Jersey, our port of embarkation. We got on the *Queen Mary* about two days before Christmas. We headed out into the Ocean to make a straight shot to England. One night the sonar detected a German submarine, so the captain made an extreme turn to the left. We could tell because this one night we noticed that all of a sudden, everybody fell to the other side of the cabin. We outran the submarine and went up toward Iceland. From there we went into the Firth of Forth and Scotland. Then we rode a train down to Braintree.

Braintree is where we were on detached service while they put up our hospital. Our first night in the ETO, first night in England, we got the alert to get in the bomb shelter. So that was exciting. We'd just got there and we already were in the bomb shelter. From Braintree we went north to Newport, where the train station was called Oddly End. The hospital was located in an area called Shortgrove Park, which was owned by a wealthy Englishman. He allowed the Americans to build it on his property.

I was assigned to the 280th Station Hospital, which was the first tent hospital in the ETO. Our commanding officer was Colonel Zellhoffer; he was from West Point It was a 250-bed hospital. There were thirty doctors and 150 nurses. We lived in tents and we worked in tents. That was all through the winter, which was just gloomy. There's a song, "It's Always So Cold and Damp."

I worked on the medical ward giving out medications and taking temperatures and blood pressures, but ward boys changed the guys' beds and helped them with their baths. In England most of our patients had been wounded on bombing missions with the RAF and the Air Force.

The English civilians were in a tough way. They had rationing and they'd ask us for stockings and things like that. I'd meet the English girls at parties who were dating our pilots.

They'd ask, "Ooh, can you get me some stockings? Can you get me this, get me that?"

We had more than they had, that was true. The civilians in France, well, they tried to be polite. You know, they were charming, but, really, we didn't understand them, and we didn't have much to do with them.

I knew some of the pilots who'd shot down a lot of enemy planes. I dated John Godfrey.[120] Godfrey was a prisoner of war for a while. He was handsome. He went home and married a rich girl. It was the best thing that ever happened to me, because he died at the age of thirty-six of Lou Gehrig's disease. I felt bad about that. And I knew Don Gentile[121] who was dating one of my friends. Gentile died in a plane crash after the War. They flew P–47s and then they switched to P–51s, fighter planes. Debden Air Base was two miles from our hospital, and we saw a lot of the pilots because the parties were held over at their place. We'd go to their parties because they had ice cream, and we didn't!

We went to London at least six times. We'd get a Jeep and a driver, and about four of us would go in together and we'd walk around, look at all the stores, have tea, have dinner and then get home around eight-o'clock at night. We didn't have any interest in buying any clothes because we couldn't wear them anyway.

I was in London one night when eight buzz bombs fell. Thank goodness one didn't hit us. When the engines on them stopped, we knew they were coming down. One week after we left England to go to France, a buzz bomb fell on our hospital and leveled it. We left just in time. They hadn't even bothered to take the tents down. They just left them. There was a lot of waste in the Army.

We landed at OMAHA Beach on D+120, roughly the first week of October 1944. They dropped the ramp of the LSM and we waded ashore. The French were there to give each one of us a loaf of bread.

They said, "You won't have bad luck with a loaf of bread under your arm."

It was rainy weather when we arrived. We went on detached service to a cow pasture that was near Ste. Mère-Église. It was muddy, and, being young, we laughed a lot. We lived twenty nurses in one tent, with two pot-bellied stoves. Wouldn't you know, the tent over my cot leaked. I wrote a lot of letters home. There was nothing to do for about two months while we got organized. The 198th had to clear out of the hospital in Cherbourg to let us use it. Things moved slowly. Hurry up and wait!

We'd walk from our tent to Ste. Mère-Église, where there was a pump. We'd pump water into our helmets and bathed from them. They set up a mess tent, and we lined up with our mess kits. After we ate we washed our kits in boiling water so no germs would form in them. I don't remember anyone getting sick. It was average food; if we didn't eat it, we'd go hungry. We got used to it; powdered eggs and all that stuff, but it wasn't bad.

The hospital in Cherbourg was a fairly large building, and it was a permanent hospital. We lived in a manor house, which was really big, you know. It was close enough that we could walk to the hospital. Rosie Grady (McDonald), Ruth Lawlor, Mary Blount (Ludwig), Joey Gordon and Helen Robb were my best friends. I was in the medical ward. It was just like every other hospital. And it ran well, thanks to Colonel Zellhoffer. We had Red Cross girls with us, too. They mostly served doughnuts. They were okay.

We went to Paris a lot, maybe five times. There was one little black soldier that kept following me, so I had to report that. I was scared to death. He was in the Army, but he'd follow me to where I lived in the manor house. Finally I reported him, and they did something about it. After that we always traveled in twos. That was the only scare I ever had.

We treated lots of gunshot wounds. Some wounds were very severe, almost like accident cases, missing a hand or a foot. Some of them were in bad shape.

On Christmas Eve I'd just gone off duty. Soon after that they ordered us all back to work. The *Leopoldville*[122] had been sunk by a submarine in the English Channel. Eight hundred were lost at sea. We trooped back and we worked a long time. I don't know where we got the stretchers; they must have been in storage—but we had patients on stretchers in the halls, in the stairway landings, in the offices. The place was loaded with cots, and all the patients were hypothermia victims. They had been in the cold water for a long time. We got them warmed up and gave them hot drinks, fed them intravenously, and covered them up with lots of blankets. They eventually came around.

Also in France I was in a ward of paratroopers who were not allowed out of bed because of trenchfoot and frostbite. They had exercises to do, so I directed the exercises. When the food cart came up, we'd fill a tray with food and give it to the first guy, and he'd pass it clear down to the last guy on each side; it went fast. Every third day they got their beds changed; the ward boys did all that. One patient would hop to the next bed while his bed was being made. The paratroopers were healthy except for frostbite and trenchfoot, but we had a lot of fun with them then because they were young. They were nineteen, twenty, and they wrote a lot of poetry.

On 8 May 1945, my best friend, Ruth Lawlor and I were listening to the radio with Joe Kelly. He was our mess officer. About one o'clock in the morning, an announcement came over that Germany had capitulated. So we woke everybody up. Joe took the nurses' department and we took the doctors'.

We opened the bar and we partied and partied. The girls were in chenille bathrobes with curlers in their hair. Everybody had a good time. The War was over!

I had my picture taken with Bob Hope on the French Riviera. Ruth Lawlor and I had gone down to Eden Rock for four days of R and R. Bob Hope and his group were there. We stayed at the Provençal Hotel, very fancy living. We were at the pool, and I said to Ruth, "I'm going to get dressed."

She was down there, still on the beach, and as I was coming up to get dressed I stopped to lean over the rail, looking at Ruth and the scenery.

Behind me, someone said, "Are you having a good time?"

I almost fainted when I turned around.

"Yes," I answered. And then I said, "Oh, you're Bob Hope!"

Ruth took our picture.

In September 1945 the 280th moved to Marburg, Germany for four months. We set up our hospital in a school house there. We had German soldiers working for us. They were very humble and very docile. They'd clean up, shine our shoes, things like that. Those were the good old days, when somebody would shine your shoes for you! We shopped in Wiesbaden and Bad Nauheim. I bought a big piece of black leather at Offenbach; it was the leather center of the world. I brought it home and when I worked at the VA, one of my patients said, "Oh, I do a lot of work with leather. I'll make you a purse out of that."

He took the leather, but I never saw it again.

I met both Eisenhower and Patton when we were on occupation duty. We'd go to Frankfurt for the football games, and it would be the "Hypos," which were the

Charlotte Lally and Bob Hope. This photo was taken on the balcony of the Provencal Hotel during Nurse Lally's visit to the French Riviera.

Charlotte Lally at
Camp Pickett, *1943*.

medical players, against some other team. Patton and Eisenhower came to the games. Eisenhower sat on one side of the field and Patton sat on the other. Then at halftime they'd switch. We got to sit next to them. It was a big thrill talking with them. Patton was the big hero.

I boarded a Liberty ship in Le Havre about a week before Christmas 1945. It was just packed with people; we could hardly find a place to sit. The trip took a little bit longer. We went over in four days on the *Queen Mary*, but coming home I think it was a week. We landed in New York Harbor, and then went to Camp Kilmer where we were discharged. That's where I signed up with the Veterans' Administration.

We went from there to Philadelphia and spent a night in a big hotel. Next morning we got on the train from Philly to Pittsburgh. It was so packed with GIs that I couldn't find a seat. I sat on my suitcase.

I came into Penn Station in Pittsburgh where I got cleaned up because I was all night on the train. Then I took a street car out to Presby to see my sister who was in training, and then my mum and dad came up there. When I saw my mother, it was a shock. I hadn't seen her for two and a half years. She was diabetic and she'd lost almost sixty pounds of weight. I went home and I hung around for a month then in January I left for the VA.

I worked at the VA hospital in Aspinwall until late 1947. I was on the medical ward there. Gastroenterology was my department. I started on the GI ward, then I was on the ear, nose and throat ward. It was very well-run. Three weeks after I started, Frank showed up.

I thought, *'This is the man of my dreams! This is the guy for me!'*

Frank was in residency at the VA. His specialty was internal medicine. He had been interning at Mercy Hospital in Pittsburgh, and they shortened the internship. It used to be a year, but during the War they made it nine months because they needed doctors in the service. So he left after nine months and went in the service.

My husband was one of the first into Dachau. He was with the 47th Regiment, 9th Infantry Division. When the War ended, the prisoners were still there, half-alive. It was pathetic. He was in the Battle of the Bulge and had been surrounded by the Germans. His was a medical unit and he was the battalion surgeon. They slept in foxholes. He and his aide man slept head to foot, because the breath of one would keep the feet of the other warm. We were losing the battle and then Patton came up from the south and saved the day.

Frank's hometown was Sharpsville, near Sharon. We were married in February 1948. He was still in residency, so he'd drive down, stay for the week and then come back up to Sharpsville for the weekend. That was just for a couple of months. His family was around there and we all got along fine. They helped out.

I belong to the Women's Overseas League.[123] Everybody wanted to go in the service and everybody respected the service. It was a whole different attitude than what there is today. We were so proud to be part of the Army. It was an honor to serve my country.

"He Still Called Me 'Kid'."

Norman Larson
United States Sixth Army
33rd Infantry Division
130th Infantry Regiment, 1st Battalion, Company A
(Post-war Service: 24th Infantry Division, 21st Regiment)
Born in Cleveland, Ohio, 13 July 1926
Cumming, Georgia

"Our captain singled me out and told me to check one of the dead Japanese. He wanted to get me exposed to this kind of thing and get me hardened as quickly as I could. He said, 'Number One, make sure this guy is dead. Number Two go through his pockets and bring me back what you find.' I felt a little sick about it, but I had to carry out the order. When I got close enough, I saw that the soldier was indeed dead, and that he was around my age. He was a kid, too. I couldn't help but realize that our situations might have been reversed had they attacked us when we ran into them on the trail. I reached into his breast pocket and found a wallet. Inside were pictures of his family. At the time I really wasn't feeling too much compassion, as I said, this could have been the other way around. That was my introduction to combat."

THERE'S NO DOUBT about it. The early 1930s were difficult times financially. We were fortunate to be able to struggle through it. At one time, my parents were concerned that they may have to lose the house that they had just built in 1931 in Cleveland Heights and move in with Dad's parents down in the heart of Cleveland. But Dad was able to hang on and be able to satisfy the needs for the mortgage payment. They lived in that house all the way through. Mother died in 1985, and Dad still stayed in the house until he went into a retirement home.

My father was Oscar Fredrick Larson and my mother was Lovina Wells Larson. My father's parents were both born in Norway and immigrated to the States late in the 1800s. My father was born in 1896 in Ohio. My father wasn't a World War I veteran because he worked on freighters on the Great Lakes. He worked there for seven years and as such his job was considered vital, so he was deferred from military service. My parents were married in 1920. At the time, my father wanted to continue on the Lakes and she said "NO" in no uncertain terms because in that capacity he was gone throughout all the summer months and much of the fall, so he gave that up. After that he started work in the Rockefeller Building in downtown Cleveland in a lower-level administrative capacity and worked up to building manager. He was at that location and with the same company until he retired at sixty-five.

When I was eleven I got my first job. I had a paper route. I also worked at a golf driving range near our house. The owners hired a bunch of us. Each hour on the hour they'd ring a bell and we'd grab buckets and collect golf balls. When I filled a bucket, I'd bring that in and get a nickel. I'd spend five hours doing that, and then go home with twenty-five cents in my pocket. Back then I could actually buy something with twenty-five cents. Parents felt the impact of the Depression more than the offspring, at least in my case. Up to the time he died at ninety-eight, Dad thought a five-dollar bill was still a lot of money.

I was fifteen when Pearl Harbor was attacked. I was just going into high school, but we all got pretty Gung-Ho about it.

I said to my mother, "Boy, I hope this lasts until I get out of high school so I can go in!"

She said, "Don't you say that kind of thing!"

But that's the way we felt. We all wanted to get involved.

Rationing was on. That was mainly for the parents and other adults. My friends and I collected any kind of metal object that we could deliver to a designated place.[124] My dad was proud of his lawn and his backyard, but he dug up the whole place and put in a Victory Garden.

I have an older brother who went into the service before me in late 1942. He became a navigator in the Air Force and served in the Pacific. He was in the States for a period of time; then he went overseas and was on the island of Tinian. Because he was older, and had gone in before me, he was discharged from the service and was home before me.

My parents were supportive of the war effort, but it was a two-edged sword for them. They were proud to have their sons in the military, but at the same time there was obviously an awful lot of apprehension on their part. They never knew if we were going to come back alive. My parents had two Blue Star banners hanging in their windows.[125]

When I graduated from high school in 1944, it was about a month before my eighteenth birthday, so I registered for the draft that July. A lot of close buddies were already gone, and I was ready to go. I went down to the induction center, went through the screening process and went to a reviewing board. There were officers there from the Marine Corps, the Navy and the Army.

They said, "We see by your record that you have enlisted rather than waiting to be drafted so we'll give you your choice of which service you want."

I didn't know if it was a smart thing or not, but I said, "I want the Army."

There was a huge group of us there to be sworn in. They then told us all we'd be leaving immediately. Dad had driven me down to the induction center that morning on his way to work. When I found out I'd be leaving I called Mother. She told Dad. They met me at the train station, and we were able to say goodbye.

From the induction center, we all marched down to the train station in downtown

Cleveland. There was a small band there and a local politician made a speech. This was a big thing in those days. As we boarded the train, a gal passed out Philip Morris cigarettes.

The first thing everyone did was light up. *'I guess this is the thing you do now,'* I thought.

So I lit up, too. Stupid!

Sitting there on that train, I didn't have the feeling that I wouldn't come back. I guess it was too early. There was definitely some apprehension as to what I was getting into but everyone was serving their country, and I was glad to be a part of it. I'd have felt horrible if I had been declared 4-F or for some other reason wouldn't have been accepted.

The train took us over night to Camp Atterbury, outside Indianapolis, a staging location where we were issued uniforms. Then they briefed us on what would happen next. We were there about ten days, and then we were all sent out to different locations. I was sent to Camp Wolters, Texas, for basic training.

A typical day of basic training at Camp Wolters started with the sergeant coming into the barracks, turning on the lights and saying in no uncertain terms, "Rise and shine!"

Then we really had to hustle; go to the latrine, get a shower and shave—if we had time for a shower and shave—brush our teeth, and then fall in for roll call. They kept us going all day long. It was pretty demanding. We had to go out and simulate the kinds of conditions that we would encounter. He had to dig foxholes and spend the night out in the foxholes on more than one night. Then we went through different kinds of mock battles in the day time. We were introduced to flame throwers and we went out and spent a lot of time on the rifle range. They trained us using hand grenades. We started by using dummy grenades and then worked up to live grenades. We were told time and time again that our best buddy would be our M1 rifles and that before we left there we would be able, with a blindfold, to strip the M1 down, clean it and put it back together again. We wound up our basic training with a twenty-mile march. They wanted to get us as prepared for combat as well as they could. We were not training as a part of a division. We were segregated as to the type of training we would get. I mostly trained in heavy weapons–mortars and the heavy .50-caliber machine gun. However, I didn't use any of these once I got to the 33rd Division overseas because they made me an M1 rifleman.

Events in the War caught up with us, and they reduced our training from eighteen to fifteen weeks because of the Battle of the Bulge, and they needed replacements. We didn't know if the abbreviated training would affect our ability as combat troops. As a result, almost everyone I trained with went to Europe. In retrospect, I feel I was lucky that I went to the Pacific. The conditions in Europe, at that time, were unbearable because it was mid-winter and those poor guys were subjected to the worst elements. It was miserably hot where I ended up, but the heat was probably more bearable than the cold.

Once training was over we got a ten-day furlough. I took the train from Texas back home to Cleveland. I had a week or so there, and then got orders to report to

Fort Ord, California. Trains were extremely crowded in those days. I shared a coach seat from Cleveland to California with a sailor. He was older than I and really a great guy. I don't recall his name. I'd sleep for a while, then he'd wake me up, and we'd change places. I'd walk around or go wherever I could. That wasn't the most pleasant arrangement by any means.

Fort Ord was our point of embarkation. We shipped out on 23 February 1945 on the USS *Sea Pike*, a large troop transport. We went over separately; no convoy, and we were a sitting duck, to tell the truth. There must have been several thousand of us on board, jammed in the hold like sardines. The sea was rocking and rolling and a lot of guys got sick. Fortunately, I didn't. The bunks were pieces of canvas stacked four or five high and supported by ropes. They could be raised for stowage and lowered for use.

Around the Equator it got beastly hot. We slept only in a pair of GI shorts. The stench in the hold was terrible. All we had to wash in was cold saltwater. The officers had it all. We were just a bunch of grunts, just a bunch of numbers. None of us felt we had an identity anymore. To make matters worse, we were out in the middle of the Pacific Ocean, and I came down with malaria.

At the dispensary I asked, "How can I be out in the middle of the ocean and get malaria?"

They asked me where I took my basic training.

When they found out they said, "We've had cases of this. Soldiers who had been in Texas contracted it from the Anopheles mosquito."

To tell you the truth it was a blessing, because I was in the hospital on the ship for about seven days and I got fresh water. I hated to leave the hospital once I got better.

It was so bad down in that hold. Sometimes, at night, I'd take an Army blanket, which we sure didn't need down below, and go up on deck. I'd throw it down and sleep on that. The deck was hard as a rock, but at least I had some fresh air. They'd have music playing, and there were all these stars out, and I thought, *'God, it could be so nice here!'*

But then I realized I was going to the War.

Our first stop was in Finchaven, New Guinea. They said it was something like seventy-five-hundred miles from the States and that's when I thought, *'Oh my God, will I ever see home again?'*

After Finchaven, we went up the coast to Hollandia and unloaded supplies. Then we took off and went through the Solomon Islands. We went past Guadalcanal and Bougainville. We all knew these were great battles from earlier in the War. Then we docked in Tacloban, Leyte, in the Philippines. The thing that really stood out to me about Leyte was the destruction along the coast. The Army had invaded Leyte in October 1944, and this was now March 1945. After I saw all that destruction I knew this was all for real.

From Leyte, we went up to Luzon and landed in Manila on 1 April 1945. It was a hot, humid morning when we finally got off the troop ship. We waited at the dock for a convoy of Army trucks to transport us to a staging area on the outskirts of Manila. Most of the area around Manila had been recaptured by the Allies, but the Japanese were still heavily entrenched in the walled city area of inner Manila and in the city of Baguio, the Philippine summer capitol in the hills of Northern Luzon.

While I waited for the trucks, I walked down to the shore to watch some Filipino boys swim in the dirty water. In the harbor were the partially submerged ships that had been destroyed by both sides. My buddies later told me that while I was sight-seeing, General MacArthur drove past in his black limousine. I missed seeing him. I did see the Hotel Manila where General MacArthur had established his headquarters before he fled to Corregidor, and then to Australia early in the War.[126] The hotel, by the time I saw it, was a destroyed mess.

The convoy finally came, and as we were being transported to our camp, hundreds of Filipinos lined our route and greeted us with applause, fresh pineapples and bananas. I spent about four weeks at this staging area not really doing much of anything. We were just waiting for an assignment. On 28 April, I was assigned to the 33rd Division. I felt both apprehension and some excitement, but more of the former. I was a raw recruit, eighteen-years-old, and I really didn't know what I was getting into. Of course I had training and a lot of simulation as to what it would be like, but this was going to be the real thing. I didn't go in as a Gung-Ho young guy saying, "Let me at 'em!" No way!

My unit was down in the low-land area around Manila. The same day I joined them, we went by truck convoy up into the hills. That's when I got my baptism of fire. On our way up to the front it was pretty quiet. We put a perimeter at the top of this one hill that we were to hold and use as base for a period of time.

The twelve-man squad I was assigned to, however, was tapped to go out and set up an ambush. As a replacement, I was assigned to a more experienced veteran, Staff Sergeant Mike Murphy from New York City. He was our squad leader and a really great guy. An Irishman, of course, and Gung-Ho up to a point.

Everyone dug a foxhole to use as a "home" for the night, everyone, that is, except my squad. We left at dusk and headed down a mountain trail to where it formed a junction with a dirt road. There we set up an ambush on the high ground that overlooked the junction. As we proceeded down the trail at dusk, we saw a number of Japanese soldiers silhouetted against the skyline on a hill to our left. We were on an embankment down which, to our left, was a stream.

Murphy said, "Okay. Change of plans. If we could see them, they probably saw us! Pair off in twos and wait and see if the Japs advance. Get in position along the bank of that stream."

I paired with Mike. We synchronized our watches. Mike took the first two-hour watch.

"Hell, Mike, there's no damned way I can sleep with what's out in front of us."

Mike was twenty-two years old, but he still called me "Kid."

"Kid, you gotta learn in a hurry to sleep when you can."

I understood what he said, but there was no way I could relax enough to fall asleep. As time went on, and I gained some experience at the front, things got a little easier for me, but we never did get a lot of sleep. Very soon after we got into position, we heard the rustling of bushes and the rattling of stones and branches. The Japs were advancing, but we had no idea how many were coming. Mike told us to regroup, work our way back to the perimeter, and warn the company about a possible attack. On the way back we had to scale a stone wall not more than six-feet high. This was my first night out, and I was as nervous as one could be. I stumbled all over myself. A couple older guys got up on top of the wall, grabbed my arms and yanked me up.

As we continued on our way back to the perimeter, a group of Japs, who had apparently crossed the stream unseen by us, came at us from an angle ahead and to our right. They came within twenty feet and stopped. There was no fighting, and nothing was said. We continued on in a hurry back to camp. Shortly after that, the Japs attacked and all hell broke loose. We figured later that what they really wanted was our food and other supplies, and they knew they had to go through the company to get at what they wanted. Had they engaged us on the trail, they'd have invited an attack by our company.

None of us in the squad had a foxhole, so we sought any means of cover when the Japs attacked. I crawled under a Jeep, and later found it to be a good place to spend the night under. We repelled the attack and there were a number of dead bodies strewn outside our perimeter. Our captain singled me out and told me to check one of the dead Japanese. He wanted to get me exposed to this kind of thing and get me hardened as quickly as I could.

He said, "Number One, make sure this guy is dead. Number Two go through his pockets and bring me back what you find."

I felt a little sick about it, but I had to carry out the order. When I got close enough, I saw that the soldier was indeed dead, and that he was around my age. He was a kid, too. I couldn't help but realize that our situations might have been reversed had they attacked us when we ran into them on the trail. I reached into his breast pocket and found a wallet. Inside were pictures of his family. At the time I really wasn't feeling too much compassion, as I said, this could have been the other way around. That was my introduction to combat.

For most of the next month, most of our activity was confined to squad or platoon-sized reconnaissance patrols. In late May, we prepared for another full-company advance.

On one occasion, we were camped on one hill, and the Japanese were camped on an adjacent hill. Their hill was our objective. Through binoculars, we watched them playing volleyball. They were apparently having a lot of fun. We realized again that they could see us, just as readily as we could see them.

We assumed that they'd be well-positioned in bunkers and pill boxes, and our captain made sure we were armed with a bazooka to use against their defenses. No one was designated "Bazooka Man," so a couple of us were assigned to practice a bit by shooting at a designated target. I was the only one to score a direct hit, and that's how I became our "Bazooka Man." I still think the others missed on purpose! They gave me a Filipino ammo carrier and a .45 pistol to use in case I ran into a hand-to-hand situation.

The path of our attack was difficult because of a thick growth of trees and underbrush. As we expected, we ran into opposition in the form of two well-camouflaged machine-gun nests located diagonally to our right and left. The gunners wounded some of our forward men, but none seriously. The first one to get hit was Tony Peters from California, and so we named the place "Peters' Knob."

We never did find the machine gunners, so there was no need for me to use the bazooka. Anyway, my ammunition carrier panicked and dropped the ammo pack and scurried back down the hill. That left me to carry my combat pack, the bazooka and the ammo.

That night we set up another perimeter. This time we all dug one-man foxholes. We tried to get some sleep, but guys were so jittery from the day's action that some of them fired their weapons or lobbed grenades at "mirages" that they thought were oncoming Japs. Once one started, we all got into the act. I threw a few grenades into the brush myself. It was all wasted ammunition, really. It was all make believe. The only attack we got that night was from the mosquitoes. Even though we slept in our fatigues, kept our shoes on, and covered our helmets and faces with mosquito netting, the bugs always found a way to penetrate.

Our next objective was to take control of an area called Totem Pole Ridge, and then to push forward to an airfield called Daklan Airstrip. Our point of origin was Acop's Place, and the airstrip was thirty-two miles away. The dirt airstrip was small and could be used only by light, daytime reconnaissance planes. We met no resistance on our approach. We crossed in single-file, allowing about thirty feet between each soldier. I had no bazooka this time! I was back to my M1 rifle. We didn't walk across, we ran. I was one of the first to cross the airstrip. Seconds after I reached the other side, a machine gun opened up. The man behind me was killed. His name was Norman Hubbard. He was one of the guys who had been with the unit from way back. When he went down, that's when we all took cover.

I was sitting on the ground next to a fella that had preceded me when a sniper took a shot at us. The round landed between us, and we immediately took cover. We never located the sniper. We moved forward and dug in.

Each day after that, we skirmished with the enemy, but they were definitely on the defensive and short on food. We did take some prisoners, but it was a limited number. It was unusual to take prisoners because many of them wouldn't subject themselves to captivity. One fella had a Japanese/English dictionary and he'd thumb through it and come up with a word and yell it at them, but they didn't understand what the heck he was saying.

Rather than surrender, others committed suicide. When we had the upper hand on them in combat, they'd scurry into some of the many caves. We'd yell to flush them out, but that didn't work. Soon after we'd hear a grenade go off or they'd use a knife and do the traditional Hara-Kiri disembowelment. We'd hear them screaming.

In mid-June we were certain the War was winding down, but the enemy remained tenacious, and they were prepared to fight to the end, no matter the odds against them. While we were on a brief period of R&R, our officers told us to prepare for a short "mopping-up" exercise. Because we were to be out for a period of two days, they told us to pack clothing and rations only for that amount of time. The two days turned into eighteen, and they were the most grueling that I ever encountered.

On the first day, we took another hill, but got cut off from behind. We were heavily dug-in, and this time I was assistant BAR man. That meant that I not only had to carry my M1 but also the ammunition for the Browning Automatic Rifle (BAR). The gunner was Arturo Lopez, a Mexican from Texas. We shared the same foxhole, and talked about our different backgrounds and our ages. He was a seasoned veteran, and he was compassionate and protective toward me, a rookie. He was thirty-six, and I was eighteen. I learned a lot from Arturo.

We were shelled with artillery and mortar fire from the Japanese unmercifully at night. The sky was filled with flares and tracers. We listened to the incoming shells whistle before they hit and crouched down in our foxholes. It was like the Fourth of July. The sky would be all lit so they could see the effects of their shelling. I've hated fireworks ever since. Our only defense was prayer.

One night the Japs attacked our position, but we held them off. They lost a number of men, and their dead lay out in the heat and humidity. By the second or third day, the stench of rotting flesh became unbearable. Our captain picked seven men, including me, for a burial detail. Four of us dug the graves, while the others stood guard. We rotated duties at intervals. It wasn't a pleasant assignment, and it grieves me to this day. The families of the dead Japanese would never know what happened to them, and even if their graves were to have been discovered at a later time, no identification seemed possible.

Eventually, we advanced and overtook a Japanese camp that they had hastily abandoned after they realized the strength of our unit. They obviously scuttled out in a hurry because we came across large bags of rice, which in view of their hunger, I knew the rice would've been more valuable to them than a lot of money. I found a Japanese battle flag almost buried in the mud along the trail. One of our fellas found a Samurai sword, and we had our picture taken together with our "loot" when we got back to base camp. Unfortunately, when I got to Japan after the War, the cargo nets in which my barracks bag was carried to shore broke, and all of my belongings fell into the sea and sank.

We found lots of stuff at the abandoned camp. Since we had no toilet articles with us and had been out by that time for twelve days, I was lucky enough to find a Japanese razor, a bar of soap and piece of mirror. Using those, I got rid of a heavy growth of beard. A beard was a bad thing to have in the humidity, especially if there was no chance to wash. Beards were a prime target for tropical sores; large, red pimples that oozed from the center. They left pock marks after they healed, but these disappeared over time.

Since we were isolated, rations, ammunition and mail were parachuted to us by C-47s. The problem was we had to fight for the stuff when it landed, because the Japanese came out to collect it as well. The mail was a good thing. My dad always mailed me copies of the Cleveland *Plain Dealer* so I could catch up on the baseball summaries. We did not get mail at the front. We might have a mail call and get nothing. Then other times we would get seven or eight letters at a time. I had a steady gal at home and she wrote all the time. I had buddies of mine from high school that I wrote to. We were all in the service in different areas and theaters.

We had some men who broke down as a result of combat. I saw some of that at the end. In the squad we had a couple of forward guys, or scouts. They were out in front, and from what I was told one guy was outstanding in that responsibility. But toward the end of the War, he was a nervous wreck. If he had been an athlete, we'd say he was benched. Everyone had a breaking point, and an awful lot of these guys had been overseas a long time. The War wasn't going to last much longer and I guess the realization in everyone's mind was, *'I made it this far, but how many more chances can I take?'*

Finally, after eighteen days, another company broke through from the rear relieving us, and we returned to base camp.

In early July, we were ordered to take a hill heavily defended by entrenched Japanese. Company A was to attack at daybreak, and then be relieved by Company K. With artillery support, we made our approach before daybreak through a low area leading to the hillside. A heavy fog rolled in, making visibility virtually zero. As a result, we had to wait for the fog to lift, but it wouldn't. Eventually, Company K arrived to relieve us. As we started to pull back, the fog lifted and all hell broke loose between the well-positioned Japs and Company K. We learned later that seven members of Company K had been killed.

After that action we were transported by trucks to the seaside near the city of Aringay for R&R, and after that to prepare for our next assignment, the invasion of Japan. We practiced amphibious assaults every morning in full combat gear. They loaded us up on ships, and we climbed down rope ladders to landing craft. We made simulated assaults on the beach and moved ten miles inland, and then regrouped, returned to the ship, and did it all over again. We continued into mid-August, and then the miracle happened. One morning, as we were climbing down to the landing craft, there came an announcement over the ship's loudspeaker that the United States Air Force had dropped some sort of mega-bomb on the cities of Hiroshima and Nagasaki, and that the Japanese had surrendered. We learned later that the invasion of Japan had been scheduled for 1 November 1945. Our division was to attack a southeastern sector of the Island of Kyushu. I doubt that I would've survived.

After the surrender, we were assigned to "invade" the port city of Wakayama on the main island of Honshu on 25 September. It wasn't known if we would still meet resistance, but we were still ordered to make a full beachhead landing in full-combat readiness. Still, we were ordered to fire only if we were fired upon. We landed without incident, and went from Wakayama to Kobe and then to Himeji where we set up in a camp that had been used by the Japanese.

Most of the men of the 33rd had earned enough points to be discharged. Because of this, the Division was deactivated, and I was transferred to the 24th Division. I was promoted from corporal to sergeant, and put in charge of the post office for the 21st Regiment. I eventually accumulated enough points to come home in September 1946. I came home on a Victory Ship and we were all jammed in there again! After a while I put two and two together and I noticed where the officers on board ship had their latrines. They had the fresh water. I recalled my miserable trip overseas on the

Sea Pike and it looked like things were going to be the same again on this ship. These officers, when they took a shower, would strip down to their GI shorts and combat boots, and go into the officer's latrine with a towel. I thought to myself, *"I wonder if I could do that too?"*

So I did! I never got caught and I certainly didn't talk to anyone while I was in there. I was dressed the way they were. Just to get fresh water like that made a big difference!

After arriving in the States, I took a train across the country to Cleveland. When I got home it was a joyous occasion. My parents and my brother who had been discharged by that point, and his wife, met me at the train station. Because of my nineteen months overseas, I had considerable furlough time. I spent a military leave at home from 25 September to 22 November 1946. I was officially discharged at Fort Benjamin Harrison in Illinois. My total time in the service was almost exactly two years and two months. Little by little I worked my way back into civilian life. I didn't do it over night. It took some time.

I started college and graduated after four years. I met my future wife my senior year in college and we got married two months after I graduated. I went to work for a company called TRW which in time became a very large multinational company with over one-hundred-thousand employees. I stayed with them my whole career. I started out in sales, then sales management and then general management. I was transferred to different parts of the country and then back to home base which was Cleveland. I actually retired on my fifty-eighth birthday, but then I wasn't totally ready to hang it up so then I went into private consulting until I was seventy. My wife's name was Roberta. She wasn't the girl I had been corresponding with overseas. You know how those things work out sometimes! Roberta and I had fifty-four great years together until 2004, when cancer claimed her.

When we were overseas we got the ribbons to put on our blouse front. When I got out I didn't care at all, I just wanted to get out. But about twenty years later I felt I really wanted to get those medals. I got hold of an outfit in St. Louis. I waited and I waited and then one day a package arrived with the goodies in it.

I struggled with the malaria for a while. Besides the attack I had going overseas, I had it in the Philippines, and then I had it again in Japan. In fact, I had it so many times that when I was discharged, I was considered to be ten-percent disabled. This really turned out to be a blessing.

They said, "You're ten-percent disabled. So as long as the malaria is in your system we are going to send you a paycheck every month for ten-percent of your salary."

Well my salary as a T4, which was a buck sergeant, plus combat pay, plus overseas pay came to $128.00 a month so that worked out to an additional twelve dollars and eighty cents every month. The beauty of it all was, when I went to college, I was put under Public Law 16 because of the malaria. As a result, not only did I get all my tuition paid for, but I got all of my books, all of my supplies and all I had to do was go to the campus book store, pick out everything that I needed, sign for it and away I went. In addition, I got a check every month for $110.00 for incidental spending money! It worked out well! The last attack I had of malaria was about five years after getting out of the service. Fortunately, I never got malaria when I was on the line. I got it when we were having a period of R&R before going to Japan. I'd get this terrible fever and chills. I remember they took me to a hospital in Japan.

The attending doctor looked at me and said, "You're not feeling very well are you?"

That was an understatement because I had a fever of 105!

I feel tremendous pride having been a part of the 33rd Infantry Division and having served in World War II. Those were different times. In those days, when the United States was provoked, watch out, because we, as a country, were able to react and the final result that we got in World War II was indicative of the abilities that we had. In other words, don't mess with us or by God watch out!

Looking back on World War II it seems like I was hardened to some things, and today, it seems difficult to rationalize. I did not take part in any operations where we used the flame thrower, but I did come across some dead Japs who had been killed with a flame thrower. We saw so much mutilation of bodies as a result of combat. We just got hardened to seeing this kind of thing. We were on this mountain trail and we took a break. When we stopped for a break we took out rations. I took my helmet off and sat down on it for a chair and there was a dead Jap, and I bet he was no more than fifteen feet away from me, totally charred by a flame thrower. I have to admit I just sat there and ate my dinner. Then when I got back to a civilized way of living I reflected on that and thought, *'Okay, I did it then, but there's no way I could do that today.'*

Norman Larson and buddies clown using a captured Japanese flag. Low pitches were the order of the day.

Norman Larson in Kyushu, Japan, after the War.

"This Country Gave Me Life!"

Eric Leiseroff
89th Infantry Division
353rd Infantry Regiment
2nd Battalion
Company E
Born in Dresden, Germany, 10 October 1925
White Plains, New York

"The living prisoners were bad, but the dead ones were worse. They were left with their heads lying around and unburied. If I had wanted to, I could have gone and touched the dead bodies! They just lay in the ditches where they were supposed to be buried. It moved me very deeply. I believe that Ohrdruf was a landmark in my life! And I was so near my old home! At the end of the war I was maybe fifty or sixty miles from where we used to live!"

I WAS BORN IN DRESDEN, Germany. My mother's family owned a cigarette factory, and my father was one of three Jewish national soccer players. My parents named me Eric Arnold Ishmael Leiserowitsch, but I changed my name to Leiseroff when I came to the United States. The customs officer said it would be easier for me if I did.

My father was very different from my mother. He was very social and liked to entertain people. He was a sportsman and his friends were sportsmen, and he threw parties for them. Once he invited a Finnish five-time Olympic gold medalist over to the house. They were kind of cheap, these celebrities. They'd come over and my father would feed them and amuse them all for nothing, but my father didn't mind. He liked these people.

When I was two years old, my parents got divorced. My father went to Palestine, where he remarried, and my mother and I moved to a little town called Stendt, near Dresden. She owned a plant nursery there. My mother didn't raise me in the Jewish faith. I was brought up like a German. We were the only Jews in town, and for a long time, I didn't even know what a Jew was. In Stendt, though, everybody else knew who was German and who wasn't. If I went to the toilet, they knew! But they knew mostly because of all the records. Wherever I went, I had to have my ID. Since I was Jewish, the identification said, "Jewish." And then people knew by the names as well. For me it was Ishmael. For a woman it might be Sarah. So everybody knew.

From 1932 to 1936, I went to a German school. In class, the teacher asked questions while everyone stood. We couldn't sit until we answered a question. I'd raise my hand, like all the other children, but the teacher never called on me. Finally, when I was the only one left standing, the teacher would say, "You can sit down now."

It was very humiliating. During recess, the other children walked in a circle around me and taunted me because I was Jewish. There was no escape from this kind of torment.

Halloween was a big deal in Germany. On that night, all the people in the town, young and old, gathered outside our house in costumes yelling, "Kill the Jews! Kill the Jews!"

All my mother and I could do was to sit in our house and shiver. It was horrible! We walked around in fear from morning until night. As a Jew, my mother couldn't complain to anyone. The police were on the Germans' side.

Not all the Germans were bad, though. The ones that knew us were very helpful. Unfortunately, they didn't go unpunished for this kindness. One of my close friends was German and he got fined for playing with me. He was killed shortly before the war ended. It was a sad time.

I had to have a sinus operation and the doctor in Dresden wouldn't operate on me because Jews weren't allowed in the hospital. So I had to go to a private hospital. This was a seven or eight-hour operation in those days and, low and behold, the lights went out right in the middle of it! They got it done somehow, though. The doctor was very kind. Later, he went into the service and became a colonel. My mother and I saw him on the bus once and he came over and talked to us. If it weren't for the good Germans, I wouldn't be here today!

When the war started in 1939, the German government issued ration stamps. Because we were Jewish, we didn't get the same stamps as everyone else. Once, they gave us chocolate stamps by mistake, and a German policeman came over and cut them out. Later in the war, they started issuing special stamps for Jews marked with a "J" for *Jude*. When I went to the store for some meat, the shopkeeper saw the J and instead of giving me the good meat, he gave me the lousy meat.

My mother wanted me to get a better education, so in 1936 I went to a school in Berlin. I only went there for one or two years, though. Then I had to come back to Stendt because the Jews weren't allowed to attend school anymore. For a few years, I had no education whatsoever until 1939 when the Jews were allowed to go to school again. This time, I went to an institution in Dresden. I had to take a train every morning, because Dresden was about thirty miles away from Stendt. I continued to go to school there until 1941 when I left Germany.

Sometimes, trains would come through Dresden packed with Polish Jews who were being deported. They traveled in second class compartments with an SS officer riding with them. When a train came through, my mother and I made arrangements to see the people. We brought them food and hot drinks. I gave out cocoa to the children and the elderly. Once we came down to the train and one of the officers came running out. "I've got women and children in this car. Please, you've got to give us something!"

So we gave what we had. Seeing the happiness I created by giving these Jewish children a hot drink was one of the highlights of my experiences during that dismal time.

Although I wasn't raised with a strong awareness of my Jewish faith, my mother did make a point of having a Bar Mitzvah for me. We had it at the synagogue in Dresden in 1938. Two weeks later, that synagogue was burned down during *Kristallnacht.*[127] What a horrible name to call that night of fear and destruction—the "Night of Crystal!" We weren't there, my mother and I, but we saw the destruction afterwards. All the Jewish shops were destroyed and the windows were all broken. We read about it in a German paper called *Der Sturmer.* Julius Streicher[128] ran that newspaper, and he'd talk about the physical appearance of Jews. He'd show a half-dead Jew and then he'd show the young SS officers looking like one of the United States Marines!

Before Hitler came to power, Jewish people were quite easily assimilated into German government. In 1927 there were even high Jewish officials. When Hitler gained control, many Jews thought that he was the answer to all of Germany's problems. Hitler spoke about a free Germany and moving forward like France and England. He promised the Germans that he'd restore the old glory. He fooled a lot of people.

No one shook hands anymore, they just said, *Heil Hitler!*

When I would go into a store, the shopkeeper wouldn't say, "Hello," he'd say, Heil Hitler!

Thousands of people listened to him speak and they'd yell, *Heil Hitler!*

Eventually, it became ingrained into me. I'd come home from school and say to my mother, Heil Hitler!

I would get onto a bus and say, *Heil Hitler!*

I didn't want to say it, but I didn't know who was on that bus!

My mother took take care of some buildings in Dresden her brother-in-law owned. Once, my mother went to collect the rent from a Jewish lady.

The lady asked her, "Do you see my husband here?"

She showed my mother an urn full of ashes. The Nazis had sent her husband to a concentration camp where he was killed. They sent him back to his wife in an urn.

They'd poison the minds of young kids as well! I was skiing in Stendt once and some other skiers who knew that I was Jewish saw me. They came up to me and started calling me a "goddamned Jew." They even tried to stab me with their ski poles. Finally, someone else came along and told them to leave me alone. It was scary!

My mother belonged to an association of businesses because she owned the plant nursery. One day in 1935, when she came home from a meeting, she said that a man there had said, "We're gonna walk in the blood of the Jews."

And that was in 1935! Hitler did a good job. A really tremendous job! I hate to say it, but some days I get scared even over here. Sometimes when the telephone or the doorbell rings, I get worried for a minute. Even now, safe in America!

This was the end of the road for my mother. She knew it was time to get out. In 1936 we got our visa application. It was a long process. Every so often we'd have to go into Berlin to the American Consulate. With all due respect, the American Consulate treated us just as badly as the Germans did! We'd wait in line for hours, and then they'd question us. Sometimes, we had to wait for five hours before someone would see us. It was like they didn't understand that it was a matter of life or death for us!

We waited and we waited and we waited. We had to get all these papers. My mother's brothers already lived in the United States, so they helped us get affidavits. I had an uncle who didn't want to give an affidavit because they asked how much money he had and he didn't want to say. Then if my mother or I got sick in the United States, our relatives would have to pay for the hospital. In those days there was no insurance to take care of that sort of thing. So it took a long time, but in 1941, we finally got our visas.

I remember in school in Dresden one day I said to the kids and the teacher, "I'm leaving. I'm going to the United States."

They looked at me like I was full of it. They didn't believe me. Soon after, my father's brothers came and took us to the Berlin station. We went by train from Berlin in sealed cars through France and Spain. In Spain we saw the effects of the Civil War. We saw bombed buildings all the way to Portugal.

In Portugal we took a freighter called the *Excalibur* to the United States. When we landed in New York, my aunt picked us up and brought us to the Bronx, where my mother's family lived. The first chance they got, my two boy cousins took me out to get hotdogs and ice cream. It was wonderful! In Germany we didn't have food like that. My uncle owned a house in that area where we stayed until we moved to Port Chester. There were seven in my mother's family. None of her brothers or sisters got killed, but in my father's family, everybody got wiped out; all except one of my father's brothers. He was a concertmaster in Germany, and he lived because somebody hid him.

We lived in a three-storey apartment in Port Chester that's still standing today. Once it was a family estate, and the street that it's on was named after the people who used to own it.

It was unbelievable to be able to come to the United States. For me, it was like I was in prison for no reason at all and then suddenly the police found the DNA to prove that I was innocent! I came here and suddenly everything was free!

As soon as we moved to Port Chester my mother went to the school and signed me up for classes. I started in October, but because I didn't speak English, they put me in first grade. When I came into the classroom all the little kids started to snicker. The chairs were much too small for me. It was horrible! Just as bad as Germany! I went home and told my mother that I couldn't go to school if it was like that. So the next day she took me and we went to see the principal of the middle school. They said it was a mistake and transferred me the next day.

I still had trouble with my English, though. There was one very nice teacher who kept me after school to tutor me. I'm so thankful for everything she did for me. Because of her, I was able to learn English quickly and catch up in school. I also took some night classes to help me learn the language. Pretty soon I got the hang of it, though, and I started to make friends.

I got involved with sports. I liked to run, so I joined the track team. The football games were a big excitement for me. In those days it was thirty or forty cents to get in and watch the match. Before the game started, they had a couple of us track guys run across the field with American flags. It was a kind of a salute because it was wartime.

Sometimes, American people would make fun of me because I was from Germany. I would go to school and some of the other students would see me and say, *Heil Hitler!*

In the Port Chester school system in I don't think there was anybody else who was a refugee. There were some German Jews who came over in 1936 or 1937, but they already spoke English. A lot of Italians came over, but they also came over earlier. I really stood out. All the Jewish people who played cards would go to a certain house on Friday nights. Every week we'd go to a different place and play cards and there was this one guy who would mimic my accent. It bothered me so much that I quit the club! Sometimes people would even cry "Here comes the Kraut!"

It stung my feelings.

I think I was listening to the New York Symphony on the radio when I heard about Pearl Harbor.

I remember my mother's brother, my Uncle Frank said, "We're gonna have these guys on their behind in six to eight weeks."

I just shook my head and said, "I don't believe it!"

In Germany, we lived near an army camp. They had thousands and thousands of tanks and tons of heavy machinery. I thought for sure the Germans would invade Great Britain, and I figured once Great Britain falls, that's it!

I had to do something. This country gave me life! It saved me! When the war broke out, I knew I would volunteer for the service. I felt it'd be my duty. In addition, I lived in a small town where everybody knew when someone was in the service. From 1941 on, if a man were my age or a little older, the next thing for him was the service. I certainly couldn't say, "Let me try not to get in."

I considered it a great honor for me to go. I didn't even think, *'When is that War gonna end?'*

I didn't think too much about it at all. I'm still not sure whether I really enlisted or not though, because two days later I got the draft papers. They came three or four days after my eighteenth birthday. So I feel like I volunteered. But who knows?

When I got into the service in 1944, Roosevelt was running for his last term and our soldiers were being killed by the thousands. I was supposed to go overseas in June; the same week the Allies landed in Normandy. I was supposed to go overseas as a replacement. But since Roosevelt was running for reelection, he came out with a directive that nobody under nineteen would go overseas. So I waited a year, and we went over to Canterbury, England, in October.

I went to Fort Dix for my Army physical. I went through the whole thing; the short-arm inspections and the hearing test and everything else. But I stayed with it. I wanted to get in!

When I went to the doctor, he checked my hearing and said, "You know they'll never take you, your hearing is no good!"

But they did take me.

It was very important for me to show that I was one of the men. We became like a family. Once we were running an obstacle course. They shot the guns over us and we climbed over walls and everything else. This would have been fine, except that I was afraid of heights. I started climbing this twenty or thirty foot wall when I suddenly realized what I was doing and froze up!

"You gotta get up there!" the staff sergeant yelled. "You can't stop and sit!"

When I got up to the top of the wall, there was a very narrow platform to rest on. All the other guys were there standing and walking around with only these little railings to hold on to. I wasn't taking any chances, however. I was laying flat! There was another guy who helped me down and I was very grateful to him for that. My fear didn't keep me in the States, though. I still went overseas!

In Camp Croft we had our basic training. It wasn't easy. We'd go out on twenty-mile hikes in the summer heat with heavy clothing on and the noncoms would lash into us. Then we had rifle training, along with the daily routines: cleaning, taking care of the toilets; those sorts of things. Then we had the PXs. We'd go to the PXs for entertainment. I must've seen a lot of movies in those days. I can't remember any of them, but the letters I sent home are full of them.

Next we had weapons training. We learned how to use a BAR, how to throw a hand grenade, how to put on the gas masks and go into the gas chamber, and how to use mortars. I would get really scared sometimes. These weapons gave a guy a lot of power!

I was only eighteen. I didn't know what was going on. I had never handled a gun before I got to training camp. This was all new for me. I learned how to shoot a carbine, and the M1. When I went on patrol I would go with the carbine, which was lighter. I usually went on patrol because I spoke German.

They kept me busy. Other than as a translator, I didn't get singled out much for being German. Our outfit was from Oklahoma originally. Most of the people in it were from out west. The nickname of the 89th Division was "The Midwest Division," or "The Rolling W." A lot of them came from Kentucky. Many of them didn't know what a Jew was. So, I was again an outsider. We had another Jewish guy in the outfit who was very friendly. But when he took off his shoes, his feet smelled terrible!

So the next thing I know, everybody was saying, "Look at these Jews, their feet smell!"

I was assigned to the 89th Division's 353rd Regiment, 2nd Battalion, Company E. It was a rifle company. I was in the 2nd squad. I was with the 89th Division for about half a year before we went overseas. Our division was stationed at Camp Butner near Raleigh, North Carolina.

I did a lot of training with the 89th. I liked the captain. In today's market, I would call him a friend. The lieutenant we had was a different story. He was a dumb individual, and a very bitter man. The things he'd order me to do when we were overseas! We were on patrol in the woods once and we found an old German guy walking around. He wasn't even in the German Army. He was an air raid warden.

The lieutenant said to me, "Shoot this guy!"

"Shoot him?" I asked. "For what? He's just an old man!"

I don't know what was wrong with that lieutenant. He was a bitter man, I think. He might have thought he should've been a captain. I don't remember if he was a 90-Day Wonder or not. I didn't like him. There was something about him. I didn't think he was very competent. There were a lot of those guys around. Some of them got a better job than they deserved. They got to be officers because they went to college. They were a little older, but that didn't mean that they were smarter.

In October or November of 1944 I found out we were going overseas. We left from Boston on 9 January 1945. My mother knew I was leaving, but I didn't get to see her before I left. She actually made a trip to come see me in Camp Croft earlier. I must've been the only kid in training camp whose mother came to visit him! She came down to see me because she was lonely. She was a single mother who had come through a lot, and I was her only child.

It was kind of ironic, because when we left to go to Boston, we had to go through Port Chester, my old town. In Port Chester they made butterscotch Life Savers candy, and when they were making them the town used to smell of it. The day we went by, they were making butterscotch! We could smell it from the train! It was sad. I wanted to jump off. We couldn't go into the city, though. Everything had to be kept secret.

Going back to Europe gave me a very, very strange feeling. By then I spoke good English and I wanted to contribute something to the war. I felt elated that I was able to be a part of it, even though we were losing tons and tons of guys. It was right around the time of the Battle of the Bulge and they needed bodies. They took anybody.

The trip overseas was really awful. We went over on a freighter, a Liberty ship. We lived in the hold. Since I had a top bunk, I was always cold because the air would come right on top of where I was supposed to sleep. The mess hall was basically just a long line. There must've been thousands and thousands of us up there. The only advantage I had was that when I came off guard duty at twelve o'clock or so, and I could go down to the mess and get something to eat. I was lucky I could eat at all. Most of the guys were sick. That boat went up and down, up and down. It was rough! We must have zigzagged the whole way across, because it took days. And all the time we heard depth charges going off to make sure that we weren't being attacked. We were packed onto that ship so tightly. For all I know, it might've been the whole division!

We landed in Le Havre, and from there we went to St. Valery-en-Caux and Camp Lucky Strike. We arrived on 22 January 1945 and left for Luxembourg on 20 February. At Camp Lucky Strike we spent most of our time just waiting for an assignment. While we were waiting, we'd go to the little French towns to get bread. They had some German prisoners there who would do the baking.

In Luxembourg I saw lots of dead people. There were German dead and American dead. Seeing the combat boots on the dead GIs really got to me. It was like the boots could talk and they were saying to me, "Hey, that could be you tomorrow!"

It was something I didn't like to think about.

Apart from that, there was very little fighting. We did see some of the veterans as they came back from combat. They looked like ghosts, and there we were with clean uniforms and everything else! They were so happy to see us. They were probably there from the beginning of the fighting, so they just wanted to get out of there and let us replacements do something for a change.

They didn't try to warn us about what we were going into or anything, they just said, "Hey, you're going to Hell!"

After a few days we crossed the Moselle River and attacked a town called Zell. It was the first time we really got shot at. I walked by the dead body of one of our guys. When we came back to Zell after patrol, we saw four young, blond guys in civilian clothes.

I said to the lieutenant, "These are Germans."

But he wouldn't believe me! He said, "No, they're civilians." So we didn't arrest them. It wasn't like we could go and say, "Here's a German. Shoot him."

But they were German soldiers. I'm so sure of that to this day.

In Zell, the Germans were safely entrenched in the hills around the town. They were shooting at us with 88s. I remember walking by houses in Zell at eight or nine o'clock during a blackout. The Germans were so shocked to see us! They couldn't believe it! The German radio kept telling them that the American forces were in France, and here we were deep in Germany in little towns like the one where I used to live!

Most days we weren't fighting. We walked. And then suddenly we'd hear something and flop down and wait, feeling cold. Then somebody would yell, "First squad, go to the left, 2nd squad to the right!"

With all due respect to our officers, they didn't know anything! Everybody was a rookie. Even our division commander was new. So that was what we'd do day to day. We'd walk in the squad and if someone heard something everybody flopped down.

My biggest worry was that I would have to go to the toilet. I had a problem, even in those days. Most of the time when we were walking and one of us had to go, we just stopped and went. But it was different at midnight in a foxhole.

I'd say, "Oh, I gotta go and take a piss!"

Then I would have to crawl out and find a place to go. We didn't go in a house or anything! It was bad if we had to do more than just a piss because the paper they gave us was horrible! Newspapers are better! So the personal things were not easy.

We waited for the mail. When we were in an advanced part of the Division we had no contact with the rear. We didn't like to be near the tanks either, because if the Germans saw a tank they'd fire artillery on them. When we were near a tank, all we could think was, *"Oh my God! Why don't the tanks go?"*

It was a confused war! There were these few guys making decisions for other people's lives. It was a big responsibility, and some of them didn't take it seriously. They thought they were cowboys or something! Like the captain from Company F. I don't know what he was thinking, but he ran up a hill into enemy fire. It was a stupid thing! He got a bunch of guys killed. There were enough guys getting killed without idiots like him!

One day we were attacked from the air. They came with a plane or two and tried to stop us from getting through. They'd shoot and hit somebody, and then fly away fast! We had no time to shoot back. We were really very lucky, though. We didn't have a hundred people killed at one shot, or anything like that.

At night we tried to sleep, survive and keep quiet. We'd either dig in somewhere or, if we were in a town, we'd take over a house and sleep in there. I was mostly out on patrol at night. We didn't know what was going on most of the time. We didn't have maps or anything.

I knew a little bit more, because I spoke German and I'd ask the people we met, "Where's the next town?"

They'd tell me and then I'd ask, "Are there any soldiers there?"

"No soldiers around here!" was their usual answer.

Our company liked me. One day we had to get into this place and the door was locked. Well, he just took out his pistol and shot the lock.

He said, "I always wanted to do that!"

He was like John Wayne. He was a real human being. When we captured Germans, the captain asked questions and I would interpret. Then we sent the Germans back down the line. I don't know what happened after we captured them. We captured a lot of Germans who helped us capture more because of the information they gave. Most of them wanted to be captured because they were worried about the Russians getting them.

They came with their hands up and said, "Don't shoot! Don't shoot!"

I don't blame them. As prisoners they lived better than we did!

One midnight three or four of us were on a patrol near one of the docks on the Rhine River. When we crossed to the other side there were no Americans there. Suddenly, we came under fire. Luckily, we weren't hit. We got under cover. I don't think we were more than twenty yards away from the Germans. We could hear them talking! At four or five in the morning, the whole division started to cross. The Germans opened up with the 88s. But we got across.

On the other side it was all mountains! Occasionally, the Germans opened fire, but then they gave up. We captured a lot of people. When we did, they'd ask us what division we were in and stuff like that. I'd answer their questions and then send them back. Being able to speak German was helpful. I got a completely different picture of the war but it put a lot of strain on me, too.

Patrols were something. I was not a scout, though. The scouts were supposed to tell us where to shoot the artillery. I went because we'd certainly find Germans and they needed me to translate.

I'd ask, "Are there any German soldiers here? Any guns?"

The usual answer was, "I don't know."

Sometimes, one of the guys would say, "Be careful. There must be someone out there. I heard gunfire."

We'd report it to the captain and he'd say, "Don't do anything now. Wait until the morning. We think there might be a German entrenchment, machine guns or something like that."

So we'd wait. Sometimes, I interrogated guys and they wouldn't say anything. We captured these SS and we'd ask them a question and they'd just give their name, their serial number and that was it!

One day the captain sent us to Ohrdruf. He didn't know there was a concentration camp there. He told us to take the Jeep and check it out. Two of us went into town and eventually came upon the camp. It was the worst experience I ever had! When I walked in, I saw the ditches, I saw the dead. And then the live ones came out.

When the survivors embraced us, my buddy said to me, "I hope they don't have lice!"

We gave them cigarettes, candy, anything good we had. There was an English soldier who had killed a couple of the guards.

Even today, I go to the schools, and talk to classes about Ohrdruf and I can't sleep for days afterwards. The movies and pictures are awful, but to see it live!

When I saw their clothing, I thought, "Is this true? Could that have been me?"

None of my family was in that camp, although some of them died in similar places. The strangest thing about it all was that no one in the town knew what was really going on. The mayor might have known because he committed suicide, but no one else knew! It was a strange, strange feeling. It would be like having an ammunition factory next door and never knowing about it. I suppose it's understandable. The Germans called these camps "Work Camps."

They didn't say, "We bring these people here to die."

It gets to me sometimes that some people don't believe the Holocaust happened.

I had a friend, years ago, who came up to our house one day and said, "Oh, this didn't happen. This whole Holocaust thing is all made up."

That made me mad. People don't want to hear the truth. I was there, though! I saw these things! I can only hope that wars will be eliminated by the force of my testimony. But this is not going to happen. The German Jews were like sheep.

I remember asking my mother after the war, "How could they have allowed this? Killing all these Jews. Why didn't we fight back?"

We were helpless!

After that experience, I began to have such a hatred for the Germans! I wouldn't say that this was good that I saw the concentration camp, but it certainly made my purpose in the Army clearer than ever. But people in the United States didn't seem to understand this purpose. I couldn't understand why the United States didn't bomb the railroads. You would think they'd do a little bit more. But no one understood.

The officers didn't get it either. There was no concerted effort with one officer in charge to help these people. It's like they didn't know why they were over there. I guess that's why we saw the camp. Ike wanted to make sure that the GIs saw this to show us what we were fighting for. It was almost like Times Square; everybody who heard something about the concentration camp came to see it. The living prisoners were bad, but the dead ones were worse. They were left with their heads lying around and unburied. If I had wanted to, I could have gone and touched the dead bodies! They just lay in the ditches where they were supposed to be buried. It moved me very deeply. I believe that Ohrdruf was a landmark in my life! And I was so near my old home! At the end of the war I was maybe fifty or sixty miles from where we used to live!

We had a little compound where we put Germans prisoners. Every time I walked by, one of the guys would yell, "Eric! Eric! Eric!"

I wouldn't stop, though. I just looked away and didn't stop. I'm sure he knew me from before, but I didn't want to get involved.

Despite all the atrocities we witnessed, I don't remember ever even hearing of an American shooting a German prisoner. It was never even thought of! I interrogated the Germans, but nobody ever shot them. Never![129] We were taught in those days just to give our name and serial number and that was it! The Germans were taught the same. I talked to German SS guys as a translator. I saw them as walking around with blood on their hands, but I never thought of trying to punish them myself. I only got involved because I spoke German.

In early April, we went to Eisenach to take the Würzburg Castle where Martin Luther started the Protestant movement. We didn't want to damage the castle and destroy its history if we could possibly help it. The Germans there refused to surrender so we had to use artillery. There was a lot of fighting in Eisenach.

The day Roosevelt died, we had just captured a bunch of German soldiers. I was standing up on a hill and one came over to me and said, "Your President died."

I didn't believe him. I just said, "Come on."

When the war was over, our division went back to France to go to Japan. I stayed in France for five days and then they sent me back to Austria, because I spoke German. When the Atomic Bomb was dropped, we celebrated. I mean we were really happy! We didn't care that thousands of Japanese had died. We were done fighting!

After the war, the American Army sent me to a Displaced Persons camp to look for Germans. There were a lot of Polish DPs there, but I was supposed to see if there were any German soldiers hiding there. It was a real fiasco! The guys knew right away that I wasn't one of them. I only stayed there one or two nights. It didn't really work out.

My time in Germany was not so much fun as it was relaxing. First of all, there were a lot of German girls. I spoke German so I had an advantage. I was in the prime of my life! To top it all off, they made me a corporal. So I taught in Germany for the Army, but first they sent me to Salzburg, Austria. I interrogated people and acted as a translator. The Austrians came to me with their problems and I'd send them to the appropriate officers. I was kind of a Man for All Seasons.

At this time, it was important to me to see who was still alive in my family. We had no contact since before the war. I went to the Red Cross and got all the information I could from them. Then I went to visit my mother's sister near Nuremburg to make sure that she was all right. I got very deeply involved. I also helped some of the guys who came out of hiding. When I came back to the States, I went to look for their families over here. But wherever I went I found that they were dead.

I was able to get some pictures of my little cousin. She was born in 1939 to one of the soccer players. But she was gone. Everybody was gone.

Every time I learned about a family member, I would write to my mother and say, "I just found out Uncle Fritz died somewhere."

It was awful. My mother figured out that she personally knew twenty-seven people who perished in concentration camps in Germany. I remember searching for one uncle, but then I forgot to look for the other uncle.

When I came back to the United States the uncle I had forgotten wrote me a letter saying, "You didn't look for me! Why didn't you look?"

I wrote back and told him that according to the Red Cross, he wasn't alive!

In May of 1946 I came back to Port Chester after being discharged from Fort

Dix. It was kind of sad to walk out of Fort Dix. Suddenly, the Army wasn't taking care of me anymore. I took a bus to New York and I sat there by myself. My mother was happy to see me, of course. I was happy too, but the war left scars on me. First of all, I got older. People age fast when they go through a war. Suddenly I found all my friends had been killed or didn't live in Port Chester anymore. I had to remake my old friends who were still alive.

After the constant the fighting, civilian life was a hard adjustment. Suddenly, there was peace. I came back and I had to look for a job. There was a 52/20 club in New York where I got a job, but I had to start on the ground floor. In those days I worked five and a half days. And if they wanted me to stay until nine o'clock at night I worked until nine. Slowly, I started to reestablish myself. I wanted to get a car. I wanted to get married.

About half a year after I came home, I got a letter from a guy by the name of Simon. It said, "Would you be interested in doing additional service? Can you stop by and let us know?"

I went there and they wanted me to learn Morse code. They asked me if I was interested in going back to Germany as a spy for the United States. I was supposed to denounce the United States and go back and live in Germany. They offered to pay me an annual salary of ten-thousand-dollars, a tremendous amount of money in 1947. My mother thought it was crazy, so I told them I wasn't interested.

Instead I got a job working for a very fancy paper company. After a while, I had enough money to buy a car. Before the paper company, I had a job carrying golf bags at a country club until one day the manager came over to me and said, "You know, you're doing a good job, but somebody complained because you're Jewish. There are no Jews allowed here."

That was right here in Port Chester! I go by there every now and then, and every time I do I think of that incident. I went and lived in New York for a while. I wanted to meet people, primarily girls. I started to date. The big thing then was to go to the movies on Friday night or Saturday night, then go out and have a Chinese meal. I met my wife, Cecilia, in 1947, and by 1950 we were married. She taught me how to dance. We have one daughter and one granddaughter now.

In those days, I didn't look back on my experiences and wonder why or how I survived. Instead I tried to forget it. I didn't talk about it. I only joined the American Legion because they had a shooting range. I didn't like the guys there. They'd talk and they'd drink. That wasn't for me. And then they'd brag that they were in here or in there and they did this or that! To me that was all BS. I considered myself to be nothing, but according to them, these guys all won the war! So I left them. I couldn't take it any more.

Around that time, I tried to get recompense from the government because I had lost some more of my hearing because of all the shooting. The government rejected my request, though. This was kind of ironic, because they almost rejected me for the service because of my hearing!

"God Bless My Buddies!"

Jesse Lesico

United States Sixth Army
32nd Infantry Division
Wisconsin National Guard
"The Red Arrow Division" "Les Terribles"
120th Field Artillery Battalion
"The Red Fox Battalion"
Battery A
Born in Koloa, Island of Kauai, Hawaii, 26 April 1913
Castro Valley, California

> *"We counted on it raining about three or four o'clock in the afternoon every day on New Guinea. It'd rain so much that some of the camps would fill up with water and we couldn't get trucks through. They'd get stuck in the mud and we had to get tractors to pull them out. Just before night we'd try to get something to eat, but we didn't have any fresh vegetables, we didn't have nothing but what was canned. In fact, one time my buddy, Herb Delveck, and I were hauling supplies from the ship to the camp with a TD6 tractor, and we got stuck in the mud. We threw big cans of GI rations under the tracks to get out of the mud."*

My parents and one brother came to Hawaii from Lisbon, Portugal. They settled in Hawaii and worked cutting sugar cane. Then we came to San Francisco and lived in Hayward, just across the bay. I lived there most of my life. In 1930 I went out to work on a cattle ranch for a dollar a day. That was a silver dollar, not paper! I got into the oil business before I went into the War. I volunteered and I was in the Army until June 1945.

Right away after Pearl Harbor, my two brothers joined up, and then I volunteered later. The Army didn't want all three brothers in the service because of what happened to the Sullivan Brothers[130] later in the War, but they did end up taking all of us. In the window of my parents' house we had a little flag with three stars, one for each son in the service. My youngest brother went into the Army and went to France, and the other went to a camp in California. He broke his leg when he was younger and had a little bit of a limp so they kept him for about sixty days and then let him go. I went to Camp Roberts, California for about three or four weeks.[131] But I did most of my training with the 32nd Division overseas at Camp Cable in Australia. I went over as a replacement.

Some of the guys picked up this dog in Vicksburg, Mississippi. They named him "Vicksburg" after the town. Well, we stuck him into a bag. We were loading up on the ship in San Francisco and they were asking us our last name as we were boarding.

I told the guys, "Just keep walking once you get on."

We figured he'd bark, but he kept quiet. He went overseas with us.

Vicksburg got killed later in 1942 and is buried in Australia. My neighbor, who is a mining engineer, goes all over the world. He was in Australia two years ago and he was talking with a friend of his over there who said, "Yeah, those Yankee boys had a camp up there, but there's nothing up there now but a tombstone for this dog."

He took pictures of Vicksburg's tombstone. That little dog, he was a devil. He'd be out there with us when Reveille sounded. We missed him when he was killed. It was an accident. They were building what they called a corduroy road, and a gum tree they were cutting down fell on Vicksburg and killed him.

We went overseas on the SS *Monterey* and left San Francisco on 22nd April 1942. We got to Australia in 14 May 1942. We were in a convoy of ten ships and we zigzagged the whole way across the Pacific because of the Jap submarines. There were five-thousand of us on the *Monterey*. It was an old luxury liner and they took all the beds out and put bunks in so they'd get more people on board, but it was still pretty crowded. I was only in the Army for about four weeks, and this was all new to me. We had some submarine alarms. When that sounded everyone had to get on deck, they didn't want anyone below decks in case we were hit with a torpedo. That was scary because I don't think I could swim too far!

We arrived in Port Adelaide, Australia and then we went to Camp Cable, named after Sergeant Gerald O. Cable, the first American soldier killed in Australia when his ship got torpedoed. The thing I remember about Australia was the Australians always said we talked funny. Every Friday, a farmer came by with a horse-cart carrying an eighteen-gallon keg of beer.They were a real good bunch of people, and they were good soldiers.

One time I was having a few beers with two Aussie soldiers, and we decided to take a tank for a ride. The MPs caught us and put us in a jail that was actually an old horse stall. We stayed there overnight. I got sent back to camp the next morning, and I didn't get into any more trouble over the tank thing.

I was a replacement for the 32nd Division to fill up their ranks. They were mostly Wisconsin National Guard, but I was from California. So initially it was hard to get a promotion because these guys had it all set up, but I made it to staff sergeant as the War went on.

After training I went into Battery A of the 120th Field Artillery, 32nd Division. I stuck with them from the beginning to the end. The training was great. We went out on this twenty-five-mile hike with a forty-pound pack. It toughened us up. They'd get us up at two in the morning for these hikes. We'd march for hours before they'd give us something to eat. I trained a lot on .50-caliber machine guns which we used in the 120th. We also used 105mm howitzers.

Part of the division went up to New Guinea before us and fought at Buna.[132] We stayed in Camp Cable training, and then we went to New Guinea, too. I was in several battles there: Saidor, Aitape, and the Driniumor River. Later I went to Morotai Island. Some of the battles were tough but there were others where we were just too strong for the Japanese.[133]

Our first landing was on Saidor in New Guinea.[134] We went over on a troop ship and our landing craft went to the wrong beach. There was a mix-up between the Blue

Beach and Red Beach, and we were fired at by our own men. They didn't know and we didn't know. We turned around and went back and got straightened out and then went back in. No one was killed from that "friendly fire."

We approached the beach and the landing craft dropped the doors down and we took ashore our 105mm howitzers and later they brought in the bigger 155s. It was awful on New Guinea. We'd hear drums in the jungle banging. We called the natives "Fuzzy-Wuzzies." We'd see them and then we wouldn't see them. They never got too close to the camp; in fact, we wouldn't let them. We heard there were still some cannibals there.[135]

We counted on it raining about three or four o'clock in the afternoon every day on New Guinea. It'd rain so much that some of the camps would fill up with water and we couldn't get trucks through. They'd get stuck in the mud and we had to get tractors to pull them out. Just before night we'd try to get something to eat, but we didn't have any fresh vegetables, we didn't have nothing but what was canned. In fact, one time my buddy, Herb Delveck, and I were hauling supplies from the ship to the camp with a TD6 tractor, and we got stuck in the mud. We threw big cans of GI rations under the tracks to get out of the mud.

Water poured into our foxholes, and the temperatures went high. We'd get soaking wet. We didn't take our boots off for a week, or our socks. We didn't have clean clothes. It was miserable living! We lost so many men from the environment. The jungle was so thick we hacked our way through with machetes. We had to be very careful, though because the Jap snipers waited for us on those jungle trails.

The nights were long on New Guinea. I'd chew tobacco and I sat there at night in my foxhole and spit out over the top of the hole.

The guy in the next hole could hear that and he'd say, "Jess, don't make so much noise!"

I said, "Naw, they can't hear that!"

I'll tell you we were so scared, that sometimes just kidding around helped.

The infantry advanced and radioed back to us to adjust our guns so many degrees here and so many degrees there. That's how they'd direct our fire. We found out that carrying a radio was one of the most dangerous things a guy could do because the Japs would try to pick him off. They wanted that radio out of commission so we couldn't call up the artillery. It got to the point where no one wanted to carry the radio!

The Japs would also put out booby-trapped hand grenades. They knew American soldiers would be looking for souvenirs. They'd put a hand grenade under the elbow of one of their dead soldiers and when one of our guys would start to move that body, that grenade would go off.

We had some Banzai attacks, but other times we'd be out in the jungle and they'd practically go by us and the rule was, "If you don't see them, don't shoot them."

We wouldn't fire but we'd keep our guns real close. If we fired, we'd give our position away. That was scary!

After the New Guinea campaigns and Morotai, we went to Leyte. The invasion of Leyte was big.[136] While I was on that troop transport, I could look in either direction out on the ocean and I couldn't see the end of all the ships! A Japanese torpedo skipped right by the ship next to ours, just missing it! Then we got into the landing craft and circled the mother ship until they gave us the signal to go in. Leyte was really scary because the Japs had a lot of fire power there. They'd get up in the trees at night and they'd put snipers up there. They'd sleep up there and wait for us to come up the trail.

After the battle for Leyte, I went to rest camp where I came down with malaria. They took me in a Jeep to a field hospital. After three weeks, I got tired of the hospital, but they wouldn't let me go. I decided to sneak out and get back to my outfit. I didn't want to lose them. There was a supply tent and I went in there. I got my pack and my .38 pistol. This was my own pistol. I snuck down this creek bed and saw this road. There were some Army trucks and Jeeps coming up the road. I flagged a Jeep with a second lieutenant in it. He gave me a ride to this airfield. He didn't question me where I was going, which is strange because I was the only one walking on that road. I couldn't get a ride that night at the airfield because they were going to bomb Corregidor.

This pilot said, "Wait here, and tomorrow we'll take you up to your outfit."

I got a ride on an airplane that took me to Mindoro and then I went over to Luzon. It was raining like hell when I got there and some Marines were in a tent raising hell laughing and singing and I went in there and we had some beers. I was there for two days. I went from camp to camp looking for my outfit. No one knew where Battery A was. One day, early in the morning, an LST came into the port. The ramp dropped in front of the ship and out came my outfit! I met my captain and my major and I told them that I was trying to find them for three weeks![137] A lot of guys go AWOL to go see a girl or something like that. I was going AWOL to get back to my unit!

Our next campaign was on the Villa Verde Trail in Luzon. So many boys got killed there, 850 of them. Coming up that damn mountain side there were no trees; it was rocks and no brush. The Japs were hiding in caves and really raised hell with us. I came face to face with some Japs. I got close to them. I shot at them. We didn't take too many prisoners. Once we were trapped for five or six hours but were able to sneak down this creek bed and got the hell out of there.

About half way through the Villa Verde Trail campaign, it was one o'clock in the morning and this officer called me.

I said, "What you do you want?"

He said, "Get on that truck right now."

I said, "What for?"

He said, "There's a plane waiting for you. You can go home."

That was all I needed to hear. I grabbed my things and went.

Before I went home the captain called me into his office and asked me if I wanted to be a second lieutenant.

I said, "No, I just want to go home."

It got to me, being over there and I got to thinking of home more and more and I just wanted to get away from it.

By 11 June 1945 I was back home and discharged out of Sacramento. I went back with my oil business. I was going through town in an oil tanker and I heard on the radio that the War was over. It hit me hard. God almighty that was a happy day!

I got married in 1961. We have a ranch up here twenty miles from Livermore, California. I bought the ranch in 1955. It's a cattle ranch; beef cattle. I enjoy the outdoors. I hunted a lot when I was younger but after the War I didn't want to be around guns.

I have some medals for my service in World War II. I got the campaign medals, some Bronze Stars, the Victory Medal and I got the Good Conduct Medal. I think that was the last one I earned!

The 32nd Division had 654 days of combat, more than any US division in any war. After going through about a dozen of those battles myself I can see how it can really ruin a person's life! It was a sad thing to see so many young kids get killed. I remember trucks came down from the Villa Verde Trail with bodies stacked like wood in the back. Those were men from the 32nd dead in those trucks. That stays with me and I'll be ninety-four years old soon. I'll never forget that as long as I live. All I have to say is, "God bless my buddies!"

The tombstone of "Vicksburg," the mascot who went to Australia with Jesse Lesico's 32nd Division.

Jesse Lesico (right) with Herb Elsen and (?) Bjerke.

"It Wasn't a Shell, John. It Was a Plane!"

Jonathan Lukowsky

United States Seventh Fleet
Escort Carrier USS *Santee* (CVE–29)
Born in Ford City, Pennsylvania, 14 February 1924
† 21 August 2006

"I looked up but I couldn't see the Kamikaze until it hit one of our sister ships about a quarter of a mile away. The explosion from the impact turned the ship into a ball of fire. One of the ship's planes had landed just before the Kamikaze hit and was being taxied up to the front. The men who were taxiing the plane got trapped in the fire and were scrambling to get off the ship."

I was born on Valentine's day 1924 to Michael and Paulie Lukowsky. Like many children my age, my parents were immigrants. My father was a Ukrainian immigrant and my mother was a Ukrainian-Polish immigrant. I was born in Ford City and while I was still young we moved to Lyndora. A few years later we moved back to Ford City. I had one sister Olga and two brothers, Morris and Nicholas. My family owned the Ford City National Bakery.

I played football on Ford City High School's only undefeated football team in the school's history. I graduated from there in 1942, and then I went to the University of Pittsburgh for one year before I got drafted. In the summer of 1943 I went to the Naval Training Station in Sampson, New York, for boot camp. When I finished boot camp, I played football for them for one season.

When the football season ended I was assigned to a small carrier, the USS *Santee*, an escort carrier, also called a "Jeep carrier."[138] Escort carriers were converted oil tankers that had flight decks built on top of them, and they could carry fuel and supplies as well as airplanes. A regular carrier was about two or three times bigger than ours, but the landing area on our carrier was just as big as theirs. There were four ships in our class: the *Santee*, the *Sangamon*, the *Suwanee*, and the *Chenango*. They were all named after rivers. The Santee was a river down in Georgia, and the *Chenango* was a river up north in Pennsylvania. We operated in the Atlantic for some time before joining those three sister ships that were already in the Pacific. Before I came aboard the *Santee*, it had been part of the invasion of Africa and it had also done antisubmarine duty off the coast of Brazil.

The *Santee* carried a mix of fighters and torpedo bombers. The torpedo bombers were TBM and TBF Avengers, exactly the same type, but the TBMs were General Motors produced and the TBFs were Grumman produced.

I went aboard the *Santee* in Norfolk, Virginia, and sailed north to the Brooklyn Naval Base. We were out at sea about three or four days going up to New York and, I was sick as a dog the whole time. It was so bad that I just wanted to curl-up and die. That was my first "trip" you could say.

We stayed in New York City about a week where they loaded us up with P–38s that we were to take to Scotland.

The War was well under way by then so for safety we sailed in the middle of a small convoy. One of the ships with us was the USS *Texas*, a World War I-era battleship. It was winter in the North Atlantic and very rough going. That big old battleship got thrown up and down like a toy. Our ship was doing the same thing—up and down, up and down.

We were actually three days late in getting to Scotland because of the weather, and when we arrived they said they had given up on us. They thought we had been sunk by German U-Boats while crossing because the whole area was just full of them.

When we arrived in Scotland, we went through some kind of a canal up around Glasgow. We unloaded our supplies and spent the next two or three days docked there.

We were given liberty, and I went ashore and met a Scottish girl. We got to talking a bit, and we decided to meet up again the next day.

The second time I met her was at nighttime. She was on her way home from work, and of course everything was blacked out and dark.

I kept bumping into people and saying, "I'm sorry, I'm sorry!"

She said, "John, you don't have to say that. These people understand that you're not doing that intentionally."

She was very nice and I bought her some beer or a bottle of booze (I can't remember which) to take home with her.

After two days in Scotland, we set to sea again and headed back to Norfolk, Virginia, to repair damage caused by stormy seas. Once the repairs were made, in about May, we set out and went down to Panama. It was a pretty tight fit for even our small carrier to get through the Canal. The plates around the gun mounts kept sticking and scraping the sides of the locks. Finally, to get through them we cut those parts of the gun mounts off and then welded them back on in San Diego.

Once on the western side of the Canal, we were given a two-day liberty in Panama City. The medical officer wanted all the guys to take condoms with them, but the Chaplain put up a fuss saying that the MO was encouraging us to go out and use them. It was a good idea, though, because there were guys that seemed like every time we went to port, they came down with Gonorrhea. I had a buddy like that. He seemed to get it everywhere we went.

At San Diego we loaded up with a squadron of fighters and torpedo bombers. From there we went to Pearl Harbor, and we stayed there about two or three days. After that we left and met up with our sister ships. We were all assigned to the Seventh Fleet.[139] The Third and Fifth Fleets had all the modern ships. Our Seventh Fleet had Jeep carriers, destroyer escorts and World War I-era cruisers and battleships.

Our big part in the War was our return to the Philippines. On our way there, we hit a typhoon. The waves were huge and sometimes the destroyers that were with us were practically under water! Nobody went out on the deck because the waves would have swept them into the sea.

We got through that storm and made it to Leyte Gulf. We fought a big battle there. The *Santee* was one of sixteen escort carriers that were involved in the operation. They were split into groups to the north, the middle, and the south. The escort carriers in the north kept moving around to trick the enemy into thinking we had more ships than we really had.

That's how the battle was won, really, through different tricks. One trick was to send radio messages like, "The Fifth Fleet is going to replace the Third Fleet."

Actually it wasn't a change of fleets, just a change of commands. But the Japanese didn't know that. It was just a change of commands. Admiral Halsey was in command of one and Spruance was in command of the other. Every so often they'd just switch places.

At one point we got word that Japs had sent some of their carriers south, toward the Philippines. After that report came in, Admiral Halsey took all of his battleships and carriers up to meet the threat, but it turned out to be a decoy.

While he was headed north, the Japanese fleet, or what was left of their fleet, came down through the Surigao Straits to the eastern side of the Philippines and into Gulf. There they started their attack.

Fortunately, we had a lot of squalls brew up and the Jeep carriers went into the squalls and hid. If the Japs had only known what was out there opposing them, they could have crushed us. We had our destroyers with us, but our fleet's battleships were in the southern part of the Philippines.

At some point we were told that two groups of Japanese battleships were coming after us. We were between the islands and the Japs and it would have been nothing for them to annihilate us if they had tried. When they found us, I don't think that they could believe that we were by ourselves. I think they thought that they were being sucked in by a decoy. As a result, they turned tail and started going back up the strait.

As they were fleeing, our big carriers got wind of it and sent all their fighters and bombers to destroy them. The Japs lost several ships in that strait. In the end I think that ships like the *Santee* survived through luck.

Ours was one of the first ships ever hit by a Kamikaze attack, and it was during the operations in the Philippines. I was at my station when the plane hit.[140]

I was a weather man. There were three guys with me in the weather shack and we had our headphones on at the time the plane hit. I was sending up information to the flight officer on the flight deck about where the wind was coming from and at how many knots per hour it was blowing. He needed to know that because when we launched or landed planes, they had to be headed with the wind at all times. If the wind came from behind and they tried to land, they'd crash.

All of a sudden, as we were sending these reports to the flight deck, we heard a loud crash. I thought we were being hit by shell fire from the Japanese fleet. About a half an hour later I sneaked out onto the flight deck. I wasn't supposed to, but I wanted to know what the hell was going on. I went over to a guy I knew. His name ended in a "sky" like mine. They called him "Ski" and they called me "Lukow," so as not to get us mixed up.

I said "Hey, Ski, where the hell did that shell hit?"

"Shell!? It wasn't a shell, John. It was plane!"

"Oh bullshit! What do you mean a plane?"

He showed me the hole, and I walked over to where the damage was. On the flight deck there were gutters that took the rainwater off the flat area of the deck. They went down the whole flight deck crosswise from starboard to port. I looked down in the one gutter near the impact hole and saw what looked like a part of someone's neck and shoulder. It must have been the pilot's. Beside it was a huge hole, and I could see right through the flight deck. Just then the general alarm went off. I was too far from the weather shack to get back so I jumped down into one of the holds in the side of the ship where they kept ammo for the anti-aircraft gun. There were four or five other guys in there with me.

All of a sudden one guy pointed and said, "Look at that plane diving!"

I thought, *'Don't tell me there's another one diving for our ship!'*

I looked up but I couldn't see the Kamikaze until it hit one of our sister ships[141] about a quarter of a mile away. The explosion from the impact turned the ship into a ball of fire. One of the ship's planes had landed just before the Kamikaze hit and was being taxied up to the front. The men who were taxiing the plane got trapped in the fire and were scrambling to get off the ship. I could see them moving down the head line into the water to escape the flames. The head line was a rope that was a sort of emergency ladder. Eventually, they got the flames out on the ship, and the destroyer escorts came up and pulled the guys out of the water.

Earlier in the War I was talking with some people about fear, and one fellow said that he was so scared once that his knees were knocking together. I couldn't believe that anybody's knees would actually knock in fear. When that plane hit, I looked down and my knees are knocking even though my feet were about six-inches apart. I started laughing. I couldn't believe my knees were knocking just like that guy had said his had done.

About seventeen minutes after being hit by the Kamikaze, our ship got hit with a torpedo. The captain came on the intercom right away to tell us what happened, and then he signed off. The torpedo, instead of going directly into us, went off to the side because it had hit a crossbeam when it entered the ship. After it hit that beam it exploded, and it knocked off a bunch of plates on the side of the ship. The hole it left was big enough to put a two-storey house in. We took on water, and the ship started to flood and list.

A few seconds later the captain[142] came back on and said, "Be prepared to abandon ship."

Fortunately, the crew had sealed off the flooded compartments and started pumping out the water. The ship righted itself, not fully, but we were able to stay in battle formation, landing and launching planes like always.

Our destroyer escorts dropped depth charges. They claimed to have hit the sub, but later I read that the Japs reported the sub as having returned to port.

After everything cooled down, I went down to the hanger deck where our torpedoes were stored. I took the caps off of a few of the torpedoes and looked inside. All the powder inside of them had burned up. I thought they should have exploded, but they didn't. The insides just kind of melted.

The Navy never gave the Seventh Fleet too much credit despite everything. Whether they were ashamed to say the Seventh Fleet, with its old battleships and jeep carriers, beat the Japs in the biggest naval battle that was ever fought or not, I'll never know.

After the battle our admiral ordered our carrier back to Pearl Harbor for repairs. We went back at about half of our normal speed because of damage.

When we got to Pearl Harbor, they said, "We can't repair you here because we have bigger ships than you coming in that have priority."

Instead of doing a permanent repair, they put a big steel blister around the hole and they sent us back to the States for repairs. Once they repaired the ship, they sent us to the South China Sea between the Asian mainland and Japan. We were to be part of the planned invasion of Japan. Since we were so close to Japan, we were in a constant threat of Kamikaze attack. Our gunners knocked a lot of planes out of the sky. They knew what could happen if they failed.

From there they sent us to Guam for a bit, and then they sent us back to Japanese waters. On our way, the War ended. We ended up in Japan, where I had a one-day liberty on the mainland.

From Japan we went to Taiwan to pick up Allied prisoners of war—American, British and Australian—and take them to the Philippines.

Finally, I came home. It was a full circle. I was discharged from the Sampson Naval Training Center. I began and ended my war in the exact same place.

After the War I returned to Ford City and went back to college. I didn't go back to Pitt, though. I used my GI Bill and went to Washington and Jefferson college instead. I graduated from there in 1949.

After I graduated, I became a part owner of my parents' bakery. Within a short period of time, I returned my ownership in the bakery to my father and went to work for Harleysville Insurance Company as a claims man until 1987, the year I retired.

I was single until I was forty-four. In 1968 I married my wife Eileen and we had four children, two daughters, Ann and Michelle, and two sons, John and James Matthew. All four children are graduates of Saint Vincent College. I also have six grandchildren.

Life moved on after the War as it always does. In my retirement I have enjoyed raising gladiolas, gardening and babysitting grandchildren.

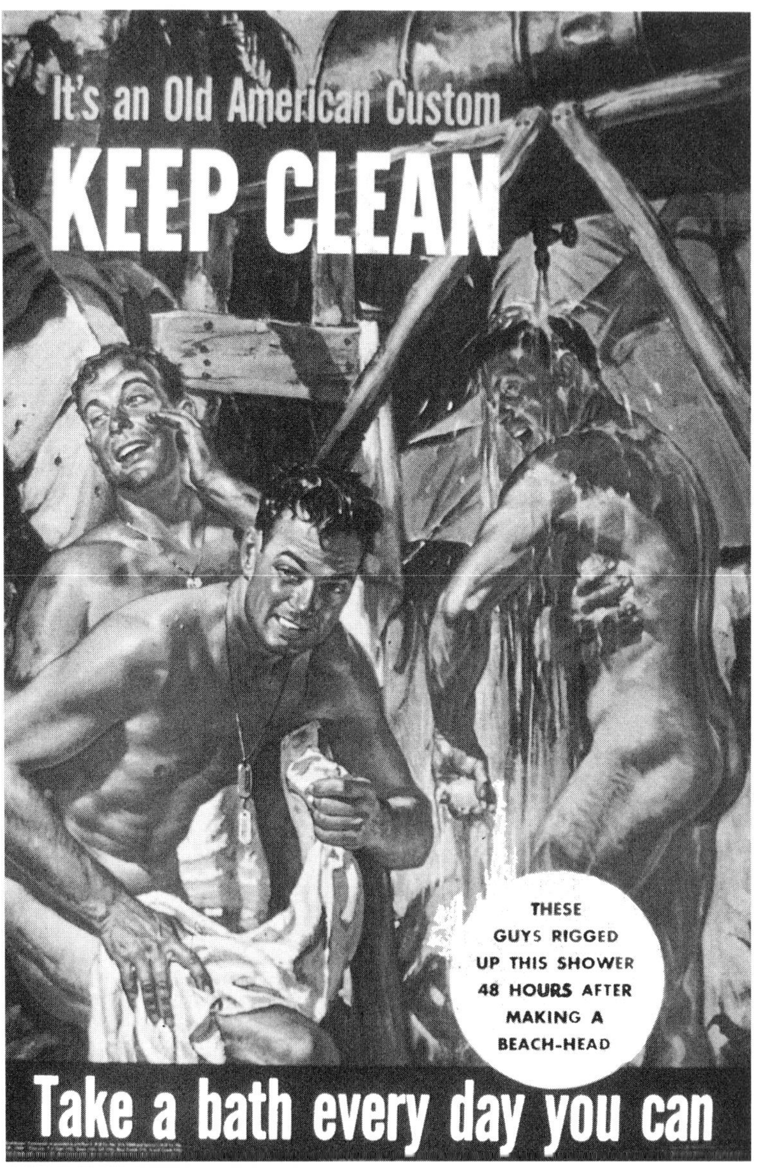
It's an Old American Custom
KEEP CLEAN
THESE
GUYS RIGGED
UP THIS SHOWER
48 HOURS AFTER
MAKING A
BEACH-HEAD
Take a bath every day you can

"At Our Young Age, We Could Handle It."

John Paul Luther

28th Infantry Division
"Keystone Division," "Iron Division,"
"Bloody Bucket"
Pennsylvania National Guard
103rd Medical Battalion, Company D
Born in Fairfield Township, Pennsylvania, 3 October 1922
Ligonier, Pennsylvania

"Sometime after lunch, we stopped along the road and joined a group gathered around a car radio to learn about the bombing of Pearl Harbor. Most of us had no idea where that place was. The whole atmosphere changed because war had come and we were saddened by the news. We all knew it was coming someday, but were we ready for this? Our equipment was minimal, as was our training. The trip home changed now as well; instead of rotten tomatoes, the people were throwing candy bars, cigarettes and other goodies at the passing convoy."

My Grandfather, Joseph G. Luther, was a carpenter's apprentice when the Civil War broke out. He enlisted as a private in the Union Army on 1 August 1862 as a member of Company F, 135th Pennsylvania Volunteer Infantry under Captain George Mabon. The unit became part of the Army of the Potomac and they participated in the battle of Fredericksburg, 12 to 15 December 1862 and the battle of Chancellorsville, 2 to 6 May 1863. He was honorably discharged from service following Chancellorsville. He reenlisted in Company D, 5th Regiment, Pennsylvania Heavy Artillery under Colonel George S. Gallupe in August 1864. He was promoted to fifth sergeant, then subsequently to first sergeant. He was present at the battle of Piedmont, near Lynchburg and then took part in the battle of Fishers Hill, Shenandoah Valley, Virginia. There, the Confederates took him prisoner on 5 October 1864. He was in Belle Isle and Piedmont Prisons and eventually Libby Prison. He was released 17 February 1865 and was honorably discharged 1 June 1865.

After the War, he married and used his carpentry skills to begin a business in undertaking from the homestead he built. In those days, undertakers conducted burial services from private homes. Horse-drawn carriages transported the caskets to the cemetery. He served his township as assessor for six years, tax collector for four years, justice of the peace for twelve years and school director for fifteen years.

My life began on 3 October 1922 in the old family farmhouse in West Fairfield,

Fairfield Township, Pennsylvania, where my father was born in 1884. Our old home was typical of farmhouses of the early days, no running water, no electricity, or inside plumbing; our lighting was by kerosene lamps and the "Aladdin" table lamp. The home, however, with its living room, dining room, kitchen and four bedrooms on two storeys was better than some in the area. The kitchen had a coal fire cook stove with a big oven and warming cabinet above, along with a tank on the side for heating water. A small hand pump drew water from the cistern beside the house and we had a sink with a drain to a sump outside.

Our daily water needs came from runoff rainwater from the roof which flowed into three underground brick cisterns with a cement plaster lining and a concrete platform top. We filtered the water through charcoal as well. Water was our biggest inconvenience and when our water was low, even before I had a license, I'd take our 1931 Chevrolet pickup truck loaded with five-gallon milk cans to a spring in a place called "Midget Camp" and fill them. When the cisterns were empty, we scrubbed them before we filled them with water.

A large "back kitchen" was at the rear of our kitchen and down two steps. In here, there was a large brick structure containing a brick bake oven with a large cast-iron door and a firebox below. A thick cast-iron plate with a hole sat over the firebox and over it was suspended a large copper kettle in which we heated water for baths and washing clothes. Our kerosene cooking stove and a small sink with a hand pump for the cistern were in the same room.

Our cellar had a dirt floor and housed the furnace with a coal bin and a large metal tank for kerosene. We often kept orphaned lambs near the furnace during the birthing season until they could join the flock. We used the sheep as a "cash crop" to pay taxes. We also kept cows for milking and a few pigs that we butchered for ham, bacon and sausage. Hay was the main crop, but we also grew corn, wheat and oats for the horses and chickens.

On the homestead, we had a two-hole seat privy, a grape arbor, two smokehouses, a chicken coop and a large barn. We also had a large, two-storey building where my grandfather's carpenter shop was located. Outside of that there sat a large, stationary steam engine with a big smokestack. My grandfather used this to power his wood working tools.

We were a very small village of about fifteen homes, three churches, a small gasoline station with a store and a school with a softball field; there may have been 125 people, counting dogs!

Our school was a large, one room building for all eight grades and was on our dirt road, past our church, three-hundred yards from my house. We might have had thirty kids there at one time. It was set up like our homestead: outhouses, one for boys and another for girls, rainwater runoff from a cistern for hand washing and a five-gallon milk can with a community dipper for drinking water, but we had our own cups.

Our United Presbyterian Church was the social center of our neighborhood. It had a small congregation, but everyone seemed to go to church and we always had extra activities: young peoples' plays, Easter and Christmas Pageants, Sunday School, funerals and weddings.

The construction of the concrete highway, a link to the new road built in 1926 at the foot of the hill near the Tubmill Creek, brought many travelers though our area with new and interesting cars to watch. My father was employed as a road maintenance supervisor, and his road crew took on the maintenance of the new highway. Mowing banks, building guardrails, painting wooden guard rail posts, hand-spreading ashes on the roads in the winter so the traffic could keep moving were all his responsibility. Horses hauled the old road graders, wagons and scoops; everything else was done by hand.

When the highway was finished, they formed a parade to commemorate its opening. A truck in the parade pulled my grandfather's old horse drawn hearse. Shortly after the road opened, a fellow named John Henderson built and opened a small grocery store with gasoline pumps. We had no electric power yet, so the gasoline was pumped by hand to a glass tank on top of the pump and a valve was opened on the hose to drain into the tank.

We got our first radio in the early 1930s, a battery powered Atwater-Kent unit installed in a writing desk. The speaker was located below the desk. We'd sit under the desk against the speaker front to hear. It was a treat to hear the half-hour adventure programs like "Orphan Annie," "Terry and the Pirates," and "Jack Armstrong." We also listened to the "Amos and Andy" and "Jack Benny" shows after the news was over.

In 1936, electric power came to our area. It changed our whole world. Electric lights and appliances came to us very soon after.

My first year at Bolivar High School was also in 1936. This was before the school bus system, and for a while we got rides from friends or my mother, but when I got my license in 1938, I drove our 1933 Chevrolet sedan to school, and it was always filled with kids. In the summer of 1937, my cousin Jack and I worked at the Ross Mountain Clubhouse as busboys. We lived above the kitchen and worked at various jobs in the kitchen and dining room. We had floor- mopping duties every day, setting up tables and clearing dirty dishes from the tables. My mother also worked there, but she slept at home.

I graduated from Bolivar High School in the spring of 1940 with no thought of my future. Jobs were scarce in our area, and we had no money to go to college. The Depression was still going on and family providers consumed the few jobs in our area. I managed to get a job with the Gas Company constructing a line through the woods in the Tubmill Valley that was to provide gas service to the Ross Mountain Club community. This was hand-digging through the woods, and the tree roots and rocks made my life miserable. I decided that this life wasn't for me.

I turned eighteen on 3 October and felt completely bored with my life. Sherman (Tubby) Barnhart, a close friend of mine, felt the same way and he suggested that we check out the National Guard in Ligonier. This meant Monday evening drill, two weeks of camp during the summer in the South and a small paycheck. We joined up on 17 October 1940 and were very surprised to find that, after word had gotten out in our community, my cousin Jack, my cousin Dave Gardner, Ed Horrell, Vick Barnhart and Harry Seitz decided to join as well.

We were issued uniforms and supplies and ushered into Army life. We spent summer evenings learning "army" and how to drill and march in step. We made new friends and got to be like a family. Because I was in a medical ambulance company, I didn't have to learn how to shoot.

On 17 February, we were "federalized" into the regular Army. The war in Europe was on and our country was starting to prepare for our possible involvement. Needless to say, we were all shook up with the real possibility of going to war. We were now staying at the Armory day and night. Our stay there was short however, because on 24 February we packed up everything into trucks and convoyed to our new home at Indiantown Gap Military Reservation, near Annville, Pennsylvania.

We arrived there on a cold, wet winter day and were welcomed with muddy streets, new barracks which hadn't yet been used, no mattresses or pillows. The toilet rooms were muddy. When the weather improved, we built stone streets, duckboard walks and even flower beds around the barracks. We had a nice service center nearby where there was good entertainment: dance bands, parties and a lot of other fun things. We visited nearby Harrisburg, Lebanon and Lancaster as well. Our regimental area contained about fifteen buildings. Besides the barracks, there were kitchens with mess halls, an infirmary, day rooms and a motor pool with a vehicle service building. The barracks were wooden, two-storey, uninsulated frame buildings that were typical camp structures about twenty-five by one hundred feet with a large open room for bunks, office quarters, a day room and stairs. The first floor contained the toilet and shower room along with the furnace room. Each building housed a full company of men; in our case that meant fifty people. We were all very homesick and wondered how bad life was going to get.

When we left Ligonier, we were Company D, but shortly after arriving at the Gap, we formed into new companies. Most of us that went from Fairfield were assigned into a new F ambulance company and others became Company B. Of nine companies, A, B and C were aid companies, D, E and F were ambulance companies, and G, H, and I were hospital companies. Those nine companies, along with headquarters and service companies made up the 103rd Regiment of the 28th Infantry Division. This was known in military terminology as a "Square Division." At full strength, the Division consisted of about eighteen-thousand men, though I don't think we ever reached this total.

We settled into regular Army life: guard duty, infirmary duty, furnace room duty, parade marches, hikes, drill instruction and general basic training. In early March, we were trucked to Holmberg, Maryland to bring back a whole fleet of new trucks to the Gap from the Army supply depot there. We picked up kitchen trucks, ambulances, Jeeps and "googybuggies," open, two-seated command cars that we used for training. Our training continued into the early summer of 1941 until the Division made a maneuver trip to Camp A.P. Hill in Virginia. I failed to make the trip because I came down with appendicitis and spent fifteen days in bed and fifteen days recuperating in the base hospital. In the meantime, the company had come home from Virginia.

At the close of May, we were trucked to Lancaster for a big Memorial Day parade on the grounds of Franklin Marshall College. We paraded at the football field in front of thousands of people. It was a spit-and-polish occasion. I went home for a short leave after my hospital stay.

We enjoyed going home on weekends following Saturday morning inspection, cramming as many as we could into Ed Horrell's 1939 Ford. We drove four hours on the Pennsylvania Turnpike from Carlisle to Donegal and came back to camp on a Sunday evening. We'd hit the road, drive four hours on the Turnpike from Carlisle to Donegal and then return to camp Sunday evening.

In September, the whole Division left for maneuvers in North Carolina. Around that time, doctors found some heart problems with Victor Barnhart, and he was discharged from the service. On the way to Camp Meade, Maryland, kids along the road threw rotten tomatoes at our convoy. We camped for the night in Maryland, then we traveled on to a tent city in Wadesboro, North Carolina. We slept in squad tents: four men to each tent with folding cots that sat on sandy ground. By morning, the cots would be almost be planted into the ground from us turning over in our sleep. We got our water supply from cold water spigots. A creek was our source. Our drinking water was treated with iodine, and it came from a Lister bag. Cooks prepared our food on kitchen trucks, and we stood to eat at an elevated plank table.

This was a big tobacco and cotton country, something we had never seen before. Wadesboro was about three miles away; nearby there was a cotton mill where the Army trucked us for our showers. We did have electricity, so we had lights and some radios. Next to the camp was a civilian soda pop and ice cream stand. We hung out there a lot. The stand had a jukebox that seemed to blare country music all the time.

My father and cousin Joe drove to visit us for a weekend. They stayed about ten miles away in Chesterfield, South Carolina. We stayed there until early December doing our maneuvers, convoy practice and hospital tent setup. At our young age, we could handle it.

We broke camp on 6 December 1941 and headed north back to Pennsylvania. Meanwhile, at the Gap, we began getting draftees to fill up the companies. Most came from Camp Croft, South Carolina, where they had taken their basic training.

We camped in pup-tents overnight at an airport near South Boston, Virginia. Sometime after lunch, we stopped along the road and joined a group gathered around a radio car to learn about the bombing of Pearl Harbor. Most of us had no idea where that place was. The whole atmosphere changed because war had come and we were saddened by the news. We all knew it was coming someday, but were we ready for this? Our equipment was minimal, as was our training.

The trip home changed now as well; instead of rotten tomatoes, the people threw candy bars, cigarettes and other goodies at the passing convoy. We arrived at the Gap the next day to a very cold barracks that hadn't been heated yet for the season.

The Army sent half of the outfit home for a week. When they came back, the other half left. We were there until late January.

Sometime in January, some of us came home with Art Johnson in his 1932 Model-A Ford. We left with Art from Ligonier at about ten in the evening for the Gap in a blinding snowstorm. His car had a bad heater, and we about froze. We made it midway at about three in the morning where we stayed until we got warm. We arrived at the Gap at about eight in the morning. The first sergeant considered us AWOL and confined us to our barracks for fifteen minutes.

The Division was ready to travel by the last week of January 1942. We took a truck convoy to Louisiana which became our new home; we sure were looking to get out of winter country. I was assigned to a fuel truck with Harry Seitz as my assistant driver. Our trip by convoy was slow and we made night camp stops at Camp Meade, Virginia, Fort Bragg, North Carolina, Columbia, South Carolina, Fort Benning, Georgia, Demopolis, Alabama, Vicksburg, Mississippi and finally Camp Livingston, Louisiana. At each night stop, the empty five-gallon gasoline cans we hauled had to be exchanged for full ones at a fuel depot and redistributed to each vehicle before our day was over. Of course we had lots of help, but it was hard work and it made us sleep well in our pup tents.

We ate well from food prepared in our kitchen trucks and we had pit stops at fire stations, gas stations and sometimes in church outhouses along the road. Stopping to use the latrine beside the truck was a no-no while in convoy, though I'm sure it happened several times. In the instance that we had to stop and go beside the trucks, we dug a slit trench and erected a canvas screen. We filled the trench with lime and covered it with earth when we moved on. We had good weather the whole trip. It was full of good experiences, but at about this time, Harry Seitz was becoming dissatisfied with our outfit and told me that when we got to Louisiana, he was asking for a transfer to some place with real action.

Camp Livingston was a very large facility. Our whole division was together like at the Gap, but now we were in pyramidal tents: eight people each, cots and mattresses, wood floor and sides up about three feet with screens above and then a canvas tent with roll up sides and a pole in the center. We had no heaters in our tents. The tents were about four feet apart and in neat rows. These quarters meant our unit was very spread out and took up a lot of land. All the buildings were good wooden structures. We were amazed to see all pine trees with no underbrush, just pine needles on the ground. It would rain very hard in a short amount of time and still remain dry, no mud.

The camp was often visited by big USO shows that had a lot of big names and celebrities. Bob Hope, Jerry Colonna, and Francis Langford[143] were a few. It seemed like there was a big show every week of some kind.

Alexandria was a large town nearby and the bus service was free, so we went often. Pineville was also a small community close by, but there wasn't much to do there, especially with thousands of GIs roaming around. There was a roadhouse called "Schlitz Canteen" just outside of camp and it really jumped with activity. They often had big bands for dancing, but the problem with the place was that there weren't enough women to go around! I got drunk for the first time at this place, and I vowed never to do it again.

Harry Seitz got his wish and was transferred to the 82nd Airborne Division. He went to Africa and then to Sicily. He was severely wounded at Anzio Beach on the Italian peninsula and died soon after from his wounds.

Not long after arriving at Camp Livingston, the units and personnel became all shook up. We now became a "Triangular Division," meaning we didn't have a regiment anymore. We became a battalion with only four companies, headquarters and a service company. Three were known as Collecting Companies A, B, C. Then we had a Clearing Company D. Jack went to B, Tubby to C, I went to D, and Ed, Dave and others went to the 30th General Hospital that was a newly formed unit. We also got new draftees from elsewhere to make up our new companies.[144]

In April, I was selected to go to Fort Sam Houston in San Antonio, Texas for six weeks Medical Technician Training School. I boarded a train in Alexandria and traveled to San Antonio where I was joined by others for the same training. We were housed in a big, beautiful, brick barracks with no air-conditioning. It was hot and uncomfortable. The Alamo, Brackenridge Park, the River Walk and other attractions made it like a vacation.

The classroom training was comprised mostly of first-aid classes, doctor assisting procedures, administering blood plasma and lessons in minor suturing under field conditions. I'm not sure how much we really learned because the instructors were never field trained; we learned from outdated textbook stuff, old war medical techniques.

After I completed training in San Antonio, I came back to Camp Livingston, was granted a two-week furlough, and I went home. That was a wonderful trip. One evening, I stopped at "The Dairy Nook" in New Florence and found a group of girls there having a good time. I joined them at the booth, and there was one girl who really caught my eye and appealed to me right away. She seemed very reserved, attractive and nearly my age. We seemed to have no problem getting acquainted. As the evening progressed, I asked if I could take her home. I learned that she lived near the Tubmill School which was in my direction home, too. I saw a lot of her the next few days until I had to return to camp. I was really hooked on her then and there. Her name was Helen. After the War, she became my wife.

Not very long after my return to camp, I received word that my Uncle John had died. Through the Red Cross, cousin Jack and I were granted a ten-day furlough. We had been on an overnight training march, arriving in camp early in the morning. We were dead tired, hungry and needing sleep when the First Sergeant informed us that we were granted leave. Our train left Alexandria at noon.

Alexandria was a rail-hub for the whole area. There were three big Army camps nearby and GIs were everywhere. We pushed through the mob onto the Southern Pacific "Sunshine Special." Of course, all the seats were full and we had to stand or sit on the floor. The toilets were crowded and smelly, and we had no drinking water and no meals. We anticipated the problem with meals, so we stored up on candy bars at the station.

The train finally made St. Louis and we thought things would improve when we transferred to the Pennsylvania Railroad. They were using baggage type coaches with a net across the door and plank benches, no toilets and no drinking water. The train stopped often at stations along the way for pit stops.

We came to Johnstown where we were met by my Dad who took us home. The funeral was very large because Uncle John was a family doctor and everyone in the valley knew him. I was happy to spend time with Helen, but we had to return to camp too soon. The trip back went well and we had seats that reclined!

On 15 January 1943 our Division moved by rail to Camp Gordon Johnson, Florida for beach training. It took three days. We had compartments that seated four, a bathroom, eating areas, and seats that converted into bunks for the night. We had nothing to do but play cards and sleep.

Camp Gordon Johnson was about fifty miles from Tallahassee, in a place called Carrabelle, right by the beach. The buildings were low, sheep-shed style, and temporary structures with no floors, just sand. We had folding cots sitting on the sand and duck board walkways between cots and down the center aisle with electric bulbs hanging from the roof framing. The mess halls and toilet rooms were more permanent buildings. Fortunately, the weather was amiable because we had no heat. It was here that we had our first encounter with chiggers, small sand fleas that got into our socks and made our feet itch.

We had a large amount of LCI boats that were manned by another outfit and we were on them daily. There's an island about ten miles out that was uninhabited, and it served as our beach landing practice area. We practiced day and night landings. Sometimes, on weekends, we went out on the boats, just for something to do. Some of the guys went fishing.

Not far from camp was a resort called Wahulla Springs that the Army had converted into a training area. The main structure had burnt down sometime before and was deserted. There was a beautiful lake nearby with very clear spring water and a seventy-five-foot-high diving tower. We were required to climb with full gear to the top, and jump off into the water that had been oiled and set afire. This exercise was to simulate "abandon ship." It was scary, but we learned to come up splashing.

The area was full of alligators. We had never seen them before coming to Florida. Our captain, Captain Applewhite, used to capture them and display them in a fenced-in pond at our camp. He'd also hunt wild pigs and dress them for an occasional Sunday barbecue.

We were at this camp until 9 June 1943. After that, we moved again by train to Camp Pickett near the town of Blackstone in southern Virginia, thirty miles west of Petersburg. This camp was much like Indiantown Gap, but with more permanent wooden buildings. The training there varied; on one occasion, we were trucked to the mountains of West Virginia for eighteen days of mountain training. We also spent seven days in the Chesapeake Bay on a large LST for ship-to-shore training. This was a pleasant area, and Jack's wife, Louise, and Had's wife, Mary, had an apartment in Blackstone for a while.

On 30 September 1943 we boarded a train and headed north. We were instructed to ride with the blinds drawn and without lights, but when we passed through the big cities, I peeked under the blind. We ended up in a camp called Camp Myles Standish near Brockton, Massachusetts. It was a heavily wooded staging area and we were confined to camp. We weren't there long, though.

Before daylight on 7 October 1943, dressed in our overcoats, rabbit hats, newly issued warmer gloves, and carrying our barracks bags with everything we had, we loaded onto tractor-trailer trucks with wooden side racks. We stood the whole way to a location in Boston Harbor, about forty miles. There, the trucks drove down onto the dock beside the SS *Henry Gibbons*, a Liberty Ship. To us who had never seen an oceangoing ship, it seemed huge. We were going overseas.

After boarding, we went down the gangway to the lower decks where we found five-high, narrow, canvas bunks that were to be our homes for the trip to England. We stowed our gear and went on deck to have a look around. We seemed to be about fifty-feet above the dock. While we looked out over the harbor, tugboats moved the ship from the docks. We had dinner late in the day in a stand-up mess area several decks down. After dinner, we went back on deck. We were no longer moving. We sat anchored all day and through the night. In the morning, we went back on deck. We saw ships everywhere. We had become part of an enormous convoy. We knew right then and there that war was a big deal.

Shipboard life was full of diesel fumes, crowded conditions, uncomfortable sleep, uncomfortable, open-type toilets, saltwater showers and long, metal wash basins with cold water only, but I managed. After all, it was a troop ship and not a luxury liner. We had two meals a day, breakfast and a late day dinner. After our meals, we scraped left-overs into garbage cans, plunged our mess gear into hot water and then dipped them into a rinse bath filled with some kind of bad-smelling disinfectant. There was always water on the floors, making them slippery. When the ship rocked, people slipped and fell. Each morning, as soon as possible, we headed for the open deck to sit on a big pile of cargo nets on top of a planked area known as Hold Number Two. There, we sat and wondered what was going to happen next.

After several days out, the weather turned very cold. Ice formed on everything, but we still stayed on the deck because the lower decks were so uncomfortable. A storm came up and the ship rolled severely. The waves looked to be thirty-feet high, and sometimes the ship's rail went under water. We all got seasick and didn't get over it until the trip was over.[145] The ship's crew told us to be grateful for the rough seas, because German U-Boats in the area had difficulty attacking. On the ninth day, we entered the Irish Sea and said it must have been called that because the water was green.

On the eleventh day, 17 October, we reached the port of Avensmouth near Portsmouth. We were serenaded by an English band. The Red Cross was there with coffee and donuts. We boarded a train for an all-night ride to Tenby, in Wales, and from there bused to Camp Penhally, two miles away. We had trouble getting used to the strange train whistle when it approached the Station at the Village of Penhally a half of a mile down the road. The village was small with one street and an alley that housed a small pub. Farther down the road, about two more miles was the town of Tenby. A nice place, sort of a vacation spot, about the size of Latrobe, Pennsylvania. We walked there often, cutting across the golf course to save time. The main attraction was a movie house.

Penhally had been a British Artillery training area and was just above the beach on Carmarthen Bay facing southeast. The area was only a battalion size with about fifteen low buildings that were covered in tar-paper. Each building housed about fifty men, or half a company. The beds were bunks with straw-filled mattresses and pillows that took some getting used to. Two potbellied coal stoves sat in the aisle and were too hot or too cold depending on one's proximity to them. Each company had its own mess hall and toilet room. High above the main camp was a recreation hall where we hung out when we weren't on duty. In the back of the building there was a small, stone home with a thatched roof and a beautiful flower garden; a setting we had never seen before. The front of camp opened to a main road, and below that a railroad, and then a wide beach. An elderly lady, the wife of a British army officer stationed in India, became friends with a few of us and would have us over for dinner several times.

In the other direction from our camp, there was a larger British army camp called Manorbier. It was in this camp that we discovered the ATS[146] girls. Glenn Shirey was lucky, and he married one of them after the War.

While we were at camp, General Eisenhower visited us and we felt very honored that he did because we were not a very important group at the time. Our training there was just a routine rehearsal for things to come. We departed our seaside haven by truck convoy on 17 April 1944, never to return. Our new camp was outside the town of Swindon, thirty miles from London. The area was crowded with hordes of soldiers and lots of traffic, much different from Wales, where we were pretty much alone.

6 June 1944 was a day I will never forget. During the night, thousands of aircraft filled the skies with a continual, deafening roar. Of course, we knew what was happening; The invasion of Normandy was on. Though we were a little disappointed that we were in reserve, we were glad that we were not going just yet.

With D-Day came casualties and our neighbors, the 130th Station Hospital and the 217th General Hospital, needed help, so some of our doctors and technicians went on detached service. We continued treating wounded as necessary, and on 18 July we went by motor convoy to a marshalling area near Southampton on the English Channel. The area was a tent city: crowded, dusty and confining. We felt very apprehensive about what was to come.

We exchanged our currency for French Francs and stayed there for three days, leaving on 21 July for the Embarkation Docks at Southampton where we boarded the HMT *Devonshire.* We sailed on 23 July in the early morning and arrived at the French coast in the afternoon where we boarded an LCT. Climbing down over the side on cargo nets with only our backpacks, we stepped ashore on OMAHA Beach, France.

We walked through de-mined paths identified by bandages tied on rifles that were stuck in the ground, and then up a hill past blown-out German pillboxes. Climbing the hill made us realize the difficulty our comrades must have had during the first hours of the invasion. When we reached the top of the hill, we looked back and could see hundreds of ships. Many had been sunk, and others were unloading supplies and troops. We marched past a graveyard in complete silence. After about nine miles, we bivouacked for several days. The War was about fifteen miles farther inland, but we were still in harm's way. We heard artillery and could see smoke.

That first evening we dug foxholes for protection from strafing planes. Ack-ack fire was intense and a German fighter plane crashed in a field near our area, reminding us that it was a war. Not very far from us an ammo dump exploded and lit up the night sky like daylight.

The quartermaster trucked our personal gear and all our equipment to us the first day. For most of the next few days, we were busy painting crosses on our helmets and tent tops. We were on Ten-in-One rations because the kitchen trucks were slow in getting to us.[147]

On the morning of 29 July, we received orders to move to the outskirts of St. Lô. It would be our first "combat," and, naturally, we were excited. Slowly, we moved along until we reached the city, where we waited for the engineers to clear mines. We were on a hill overlooking the devastation of the city below, and a Jeep drove by and kicked up some dust. Then we came under German 88 fire. Frightened, we scrambled for cover. There was a hand-painted sign near me that read "DUST BRINGS FIRE." The sign referred to exactly what happened to us at this location; German artillery waited for dust clouds that told them our vehicles were on the move, and then they opened up.

We passed through the rubble of St. Lô where, just the day before, there was an enormous air raid by thousands of planes.[148] The streets were indistinguishable as we wound through the city to a location on a hill and into an apple orchard. A small station was set up and we began to detect the strong odor of death. About seventy-five percent of German artillery at this time was pulled by horses, and everywhere we saw bloated carcases with their feet sticking up in the air. Around the hedgerows and in the meadows, people were butchering cattle.

In a lane between hedgerows, we saw two dead Germans laying by a bicycle. Shortly, a reconnaissance squad came by and fired on a nearby farmhouse where two snipers were hiding. They advised us to stay away until they cleared booby traps. We dug foxholes that night and tried to sleep.

At about three in the morning, we got orders to load up and move out. We moved under blackout a short distance when we came under an air attack by three Kraut planes.[149] The painted crosses on our canvas tops may have helped us because there was little damage, just a big scare. They dropped flares that lit up the sky, and then they bombed us. There were several near misses. Several of the trucks were damaged and had to be towed.[150]

In the early morning, we set up our hospital next to a battery of "Long-Toms" that fired all through the day and night. We received so many wounded that we were swamped beyond belief. Our hospital setup of twenty-one ward tents was the largest we were ever to have until the Battle of the Bulge.[151]

We received soldiers suffering from "shell shock," or "battle fatigue." Captain Burke, a physiologist under Major Namon, seemed to like me so he appointed me as his assistant, and then he made me a technician in charge of the wards. I hated the job, but survived it. Fortunately, the job got me out of the medical ward where the doctors performed emergency operations. Since we were a clearing company, we treated cases that could be returned fairly soon to combat. The seriously wounded were routed to the rear. Our company commander, Major Petraglia, issued Purple Hearts.

We soon got our first pay in French Francs. Big deal! We had no place to spend it! Somebody found a cache of Calvados[152] in a basement or wine cellar. Many of the guys welcomed the potent drink, and they filled several Jerry cans for future use.

On 12 August[153], near the town of La Julliere, we were again so close to a battery of Long Toms that the concussion nearly blew down our tents. Our casualties were exceptionally high here, and our Division commander, General Wharton, formerly with the 9th Division, was killed by a sniper.[154] General "Dutch" Cota then took over as our commander. He had been the commander of the 29th Division at the Normandy landing and was later depicted in the movie *The Longest Day.*

Our kitchen truck was situated near a hedgerow and the strong odor from dead cattle and some German bodies lying near us made it unbearable. A few horses full of maggots lay rotting in the sun, but that didn't stop the locals from taking the meat.

A detail led by Lieutenant Hunter had the unpleasant job of burying the dead Germans. A low-flying Piper Cub buzzed our location, signaling that there was also a dead Yank in the vicinity. The Graves Registration[155] people came and took the body away. There were many unexploded German shells in our area. We knew enough to stay clear of them.

On 20 August[156], we closed the station and got orders to move forward. We drove through an area that we learned later had been strafed by our planes that were pursuing retreating enemy. The ground was littered with burned-out German tanks, armaments of all sorts, burned troop trucks and bodies. It was raining and the weather contributed to the carnage. The area became known as the Falaise Pocket. One of our drivers became ill, and I replaced him.

We arrived in the town of Conches-en-Ouches on 24 August, and from there we moved on to Louviers where we traveled through a large railroad yard that had been heavily bombed and completely destroyed just hours before we got there. Fires were still burning from wrecked trains.

We arrived on the grounds of the Palace of Versailles on 28 August and bivouacked in the lawn area below the palace. Nothing had been damaged from the War, and it was beautiful. We were allowed to walk freely through the Palace, but all the furniture had been removed to storage, or maybe the retreating Germans had confiscated some of the items. We learned that the German Gestapo headquarters had been there for years, in the same splendor Emperor Louis XIV ruled during the Golden Era of France!

29 August was a big day for the 28th Division. The city of Paris had just been liberated and our Division was chosen to parade down the Champs Elysees, around the Arc de Triomphe, past the Notre Dame Cathedral and the Grave of the Unknown Soldier. I was lucky to see it all from the top of a truck. People jammed the streets throwing flowers and kisses. Our convoy bivouacked in the St. Denis Park. In minutes, we

were overwhelmed with happy people of all ages. The kids begged us for chocolate. A woman arrived in a big sedan that was loaded with several cases of champagne, and she began to barter for cigarettes, but our supplies were limited.

From the time we arrived on French soil until we made it to Paris, our fraternization with civilians was limited. Paris was a brief relief from the pressure of battle, and our lives seemed a little more normal, but it was war, and I knew there was more of it to come.

The next day, we moved about twenty miles to the town of Puiseux and set up in an apple orchard. A local farmer brought us early ripe apples and vegetables. It was a treat after days of K-Rations.

On 7 September, we arrived in the city of Sedan[157] which was also untouched by the War. We moved on to Pour St. Rémy on 8 September, our last stop in France. In St. Rémy we watched as angry townspeople shaved the heads of women who had collaborated with the Germans, or who had entered into romantic relationships with them. After they shaved them, they tore off their clothes and sent them running down the road. Even worse, some were flogged.

We set up in the town of Jamoigne, Belgium on 9 September. To our amazement, we got there before we were scheduled and had to backtrack out of the town because it hadn't been secured.

The next day, we moved into Habay Le Nueve. We set up station in a beautiful castle; this was the first time we were in a building instead of tents. The walls were lined with stag antlers inscribed with names and dates. One item was a large moose head cast in bronze! We had orders: "Hands off, no souvenirs allowed!"

On 11 September, we set up in Chifontain. We received several dead children that had set off a land mine.

We moved on 12 September to Trois Vierges near the northern tip of Luxembourg, right at the German border. Our Division was the first to reach the Siegfried Line. We moved into a girls' dormitory! Our building was empty, but there were a lot of girls next door. We had orders: "No Fraternization Allowed!"

On my birthday, 3 October, we moved on to Elsenborn, near Liège, where we set up in a three-storey school building. We were receiving so many wounded, we had to set up several ward tents in the schoolyard.

The second night there, the Germans fired seventy 88mm rounds, damaging the facilities severely wounding several patients. One of them died. A female nurse was killed at the nearby 45th Field Hospital, the first to die in the War.[158]

We remained in Elsenborn until 25 October, then we moved on to Rearen. It was in this area that we began getting our first large groups of refugees from Aachen, Germany. The city was under heavy shelling from more than 130 battalions of American and British artillery.

From there, we moved to Roetgen, Germany, on 2 November and into the area known as the Hurtgen Forest. We set up in a nice hunting lodge in a beautiful forest with well-trimmed shrubs and hedges. The first day there, it snowed and made the location very picturesque. The weather turned rainy soon after and made the conditions terrible for those trying to keep warm and dry while fighting the Germans.

The fighting became severe and battle casualties started pouring into our station. We registered 515 casualties in one day, the most we ever had to that date. Many GIs suffered from trenchfoot, a condition brought about by the feet continually being wet in cold weather, causing the tissue to freeze. Some cases were very severe, and their feet or toes had to be amputated. I was in charge of the wards for the "combat exhaustion" cases and it was necessary to set up at least five ward tents outside to handle them. All we could do was administer Sodium Pentothal tablets, let them rest. We sent the worst cases to the rear for further treatment. Those that improved after a couple days came back to their outfits, but many of them came back to us after a couple days combat.

I found these comments that a soldier had written and stuck in the lining of his helmet:

> To the few atheists who still claim that men have no souls and that there is no divine deity, I merely say, be at the front and see the life and souls depart from the vigorous body of a friend, when but a moment before could speak, love and create. It is a skeptical person indeed who can deny that there is a great beyond, an afterlife and a heaven. Life's process would be futile indeed, if there were no spiritual life to follow. This aspect of religion occurs to many in the course of battle.

There were two ambulance drivers that approached one day to get three Yanks who were laying out in the field. One of our guys got out of the truck—there was nothing going on and it was quiet there—and he went out to get these guys, stepped on a mine that cut him in two. The other ambulance guy took a rope and tied a bag of something heavy onto it, threw it out and dragged it back to clear the mines. They got those guys out of there. We also had two ambulance drivers that were shot and several others that were taken prisoners.

The 8th Infantry Division Clearing Company relieved us from our first real job in Germany, and we moved south to the City of Wiltz, Luxembourg at the end of November for a well-deserved R & R after our weeks in the Hurtgen Forest.

We set up our hospital in a school building in a well-kept area of town with the buildings at the edge of the street with no sidewalks; it was similar to an English town. I was billeted, along with about six other guys, on the second floor of a bakery that was still active. We slept on the floor on blankets and had access to a toilet. Again, the furniture had been moved and stored. Across the street was a pub operated by a nice family named Glessner, Helen's maiden name. They always had pastry snacks and drinks available and were friendly to everyone. The GIs had planned a Christmas party for the town kids at the pub with from home. The Glessners put up a tree decorated with ribbon. However, the party never came about because of a battle that was developing. History would call the battle, "The Battle of the Bulge." It would start on 16 December 1944.

In early December, some field positions had opened up, and Sergeants Fasig, Bryant and I had been put up for a battlefield promotion to second lieutenant. We had all passed the board examination and were expecting our promotions, but the Bulge put an end to it. Little was said about the promotions, and time passed us by.

Since it was a slow period, the company brass issued some three-day passes to Paris. We didn't all get to go, but some of us were lucky. Flack, Van Shepin and I went by truck to Liège, Belgium where we boarded a train for Paris. Once in Paris, we got free lodging in a small hotel, one that the Army had made available to visiting military personnel. The city was jammed with soldiers, and we fought the crowds everywhere we went, and the city was still in blackout. After three days, we took the train back to Liège, got on a truck and headed for "home." Or so we thought. Instead of Wiltz, we trucked to Clervaux, to an aid station along the twenty-seven-mile stretch of front that we called the "Thin Line."[159]

We were to spend the evening of 15 December in Clervaux and then go next day to Wiltz. That night all hell broke loose! We came under heavy shellfire. The German Army broke through and overflowed into the community. By noon, we could see them in the bell towers, on the tops of and in the rooms of buildings. One of the guys managed to get a truck that was parked in an orchard and we managed to get out of town. There was a lot of small-arms shooting at our truck, but we cut ass out of Clervaux safely. Lots of other guys, if they were lucky, became prisoners of war.

We made the fifteen miles back to Wiltz just ahead of the Germans, only to find our outfit preparing to evacuate. The first sergeant told everyone to climb on board the vehicles. He also told us to leave everything behind since we'd be back as soon as our troops stopped the German attack. All I had with me was a little pack of items I had with me in Paris. I lost my duffel bag and everything in it—photos, letters, blankets and winter gear.[160]

It started to snow heavily, and the weather turned colder. I could see the advancing tanks and infantry over the hillside about two miles away, far enough that I felt lucky to be getting out of harm's way.

We made our way to Bastogne, Belgium, about fifteen miles away, where we came under heavy artillery fire. The town was crowded with retreating GIs. We were about to unload and set up a station at a church in the middle of the town, when we got orders to move out before it was too late or else get captured by the Krauts.

By then it was about nine o'clock and dark, cold and snowy. It wasn't a good time to be in the back of a truck and wearing very little warm clothing. They gave us some K-Rations. We got in a large convoy of vehicles heading west out of town just in time; the Germans were closing in.

Fortunately, the Germans couldn't fly in this weather, so we were not harassed by their aircraft. We arrived in the town of Neufchâteau, and in the morning set up in a Catholic Clinic, but the German advance kept us changing the location of our aid station. For days, we kept getting GIs in our station that were not injured, but lost, cold and hungry. We moved four times in three days with what little equipment we had salvaged. I was finally able to scrounge up some warmer clothing as well.

Eventually, we ended up back in France in the town of Signey L' Abbaye on a cold and snowy 3 January 1945. Christmas and New Year's had passed without us even realizing it. Almost all of our meals were Ten-in-Ones or K-Rations, but when we stopped running, we began to get hot meals, showers, new clothing and new equipment. The German attack sure succeeded in messing up our outfits by scattering units all over the area. We had become complacent thinking the War would soon be over, but the German offensive was overwhelming, and nobody expected them to have that much equipment available for such an attack.

January 17 was departure day from the French camp for a long, cold, 226-mile trip over some very snowy roads. We arrived at one o'clock in the morning in Plainfang, near Fraize, France. We set up the station in a cold, windowless Tuberculosis Sanitarium. Snow was blowing in the wall cracks, but there was a wood stove available, and we cut and dried wood for it. Another portion of the building was still in use by some women patients. Sadly, this area was off limits to us largely because there were some nice-looking patients residing there.

Late at night, on 1 February, we moved on to Bonhomme, France. After crossing snowy, mountainous roads in Vosges, we set up a hospital which had been taken over by nuns for the care of the elderly of Alsace. It was here that we had our first contact with Moroccan mule caravans moving ammunition into the mountains. They were ill equipped for the snowy weather and we found many to be suffering from exposure and trenchfoot.

On 7 February, we moved into a French camp at Rouffach where the Moroccans there were eager to sell their German Lugers for some spending money; the French government had neglected to pay them for their efforts!

The city of Toul, the "City of Dreams," was our next location. After a cold and miserable 125-mile trip, we arrived at an area that was previously occupied by French troops who had left their billets in terrible conditions on 14 February. We soon got more habitable quarters. Here, we discovered the Navy was on hand preparing for the upcoming Rhine Crossing. We used their projectors to show some movies.

We set up the station as usual, but we treated a different kind of "wounded." The foresight of the Army had created an annex to the aid station, from which we distributed Silver Protein, Bi-Chloride of Mercury and an ointment of Mercuous Chloride, all treatments for venereal disease. We also handed out a host of prophylactics.

On 19 February, we moved into Lince, Belgium, and, in the Monschau Forest, we found ourselves back near the front lines. After several abbreviated moves, we crossed the Rhine on the night of 29 March on a pontoon bridge that was lit up like a Christmas tree; this was to increase visibility in order to detect any floating mines or demolition charges. The bridge was six miles north of Andernach and south of the Ludendorf Bridge at Remagen.[161] Our speed limit was five miles per hour, maintained at sixty-yard intervals, so it took us quite some time to cross. Several guys had the pleasure of moving to the rear of the truck to urinate in the Rhine.

Along the line somewhere, our outfit came across a big German truck that was powered by fumes from charcoal in a large tank mounted on the side by the front fender. I don't know how it worked, but our smart mechanics were able to keep it running and they brought it along with us as we traveled. They gave it a nickname, "Olive VI." I have no idea when it met its demise, but it was transferred to the Division's Special Forces.

We reached the town of Langendernbach in the late evening and set up in a hotel, but we soon had to move because an echelon from Division Headquarters was moving in and taking over. We moved three miles down the road to Elbgrund, an old castle that formally housed Hitler *Jugend*. While there, many guys got the measles, and one fellow contracted scarlet fever, but recovered from it. I didn't get ill, so I was one of the lucky ones.

On 21 April, we arrived in a pleasant town called Landstuhl, in an area of Germany known as Saarland, virtually untouched by war. A large hotel building about four-stories high, and a famous spa and health retreat facility was our new home. The locals told us that a Dr. Carl Marx operated the facility. It was set in a walled courtyard. Every guy had a nice bed and a toilet with a shower just down the hall as well as a complete kitchen and dining room; we really lucked out with this site. The people around the complex were very friendly, but non-fraternization was still in effect. Everyone was aware that the War would soon be over, and they wanted to be our friends.

In Landstuhl,[162] we administered medical help to Displaced Persons in a nearby camp. Hundreds of them of both sexes and all ages, slave laborers used by the Nazis from Eastern Russia and the Balkans, filled the shed-type buildings. The Allies were working on transporting them home in time.

I really had nothing to do because hostilities had ceased in this part of Germany, so I got lots of sleep time. That was when we started our *Clearing Company Diary*.[163] Information came from different sources, but mostly from day orders kept by the company clerk, and Major Pat, who was a nut about keeping a personal diary. We were not permitted to keep personal diaries during the War for fear that the enemy would get their hands on them, so we had to have permission from headquarters to write one. We all contributed thoughts and experiences. Each of us had his own memories to tell, but we limited the diary's length to highlights.

In late April, we left Landstuhl, moved on to Kaiserslautern, and set up in a school building. There was little to do; we weren't in war all the time, so the fraternization rule was lifted and we were free to associate with girls.

By the second week in May, the War was finally over and needless to say, I was happy and relieved. I felt more like a tourist than a soldier.

After a short time, we relocated to the city of Karlsruhe and were housed in a small hotel on the main street near the high-rise apartments. Our mission here was to help the DPs. They were traveling by train on their way back home and we were there to provide medical support. We had lots of free time, and the guys hatched many romances.

After Karlsruhe, we moved to the city of Baden-Baden sometime in early June. Once again, there wasn't much to do. We were like tourists: no restrictions, or duties except to be Orderly of the Day (OD) or do the company roster check. While we were there, the Army gave new shoulder patches for the other arm. We became part of the 106th Infantry, because the 28th was getting ready to go to the Pacific.

The Army formulated a point system to determine who would be first to return home from the European Theater. It determined the number of points according to length of service, overseas time, rank, battle stars and medals. I had 145 points; those having higher totals were flown home soon after the War's end, but they stopped the system just above me, so I had to either stay to be sorted out for the invasion of Japan, or a boat home. Any anxiety anyone had about going to the Pacific ended when they dropped the Atomic Bomb.

In mid-August, General Eisenhower issued an order allowing anybody who wanted it to visit places of interest, but only in the United States Zone of Occupation, and that meant only southwestern Germany and Austria. Ten men, an officer with enough water and Ten-in-One Rations for ten days could get a truck and venture out. We made up a group and traveled across the Bavarian region. We visited Dachau, near Munich, where we saw gas chambers, gallows, ovens. We visited Berchtesgarten, Hitler's retreat in the mountains. The lodge had been heavily bombed. There was a large picture window with no glass in it, and I looked out at the splendid view.

We then moved on to Innsbruck in western Austria where two young girls asked our officer, Captain Cottom, to visit one of their grandmothers in a village high in the mountains. The girl took us there, and the grandmother treated us like royalty, feeding us ham, eggs and fresh biscuits. We stayed in a hotel there for several days and then went on to Salzburg, where we saw Mozart's house. We saw a lot, including Konigssee Lake, the highest in the world, and the Brenner Pass. We couldn't go farther into Italy because of the rules.

We left by train sometime in mid August for Camp Lucky Strike, a hot and dusty tent city for thousands of soldiers near Le Havre, a busy port for the Allies. We slept eight to a tent and on folding cots, and we stood in long lines for everything from chow to toilets and showers. I spent my days playing cards and going to open air movies with the guys from my outfit.

After about two weeks, we finally boarded trucks for the docks. We passed fields lined with thousands of stored Army equipment; trucks, Jeeps, airplanes, tanks and guns. We were happy when we reached the docks. Our equipment now was just a small duffel bag with personal items, no packs, no helmets. The HMS *Queen Mary* was there, but it wasn't for us. Our ship was a small tub called the *Sommeldyke*, a converted cargo ship half the size. We crossed the Atlantic in six days. It was warm and calm, and we spent most of the time on deck, often shirtless, playing cards.

On one bright morning in late August, we went on deck and there before us was the Statue of Liberty in all its glory. We entered New York Harbor, and huge New York City Fireboats saluted us with great streams of water. We continued up the Hudson River for several miles and with the help of tugboats, we berthed at a temporary pier near a large Army camp known as Camp Shanks. We were only there for two or three days, then we boarded a troop train for an overnight trip to Indiantown Gap.

The barracks at the Gap were overcrowded, so the Army gave us passes to go home for a week. After that, we were supposed to get our discharge papers and $250.00 mustering out pay. "Tubby" Barnhart went home by bus, and Dad met us in Donegal.

When it was time to go back, Tubby borrowed a car. Back at the Gap they instructed us about the merits of staying in the Army. But I had had enough! I had spent five years in the Army.

When I got back to Fairfield, I moved in with Dad and Mother to a smaller house across the way from the homestead, which they had sold. I took the GI Bill and went to the University of Pittsburgh at Johnstown for classes in engineering.

I married Helen on 17 April 1946. She lost her job at Penelec Powerhouse because they didn't employ married women. She got another job while I stayed in school. After I had spent two years in school, Helen had a rough time delivering our firstborn, so I quit school and went to work at the Seward Powerhouse in 1949 as assistant field engineer. Eventually, I became superintendent. Then I went to work as a field engineer on the Johnstown War Memorial, the Johnstown Mercy Hospital and the Conemaugh Generating Station and finally in the office of Dill Construction. I retired from Dill in 1986.

In 1946, we started to have reunions. The first one was in Lancaster, Pennsylvania. We met in the armory. There were three-hundred of us, all guys. We slept on cots! That was our reunion!

Finally, we said, "That's enough of this horseshit!"

The next year we brought our wives and had a nice "to do" at a hotel.

I was president of the group for a long time. I was also the secretary, so I'd keep track of all those who had passed on. It got to the point where so many had died, and for some travel was difficult. So we stopped having reunions. The last one we had was in Ligonier, Pennsylvania. There were eighty-two people there. Only thirty-three of them were veterans. After sixty years, we disbanded.

Three of Paul Luther's buddies. Left to right: Pooch, Young, Wallo.

Paul Luther with a souvenir Swastika (*Hakenkreuz*) atop a castle wall in Landstuhl, Germany, in 1945.

"I'll Be in This Thing Before It's Over."

Paul R. Maher, O.S.B.

Fifteenth Air Force
454th Bomb Group
739th Squadron
Born in Latrobe, Pennsylvania, 30 November 1925
Saint Vincent Archabbey and College, Latrobe, Pennsylvania

"It was rumored that the major told his ground crews that he wanted thirteen planes in the air every day, and if they didn't succeed they'd lose their passes to town. So we got the feeling, and I think it was partially justified, that we were flying planes that weren't always ready to fly; but rather than lose their passes to town, the ground crews would sign off on the planes. Once, while we were landing, there were four, crashed B–24s still on the side of the runway. That hadn't happened all that same day; they just hadn't been cleaned up yet. On another occasion during night training, we went out to the line to our plane, and our pilot asked the crew chief, 'Is this thing ready to go?' And the crew chief answered, 'Yeah, it's ready to go, but I wouldn't fly in it!' We flew in it anyway—for the practice."

MOST OF MY FAMILY was born in a brewery! My father worked as the bookkeeper in the old Latrobe Brewery that much later became Rolling Rock, and during Prohibition he was the caretaker of the property. We lived in the Brewmaster's apartment. My parents raised eleven children, eight boys and three girls. Most of them went to Latrobe High School. My oldest brother, by the time the War came along, was a diocesan priest.

On 1 September 1939, when Hitler invaded Poland, I was just finishing eighth grade and getting ready to go to high school. My second-oldest brother, a postal worker, was already in the military, because they had the peacetime draft back around 1940, and he was caught up in that. He ended up at Fort Knox, Kentucky with the tankers, and they put him in the postal service there, too.

When we got into the War on 8 December 1941, I was in my third year of high school. I didn't go to Latrobe High School because I had a scholarship to the Saint Vincent Prep School. Two of my older brothers were already day students at the college. Once we got into the War, it was sort of rapid-fire drafting into the service, so three more brothers went into the service rather quickly. When I finished high school in June 1943, I was still only seventeen years old, one year from draft age. I had an interest in history and geography, so from the beginning of the war in Europe I sort of followed the developments in the newspapers, magazines and radio. I can still hear Edward R. Murrow saying, "This is London calling." By 1943, we were deeply involved in the War. One evening at dinner I said, "I'll be in this thing before it's over."

My mother got a little excited by that remark, mostly because I was just a high-school kid, just seventeen and one year from draft age. At the time, seminarians were being given exemptions from military service. Father Edmund Cuneo, Headmaster of the prep school said to me, "Why don't you join the Scholasticate, the minor seminary? You can be exempted."

I didn't want to do that. It didn't feel right; I already had four brothers in the service, and to me that would look like I was just trying to get out of serving. Though I had thought about becoming a diocesan priest, I wasn't certain about it, so I didn't take Father Edmund's advice. I worked in the local post office until I was eighteen, and then I was drafted. Right after my birthday, I wrote to the draft board, notifying them I was eighteen and the sooner the better, so to speak. In January 1944 I was admitted to the military.

The recruit train began in Pittsburgh and picked up fellows as it went along. It picked up a group of us in Latrobe and took us to the induction center at Fort Meade, Maryland. While we were being processed, one of my buddies from Latrobe said, "You know, we probably ought to volunteer for this Air Cadet Program, otherwise we'll end up in the infantry."

The Air Cadet Program was still one of the only things you could volunteer for. I hadn't planned on doing that, but he talked me into it. So we volunteered.

We went through the usual processing, coordination tests, physical exams, and the like. At one place was a fellow who had a book set out in front of him. He flipped pages that looked like camouflage. He'd ask, "What do you see on this page?"

And we'd answer some number or other. It was the color-blindness test. I had no problem, but my buddy who got me to volunteer couldn't make out the numbers, and he flunked out right on the spot.

I went to BTC 10 (Basic Training Center) in Greensboro, North Carolina. We were still there when the Army higher-ups dropped the Air Cadet Program. The men who were in the program but had come from other outfits—the infantry or artillery—were sent back to their units. We heard, but I didn't know if it was true, that forty-thousand infantrymen went back to their units. Fellows like me, who had never been in another outfit, had come from civilian life, they made us gunners in the Air Force.

I was sent to Laredo, Texas, for gunnery school, but they also trained me for a particular turret. I was trained for the tail turret of a B–24, but not yet assigned to a crew. They didn't ask if anyone wanted to be a gunner. They just assigned us. There was a cable and pulley system to close the turret doors behind me, but the system didn't work perfectly. I was actually too tall to be a tail gunner, and I soon realized that I might be stuck if I squeezed up and got those doors closed. I never consulted anyone, but I just adopted a personal policy never to close them when I was on a combat mission. So when I swung the turret around—it was hydraulic—there was an opening about ten-inches wide where I'd be looking out into space. It wasn't enough to allow me to fall out, but it was interesting!

I had a ten-day furlough before I reported to Lincoln, Nebraska, one of the staging areas for the Second Air Force, the Air Force Training Command, which had about a dozen training bases located throughout the United States. That's where I was assigned to a crew, ten men in a B–24. We went to Casper, Wyoming for a couple months training.

It wasn't in combat that I first became aware of death's reality in war. It was at Casper. I was there only a couple months, and in my last nineteen days of training, twenty-one men were killed. Later, in Italy, we kidded, "This war isn't as bad as Casper."

And in no one case was it ten men at one time; it took more than a couple of crashes. First of all, there were pilots who were still training; second, the planes tended to be old, combat-weary machines that had been brought back specifically for training.

When we got to Casper, they got our group into a big theater, something like a thousand men. A major, the head of the base, right from the start chewed us out, saying we were the scrapings from the bottom of the barrel; he really put us down.

I said to myself, *'I'm eighteen years old, I just finished high school, what are you talking about?'*

It was rumored that the major told his ground crews that he wanted thirteen planes in the air every day, and if they didn't succeed they'd lose their passes to town. So we got the feeling, and I think it was partially justified, that we were flying planes that weren't always ready to fly; but rather than lose their passes to town, the ground crews would sign off on the planes. Once, while we were landing, there were four, crashed B–24s still on the side of the runway. That hadn't happened all that same day; they just hadn't been cleaned up yet.

On another occasion during night training, we went out to the line to our plane, and our pilot asked the crew chief, "Is this thing ready to go?"

And the crew chief answered, "Yeah, it's ready to go, but I wouldn't fly in it!"

We flew in it anyway—for the practice.

Once we were landing after a night flight. The cabin wasn't enclosed, and there was a strict no-smoking rule because of fuel fumes. We were up two-hundred feet or so, when a fire broke out in the electrical equipment in the waist. It was a four-by-four area, and the sparks were falling.

I thought, 'We're not allowed to smoke, and here's all these sparks coming down!'

We really sweated out those last thirty seconds before we landed.

One day we were supposed to go to the gunnery range for practice, and then, while still flying, to the bombing range for practice with dummy bombs. We finished up gunnery practice, but before we got to the bombing range the plane's engineer, an enlisted man who did fuel transfers and other stuff, checked the fuel gauges and told us not to go because our plane was too low on fuel. Now the gauges weren't perfect, but the engineer knew.

Our pilot was like, "Oh, no, no, we've only been up so long; I'm sure we have enough."

"Yeah. It's ready to go,
but I wouldn't fly in her."
Michael Wilkey 2006

All of this was between the engineer, who was a sergeant, and the pilot, who was a second lieutenant, so the engineer backed off, but only after he warned, "I don't think we should do this."

We dropped some bombs over the bombing range and then came back to base. Once the plane set down, they had to bring out a tractor to pull us off the runway. We had no fuel left! Who knows what would've happened thirty seconds sooner! We didn't complain, but we were a little nervous! Our pilot got chewed out, and at the next day's officers' briefing, his superiors referred to the incident, adding that pilots weren't to be taking similar chances.

After Casper, we went to another staging area in Topeka, Kansas. Ten days later we left for Camp Patrick Henry in Virginia. At mealtime there we were served by German POWs. They had it made!

Then they put us in a French ship that had a French-speaking crew. It was a little convoy of about seven ships, three transports and four destroyers. It was well into November 1944, so the nitty-gritty stuff was pretty well behind us, but everything was still blacked out. We were stacked up in three layers of bunks. The best bunks were the ones on top, in case anyone got sick and threw up. It was a thirteen-day trip. We knew there was a remote chance of U-Boat attacks, but nothing happened. At night we went up on deck. It was pitch black, and there was always a beautiful night sky. We saw porpoises running alongside the ship, something we never could have seen if the lights had been on.

We landed in Naples, Italy, and went from the ship into the shore over planks that actually led over another ship which was sunk on its side, either on purpose to avoid being captured or by aerial bombardment. Then they put us onto another ship, a coastal ship called the *Arundel Castle*, a British ship and took us to Taranto, a big Italian naval base inside the heel of the Italian boot. When we landed, they put us on trucks and took us to Gioia del Colle, about forty miles inland, and a staging area for the Fifteenth, where we were processed. After that, we got on trucks again and went to the 739th Squadron, 454th Bomb Group, about seven miles outside the city of Cerignola, a flat, wheat-growing area known as the "Breadbasket of Italy." It was the same place where Mussolini had situated his airfields.

We had two runways, parallel with each other, and they were about three-thousand-feet long. At each end there was a stretch of about one-hundred yards of steel matting, sheets that were about twenty-feet long, maybe four-feet wide, with holes in it, hooked together, making a relatively solid surface there for landing. The rest of the runway was just hard dirt, stone, stuff like that. The four squadrons, the 736th, 737th, 738th and 739th, were clustered around these two runways, and the headquarters for the 454th Group was ten or fifteen minutes walking distance from the 739th tent area. By this time I had my nineteenth birthday. It was 30 November 1944. The front line was above Florence, around Bologna.

To "get our feet wet" new crews were split up, five and five and flew the first couple missions with five men from a veteran crew. After that, the split crews rejoined and flew together. I wasn't on the first mission, but my pilot was flying copilot. They ran into Flak, and my pilot took shrapnel in his right arm. The plane also lost half

Paul Maher's Air Force ID card to be handed to the Russians in the event of a landing in Russian-held territory.

U.S. ARMY AIR FORCE

IDENTIFICATION CARD
УДОСТОВЕРЕНИЕ ЛИЧНОСТИ
DOWOD OSOBISTY
LEGITIMACE
LEGITIMACIJA
SZEMÉLYAZONOSSÁGI IGAZOLVÁNY
LEGITIMATION

Paul R. Maher
SIGNATURE

I AM AN AMERICAN AIRMAN.
PLEASE TAKE ME TO YOUR COMMANDING OFFICER AND NOTIFY NEAREST AMERICAN OR BRITISH MILITARY MISSION IN BELGRADE, BUCHAREST, POLTAVA OR OTHER NEARBY PLACE. ALSO, PLEASE ARRANGE FOR TRANSPORTATION.

Paul R. Maher THANK YOU

SHOW THIS TO RUSSIANS:

Я АМЕРИКАНСКИЙ ЛЕТЧИК
ПОЖАЛУЙСТА ПРЕДСТАВТЕ МЕНЯ ВАШЕМУ КОМАНДИРУ И УВЕДОМИТЕ БЛИЖАЙШУЮ АМЕРИКАНСКУЮ ИЛИ БРИТАНСКУЮ ВОЕННУЮ МИССИЮ В БЕЛГРАДЕ, БУХАРЕСТЕ, ПОЛТАВЕ ИЛИ В ДРУГОМ БЛИЖАЙШЕМ МЕСТЕ. ТАКЖЕ РАСПОРЯДИТЕСЬ О ПЕРЕДВИЖЕНИИ.
БОЛЬШОЕ СПАСИБО!

Reverse side of Paul Maher's ID card in Polish, Czech, Croatian, Hungarian, and German.

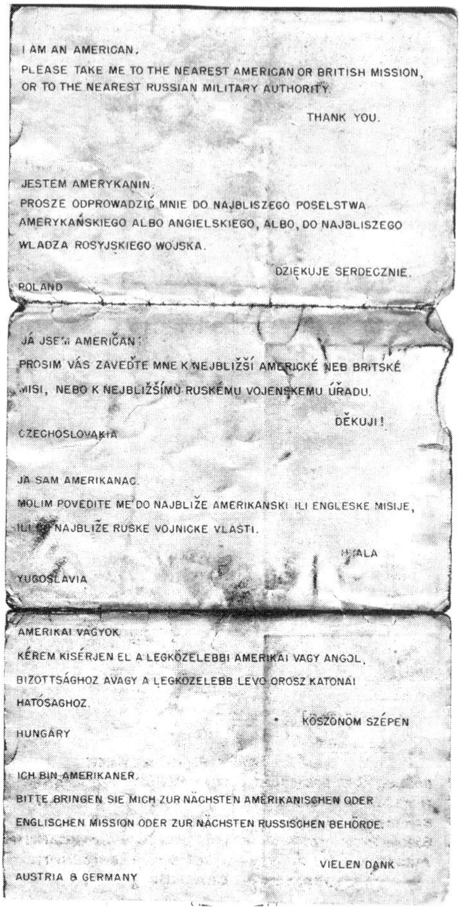

I AM AN AMERICAN.
PLEASE TAKE ME TO THE NEAREST AMERICAN OR BRITISH MISSION, OR TO THE NEAREST RUSSIAN MILITARY AUTHORITY.
THANK YOU.

JESTEM AMERYKANIN.
PROSZE ODPROWADZIĆ MNIE DO NAJBLISZEGO POSELSTWA AMERYKAŃSKIEGO ALBO ANGIELSKIEGO, ALBO, DO NAJBLISZEGO WLADZA ROSYJSKIEGO WOJSKA.
DZIĘKUJE SERDECZNIE.
POLAND

JÁ JSEM AMERIČAN.
PROSIM VÁS ZAVEĎTE MNE K NEJBLIŽŠÍ AMERICKÉ NEB BRITSKÉ MISI, NEBO K NEJBLIŽŠÍMU RUSKÉMU VOJENSKEMU ÚŘADU.
DĚKUJI!
CZECHOSLOVAKIA

JA SAM AMERIKANAC.
MOLIM POVEDITE ME DO NAJBLIŽE AMERIKANSKI ILI ENGLESKE MISIJE, ILI DO NAJBLIŽE RUSKE VOJNICKE VLASTI.
HVALA
YUGOSLAVIA

AMERIKAI VAGYOK.
KÉREM KISÉRJEN EL A LEGKÖZELEBBI AMERIKAI VAGY ANGOL BIZOTTSÁGHOZ AVAGY A LEGKÖZELEBB LEVŐ OROSZ KATONAI HATÓSAGHOZ.
KÖSZÖNÖM SZÉPEN
HUNGARY

ICH BIN AMERIKANER.
BITTE BRINGEN SIE MICH ZUR NÄCHSTEN AMERIKANISCHEN ODER ENGLISCHEN MISSION ODER ZUR NÄCHSTEN RUSSISCHEN BEHÖRDE.
VIELEN DANK
AUSTRIA & GERMANY

Paul Maher (left) and nose-gunner Bill Kearney after a mission.

Paul Maher and Consolitaded B-24 Liberator, "Miss America." This aircraft was the oldest in the 739th Squadron, and flew many missions before Father Maher flew in it. The plane's bombing missions and score of destroyed enemy fighter planes have been painted on the fuselage.

May 1945. Paul Maher on the Isle of Capri sitting on a pedestal that was part of 2,000-year-old Tiberian castle.

Paul Maher poses in front of his tent in Italy.

its oxygen supply. Our navigator was also in the crew, and he had to share his oxygen mask with a buddy. The veteran pilot was very good. He put the ship on a 180-degree, due-south course and brought the ship home. My pilot was in the hospital for two or three weeks, and we didn't fly as a crew until he was strong enough to come back. We weren't complaining about the delay. Our pilot was a little eager, but we weren't. When he finally came back, we began to fly missions.

On our missions we had P–51 escorts, the black pilots, the Tuskegee Airmen. We were very happy they were there with us. They were very fine fighter pilots. The Germans weren't any longer able to put up many fighters, but they were using jets. One of our missions was to the Munich area[164] where the Germans had three airfields where they had based some of their jet fighters. The briefing officers told us, "We don't think they'll come up, because as far as we know they don't have any fuel."

I can't say for sure that I ever saw an enemy plane, though there were a couple of times when we saw a plane off in the distance, perhaps a German measuring our altitude for their anti-aircraft. We were always on alert because we couldn't be sure. Flak was always our worry. Most of the anti-aircraft guns were 88s, but they were beginning to use 120s. The 88 bursts were, as I recall, a grayish-white puff, while the 120 bursts were great, black things. We could always tell which was which and whether they were using a mix.

Even then, many of my missions weren't heavy on Flak, except for my first mission to Verona with half my crew and a veteran crew. We were after some marshalling yards, and we seemed to stay in the Flak a long time. It seemed like half an hour. Our exit route took us over the Adriatic in a direct line over Venice, so they must have had guns all along the way. We came back okay, but it was scary. That evening a big, extroverted fellow from Chicago, who already had fifteen or twenty missions, was impressed! He came into our tents laughing, "I hear you guys had a real baptism of fire today."

We were over Vienna a couple of times. One time I think the whole Fifteenth was with us. Half of them bombed marshaling yards in the north, and the other half bombed in the south. Vienna was a big city. My toughest mission was to Linz, the St. Valentin s uburb and the Herman Goering Tank Works. At briefing, they told us there were four-hundred anti-aircraft guns at Linz. On these missions not every group or squadron suffered equally. This day, our squadron of seven planes suffered. The first two planes went down over the target; the third plane made an emergency landing halfway home, on an emergency strip on an island off the coast of Yugoslavia. Four of us got back, one on two engines. Now a B–24 didn't maintain altitude very long on two engines, so I guess the second of the four engines failed when he was pretty close to home. Two of the squadron came back on three engines. Ours was the only plane to come home on all four.

In Italy, we had a lot of respect for ground crews. Over there, as opposed to when we were in training, the planes were better, later models, and our pilot was by then more experienced. When did I start to get scared? Well, fear was a gradual thing. I was a believing Catholic. With that being understood, there's a certain element of fatalism attached. When it was your time, it was your time. I was thankful I didn't go over a year or two before, when they were bombing Ploesti and other places badly. In our case, if seven hundred planes went up on a mission or a combination of missions, maybe a day or so later we'd hear or read that maybe sixteen planes went down. Well, sixteen out of seven hundred wasn't bad, unless you were one of the sixteen! Guys would go out on thirty-second or thirty-third missions and not come back. I got in when it was less dangerous, but scary enough.

There was a rule that we could go home after thirty-five missions. On 8 May 1945, when the war in Europe ended, I had twenty-one. Some of the final missions tended to be "milk runs," maybe bombing troop concentrations above the front lines. It would be "Angel" area or "Charlie" area, but not a city. There was also a rule that if our mission was canceled and we were on the southern side of the Alps away from German territory, we were supposed to bring our bombs home, not jettison them in the sea. We didn't get credit for canceled missions. One time we had a mission to northern Italy canceled because of cloud cover, so we came back to Cerignola. Routinely, planes landed one after another; my plane landed, and then we pulled off the end of the runway and taxied to our parking space. The plane after us landed and was pulling off the runway, and just as the next plane touched the runway it blew up. We heard this BOOM, and turned around. A few hundred yards away we saw this big cloud of smoke. Ten men dead, gone; I mean, no chance in the world. That was just two planes behind us, and we had landed with all our bombs, too.

During the last couple days of the War, everyone knew it was winding down. It was V-E Day for the west, but not for the Russians. Their date for the ending was 9 May. On a field right next to our tent area we had a big picnic with hotdogs and beer to celebrate the end of the War. We all thought that we'd get a thirty-day leave, go home to the States and then (especially me, who hadn't completed the required number of missions) ship to the Pacific where the war with Japan was still going on.

Meanwhile, we had been routinely scheduled for R&R, rest and relaxation. A truck took us off for Naples, and from there we went to the Isle of Capri for a week. It was a special time. The officers got their R&R in Rome. After leave we returned to Cerignola. My crew and I didn't leave Italy until 6 July. At first, it was just killing time, and they didn't have us on parade or stuff like that, but then they started these PT, physical training sessions and parades. That wasn't pleasant, but for us the war in Europe, at least, was over.

We flew once or twice when the pilot wanted to get in some flying time, and once we flew up over Mount Vesuvius, but not over northern Italy or Germany.

Eventually they wanted to get the planes back to the States, and they had this route for flying the planes home. Each B–24 would have its crew of ten and five extra men, maybe some ground crew, for a total of fifteen. We went from Cerignola to Marrakech in Morocco the first day; we only flew during the daytime, seven or eight hours, something like that. We did an overnight in Marrakech; we stayed in a tent and we didn't get to go into the town. Second day, Marrakesh to Dakar; now we were on the west coast of Africa. The next hop was across the south Atlantic. We heard that the night before a C–54 had taken off from Dakar and wasn't heard from again. We were to fly the next day!

From Dakar we went to Fortaliza, Brazil and from there to Georgetown in British Guiana (now it's just Guyana) and next day from Georgetown to Puerto Rico. Then we flew from Puerto Rico to a base in Florida. Up to that point we were flying a B–24, bringing it home, but there we left it and they put us on a C–47 and flew us up to Indiantown Gap, near Harrisburg, Pennsylvania, where we were given our thirty-day leave.

I came home to Latrobe, and three of my brothers who were in the military were there. A fifth brother was still a ground crewman with the Second Air Force in Ardmore, Oklahoma. While I was home, the United States dropped the Atomic Bomb on Japan and 15 August, the Feast of the Assumption, was proclaimed Victory over Japan Day. After that, the whole war was over, but I was still in the Army. I went back to Indiantown Gap, and they sent me out to Sioux Falls, South Dakota, just to wait to out-process. I was discharged on 4 November 1945.

By the time of my discharge, I had pretty much made up my mind to give the Benedictine monastery at Saint Vincent a try because I had been impressed by the men who had taught me in prep school there. I still wasn't sure, but I started college in February and got in the second semester in the summer on their accelerated schedule. After my second year, I joined the Novitiate.

My time in the service helped mature my decision to become a priest, though I probably would have made the same decision anyway. At least while I was in the service I realized that I wouldn't be happy doing anything else unless I tried training for the priesthood. Once I started to study, I never had a serious vocation problem. I might have been frustrated with a particular job or superior, but never with my vocation.

I began teaching philosophy in 1957. A confrere, Father Sebastian Samay, taught with me. In 1962, we attended a one-day philosophy conference at Penn State University. On the way home, Sebastian and I were in the back seat of the car, having a conversation. It just happened to be 8 May.

I said to Sebastian, "Do you know what day this is?"

"No."

"Well, it's V-E Day."

Anyway, that got us talking about the War. During the War, Sebastian was a young Hungarian refugee, about seventeen. Hungary was allied with Germany then, and they began to draft young Hungarians. In the closing months of the War, a group of them was being marched off to Germany for training. They'd march so many miles a day, then stop for the night. One day they stopped in Graz, Austria, where they had to take shelter from a bombing raid. Sebastian got into a basement with his group and some civilians, women and children. The building was hit and it collapsed. No one was killed, but they were trapped in the basement and had to dig themselves out. Eventually, the group got underway again.

When Sebastian mentioned the bombing, I thought, *'Graz, Graz?'*

I remembered having been over Graz on one of our raids, at least once, maybe three times. It wasn't a big city, and ordinarily we didn't bother with small towns like that unless it had marshalling yards, and it did. So, we bombed Graz in Spring 1945,[165] and there was a good chance Sebastian was beneath us taking shelter in that basement. We still kid around about that.

When we select a new abbot, we have a step in the process called the *scrutinium*, a secret examination of the candidate. Before I was elected Abbot, Sebastian got up and said, "Father Paul bombed me, and now I'm going to bomb him!"

Or so I'm told.

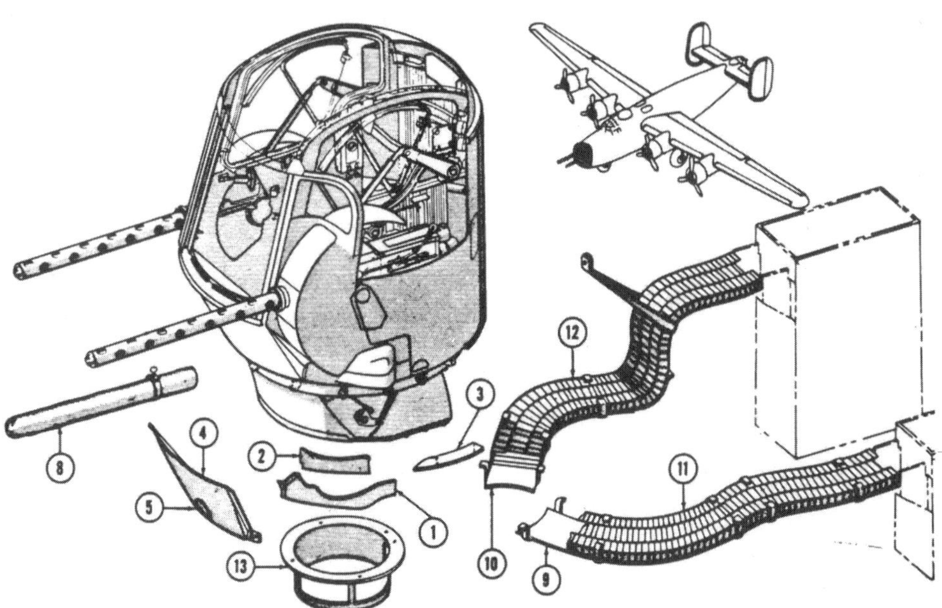

B-24 rear gun turret. US Government publication

Paul Maher, now Abbot Paul Maher, O.S.B., Saint Vincent Archabbey, poses beneath the tail gun of a B-24 at the Arnold Palmer Regional Airport in Latrobe, Pennsylvanial. In the background is a Boeing B-17. The day brought numerous area veterans to the airport to visit and reminisce about the kinds of planes in which they once flew.

"Don't Volunteer for Anything."

Denny D. Matsik

United States Naval Reserve
Escort Carrier USS *Cape Esperance* (CVE–88)
Born in Cuddy, Pennsylvania, 29 April 1916
Natrona Heights, Pennsylvania

"When I was drafted, they called me into the office and said, 'We can get you a deferment if you want, we could declare you necessary to the war effort here at home.' I said, 'Don't bother, all my buddies are in now, there's nobody left around here.'"

FOR A WHILE I wasn't eligible to go into the service because I had a hernia, and I wouldn't have been able to pass the physical with that. So in 1942, I made an appointment with a doctor and he repaired the hernia. That made me eligible to be drafted. Eventually, I was notified to report to Greensburg for my physical.

When I was drafted, they called me into the office and said, "We can get you a deferment if you want, we could declare you necessary to the war effort here at home."

I said, "Don't bother, all my buddies are in now, there's nobody left around here."

After we passed the physical, we had seven days to clean up any odds and ends, and then we caught a bus to Pittsburgh. The day I was sworn in was the day Mussolini surrendered.

We were then sent from Pittsburgh with a contingent of around sixty men to the Great Lakes Naval Training Station. It was the biggest contingent ever to go to Great Lakes from Pittsburgh. I was at Great Lakes for eight weeks of boot training and a basic engineering course. I got a leave of absence after the eight weeks, and then I was sent to advanced school in Milwaukee.

Those of us there were scheduled for escort carrier service right from the start because those types of ships were getting hammered pretty badly by the Japs and they needed replacements. The escort carriers or CVEs were smaller carriers used for transporting goods. So, we were sent to school in Northberg, Milwaukee, right where they built the engines we had onboard. There we got to see how they built the engines from the ground up, in all the various stages of construction, and that gave us a better understanding of them.

During our second week there we were assigned to a ferry ship that crossed Lake

Michigan, from Milwaukee to the Lovington Ferry. That ship had the same engine that we were learning about. We took turns on the throttle watch, learning how to handle the engine and everything else. That was good hands-on experience for us.

After our two weeks there were completed, we got on a train and went out to Bremerton, Washington. I was on a sleeper car, traveling first class on the Milwaukee/ St. Paul Pacific. It took us a couple days to get out to Bremerton and then we had to stay there a bit because our ship wasn't even built yet.

Eventually it was completed and designated CVE–88. It was named the USS *Cape Esperance*, which meant "Cape of the Spirits," and there were lots of good and evil spirits and a lot of sunken ships left there after the Battle of Cape Esperance, the first engagement where we matched Japanese firepower.

Eventually they finished our ship and they floated it down the Columbia River to Astoria, Oregon and we picked her up there on 9 May 1944. There we commissioned the ship, and then we went up the coast into Puget Sound. That's where we had a short provisioning and preparation period to get the ship ready for the war zone. That included degaussing which protected the hull from anything magnetic like mines or torpedoes. We also made trial runs, "shakedown trips" as we called them, to see if everything could handle the stress of operation.

From Puget Sound we were sent to Frisco and we left from there for our first trip into the Pacific. On that first trip we traveled about fifty-five hundred miles. From that point on we were continually coming in and out of the west coast for various transport duties.

On a typical trip we'd pick up a load and go to Hawaii to deliver the stuff or maybe rendezvous with the fleet and take ammunition, equipment or planes and pilots to wherever the fleet needed them. We were part of what they called the "ferry system." The nice thing was that we were in and out of the States pretty often. The longest time we were out to sea was five months. We supplied materials and men out to the fleet until the very end. After the War ended, we were given the duty of bringing back material and men.

While out at sea we had a lot of general quarters because they never knew if an incoming plane was a friendly or a "bogey." Most of the time the general quarters were false alarms.

Our carrier was built on top of the hull of a transport ship. They put flight decks on it with a hangar deck below the flight deck. To launch planes we used a steam catapult that worked on hydraulic jets. That would give the plane a quick start off and once in the air they'd fly to where they were assigned.

Usually planes would take off, attack a position and then land on an airfield or a larger carrier, whichever they were assigned to. That's actually how we got our battle stars. Some of the planes from our ship made hits on enemy positions before they reported to their mother carrier, and that counted for combat for us.

We carried all manner of planes—fighter planes, torpedo planes and light bombers. All of them were planes that could take off on our shorter deck. Sometimes we delivered Army planes to the Marines, sometimes to the Aussies. It was different every time. We delivered what was needed and where it was needed—the Philippines, Guadalcanal. We had extra oil tanks so we could fuel destroyers and destroyer escorts, the smaller ships. We had a good freezer capacity because we took supplies out to the fleet all the time.

On board they tried to make life as easy as possible. We were on twenty-four hour duties so that there would always be someone on watch. Our engine-room crew took turns standing watches that ran four hours on and eight off, then back on four again and off eight again. It wasn't bad, but sometimes it was quite hard to find time to get rest. Of course, we rotated the schedule to make it fair for everyone.

My sideline job was as a ram-truck operator. When we commissioned the ship, they got all the engineering people together and asked if anybody had experience on high-lift ram trucks. The buzz word was always, "Don't volunteer for anything!"

I knew some of the guys could operate ram trucks, but they adhered to the old adage and didn't volunteer. When they couldn't get anybody I spoke up and said, "Let me take a look at it; I think I can run that thing."

In civilian life I had just gotten my license to drive coal trucks, and I figured if I could do that, I could run a high-lift. The controls were plainly marked so it seemed no problem. I got on and tried everything out. There was no problem. I was glad I volunteered, because it saved me from KP. One day they brought a one-hundred-pound bag of potatoes for us to peel. The master-at-arms came over and asked, "Which one of you is Denny Matsik?"

I said, "I am."

He said, "You're wanted on the flight deck to run the ram truck."

That rescued me from KP duty, and after that the commander said I wasn't to be put on KP in case I was needed to run the ram.

So it worked out for me! Some of the guys didn't like it that I broke the rules, but I was glad I did! I'd be sitting up there on the ram truck and they'd be sweating, carrying boxes and stuff.

We were always assigned to a task force. For a while we were attached to the Third Fleet, another time we were attached to the Fifth Fleet. One was headed by Halsey. One was headed by Nimitz. The flag ship for the Third Fleet was the carrier *Yorktown.*

There were just an incredible amount of ships involved in fleet operations—big carriers, battleships, cruisers, destroyers, just every kind of ship I could imagine.

We were close to real action only once. We were going through the Surigao Straits in the Philippines and a Japanese submarine surfaced along the shoreline. A couple PBYs came out and dropped depth charges and hit the sub. It was in rather shallow water along the coast so they got it very easy.

We were, of course, aware of the Kamikazes because we'd talk to people from other ships that had been attacked by them but we never experienced a Kamikaze attack ourselves, fortunately. The escort carriers were at the mercy of them, and if they hit any part of one it usually sank.

Of course we had a few defensive guns, one 5-inch gun on the fantail and around the flight deck they had 40mm cannons, 20mm cannons and machine guns. All of those were for defense against Kamikaze attacks.

We were in the great typhoon which hit our fleet on 18 December 1944. It was survival of the fittest at that time and a weather officer at one of our reunions explained that the last weather report he had gotten said the typhoon was headed almost due north. He relayed that information to the captain and the captain said, "Okay, we'll go due west."[166]

What we didn't know and what the weather officer didn't know was that typhoons changed course, like any storm, and this one turned northwest. We ended up traveling along with it, about nine miles from the eye. We were lucky to have survived. In fact, we lost three destroyers in that storm because they ran out of fuel. We had been refueling destroyers the morning the storm blew up, and it became too rough for us to finish. The ship beside us would roll one way and our ship the other, and that would pull the refueling hoses apart like they were strings. When those three destroyers ran out of fuel they lost all power and were at the mercy of the storm. They sent search parties to find survivors, but the searches were unsuccessful.

During the typhoon we were carrying planes on the top deck of the ship and the ship was pitching and rolling far past the point of roll advised by the Kaiser Company who had built it. So it was a good thing that the planes on top broke their cables and went into the ocean because if they had still been attached we'd have rolled past the point of return and most likely would have gone under the water. The planes were tied down with wire cable instead of the rope which we usually used. The rope would have been useless in the storm, but it didn't matter. The wind snapped the cable like thread.

Eventually the War wrapped up for us and the supplies were no longer needed. I was discharged on 6 May 1946 after thirty-five months in service.

When I came home and went back to the mill I found out that they were discontinuing my department. As a result, I was put on as extra labor in another department. They were obligated to give me a job. I worked there for a year in the sheet department.

I wasn't getting anywhere, so I said, "This isn't working."

I took a leave of absence from work and enrolled at the University of Pittsburgh in the engineering program. We went by trimesters at the time, nine in total. By going three summers and six regular fall and spring trimesters, I was able to complete the degree in three years. Work was kind of scarce after I graduated and I had a little difficulty getting back in because of the leave of absence. Then I got a letter saying I either had to return to work or take severance pay. I took the severance pay, and that made it difficult to break back in. Fortunately, things picked up a little bit, and they started hiring. I was quality control for the rest of my time with Allegheny Ludlum. I did the right thing when I took off and went to school.

Our ship was moth-balled twice after April of 1946. They decommissioned it and then they recommissioned it for the Korean War. Then they put it back into mothballs again in Puget Sound and then they recommissioned it again for the Vietnam War. Our ship had about fifteen years of service, but it's scheduled to be scrapped now.

There are a lot of veterans that don't want to talk about their experiences. They'd rather forget the whole mess. A young fellow from New Jersey called me one day; he was at the Smithsonian looking at the old records of our ship because his dad served on it as a radio man. His father's name was Martin, right next to mine on the list. The dad never told his son about the War.

I wouldn't trade my experience in the Navy for anything, but I wouldn't want to do it again.

Together Again. June 15-18 2006 reunion of CVE 88 - *USS Cape Esperance*, San Antonio, Texas. Four of the original "Plank Oweners." LR: Denny D. Matsik (Foward Engine Room); Dominic Shemo (After Engine Room); Wilbur Green (Motor Launch Operator); Harold Daum (Pharmacist Mate). *Courtesy: Denny Matsik.*

USS Cape Esperance. US Navy photo.

All Together, Mates!
Let's Sink 'Em!

"For You Der Var Ist Ofer!"

John "Jack" McCracken

Eighth Air Force
390th Bomb Group
570th Squadron
Born in Pittsburgh, Pennsylvania, 26 November 1922
Ligonier, Pennsylvania

F - is for the fighter that flew by our sides. O - means only that we love to fly. R - is for the risks we take while up on high. T- is for the target we seldom missed. R - is for the Radar to score the hits. E - is for the enemy that fought us while we flew. S - is for the shots that come to us untrue. S - is for the ship which is master of the blue. Put them all together and they spell "FORTRESS" - the pride of the Red, White and Blue.—Anonymous.

I GREW UP ON a 180-acre farm. My dad farmed and was a township supervisor. Around 1936 we converted the barn to dairy and sold milk to the Otto Milk Company in Pittsburgh. He also mined eight acres of good Pittsburgh coal on the south hill for the farm and sold the coal to families and businesses. The coal money helped pay expenses on the farm.

I wasn't aware of the Depression as much many other people because we always had enough to eat from the farm.

I went to a one-room school. I could only study on Saturday nights and all day Sunday, because I had to help with the milking and other chores, plus I worked the coal mine. I wouldn't get washed up until ten at night, and I washed in a tub and spring water.

By late 1942, all my friends were in the service, so my friend Don and I went to the local draft board to see if we could volunteer for the service we wanted, the Air Force. There was no problem with that, and by 23 January 1943, we were on our way to Fort Meade, Maryland. We got in late at night. There were four trucks there, one for the Army, one for the Navy, one for the Air Force and one for the Marines. Don got called to go on the Air Force truck, and I didn't.

I went over to a first sergeant and said, "Sir, I was supposed to be called for the Air Force truck, but I didn't."

The sergeant introduced me to the military with a chewing out, my first. He said, "You never call a sergeant 'Sir'!"

Then he told me to go back to the barracks and stay. After a while, a clerk came by and told me to get on the Air Force truck.

At first, they wanted to put me in transport because I was six-feet tall, but I managed to pass the physical for gunnery school. I was a pretty good hunter back home so I knew how to shoot and lead with a shotgun, but because a lot of the guys never had any firearms experience we all started with BB guns, then went to .22s, then shotguns and so on.

Tampa, Florida, is were we finally go assigned to crews. We also took combat training there, practicing bomb runs and different drills. That's were I bombed Tallahassee.

I was on my eighteenth bombing mission in a new B–17G.[167] It was a Saturday, 9 September 1944, and we were on a high-altitude mission to the Rheinmetall-Borsig arsenal in Dusseldorf, Germany. The flight was pretty uneventful until I heard Lieutenant Zieff's "Bombs away" over the plane's intercom.[168]

Immediately after that the German anti-aircraft guns opened up. Their Flak was deadly accurate. Our plane took two hits through the left wing and one through the right. A plane off to our right simply exploded. It must have taken a hit in the bomb bay just as bombs were trailing out.

We lost engines one, two and four. Engine three trailed white smoke. The Flak also damaged most of our flight controls, and our pilot, Don Harris, had great difficulty controlling the plane. Don managed a right turn down and away from the formation and target area and headed west in a fast, gliding descent.

Concussion from the exploding plane off our right wing blew out the plexiglass dome window panels in the top turret and created a strong suction that made it difficult for me to get down out of the turret. The intercom was inoperative. As I struggled to get out of the turret I felt Don Harris, the pilot, pull at one leg of my flight suit, trying to get my attention. I finally managed to get free of the turret, I turned to Don who advised me of the extensive damage the plane had suffered. He told me to go to the rear of the plane and check on other damage and to see if anyone was wounded. He also told me to tell the enlisted crew members to throw all the guns, ammo, Flak vests and anything we could get loose out of the plane and prepare for bailout.

I raced through the open bomb bay into the radio room where I found Sergeant Curtis Anderson sitting in his chair looking like he was in a state of shock. He pointed to his foot, showing me a quarter-sized shrapnel hole where shrapnel had hit. Carefully, I removed his boot and sock and saw a puncture wound in the top of his foot. Since it wasn't bleeding, I told Curtis to stay put until I returned.

Right after that I went into the fuselage area and pounded the top of the ball turret, got Sergeant Carnahan's[169] attention and told him to evacuate his position. At the same time, I told the waist gunner, Sergeant Virgil Gordon[170], to start throwing everything he could out of the plane. A lighter plane would make it easier for Don to get farther away from the target area before we bailed out. The civilians living around a place that had just been bombed usually didn't appreciate what happened and often killed or seriously injured captured airmen.

When I got back to the tail section, I gave Sergeant Jarszynka's[171] foot a good jerk.

He sensed we were in trouble as soon as he saw me. He crawled out of his position, and I gave him the same instructions I gave the waist gunner. His two .50-caliber machine guns and ammo would lighten the plane quite a bit.

I got back to Carnahan's position, repeated my bailout instructions and then told him to go to the radio room to administer First Aid to Anderson.

I knew that jettisoning the ball-turret would lighten the plane by several hundred pounds. I grabbed a wrench that was designed to the job and tried to remove nuts on the turret suspension post. The metal of the wrench, however, was softer than the metal on the nuts. It stripped so badly that I couldn't turn the nuts with it. I threw down the wrench and then went to help out with Anderson.

Before returning to the cockpit to report to Don, I told the men to line up at the fuselage door in proper sequence. Anderson was the exception because he was wounded, and I moved him from fourth position to first. Wounded crew members were always the first to go out, providing there was ample time for an orderly bailout.

After that, I reported to Don who told me we needed to bail out, not only because we were getting closer to ground, but also that number-three engine was now on fire. I returned to the rear and waited for the bailout signal. Because the bailout bell wasn't functioning, we had to wait until the copilot, Howard Ford, gave us the signal. It wasn't long until he came through the bomb bay and motioned for us to go.

We were near the city of Bonn at about four-thousand feet when we jumped.

Just as Anderson left the plane, I realized I wasn't wearing my parachute! All I had on was the harness that held the parachute on. Because the space in my turret was so confining, I always kept my parachute on the floor of the cockpit near the turret so I could grab it as I left the turret, but with all the excitement I forgot. I picked up the spare parachute on the fuselage door, but it was full of Flak holes. I ran back through the radio room, through the bomb bay, reached into the cockpit, grabbed my parachute, put it on and ran back through the bomb bay, through the radio room and into the fuselage. When I passed Ford, his face was as white as a ghost's. I hesitated to ask him if he was Okay. He told me to get out, and I did.

When I jumped, I remembered in great detail what I learned in bailout class just the day before. To equalize the pressure on my eardrums, I yelled "GERONIMO!"[172]

On the way down, I counted to ten, straightened out my body, put my arms down at my sides, turned my head to the right and pulled the rip cord with my right hand. The chute opened "as advertised." I felt a jerk when the chuted filled with air and snapped open. The canopy slowed my free-fall speed.

As I floated down, I noticed an unbelievable silence. Then I heard our plane explode. I didn't know if it exploded in the air, or if it hit the ground and exploded. Later, Don told me the plane exploded in midair shortly after he jumped. My first thought was whether or not the crew got out safely, but I wouldn't know for sure until much later.

I was still in the air when I heard gunfire and bullets whizzing by me counterclockwise. The shots seemed to come from a village below. I pulled on my right shroud lines, trying to "dump" air, hoping that I could drift away from the village. It

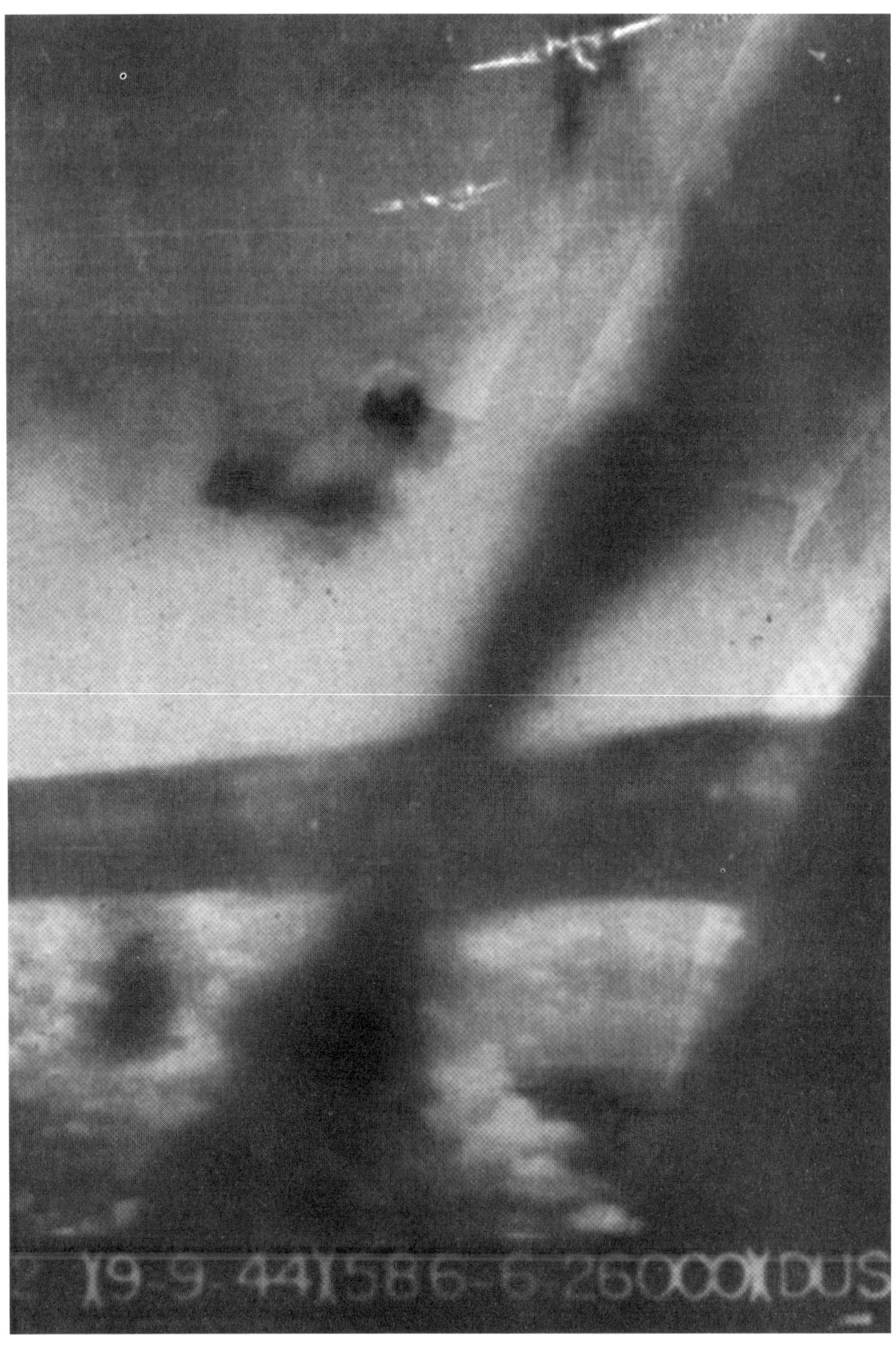

Over Dusseldorf, 9 September 1944. The B-17 at the top of the photo was identified by the Unit Photographer as that of Jack McCracken's plane just after bombs were released. *United States Army Photo.*

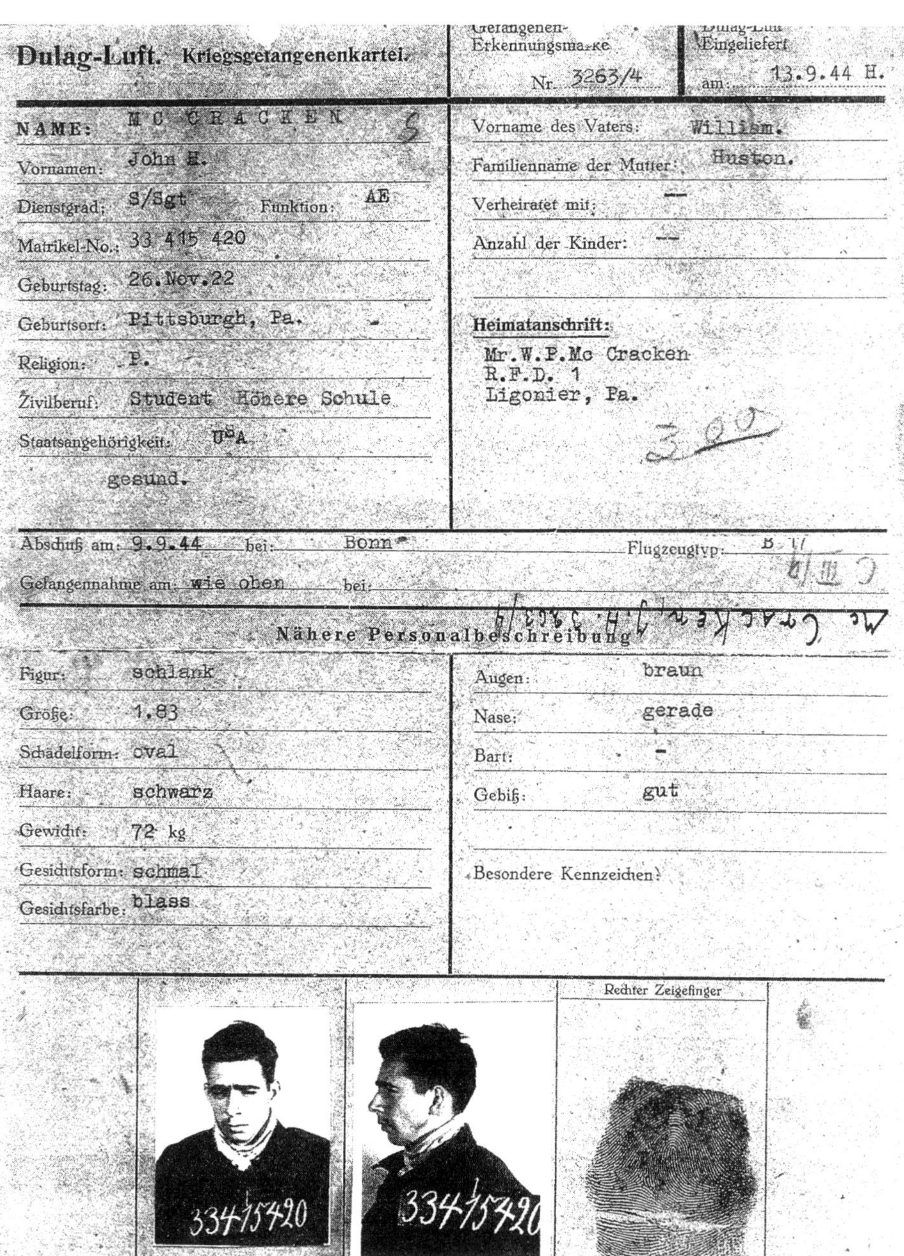

Dulag-Luft. Kriegsgefangenenkartei.

Gefangenen-Erkennungsmarke Nr. 3263/4

Dulag-Luft Eingeliefert am: 13.9.44 H.

NAME: MC CRACKEN

Vornamen: John H.

Dienstgrad: S/Sgt Funktion: AE

Matrikel-No.: 33 415 420

Geburtstag: 26.Nov.22

Geburtsort: Pittsburgh, Pa.

Religion: P.

Zivilberuf: Student Höhere Schule

Staatsangehörigkeit: USA

gesund.

Vorname des Vaters: William.

Familienname der Mutter: Huston.

Verheiratet mit: —

Anzahl der Kinder: —

Heimatanschrift:
Mr.W.P.Mc Cracken
R.F.D. 1
Ligonier, Pa.

300

Abschuß am: 9.9.44 bei: Bonn Flugzeugtyp: B 17

Gefangennahme am: wie oben bei:

Nähere Personalbeschreibung

Figur: schlank

Größe: 1,83

Schädelform: oval

Haare: schwarz

Gewicht: 72 kg

Gesichtsform: schmal

Gesichtsfarbe: blass

Augen: braun

Nase: gerade

Bart: -

Gebiß: gut

Besondere Kennzeichen:

Rechter Zeigefinger

33415420

33415420

Jack McCracken's POW I.D. card

did, but it also caused my body and chute to spin. I tried to stop the spin by crossing my arms above my head and pulling the shroud lines in opposite directions. It didn't help. I pulled too hard and spun faster in the opposite direction.

By now, I was so close to the ground that I could hear birds chirping. I looked to see where I was going to land. I drifted over a narrow forest and then caught a glimpse of a team of horses pulling a farm implement across a plowed field. The ground was coming up fast, and I was still spinning out of control. Then I hit the left side of the horse with the right side of my back, my heels and buttocks struck the ground, my head hit something hard, maybe the ground or the harrow, my feet flew over my head. I lost consciousness.

When I came to, a farmer was holding and twisting my left foot and leg, trying to straighten my legs, both of which were in great pain. The farmer had removed my parachute and harness and placed them on the ground about twenty feet away. I sat on the ground for a while rubbing my knees until the farmer helped me to my feed and walked me over to the horse so I could its harness for support. I noticed that it wasn't a team of horses after all, but a horse and ox yoked together. I had difficulty standing and thought that I might have fractured by knees, especially the left one.

I wasn't sure if the farmer was French or German. I sat down and got the language dictionary from the escape kit we all carried in our flight suits. I turned first to the French section and indicated my identity and need for help. The farmer gently took the dictionary from me, turned to the German section and advised me that, "For you der Var ist ofer!"

The plowed field was about ten acres in size. Along the southern side was a fruit orchard and, beyond that, a farm house. Down a hill, to the east, was the forest that I had drifted over. I thought about making a break for the forest, but wasn't sure my knees were up to it. I knew that if I wanted to escape I had better do it before more Germans arrived on the scene. I decided to push the farmer over onto the harrow and then make a dash for the forest. While I tried to get in position to push him, a small boy and a woman came into the field from the orchard. When they arrived on the scene, I gave the boy my penknife, motioned for the woman to take the silk parachute and then motioned for them to leave. The farmer said something to them that I didn't understand, and the boy and woman headed for the farmhouse.

I tried again to position the farmer between me and the harrow. I bent down to make the farmer believe I was just rubbing my knees. Just as I was about to lurch forward, a truckload of German soldiers drove into the field between me and the forest. It was then I realized the truth of what the farmer had said to me. He was right. For me the War was over.

A German sergeant sent three soldiers down into the forest and then walked up to me and said in good English, "Are you going to be my prisoner?"

I looked at him for a few seconds and said, "Do I have a choice?"

"You do not," he replied.

"Then, I'll go with you," I said.

On my way to the truck I suddenly realized that I was a prisoner of war, alone in a strange land. I had no personal belongings other than the wrist watch my mother had given me when I left for the service. Everything else belonged to the United States government or the Royal Air Force.

I wondered what was going to happen to me. Where was the sergeant taking me? Will I be beaten? Killed? Imprisoned? I knew my odds of completing my required missions were against me; still, I never thought I'd be shot down or even injured. I remembered the stories they told us in England about how Hitler told the German people that all American bomber crews were "Chicago gangsters," and how we would be treated if we were captured.[173]

The sergeant never removed his sidearm from its holster. In fact, he never even put his hand on the holstered gun as he approached me earlier. I felt a little safer because of that, but especially because the sergeant was wearing a *Luftwaffe* uniform and not an SS one.

The sergeant told me to stand beside the truck bed while he went around to the other side to watch for the soldiers he had sent there. While we waited, a dozen or so civilians gathered around me shouting and calling me names. I couldn't make out what they were calling me, but I was sure the words were choice ones. I turned my back to them. One called me a "Baby Killer," and I sensed that he was getting close. I turned my head slightly to the right and saw a man swinging a club. Instinctively, I turned my right shoulder toward the truck bed, and the truck took most of the force of the blow. I got bruised just a bit. At that instant the sergeant came back around, his pistol out and cocked. I had both hands on top of the truck bed so he'd see that I wasn't up to something. He dispersed the crowd and made me get on the truck.

The three soldiers came back out of the forest. With them was our bombardier, Lieutenant Zieff![174]

The truck started off. Zieff sat in the right rear corner, and I sat in the left front. Guards stood in the other two corners, rifles slung over their shoulders. The sergeant ordered us not to talk. We rode through a pine forest. The trees were set out straight and even, and we could see far back into the forest. Zieff and I signaled escape plans to each other. At his signal, we'd jump the guards, get a rifle and force the sergeant and driver to stop the truck and surrender. Zieff and I got into squatting positions. The guards didn't notice. They seemed to be more interested in the forest than in us.

I looked into the forest on both sides of the road, trying to find the best way to run. The forest was full of German soldiers and camouflaged anti-aircraft guns. I slid my feet from under me and sat back down on the floor. I told Zieff that the woods were full of Germans. A guard turned and told me to stop talking. There was no chance of escape.

We arrived at the airdrome at Bonn. They put Zieff and me in a large, empty room. A German officer came in and interrogated us, but we gave him only our name, rank and serial number. He left in frustration.

Later that afternoon, at different times, they brought in five more crew members. By nightfall all the crew was there except Ford and Anderson. We were taken out and questioned individually. Again, we gave only our name, rank and serial number.

The first afternoon, two young boys, with rifles longer than the boys were tall, were our guards. We wondered if they could really shoot the rifles if they had to. The boys started fooling around and accidentally fired one of the rifles. The bullet went into the ceiling. We all sat down on the floor expecting the worst. A sergeant and several soldiers rushed in to see what was happening. They seemed surprised to see us all seated on the floor, not attempting to escape. They relieved the boys and sent in a more mature guard.

Around four o'clock in the afternoon, they took me and another prisoner and put us on a horsedrawn wagon. We had no idea what was happening or where we were going. We rode out into farming country following a wagon trail. After passing several fields, we came to a small building that looked like an American farmer's corn crib. The sides were made of slats spaced several inches apart to allow for air flow. It was filled with unwrapped loaves of German black bread. I couldn't believe that they stored unwrapped bread that way, unprotected from the weather. A guard opened the door and ordered us to load the wagon. When we got back to the airdrome, they gave each one of us a hunk of black bread for dinner. It was sour, moist from rain and inedible, but we learned to eat it, because it was our main diet for the remainder of our captivity. I think the bread had a lot of sawdust in it.

We slept on the wooden floor for the first night. We had no bedding. Most of us were still wearing our heavy flight clothing, and that provided some warmth.

The next morning[175] they gave us another piece of black bread and some *ersatz* coffee. I still couldn't eat the bread, but still kept it in my flight suit until I got hungry enough. Later in the morning they loaded us on a truck and took us to the Bonn train station. They told us we were to be taken to an interrogation center in Frankfurt.

After we boarded the truck, we heard the sound of approaching aircraft, machine-gun fire and a lot of confused shouting from nearby soldiers that were running into a bomb shelter. They left one outside to keep an eye on us. Two P–47s flew by and strafed the airdrome. On their second pass, I saw black smoke trailing one of the planes. One of the crew yelled something in support of the fighters, but when the guard pointed his rifle at us, we thought it best to keep our feelings to ourselves. I didn't hear a plane crash, so I hoped that the pilot made it back to friendly territory.

We got into Frankfurt near dusk. We saw the results of our bombings there. Much of the rail yard and buildings had been damaged or destroyed. They marched us through the crowded station to a nearby street car. People called us names, threw things and spit at us. Fortunately, the guards did their best to protect us.

We rode the street car for about twenty minutes. When we got to the interrogation center, it was during a blackout. We were hungry. I took a couple bites out of the black bread I was carrying.

We agreed among us that no one except Harris, the pilot, would answer questions about Ford nor Anderson, but would give no more than their name, rank and serial number so that family members could receive information about their fate from the International Red Cross. We knew Anderson had jumped, but Ford was the last to leave the plane, and no one saw him bail out.

Each of us went through a short interrogation. After that they placed us in solitary confinement cells about six-feet wide and ten or twelve-feet long. My room had a six-foot by two-and-a-half foot box nailed to the wall to serve as a bed. There were bed slats about five-inches apart. Cardboard covered the slats to hold the loose wood excelsior that was the mattress. There was one German army blanket but no pillow.

When the guard escorted me into my room, I had to remove my shoes and place them outside the door. They locked me in and turned out the light. I was exhausted from the trip. In the darkness, I groped around for the bed. I laid down and fell asleep. In the morning, light streamed through a small window, but the window was too high up for me to see anything but the sky.

The next morning, a Monday, we were interrogated by a *Luftwaffe* officer. After my first session they took me to a large room that had a full-sized bed, a table and three chairs. There were two big windows with bars in the room. I looked out and watched Germans walking through the courtyard, sometimes escorting American, British, or Canadian POWs from one building to another.

I had two interrogation sessions a day. On a Wednesday morning, I noticed that the guard hadn't locked my door when he left. I waited a few minutes, and then I opened the door. I looked down a long hallway, but didn't see anyone or anything except pairs of shoes and boots of all types on the floor outside most of the rooms. I reached down, grabbed by flight boots and put them on. I worked up my nerve and walked down to an intersecting hallway where I heard people speaking with English accents. I looked around a corner and saw no one, but I could still hear the voices. I walked a little farther and came upon two British prisoners working in a canteen that was across from the latrine where I was taken for relief twice a day.

No Germans were in sight, so I asked if I could shower and shave, not having done either since I left England. A little anxiously, they provided me with a towel, soap and razor. Once in the shower, I checked all of the windows to see if there was a way I could slip out, but all of the windows had bars. I returned the things to the Englishmen, went back to my room, took off my boots and placed them on the floor. I went in and closed the door. As far as I knew, the guards never knew I left.

My mind started working on an escape plan. I decided to wait until late that night and then go out the door where we had originally entered the building. I knew there was a blackout, and I hoped to use the darkness to slip away into the unknown. A guard, assigned to take me to my eighth interrogation, interrupted my thoughts. All the others had finished being interrogated, and I wondered why they were still questioning me. Then I figured out why. As the engineer, I was supposed to know the plane's serial number, but because the plane had been new, I didn't have time to memorize it, and the explosion had destroyed all of my records.

After the interrogation, they took me back to my room. Again, the guard didn't lock the door, and that gave me some hope that I could escape that night. I wondered if the guard would lock the door when he brought me my evening meal.

After a few minutes, the door opened, a guard stuck his head inside and asked, "What is your rank?"

I answered, "Staff Sergeant."

With a surprised look, he slammed the door and locked it. I realized then something I had suspected all week. The room I was in was usually reserved for high-ranking Allied officers. The guard from my first interrogation had mistakenly placed me in the wrong room. My escape plans were thwarted. Later that night, a guard moved me to a small, solitary confinement cell like the one in which I had spent my first night.

My ninth session was the next morning. Again, I wouldn't fill out some blank spaces on a form and sign it. All I filled in were my name, rank and serial number. The officer asked me how I liked being sent back to the solitary confinement room. I just shrugged and said nothing.

I didn't see the crew for several days until the officer finished questioning each of us. After my ninth session, they took me to another building where I found them. We were in a holding area, awaiting transport to the *Dulag Luft* in Wetzler. The crew had been concerned about me because of my extended interrogation. I told them about my "luxury" accommodations, my unlocked door, my trip to the latrine and my shower and shave. None of them had been given the same opportunity.

On Friday night, we were placed in a community room with other Allied POWs. That night we had a nerve-wracking experience. The RAF and RCAF[176] chose that night to bomb Frankfurt. Unlike the Eighth Air Force that bombed from a tight formation for a few minutes over the target, the British bombed from different directions and altitudes. Because of that, only one plane would be over a target at the same time. Otherwise, they ran the risk of bombing friendly planes flying below them. Their technique created very long raids, depending on the number of planes. They were dropping Block Busters.[177] None hit us, fortunately, but the buildings shook from the concussions.

On Saturday morning[178], they marched a large group of us from the interrogation center, back through the results of the previous night's raid, to the railway station. We were again treated to name-calling, spit, stones and other debris. In anticipation of this, I made sure that I marched inside the formation. The guards were very concerned about our safety.

We got on the train and got to Wetzler without incident. As we marched through the town, we heard someone whistling "Yankee Doodle." Those of us who saw the person concluded that he was an American evadee working his way back to friendly territory. We hoped he was, and that he'd make it.

They gave us a suit case made of compressed cardboard filled with American Red Cross items that came through the International Red Cross. They also took away some of our flight clothing. They gave me an Army overcoat, and that came in handy that cold winter.

At the *Dulag Luft* I ran into our crew toggelier, Sergeant Cecil Smith, who had been with another crew and who was shot down the same day as we were. We stayed at the *Dulag* for several days while we waited for transfer to a permanent camp. We were all given several post cards and one or two letter forms so we could write a note back home to our families.

The enlisted men were separated from the officers and sent to a camp in East Prussia. We were again issued Red Cross food parcels, one for every two men. Then they marched us to the Wetzler railway station where they herded us into box cars like a bunch of cattle, more than fifty men to a car. We went through Berlin and stopped at the rail yards because there was a bombing raid. Fortunately, our train wasn't hit. We were delayed for several hours because the bombing severely damaged the tracks. We ended up at *Stalag Luft IV* in Grosschow, Germany. It's now a part of Poland.[179]

They unloaded us from the cars and marched us a mile or so to the camp where they herded us into a long room with tables set end to end through the center. There were benches lined up along the walls. They told us to undress and place all of our belongings on the tables. Then they took us into a large shower room. Some of us were leery because there were rumors about the gas chambers. Having no other choice, we stepped in and enjoyed a good, hot shower, my second in three weeks.

While we were showering, the guards searched our belongings and confiscated our food, cigarettes and anything else they wanted. Before I got into the shower, I slipped a small compass into my mouth to conceal it from them. We called it an "Anal" compass. Some called it by another name, but the "location" remained the same. I thought my mouth was the better place to hide it. What's more, I didn't have time to put it in the other end.

We returned to our clothing, and they told us to dress. The guards yelled at us to hurry. There was one particular loudmouth next to me, and while I hurried, trying to tie a shoe, he struck me across my bare back with a leather belt. I straightened up from the pain, and out came the compass. The Loudmouth saw it and hit me several more times across the back. Then he turned to some of the other guards and said something to them. He escorted another guard from the building. I assumed that he was the one who was supposed to search me and my belongings.

Hurriedly, I finished dressing, grabbed what remained of my property and then moved down the line of men, hoping the Loudmouth wouldn't find me in case he came around. They marched us out of the building without further incident.

They took us to Compound A (*Lager* in German) where they assigned us to the tents that would be our home for several weeks. I later learned that the guard who struck me was called "Big Stoop"[180] after a comic-strip character from *Terry and the Pirates.* "Big Stoop" was the sergeant in charge of the camp's *Gestapo* Detachment. He looked like he was six-nine and had hands as big as a full-grown elephant's foot. A big and mean man he was.

After several weeks in a tent, I moved into Compound C, Barracks 3, Room 9, with twenty other noncommissioned officers. The barracks buildings were constructed of wood and set on posts thirty inches above ground level. The open area under the barracks was forbidden territory, and the guards kept a close watch there for tunnelers. There were nine or ten rooms along each side of the barracks with a hallway running through the center from end to end. One end room was reserved as a community washroom and latrine, though there was no running water. We also used the latrine during the night after they locked us in. We were issued a large serving bowl to use for eating, washing and shaving. There were no showers. We had no hot water other than what we heated in small food cans on a burning charcoal brick inside a pot-bellied stove.

Each room was twenty-feet square and had one outside window in the center and one door to the hallway. The Germans closed the wooden shutters each dusk or when there was a real or practice air-raid drill. The double doors at both ends of the barracks were also locked at night, or when we were being locked in as punishment. There was a table and two or three stools in each barracks, but no beds.

The furniture and stove were located in the narrow community area, so there was little room for twenty-two men. Because of the limited space, we spent much of our daylight time outdoors playing games, milling around aimlessly, or walking the perimeter for exercise or just to get warm. We played cards, softball, football—sometimes with homemade balls—or we read books by the YMCA. We also spent some time playing tricks on the "Goons," the name we gave to the guards.

There was a single strand of barbed wire located about eighteen inches above ground and about twenty-feet in from the main fence. It was a warning wire, and anyone crossing it would be shot by the tower guards. After each roll call, the *Apel*, there was an endless line of men walking along the warning wire. Most of us would walk around the compound one way and then the other, hoping to find a friend who might just have arrived. One prisoner found a relative this way.

When the weather was really cold, we were given several charcoal bricks, about the size of a standard American building brick, to burn in the stove. Needless to say, the bricks didn't give off much heat, and it was the coldest German winter in more than fifty years. In my barracks we burned the bricks only at meal time so we could heat our food. We placed one lighted brick on the stove grate and drew cards to determine how we would all line up to use the brick. It was a slow process, but we had a lot of time on our hands. After we ate, we heated shaving water on the brick—if it was still burning, that is.

We elected Vincent Landolfi as our room chief. He divided us into teams of eleven each and assigned one team to each side of the barracks. Each of us had two thin German army blankets. We made beds by removing the thread from the hem of one blanket and with the thread made one long blanket that reached from one wall to the other. We removed every other nail in a section of wall and tacked down the part of the blanket that ran down the center of the room. We put wood excelsior on the floor and pulled the blanket up over it to the wall, making a long mattress for eleven men. Each night before retiring, we'd pull the blanket to the center of the room and shake up the excelsior to form a softer bed. We slept in our clothes and covered ourselves with the remaining blanket and overcoats. It was so cold that winter that several of my toes on each foot got frostbite. The worst was the fourth toe on my right foot. The flesh had rotted away to the extent I could see the bone.

The Germans gave each one of us a large serving bowl, a cup and utensils. Food wasn't plentiful, but it was enough to keep the recently arrived prisoners in fairly good shape. Most of the time, we got the equivalent of what the German soldiers got, which wasn't much compared to what our GI rations were. We supplemented our food with what was in Red Cross parcels. Because there were British and Canadian prisoners in the compound next to mine, we sometimes got British or Canadian parcels. Usually, we got one parcel for every two men. At Christmas 1944 we each received an American parcel plus one British parcel that we divided among four men. It was a feast!

Cigarettes were money and the better the brand, the higher the price. Lucky Strike was the preferred brand, followed by Camel. I didn't smoke, so I used my Red Cross cigarettes to barter for more food, but I gave most of them to a good buddy who was a chain smoker.

But we spent most of the time talking about food, our families and what we planned on doing once we got back home, if we got back. Loss of weight was our great concern, as was the constant tension we were under from the guards' threats. We were all under emotional stress and frustration. Oftentimes, a simple innocent remark among friends would incite a violent verbal or physical encounter.

I started to lose weight around the middle of December, and I craved for more food than I was getting. I told my buddy that I was going to use all of my cigarettes to buy food, so there wouldn't be any more freebies. I didn't want to buy his food; I knew he needed all that he had. He got really mad at me, so I promised him one full pack, but that I'd use the rest to barter with. He got even madder, and he wouldn't speak to me for several weeks. After that, I didn't even give him the one pack. Just before Christmas, he apologized and we became good buddies again.

The Germans opened all food parcels and removed everything they thought would assist in an escape. This included pepper and metal can openers. They often confiscated a pack of American cigarettes as well. That would leave us with only a couple packs to use as barter instead of the usual five

Our captors never issued enough parcels at a time to insure that each prisoner got one each week. They'd issue about one third the number so as to stretch the process over three or four days. We devised a room plan to assure that a food parcel would be given to each occupant on a fair rotation basis. One member of each team drew a card to establish positions on the Ration Issue list. I was placed in charge of the ration issues largely because I was the only one with a YMCA note book. Each room in the barracks had been given one of these note books, and I won mine in a lottery. I still have the book. My job was to pick up all food parcels at the kitchen when the Germans issued them. After each team drew a position card, I entered their names in the note book. The highest card holder got to be first on the list and so on down the list of eleven teams.

The prisoners of Compound C agreed that our American kitchen people should remove all cans of Spam and corned beef from the parcels and cook the meat with potatoes or turnips to make a hash. This way the meat went farther, and the potatoes and turnips tasted better. They issued the hash by the half or three-quarters-full regular scrub bucket, one bucket per barracks room. The kitchen staff set up a barracks rotation system so that each of the ten barracks had a turn at the front of the line. A separate rotation system was set up for the ten barracks to get a chance at second helpings. Second helpings didn't happen very often. They happened even less when we were transferred to *Stalag Luft I* in Barth, Germany.[181]

In early January 1945, the Russians were advancing into our area. Rumors started to float around that we were going to be evacuated. I was getting treatment for my frostbitten toes, and the doctor told me that I'd be evacuated from the camp by train. He told me to return to my barracks and prepare to leave on a moment's notice.

Several days later, fifteen hundred of us sick and wounded prisoners were taken to the Keifheide railroad station and herded into small freight cars. There were fifty-two prisoners and one guard stacked in my car. The last time I'd see my crew was the day I left. What I didn't know was that Anderson was on the same train. He had injured his foot and had spent time in a German hospital. He was also on sent to *Stalag Luft IV*, but he'd been placed in a different compound. I didn't even know he was in the same camp.

The box car had two side doors, one on each side and one small door at the rear. The floor was covered with wood excelsior, and that meant "No Smoking." A German guard, probably in his mid-sixties sat on a stool inside the rear door. He had hung his rifle on a nail protruding from the wall. He also had a toilet-bucket for his and our use. It was supposed to be a three or four-day trip, but it lasted nine days. There was hardly any food, and sometimes we would have to stop for hours while German troop trains passed, or for unknown reasons. Only once were we allowed off the train for fresh air and some stretching. Some of us washed our faces and hands in the dirty snow we found between the rails.

We were so packed in the guard couldn't empty the bucket. It was overflowing for most of the time. We couldn't lie down to sleep, nor could all of us could sit at the same time. For almost nine days we took turns to sit down and sleep. After several days, the excelsior got wet from urine, vomit and excrement. Our shoes were covered in the filth. Our clothing was filthy and the stench was terrible. Many, including myself, got dysentery and couldn't make it through the crowded car to the bucket. The floor was the only place to go.

The car locked from the outside, and the guard could only empty the bucket when the train stopped and the guards outside opened the door. After a few days, we found a rotted floor plank. We chipped away at the wood and made a hole about two-inches wide and seven- inches long and used that to squat over for our "outhouse." This was a little relief.

We heard German and Russian artillery most of the time. Our German guard spoke fairly good English, and he told us he wouldn't prevent anyone from escaping since he knew the War would be over soon. He asked us not to harm him, and he'd do no harm to us. Anyway, the thought of escaping in harsh weather and in our condition never occurred to us. We also knew the War would be over, and that our best chance of surviving was as a group. The guard left his rifle on the nail, except when he had to get off the train. No one even tried to touch the rifle, and the guard only took it with him to avoid getting into trouble with his superiors.

We got to the new camp around 11 February 1945. We were herded into a large room, searched and then assigned to a barracks. When they searched us, the guards took whatever food we had left. I was assigned to Compound D, Barracks 204, Room 13. The barracks were pretty much like the ones in our previous camp, except it had three-tier beds along the two walls. There was excelsior as usual, and those who slept on the lower bunks complained about small pieces of excelsior falling on them from the bunks above them. English officers were housed in the rooms along one side of the barracks, and Americans, mostly non-coms like me, were housed on the opposite side. Room 13 housed twenty-four men. Lieutenant Colonel Francis "Gabby" Gabreski was our American commander.[182]

At *Stalag Luft IV*, the Germans respected our rank and didn't require us to do any type of manual labor. The new camp was different. We were sometimes detailed to do manual labor within the compound. On one occasion, I was detailed with some officers and other non-coms to dig a drainage ditch to drain the ground water away from the latrine building. I objected not to the work, but that we were required to do it. On another occasion, officers and non-coms were detailed, by our senior officers, to wash down the outside latrines, a job that was usually done by guards or Russian POWs at my first camp.

After I got settled, I went to the warning wire between Compound C and Compound D and asked the prisoners on the other side of the fence if anyone knew Lieutenant Donald Harris. Someone did, and he went to get Harris. It would be the first time we saw each other since being separated at *Dulag Luft* the previous September. Don informed me that Jest, the navigator, and Zieff, the bombardier, were in Compound C and that Anderson was in the south compound. That's when I found out that everyone had survived the bail out except Howard Ford, the copilot.

Anderson had eluded the Germans for eight or nine days before he got captured late one night climbing into an empty freight car. He had lain in wait for a long time watching for workers or German troops. Not seeing anyone, he boarded the car, hoping the train would cross the bridge on a nearby river. What he didn't know was that the train was a troop train and troops were asleep in adjacent cars. When Anderson closed the door of the car, it made a loud noise and awakened the sleeping soldiers. They came to investigate, and they found him. So, for Anderson, "The War was Over!"

Some time later, I got to talk to a new acquaintance from Emporium, Pennsylvania. I mentioned that my copilot was from Olean, New York, but that he had worked in Emporium before the War. Immediately he told me that Ford had injured his back when he landed in a forest. The Germans found him three days after the bail out. I went back to the fence and, summoning Don Harris, I told him the good news. Now we knew that the whole crew had survived the bail out!

At the new camp, we were not permitted to trade or buy items from the German guards. Trading was the responsibility of one appointee from each barracks. In ours, the senior British officer was the designated "trader." If we wanted to trade anything, we wrote down what it was we wanted and the item we were trading. Seldom did we receive what we wanted, and we often lost the use of our trade item.

Rations and parcels were scarce at the new camp. The few parcels were usually kept for sick and wounded comrades. Occasionally, the Germans would bring a farm wagon load of potatoes and unload them with a shovel through a window of the kitchen building. The shovel cut chips off the potatoes, and I crawled under the wagon to

Jack McCracken and his crew. L/R, top row: Ernest Stoneipher, Virgil Gordon, Jack McCracken, Davey Jones, Curtis Anderson, Leonard Garzynha, Buck Petre, Marvin Jest, Don ?, Howard Ford.

An Unexpected Visit With a German Farmer

by SMSgt John H. McCracken, USAF (Ret)
Belleville, IL

SMSgt John H. McCracken USAF (Ret)

pick up as many of the chips as we could find to boil in a tin can. As they cooked, they grew blacker and blacker. I was tempted to throw the mess away, but I ate it anyway because I was so hungry.

One night I was cooking food, and reaching down through the stove lid, I picked up the hot can and accidentally dropped it on the hot charcoal brick. The brick let off steam that burned the inside of my wrist. The English officer in charge of the barracks summoned a guard by pounding on the locked barracks door and arranged to have me taken to the medical room where they treated my burn.

At night, the compound was "No-Man's-Land," and any prisoner out at night could be shot. After I was treated, the guard and I went back outside. While he paused to lock the door, I stood at the bottom of the porch steps. He told me to keep going. After thirty feet or so I realized the guard wasn't following me. The tower guards turned a searchlight on me and started laughing. I stopped, turned around and walked back toward the guard, who told me to turn around and head back to my barracks. I did as I was told, and he followed me with his guard dog. As we crossed the grounds the guard and the tower guards laughed, knowing that they had tricked me into thinking that I was going to be shot!

There were several motorcycle enthusiasts in Room 13 who spent a lot of leisure time discussing a motorcycle club they were going to form after liberation that would restrict membership to former American POWs. The plan was to tour the United States before we entered school or started a career. I had never driven a motorcycle nor ridden one, but I thought the idea was great, so I joined as a prospective member. Our leader, Bill Beadle, from Indiana, had a GI artist design a club logo. I made a copy of the design and put it in my YMCA record book. I gave the original to Bill.

All of us had plans for after the War. With one of my roommates, I got interested in opening a large bowling alley somewhere in New Jersey, or opening and operating a combination barber shop and beauty salon, complete with private shower rooms for the customers. All of those "Kriegie"[183] plans were forgotten once we were liberated.

We awoke one morning to open barracks' doors and our own people. The Germans had fled during the night because they didn't want to be captured by the Russians. One guard had remained behind and was found hiding in one of the kitchen buildings. I never found out what happened to him.

Colonel Zemke[184], the senior American officer, had placed American guards at the gates to prevent us from leaving the camp. He had orders to stay put until Allied forces arrived. I thought it was a good idea since the Germans might have mined the area outside the camp. Many of the guys didn't like the order, though. They were anxious to get out and go home. The inner gates were left open, and we could visit each other. I found Anderson, and we decided to stay together in the same room, so we could leave together.

Over the next three days, several junior officers and non-coms went out to forage for food and find the approaching Russians. They came back with several cattle that we butchered. One day, the first Russian soldier came riding in on a white stallion. After him came more Russians on foot, horsedrawn wagons and horseback. The Russian commander was surprised that we hadn't torn down the fences. Then, someone started to tear down the barbed wire, and it wasn't long until thousands of my comrades broke off tall posts and used them as ramrods to break down the fences. I didn't participate because I still felt obliged to obey Zemke's orders.

With the fences down, many of the former prisoners headed west to meet the Allies. Some of our men even joined the Russians and were killed in skirmishes with German soldiers. Most of the Russians were drunk, and I didn't feel too safe around them.

One day Curtis Anderson and I joined a group that was forming to tour the town of Barth, something I did on several occasions. By that time the road was cleared of mines. We went in a loose formation led by a captain. In town, we saw a former *Stalag Luft IV* guard wearing civilian clothing. It was the good-looking, tall blonde with a patch over one eye we called "Hollywood." It was said that he lost an eye on the Eastern Front fighting the Russians. Hollywood gave us a rough time in camp, and we told the captain about him and the captain told the Russians who found Hollywood hiding in a nearby building. We found out later that the Russians put him on a train with other German POWs bound for Russia.

I went for a walk one day alongside a dike just outside the camp and came upon four dead German women. They appeared to be four generations from one family—a baby in a buggy, a woman apparently in her twenties, a woman about fifty and a woman about seventy or eighty. It might have been suicide or murder; each of them had been shot in the right temple. I saw no weapons, at any rate. Even if there had been a weapon, it was probably picked up by someone. The baby and women were the only casualties of war I saw during my combat experience.

During our time under Russian control, it was our understanding that the Russians wanted to march us to Odessa and from there send us home on a Russian ship. Colonel Zemke, however, was able to hold us at the camp until other arrangements could be made. We thanked him for that.

In early May 1945, B–17s from the 91st Bomb Group began arriving to transport us to France. As I remember, Curtis Anderson and I left on 13 May. The pilot took us on a low-altitude flight so we could see the devastation Allied bombing had inflicted on the German cities. It was then that I felt some compassion for the innocent people who had been killed, injured or made homeless.

We landed in France near Camp Lucky Strike after dark. Everyone got off the plane, but there was no one there to meet us, and the plane took off immediately to get more POWs. We milled around for fifteen minutes or so until a long line of Army trucks came roaring in to take us to the camp.

At Camp Lucky Strike they herded us into a large tent where we undressed and threw our clothes into a huge pile that would later be burned. We all took a long-welcomed shower and got four new uniforms and went for a medical exam.

A visit to the mess hall came next. It was to be my first American meal in eight months, and we could eat as much as we wanted—freshly-baked bread, Longhorn cheese, rich egg nog, whatever! I, along with many others, ate far too much at one sitting and ruined our stomachs and esophagi. Our stomachs had shrunk so much from starvation that so much food too fast stretched the stomach more than it should have been.

General Eisenhower visited us at Camp Lucky Strike and told us he'd get us home as soon as possible. He also told us that ships were scarce because they were needed in the Pacific, and that we might have to share a bunk with one or two others. He suggested that the Air Force people get back to their groups and return home with them.

Curtis and I hopped a plane to London where we discovered that the 390th had already left. They told us there to go to the Debarkation Center in Southampton to get transport back home. We didn't have any official orders, so we stayed in London until our money ran out. That took only a week.

We traveled to Southampton by rail. We found out from an American soldier that, as ex-POWs, we were eligible for some money from the American Red Cross. We went to the Red Cross office and got one English pound each.

We did a lot of sightseeing in London and financed our travels from camp to London by buying stuff from the Post Exchange with our pound, then selling what we didn't want at a small profit outside the camp gate, something we were allowed to do. This routine went on for about six weeks.

One day we got back to camp and found our names had been put on a supplemental shipping list several days earlier. We decided we had better stay in camp in case the MPs were looking for us. Eventually we got to the top of the list, and we were homeward bound.

We got into Boston around 25 July 1945 and immediately went to Camp Myles Standish. Our first meal there was steak served by German POWs! We noticed that the Germans got the same dinner we got. Our minds went back to the meals we were given while we were in the prison camps. I thought that a riot might break out. We all shouted at the Germans about how well they were living and eating! They had to call in the MPs to quiet us down.

I arrived at Indiantown Gap on 26 July where I got *another* set of uniforms, my fourth since liberation. I told the supply sergeant that I already had three sets, but he said that they were trying to get rid of surplus uniforms.

At Indiantown Gap they gave me partial pay and a seventy-five-day recuperation leave. I took a Greyhound bus down the Pennsylvania Turnpike to Donegal where my parents and Aunt Mame Huston were waiting to meet me. By then I was up to 180 pounds. They expected to see a skin-and-bones son, but after two months at Camp Lucky Strike I'd eaten so much that I gained fifty-six pounds. We drove to the family farm, and when we arrived my two younger brothers ran from the dairy barn to meet me. I was happy to be home.

I remembered my thoughts as my parachute spun down over the landscape of Germany eleven months earlier: *'Would I ever see my family again?'*

The Aluminum Trail

John Means

Fourteenth Air Force "Flying Tigers"
308th Bomb Group
373rd and 375th Squadrons
Born in Pittsburgh, Pennsylvania, 27 February 1925
† 9 December 2006

"Martin came to India with us, and we were staying in some godforsaken camp in the jungle. One day they found a flight for Martin and up he went. The pilot decided to have some fun. He was following a river, so he decided to fly down low and check out the jungle along the banks. There was a cable stretched across the river. The plane hit it and crashed. Everyone in the plane died. Martin died for a lousy seven hours. All for military bullshit. Martin was nineteen, and he was the youngest of our crew."

IN 1942 I WAS at Alderdice High School in Pittsburgh; the War was on and I wanted to be in it.

The Army Air Force[185] had a program for pre-enlistment for high-school students. When we turned eighteen, if we passed all the Air Cadet exams, we were guaranteed a spot in the Air Force. I passed all tests. My school system decreed that if anyone enlisted in his senior year, he'd graduate even if he didn't finish all of his school work.

I turned eighteen in February and was called in. In a month or so I was sent to Maxwell Field in Montgomery, Alabama, where I went through the Air Force cadet school. From there I was sent on to Clarksville, Mississippi to learn to fly on Boeing (Stearman)PT–17s.That's as far as I got. I got caught mock dive-bombing a barge on the Mississippi River and that got me washed out of pilot training. After that I went to radio school in Sioux Falls, South Dakota. From October to March I learned to be a radio operator. Then I went to Aerial Gunner School in Yuma, Arizona.

At Yuma, they flew B–25s or B–26s with big, white, target sleeves behind them. We'd be in B–17s, parallel, shooting .50-caliber machine guns at the targets. They'd have maybe five different gunners practicing with one target. Each gunner had ammunition with different colored tips, red, orange, white, yellow, purple, black. They could tell who had how many hits in the target by looking at the colors in the holes of the target.

From Yuma, we went to Fresno, California, to a sort of holding area, where we got a ten-day furlough. It wasn't much of a leave, really. I spent six of my ten days on a train traveling to and from Pittsburgh. After the leave, I went to Walla-Walla, Washington, where they were training B–24 crews. When we were ready, we went to San Francisco, where they gave us a brand-new B–24. It was so new our crew was the first to do flight checks on it. Eventually, we got orders to fly the plane to Kunming, China, by way of the Atlantic Ocean.

After we crossed the ocean, we spent a week in Marrakech, French Morocco. They had a walled city there (a *Medina*) where the Arabs lived. We were near there one day when MPs came past dragging two guys who were wearing white Arab robes.

We asked, "What the hell is going on?"

One of the MPs answered, "They went AWOL and they figured they'd hide in the market city. So they put these things on, and they're all suntanned, so we caught them in a minute."

"How?"

"They kept waving the flies off their nose and their lips. The Arabs don't do that."

We were not under orders at the time. We had the aircraft but we were getting paid per diem and we could sort of stay longer at a place that we wanted to. By "we" I mean Hugh Kelly, the pilot and commander of the aircraft. It was his decision to make. Anyway, after Morocco, we flew to Tunis, Tunisia. We didn't like it too much there, so we went on to Cairo, Egypt. We hung around there for about ten days, then flew to Abadan, which is now in Iran.

When we knew we were going to fly to Abadan, they told us, "You've got to leave at three in the morning."

We said, "Why?"

"Where you're going you have to be there before nine because the runway is asphalt and it melts after that time."

It was true! We got there and it was a hundred and twenty some degrees after we landed and the runway just melted. We only stayed there one day.

From Abadan we went to Karachi, India (now it's in Pakistan), and then to Bengal. An interesting thing happened while we were in Bengal. We never knew why certain things happened the way they did. In fact, a lot of it I never understood until I read about it much later. After Pearl Harbor happened, Claire Chennault[186] was in China with his bunch, the "Flying Tigers." They were all told that they were going to be inducted into the Army Air Force after Pearl Harbor and most of them refused.

They were told, "Okay, you're going back home, and you'll be put into the draft and drafted into the infantry."

Well, many of them then changed their mind right then, and those that were inducted were made into the only United States Air Force group in history created overseas. They were formed into the Fourteenth Air Force in early 1942. Chennault, their leader, was made a brigadier general. This maverick who had quit the military became a brigadier general and I'm sure that Madame Chang had something to do with that. There was another brigadier general commissioned at the same time, but he was named in the morning and Chennault was named in the afternoon, so the other guy would have seniority.

In my opinion that was the government getting even with this dude, who became a brigadier general without going beyond captain during his previous military career.

They were going to fix his ass, and one of the ways they did that affected us directly. They took our plane.

The aircraft that we picked up in San Francisco, was called a B–24 H. The first B–24s were A, and then B, C, D, E, F, G, H. The difference between the H and, say, a D, was that we could run the heat from the exhaust from the engine into the wing tips and melt the ice on the wing tips. The cabins were also heated. In the D I wore an electric blanket suit and there were deicing boots on the wing. That H was really top of the line because of the little things like that.

Well, when we got to Bengal with this H, a major came along and said, "Get all your gear off this aircraft."

Kelly said, "But I have orders to take this to Kunming."

"Lieutenant, you got fifteen minutes to get your gear and your people out of here, or you're going to jail."

So they took our B–24 H and headed to China, leaving us without a plane. Then they sent us by air transport to Calcutta and then to Chadua, India, at the base of the Himalayas. From Chadua they flew us over to Kunming and from Kunming to Luliang Airfield. Each Fourteenth Air Force base had twelve to fifteen bombers plus fighters. We were part of the 308th Heavy Bomb Group.

Once we got situated, we were sent on a five-hour mission bomb a Japanese motor pool in a city called Changsha, near the Yangtze River. We all had stuffed our parachutes under our seats somewhere. We also had Flak jackets, full of lead bars sewn into canvas pockets. They weighed sixty or seventy pounds. They were also under seats in various places. We didn't pay any attention to the parachutes or the jackets.

Over Changsha we heard noises like a dog barking. It was anti-aircraft shells going off. Pretty soon we saw the smoke out there and heard this bark, and everybody's running like hell to put on jackets and parachutes! It took awhile to find them all; it was chaos, really. That taught us after that to know where the parachutes and combat jackets were at all times.

Our function mainly was the bombing of Japanese facilities. The problem was we were always under-supplied. This, in my opinion, was because the powers at home wanted Chennault to fail; they didn't give us enough bombs, gasoline and all the other stuff we needed to support a bomb group. In order to get what we needed we had to fly the "Hump" over the Himalayas from China to India a couple times a month and pick up bombs and gasoline and other supplies and fly them back to Luliang.

I didn't think there was any reason a bombing/combat crew should have been doing that. They had Air Transport there for that job. They were prevalent in India and flew supplies and personnel often. Why in the hell they didn't have them fly any supplies to us is anybody's guess.

"Flying the Hump" was at least as dangerous as actual combat missions. We called parts of the Hump "The Aluminum Trail" because it was full of crashed C–46s and C–47s. The pilots never knew what they'd run into in terms of weather, and there were no navigation aids except for shooting calculations off the sun and the stars.

We always had to fly very high because Mount Everest, more than twenty-nine-thousand-feet high, was there. And there were others almost as high. The wings would

"A major came along and said, "Get your gear off this aircraft."

ice up. The way we handled that was pump up a rubber boot that ran along the entire edge of the wing. It was supposed to crack off the ice. The problem was that when the boot got blown up it would often freeze in place and we couldn't retract it. We had that happen once, but fortunately it occurred when we were out of the bad weather, and we had time to get over the worst of the Hump and get down to a lower altitude. A lot of folks didn't have that chance.

We flew several missions before we ever saw a Japanese fighter plane. Sometimes we had air cover and sometimes we didn't. Most of the time we ran into anti-aircraft. We did a lot of bombing over Hankow on the Yangtze, where the Japanese had huge warehouses filled with supplies and equipment. There were plenty of anti-aircraft guns to worry about, so we flew mostly night missions.

We also had one mission to bomb Hong Kong, a fourteen-hour round trip from Kunming. We flew all the way across China to the coast of the China Sea. When we got to the coast, there must have been five hundred islands in that area, any one of which could have been Hong Kong. We flew up and down that coast several times but couldn't find Hong Kong. We couldn't keep doing that because of gas. Finally, we found Hong Kong, bombed it and flew back. After we landed, the mechanics put a pole into the gas tanks to see how much gas we had left. According to them, we had only ten minutes of fuel left.

The next morning the colonel called us in. He had received a telegram from somewhere in the States raising all kind of hell. It turned out we had bombed Macao instead of Hong Kong and the Portuguese were quite upset about it.

The Colonel read us the telegram, and said, "Well? What do you have to say?"

Everybody shrugged their shoulders.

Then the colonel said, "Okay."

What could be done about it, anyway?

One of our most dangerous missions was a non-combat flight. There was an airfield that the Fourteenth Air Force had in Central China on top of a mountain. The Japanese were still bombing that airfield and the base lost a generator that they used to produce electricity. They had us fly a new one up in a B–24, but we didn't use our regular plane. The generator was probably five-feet-long and three-feet-wide and probably weighed seven or eight-hundred pounds; that's two problems right there. It was hard to find a place to put something that size on a B–24, but up in the nose area there was an open space. That's where they put it.

The B–24 had a nose wheel and when that wheel dropped down, it locked into place. There was a yellow line on the shaft of the wheel and a yellow line on a metal beam that matched up when the wheel locked. When that line was perfectly level the wheel was in place. The engineer would usually go down there before every landing and look at that line to make sure it was locked.

They strapped that generator on the lower walkway. That blocked passage to the nose wheel so we couldn't see if it was locked or not. We flew over to that base at about midnight and we landed. The weight of the generator, apparently, had affected the ability of the nose wheel lock in but there was no way we could have known that. When we landed the nose wheel just kept collapsing slowly and we slid fifteen-hundred feet down the runway, tore the props off the engines and destroyed the nose.

You can imagine the pilot and the copilot sitting up there watching the front of the aircraft disintegrate! When we finally stopped, the radio was still working, and I was able to radio the tower and tell them we were on the runway and that we had crash-landed. They had to warn off other planes that were coming in. That plane could've flipped forward, it could've flipped sideways, it could've started a fire in the tank but we all got up and walked out without a scratch. It was just an oddity of war.

A captain there joked, "Get your wallets ready. You'll have to pay for that!"

A mission that really scared hell out of me was one to Hankow. We were going to the Hankow docks, and when we got near the target, it was my job to leave the radio operator's station up in the flight deck and walk back through the bomb bay to the waist and stand by the two guns there. I never made it back there. On my harness strap were two round metal clips on a round thing like a dog's leash on which I hooked my parachute. The way through the bomb bay was very narrow and full of hydraulic hoses, quarter-inch tubing going to different places. Everything on the B–24 worked on hydraulics.

In the bomb bay were metal struts that held the airplane together, and they were all along the walkway. As I was walking through, I kept touching the frame of the plane, because it wasn't wide enough what with all I was wearing. All of a sudden I heard a click, and I'm clicked onto one of these quarter-inch hydraulic hoses. I can't get to it in order to loosen it, because I got wedged between the struts. I was stuck, and nobody knew I was there. The people up front didn't know I had left, and the people in the back knew I was on my way, but for some reason hadn't yet arrived.

I'm standing there on this bridge, and they opened the bomb bay doors; it was no real danger, but they released the bombs and down they went. The air came rushing in, and the defender's search lights were shining up through, and I could see our fighters diving down toward the lights trying to shoot them out. I kept thinking that I was just going to down with the plane if something bad happened.

Our mission to the Yellow River Bridge was another scary one. It was a mile-long bridge and probably the only one across that river for hundreds of miles. The Japanese used it to get from the part of China they occupied to the part they were fighting in. We had already tried to destroy the bridge a couple of times. Of course, they had a hundred and some anti-aircraft guns around it.

Our side tried to bomb it flying lengthwise, like down an alley, but they lost so many aircraft that way they quit trying. When they told us we're going to bomb the bridge, we said, "What the hell are they we going to do that for? You know we can't do that!"

They said, "Well, you're going to go this way."

That meant we were going to attack from the side. It was a small target, only ten-feet wide, but our bombardier hit it. He had been in the doghouse with the "Powers That Be" at Luilang up to that point. He was still a second lieutenant after everybody else had been promoted. Two days after the bridge was hit he was promoted. It made the newspapers in the States.

He came and visited sometime back and brought pictures of the raid and the hit. A couple years after I got out of the service there was a magazine article in *Esquire Magazine* titled "I Blew the Yellow River Bridge." It was about a guy whose specialty was setting off bombs behind enemy lines. He told how the bridge had been destroyed by the Fourteenth Air Force, but repaired in ten days by the Japanese. To finally take care of the bridge, they sent this guy. With a couple Chinese guides and a bunch of explosive he hiked over to the area, climbed the bridge, wired it, and then blew it up. That was quite a revelation to me. It was the first time I had heard that what we had done was repaired.

Originally we were in the 373rd Bomb Squadron, 308th Bomb Group but they moved us to Qingtu, up in the northern part of China where we became part of the 375th Bomb Squadron. The Japanese had an airfield there with a lot of fighters and bombers. They were just raising hell in China from that base. The brass decided to take the base out once and for all, and they were going to do it with a ruse of which we were a part.

B–29s were to fly and bomb some Japanese position that was three hundred miles north of Hankow. The thought being that Japanese would send their fighter planes up there to take them on and we'd then get to Hankow unharmed. The B–29s would bomb at eleven and at noon we'd fly over Hankow, the whole group, twenty-eight B–24s, fifteen P–51s, twenty P–40s, some P–38s as cover and hammer them.

We got to Hankow, and all but five Japanese fighters had left. The ruse had worked. The idea behind the ruse was that when the enemy planes came back they'd be out of gasoline and they wouldn't have an airfield left to land on.

The five Japanese fighter pilots we encountered were about the bravest men in the world. They came up to take on this whole armada. Instead of diving on us, they got right in the middle of the formation so our gunners couldn't shoot at them for fear of hitting one of the bombers. Our fighter guys took care of them, though. They got above them and dove down. I saw one enemy fighter in the formation next to us and the next thing he was gone. A P–51 came right down through where the enemy had been.

After the mission our group found out that we had set down a perfect pattern of bombs, but two hundred yards to the side. We completely missed the target! Not one damn bomb hit on that airfield. Of course, that never made it to the papers.

The regulation was that when we got three hundred combat hours in China we'd be sent home, and I had three hundred and some in the end. We all finished our hours at the same time except for our one gunner named Martin Steer from Boston. Most of us were nineteen or twenty. A couple were twenty-one. There were two old guys. The bombardier was twenty-five and a gunner was twenty-six. His name was Dave, and he was a real cowboy.

The reason Martin didn't finish at the same time as we did is because on one mission he had the flu and he didn't go. When it came time to go home, Martin was about seven hours short. So they said, "Okay, you can go home too. You're going to India and you'll be there a while waiting for transportation so we'll arrange for you to have a cargo flight or something to get your hours in."

Martin came to India with us, and we were staying in some godforsaken camp in the jungle. One day they found a flight for Martin, and up he went. The pilot decided to have some fun. He was following a river, so he decided to fly down low and check out the jungle along the banks. There was a cable stretched across the river. The plane hit it and crashed. Everyone in the plane died. Martin died for a lousy seven hours. All for military bullshit. Martin was nineteen and he was the youngest of our crew.

We were down in that jungle for about a month then they sent us to Calcutta. Once you've been to a place like Calcutta, you feel fortunate to live in America. Guys would walk down the street with sticks early in the morning prodding people who had slept in the street or wherever the night before. The prodding was to see who was alive or dead. I saw women sitting along scooping water out of the gutter and giving it to their children. It was just total poverty.

We finally got onboard a troop ship on 6 August and left India for Perth, Australia. We stayed in Perth for about a week and then went on to Leyte in the Philippines to pick up some medical personnel. Along the way, we picked up some Army infantry that had been at Guadalcanal since 1942. They wore pirate scarves, had rings in their ears, they wore necklaces made out of Japanese ears. That's how Asian they had become. It was kinda of scary seeing what these young guys turned into. They'd have killed as soon as look at somebody.

From Leyte they sent us to New Guinea and from New Guinea we went to Okinawa to drop off the medical group. We weren't at Okinawa more than a couple hours and they said, "There's a typhoon heading this way, you got to leave immediately."

So, without dropping the medics off, we put to sea, but ran into the typhoon anyway. We were on a thirty-thousand-ton ship, the *General Collins*, and it was taking a pounding. I went up a couple of times to look through the portholes, and it was just sea everywhere. There were waves forty feet above the deck. The waves actually broke the anchor that was fifteen or twenty-feet long. God knows how much it weighed. It broke loose and caved in the plates on the bow of the ship. That's how powerful that typhoon was.

It took us twelve days to cross and get to San Pedro Harbor in Los Angeles. From there we wended our way across the United States to Greensboro, North Carolina, where we were discharged.

On the way there I passed through Pittsburgh. I couldn't understand why they just didn't discharge me there since there were military facilities in Allegheny County, but that was the military.

I think I was one of the luckiest young men alive. I really grew up in the service, and it only took about six months to do so. I didn't mind the discipline, the conditioning and the schooling, either. By the time I was twenty-one I'd traveled all the way around the world, came through some dangerous work without getting hurt, seen things that most kids my age would never see in their lifetimes, and I enjoyed it.

Someone said to me, "Oh, you made a big sacrifice."

I didn't make any sacrifice at all.

In the law firm that I worked in, we had a Chinese lawyer who was brought up in China. They sent him over here to learn American law. He was a regular lawyer in the firm and spoke excellent English. His name was Jack Zao. Jack told me one time after he found out I had been in the Flying Tigers, "You know, when I was growing up, we were taught in school that the United States was a bad, evil country, and that Americans were not good people except for the Flying Tigers. If you ever go over there and they know that you were in that group, they'll do anything for you."

We went over wearing our CBI caps, and what Jack said turned out to be true.

Nose art on a B-24 from John Means' 375th Bombardment Squadron. The aircraft retains the shark teeth that distinguished the P-40s of General Claire Chennault's prewar AVG (American Volunteer Group).

Boeing PT-17 Stearman trainer. Originally PT-13 with a Lycoming engine, the PT-17 had a Continental engine. The PT-18 featured the Jacobs engine, and the P-27 bore a cockpit canopy. *Courtesy: USAF*

Curtiss C-46 "Flying the Hump" *Courtesy: USAF*

C-47 Skytrain (Douglas DC-3 "Gooney Bird," also called "Dakota" by the British)/ The first C-47s were ordered in 1940 and by the end of World War II. 9.348 produced for the USAAF They carried personnel and cargo, and in a combat role, towed troop-carrying gliders and dropped paratroops into enemy territory. Few aircraft are as well known or were so widely used. Courtesy: USAF

Maj. Paul Cyr, United States Office of Strategic Services (OSS, forerunner of the CIA) training with Chinese guerillas for MISSION HOUND On 9 August 1945 —t he day that Nagasaki was destroyed by an atomic bomb, Cyr destroyed two spans of the Yellow River Bridge just as a Japanese troop train was crossing. *Courtesy: Paul Viau/CIA.gov.*

10-Foot Target Hit From 14,000 Feet

BRIDGE SEVERED—Bombs from Liberators of the 308th Bomb Group of the Fourteenth Air Force flying at 14,000 feet have just landed on a hairline target, the 10-foot-wide "Old Yellow River Bridge." The 9620-foot structure is China's longest bridge and the most difficult of all Jap targets to hit. Three automatic weapons towers and three flak towers sent up a heavy barrage preventing the bombers from dropping to a range closer than 14,000 feet

326

Newsclipping describing the bombing of the Yellow River Bridge by the Fourteenth Air Force.

John Means

"Oh, He's a Good German."

Peter Patrick Muse
United States Eighth Air Force
94th Bomb Group (Heavy)
410th Bomb Squadron
Radar Countermeasures Operator ("Spot Jammer")
Born in Leechburg, Pennsylvania, 25 December 1922
Greensburg, Pennsylvania

"We were hitting the oil refinery at a target called Plauen, which is in the eastern part of Germany close to the Russian lines. We began our bomb run at 0930. I felt the blast of freezing air just behind me as the big bomb bay doors opened. We were hit by Flak. I heard the thump and felt the ship jump a little bit and begin to vibrate badly. The Germans were aiming their radar at us and I was pretty busy with my equipment. I happened to notice the flight engineer come back into the radio compartment. He looked kind of scared so I figured there was some sort of problem. I looked up through the radio compartment hatch and could see that we were going in one direction and the rest of the group was going in another direction. I knew we were in trouble then."

LEECHBURG, PENNSYLVANIA, where I grew up, was a small town. It was a peaceful town with no crime. It was a pretty good place to grow up. Allegheny-Ludlum had a steel mill just across the river. The mill and the coal mines were the town's chief employers, but jobs were scarce because of the Depression. Our family didn't have a car, but everything in town was within walking distance. We spent a lot of time in the woods near our home. We played a lot of street games. We made rubber band guns, had snowball battles, and played sandlot baseball and football. We found things to keep us occupied.

My father, Joseph Musso, was a steel worker and a coal miner at different times. He was born in Italy and came over here in 1910. My mother's name was Domenica Maridon. Her first husband died, leaving her with three kids. She married my father and had four more kids. I grew up in Leechburg and graduated from Leechburg High School in 1940. I took general classes, but my favorite was history.

After high school I worked at Fiori's drug store for a couple years as a clerk and soda-jerk. The owner had two stores, and for a while I managed the second store. I started at ten dollars a week and was making twelve when I left.

One Sunday afternoon in 1939, my brother and I were hitchhiking to the swimming hole at Crooked Creek, which is near Ford City. On the way, we picked up a newspaper. On the front page was a picture of Polish cavalry charging the Germans. We were pretty fascinated by that.

Early in the War, the government needed defense plant workers, and they were offering free training on how to operate machine-shop equipment. My twin brother,

Patrick, and I took this three or four month course and ended up working as machine-shop operators in a defense plant in Erie. We were registered for the draft, and the Navy was desperately looking for machine-shop operators to help repair the ships at Pearl Harbor. We thought that sounded pretty exciting, so we signed up for it.

We passed all sorts of tests and an FBI investigation. We were all set to go; we'd said our goodbyes and we even had airline tickets to the west coast. The Navy told us that the last formality we had to go through was to get a release from the Draft Board to leave the country. They told us not to worry about it, since we were going to a war zone, no draft board would ever deny our request. Well, this Draft Board did deny us.

I said to Patrick, "Now they're going to draft us. Let's enlist."

And we did.

After we got uniforms and such at Fort Meade, we went to Miami Beach for a couple weeks basic training. It was after that my brother and I accidentally got separated from each other. We went to different tech schools. He went to Texas for Engineering-Mechanic and Gunnery School, and I went to Lowry Field outside Denver for Armorer and Gunnery School. My brother didn't like the idea of us being separated, so he wrote a letter to President Roosevelt. By gosh, some months later, orders came through reuniting us.

In 1943, after I finished at Denver, I volunteered to go to Aerial Gunnery School in Laredo, Texas, because I wanted those silver wings. In Texas, I flew in the rear open cockpit of an AT–6 trainer. The pilots took the gunners up. There were .30-caliber machine guns mounted on the edge of the cockpit. We fired at sleeve targets towed by other aircraft. The bullets had different-colored paints on the tips so that they would mark the sleeves and show how many hits we got. I guess my shooting was good enough because I got my silver wings!

After gunnery training I was sent to Gowan Field in Idaho. When I got there, I reported to this tall, skinny lieutenant in the orderly room. It was the actor, Jimmy Stewart, but I had no idea who he was at the time.

I was assigned to a B–17 crew and we started our overseas training. We had only flown a few training missions when orders came from Washington freezing me and ordering my brother to join me. I was taken off that crew while I waited for Patrick to get there. His training was longer than mine had been, and I had to wait for him to finish. They gave me work details on the base while I waited. I often wonder what happened to that crew. At that time the B–17s were getting hit really badly overseas. I wonder if that crew survived.

Patrick and I signed up for the Air Cadets at Grand Forks, North Dakota. From there we went to California. But by that time the Air Force had overestimated our pilot losses, so they began cutting back on the Air Cadet program. It didn't bother us too much. We still had our sergeant's stripes on our sleeves and our gunnery wings.

We were assigned to a crew and went overseas in Spring of 1944. We flew over in a brand-new B–17G. We were assigned to the 410th Bomb Squadron in the 94th Bomb Group.[187] Our base was Bury St. Edmunds.[188]

Originally, there were ten men in a crew, but when we got overseas they were flying missions with only nine men. They eliminated one waist gunner. In combat, if they were attacked, the radio operator would man the other waist gun. So, I was taken off the crew and made a spare gunner. That was OK, because my brother and I had hoped not to fly on the same plane in combat. Our father was still living and we thought it would be better for his sake, just in case. There was another set of twins that trained with us. They were in the same group, but a different squadron. They were each killed, one at a time.

We weren't too far from London, so we'd often go there on a two or three-day pass. Being young and single, we'd mostly chase girls. Bury St. Edmunds was a good-sized town, and I met quite a few British people. When we'd meet a British girl, we'd usually get acquainted with her family. The buzz bombs were still coming over pretty frequently. One of the first nights we were there, I heard this roaring sound, almost like a radial-engine plane doing stunts. I asked one of the guys what idiot was up there flying around in the middle of the night. It turned out it was a V–1. We got strafed once. A German plane came over in the night and shot up a field near our hut.

I had been taken off of my brother's crew, and they had already flown nine missions. I went along with them on a furlough and they all told me what combat was like. They suggested that I switch places with my brother for the next mission so I could see for myself. So I did it; I flew my first mission in his place as a waist gunner. We went to Hamburg that day. We took a few Flak hits on the plane, but nothing really bad.

Typically at two or three o'clock in the morning someone would come into the barracks with a flashlight and call out the names of everyone who was supposed to fly that day. We'd get dressed and go outside, where trucks would be waiting to take us to the mess hall. Then we'd go to briefing where we were told about the mission and the weather. From there we'd go to our individual planes and got ready to go. Each crew member had his own responsibility. As a waist gunner, all I had to do was carry my .50-caliber gun to the plane and set it up. As an armorer-gunner, it was also my job to pull the safety wires out of the bombs. The safety wires kept the little propellers on the bombs from rotating. The rotation is what armed the fuses as the bombs fell. I'd do that as we crossed the Channel, just before we hit enemy territory. I flew six missions as a waist gunner.

The Air Force had developed a new radar jammer to counteract the German gun-aiming radar. A lot of the time we were not visible from the ground. We'd fly above the cloud layer, so they used radar to aim their Flak guns at us. I was given a short training course on this new equipment, just a few days. We'd pick up the German radar signals audibly, then find that signal on our receiver and jam it with one of three transmitters.[189]

The transmitters produced static that prevented the Germans from getting a clear signal. It was kind of nerve-wracking because all they had to do was shift their signal left or right a little bit and they'd get out from under my jamming.[190] So I had to keep checking the frequency band to make sure they hadn't shifted. Sometimes there were just too many radar signals coming in and I couldn't cover them all. I had to monitor their radar the entire time we were over enemy territory. When I was working the jammer I wore headphones, so I wasn't able to hear any of the crew on the intercom. The jammer was a little taller than a two-drawer file cabinet and consisted of three transmitters and one receiver.[191] It ran off the plane's power. We were called "spot jammers." It was properly called "radar countermeasures." It wasn't really that complicated, in terms of today's electronics. It was fairly easy to learn. They taught us how to operate the system, but not to repair it. One plane in each squadron would be equipped with the jammer. So each group would have three on a mission.

For six consecutive missions Walt Tejan's crew had been flying my radar plane and I was scheduled to fly my next mission with them on 24 February 1945. My brother's crew had flown enough missions to earn them a week-long rest leave to Southport, a seaside resort. Our flight surgeon, a considerate man, offered to arrange it so I could go with them despite my shortage of missions.

We had a great time at the resort and were in high spirits during the train ride back. Our euphoria quickly vanished when we arrived at the base. Walt Tejan's plane had received a direct hit from an 88mm shell and had gone down. Some 'chutes were seen. I found out later that the shell had exploded in the radio compartment, instantly killing the radio operator. But for the kindness of the flight surgeon, I'd have died with him.

The mission I remember most was my last.[192] On this mission the ship was manned by Lieutenant Dale Nahrstedt's 410th Bomb Squadron crew.[193] Robert Knott was copilot; Art Jannek, the navigator; Ben Vitale, the bombardier; Flavis Hiers, the flight engineer; Tom Kitts, ball turret gunner; John Willey, radio operator; William Kirby, tail gunner; and Frank Camp, waist gunner. This crew had nine missions in and this was my first trip with them.[194]

We were hitting the oil refinery at a target called Plauen, which is in the eastern part of Germany close to the Russian lines. We began our bomb run at 0930. I felt the blast of freezing air just behind me as the big bomb bay doors opened. We were hit by Flak. I heard the thump and felt the ship jump a little bit and begin to vibrate badly. The Germans were aiming their radar at us and I was pretty busy with my equipment. I happened to notice the flight engineer come back into the radio compartment. He looked kind of scared so I figured there was some sort of problem. I looked up through the radio compartment hatch and could see that we were going in one direction and the rest of the group was going in another direction. I knew we were in trouble then.

Flak had killed one engine, and we were losing power in another. We knew we weren't going to make it back to England with the crippled engine. We were getting ready to bail out, but when the pilot dropped below a certain altitude, the air pressure changed and the second engine started to perform a little better. So we didn't have to jump out. We had a couple of P–51s escorting us and by that time we were over the Russian lines in Poland. The pilot happened to spot a fighter airstrip and he was able to land the plane.[195]

We had plastic-covered cardboard tags written in Russian that identified us as

Americans and asking that we be taken to the shuttle base in Poltava, one of our shuttle-bases.[196] That's what we thought was going to happen. But it didn't work out that way.

The Russian and Polish soldiers were friendly enough. They took us in and fed us. Then a Russian officer started to question us. They seemed very suspicious of us. They'd ask the same questions over and over, and ignored the answers. It was kind of strange. At one point when they were questioning our navigator on the other side of the room, I looked over and there was a German soldier standing there questioning the navigator alongside the Russian officer. The navigator had only been overseas for a few days and it was clear that he didn't recognize the uniform. I went over and asked the Russian colonel what this German was doing there.

He said, "Oh, he's a good German."

Whatever that meant!

After questioning, they put us on a gondola car for a hundred-mile train ride to a town called Oels, a hospital town. On the way we had one overnight stop at Krotoszyn. There was a castle at Oels that once had been a summer home for a crown prince of Germany. We were there for three days. There were a lot of wounded Russian soldiers recovering there. When we left Oels, we were put in a small boxcar and traveled the whole length of Poland. It took nine days, because the train stopped often, and we were bombed a few times. Our Russian escort wasn't armed. He carried the paperwork necessary to get us where we needed to go.

When we arrived at the city of Lvov in Poland, we were turned over to the Allied Military Mission offices at a hotel. We were there for a few days while we expected the Russians to arrange for transportation back to our base. Some Russians came with a big truck and said they were going to take us to the airport. We went willingly. At the airport we were taken to a second floor room in a bombed-out building. There were ten other American crew members there already. The Russians had an armed guard outside the door. We were prisoners from that point on.

They wouldn't tell us anything, but at the time it was clear their orders were coming straight from Moscow. In any contact we had with the Russian soldiers and officers they were very clearly pro-American. They liked Americans, but they had their orders and they carried them out.

We only stayed there for a short time. They flew us eastward, farther into Russia. We ended up in a regular camp with guards and barbed wire near Kiev. We were still treated well, but it was obvious that we were prisoners. Two of the other crewmen escaped from the camp. They were trying to make it to Odessa on the Black Sea. In the middle of the night they stumbled onto a Russian Flak battery and were captured. They were brought back the next day, escorted by a Russian pointing a pistol at each guy. They were kept in a room by themselves for three days and then they were released to us.

There were two Canadians with us, and they were released by the Russians. We were pretty suspicious by this time, so the Canadians said if they did get out, they'd notify the American authorities of our whereabouts. A week or so later, we were all put on a train and taken to Odessa and turned over to American authorities. That was during the last part of April 1945. We were maybe three or four days by ship from Naples, Italy. While we were in Naples, the Germans surrendered.

After a week in Naples, they put us on an old tramp steamer with an Italian crew and we went to Marseilles, France. From there we went by train to a repple-depo near Paris. Then we crossed the Channel and ended up back at Bury St. Edmunds. My brother's crew had finished all of their missions and gone home, but he had gotten permission to stay until he could find out what had happened to me. So he was still there. We came home together.

Years later I found out why the Russians had been so suspicious and why we were imprisoned. Ten years after Roosevelt died, his papers were made public. It turned out that during one of the Big Three meetings with Churchill and Stalin, they got into a serious argument about the postwar disposition of Poland. The Russians wanted to keep Poland in their sphere. The result of that argument was that anyone who ended up in their territory, British, American, Canadian, it didn't matter, was interned and put in a camp.

Because I was shot down, I wound up with only twenty-three missions. My brother flew the full thirty-five missions, flying his final mission on the day I was shot down.[197]

While we were home on furlough, the point system requirements dropped so low that we were able to be discharged. We planned on joining the reserve, but when we were discharged in North Carolina, we were hurried through the procedure so fast, they never gave us a chance to join the reserve. Later on, when the Korean War started, we were both glad we hadn't.

Both of us went to art school after the War. I became a commercial artist. I worked for the *Pittsburgh Press* for about nine years, and worked for WearEver Cookware company in New Kensington. My last job was with a printing company in New Kensington. I retired from there. I married Louise Coquillard from Greensburg in 1947. We met in art school.

I've been to quite a few of our bomb group reunions. We had our final reunion in 1999 in Seattle. My brother and I went back to the old airfield at Bury St. Edmunds in 1978. By then only a few of the buildings were still standing. These air bases were located on some of England's finest farmland.[198] By 1978 the land had reverted to farming and there wasn't much of the base left. Out of the ten men on the crew, there are five of us left. We still keep in touch.

Peter Muse (center, kneeling) and friends. Poland, 1945.

The Muse twins. Patrick (left) and Peter in London, 1945.

NOW—FOR COLLEGE MEN—A NEW OFFICERS' TRAINING PLAN

★ *New Deferred Service Plan Allows You to Continue Your Education* ★

FROM coast to coast—in the skies over America—there is a thundering drone of fighting ships. The mightiest air fleet in the history of the world is mobilizing for victory!

So fast is it growing that there is a place here—an *urgent need* here—for every college man in America who can qualify for Officer's Training.

The U. S. Army Air Forces need Officers . . . Flying Officers and Ground Crew Officers. And many of them must come from the ranks of today's college students—men who make their plans now for the necessary Aviation Cadet training.

Thanks to a newly created Air Force Reserve plan, men of all classes—within the ages of 18 to 26, inclusive—can enlist for immediate service or continue the scholastic work required for graduation before being called for active duty.

You must meet the requirements for physical fitness, of course. In addition, you take a new simplified test to determine your ability to grasp the training. A college man should pass it easily.

$75 A MONTH DURING TRAINING

Those accepted who wish immediate duty will go into training as rapidly as facilities permit. As an Aviation Cadet, you are paid $75 per month, with $1.00 a day for subsistence, with quarters, medical care, necessary uniforms, clothing, equipment, traveling expenses.

In 8 months you can win an officer's commission on the basis of your training record in competition with other Aviation Cadets. You can become one of the musketeers of the air—a bombardier, navigator, or a pilot—and be well started on your way to serve America and advance yourself in aviation.

MANY BRANCHES OF SERVICE

There are also commissions awarded in ground crew service. College men particularly will be interested in the requirements for Armaments, Communications, Engineering, Meteorology, Photography. If you have extensive engineering experience your chances of getting a commission are excellent.

This past year about 80% of all Aviation Cadets were commissioned as Second Lieutenants—about 67% as flying officers. Those who do not qualify remain in the Air Forces on an enlisted status and have further opportunities.

As a Second Lieutenant on active duty with the Army Air Forces, your pay ranges from $183 to $245 a month.

AVIATION — THE COMING INDUSTRY

The opportunities for aviation in civilian life have barely been touched. You will bring to those opportunities not only the best training in the world—but the executive ability of an Army officer's training and experience, which have always commanded a premium in business life.

ACT AT ONCE

If you want to fight for America, this is where you can strike deadly blows against our enemies.

If you want advancement—years of solid achievement and education that can never be duplicated—this is where you belong.

If you want to be up there in the middle of things—when the enemy cries quits—your place is *here*—in the Army Air Forces.

FLY WITH YOUR FRIENDS

A special squadron for training is now forming at this college. You and your friends can share together the work and fun of training. If you plan to enlist immediately, start getting your necessary papers ready for the Aviation Cadet Examining Board when it meets in your locality. For complete information, see your Faculty Air Force Advisor. You can take your mental and physical examinations the same day you apply. Get further information now.

* * *

NOTE: *If you wish to enlist, and you are under 21, you will need your parents' or guardian's consent. Birth certificates and three letters of recommendation will be required of all applicants. Obtain the forms and send them home today—you can then complete your enlistment before any Aviation Cadet Examining Board.*

THREE ENLISTMENT PLANS FOR COLLEGE MEN

Juniors • Sophomores • Freshmen May Continue Their Education

1. A new plan allows Juniors, Sophomores and Freshmen in college, aged 18 to 26, inclusive, to enlist in the Air Force Enlisted Reserve and continue their schooling, provided they maintain satisfactory scholastic standings.

All College Men May Enlist for Immediate Service

2. All college students may enlist as privates in the Army Air Forces (unassigned) and serve there until their turns come for Aviation Cadet training.

3. All college students may enlist in the Air Force Enlisted Reserve and wait until they are ordered to report for Aviation Cadet training.

Upon graduation or withdrawal from college, men will be assigned to active duty at a training center as facilities become available.

If the necessity of war demands, the deferred status in the Army Reserve may be terminated at any time by the Secretary of War.

The new Army Air Force Enlisted Reserve Plan is part of an over-all Army Enlisted Reserve Corps program shortly to be announced. This program will provide opportunities for college men to enlist in other branches of the Army on a deferred basis and to continue their education through graduation if a satisfactory standard of work is maintained. In case of necessity the Secretary of War shall determine when they be called to active duty.

It is understood that men so enlisted will have the opportunity of competing for vacancies in officer's candidate schools.

This plan has been approved in the belief that continuance of education will develop capacities for leadership. (Reserve enlistment will not alter regulations regarding established R.O.T.C. plans.)

LET'S GO! U.S.A. KEEP 'EM FLYING!

SEE YOUR FACULTY AIR FORCE ADVISOR FOR FULL INFORMATION

(*Or Apply to Your Local Recruiting and Induction Station*)

THE SPECIAL EXAMINING BOARD WILL VISIT YOUR CAMPUS SOON

"I Propped My Razor and Shaving Cream on a Convenient, Shroud-Covered Cadaver."

E. Kay Myers
Landing Craft, Tank USS *LCT–1420*
Born in Huntingdon, Pennsylvania, 22 June 1925
Ligonier, Pennsylvania

"Then there was one time I read in The Daily Okinawan, a recently established Armed Forces newsletter, that Admiral Chester Nimitz, the Commander-in-Chief of the Pacific Fleet had visited the island. One of my crew heard me remark on that and said, 'Yes, and he came on board the 694.' My eyes bugged out as I queried him when and where. 'It was Sunday morning. We were all asleep. His barge pulled up alongside and he crawled over the side and walked across the main deck, passing about six feet from your cabin. Then he crawled over the side and stepped onto the dock where a Jeep was waiting.' Now you must realize there was a rigid protocol to be observed when a ranking officer boarded a Navy vessel. Side boys in dress uniform should be lined up and saluted when the bosun piped the officer on board. Well, I was shocked, but realized my bosun probably didn't even own a pipe, and no one wore dress uniforms. I then asked him what the man on watch did. He relied that Eppley, the quartermaster, was on duty, and when he saw the Admiral's barge come alongside, he hid in the pilot house. At that point, I laughed and agreed he was wise to lay low."

I AM PLEASED TO BE recognized as a member of the "Greatest Generation" that fought and won the Second World War from 1941 until 1945. But there's one problem with my military career, I was no hero! While many of my classmates fought bravely and perished during those troubled times, I spent sixteen months of my service time attending college and another six months earning a commission in the USNR and qualifying as a trained deck officer. It wasn't a very exciting, dangerous or tough military career. I was very lucky for many of my friends and classmates didn't survive that terrible time.

It all began in the spring of 1943, my senior year at Latrobe High School. The Navy, in preparation for Operation OLYMPIC,[199] anticipated a shortage of officers and came up with the idea of a national intelligence test, which they gave to all interested high school seniors. Those who passed were given an opportunity to attend college for at least four semesters to qualify for a commission in the USNR. This was called the Navy V–12 program. There were other versions such as V–5 for potential naval aviators and another for young men interested in pursuing medical careers. I passed and in mid-May 1943, I went to Pittsburgh and took a physical and was sworn into the USNR as an apprentice seaman. For some reason, I was the first from the class, but more followed.

On 1 July 1943, with my classmates Robert K. "Chis" McCormick and Larry E. Moore, we went to Pittsburgh where we boarded a Pennsylvania Railroad troop train of V–12 students bound for colleges in the East. We three were assigned to Princeton University. The fact that Larry's aunt was the secretary for Commander Lynch, CO of the Pittsburgh Navy Recruiting Station probably helped our college selection.[200]

At Penn Station, we met a friend Marcus W. Saxman, III, who was headed to the Massachusetts Institute of Technology. Mark, who lived only a few blocks from us, had already completed a year at Lehigh, but the Navy assigned him to the New England school.

As apprentice seamen, we attended classes in uniform and were subject to military discipline that included plenty of close-order drills. We also were assigned courses such as calculus, thermodynamics, astronomy, navigation and physics that the Navy deemed appropriate for future officers. Attending college was a wonderful way to serve our country! Two other of my classmates at Latrobe High went through the same program. Adolph "Abby" Lena went to Penn State and Dick McHenry became a naval aviator, but I'm not sure where he received his college work.

After four semesters of college, in late November, Larry and I were assigned to Pre-Midshipman School at Asbury Park, New Jersey. After a month, Larry went off to the Notre Dame Midshipman School. He earned his commission and got assigned to a Naval destroyer in the Pacific and actually saw some action on a picket ship off Okinawa. After two semesters at Princeton, Chis, who had been my roommate, transferred to the V–5 to become an aviator like his brother, Eddie. Edward McCormick, a football star at Princeton had become a pilot, he was lost at sea in early 1944. He flew off of his a carrier and was never seen again. It's because Eddie had been to Princeton, that the three of us requested that particular school. Chis washed out of pilot training, but went to become an aerial navigator.

In late January 1944, I was ordered to board a troop train to Chicago where we were assigned to the Abbott-Hall Midshipman School in the downtown. As soon as we arrived in the Windy City, we realized we were special. From the train we were packed into buses and escorted to Tower Hall by a police motorcycle escort complete with screaming sirens. Our barracks, Tower Hall, was in a twenty-storey building close to the landmark Water Tower and the Navy had built a bridge so we could march across Michigan Boulevard to classes at the National Guard Armory and Northwestern's downtown campus. One of the first graduates of Abbott Hall was Ensign John F. Kennedy, who later distinguished himself as a PT boat skipper in the Solomon Islands. Several of our instructors were classmates of Kennedy.

The people in Chicago loved servicemen and it was a great life. Classes were hard, but we were treated as potential officers and treated royally. Once I picked up a neat young lady in a loop bar who took me home to dinner in the suburbs. She turned out to be the niece of my Latrobe dentist. It was surely a tough war and even we had casualties. One day on a training cruise in Lake Michigan, one of my suite mates fell overboard and the seas were so rough, they couldn't pick him up, and he drowned. The irony is that a short while before his accident he had pointed out to me his family home less than a half-mile from where he perished.

As a side note, in Chicago I got together with my roommate from Princeton, Wally Good. Wally was super-smart. The only person I knew who was exempted from all math homework by the professor. He also was a good friend of Larry Moore and visited Latrobe on one of our leaves. Unfortunately, Wally was flunked out of midshipman school for lack of military aptitude despite the fact that all his grades were 4.0. He was a little chunky and maybe a bit slovenly, but I was shocked when I found out. His father had been the Secretary of the Navy Forrestal's roommate at Princeton. The Navy did, however, recognize Wally's brain sent him to Chicago to a special radar/electronic school for whiz kids.

On 12 April, Franklin Roosevelt, our president, died. That Sunday, we were called back early from our weekend liberty to stand at attention for two hours in the Armory honoring our fallen Commander. That just happened to be the weekend my buddy, Dick Turnbull from Meadville, Pennsylvania and I had a big time with our Chicago girls and I didn't get much sleep. Midshipmen began to drop out of rank right and left from exhaustion. I was ready to fall myself when we were finally dismissed, but I used that occasion to stop by the sickbay. All I really wanted to do was check out the Navy eye-examination chart because I was slated for my officer's physical the next day. My eyes had been just a tad off ever since Larry Moore caught me one day with an ice ball to my left eye. I've worn glasses ever since.

Everything went well at the physical, until the doctor caught me.

"Myers, you've got that chart memorized. You don't need to do that. I'll get you a waiver and you'll still get commissioned."

He was right. Dr. Smith came through and I got my waiver on the morning of our graduation ceremony. Because it was slow in coming, I hadn't had my gold stripe sewn on my uniform coat. Somehow, my mother managed to do it. My parents were in Chicago to see me become "an officer and a gentleman" at Chicago's Navy Pier. Secretary of the Navy Forrestal[201] gave the graduation address. I was nineteen when I got my gold bar.

After graduating as an Ensign, one of twenty-five hundred in the twenty-fourth and last class at Tower Hall, I was sent to Miami, Florida, to General Line Officer's Training Center. There we lived in a luxury hotel BOQ (Bachelor Officers' Quarters) close to the Miami Beach causeway. Our training included cruises on USS Destroyer Escort 595,[202] which just happened to be manned by a fellow classmate and Spring Street neighbor, Robert "Cheese" Switzer. He was a machinist mate. While at Princeton, Cheese met me in New York City about a year before for a weekend cruising 52nd Street and the Village.

I was at sea studying Anti-Submarine Warfare in early August on an AK(cargo ship) in the Caribbean when the ship's news reported a bomb had been dropped on Hiroshima that wiped out the whole city. By the time we returned to port in Miami, we learned it was the Atom bomb. At this time I was due to graduate, and while awaiting orders, I lined up a part-time job as a singing waiter at Zissan's Bowery on Miami Beach. It was expensive to enjoy the Miami night life so this job was a big help.

Sometimes officers waited for weeks for new orders, so I was prepping for the worst. After one night on the job, my orders transferred me to Coronado, California for amphibious training. I was able to come home on leave in Latrobe when the Japanese surrendered and the World went wild. We raced all over town, horns blowing and people screaming. The streets were packed with people. The Mahady family hired a polka band to play on the front porch of their Ligonier Street home. Townspeople who had been working overtime for years in local plants were relieved as were the many families with boys overseas. Joy was blatant, not only in Latrobe, but all across the nation.

At Coronado, we'd hike a half-mile from our BOQ to the exclusive Hotel Del Coronado where we used their beach to swim in the Pacific. We also took advantage of the bar, but it was cheaper to drink in Officers' Club at the base. Coronado is just across the bay from San Diego so I looked up my old high school journalism teacher, Don "Doc" Benford, who was a training officer at the San Diego Naval Base. Doc took me to the Navy Officers' Club located in the middle of the San Diego Zoo. At Coronado I ran into my old high school debating partner, Abby Lena, who had just been commissioned. Doc took the two of us to Tijuana, Mexico, to see the sights.

The way the Navy does things, the morning train to San Francisco was held up so Marshall Raymond, a fellow graduate of Tower Hall, and I could get our orders written and make the train. The WAVE typing our orders loved holding up the train. In San Francisco we were put up at the former German-American Club, now a Navy BOQ. We had a wonderful time in Frisco. Nothing to do but loaf around and go out on the town. We met some neat gals from San Francisco College for Women and really lived it up each night while awaiting transportation across the Pacific.

The War was over, but we were still shipping out to be replacements getting ready for the big occupation of Japan. After a week, orders came through and we shipped out on an APA (Attack Transport). My San Francisco girlfriend took the day off and came down to the dock to wave me off. That got me a big cheer from the sailors lining the dock. We officers shared a large cabin on the main deck. As a junior officer, I was assigned to be in charge of one compartment of Navy seaman. It was an easy job, except I had a problem. The men complained one sailor refused to shower and smelled bad. I advised them to get a gang and take him into the shower where they could scrub him down, and they did. Another time I awoke to discover that one of my men had received a "Dear John" letter from his girl and was so despondent that he hung himself. As his Commanding Officer, I had to participate at his funeral. Fortunately, the APA captain opted to read the burial service as his flag-draped casket, with the ship's company lined up at attention, was tipped into the Pacific. My job was to grab the flag and send it with a letter of condolence to his family.

While we were sailing across the Pacific, the official Japanese surrender ceremony took place on board battleship USS *Missouri* in Tokyo Bay. We arrived in Buckner Bay, Okinawa, in mid-September and it wasn't long until an LCT, really not much more than an overgrown barge, pulled along side to start unloading the APA.[203]

Ensign H. Edward Patterson, my Latrobe neighbor from across Spring Street, had written to me that he was on an LCT, but wartime censorship didn't permit him to say where.

On a hunch, I hollered across to the LCT Skipper standing on the conning tower, "Do you know where the USS *LCT–689* is?"

"Sure. That's Ed Patterson's boat. He's probably at Brown Beach."

On our own, Curley Raymond and I hitched a ride ashore with the LCT where we disembarked on the steel causeway assembled by the Seabees. As we looked around we saw something was going on. An ambulance lurched past us and stopped in front of a bunch of scraggly sailors. It turned out they were playing pickup basketball with a steel bank-board stuck along the edge of the dock. It seems the bank-board had been jostled and crashed down breaking the neck of one of the players. Death on the causeway was our introduction to Okinawa. So we reported to the Navy repple-depple located in a nearby tent.

There I discovered my assignment was to the USS *LCT–1420*, but I'd need to wait while they figured out where it was and processed my orders. They figured we'd be living in a nearby tent city eating K-rations for a couple of days until things were sorted out.

With nothing else to do, Curley and I decided to hitchhike around the island to see the sights. It was easy to snare a ride on a Jeep or half-track since they were cruising back and forth. We decided to see Naha, the capitol, but were stopped at a roadblock several miles north. The Jeep driver told us the Marines were digging Japs out of caves nearby and if we were careful, we might see something interesting. That we did! As we walked toward the action, a Marine suggested that was as close as we should go. Suddenly, the air was full of the acrid smoke of burning flesh and a few minutes later, a handful of scraggly Japanese soldiers wearing loin cloths came marching by with their hands held high. That was our introduction to Okinawa.

Even a year later, emaciated and starving Japs continued to be flushed out of the Island's warren of caves. One May 1946 morning, while Seabees loaded my LCT with defective ammunition, I saw a Marine patrol walk by with some twenty prisoners who had just surrendered. They still were carrying their rifles. One shot on my deck full of defective bombs and stuff could have made an interesting day.

When Ed Patterson heard I was on the island, he went up to "LCTville" where he checked with the Squadron 35 CO and discovered I was assigned to the *1420*. It just happened that the *LCT–1420* was at that time attached to a repair ship at Gray Beach where they were installing an A-frame crane on the bow. Ed borrowed a squadron Jeep and picked Curley and I up at the tented repple-depple BOQ and took us to flotilla headquarters where they expedited our orders. It seemed the *1420* was to become a repair ship to help clean up all the sunken ships and boats littering Buckner Bay after a typhoon that blew through a week before we arrived.[204] Curley was slated to be an executive officer of another LCT.

The Captain of the *1420* was so happy to see me; he immediately held a welcoming ceremony with the whole crew, all twenty of them drawn up at attention. That's when I learned that I was the new Executive Officer. Later, the full story came out. Once I learned how to handle an LCT, he'd be allowed to return to the states to see his wife and baby daughter. It seems LTJG Welsh had been overseas for two years and was most anxious to head home. He'd been in the Philippines when his wife had the baby. It had been more than a year, and he hadn't seen her yet. One strange thing I learned about the Skipper was that he came down with sympathetic morning sickness when his wife was pregnant, but he still suffered from the psychological malady a year after his wife had the child. Another thing I noticed, for lack of any proper reading material, he was reading the dictionary from A to Z. Every now and then he'd look over at me and chuckled, "Here's a good word" and read the definition. Once he admitted to me that this was the third time he was reading through the book.

Needless to say after one week on board, he was happy to turn over the command of the ship to me. At the age of twenty, I was the youngest guy on the ship and assumed the post of officer-in-charge. The *1420* was one-hundred-twenty-feet long and thirty-three-and one-half-feet wide. With a full load, she drew eighteen inches at the bow and three and a half feet in the stern. She was powered with three 225 HP Gray Marine Diesel engines. On a fair day, we could clip down the channel at a flank speed of six knots. That meant if we had a tail wind, the flag on the stern would be flying in the direction the wind blew. But with three engines and three screws, she was very maneuverable.

There was one other problem with the *1420.* There was a full load of deep sea diving equipment on the main deck. The gear belonged to a Seabee unit that had suddenly been pulled off the Island and shipped to Japan when the surrender was signed and no one knew what to do with a deck load of diving gear. That meant we couldn't operate. The squadron commander solved that problem by assigning the *1420* to tie up along side Ed Patterson's *689.* It seems Ed's LCT had gone aground on a coral reef during the invasion of Okinawa, and despite time in a repair LSD her bottom still had serious leaks. My ship was ordered to help keep Ed's LCT afloat with our pumps. So, we two residents of Spring Street, Latrobe, tied up our ships and integrated the crews. That situation lasted until mid-January 1946, when Ed's ship was ordered back to the States. A huge crane lifted the *LCT–689* out of the water and loaded her on the deck of an LST, destination Pearl Harbor. When they got to Pearl Harbor, the captain of the LST had enough points to be sent home and discharged. As the senior officer on board, Ed was made CO of the LST and sailed her back to the States where she and the *LCT–689* were decommissioned under his command. Do you see why I laugh when I repeat "War is Hell."

Meanwhile, back at Buckner Bay with nothing to do, Ed and I spent many a night at the Brown Beach Navy Officer's Club. It was in a Quonset hut with a dirt floor. The bar was a trestle table and there were no seats. The only glasses were the standard USN water glass. Hours were five o'clock in the afternoon to seven o'clock in the evening. We had to use the Occupation money. A bottle of beer, variety whatever popped up, cost five cents. A shot of whisky was ten cents and since there were no shot glasses, it was measured by eye as one-third of a water glass. What we'd do is buy four or five whiskeys and pour them into a Coke bottle for later consumption, usually at the night's poker game. War is not a joke, but some of us were lucky and made the best of our situation.

They had erected an outdoor stage and movie screen near Brown Beach, and there would be a movie a couple nights each week. That was the highlight of the day. One time, everyone was excited to hear there would be a USO show. After stoking up at the officer's club, a group of LCT skippers walked over to see the show. There was a lot of the usual banter between everyone when an officer sitting in front of me jumped up and ordered us to stop using foul language.

Figuring it was some self-important LST Skipper, I said, "Stow it, Mate."

The man erupted and slugged me in the left eye with his right fist.

Immediately, my fellow LCT guys jumped up and were ready to fight with shouts of, "Who hit Myers?"

I could see my antagonist was really worked up, and I tried to calm the boys down. When he hit me, the guy broke the lens of my glasses and the glass cut my eye so I was bleeding. Ed grabbed my arm and told me we were going to the infirmary, which was just above the theater amphitheater. In the meantime, Curley obtained the name, rank and serial number of the officer who slugged me. He was Lt. Commander B_____, a Baptist chaplain!

The Shore Patrol showed up and took him into custody and interviewed me in the Emergency Room while the corpsman treated my eye.

Asked if I wanted to prosecute, I said "No."

What chance would a lowly Ensign have in a court against a chaplain? Actually, someone determined the chaplain was suffering from battle fatigue and the next day he was on a flight back to the Naval Hospital in Pearl.

The outcome of the situation was that I had pieces of glass in my eye, and the next day they shipped me down to the big Naval Hospital at Gray Beach where they operated. The first MD, it turned out, had the serious shakes ever since the Jeep he was riding in earlier in December was run over by a DUKW, killing his three fellow doctors.

The head MD, anticipating a problem, took over the eye operation at that point and as he delicately plucked out the shards of glass from the left eye, asked "Ensign Myers, do you remember me? I'm the guy who gave you the eye waiver in Chicago."

Small world!

It cost me a case of beer to get my glasses repaired and new lenses installed, and I spent the next three weeks in the Brown Beach Hospital. Since I was the only officer there, the officers' head doubled as a morgue. More than once when shaving in the morning, I had to prop my razor and shaving cream on a convenient, shroud-covered cadaver. The hospital was busy. Sometimes men cleaning up the debris of the fighting came across phosphorous bombs and received bad burns. The hospital ward often reeked of burning flesh. My crew would drop off the Jeep in the evening after they used it during the day and I'd pick up Ed and my other buddies and we'd go off to various Officers' Clubs scattered about the island. I still recall one night over at the White Beach Club, when I felt the need to relieve myself, walking out to the smelly outdoor head, I decided it was far more pleasant to urinate in the bushes when a guard carrying a carbine came up and told me, "Sir, will you please not urinate outside. You are to use the head."

I responded with a chuckle, "Too late buddy, I can't stop now."

Jeeps were in a great demand, but none were issued to the amphibs. This bothered the crews of the *689* and *1420*, so the boys scouted around and found a field full of Jeeps and other surplus vehicles. They selected one that was near a road and, in the dead of night, checked it out, making certain it would run. They even replaced the battery. Finally, one night they said they were ready to "liberate" the vehicle. Ed's bosun's mate had somehow gotten a hold of an LCVP and a couple guys plus Ed and I climbed aboard and headed to the causeway where we tied up with the ramp partially down. Suddenly, the Jeep zoomed onto the dock and headed toward us. Just as they began to back it up to the ramp, the Jeep stalled. At that moment, an Army MP Jeep with red flashing lights and siren blaring raced toward us.

"The jig's up," shouted Ed. "We'd better vamoose."

Everyone jumped into the LCVP, while Ed on one side and me on the other surreptitiously uncoiled the bow lines and slipped into the LCVP as the MPs swarmed over the abandoned Jeep. With a roar, the coxswain threw the LCVP in reverse and we roared away from the causeway unscathed.

From our officer club travels, we got to meet other units. In fact, one unit had traveled to the Okinawa invasion on Ed's ship. That's how we met Colonel Wilson from Little Rock, Arkansas, where he was a car dealer. His executive officer was a Captain Smith and every now and then they'd show up for cocktails and dinner on our LCTs. They loved our food. Sometimes Captain Smith brought along a real, live Army nurse. When she showed up, the crew went "gaga." So did I.

One night the Colonel told us they were in charge of all vehicles on the island and it was getting to be a problem. A couple of days ago, some enterprising sailors had tried to steal one of their Jeeps. Ed and blinked and I told him it would surely be handy to own a Jeep.

"Hey, no problem! I'll be happy to give you a Jeep, complete with Navy serial numbers and registration. I'll even get you boys Okinawa driver's licenses."

That Jeep was my pride and joy.

In mid-January, while I was still in the Navy Hospital recovering from my eye operation, Ed's ship was ordered back to Pearl. At the same time, the *1420* was ordered to Eniwetok for the atomic bomb tests. Since I wasn't available, another officer took over, so I missed all that excitement. With orders, the load on the deck was suddenly removed. I later learned my crew went to Eniwetok with a hold full of beer, which I bet they were able to unload at a great profit.

LCT men were very resourceful. Since we hauled cargo from ships in the harbor to the shore, if it was useful stuff, a few items would disappear into the bowels of the boat and later be shared with other crews. When I finally was released from the hospital, I was sent to White Beach to take charge of the USS *LCT–1328*. It had a problem. During a typhoon, the bow ramp had fallen off and thus the vessel couldn't be operated. I was delighted to wake up my first morning on board and reaching up, pulled out of a bookcase left by the old Skipper, a copy of Agnes Sligh Turnbull's[205] wonderful history of the Colonial times around the Loyalhanna Creek. It made me homesick. I also discovered two volumes of War and Peace, which I read with one eye in a week. When I had to move the ship, I had my Quartermaster stand near me in the conning tower pointing out the buoys and channel markers.

The squadron lost so many officers in the spring of 1946. At one time I was Skipper of the *694* and *1328*, and I also operated three times a week another LCT, whose Captain was in the Naval Hospital with a bad case of malaria. It just happened at that time with pullbacks to the states and a frequent turnover of men, we landing-craft folk lived quite well. Once I was down to a crew of five men. Two of them were cooks and the third was a baker. Another time I happened to check the payroll and discovered my bosun's mate (and a good one too) was really a 1st class petty officer with a mess cook specialty.

When I faced him with the fact, he explained, "Skipper, I've got a problem. I don't mind cooking, but I can't eat any food I cooked. If someone else cooks it, everything is fine. Well, on a small ship like this, that's a problem, so I bribed the squadron yeoman with a birthday cake to put me down on the muster as a coxswain."

The acting-chief cook did have a penchant for every now and then stepping out to the stern of the ship from his galley and shooting out to sea. Sometimes, he'd use a .45 pistol and other times a rifle. He claimed it relaxed him and except for the noise, never bothered anyone.

As a working Navy, we had little to do with the native Okinawans. Although officialdom frowned on the term, we all called them "Gooks." Sometimes they came around our anchorage in small, wooden canoes to fish. They dropped nets and make a circle fifty to one-hundred-feet across and then one of the men would drop a small charge, probably a hand grenade, into the water. That would kill a school of small fish and, with great glee, the canoes would paddle toward the center as they pulled in their nets.

Many times our work consisted of going out to the Bay and meeting a ship returning natives that the Japanese had sent as laborers to other islands. Once I came alongside a Japanese destroyer packed with Gooks. I know now it was silly, but I wanted to show the enemy we were the conquerors. As I stepped aboard the destroyer, I deliberately spit a big hawker at the feet of the commanding officer who greeted me at the head of the ladder. I later learned more civil skippers were invited into the Captain's Quarters and given tea or saki and a small token, such as a silver mustache trimmer. My guy did tell me he had been on the *Yamato*[206] when the Navy sunk it in the China Sea. After we hauled that dirty, smelly load of humanity to port, we had to hose down our decks to get rid of the debris, excrement and garbage they left behind.

The US Navy didn't quite know how to treat our amphibs. For instance, when a "reefer" ship (refrigerator ship) showed up in Buckner Bay, we'd sail out to it and requisition meat. To the Navy, we were considered a small ship like a destroyer escort and that was the ration they'd give us. Enough meat to feed a crew of 350 men. We'd take the best, the "roasting and fryers," some chicken maybe and hamburger for variety. Then we'd share the bonanza with fellow ships and what no one wanted, mutton, two-year-old cold storage eggs, we'd give to the Gooks. Some guys got excited by the women, but they were generally chunky and most sported gold teeth which turned me off.

When I was awaiting a ship back to the states back in the repple-depple, we had native gals who straightened our Quonset hut quarters and even made our beds. They giggled a lot, but most of us were holding out for stateside feminine pulchritude. I was somewhat chagrined when I went to the flotilla headquarters in the *LCT–1415* to discover LTJG R______ was the CO and had to sign my release papers. I had been offered that post with an advance in rank, but was too homesick to want to spend another six months on the island. I knew R______, a smiling Irishman from Boston, from Asbury Park, and I considered him a poor officer. Once I came across his ship aground in the middle of a channel and pulled alongside to help get the vessel free. One look around the *1415* underlined my opinion for he had integrated the crew with young Gook females. I had to admit that the one that seemed to be his was a beauty, but the ship was filthy and the condition of the vessel shocked me.

Okinawa was a beautiful, hilly, wooded island. One thing we couldn't miss was the ancestral tombs. Nearly every hillside in the settled sections was dotted with these tombs made of cement and stone. They often had pillars in front and fancy doors, and they made great hiding places for the hundreds of holdout Japs. Another feature of the island, was the row after row of rice paddies frequently filled with water. A popular shortcut from the causeway at Brown Beach was to cut through a rice paddy and many of us rued that trip because the banks of the paddies were narrow and often slippery. Anyone who fell into a paddy was covered with slimy, stinking mud. The Okinawans used human waste for fertilizer adding to the putrid mess.

Then there was one time I read in *The Daily Okinawan*, a recently established Armed Forces newsletter, that Admiral Chester Nimitz, the Commander-in-Chief of the Pacific Fleet had visited the island.

One of my crew heard me remark on that and said, "Yes, and he came on board the *694*."

My eyes bugged out as I queried him when and where.

"It was Sunday morning. We were all asleep. His barge pulled up alongside and he crawled over the side and walked across the main deck, passing about six-feet from your cabin. Then he crawled over the side and stepped onto the dock where a Jeep was waiting."

Now you must realize there was a rigid protocol to be observed when a ranking officer boarded a Navy vessel. Side boys in dress uniform should be lined up and saluted when the bosun piped the officer on board. Well, I was shocked, but realized my bosun probably didn't even own a pipe, and no one wore dress uniforms. I then asked him what the man on watch did. He replied that Eppley, the quartermaster, was on duty, and when he saw the Admiral's barge come alongside, he hid in the pilot house. At that point, I laughed and agreed he was wise to lay low.

Another time I decided my crew did care about me. One morning while I was showering, the man on watch stuck his head in the stall and said, "Skipper, you've got to hear this." As I grabbed my towel to dry off, he told me he heard a priority radio message that a Tsunami was spotted at sea heading to Okinawa and that 250-foot tidal wave would hit the island in ten minutes.

As I shook my head to clear my hearing, I said "go back and verify the message and then pass the word to all ships."

At that point, I realized the *694* was the only ship that had a twenty-four-hour watch. With peacetime, most LCTs were in a relaxed mode.

Then I headed to my cabin to grab some clothes and a copy of my seamanship manual to look up "Tsunami." That would be a large, high wave initiated by an underwater disturbance such as an earthquake and be followed by smaller high waves and a high tide. With that information, I ordered "all hands on deck" and commanded that the ship's engines should be started. Then I ran on deck and realized that I was the inboard LCT with three others tied up toward the harbor.

By now the sleeping lineup of ships had come to life and people were scurrying about, starting motors and battening down the hatches. We had a quick huddle of skippers, and they agreed with me that our best course of action would be to head out in the channel and anchor with our bows headed to shore. If we were lucky, our ships would be carried ashore by the wave. There was one problem. As the inboard vessel I had to wait until all the other ships left the dock. After about fifteen minutes, the coast was clear, and I manned the con ordering the lines untied and the engines back one-third. Nothing happened. The *694* was aground. We needed to wait until the tide came in to lift the ship. Two hours later, we floated free and headed out to the harbor. In the meantime, I knew one of the cooks had vowed he'd never spend another typhoon at sea so anticipating trouble, I strapped on my .45 and went and stood on the bow. Sure enough the guy wanted to jump ship, but when he saw I meant business, he backed off. He also saw my logic that he was safer on board than trying to get to high ground at White Beach.

We anchored out in the harbor and received another message that apparently the Tsunami had dissipated at sea, but we were warned to expect a higher than usual tide. It was all of six-inches above normal. Meanwhile, anchored out, I decided to swim over to visit with my buddy, Chuck Harrison. I told the watch where I was going and said I'd be back in an hour. No problems swimming over, but when I started to swim back, I found out the tide was coming in, and it was tough to swim against the current.

That's when the ship's dingy put-putted up, and Eppley pulled me out of the water. "Skipper, I was watching for you and figured you needed a ride."

God bless Eppley!

Homeward bound, I caught an APA headed to San Diego by way of Tokyo Bay where we picked up a battalion of Marines in Yokosuka. Their Gung-Ho officers who shared our cabin made the voyage home a pain. From San Diego, I ended up in Philadelphia where I received my release to inactive duty after thirty-seven months in the Navy.

I was called back for the Korean War, but the medics turned me down because I still had glass in my eye, though it didn't interfere with my vision.

After my release to inactive duty in September 1946, I wanted to finish college at Princeton, but my application had disappeared in a 1945 Christmas package I never received. With colleges packed with returning servicemen, I couldn't be admitted until 1947. Instead, I enrolled at Saint Vincent College and later graduated from Dickinson College, Carlisle, Pennsylvania, after earning summer credits at Penn State University. It was at Penn State where I met my wife Gertrude, a native of Shamokin, Pennsylvania.

Following a short romance, we got married, and I went to work for United Press in Frankfort, Kentucky. I lost my job after a transfer to Harrisburg, Pennsylvania, because I refused to join a Guild strike. What I didn't know was that my boss and Harrisburg Bureau Chief was also head of the local Guild.

Next, I worked in radio in Shamokin, Bloomsburg and Reading, before returning home to Latrobe as advertising manager/PR director for Vanadium-Alloys Steel. I worked there from 1954 to 1966, when I went into advertising. Since 1989, my wife and I publish *Around Latrobe* and the *Ligonier Free Gazette*.

E. Kay Meyers (right) and friend on Okinawa after the War.

Ships in Buckner Bay while Typhoon Louise rages, 9 October 1945. *National Archives.*

Buckner Bay, Okinawa, after Typhoon Louise that hit 9 October 1945. *National Archives.*

"It Was All Unreal to Me."

Gordon Mickley

USS *LCG(L)–426*
USS *LCT–1224*[207]
Born in Evans City, Pennsylvania, 9 May 1921
† 9 April 2007

"On our way in, a landing craft full of troops passed us. We hadn't yet turned to go into our firing position at that point. The troops on the landing craft waved to us. I was in the front of our boat at the time because I was supposed to stay on end opposite the captain. That way we both wouldn't be hit at the same time and I could take over command if he were killed or injured. As I stood there, I waved back at them. All of a sudden they swerved and went under our bow. As soon as they did that, they exploded. The troops in that craft flew all over the place. It didn't hurt our boat at all but it destroyed their landing craft. I'm sure some of those men were killed by our propellers. We kept moving because we had orders not to stop for any reason. I think they tried to avoid a mine, but hit another one. It was just lucky for us that they hit the mine before we did."

I WAS STILL IN college in 1943, the year I signed up for the Navy. The Navy program I enlisted in allowed me to stay in school until I graduated, and since the Navy wanted us to graduate as soon as possible, we didn't have to take final exams. As soon as I graduated the Navy assigned me to Notre Dame University as an apprentice seaman. After thirty days I was promoted to Navy cadet. I graduated from cadet training after ninety days, and was sent to Sullivan Cove, Maryland, to be trained as an officer on landing craft and small boats.

My training at Sullivan Cove, however, went for nothing, because we were all transferred to England to train on boats that were going to provide fire support for the infantry that would be involved in the invasion of Normandy. They were larger than the ones we trained on in Maryland, and we were sent to England even before they were completed. We left the United States for England on 1 January 1944 and landed in Scotland at Rosen Heath. We stayed there until the boats were ready.

There were three different kinds of craft in our support group.[208] They were all manufactured by the British, and they were all built on the hull of existing landing craft. The boat I served on as executive officer had old-fashioned British 5-inch guns and 20 and 40mm guns. A second version carried a rocket platform, and a third version was converted into an antiaircraft platform.

Once the boats were ready, we took them to Southern England for training exercises. We were based beside a little town, near the mouth of a river that flowed out to the open water. We arrived there five months before the invasion. While we were there, we would go out to the open water and do extensive fire training on targets that were set up to like the actual targets we would be firing on during the invasion.

We knew the time had come for the invasion when we were no longer allowed to get off the boat for liberty. We stayed on the boat, at the ready, until 4 June 1944, the day we started across the English Channel for the Normandy coast. We left ahead of time because we were slower than the rest of the convoy. We were already halfway across the Channel when Eisenhower called back the invasion because of bad weather.[209]

We turned around and put at the Isle of Wight, just off England's southern coast. We spent the night there and the next day started another Channel crossing. Our area was UTAH Beach.[210]

The landings were timed very closely so that the landing parties could get to shore on schedule. There wasn't much room in that water and there were a lot of coxswains doing a lot of signal work back and forth so there wouldn't be any problems or backups.

The landing craft taking in the infantry circled after they loaded up and waited until they got the signal to go. Then, in intervals because there were so many places on the beach to land troops, they broke out of the circle and headed toward shore.

On our way in, a landing craft full of troops passed us. We hadn't yet turned to go into our firing position at that point. The troops on the landing craft waved to us. I was in the front of our boat at the time because I was supposed to stay on end opposite the captain. That way we both wouldn't be hit at the same time and I could take over command if he were killed or injured. As I stood there, I waved back at them. All of a sudden they swerved and went under our bow. As soon as they did that, they exploded. The troops in that craft flew all over the place. It didn't hurt our boat at all but it destroyed their landing craft. I'm sure some of those men were killed by our propellers. We kept moving because we had orders not to stop for any reason. I think they tried to avoid a mine, but hit another one. It was just lucky for us that they hit the mine before we did.

After the invasion, we stayed anchored near UTAH Beach for a time. We had nothing to do there but sit. To pass the time, we listened to our radio to get reports on how everything was going inland. A few days after D-Day the top command decided that there would be a second invasion in southern France.[211] They only took the rocket boats for that operation and sent us back to Scotland where we waited until they refitted our boats with larger guns.

In September, when our boats were ready, we were ordered back to the States. Churchill wanted to go, but for some reason he didn't want to fly, so he came with us on the *Queen Mary*.[212] We dropped him off in Halifax, Nova Scotia. I didn't see him get on or off the boat. He must have gotten off in the dead of night. Once we reached New York, we were all given leave.

While on leave I bought my future wife a ring, and we got married. Shortly thereafter I received orders to return to New York. There I was assigned to an LCT which was a smaller landing craft than the one I had been on. I was the skipper of that boat, and I had a crew of twelve.

In New York, our LCT was placed onboard an LST for transportation to the Pacific via the Panama Canal. Our first stop in the Pacific was to be San Francisco, but we had an incident before we got there. One of the sailors developed appendicitis. Luckily, we had a doctor on board who told us that an operation was immediately necessary but that he couldn't do it because the sea as too rough. We received permission to go into a harbor in a central American state. Once there the sailor and doctor left the ship and found a local hospital where they performed surgery. We left the sailor there to recover. We stayed moored in the harbor overnight tied up alongside the banana boats. We had quite a few bananas to eat in the days after.

In San Francisco, we had practice exercises. During the course of the exercises, I decided to go under the Golden Gate Bridge as a challenge. I shot for an open space, but didn't realize that we were being pushed off course by the wind. Luckily, I caught the danger in time and backed off.

They had raised the bridge for us to go under. It was about the time that people were heading home from work so there was quite a backup. The people from those cars were all looking over the railing and yelling at me. It was very embarrassing. After we backed up, we went in for another run. We made it the second time. Once we were through they put the bridge back down and the cars went on their way.

After our two weeks in San Francisco was up I sent my wife home and we sailed for the Pacific.

We left on April Fool's Day 1945. That was the day the invasion of Okinawa began. Okinawa was our final destination.

We went across the Pacific on a different LST than the one we had gone through the canal on. I enjoyed myself on the LST because I didn't have any responsibilities. My crew and I were just catching a ride across the ocean.

On the way across we stopped at a place called Ulithi. It was a small natural harbor formed by the top of a dead volcano. It was, in fact, just the very top ring and crater of the volcano. There were hundreds of places where a ship our size could find protection.

The first thing I noticed when I got off the boat on what land there was, was a row of pipes sticking in the ground. The island had palm trees but no lower growth, just sand. So, I wondered why all those pipes were in the ground. Each one had a funnel on the end of it.

It turned out they were for us to urinate into. There was a bunch of sailors there that were having a beer party so they got quite a bit of use. Eventually we left Ulithi and headed to Okinawa.

We arrived there on 15 April to haul freight from the cargo ships to the western side of the island.

Before we started hauling freight, we were temporarily anchored in a bay on the eastern side of the island called Buckner Bay. It was named after General Buckner who had been killed in the battle.[213]

While we were anchored there, a severe typhoon hit. The battleships, cruisers and destroyers went out to sea to ride out the storm but we couldn't, we were too small to do that. We would have just rolled right over out in the deep waters. We had to stay anchored right where we were. The winds reached around one-hundred-forty miles an hour. It blew in from the sea toward the land.

Throughout the course of the storm we just sat, hoping that the anchor would stay set and the cables remain intact. We were loaded with boxes of food at the time. They had just been dropped in with a cargo net so, they were just all over the place. As skipper I had to go out from time to time and check the anchor and anchor cable. It was quite the job having to step over all those scattered boxes in those the high winds.

Thankfully, the cable and the anchor held throughout the storm and we survived. I often said, after the War, that I was going to write to the manufacturer of that cable and tell them how good it was but I never did. After the storm we started our job of hauling freight inland.

At one point we were ordered to beach at a small island just off of the northwest coast of Okinawa called Ie Shima. It had been declared secure only a few hours before we got there. It was there that I saw the aftermath of a battlefield up close.

Our second day there we found out that Ernie Pyle had been killed on the island during the night by a sniper not far from where we were beached.[214] I wanted to go see where he was killed. We took our .45s, left the boat and went to look around.

I remember seeing a soldier who had been blown right in half. There was no blood around him. He had been cut right at the diaphragm. At about the time we came upon him I saw some women up ahead of us. They saw we had our pistols and they started bowing down in front of us. I think they thought we were going to kill them.

Just after that happened a black soldier came down the hill toward us. He was a huge guy and he had a little baby in his arms.

He said, "Look what I have!"

I said, "What are you going to do with it?"

He said, "I'm going to take it with me and turn it into the nurses down over the hill."

After that we went back to the ship. It was all unreal to me. I couldn't believe the damage and the ugliness of it.

We stayed at Ie Shima from that time on hauling freight. We worked constantly, day and night. It got monotonous after awhile.

During our time there we had the privilege, if you want to call it that, of losing our ramp. There was a ramp on the front of the landing craft could be lowered to move supplies or troops on and off. That broke off on one of our trips in and for a while, until we got another ramp, we could only haul certain things that were light so we wouldn't get swamped.

Around that time we had a second accident. When we beached that kind of boat, we had to make sure of a few things like making sure it wasn't high-tide. And we had to make sure to drop anchor out far enough to use it to help back us off if we needed to. We'd been told to beach at a certain spot where we shouldn't have. It turned out that the tide wasn't right there and we got stuck. In the process of trying to back up, we hit our anchor and tore a hole in the bottom of the boat. Within a very short period of time the engine room flooded.

They brought in a repair ship to fix it. Our boat went into a mobile dry dock and we had a nice vacation for about a week just sitting and watching the repairs being made.

We were at Okinawa when the War ended. It was at that time that another officer came aboard to replace me. I was the first one on our boat to be shipped home.

I came back by ship and docked in Seattle. I was discharged there. From there I took a train home.

★ SILENCE MEANS SECURITY ★

“I Just Loved the Marine Corps!”

Dora May Morgan

United States Marine Corps Women’s Reserve
Born in Fairmont, West Virginia, 23 June 1925
Beaver, Pennsylvania

“. . . I started dating an Italian boy. My father was dead set against Italians. When he found out, I was dating an Italian he got really mad and things got rough. The boy wanted to get engaged, but I didn’t because my dad had said it would sever the family if I did. I didn’t know what to do. If I stayed, I’d keep seeing him, but I couldn’t disobey my family. The problem resolved itself really. I was out walking around one afternoon, and I went by the post office and saw a recruiting poster for the Women Marines. I thought, ‘Man, that’s what I’ll do!’”

When I was fifteen I dated a young man who went overseas with the Air Force as a gunner on a B–17. In the summer of 1944, his plane got hit over Hamburg, Germany. He was killed when he went back to help the tail-gunner when the plane exploded. That was very traumatic for me, and I didn’t date for a while after that.

Then I started dating an Italian boy. When my father found out I was dating an Italian he got mad. The boy wanted to get engaged, but I didn’t because my dad had said it would sever the family if I did. I didn’t know what to do. If I stayed, I’d keep seeing him, but I couldn’t disobey my family. The problem resolved itself really.

I was out walking around one afternoon, and I went by the post office and saw this poster for the Women Marines.

I thought, *‘Man, that’s what I’ll do!’*

So I went up to enlist, but I was too young. I had to wait a year, and once I came of age I went back and enlisted. I left for boot camp on 8 August 1945. Would you believe it? The Japanese surrendered on the fourteenth! My father laughingly told me, “Well, it took a while for them to hear you enlisted!”

That was a big joke in our house. I was a member of the Marine Corps Women’s Reserve. I loved it!

We did our boot at Camp LeJeune; in those days women weren’t trained at Parris Island. They had a special area for just women at LeJeune, separated from the men. I loved boot camp, and I loved the girls I met there. Maybe it was because I was an only child but I really enjoyed the fellowship. There were a lot of funny things that happened.

One time we were marching down The Grinder.[215] The drill instructor said,

"Halt! I want everyone to do an eyes left when I tell them, and I don't want to see a smile in this group."

So he stood there for a minute, and he said, "Attention! Eyes left!"

We looked, and there was a girl marching by herself a block or two away. He put his hands up to his mouth and yelled, "About face!"

And this girl turned around and found that she was all by herself. She almost died of embarrassment. She marched all the way back up, and the DI read her the riot act up one side and down the other. We were just dying to laugh, but, of course, we couldn't even smile; we were Marines! Needless to say, that girl never missed an order again!

We lived in a barracks with four rooms and a hundred girls in each room. With that many girls there was no privacy. The shower room was just a room with open faucets, no curtains around or anything. It was real community living, just like the men had. It took a while to get used to that kind of stuff but after I did, I think it made us closer. After a while, we didn't pay any attention to it. We did what we were told. In some ways, our minds became like computers, and we reacted to things without thinking.

A typical day started with the DIs coming in and banging a garbage can to wake us up. After that we made our beds. That was a big deal! We even had to lie on the floor and make sure that the bed was as neat underneath as it was on top. There couldn't even be a wrinkle. If there was, they'd rip that bed apart, and we'd have to do it again. Then we fell out for muster and chow. After that it was classes on Marine history, especially famous Marines.

We had a lot of inspections, and they were very strict. Our uniforms had to be on hangers, and the ones we were wearing had to have every button buttoned. We were not allowed to have any treats, no candy, no cookies, no packages, nothing like that. If they found anything like that in anyone's foot locker, God help that person!

There was a girl whose husband had been killed in action. Every night when they played Taps, she cried. We took turns sneaking over to her bed. We weren't supposed to be out of our bunks, but we felt so sorry for her.

There was another girl who wouldn't wear pajamas. She was from the South. She said "I never slept in nightclothes my whole life, and I'm not sleeping in them now!"

We said, "You're not running around this barracks naked!" Eventually, she turned out all right.

Whenever we were in boot camp, we had something called "quiet hour," from seven to eight; we could write letters, polish shoes, rest, read, but we had to be in our bunks, and we weren't allowed to even whisper to those around us.

After we graduated, we got our orders. I was hoping they'd give me anything but a typewriter. Well, what did they do? They made me a secretary at Henderson Hall in Arlington, Virginia, just behind the National Cemetery. Today, Henderson Hall is Headquarters Marine Corps. Every day, when I looked out from the back of the barracks into the cemetery, I saw a steady stream of horses pulling the caissons of dead boys in for burial.

I worked the three-to-eleven shifts. That was nice because I could sleep in the morning a little bit, and chow lines weren't too long during the off hours. Best of all, I got late liberty! The other girls had to be in at twelve, but I could stay out until two. We used to aggravate the girls who had to be in early.

They'd just be coming in with their boyfriends, and we'd say to their boyfriends, "We'll be right back out!"

Most of the time I came home on weekends, and I'd bring with me girls from other states who couldn't go home. Pittsburgh wasn't that far from Washington, D.C., and the bus fare to Pittsburgh was twelve dollars. I made fifty dollars a month. I'd come home for twelve dollars, then my dad would give me the money to go back.

During World War II, we weren't permitted to ever be out of uniform. What I used to do was come home and put on my fatigues, and then my dad would take my uniform up the street and get it cleaned while I was sleeping or eating. My uniform would be done in an hour or so, and I'd have it for the evening.

Washington was a little scary back then. There were lots of strange people around, but there were a lot of military as well, and they took precautions with us. If we had visitors from out of town who happened to be staying in a D.C. hotel, we had to visit with them only in the lobby, not in their rooms. The Marines were very protective of their girls. Once I was going to the railroad station in Washington, D.C., and a sailor grabbed hold of me and started pulling toward some bushes. Just then two Marines appeared from I don't know where, and they took care of the situation.

After two years of service I was discharged, and I came home. I would've made it a career if I could have. We were forced out, disbanded or cut to the bare minimum, and that meant most of us had to go.

I got $200 upon discharge, and I joined the 52/20 club. I looked for work right away and got a job with Westinghouse. If I had stayed I probably would've advanced, but I got married and had children instead. Sometime later we got a $600 bonus from the State for our service.

One day at Westinghouse I was sitting there typing, and this guy came by hauling this tote of scrap metal or whatever.

First I see the bulging muscles, you know, then I see the crew cut, the high and tight haircut and I thought, *'Oh, my goodness. Who is that?'*

Then I checked out his shirt and thought, *'That's got to be a Marine!'*

So I made it my business to meet him. I did, and eventually we married; we celebrated our fiftieth wedding anniversary and had five children, four boys and a girl and had a very happy life.

He was one great Marine. He was on Saipan, Okinawa, Iwo Jima. I don't know what to say about our marriage. It wasn't a regular marriage. My mother used to say, "I never see you two hold hands or anything."

I'd reply "That's because we're both Marines! We don't do that kind of stuff out in public."

We were both trained the same way, and I think that's why it worked so well.

When Korea started, they made women a permanent part of the Marines. Then the girls could make a career out of it. I wish I had had that opportunity.

I've been back to Washington, D.C.; the barracks are still there, and they sort of look the same, but the PX, and what we used to call the "slop shoots," the Beer Gardens are all different. The PX is now a big department store.

It was hysterical when I went up to go in the barracks to visit. I pulled out my ID card, and the guard said, "What's that?"

I said, "It's my ID card!"

"Never saw one like that."

"That's because that was way before you were born!"

With that, he let me in, but I don't think he believed me.

"They did take us to the rifle range."

"I'm Still a Deer Hunter..."

Theodore "Teddy" M. Pajak

6th Army (New Guinea, Philippines)
47th General Hospital
Born in Alverton, Pennsylvania
3 October 1921

"Once a GI came to us without a nose, simply two holes on his face where the nose would have been. Dr. Rosenvold had to conduct reconstructive surgery. We removed a piece of boney cartilage from the soldier's rib and set that as a nasal septum. We then retracted a piece of skin from his forehead and molded that to cover the new septum. It was not pretty but it worked, and he was then stable enough to ship home."

MY PARENTS WERE IMMIGRANTS from Poland and we grew up in a home with an outhouse, gas lamps for lighting, a wood stove for heat, and a reliance on the "fat of the land" to meet our dietary needs. At a young age, my brothers and I were sent up the road to work for a local farmer to pay off a side of beef, kerosene, or other goods my family bought. This daily work was something I came to dislike because it was very hard physical work for which I received no direct pay, but to help my parents it was our responsibility.

I graduated from East Huntington High School in May 1940. Our school started earlier in the year than most, so we were let out early. I moved to Pittsburgh and worked as a short order cook in a restaurant making eggs and omelets, my pay was thirteen dollars a week and three of which were taken out for social security, which made living tough.

I worked at the restaurant through the end of 1940, but in early 1941 I took a job in McKeesport at a bomb/shell factory. McKeesport was twenty-five miles from my home and I didn't have a car, but it was not a problem because I could walk to the main road not too far away and catch a ride. The same guys drove each day; I paid them a little for gas and it worked out fine. We made the casings for bombs; the factory had a hot-mill to shape the nose, tail, and body of the bombs. We would drill the holes in them so the explosives could be later added. I had a much better pay than my restaurant work because I was now making one dollar an hour, and only one percent was taken out for taxes.

In December of 1941 I was walking down the dirt road to my home when a man came out of his house and yelled, "Pearl Harbor has been bombed!" At this time Hawaii was not yet a state, but I knew where it was. Because of this attack, we were willing to defend the United States. Few complained about the Draft.

I worked at the bomb casing factory until July of 1942. Three of my older brothers, Steve, John, and Andy, had already been drafted, so I decided to enlist to have some say in the type of duty I would perform.

I took the train alone from Scottdale to Pittsburgh. Back then, you could take a train almost anywhere, not like today.

When I got to the place of enlistment in Pittsburgh, I tried to join the Navy, but I was denied. You had to be five-feet-four-inches tall to be in the Navy, and I was five three and a half inches. My next choice was the Army Air Force. For some reason I had it in my head that I wanted to be a gunner, a tail gunner or turret gunner. It is probably best that I didn't end up there or I would have found my self as fish-bait in the English Channel.

Within a day or two of enlisting I was on a train to Cumberland, Maryland with seventy other enlisted volunteers. I didn't know any of the men except Jackie Conn, the younger brother of the famous boxer Billy Conn, from Pittsburgh, who almost beat Joe Louis for the heavyweight title.

In Cumberland we were fitted with uniforms and listened to speeches about being in the military. From there we boarded trains. We had no idea where we were going.

We ended up at Camp Forest in Tullahoma, Tennessee. I became part of the 80th Infantry Division, 318th Regiment, Company F, 2nd Battalion. The 80th had been recently reactivated and was comprised of many men from Pennsylvania. So much for picking my own service; so much for becoming a gunner. I was infantry. I wasn't happy so I went to my company commander and asked why my placement had been such. He said that on my enlistment questionnaire I had put down hunting as a hobby and that got me there. I suppose they thought I could shoot straight.

But since I had volunteered, I felt I had no responsibility to the infantry. I went again to my company commander and asked for a reassignment. I needed a reason to be reassigned, and my knees were it. I had exosteosis, and after a few X-Rays and after thirteen weeks hiking and shooting and hiking and shooting, my days in the infantry were over.

I ended up then on a train south to Fort Oglethorpe, Georgia, a reassignment location. I was sent from there on a five-day train ride to Camp White in Medford, Oregon, and the 77th General Hospital where I began training as part of the Medical Corps. This training also was very physically demanding. We went on long hikes through the mountains. One hike with all our gear was thirteen-miles long going at three or four miles per hour, which is pretty fast.

In November 1942, after my training at Camp White, I went to Modesto, California, to be part of the 47th General Hospital. The 47th was initially connected with Hammon General Hospital. All of doctors and nurses came from a religious group, The Seventh Day Adventists, all of whom at been trained at Loma Linda University in San Bernadino, California. The hospital needed staff support, so the enlisted Army members were medical technicians, cooks, guards, laundry personnel, and everything else a hospital needed to function properly. In total, the 47th had five hundred members.

I spent over a year in Modesto working at the 47th and learning the skills of a surgical technician. While working and training here I enjoyed myself. At first I worked as a ward man taking temperatures and giving baths to the patients. Our first casualties of the war were soldiers coming down from the Aleutian Islands, Attu and Kiska. They did not have combat wounds, but instead had frostbitten hands, feet, toes, and fingers that needed to be amputated. I worked with a good group of people and was glad to be serving the Army in this capacity.

As the 47th became more and more specialized, my work there allowed me to establish a life-long relationship with Captain Lloyd K. Rosenvold, M.D. He was a plastic surgeon who specialized in Ear, Eyes, Nose, and Throat (EENT) surgery. I also got along well with the other staff members as we would have time to rest and recreate after work, and sometimes even get weekend passes to out of town to places like Sacramento. The civilians of the town were very supportive and during the Christmas of 1942 I was invited into one family's home for dinner.

Dr. Rosenvold or the other doctors and nurses never pushed their religion on me. They accepted me as a Catholic. We even had a Catholic church near the hospital with a military Chaplain, Father Straub. He left Modesto to be a combat chaplain, and was killed in action when the forces landed in the Philippines at Leyte.

During Christmas of 1943, I was issued a fourteen-day pass, the only one I ever got up to that time. I went home. It was nice, but it was a tough time for my family. My mother had five of her sons, Steve, John, Andy, myself, and Walter, all over the world fighting a war, so she cried much of my visit. Later, in 1945, my brother Frank got drafted right out of high school. That made six of us in the service. My mother didn't speak any English, so my younger sisters had to read to her the letters my brothers and I sent home. My father didn't say much about the War, mostly because he was a quiet man and only spoke some English.

When I came home, Dad had no job. He was only fifty and could have gotten a job at the bombshell factory. I was sending home twenty-eight dollars a month, most of my pay, and he was using it as his only income. He was not lazy, as he worked around the house all day with the cow, chickens, and gardening, but I still thought he could have had a job to make some money to support my mother and younger brothers and sisters.

It was good to have the fourteen-day pass because soon after my return I left the States. Everyone of the 47th general hospital took the short train ride north to San Francisco. We boarded the USS *Mt. Vernon*, a converted passenger liner. There were five-thousand troops on board. Initially upon boarding the ship we were issued heavy wool coats and fatigues, so we thought we must be heading north to the Aleutians. Instead, we zigzagged for seventeen-days across the Pacific to New Guinea. Some troops were seasick and just laid on their bunks, throwing up into their steel helmets. I had no problem with the journey, and had the responsibility to work in the hold of the ship brining up the food supplies to be prepared for all of the troops.

Our cruiser arrived unharmed to Milne Bay on the South East side of New Guinea. We crawled down ladders into DUKWs. I wasn't especially scared because the Japanese all had been pushed to the northern end of the island. On shore a convoy of trucks waited to take us to a station hospital where we stayed for awhile, and then worked our way into the mountains to establish the 47th General. We set up tents on nine poles, and laid plywood floors. We lived in those, five men to a tent while we built the hospital out of pre-fabricated frames made in Australia. The floors were concrete. The first month or so I worked all day every day carrying sixty-pound cement bags from the truck to where we would mix them. I was a strong worker, and now that I was getting paid for the same type of work I had done my entire life, it didn't seem too bad. I weighed 123-pounds when I went into the Army, and I weighed the same when I left. With the help of the Army Corps of Engineers and their heavy equipment the hospital was completed and we started to take on patients.

All our patients were strictly Army, as the Marines went out to a Naval Hospital Ship for treatment. At this point I was promoted to Technical Sergeant and my good friend Corporal Chris Wilcox was my surgical assistant. We worked with Dr. Rosenvold in the Operating Room. Many of the casualties came from the Army's 25th Infantry Division. Our hospital functioned well, despite a period of sixty-one straight days of rain; we had all the medical necessities, Operating Room, Pharmacy, laundry, kitchen and mess hall.

I spent my time with Dr. Rosenvold's patients as we worked in the EENT clinic. Some cases were as simple as removing tonsils or adenoids. Other cases were not as simple: severe facial combat injuries called for plastic surgery. Once a GI came to us without a nose, simply two holes on his face where the nose would have been. Dr. Rosenvold had to conduct reconstructive surgery. We removed a piece of boney cartilage from the soldier's rib and set that as a nasal septum. We then retracted a piece of skin from his forehead and molded that to cover the new septum. It was not pretty but it worked, and he was then stable enough to ship home. Many surgeries took place like this, especially in attempt to repair burn injuries. We had a tool that would remove a thin piece of skin from the leg to cover the burned area on the neck or torso.

I worked in reconstructive surgery until early summer of 1945 when Dr. Rosenvold was reassigned to work in the Philippines. I was assigned to general surgery worked there until the end of the war in August 1945. Work in general surgery was not much different for me; I assisted the surgeons with instruments and sponges. New Guinea was not all that bad for me. We lived in the vast coconut groves, and interacted with the native people. We called them "Fuzzy-Wuzzies." They wore grass skirts or loin cloths and were always carrying some kind of spear to kill wild hogs with. Some of them worked in Australian saw mills, they'd come in missing half a hand and we'd have to sew them up. Someone got the idea to give them peroxide to dye their hair, so before long we'd see these guys walking around in their grass skirts with orange hair! We probably did things like this just to pass the time.

At the end of the Pacific War in August of 1945, the entire 47th General hospital was moved to the Manila in the Philippines. We took all of our supplies and boarded ships to head north. Once in Manila we boarded trucks, for the coastal town of Villisies. This town had mud and wooden buildings waiting for us in which. Twenty men lived in each while we set up our hospital.

I had the chance to take a weekend while in Manila and head north to the town of Baguio. There they had a large Catholic church, but they must have been short on wood and other supplies, because there were no pews to sit on, so we sat on the floor. But despite this lack of seating, the decorations of the church were all gold! The Spanish settlers must have brought that stuff over years before.

At this point we were nearing two years away from the United States; some men had problems and resorted to alcohol. While in the Philippines the soldiers would go out into the local villages to buy drinks other than American beer and liquor, which was wood grain alcohol. This drink was so strong that people went blind drinking it. In one case, a soldier got so drunk he went running out of camp one night into the dark forest and collided below the waist with a tree stump. He was sent back to the States with an injury hard to repair, if you know what I mean. The Army finally issued an alcohol ration to keep the men away from the wood-grain stuff. The men were allowed to fill a canteen one time each month with Army-issued liquor.

Most of us stayed away from alcohol by playing cards and finding other ways to beat the "down time." As a medical technician I kept myself busy by doing work for the locals, setting bones or suturing. One day, a native came in had gotten his foot caught in some kind of machine and pulled the entire plantar surface of his foot back to the ankle. It was a big job but I did my best to sew it up and send him on his way. I was also able to use my wood working skills to make Dr. Rosenvold an examining table that we were not issued with our hospital supplies, plus a dresser for his personal use.

My time overseas ended on 10 January 1946, almost two years after I had left San Francisco. We loaded-up on the USS *Brazil.* We got back in five days because we didn't have to zigzag. The Japanese submarine threat was no longer there. This time the food was fresh. Steaks, eggs, vegetables. No dehydrated stuff.

A few days after my arrival in the United States, I was on a train to Camp Campbell, Kentucky, where I was discharged in January 1946. I then took a train back to Pittsburgh and home. I stayed with my parents for a few months, and then worked for a few months for U.S. Steel in Homestead, PA. During this time I kept in touch with my former assistant Corporal Chris Wilcox who was living in Hollywood. He suggested that I use the GI bill to go to school, and this is what I did. I moved to California in January 1947 and worked in a tool shop on a grinding machine for a little while. Then I went to Los Angeles State College for a year studying anatomy and physiology. I also kept in touch with Dr. Rosenvold, and he was able to write me a letter of recommendation in 1948 that got me into technical school in San Gabriel, California, where I trained to be an X-Ray technician. After I came back from California I first worked at Mercy Hospital in Pittsburgh, but then landed a well paying job in the medical department at J&L (Jones and Laughlin) in Pittsburgh. I worked there until I retired in 1983.

Now I'm in my late eighties and I've been married to Shirley for more than fifty years. We have six children and seventeen grandchildren. I'm still a deer hunter and trout fisherman. I like to work in my garden and play golf.

I kept in touch with Chris Wilcox and Dr. Rosenvold until their deaths. Dr. Rosenvold lived to be ninety-two. I can still see him running through the forests of New Guinea chasing butterflies with a net.

"Teddy" Pajak in New Guinea looking fit after a month of carrying sixty-pound bags of cement that would be used to make concrete floors for the hospital.

"Teddy" Pajak wearing uniform of the day in New Guinea.

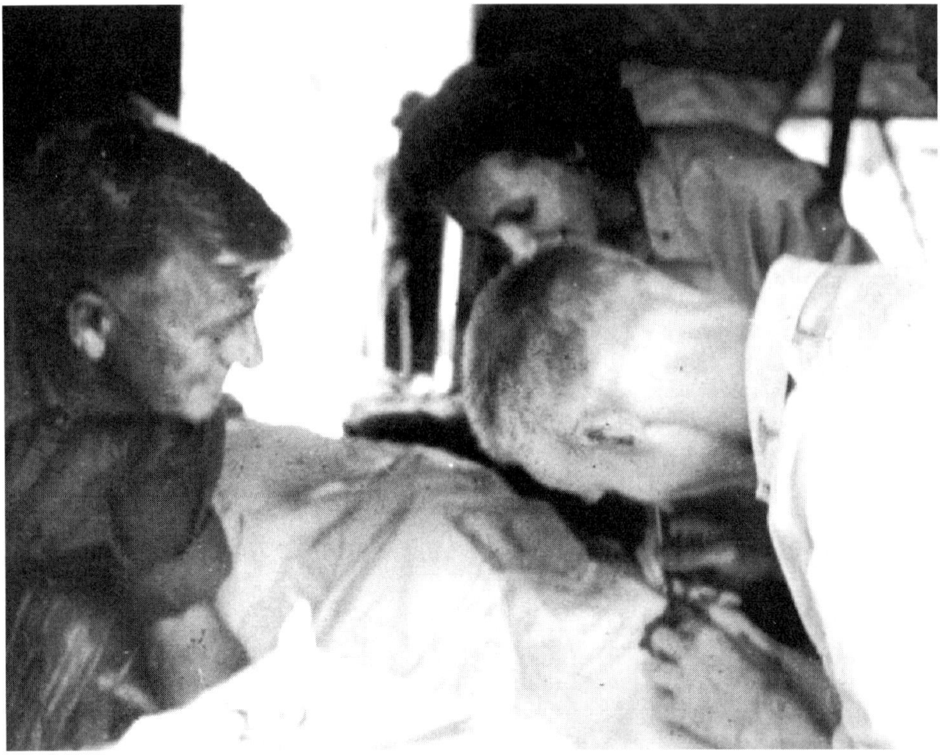

Doctor Lloyd Rosenvald performs surgery on a soldier in New Guinea while his nurse, Viola, assists. *Courtesy: Theodore Pajak*

"Teddy" Pajak at Camp Forrest, Tennessee, August 1942 when he was attached to the 80th Division, 318th Regiment.

"There Was Only One Country to Fight For."

Gottfried Pletzer

United States Seventh Army
100th Infantry Division, 398th Infantry Regiment
"The Century Division," "Sons of Bitche"
Motto: "Success in Battle"
2nd Battalion, Company E
Post-War Graves Registration, Europe
24th Infantry Division, Korea, 1953
Born in Turtle Creek, Pennsylvania, 11 January 1922
Glen Gardner, New Jersey

"Our tanks started advancing with us up the road. They took the lead, and we moved in close behind them. Unfortunately, the road was very narrow making it impossible for the tanks to maneuver. There was a high embankment on one side and a steep drop on the other. There was a dead GI lying in the road. We were under fire at the time, and the lead Sherman couldn't go anywhere but straight ahead. The driver drove that tank right over the dead GI. Even though the body was frozen, it was still ground into a pulp. A terrible mess! That was a hard thing to see. Just behind us they were picking up frozen bodies and throwing them into a trailer like they were cordwood. I looked at those bodies, and I thought, 'That was a hell of a price to pay!'"

RIGHT UP THE ROAD from us lived a Nazi *Bund*[216] leader. I'm not sure how high of a rank he was, but when I was a kid, this *Bund* leader came down to visit Mother one day.

"Could Gottfried come with us to our next meeting?" he asked.

Mom picked up a frying pan. I never saw her do anything like this before, and she said, "If you don't get out of here right now I'm gonna break your head open with this pan."

I said, "Mom!"

She said, "You shut up!"

She knew what she was doing! From that point on, this Nazi group caused great friction within our community. One time there was a grass fire at the Boy Scout camp, and my brother and I and all the neighbors went down with burlap bags and stamped it out, and that gave us the privilege of swimming at the great, big, beautiful pond they had. They invited us from time to time when there was something going on with the Boy Scouts. Now I don't know if they invited or the Nazis invited themselves, but they came marching in with their fife and drum and their swastikas and their brown uniforms when we were there with the scouts. Later, there was a bit of a rumble between them and the scouts. After the War started, though, there wasn't any trouble from them.

When I got into the Army, I saw a lot of German names. I personally didn't run into any animosity or prejudice because of my name, or theirs. There was no question in my mind that there was only one country to fight for.

I'm the only one from my family born in this country. My brother and three sisters were born in Austria. My father was Johan Pletzer and my mother was Cecilia Pletzer. They operated a small restaurant and guest house in Tyrol, west of Salzburg. Dad had a butcher shop, and mom ran the guest house and did the cooking. Dad came over here around 1911 and settled in Turtle Creek, Pennsylvania. He got a job in a slaughterhouse. Mom came over later. After working in the slaughterhouse for a while, Dad learned how to be a tool-and-die maker, and a friend of his helped him get a job at Westinghouse. In 1922, Dad's health began to fail, and the doctor suggested he find a place in the open. How Dad finally decided to move to this part of New Jersey I have no idea. I was two years old when my parents moved from Turtle Creek to a farm up the road a bit from where we are now. All I remember is this area.

My parents talked about the Old Country, but young people didn't care much about family history. After the parents are gone, I guess the young wished they had talked to them more about the family and the Old Country. Dad had brothers and sisters over there. I'm not sure how many there were, but I think there were nine or eleven cousins in the German Army! After the War, when I worked with Graves Registration, I found some bones and a helmet in the woods. The helmet had the name Platzer with the *Umlaut* over the "A" which makes the "E" sound. So, I don't know if this was anyone who was related to me, but a chill went up my back when I read that name.

I didn't learn English until I went to school. I spoke Austrian, which is a dialect of German. When I was six-years-old, I went to a two-room-school house in Changewater, New Jersey. I went there until the eighth grade, and then Dad wanted me to work on the farm. We all had a job on the farm, even me, and I was just six.

I had to carry kindling wood and water because we had no electricity. The water was about one-hundred yards away, and this is where we got all the water for the house, for the laundry and everything. We had about thirty or forty acres, so there was a lot to take care of. It was difficult to farm up here. It was "hardscrabble" farming. There were a lot of rocks, and we had to dynamite a lot of them out.

I was kind of the gofer for Mom because she didn't have any of the girls at home anymore. I'd have to chop the wood and bring in the cows. Later on I learned to milk. I'd also drive the team of horses. To supplement our summer income, Mom rented a room to some people from New York. One couple were the Nicolettis.

The wife was a ballerina and the husband played the oboe in the opera. She was an interesting lady. She had been in the 1906 San Francisco earthquake. In 1934, when I was twelve, my parents sent me to New York City and I stayed at the Nicoletti home for a week. Being a country boy, I guess my mouth got sunburned looking at all those tall buildings! They took me to the museums, the planetarium and the aquarium. It was an eye-opening experience. I got to meet a lot of city people who stayed at our farm, and they had an influence on me early in life. And because of my family's European background, when I got overseas, I wasn't totally out of the water.

When the Depression hit in 1929, nobody had any money. I can remember going over to the Pando sisters who didn't live very far from us, and I'd weed their garden for ten-cents-an-hour. They'd buy milk from us for five-cents-a-quart. I'd carry two quarts to them. I'd walk all that way for a dime, and I was glad to get it. The fact that we had the farm, we were nutritionally much better off than city people. We had chickens and a big garden for potatoes and sweet corn and tomatoes. The little garden had peas, carrots, beets, rhubarb and strawberries. We ate well, and every once in a while Dad would slaughter a calf, then sell the meat to the neighbors.

Even though we had no electricity, we still were able to listen to the radio, which was a favorite pastime. We used to have an Atwater-Kent hooked up to a car battery that we charged using a wind mill. We'd listen to the *Lone Ranger* and the *Green Hornet* and Lowell Thomas and Edward R. Murrow. We even heard a lot of Hitler's broadcasts! And the radio is where we heard about the attack on Pearl Harbor. I was nineteen at the time, and I wanted to go into the service but Mom was opposed to me going in. At the time I was angrier at the Japanese than the Germans. Then, when I realized more of what the Germans were doing, my anger was equal. I didn't find out about the concentration camps until later in the War.

I was drafted in March 1943. Before I left home, Dad sold the big farm and bought a smaller farm down the road. He came up short on the mortgage and needed twenty-five-hundred dollars.

I said, "I'm going into the Army, and I'll have life insurance for ten-thousand dollars, which will pay for this place three times over."

The bank said, "Are you willing to cosign?"

I said, "Yes."

They didn't kill me in the War, obviously, but I sent my checks home to Mom and Dad.

The Army paid me thirty-five-dollars a month, and I thought, *'Now that's money!'*

The day I left home my mother was in tears, and my father said, "Be a good boy."

There was no party or anything. Our neighbor took me and my friend Jack to the railroad station in High Bridge, New Jersey, and we ended up in Fort Dix. It was March, and it was cold. We slept in these little squad tents heated by coal fires. There were duck boards because the streets weren't paved, and they gave us something to eat, which I swear was eaten once before. Horrible! It was cold stew, and there's nothing worse on this God's green earth than cold stew with fat. Then we got on a train to go to Camp McQuade, California near Monterey Bay. It took us more than five days to get there because we were not high priority. Every time a high-priority train came through we were shunted off to the side. California was so different from here. Before this, I had only been to New York, and now I was going all over the country.

In basic training we got up at five in the morning, but me being a farm boy, I always got up way before that, so this was like sleeping in for me! I had never fired a .30-caliber before, but we had done a lot of hunting back home so shooting was pretty easy for me.

Initially, I trained on coast artillery, the old, World War I 155mms, "The Schneiders." I did the aiming. The big target was wood and canvas and painted red, and it was towed by a tugboat far out in the water. This old sergeant took me under his wing. We were supposed to take the information that we got about the distance to the target and put it on our guns and then shoot.

The old sergeant said, "When you see the target, put your cross hairs on it and fire. When you see the splash, bring the cross hairs to the flash, and the next round will hit."

The lieutenant caught on to what we were doing, and he said, "Pletzer, you sonofabitch, you're not supposed to do that—but that's good shoot'n!"

After training at Fort McQuade, we went to Fort Kamehameha in Pearl Harbor. We had the coast artillery guns that would fire and fall back behind the barriers. But coast artillery at the time was passé. We were there just a short time. On the other side of the bay at Point Weaver they had 90mm anti-aircraft guns, very similar to the German 88, but not as powerful. We never trained on those but they sent us over to man a battery of four guns.

I had an experience there that scared the living hell out of me. I was the loader, and I'd cut the fuse and ram the shell in. One time the gunner fired, and we had a hang fire. That means the round didn't go off, and we had to wait a period of time because there was still a chance that it would. Well, it didn't, and we had to get that round out of the gun. I had to catch the round as it came out of the breech. When the round popped out, I caught it, and the shell was smoking around the edge where the shell goes into the casing.

I said, "Oh, Jesus!"

I ran out of the bunker, down to the beach and laid that round in the water fully expecting that shell to blow up any time. The engineers came out later and got rid of it.

At Pearl Harbor, we saw a lot of aircraft taking off and landing all the time. I'd watch the Liberator bombers and B–17s flying around Hickam Field, and I really wanted to get into the Air Corps. But I only had an eighth-grade education, and every time I tried to get into something, they told me I didn't have enough education.

But our sergeant said to me, "You like airplanes, don't you?"

I said, "I sure do."

He said, "Why don't you try for the Air Force?"

I said, "I don't have enough education to take the test."

He said, "Why don't you try anyway?"

So I did, and I passed the test, and I came back to the States in March 1944 to Keesler Field, Mississippi, as an Air Cadet. I had just finished three weeks of ground school when one day the Major came in and said, "Well, gentlemen I got news for you. You're all transferred to the infantry."

We all laughed because we thought it was a joke.

He said, "This is no joke."

I was so crushed when I had to go to the infantry.

After the War I went back over to Europe as a part of Graves Registration looking for air crew all over Germany, Austria, Czechoslovakia, and I thought, *'Wow, I wonder if I'd have been one of them if I had stayed in the Air Force?'*

After learning I was in the infantry, I went to Fort Bragg in May 1944. I was assigned to the 100th Infantry Division's 398th Regiment, 2nd Battalion, Company E. When I got to the 100th Division, there were a lot of ASTP[217] guys. They were the brains, but they fought right along side of us.

The 100th Division had already completed their maneuvers, and they had to fill up their man power.[218] I guess that's where we came in. We then trained at platoon, company and division level and then we were ready to go. I got training on the Browning Automatic Rifle (BAR), the weapon I carried overseas. Our training was more on tactics. We learned to work with other units and when to call upon heavy weapons and air power.

We left for overseas from Camp Kilmer, New York, in October 1944. One bad thing happened there. We started to board this transport, it was cold out, and the Red Cross had coffee and donuts for us, but they charged us for it! Here we were going overseas, we might not come back, and they're gonna charge us for it? A lot of guys resented that, even to this day.

I thought, *'That's a hell of a thing to do!'*

The idea that we might not come back became greater as we left the port. I stood on deck. I looked at the Lady in the Harbor.

I thought, *'Oh, God! I hope we see you again!'*

We had a rough time crossing the Atlantic.[219] We ran into a hurricane, and none of us were allowed on deck. I think it took about fourteen days to get over. Our speed was the speed of the slowest vessel in the convoy of about twenty ships. After we got out of the hurricane, there were submarine alerts. The corvettes and destroyers were zipping in and out of the convoy.

We had a Navy crew. One time their cooks made us spaghetti and meat balls.

I don't know if they didn't like us or what but I waited until everyone was done, and I went up and asked these fellas, "Are there seconds?"

They said, "No, get outta here!"

And then the sonsofbitches threw out the rest of the spaghetti and meat balls into the garbage can. So I went out there, got my mess kit and fork and took some of it out of the garbage can and put it in my mess kit. Well, the captain of the ship caught me.

He said, "Soldier, what're you doing?"

"Sir, I'm hungry."

"Didn't you get anything to eat?"

"Yes, but I wanted seconds, and they wouldn't give me any, and they threw it all away."

He must have reamed those guys out because after that it wasn't safe to travel alone!

At Marseilles we couldn't dock because Germans blocked the harbor with derelict ships. We anchored and disembarked on gangplanks. Marseilles was the rectum of the earth. It was a dangerous and dirty place!

In November 1944 we moved up to the front through the Rhône Valley in 40x8 rail cars that were designed to hold forty men or eight horses. Every so many hours we stopped for a piss call. One guy was a little late getting back. He ran to catch the train, slipped and fell underneath the car and the wheels cut his leg off. That was the beginning of the gore.

We traveled by train so far then we had to march. We hadn't had much physical training coming across the Atlantic or at the staging area. We marched with full packs, and the more we marched, the less equipment we had. Quartermasters followed us, gathering up everything we threw away.

We relieved the 45th Division in the Vosges Mountains at night. I never saw darkness like that in my life! We had to be as quiet as possible. We wrapped up our mess kits so they wouldn't rattle. Guides came out and led us to their foxholes. We heard explosions but couldn't tell if they were incoming or outgoing shells.

Back in Marseilles, I ran into some wise guys. I was carrying my BAR, and they yelled, "Hey, BAR man, you're gonna last about two days!"

When we got to the front, there wasn't a word from those guys. The poor devils were haggard. As dumb as we were, we were a godsend to them. They told us what to look out for. They told us to make sure to have a revetment behind our foxholes so we wouldn't make a silhouette. They told us not to go moving around at night because our guys might mistake us for the enemy and shoot.

The next day we got our first real taste of combat. A lieutenant from another outfit stepped on a *Schu* mine and blew off half his foot. We heard the explosion and his screams. That was a chilling feeling. After that, we knew we were really at the front and the pucker factor became very high!

Soon after getting to the front, we went on the offensive. The Germans had the advantage over us in the Vosges Mountains. They had the high ground, and they had their artillery registered on key points. Whenever we made a move, in would come their shells.

When that moment came to get up and move forward I thought, *'Are they gonna hit me? When is it gonna happen?'*

It was always in my mind; *when is it going to happen?* In the mountains I could never tell where the firing was coming from, which made the feeling even worse. I'll never forget the first time I heard the German MG–42. It had a rate of fire of about twelve-hundred-rounds-per minute. It sounded like ripping burlap. I never wore a hood over my helmet in the Vosges because it was hard to hear or see the Germans when I did wear it.

It was a rotten winter! We lost track of time at the front. Days of the week didn't mean much. One day was like another. It stayed dark until seven in the morning, and it got dark again around four in the afternoon. Generally, our attacks were in the daylight so it gave us a chance to dig in at night. We really saw only what is going on ahead of us, and we had very little knowledge of what was going on around us. We assaulted machine-gun nests that were holes covered with logs. We moved forward, so we knew we were winning, but it was confusing. A battle plan is only exact until the first shot is fired. After that, all bets are off!

In the mountains we didn't have any tank support. The Germans didn't have any tanks either, thank God. It was strictly infantry versus infantry. It was cold and muddy. Our foxholes filled up with water and then froze. Our feet were always wet. Sometimes we'd be ankle-deep or worse in water because we were afraid to be outside our holes. One thing the medics told us to do was to take off our boots and socks and rub our feet, and if we couldn't rub them, to get a buddy to do it. We had an extra pair of socks under our shirts, but they were damp, too. They were just another pair of dirty socks! As far as hygiene goes, we did brush our teeth, but I got bleeding gums a lot, as did many of us. Once in a while we had tooth paste, but generally we took a little water from our canteens and brushed our teeth. We didn't suffer too much from lice because we put DDT powder in our hair, our clothes and our sleeping bags. When nature called, we'd sneak out with our entrenching tools. Sometimes we'd pee in a ration can. The defecation wasn't as much because we didn't eat as much.

We had a nasty fight one day. There were wounded on both sides. The Germans put up a white flag, not to surrender, but to ask for a two-hour truce. They had more medics, but we had more medical supplies. We put the supplies down in the middle, and all the medics went to work. Our job was to make sure everything was secure.

I saw a German lying there with a bullet hole in his head. He was still alive calling out for his mother, *Mutti! Mutti!*

I didn't know what to do for him. I didn't want to kill him, but he died before we were finished there. They patched up everyone and brought the wounded and dead back, and two hours later they started up the battle again. It reminded me of the World War I Christmas truce.[220]

Just before we got out of the mountains we got trapped. Our troops couldn't get us food, and the Germans couldn't overpower us. We were getting water from these ruts in the road, and since we were in a static position, urine and feces came in contact with the water. We didn't boil the water, and we all got dysentery. I got so weak I had to pull myself out of the foxhole by a little scrub pine that was growing on the outside. Even then, it was a struggle. If we had to really run or advance, I don't think we could have done it. We lost a lot of weight from dysentery, and we were only on two rations a day. But then our troops broke through, and we were removed to this open area where our cooks were making hamburgers.

The doctors said, "Fellas, eat real slow!"

We didn't listen, and we puked it all right up! It took us a week or two to get over it. By then we started an advance toward the Maginot Line.[221]

One time I was standing by the steel doors of one of the bunkers on the Maginot Line. I was looking toward the town of Bitche. A phosphorous round hit, and it just rained down in front of me, but I didn't get touched. I went around the other side of

Final Trip. This is what was left of a B-17 bomber that crashed in the Alps after a mission. Graves Registration searched for dead crew at many such sites after the war. *Courtesy: Gottfried Pletzer.*

Knocked Out Sherman Tank. A French woman atop a knocked-out Sherman tank, and showing where an armor-piercing round entered the hull. *Courtesy: Gottfried Pletzer.*

German SS troops hanged these members of the FFI (Free French Forces) near Paris. The hanging ropes had stretched, lowering the bodies to the ground. *Courtesy: Gottfried Pletzer*

French Defenses. Gottfried Pletzer at the Maginot Line in France, near the German Siegfried Line. The French, expecting the same sort of static front line that characterized the trench warfare of the First World War, built this chain of 'impregnable" fortresses along its border with Germany. The Maginot line was inneffective. The German Army, violating Belgian neutrality and using Blitzkrieg tactics, easily bypassed the French defenses.

"Fire It That Way!" Gottfried Pletzer clowns with a buddy as he "directs" fire toward Germany.

American soldiers exhume bodies for Graves Registration. *Courtesy: Gottfried Pletzer*

German POWS dig up remains for Graves Registration. *Courtesy: Gottfried Pletzer.*

Gottfried Pletzer wih a German soldier's remains.

Gottfried Pletzer's Den of Thieves in Traunstein, Germany. No one checked the Graves' Registration rosters to see if all of the men listed were dead, living or missing. Pletzer used that as loophole to obtain extra supplies and food.

R&R. Gottfried Pletzer (left and above right) in Paris for rest and relaxation.

the bunker, and there were about twenty Germans standing there with their weapons looking at me. I looked at them. They could have turned me into a sieve, but instead they surrendered peacefully.

The German soldiers in Bitche were very different. The Germans had driven us back there because our lines were spread out so much. They stormed us like mad men and broke through, shooting and screaming. I think they were doped up. It looked like there were hundreds of them. We got the order to withdraw. I was moving up the forward slope of a hill when a round came in, maybe from a 75 or 88mm. It must have been armor-piercing because it didn't explode like an ordinary shell. The round hit the ground, bounced up in the air and then tumbled past me. It made a horrible sound. Scared the hell out of me! I scrambled up the hill farther, and he fired again and missed. When I reached the top of the hill, he fired again and missed me again. I just wanted to get the hell out of there! Imagine getting shot at by an antitank gunner! I didn't think I rated that high!

Later that day we were able to establish a better defense, and their attack petered out. Then we pounded that place with Corps artillery. The next day we tried to take the town again.[222] My company was the first one in. My platoon was the lead platoon, and I was the second man in, ahead of the scout. We ran up the road toward the town.

I thought, *'This sure as hell is it!'*

Not one shot fired. They had evacuated the town!

Our tanks started advancing with us up the road. They took the lead, and we moved in close behind them. Unfortunately, the road was very narrow making it impossible for the tanks to maneuver. There was a high embankment on one side and a steep drop on the other. There was a dead GI lying in the road. We were under fire at the time, and the lead Sherman couldn't go anywhere but straight ahead. The driver drove that tank right over the dead GI. Even though the body was frozen, it was still ground into a pulp. A terrible mess! That was a hard thing to see. Just behind us they were picking up frozen bodies and throwing them into a trailer like they were cordwood.

I looked at those bodies and I thought, *'That was a hell of a price to pay!'*

This Sherman then went through an orchard to an area called Friedenburg Farms where it hit a mine and caught fire. The tank commander climbed out of the turret and jumped down to the ground onto another mine and got blown into the air. I don't know how high. Then a second tank hit a mine, but we started to go across that same ground anyway. We were getting small-arms fire all the way across. Suddenly the Germans opened up with a *Nebelwerfer,* a rocket launcher that sent over what we called "Screaming Meemies." That was the first time I heard those. I hit the ground and watched them go over me and explode a couple hundred yards behind us. The damage they did to our immediate unit was nothing, but the sound was frightening. We continued with our attack and took Friedenburg Farms.[223]

There were many narrow roads leading up to the fortifications. My buddy Joe Wagner and I were in this open column on one of these roads. A round came in, I think a mortar round because I heard nothing, and we hit the ground after it hit. Joe didn't get up.

I said, "Come on, Joe, let's move!"

He just laid there. He was dead. We couldn't find any wounds on him. We opened up his field jacket, and under his shirt we found this tiny little hole like someone jabbed him with a pencil. There was hardly any blood. A tiny piece of shrapnel must have gotten him.

Before coming overseas Joe was the one who said, "I'm not gonna make it."

I said, "Come on, Joe, don't talk that way!"

He must have had a premonition.

A little farther down that road, the ground sloped up, and there was a ditch on the right side of the road. An embankment was above the ditch, and there was this big, old, rotten tree stump. I was walking past this tree stump, and I heard one coming in. I hit that ditch. Of course, there was water in it! That round hit right in the middle of the road. It was a big one. The concussion lifted me up, took the air out of me and shattered that old tree stump. I looked at it and thought it could have been me.

Years later, when I was in Dachau with a Labor Service Company, I met the German commander of another Labor Service Company. Meisock was his name. He and I went into the canteen one day. We proceeded to demolish a couple bottles of beer. Somehow we got on the subject of Friedenburg Farms.

He said, "Oh, I was there."

I said, "I remember we lost some tanks, and then those damn Screaming Meemies came over."

"Those were mine. I fired those."

He fired them! I thought, *'Oh, boy!'*

So we clinked our beer bottles together, and that was it.

We often had the tanks with us in our attacks. Every night we'd dig in, and the tanks rumbled in behind us. The tankers would move up so they'd have infantry support. They felt safer with us around because they were scared that the Germans would sneak up with a *Panzerfaust* or put a grenade down the muzzles of their cannons. On the other hand, we felt more terrified with the tanks around because they drew artillery fire. It wouldn't be long before the Germans triangulated the sound of the tanks and opened up with their 88s. We cussed those tankers!

We said to them, "Suppose we give you boxes of Ten-in-One Rations and you stay back from us at night?"

Those rations had good stuff in them. They took the bribe.

We went on patrols looking for mines and trip wires. I found a mine once, marked it and left it for the engineers. Usually, we did this type of thing at night, so we wouldn't be too visible. Sometimes we made artificial moonlight by shining spotlights into the cloud cover. That really lit up the battlefield. A couple times we were advancing in the dark, and flares went up. God, but they were bright! We just froze and waited for darkness to come again.

Besides tank support, we had air support, P–47 Thunderbolts. They had eight .50-caliber machine guns, and they did ungodly damage on German columns. The

Germans used horses for transport, and it was pitiful to see all the dead horses after a strafing attack, especially because I was a farmer. Those animals were innocent.

Now, in the Army there was always one guy who said he was an atheist. The one in my platoon was named Strickland. Before we went overseas we had this discussion.

Strickland said, "There is no God."

"Well, I don't know if there is or isn't but when I get in real bad trouble I call out to someone."

"Naw, that's a bunch of baloney."

Once overseas, Strickland and I were in the same foxhole getting shelled.

I said, "Lord, please, if you get me through this one time more I'll be good!"

Of course, hypocrite that I am, I wasn't good, but Strickland, he was praying too! We didn't say a word to each other. We just looked at one another, and that look was all that was needed.

One time this fella named Chick and I were sort of tired. We put down our packs, looked at our foxhole and debated whether or not to put a cover over it.

I said, "Maybe we better."

We got together some small limbs. Then we put earth over them and the tarp over that. We laid our gas masks outside the hole. I don't know why we did that. During the night a mortar round hit smack on top of our hole. It completely shredded our gas masks and shattered the roof we built, but we were okay. What that round would have done had we not had that cover over our hole I don't know. Taken our legs off, killed us, I don't know. Some things happened to me that I can't explain. During shelling I'd try to get as close to the ground as possible. I'd end up with holes in my clothing and never got a scratch. I had a BAR shot right off my back. A sniper hit the BAR, split the hand guard and bent the operating rod. The gun was useless, but the bullet didn't touch me!

Once, in the town of Goetzenbruck, I was very tired. We had been on the advance for days. I was a sergeant by this time, and I had to check on my men. I was walking down this road that had a stone wall about three-feet high on the right. On the other side of this wall, on the opposite side of the town, were the Germans.

I should have crouched down behind this wall but I was so tired I said, "The hell with it."

A round came from somewhere and snapped right past me. Boy, I got energy real fast!

One time, in the woods, after a hellish artillery barrage that we laid down, this German came walking toward us. I commanded him to halt, but he wouldn't. I couldn't tell whether he was armed or not, so I put a round past his head, and that woke him up a bit, and he put up his hands and surrendered.

Afterwards we learned he was out of it from the artillery barrage we had laid down. Like that German, we all wanted the War to be over with. We wondered if it would ever end. We joked around and talked about going to Switzerland, a neutral country and get interned. But that was just a joke.

A river crossing was another thing that was always dangerous. We were in Germany guarding a river called the Jagst. That was the first time we saw an Me–262 jet. He was streaking across, and the anti-aircraft fire was about eight-hundred yards behind him. They couldn't compute his speed fast enough. There were troops and vehicles crossing, and that jet lined up with the bridgehead. He was carrying two bombs. He let one go, and it hit about four-hundred yards off. It took him a long time to come back around because those jets couldn't turn very tightly. He lined up again, dropped his last bomb, and again dropped short. Now he was out of bombs and probably almost out of fuel, and he turned and left.

One time in Germany our unit had the usual formation out, and we were dug in, and a forward observer called back to the company and said he couldn't get back because he was under fire.

The captain said, "Pletzer, take a couple of men, go around and bring him in."

As we were moving in to outflank the Germans that had this guy pinned down, someone fired a shot from a couple hundred yards away.

The guy next to me said, "I'm hit!"

I got up to him, and I said, "Where are you hit?"

"In the arm."

I pulled his sleeve up, and there was a little hole in his forearm. It wasn't even bleeding, probably because of the cold. I was amazed at how small the hole was. Then another round came in. This time it was a tracer. I don't know why the guy fired that, because I could follow where it came from. I laid the BAR down and peppered the spot. In the meantime, we managed to rescue the forward observer. I never found out if I killed whoever shot at us.

The first thing we did when we hit a town was see if there was a chicken coop where we could find eggs. Then we'd look in houses for bread and jelly. Of course, the food could have been booby-trapped with poison. Besides that, the most important commodity was *Schnapps*. I carried a little with me, and every night I'd go through the squad and give each guy a thimble full. Some of the cellars in the German homes had another cellar underneath them.

As far as the food the Army gave us went, we got these D-Bars; hard as rocks. What we did with those was we took a mess kit knife or bayonet and scraped at them and got slivers off, and we'd put the slivers in water. We couldn't bite one; we'd break our teeth. We called it "tropical chocolate."

I'd get food from home. Mom would make *Linzer Torte*, which is an Austrian cake. It lasted forever. Sometimes I'd get a box of cookies. Anyone who got a package in the Army was very popular. We didn't save it for ourselves. It was there for everybody.

One time I wrote home I said, "See if you can send me a bottle of whiskey, and hide it in a loaf of bread."

The whiskey never got to me but the bread did. Someone else got the whiskey!

We got mail, but only if the front line wasn't really hot. We'd alternated going about five-hundred yards to the rear for chow and mail. One time they took us back for showers. We had to get rid of all our old clothes, because they could stand up on their own. They took us to Belgium where these old Belgian women wearing raincoats scrubbed us down with scrub brushes.

Deeper and deeper into Germany more and more Germans surrendered. The German people would come out of their houses terrified because they were told we were going to do all kinds of things to them. But then once they realized we weren't they were more at ease with us.

In one town a lady came out and said, "There's an SS man in the barn."

I said, "Okay."

I went into the barn. That was a dumb thing for me to do. I laid down the BAR, took out my .45 and started up the ladder to the hay loft. As I was going up, the guy came out of the hay with his hands up. I had a guardian angel. He came down peacefully.

Afterward I thought, *'I'd have been better off just shooting up through the hay loft with my BAR.'*

We did have some SS against us, and they were determined. But most of these guys were just regular soldiers. We faced a lot of the *Volkssturm* at the end; the old men and young boys, but generally speaking they were relatively easy to handle. Some of them were pretty well-armed, and some of the young ones were a little feisty.

About two weeks before the end of the War, we went into this town called Blaubeuren. The first thing they asked us to do was to look for a suitable headquarters for the X Corps. I walked towards this great big building and saw a red cross on it. Out came this German colonel. He looked like seven-feet tall. He saluted us. After that, he surrendered his hospital.

They never told us how to accept a surrender like this before, so I saluted back at him and said, "Surrender is accepted! Proceed as normal!"

He took me inside and showed me this weapons room, and the first thing I did was take about five or six pistols and strapped them around my belt because I was going to sell them to the officers.

Then I smelled something. The nurses were nuns, and they were cooking food for this hospital.

I said, "That smells familiar."

They had boiled potatoes, and they took fat and flour, and they blended it together on the stove top, and they put some salt in it, and that looked so good.

They said, "Do you want some?"

I said, "Could you spare it?"

They said, "Yes."

I sat down, and they brought me some. Soon after here came dozens of German walking wounded.

I thought, *'Am I in trouble?'*

But they started asking me all kinds of questions about how the War was going and whether or not I had been to a certain town or other. The fellas were just like we were. They had the same values and concerns. I walked a little farther around that town. The Blau River came out of a pond, and a spring gushed up. There was a mill there. I saw some trout in the spillway. After months on C-Rations, the trout looked good. I pulled the pin on one of my grenades, dropped it in the water and then hit the ground. The grenade exploded, and the fish came to the surface. I gathered them up and got them cooked.

Years later, when I went back to Germany as a hunting and fishing officer, I was at a meeting, and the fella who lived near that stream invited me to go fishing. He didn't recognize me, and I didn't offer any information because when I threw that grenade in the concussion cracked the wall of mill!

In Traunstein, there's a river called the Traun, which is one of the finest trout streams in all of Europe. It was owned by a baron, whose name I don't recall.[224] We were not allowed to fish there but it wasn't properly posted so we fished there anyway.

The warden came by and said, *Nein, nein! Es ist Verboten!*

Years later, when they introduced me as the hunting and fishing officer at the division's first convention in Berchtesgaden, who do you suppose was present but that game warden and his wife.

When I first got my commission, this old colonel told me, "Remember the people when you climb the ladder of success, because you are gonna meet them as you climb back down."

And how right he was!

One bad thing that happened near the end of the War was when we were advancing on Stuttgart. We had the Free French forces on our right. It was foggy out, and a fire fight broke out between them and our guys. We were thinking they were the Germans and the French thought we were the Germans. It took about twenty minutes to straighten that all out, but some guys got killed. That's where the War ended for the 100th Division.

For the invasion of Japan they needed enlisted men to become officers. Captain Thomas Garahan, our company commander, thought perhaps I'd make a good officer, and he sent me to Fontainebleau, France, for OCS training. They were going to make us all second lieutenants with the stroke of a pen.

I left on 6 May. Two days later we got the news that the War was over in Europe. But Japan was still in the picture. I got my commission on 7 July 1945 and got ready for the Pacific. This is where I thank Harry Truman from the bottom of my heart for the decision he made to drop the Atomic Bomb. How would you like to be in the position, "Do I drop the bomb or don't I?" To tell you the truth, I don't think I'd have made it if I had to go to Japan. God got me through once, and maybe he'd have done it again, but that was asking an awful lot!

After the Japanese surrendered the Army sent me to Camp Robinson, Arkansas. It was boring there, and I wanted to get out desperately. One day a captain came around looking for people for repatriation. Being a country boy and not too smart, I ran to my tent and got my dictionary. I looked up "repatriation." It said: "the replacement of displaced persons."

I thought, *'That means all these good-looking women will be coming in from Hungary and East Germany!'*

I volunteered for it. Little did I know it was Graves Registration! Replacement of displaced persons, indeed! I went to Fort Lee, Virginia for a little quartermaster training. Then I went right back to Europe, to Carentan, France, where I had my first experience with human remains.[225] There was a little building and adjoining this building were tents where they had bodies in coffins. These are not fresh bodies; these were old ones. There were civilian morticians there, and they had a ribald sense of humor. They made sure they closed all the windows, cranked up the stove so it was nice and warm in there, and they said, "Let's bring in another one."

They brought in a coffin, and they spilled it open. Inside, was a body that had been in a marsh, and the flesh just kind of melted, and the head rolled off the vertebrae. And the mortician said, "Let's see what we have here."

He started rooting around for dog tags and looking at the teeth, whatever they could find, rings, anything. They wore gloves, and they were wading through this mush.

This guy was waiting for my reaction, and he said, "Okay, time for a break!"

He pulled his gloves off, pulled an apple out of his coat and started to eat it.

I said, "You sonofabitch!" and walked out.

My job was keeping records and supervising what went on. We had a lot of French laborers who would disinter or inter whatever the case may be. Gradually I moved around France and then around Europe. Later, I got to command my own Mobile Bivouac Unit and went to Traunstein, Germany, where I set up a mortuary tent.

Every name of every soldier in our unit was put on a roster, but they didn't say they had to be alive. That was a loophole for us. So, we signed up the dead ones too! We got extra rations and supplies that way. That's how I got a reputation for being a scrounger. My men painted a sign that said, "Pletzer's Den of Forty Thieves" outside our bivouac.

We checked with the municipalities around Traunstein, especially the churches because they kept good records. Sometimes the townspeople came forward and said, "An airplane crashed in such and such a place."

We'd go look for it. If we could identify a machine gun number or an engine number or an airframe number then that would tell us the identity of the plane and crew. If we knew there was an engine or anything in the ground from an airplane, we'd plant a charge and blow it out of the ground.

There was a plane that came in on a frozen, snow-covered lake and almost got to the shore, but the plane's weight crushed the ice. The plane sank, taking the crew with it. We didn't have diving gear, so the engineers built a dam and drained the lake. There was the plane. It had been covered with sixteen-feet of water, just enough to cover it. It had been shot up, but was still fairly intact. We collected the bodies and began processing them for identification.

We looked for bodies in Czechoslovakia as well. They were under Communist rule at the time, and their police had a tail on me. They were very suspicious of us. We had a report we were following up on about a body. We had been staying at a guest house, and I got talking with the police commissioner.

We got a bottle of cognac. We talked some, and then he asked, "What are you really doing here?"

"You won't believe it but I'm looking for bodies of downed American fliers and missing soldiers."

"Are you serious?"

"Yes, I'm serious. I'm not a spy. I'm too dumb to be a spy!"

"I know where there's a body."

"Where?"

"Right across the border. You want it?"

"Hell, yes, I want it! That's what I'm here for!"

We finished the bottle, and he said, "Tomorrow I'll have the body here."

They went into East Germany. We got our vehicle, went out, met them, loaded the body up, and that was it. That is an example of just trying to get one body.

We didn't do the identification of the bodies, actually. We brought them to a collection station, and the morticians trained in that field did all that work. They had the records of these servicemen. They had dental records and information we didn't have. There were many that were identified. I don't know, but I felt sometimes we might have been tearing open old wounds. By bringing these bodies home we were certainly benefiting the undertaker industry. They were making good money on this because the hermetically sealed coffins were about eight-hundred dollars back then. We had two ships carrying bodies home. That's an economic thing I often wonder about, as well as an emotional thing.

I went to Nuremberg in 1946 and was there when the trials were taking place. I had a ticket to get in. I saw Goering, Doenitz, Keitel, Runstedt and Jodl, all these big shot Nazis. It was actually very boring. There was the testimony then the translations. It went on and on and on, but I'm glad that I saw them. It kind of put things in perspective. It was because of men like these that we fought the War.

When I was stationed in these various places, I went to school. The University of Maryland had a branch in Munich. I caught an evening train to go to school in Munich and then came back to Landshut late at night.

In combat, I received the Bronze Star and cluster, for what I don't really know. They said this was for valor. Valor, what valor? I never thought I did anything special. It might have been for that forward observer's rescue, I don't know. I did get one that I earned, the Meritorious Service Medal. This was well after the War. I was housing officer at Fort Riley, Kansas. We had a couple of exercises out there called Big Blast One and Big Blast Two, which had to do with a lot of theoretical stuff on atomic warfare. They didn't do any live testing, it was all "what if" kind of stuff.

I stayed in the Army twenty years. I went to Korea with a heavy weapons company of the 24th Infantry Division in 1953, after that war was over.

My experiences in World War II were a blend of the great and the terrible. I'm glad I did it, but I have mixed feelings. One evening about a year after the War I just broke down and cried for what must have been two hours. I really didn't know why, but I guess it was a delayed action to the stress of combat. With my mindset now, I don't think I'd have lasted a day. When I think about what we all did, when I say we, I mean all of us, I'm proud of it, and at the same time when I think of the graves of the guys who didn't come back I almost feel guilty. The emotions kind of get tangled up. When we retraced our steps in 1991, we went out to the staging area, and everything had changed. What used to be a ghost town and No-Man's-Land was now all built up. There was a town, that stuck in my mind because on the southern edge of it there were great big concrete pipes just stacked up on the side of the road, and it was a cold winter day, and the sun was shining, and here came two P–51s. The sonsofbitches started to strafe and bombs us! We dove into those pipes, and they didn't get us. I've often wondered if they were ours or if they were Germans who had fixed these downed planes up. I went back to the same spot in 1991, and I recognized nothing.

Then we went to the town square and laid a wreath. We sang Amazing Grace, and then the French played something, and then we went to the cemetery where a lot of our boys are buried, and we laid another wreath, and that's where I came unglued, and I had to leave. I broke into tears, and I couldn't handle that. They were young, they hadn't even lived yet, and there they are now.

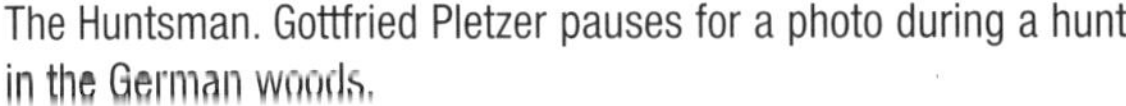

The Huntsman. Gottfried Pletzer pauses for a photo during a hunt in the German woods.

Going Native. Gottfried Pletzer in traditional German Lederhosen.

One of the *Queen's* Men
(Or the 'Battle of the Bremerton Ferry')

Wayne Shaffer
Battleship USS *New Mexico* (BB–40)
The "Queen of the Fleet"
Codename: "Ironsides"
Born in Keckshurg, Pennsylvania, 12 October 1925

"One time a Japanese plane came in very low to the water between the ships, and everyone started shooting at it. We hit one of our destroyers, and they hit us. One fellow had just come out of the head, and just as he closed the door, a 5-inch shell came through the bulkhead into the head and blew everything to pieces. He learned to smoke cigarettes that day!"

I GRADUATED FROM HURST High School in 1943, and worked that summer at the Kecks' Pepsi-Cola Bottling Works making fifty-seven cents an hour. After making "lots" of money, I decided to enlist in the United States Navy. My eighteenth birthday was 12 October, and at time they were drafting men after they reached eighteen, and then placed them where they were needed. I wanted to choose where I served, so I joined on 11 September 1943, a month before I turned eighteen.

My friends Jim Mayes and Bill Bulebosh joined the Navy at the same time, and the three of us had our physicals in Greensburg. Our next step was the Old Post Office building in downtown Pittsburgh where we had our swearing-in ceremony. We boarded the train at what is now Station Square on Pittsburgh's South Side and traveled all night, arriving at Great Lakes Naval Training Station early on the morning of 29 September. We were separated when we reached Great Lakes and didn't see each other again until we finished boot camp and came home together on a nine-day leave.

I started my training on 1 October 1943. It included a lot of marching and exercises. I was on an indoor rifle range (twice that I can remember) firing .22 caliber rifles. In the evenings I'd go to a base canteen and get some pie and ice cream. I gained about fifteen pounds in eight weeks.

The haircuts we received when we arrived at Great Lakes were something else. I was in the barber chair for about one minute and forty-five seconds. They had a clock on the wall right in front of the chair. After the haircuts, we received our first Navy pay that we called the "Flying Five." We signed a pay stub at one desk, and picked up a five-dollar bill. At a second desk, we picked up our *Bluejacket's Manual* and a shaving kit. At a third desk, we gave back the five-dollars to pay for the manual, the shaving kit and haircut, and we got back $1.25 in change. That's why we called that pay the "Flying Five."

One day I was standing on the base sidewalk doing nothing when along came a bunch of recruits marching down the street. I recognized one fellow, Joe Silvis, who was one of my teachers at Hurst High School.

I pulled him out of the group, scaring him in the process. He didn't recognize me and thought he had done something wrong, and that I was going to punish him. He felt better when I told him who I was. It felt so good to finally see someone that I knew from home.

Our barracks were right across the street from the brig. One morning when we got up, we found out there had been a jail break sometime in the early morning. We heard that a few prisoners had stolen a car that was parked in the compound and had used it to smash down the gate. I think they were caught right away because there were too many main gates to go through.

In the mornings before breakfast we had to run around the block. Every once in a while, half of us would take a shortcut through an alley, and that would cut our run in half. We never got caught doing that. If we had, we would've gotten some "Happy Hours," or extra duty.

Boot camp finally ended on 23 November, and I got ready for a nine-day leave. Before I left, I went to see Joe Silvis who was in a barracks a short distance away. I couldn't wait to show him my brand-new dress blues.

After my leave I returned to the outgoing unit at Great Lakes. We shipped out on a train to Shoemaker, California around 12 December. It took four days to get there. There were twelve Pullman cars attached to the engine and one dining car. I think we stopped to allow every cattle train to get ahead of us.

My Christmas at Shoemaker was the first I had ever spent away from home. They put on a few USO shows for us, including one with Mickey Rooney. I was at Shoemaker for at least two weeks.

One day we received word that we would be going down to the docks to be shipped out. They took several busloads of men down to the docks in San Francisco where we sat all day. Then we were taken back to Camp Shoemaker. This was the Navy's way of doing things.

A few days later we got the word again. Down to the docks we went. This time we were loaded as passengers on the aircraft carrier USS *Saratoga*. She was huge! She was 888-feet long with planes on the hanger deck and planes on the flight deck. She was carrying a full load.

On 3 January 1944 we left San Francisco, sailed out under the Golden Gate Bridge and headed out to open sea with about two-thousand passengers and a full crew. Our destination was Pearl Harbor.

The trip was very nice. I saw my first flying fish, but no whales or sharks. Of course I got seasick that first day at sea. An old salt told me to eat a big meal even though I wouldn't feel like it, to go through the line the second time if I had to and I'd never be sick again. I did what he said, and I was never sick another day.

On 8 January we arrived in Pearl Harbor and went to a Navy camp up in the hills. We were there for a few days and then got taken down to the docks. There we were assigned to several ships in the bay. On 12 January I boarded the USS *New Mexico*[226] that had been tied up to piers on Battleship Row, right next to the *Arizona*.

The *New Mexico* was six-hundred-twenty-three feet long and almost one-hundred feet wide at the beam. The crew consisted of fifty-eight officers and close to a fifteen-hundred-man crew. It took me a couple days to find my way around. The chow line formed on second deck. It didn't take me long to learn that!

I was assigned to the storekeeper's gang. My storerooms were officers' linens, towels, silverware, Silex coffee makers, and a few other items. My battle station was in what was called the ammunition passageway. We supplied ammo to the five-inch anti-aircraft guns on the port side of the ship.

We left Pearl Harbor on 22 January and headed west for the Marshall Islands. On the twenty-eighth, we crossed the International Date Line. When crossing and going west, we lost a day. When we crossed coming east, we gained a day. We almost always managed to come back across on Friday, which meant we had two Fridays in one week. That also meant we had fish two days in a row, and we didn't care much for Navy fish.

We arrived off the Kwajalein Atoll in the Marshall Island group and started to bombard the islands of Ebeye and Kwajalein so troops could land there after 31 January. Later we bombarded Wotje Island in the Wotje Atoll and Taroa Island in the Maloelap Atoll on the 20 and 21 February. These were also in the Marshall Island group and held by the Japanese before World War II. We moved into Majuro Lagoon about 270 miles southeast of Kwajalein on 23 February and later headed south.

On 2 March, we were initiated into the " Solemn Mysteries of the Ancient Order of the Deep." As we crossed the Equator, we were given chop jobs for haircuts and thrown into a swab tank which was filled with dirty water. We also had to run past a band of guys armed with wooden paddles. The officers and enlisted men were all treated alike during the initiation rites.

We continued on southward to Havana Harbor in Efate, part of the New Hebrides group. There we took on additional ammunition. On 20 March, we joined other units in one-day bombardment of Kavieng on New Ireland. This was in coordination with a United States Marine invasion of Emirau Island, seventy-five miles north of Efate.

On 23 April we sailed with the USS *Idaho*, USS *Pennsylvania* and a group of destroyers headed to Sydney, Australia for R&R. It took us six days. In Sydney, we got an education in Australian money—pence, shillings, florins and pounds. My friends and I went to a restaurant to get something to eat, and when the cashier counted our change we caught on to the system. Three pennies made one three pence, two three pence made one six pence, two six pence made one shilling and two shillings made one florin. It was easy!

I met an Australian soldier who gave me a pin from his hat. I had an ash tray made from a brass nose cone taken from a 14-inch projectile. I later put the pin on my ash tray along with three empty shells from a Japanese rifle and three six-pence coins as cigarette holders.

There was a ship's dance at a place called " Grace Brothers Hall." We went there but none of us danced, so we only stayed a little while. We met a fellow who took us to his home to meet his family. He invited us to have dinner with them. We really didn't want to but they insisted. I think they didn't have much to eat.

The Australian people were hit hard by the War. Everything was rationed. Gasoline was almost nonexistent. Every car had the trunk lid missing and there was a charcoal burner in the trunk. When they burned charcoal in it, it made a gas that was used to run the car's engine. It wasn't very good but it worked. If we were walking along, smoking a cigarette and flipped it out in front of us, someone would pick it up before we could step on it. If we did, we got dirty looks.

The crews from the USS *Idaho* and the USS *New Mexico* had a feud going on between them. We always accused the men from the *Idaho* of sitting in port somewhere drinking fresh milk while we were out on the ocean, fighting a war and drinking powdered milk.

All someone had to do was yell "milk wagon" to them, and a royal feud would take place.

While in Sydney, the *New Mexico* was tied up to the dock next to the *Idaho.* They had to cross our ship to get to the dock. One day someone yelled "milk wagon" and there was a real battle on. Potatoes flew in every direction.

On 5 May 1944, we left Sydney behind and headed back to Efate. It was just as well, for it was starting to get cold in Australia. Winter wasn't far away. Efate was much closer to the Equator and much warmer. Efate was a place we could swim in the salt water and just relax. Natives brought us small bananas and little green oranges.

Once in a while when we were anchored somewhere in deep water and there were no island beaches to swim from, we'd swim off the side of the ship from what we called torpedo blisters, extra parts of the hull from the water level on down. The blister was about three-feet wide, and the idea was that torpedoes would explode on them before they could get to the main hull.

When we brought on stores, we'd get some men from the deck forces to help. Our job was to supervise the operation. When we loaded "delicacies" like canned fruit, pineapple, canned peaches, pears or canned meats, we'd watch the men very closely. Sometimes a couple of them would take a case of food, wander off the path and hide whatever he had. Once I saw one of them go off with a case, but I let him go. I doubted if he knew what he was carrying. I'll bet he was surprised when he found out it was a case of green beans. I still wonder what he did with it.

Once we went on a small island to pick up stores. We were there all day, and the day turned into night. We were beginning to get hungry. We hadn't had anything to eat since early morning. One member of our group opened a large can of cooked beef tongues. It was very good.

Since we had access to all the food, someone opened a large can of pineapple slices, and then we sat around the open can, dipping our fingers into the juice and bringing out a slice. When the slices were all gone, we took our turn at the juice. One man would take a drink and pass the can to the next man. This went on until the can was empty. We usually got more than one turn at the can. A fried pork chop with a fried egg, some green pepper between two slices of bread made a real sandwich. McDonald's could never beat that.

We picked up our ammo at other places. One time when we were taking on ammunition, the big 14-inch projectiles were lying all over the top deck, and men were lowering them down in the ship one at a time. These projectiles weighed close to twelve-hundred pounds each. Some men were working, and some were just lying around on top of the projectiles. All of a sudden a bolt of lightning struck high up on the navigation bridge. It made an awful loud bang, and men scattered in every direction. No one got hurt.

It was something else when we took on fuel. A tanker would come along side and lift by crane some four-inch hoses across to our ship. Lots of slack was left in those hoses. When the hoses were connected to both ships, the tanker would start to pump fuel into our tanks. This was done while we were moving along in the water out on the open sea. When our tanks were full, we had 3,277 tons of fuel or 893,000 gallons. We also had aviation fuel for two seaplanes which we would shoot off the ship with a catapult. Those planes were used to direct fire for our 14-inch guns. A few days out and away from the tankers, we'd refuel destroyers from the fuel.

One time a Japanese plane came in very low to the water between the ships, and everyone started shooting at it. We hit one of our destroyers, and they hit us. One fellow had just come out of the head, and just as he closed the door, a 5-inch shell came through the bulkhead into the head and blew everything to pieces. He learned to smoke cigarettes that day!

When we shot into the destroyer, we injured a man. Since the destroyers only had a small hospital on the ship and only a few corpsmen, we sent a doctor over to their ship while the ships were moving. We sent him over on a cable drawn tight between two cranes, one crane from each ship. He examined the injured man and then brought him back to our ship. We brought the wounded sailor back the same way we sent the doctor. The sailor recovered with all that tender care, but the nurses were not the best-looking.

On 14 and 15 June, at Tinian, part of the Mariana group, Saipan, Tinian, and Guam, the *New Mexico* cut loose with an assault that sent concrete and palm trees into the sky. Troops landed on the island on 21 June. Then we shot star shells from our 5-inch guns over the island to prevent counterattacks by the Japanese. The star shells burned very brightly and they descended slowly on small parachutes.

On 30 July and sixty-five-hundred rounds of ammo later, our job at Guam ended. We left the Marianas on 2 August for Pearl Harbor. At Pearl the first time were there, we got tired of all that Hula pineapple music, but we couldn't get away from it. On the way back to Pearl and after a few months in the far Pacific, we picked up Hawaii's radio stations three days out. It really sounded great!

We left Pearl Harbor and entered Puget Sound on 18 August. At the Bremerton Navy Yard, they fitted the "Queen" with new guns, and gave us a leave. The *New Mexico* got the nickname during peacetime when the big ships competed in target practice. She won the Excellence in Firing Award more times than any other ship, and so they called her the "Queen of the Fleet."

I started my twenty-seven-day leave from Seattle on the Great Northern Railroad on a Friday night, and changed to the Pennsylvania Railroad in Chicago. I got into Pittsburgh Monday night and surprised everyone. Before I knew it, the leave was over and I had to go back to the ship.

We used to travel across Puget Sound from Bremerton to Seattle on the Black Ball Ferry Line, a pretty big boat. The lower deck was for cars and small trucks; there was room for maybe fifty vehicles. On the second deck was a lounge. Sometimes we'd go up to the roof. We always brought some peanuts or popcorn and throw the stuff into the air for the seagulls.

Anyway, on our last night in Seattle, a large number of the sailors got drunk in the city. The drunks were creating a ruckus like you wouldn't believe, hitting each other as hard as they could and then laughing about it. They didn't really hurt each other very much or do any damage to the ferry boat. They were just celebrating their last night on shore. When we arrived at Bremerton there were two-dozen Shore Police and Military Police and the whole Bremerton police force. We called that the "Battle of the Bremerton Ferry."

We left Bremerton on 26 October 1944 and arrived back in Pearl Harbor on 1 November. We tied up on Battleship Row. We put to sea again on 10 November and headed west to Ulithi in the western Carolines where we joined the light cruiser USS *Montpelier* and four destroyers and headed for Leyte Gulf in the Philippines where battle had been raging for a month. We covered the intense fighting there and Samar. After the fighting ended, we moved in closer to the shore and dropped anchor.

One day some guys went to an Army camp for a visit. Another day I went to another Army camp with a friend from our ship. The Army guys were handing out Japanese souvenirs. I still have my Japanese rifle. A few of the soldiers came aboard for a visit and ate a meal with us. I though our food was bad, but they said it was the best meal they had had in long time. Maybe our meals weren't so bad after all.

Every once in a while we'd have baked beans for breakfast and fried eggs for our evening meal. When we were going into a new engagement, we always had what was called a battle breakfast. We got up about before dawn and had a big breakfast of beef roast or meat of some kind. We had to have something that would last all day, because we might have to stay in our battle stations that long. We always had turkey with all the trimmings for Thanksgiving or Christmas. One thing I didn't like, and can't stand to this day, was orange marmalade and bread. The butter was reserved for officers.

The flour in the bake shop always got full of bugs. The cooks froze the flour to kill the bugs, and they made bread. An unidentified object on our radar screens was called a "bogey." We'd hold a slice of bread up to the light to see if there were any bogeys on the screen. I didn't eat bread for a long time after I left the Navy.

We left Leyte, and a few days later returned along with other battleships, cruisers, destroyers and several carriers. On 15 December we passed through in to the Sulu Sea to support the landings on Mindanao. After that, in early January 1945, we entered Lingayen Gulf. On board we had Admiral Bruce Frazer, Commander-in-Chief of the

British Pacific Fleet, and Lieutenant General Herbert Lumsden, the man who led the armored head that helped beat Rommel in North Africa. They were there to observe amphibious operations. We were the flagship of Admiral Bruce Frazer, commander Battleship Division 3.

William Chickering was also on board. Chickering was a reporter from *Time* magazine who had been covering MacArthur for a couple years.

On 4 January 1945, while we were moving up the west side of Luzon near Lingayen Gulf, Kamikazes attacked us. One plane hit an escort carrier and set it on fire.[227] The crew had to abandon ship, and we picked up some of the survivors. One fellow was from Greensburg. He was Sam Ankney. He said he had family that lived close to me. He left the ship later and when he came home, he visited my parents. I never saw him again after he left the ship. I don't know what became of him.

On 6 January, around noon, a Kamikaze came in on us from the starboard side through a hail of gunfire. It almost missed us but it caught something and came down onto the port side of the ship. Its five-hundred-pound bomb went off near the navigation bridge. The plane's engine went through the wood and steel on top side and ended up inside on the main deck. The rest of the plane went over the side into the water.

Captain Fleming was on the starboard side of the bridge, and when he saw the plane coming in, he ran to the port side. Thirty men died, including Fleming, William Chickering and Lt. General Lumsden. Eighty-seven men were wounded. We buried the dead at sea at midnight. After a few more days of bombarding Luzon, our troops landed.

My battle station was in an ammunition room where we sent 5-inch 25s up to the 5-inch anti-aircraft guns on the port side. When they fired the 14-inch guns up forward, we'd come out on the quarter deck and watch the projectiles go toward their target. They were big enough that we could see them if we looked up in the sky. They were close to five-feet long, and it looked like they were shooting small cars out of the barrels. One of our 14-inch guns made a smoke ring ten or twenty feet in diameter almost every time it was fired.

On 17 January we went into Lingayen Gulf and anchored. We took on ammo and gave a lot of our provisions to other ships. On 22 January we transferred the flag and headed back for Ulithi. When going past Leyte, we sent a destroyer to pick up mail that was waiting for us. The next day the destroyer caught up with us and gave us 250 bags of mail. There were a lot of happy sailors that day. We left Ulithi on 28 January for Pearl Harbor, arriving there for repairs on 7 February.

On 10 February I went to Camp Andrews, a rest camp in the hills, on the narrow gauge Oahu Railroad. There wasn't much to do there. Once in a while we'd break off a piece of sugar cane and chew on that. One fellow had a deck of cards so we started playing Black Jack with pieces of paper for money. Gambling for money wasn't allowed. The Master at Arms came in and thought we were using real money.

He said, "If I catch you doing that again, I'll give you something to do."

He came around the next day and caught us again.

Christmas card from the USS New Mexico. *Courtesy of Wayne Shaffer.*

6 January 1945., Lingayen Gulf, Philippine Islands. A Japanese Kamikaze set afire by gunners of the USS New Mexico. An instant later the suicide plane crashed into the battle ship killing Captain R.W. Fleming, Time correspondent William Chickering and British liaison officer, Lieutenant General Herbert Lumsden, along with twenty-six sailors, and wounding eighty-seven. *Courtesy of Wayne Shaffer/US Navy photograph.*

12 May 1945. The USS New Mexico an instant after being struck by a Japanese suicide plane for the third time during the War. *US Navy photograph.*

June 1945. A wounded seaman is transferred to the USS New Mexico from the destroyer USS Blaine in the waters off Tinian. The man was wounded by "friendly" fire from the New Mexico when a Japanese plane passed between the two ships. *Courtesy of Wayne Shaffer/US Navy photograph.*

16 August 1945. Sailors of the USS New Mexico celebrate the Japanese surrender. Wayne Shaffer stands top center, hand on his shoulder. *Courtesy Wayne Shaffer/US Navy photo.*

10 October 1945. Homeward bound officers and men of the USS New Mexico assembled to watch as the battleship move through the Panama Canal. *Courtesy of Wayne Shaffer/US Navy photograph.*

"Come on," he said. "I'll give you a job. You're all on garbage detail."

There was a dump truck and driver outside.

Four of us picked up garbage all over Andrews and another nearby camp. We thought it was great! The dump was on a hill, and from there we could see the ships in the bay. When we got back to camp, we asked for the job again for the next day, but he wouldn't give it to us.

We were in Andrews about a week. On 5 March, after they repaired the Kamikaze damage and replaced the guns, we moved out to sea to test the guns. On the 9th we headed west for Ulithi. On the 12th we crossed the International Dateline again. We dropped anchor at Ulithi on the 20th and worked all night loading supplies. The next day we were on the move again, this time for the Ryukyu Islands, only a few sea miles from Japan. We were scheduled to bombard Okinawa.

We traveled with the largest naval force in history. There were ten battleships, eleven cruisers and more than twenty destroyers. When we got to Okinawa, we bombarded for seven days to soften up the beachheads for our troops. On Easter Sunday morning, 1 April 1945, just after the troops went in, the Kamikaze attacks started. They came in low over the water. Bursts from anti-aircraft shells filled the sky.[228]

We stayed around Okinawa firing day and night at the Japanese-held end of the island. We fired many star shells.

Toward evening on 12 May, two Kamikazes came at us. We got the first plane, and it hit the water close to the ship. The second plane made it through the anti-aircraft and hit the small gun mounts and tore a thirty-foot hole in the stack. The plane's five-hundred-pound bomb exploded and killed fifty-five sailors and wounded 177. Later, we buried the dead on Okinawa.

The bomb also knocked out our boilers and put us dead in the water. A repair ship came alongside and worked day and night patching us up and repairing the boilers so we could get underway again. When other planes threatened us, the repair ship would pull away, leaving some of the workmen on the *New Mexico*. When the "all clear" sounded, the repair ship would come back and the work would continue.

When I went up the next morning, I saw what was left of the pilot still in the plane. One thing the Japanese pilots didn't know is that we were the flagship with Admiral Spruance on board. If they had known that, we'd have been a sitting duck for their planes.

We were off Okinawa about sixty-six days, and I doubt very much if we got more than two hours of sleep any night we were there. Japanese planes few over us every night. It was what we called nuisance raids. They were just flying around over us. They couldn't see us on the water, and we wouldn't shoot at them because it would've given away our position. Once in a while we had to call a small landing craft boat to make smoke for "Ironsides," our code name. That boat was never very far away from us, and we would call to it over the loudspeaker. We never used the radio.

We left Okinawa and put in at Guam. We left Guam on 3 June and headed back to Leyte. By this time they had established a repair base there. They sent out a repair ship, but this time the skies were clear.

While we waited for repairs to be completed, we went ashore a few times. We swam, and played softball with the Army guys. They won. We had beer, but it was only 3.2 alcohol and we had to drink it on the beach. We weren't supposed to drink it aboard ship, but if someone really had a thirst, we let him in the refrigerator room because my buddies and I had keys to all the storerooms.

It wasn't long before we got bored and thought of things to do. For instance, in one of the heads there was a trough roughly ten-feet long where sea water was pumped in one end and out a drain on the other. Some people called the exit point the "shit chute." The head had four stalls, three of them with seats where sailors could sit and do Nature's calling. Someone got the bright idea to get into a stall without a seat, wrinkle up a big piece of paper, light it, and then let it float down the trough toward the stalls that had seats. Anyone sitting there got a big raise, and I don't mean the money kind.

When our repairs were finished, we went out to sea to do some practice firing. We tore the rifling out of one of our new 14-inch guns.

A few days later we left Leyte and headed north for Ulithi again. We arrived on 11 August, but instead of stopping, we were sent to Saipan. The War had come to an end, and we had bombed two Japanese cities, Hiroshima and Nagasaki, with the Atomic Bomb. On 12 August, we arrived at Saipan. We left on the 16th for Okinawa, dropped anchor there on the 19th, left on the 24th, and on the 27th entered Sagami Wan at the entrance of Tokyo Bay.

On 2 September 1945, the surrender was signed aboard the USS *Missouri*, anchored in Tokyo Bay. We were anchored in Sagami Bay in sight of the shattered Yokosuka Naval Base. We could plainly see Fujiyama in the distance, though it was fifty miles away. Our ship's photographer rode out in the bay in a whale boat some distance from the ship where there he took a picture of our ship with Mount Fuji in the background. I still have that picture, and there's one on the Navy stone at the memorial in Fairview Cemetery.

We left Japan on 6 September. We stopped at Buckner Bay[229] for one day, then came to Pearl Harbor where we stayed five days. Leaving Pearl for the last time, we headed for the Panama Canal. It was a sight to see. We were pulled through the locks by "mules," which were actually cars that ran on tracks on both sides of the canal.

We tied up at the dock on the Atlantic side at the city of Colón. When I got off the ship, I took one shipmate with me, Don Moretz from Palmyra, Pennsylvania, near Harrisburg. We looked for a telephone. A fellow by the name of John Winclosky from Kecksburg, lived in Panama. I called him and told him who I was. He asked where I was and I told him at the train station.

He said, "You stay right there, I'll see you in a little while."

He came in on the train. It was a narrow gauge railroad. The rails were thirty-six inches apart while standard railroad tracks are four feet, eight-and-a-half-inches apart. I noticed one thing in particular; the railroad was the PRR railroad. That really caught my eye since I'd been away from home for a year. Only it wasn't the Pennsylvania Railroad, it was the Panama Railroad.

We had a very nice day's visit. John had a government job there and was in charge of building a new prison. The building was just completed and they had no customers yet, so he took my friend and me all through it. The day finally came to an end and we said our goodbyes. My friend and I went back to our ship. I learned one thing about the Panama Canal. The Atlantic side of the canal is seventeen miles farther west than the Pacific side. The canal goes from northwest on the Atlantic side to southeast on the Pacific side.

We were soon back on the high seas, this time heading north for Boston, Massachusetts. When we entered the harbor at Boston, we were met with many small boats welcoming us home. A tugboat came out to meet us with a big "WELCOME" sign on each side. The tug was carrying many girls. It was 18 October 1945, Navy Day.

The next day I left the ship for a week's furlough. I came home on an overnight train. On the return trip to Boston, the train was packed with servicemen going back to their units. The train was so crowded we had to stand on the platform outside each car's entrance. When I say "we," I mean the people who got on in Greensburg. We didn't get in the car until we were near Philadelphia. I was traveling with a Navy nurse who also got on the train in Greensburg. She was stationed at the Naval Hospital in Chelsea, Massachusetts. Her name was Virginia Shaulis. Finally after we got past New York, she got a seat and I was still standing. She turned her travel case on end out in the aisle. That made me a seat. I rode on the travel case the rest of the way to Boston.

We also learned to use the subway system in Boston. We could ride the streetcars for one nickel and the subways for a dime. In downtown, it was subways; out of the center of town it was elevated railways. I made this same trip home on weekend passes, and finally, on 3 May 1946, I was honorably discharged as Storekeeper, Second Class from the United States Navy from the Fargo Separation Center, Boston.

I entered the Navy at the age of seventeen. I made it halfway around the world; saw many places and many things. I walked on land in New Hebrides Islands, part of the Solomon Islands; several times in the Philippines; Sydney, Australia; several times in Honolulu, and Panama. I was honorably discharged from the service before I was twenty-one.

The USS *New Mexico* was decommissioned in Boston in July 1946. She was sold for scrap in October 1947.

"Every Bullet Hitting the Ground Seemed to Lift Me Up a Few Inches."

John Shultz

82nd Airborne Division
508th Parachute Infantry Regiment
Operation MARKET-GARDEN
Born in Lycippus, Pennsylvania, 13 April 1925
Greensburg, Pennsylvania

"Our planes took off one right after another, two abreast. While the last of the planes were taking off from England, the first planes were arriving back at their bases. It was a huge operation. The plane ride took about an hour. As we approached the Dutch coast the Germans started shooting at us. Our advantage there was that we were coming in fairly low, while their big guns were zeroed in for distance. Soldiers on the ground were firing at us with rifles. I started wondering again if I had the guts to get out and do it. But when the Flak started bouncing off of our plane I thought, let me out of here!"

METRO SHULTZ, MY FATHER, was a Ukrainian born in Southern Poland. He was just a child when he came to the United States, and he was naturalized as a teenager. He had the equivalent of a high school education. In the Ukraine they use the Cyrillic alphabet, and there's no letter-for-letter translation, so we translated our name phonetically. Some might spell it "Shultis" or "Soltis."

Dad was a farmer and a coal miner. He was killed in the Jamison #20 Coal Mine in Pleasant Unity in 1939. He was a switchman on the underground train. Most of the areas underground were covered with water. He switched a line of cars onto a siding and put the brake on. Then he ran to catch the train as it moved forward. He didn't realize that the cars on the siding were still moving, and his chest was crushed between two of the cars; his lungs were punctured and his ribs were broken. He lived for a few days in the hospital after the accident. I was thirteen years old at the time.

My mother was Anna Homko, and she came from the same area in Poland as my father, but ethnically she was Slavic. She never had any formal schooling. She came over with a couple of girl friends when she was thirteen years old. They were recruited as indentured servants. She worked for two years as a domestic in Ansonia, Connecticut. My grandparents had occasion to visit Connecticut after they had settled in this area. They remembered having visited the home where my mother was working. At that time, there were "fixed" marriages. When my grandparents thought my father was ready to get married, they remembered this girl that they thought of very highly. My parents married in 1918.

Dad played the violin and my mother was a good singer, so they were always invited to perform at weddings and christenings. For many years my father had a small general store next to the house. It was still there when I was growing up, but it wasn't in operation then. There was a pool table in the back, and a lot of guys would spend time there playing pool.

I had three older brothers. The second oldest, Andrew, belonged to Company M, 110th Infantry in Latrobe/Greensburg, Pennsylvania, and they were federalized in 1941.[230] He turned out to be a career man. He retired as a lieutenant colonel in the Air Force. There were eight of us all together.

We had a six-acre farm in Lycippus, right below a hardware store. We farm boys were out working in the fields all the time. We never had time to play. We grew potatoes, cabbage, corn, beets and tomatoes. We had huge fields of potatoes. We had hogs and chickens and one or two cows. The kids in the coal-mining patches had nothing to do all day, so they had time for all kinds of activities. Our childhood was work, work, work.

During the Depression, my father was out of work for a large part of those years, so we lived off of what we could raise on the farm, but we were barely self-sufficient. Our clothes were hand-me-downs. I put cardboard in the bottom of my shoes to cover the holes. When it came time to pay the real estate tax, we would kill a hog or sell a calf to get the money. The pressure was always on to keep the electricity usage down to the minimum charge. It was a rough existence.

Things started to look much better in 1939. More people had jobs because we were preparing for the war we knew was coming. My father had a car, and until he got called back into the mine, he took a job as a Maytag washing-machine salesman. He won a sales contest and as a prize got a small five- or six-tube radio. The neighbors across the street had a good radio. When Joe Louis and Max Schmeling had their title match, a gang of us boys gathered on the corner and listened to the broadcast.[231]

I attended a one-room school house until the 5th grade. The school is still standing, but it's been converted into a home. I went to Hurst High School in Norvelt and graduated in 1943. I took the commercial courses: shorthand, typing, and the basic curriculum, which might prepare me for a job following school. I never played school sports, because I had chores to do at home. I got all the physical exercise I needed on the farm. My brothers and I were made available to the local farmers if they needed field help. My grandfather had a one-horse farm of about forty acres. So I was always shucking wheat or husking corn. We all learned to drive by driving the pickup truck or a tractor across the fields.

I delivered the *Latrobe Bulletin*, which was an evening paper at that time. We split up the route among three of us brothers. I had sixteen customers and I got one penny per paper. After I finished my paper route, I stopped in the general store in town. All the World War I veterans would be there hanging around the pot-bellied stove and I felt a connection to World War I through them. I could've listened to their stories all night, but I had to get home at a reasonable time, or I'd be in trouble on the home front.

I graduated on a Monday and had a letter to report to my Draft Board for a physical on Thursday of that same week. They decided that I'd be given a deferment for six months, because of our situation at home, and with my father being dead. During that period of time I had some odd jobs, but I never made much more than five dollars a day.

I entered the service in December of 1943. I caught a street car from Norvelt to the Greensburg train station. From there I took a train to Fort Meade, Maryland. Because of my commercial experience, I was delayed from shipping out for basic training for about a month to help with processing accumulated paperwork at the Fort.

From Fort Meade I went to Fort McClellan, Alabama for basic training. This was around February 1944. I was classified as a communications specialist, wiring field phones, encoding and decoding messages, and operating a regimental message center. I did that for a couple hours a day in addition to regular field and weapons training. Basic training was nothing like what we had to endure in jump school.

From Alabama I returned to Fort Meade and then went to Fort Dix for embarkation. I was aboard ship enroute to Europe in early June when Normandy was invaded. When we boarded the ship they had us put on these big, heavy winter overcoats and all of our heavy gear, which weighed about fifty pounds. When we got to England the first thing they did was collect all of those overcoats. Someone had come up with that idea as being the most efficient method of shipping all of those overcoats to Europe. I went over on the SS *Monticello*, an Italian liner converted into a troop ship. We convoyed over in the North Atlantic and the seas were rough. I remember my mother telling me how seasick she had been when she came to the United States. At the time I thought, *'Well, what do you expect from girls!'* Well, I barfed in my steel helmet for most of my trip!

I didn't join the paratroops until I got to England. As a young kid, I was impressed by a fellow who used to make parachute jumps at Latrobe Airport on Sunday afternoons.[232] He'd pass the hat around, and when he got twenty dollars he'd go up and make a jump. Between jumps he'd have us kids help him re-pack his 'chute. So I had some exposure to parachute jumping. I thought if he can do it, I can, too. I got a weekend pass from Fort Meade, and came home, which I wasn't supposed to do, I asked my mother what she'd think if I joined the paratroops.

She looked at me and said, "Are you crazy? I wouldn't want any of my friends to say I raised dumb kids!"

I took that as a "No."

I was color blind, so I couldn't qualify for pilot training, which was what I had wanted to do. It turned out that it didn't matter, because after Normandy they closed down the pilot training to provide more replacements for the infantry units. When I got to England, I was thrown in with a hodgepodge of older Army specialists, cooks and clerks and what not. In southern England, we had to walk to and from our training areas, and these old geezers would complain about their legs and knees. The whole camp smelled of liniment!

One day a crew of paratroopers from a new jump school in England came to our unit and gave a talk about airborne warfare and said they'd be holding an endurance test in a week. I tried out, and was accepted. They were looking for soldiers in good physical condition who wouldn't give up when they got tired. Twenty or thirty volunteered, but they accepted only seven or eight of us.

Jump school was near one of the air bases in the center of England, near Manchester. Normal parachute training in the States lasted from six to eight weeks. My jump school was only four weeks. It was one big physical fitness program. We'd get up early in the morning and take a forty-minute run before breakfast. After breakfast we'd have tumbling class, where we'd jump off of an eight foot platform and hit the ground and roll instead of taking the pressure on our knees. We'd climb ropes in the airplane hangar, up and down without sliding or burning our hands and legs. We learned how to use the risers on the parachute to steer in a certain direction. The discipline was tough. Every little thing that we did wrong resulted in us having to do pushups.

In the last week of training we made actual jumps. Everyone had to have his equipment attached precisely and double-checked. We jumped with a regular parachute on our backs and reserve parachutes on our chests. In combat, we had to carry enough rations to last for ten days. There was a chocolate bar, D-Bars they were called, that was so hard I was lucky to polish off a piece an inch square at each sitting.

Our harness was supposed to be as tight as possible. If we were comfortable, we weren't doing it right. The jumpmaster would come around and try to get his hand between our harness and our body, and if he could get his hand in, the harness was too loose. There was a routine in the plane. We'd stand up, hook up and check each other's gear. Just one more thing to keep us occupied before we jumped. Then we'd sound off with, "Number Eighteen, OK. Number Seventeen, OK," and so on. Then we'd watch the red and green lights above the door. When the green light came on, the jump-master yelled, "Go!" and off we went.

My first jump was from a C–47, the first airplane I was ever in. It was aluminum-skinned with no insulation inside; the seats were a row of aluminum benches along each side with small areas dished out to sit in. We tried not to be noticeable about it, but everyone stared at everyone else to see how they were putting up with the stress. We were supposed to make five jumps to qualify, but on what was to be our last jump the winds came up too strong. We were in the plane waiting for the command to go and they canceled the jump. So my class qualified with only four jumps. I also had training jumps after I joined my unit. The requirement at the time was one jump per month to maintain our parachute qualification. We made fifty-dollars a month above our eighty-dollar regular pay. It was a hefty increase.

On my first training jump I still wasn't convinced that I could do it. I was up there, doing everything in the order I was supposed to do it, yet I wasn't sure. We jumped in "sticks," eighteen or twenty men in a stick. We were compacted tightly against the man in front of us. This was so we'd all go out the door as quickly as possible and land pretty much together. With all the equipment, I felt like I was five-feet wide. The door of the plane had been removed, and the door frame had been taped with silk to help us slide through. Coming out the door right on top of another man, there was a possibility that chutes could get tangled up. On one of my training jumps I did land on the canopy of the man below me. I sank in up to my knees, and when I did, my 'chute began to collapse. I pedaled as fast as I could to get off!

Sitting still all that time on the plane, my legs and back stiffened up. When I did stand, I felt like I weighed three-hundred pounds. Shuffling to the door, it was a help to be packed so tightly, because once I got moving I just went with the flow. There was no way to get out of it by that time! It was my third or fourth jump before I was really cognizant of what was going on. As we went through the door, the procedure was to make a half-left turn so that the propeller blast could help to open the parachute.

The first three were daylight jumps and the fourth was a night jump. On the night jump, I saw what looked like a stream, and I didn't want to land there. So I worked pretty hard to get over a row of trees next to the stream. I barely avoided the trees, but I missed the stream. When I stood up and glanced over, I saw that the "stream" was actually a wet asphalt roadway. It would've been a dangerous landing.

In training we unbuckled our parachute harness upon landing, but we were taught in combat to just cut it off with the bayonet we strapped to one of our boots. Our practice jumps were all made from two-thousand feet. We'd drop about 175 feet before our 'chutes fully opened. Going out the door, we were supposed to count to ten, then check our canopy to make sure it was open. If it wasn't, then we had to grab our reserve. Once the 'chute was fully open, we'd have to stabilize our descent and pick out our landing area. The object of a combat jump was to drop us as low as they could, giving us just enough time for the 'chute to open before we hit the ground. Some of the Normandy veterans took their reserve 'chutes off and left them on the plane during the Holland jump. They jumped from six-hundred feet, and a reserve 'chute would've been useless.

After jump training I was assigned to Nottingham, England, which was the base from which the 508th left to go to Normandy. I arrived there sometime in July. Out of 130 in my company, about fifty made it back from Normandy with the core group. Later, more trickled in from the hospitals or escaped from being taken prisoner. I realized that I was taking the place of someone who had been killed in Normandy.[233] They had some wild stories. Combat really bonds the men together. It made me wonder what the heck I'd gotten into.

I was assigned to Company A, 508th Parachute Infantry Regiment, which was an independent regiment attached to the 82nd Airborne Division. My company commander was Captain Adams.[234] He was with us for quite a while.

Before Holland, we were scheduled to make a jump into Belgium to liberate a POW camp. But before we got to the final preparations, the ground troops had already overrun the area, so that jump was canceled. On another previous alert, everyone fitted their parachutes and arranged their gear on the plane the night before. I didn't sleep too soundly. It was probably three in the morning before I fell asleep. Around nine o'clock in the morning, the sounds of vehicles and men yelling woke me up. I was still half in a dream state, and I thought we were already in combat, and I never got to fire a shot! But it was just that the jump had been called off.

About a week prior to the Holland jump, they started briefing us on our assignments. They had sand-table maps duplicating the area we were to be landing in, and they issued secret maps for us to use in the event we missed our drop zone. Those were long days. Preparing for any mission was stressful. One part of the briefings dealt with where we were to contact Dutch Underground units. They were supposed to direct us to any Nazi troops in the area.

Holland was the first airborne operation in Europe conducted in the daylight. All the others used the cover of darkness, but they decided that night jumps were not worth the losses. On the night jump in Normandy, a lot of them missed their drop zones, their planes were shot down or they landed in the water and drowned. Many were captured.[235]

I was called to Division Headquarters to be interviewed for a clerical job just before I jumped into Holland. After that, they cut orders for me to report to headquarters, but the orders didn't catch up to me before I went into combat. They listed me as AWOL, but by then I couldn't abandon my buddies on the line. Up to that time, as well, I hadn't told my mother I was in the paratroops. I finally "fessed up" in a letter I wrote from Holland.

September 17th was a Sunday. We were supposed to take off, as I recall, about three o'clock in the afternoon. The evening before, we had a special meal and listened to the regimental band. We also had a chance to go to church. Since I was a recruit, I had to spend the night in the plane guarding our equipment.

Like everything else in the Army, it was "hurry up and wait." We probably would've been ready to take off for the Holland jump around noon, but we didn't take off until around two or three o'clock.[236] The object was to jump in the daylight, get assembled then move out under the cover of darkness. Our planes took off one right after another, two abreast. My plane was somewhere toward the front of the formation. While the last of the planes were taking off from England, the first planes were arriving back at their bases. It was a huge operation. The plane ride took about an hour. As we approached the Dutch coast the Germans started shooting at us. Our advantage there was that we were coming in fairly low, while their big guns were zeroed in for distance. Soldiers on the ground fired at us with rifles. I started wondering again if I had the guts to get out and do it. But when the Flak started bouncing off of our plane I thought, *'Let me out of here!'*

After I jumped, I drifted toward a cow pasture with a fence that separated it from what looked like a hay field. I tried to pull my risers to land in the hay field. I pulled and pulled, but I just didn't have enough strength. So I landed among the cows. I got them all stirred up. When I looked over at the "hay field," I saw that it was filled with huge sugar beets. I was glad I was unsuccessful in landing there!

I was about three miles from my objective. There were no enemy troops or gun emplacements around.[237] The Germans sent some fighter planes over to strafe us. As the planes came over, we dropped everything and jumped into a nearby ditch. I laid there trying to be as small as I could, and every bullet that hit the ground seemed to lift me up a few inches. That was my first real indication that someone didn't approve of us being there!

Somehow my hand got cut when I landed. I may have cut it myself when I was trying to cut my way out of my parachute harness. While we were being strafed in this ditch, a medic came over to me. He saw that I was losing blood, and he patched me up. He wanted to write me up for a Purple Heart.

I said, "Heck, no. Purple Hearts are for guys who've had an arm or a leg blown off!"

Later, I realized the points I would've gotten for the Purple Heart would have been helpful in getting me home sooner.

We all had a mission upon landing. We didn't just land and then wait around for orders. We'd been briefed and we all knew what we were supposed to do. I depended on the guy on my left and right, and knew that he was trained well-enough to do his job when it came time. I've seen movies where ten guys were in a ditch somewhere. If we ever got caught in a cluster like that, more than two or three men in one place, we'd get chewed out royally. They didn't want one shell to drop in and wipe out a lot of men.

My immediate assignment in Holland was to collect ammunition from the supply bundles that were dropped and help conceal all the parachutes. Everyone jumped with a land mine, and we also collected those and put them in a central location. While I did that, the rest of my company set off on their mission, which was to go into the town of Nijmegen and secure an intersection leading to the ramp for the highway bridge across the Waal River. It was a huge, elevated bridge with control towers. We were told that it was wired with explosives and the Germans would blow it up if we didn't capture it in time.

As we walked past a nearby farmhouse, the residents came outside to offer their thanks. They stored their milk in a spring house to keep it cool, and a couple young girls came out and gave us some to drink. Then, when the German resistance built up, they occupied that house and started shooting at us. We had to drop mortars on the farmhouse to get the Germans out. That was horrible.

The first unit at the intersection was able to tie up the Germans at the explosive control point.[238] Then they started cutting wires to the bridge itself. Before long the Germans started bringing reinforcements into Nijmegen and it turned into a pretty difficult two- or three-day fight for the town and the bridge.

The second day additional troops and artillery landed by glider. We had to sweep their landing zone for any mines or other obstructions. There were all kinds of actions around the levees and the bridge. After we were in control of the city, I ended up on the north shore of the Nijmegen Bridge in a defensive perimeter with my company. One of our tasks was to watch the river for any floating objects. The Germans would put explosives in fifty-five-gallon drums and float them downstream in an attempt to blow up the bridge supports. If we saw anything suspicious in the water, we shot it up.

The unique thing about Holland was we couldn't dig a proper foxhole. The whole area was below sea level. The hole would fill up with water, so we used ammo boxes in the bottom of the hole to try and keep out of the water. We used the drainage ditches along the levees to move, because German machine-gun fire was trained along the dikes.

My company was assigned to take Hill 30, right along the Dutch-German border.[239] It was one of our biggest battles. The Germans held it as an observation area. They were dug in along the crest of the hill. We had a rough time taking that hill. One of the toughest operations in Holland. This was after we'd secured the bridge, but before the ground forces could get to us. Even though we were short of ammunition, I shot at anything that moved. I couldn't take the chance that it was a German patrol, especially at night. They sent patrols out to try to infiltrate our lines after dark.[240]

The soil in the area was quite sandy, and the Germans were hitting us with mortars. When a shell hit, it would just spray everything with sand. A couple hit around my foxhole and the sand got into the action of my M1 rifle. I tried to fire again, but it was locked up. I thought, *'This is was it for me.'*

I took out my grenade, which was my last chance to save my life. I pulled the pin and there I was holding a live grenade. The longer I held it, the tighter I squeezed the release lever closed. I was staring into the darkness, waiting for the Germans. Then, I lost the pin. When daylight came I was still holding that grenade, but my hand was cramping. I finally took a safety pin from my ammunition belt and used that to secure the grenade.

Two or three days later, we were pulled off the back of Hill 30 to rest. One of the guys looked at me and said, "Wow! Somebody told me they saw your body on the hillside." It turned out to be a guy named Singer instead of one named Shultz![241] That was a shocker, to think they thought I was dead. We had to leave most of the bodies lay where they fell until we got more support.

One of the selling points for joining the paratroops was knowing the details of each operation. In the regular infantry, you're in a foxhole and someone says, "Follow me," and you move forward. You never know where you are or where you're going. In the paratroopers we were expected to use more initiative. Most airborne missions were expected to last about ten days or less, the length of time we considered ourselves to be self-sufficient. We were a valuable resource, so they tried to get us out as soon as possible and relieve us with ground units so we could get back and prepare for our next mission. As it turned out, we stayed in Holland fifty-two days.[242]

When we were relieved, we marched back about ten miles to get transportation to Sissonne, France. This was before Christmas. We were at a movie when they told us to report back to our units and prepare to move out. At that time I was in Company A Headquarters, and I had to type up a roster of all the guys we were taking with us. We loaded onto Air Force flat bed trailers.[243] We traveled at night in snow under blackout conditions. They dropped us off just a little south of Bastogne. Then we marched into Bastogne. We were ready to settle down for the night, but orders were received to march us farther north while the 101st Airborne came in behind us. As we were marching up to the line, we passed some 28th Division troops coming the other way.

They told us, "You don't want to go up there."

The Germans had broken through at so many places, there was no front line. There was a lot of confusion. We were receiving reports of German units behind us. It took several days just to secure the area and tie into units to either side and establish a front line. The company headquarters was just behind the rest of the company. My foxhole was about a hundred yards behind the front line.[244]

At one point I was sent out with a patrol to man an observation post. One of the sergeants took us out ahead of our lines just as it was getting dark. We dug in and were told to report any action we saw. Meanwhile, the higher-ups made a decision to further straighten up the lines, and our company pulled back. But they forgot about us. When the company got into their new location, someone asked about us. The sergeant was the only one who knew the location, so around midnight he made his way back out to us, in what was now enemy territory, and brought us back. It was pretty dangerous for him to have come back for us. Much later, I wrote the sergeant up for a citation and he ended up getting a Silver Star. His name was Duane Dennison.[245]

During the Battle of the Bulge, we were moving forward with a tank as our shield. With so much firepower, I thought the mission was going to be a breeze. Well, the road sloped a little bit and there was so much snow the tank just slid right into a ditch. The crew popped out and said there was nothing they could do; they were stuck. So much for our tank support!

We were always trying to find ways to keep warm. I told one group of guys I had an idea. We had on about four layers of clothes. I took my boots off and wrapped my field jacket around my feet. Then I put the heavy overcoat on and curled up and tried to get some sleep. A couple of the other guys thought that seemed like it might work, so they did it, too.

During the night I heard some rustling around and heard the guys muttering, "That damned Shultz! He ought to keep his ideas to himself!"

My idea wasn't working. They tried to put their boots back on and all the boots were frozen.

I was sent back to Liège, Belgium with frostbitten toes and a serious case of bronchitis. Just a day or two before I got there, one of the buzz-bombs had dropped on the hospital area. What I needed most for my feet was to put on some dry socks. They treated the bronchitis with some antibiotics.

We kept making headway while the Germans kept running out of gasoline and ammunition. Eventually the War just sort of tapered off. I ended up a staff sergeant for company operations. After the end of the War we were part of the Army of Occupation. Originally we were sent back to a camp in France. Then they decided that the 82nd Airborne Division would occupy Berlin and the 508th was assigned as the honor guard at Eisenhower's SHAEF Headquarters in Frankfurt, Germany.

For a couple of months we went house-to-house through the city of Frankfurt searching for pockets of resistance and ammunition. We ordered all the occupants of each house to assemble in a front room while one person with the keys accompanied us through the house, opening every door. We found a number of copies of *Mein Kampf*.[246] The Germans were rather ingenious in trying to protect their valuables. One of their tricks was to put their valuables in a copper box, and solder it closed. It wouldn't rust, and there was no key to open it. We used our bayonets to cut the boxes open. We were forbidden to take any valuables; anything we took had to have some military importance or a relationship to possible sabotage. There was also a non-fraternization rule in force.

I was eventually sent to Camp Chesterfield in France. Men with about fifty points were being sent to the States to prepare for Pacific redeployment. While I was there, the Air Force was showing off over the camp in one of their new jets. It was the first time I'd seen one of those. I was there for a few weeks waiting for available transportation. Eventually our group was shipped to Antwerp for flat-bottomed transport to England. I was in Southhampton, England for Christmas 1945. Shortly after that, I boarded the *Queen Mary* with units of the 82nd Airborne Division.

We were on the Atlantic for New Year's. During the crossing, they announced that the 82nd had been selected to march in a victory parade in New York when we returned. That was something every soldier had wished for during the War. We left our camp in New Jersey at two o'oclock in the morning and landed at the Battery on the southern tip of Manhattan Island. The parade down 5th Avenue was in the early afternoon. That was a great experience!

After the parade, I was sent to Indiantown Gap. I learned soldiers in the States with fifty points or more were eligible for discharge. They reviewed my record and asked me if I wanted to stay in or take a discharge. I had 51 points, so I said I'd go home. Less than a week after the parade in New York, I was a civilian.

When I came back home, I took a job in a stone quarry, swinging a big sledge hammer to break up the rocks so they'd go through the crusher, and I only made about six dollars a day. I also worked for a ceramics company in Latrobe.

My company commander had often spoken with me about going to college when I got back home. I valued his judgment, and thought I'd be foolish not to take advantage of the GI Bill. I couldn't afford to pay the room and board, so I walked or hitch-hiked to Saint Vincent College every day from Lycippus. In time, I was able to afford an old clunker to drive. My last year I got a room in Latrobe.

I graduated from Saint Vincent in 1949 with a degree in business administration and a minor in English.

I had worked part time at Sears-Roebuck during my senior year. The manager at Sears talked to a fellow and me about going into management training. Nineteen forty-nine was another mini-depression year, and the job market was pretty slow, so I was fortunate to have that opportunity. Sears transferred me to Williamson, West Virginia for their two year management training program.

After about a year down there, my girlfriend and I decided to get married. Her father was ill and her mother was the postmaster in Norvelt. My girlfriend was the homemaker. I agreed to give up my job in Williamson, so her mother could continue with her much-needed job. Agnes and I were married in 1950. Her mother, also named Agnes, was the postmaster until 1974. My mother-in-law was a Kendi from Mammoth, and she had a few political connections to get her job.

I managed the sporting goods department at the Sears in Greensburg for one season. Then I worked as a postal clerk in the post office for a while. But I couldn't stand the post office. It was government work, and I couldn't do anything unless it was in the manual. It was no place for initiative. I went to the placement office at Saint Vincent, and they put me in touch with Stupakoff's, which was looking to hire someone in the purchasing department. I ended up doing purchasing work for the rest of my career. I had taken some chemistry at Saint Vincent, which helped me get a job at Pittsburgh Coke and Chemical.

I helped organize the VFW in Pleasant Unity, but shortly after that Post was set up, I was transferred to Kansas City. After I retired, we lived in Pittsburgh and then Washington (PA), where I joined the American Legion. When I came back to Greensburg, I transferred my membership to the Greensburg American Legion.

We had 508th Parachute Regiment reunions every year starting in about 1966. There's a world of difference between the early reunions, when everyone was young and Gung-Ho. There were big parties then. Later, people came with canes, walkers and wheelchairs!

Finally, we formed a committee to plan how to disband our Association. We decided that 2004 would be the last year we could count on having enough healthy people for a reunion. We held it at Camp Blanding, Florida. The city and the Chamber of Commerce made us feel very welcome. The local NROTC group was our honor guard. The local VFW came out. The police gave us an escort form the hotel to the camp. They treated us like royalty.

I was in the service for twenty-five months during the War. Those months fell between my eighteenth and twenty-first birthdays. I didn't know then that those months would have such a profound effect on the rest of my life.

John Schultz in Germany, 1945.

"I Was One of the Lucky Ones."

Elmer George Slezak
United States Naval Reserve
Destroyer Escort USS *Julian Jordan* (DE–204)
Hospital Ship USS *Consolation* (AH–15) (World War II)
Destroyer USS *Lyman K. Swenson* (DD–729)
Destroyer Tender USS *Dixie* (AD–14) (Korea)
Born in Farrell, Pennsylvania, 5 June 1923
Greensburg, Pennsylvania

"When we got to Pearl Harbor, we viewed the results of the attack. The Arizona, the capsized Utah and all the debris surrounding the area of the attack brought the attack home to us. As we waited there, where the War had started, the USAAF dropped the Atomic Bomb on Japan. The night of the surrender was like the Fourth of July. There were fireworks and tracers shooting all over the place. I felt a certain poetic justice, being in the place where the Japs had started the War and hearing that it was all over."

HISTORY ISN'T JUST something one reads in books. It's very much a living thing. I've gone through much of it myself. You might say I was fortunate, a late arrival on the scene during some very dangerous times. There were many times when I was in harm's way but I always seemed to have a lucky streak. I've been on the border of danger, but I survived. That's why I always say my motto is, "Be a Survivor." I could've been caught up in D-Day, in Okinawa, or in the invasion of Japan, but I wasn't. I've been blessed really.

I was born in Farrell, Mercer County, Pennsylvania, on 5 June 1923. I remember my early childhood from the late 1920s onward. Events like Lindbergh's[247] crossing of the Atlantic stand out in my mind. The bootleg booze business and the rackets[248] were also big news at the time, especially because of the stranglehold they seemed to have on society. I remember when I was a tyke watching from the curb as barrels and cans of moonshine were poured into the gutters, much to the consternation of the older bystanders. It was a wild time in this country until the bottom dropped out.

The stock market crash of 1929 and the economic depression it caused had a severe impact on us all. My father did a lot of scrambling and held several different jobs to keep our family off of relief. I knew we were poor, but so was every other family in my neighborhood. We were all in the same boat in those days.

With the arrival of FDR and the New Deal[249], the hopes and aspiration of a new economy unfolded. As our country struggled to get back to work, the flames of future war began to envelop different parts of the world. The New Deal agencies, the Civilian Conservation Corps, Agricultural Adjustment Agency and the National Recovery Act, distracted our depressed nation from those events. Many of those agencies had a big impact in the country. My father worked for the New Deal Flood Control Reservoir Program in Pymatuming.

In 1937, at the age of fourteen, I ventured to Streator, Illinois, for a summer's worth of farm life. My mother had been born and raised in Streator but had moved to Pennsylvania with two of her sisters and a niece after she married my father.

To get to Streator, I rode solo on the Erie Railroad from Sharon to Chicago and then transferred onto the Southern Pacific, bound for Central Illinois. That meant a transfer from a steam locomotive to a super diesel train. For a kid my age, in that era, that was a big deal. We grew up young in those days, though. It was my first experience away from home, and it was exciting.

It seems in my memory that from first grade on current events in my classes were fraught with warfare. It was during that time that Hitler gained power in Germany, Mussolini gained power in Italy, and the Japanese-Chinese conflict grew in concert with the Russo-Finnish war.[250]

It was something to read of the "modern" Army of Italy attacking the natives of Abyssinia (Ethiopia) with airplanes, tanks and machine guns.[251] The Spanish Civil war was raging, and it seemed to be the testing ground for the new world war that was on the horizon.[252]

All of those events were, in some way, the foundation for the attack at Pearl Harbor. A place that came to be for a teenager very important in the course of my personal history.

As a young teenager I watched as various ethnic groups gave support to one nationalist or another during those turbulent times. Organizations such as the German-American *Bund*[253] and the Sons of Italy were familiar to those of us that lived in those days. In fact, in high school, I sat next to a pretty blonde who wore a necklace with a Swastika hanging on it!

My graduation from high school in June of 1941 didn't show much promise in a world in such turmoil. In those days it was just a matter of time before one became involved.

I tried to enlist in the Navy from the outset but they weren't taking anyone because their quota was full. Instead I registered for the draft and waited for my number to come up. In the meantime I went to work at the Farrell Ordinance U.S. Steel Plant, machining armor plate for the Grant and Sherman tanks that eventually found their way to General Montgomery in the North African campaign and to General Patton when Operation TORCH began.

Eventually my number did come up. In December of 1942 I was classified 1–A, and I was called up for induction in January. I went to Pittsburgh first and then on to

Erie where I was channeled into the Navy line. It was luck that landed me in that Navy line, and I was happy because I had wanted to be in the Navy from the very start.

I went to boot camp in Sampson, New York. About six weeks into my training there I came down with Spinal Meningitis. They put me in the Naval hospital and gave me every type of sulfa drug there was. They took throat cultures every day, and I took what seemed like a fist-full of pills daily. My legs were paralyzed, and I couldn't stand or walk for a month. I survived and finished boot camp, though I was still a little shaky at the end of it.

From boot camp the Navy sent me to the Wentworth Institute of Technology where in four months I learned everything I could about shipboard naval machinery. At the Institute, we were housed in the Somerset Hotel on Commonwealth Avenue overlooking the Charles River. Across the river from us stood Harvard and the Massachusetts Institute of Technology. It was a high-rent neighborhood. We marched to and from school through Back Bay, Boston, past the Red Sox field and the museum district. Boston was a nice city in which to have a liberty. There was plenty of history about it.

From machinist school I was sent to a pre-commissioning crew based at Newport, Rhode Island. Luck dealt me another fair hand there because many of my classmates were "volunteered" for submarine duty.

From Rhode Island, I went to Charleston, South Carolina, to the Navy yard to become part of the commissioning crew for the USS *Julian Jordan* (DE–204).

My duty station onboard the ship was in the fire and engine compartments below deck, I was never on deck in the bad weather. I had it pretty nice where I was with a good bunk and good food. I got sick my first time at sea but, after that, I never got seasick again. You could say I found my sea legs early on.

Our duty onboard the ship consisted of watches at "duty stations." The duration of our watch was usually four hours on and eight off. During the eight hours off I did other duties, general duties, like scrubbing the deck and painting and so on. I also had some free time, and I slept within that cycle.

There were times when we stood four on and four off. That was usually when we were in waters that called for more vigilance, like in the Atlantic, on submarine sweeping duty or, on convoy duty. We had to be vigilant out there because those were dangerous waters.

There was a total of three watches, and I had charge of one of them. I was the senior petty officer on my watch, and that meant I had three men under my command.

During a war, on board a ship, there's a lot of space between action and regular duty. Life goes on in between the times of caution and danger. Things are not always tense and heavy.

Our shakedown cruise on the *Jordan* took place in the waters off Bermuda. Following that trial run we sailed north to Quonset Point, Rhode Island. It was at that time that a hurricane whipped up and gave us our first real taste of stormy weather. During the storm we rescued two PT[254] boats caught in the heavy waters. We tied their boats alongside of ours and pulled them to safety. When the storm subsided, we sailed south to Norfolk.

From Norfolk we went into antisubmarine duty in the Atlantic between Norfolk, New York and the Mediterranean.

We always had to watch going past Gibralter because the Spanish had spies out watching us and reporting back to the Germans. Franco was in power by then in Spain and he was sympathetic to Hitler.

Upon our return from one of those trips we picked up a convoy that we were to escort across the Atlantic to Bizerte, Tunisia, North Africa.

For that crossing we were part of the escort screening operation. We worked in concert with the airplanes flying from the aircraft carriers attached to the convoy. They were the eyes of the air, and we were the eyes of the sea. We were the lead ship in the convoy, and as such we had the Commodore on board. The trip took a total of thirty days.

I had no idea at the time that the other convoys going across the Atlantic were headed to England for the D-Day invasion.

In fact, I was in Bizerte, Africa when D-Day took place. We didn't know that anything had happened in France at first. The day before the landings, 5 June 1944, the day of the fall of Rome, I celebrated my twenty-first birthday by swimming in the Mediterranean with my good friend Julius Nemes from Sharon, Pennsylvania. It just so happened that he was on board a minesweeper, the *YMS–43* that was docked near to my ship. We were both given liberty and met onshore to celebrate my birthday.

Once we found out about D-Day we thought we might go from Bizerte to Marseilles in support of the operations in France. That wasn't to be, though. Instead, we came back to the States and went to Fort Lauderdale, the Port of Everglades area, for further training. There we engaged in antisubmarine exercises and tested the new "Fox" sonar gear. We used an Italian and American submarine as "bait."

After that, they sent me to the Philadelphia Navy Yard's Turbine and Boiler school for advanced training. When I completed my training there, I had orders to join the commissioning crew for the USS *Consolation* (AH–15), one of the newly-built hospital ships. There were six hospital ships in our class, built in expectation of the invasion of Japan.

After our commissioning and a short shakedown cruise, we set sail from Bayonne, New Jersey, for the Panama Canal and points beyond. We had a liberty in Cristobal and a stop at Balboa before steaming for San Diego for further provisions and an additional compliment of hospital corpsmen. From there we sailed to Pearl Harbor en route to Okinawa. Things were getting pretty hot at Okinawa at the time. The Navy was losing a lot of ships there, and as a hospital ship we were greatly needed.

I was given the rank of Water Tender 2/C, a Petty Officer in charge of the watch section. I was also given the job title of "Oil King." My duty was to maintain the ship's balance and integrity. I pumped oil from the starboard side to the port side and kept control of the water system. In other words, I kept the ship on an "even keel."

We fueled at sea several times while I was in charge of the oil and water systems. That was always interesting because when the sea was rough it made for a delicate operation. We transferred oil from ship to ship by hose. We dumped some oil on a few occasions, but for the most part it was a smooth process.

It was so calm at times in the Pacific that the sea looked just like glass. I remember one time we stopped the ship and had a swimming party. Can you imagine swimming in the middle of the Pacific? They lowered a launch with a sailor with a rifle. His job was to keep watch for sharks. That was an experience to remember! How many people can say they swam in the middle of an ocean?

Often we'd go onto the deck, strip down to our skivvies and sunbathe. We'd also play cards topside and gamble from time to time. We had movies on deck to kill the time and keep us busy during any downtime. And there's a lot of downtime during wartime.

When we got to Pearl Harbor, we viewed the results of the attack. The *Arizona*, the capsized *Utah* and all the debris surrounding the area of the attack brought the attack home to us. As we waited there, where the War had started, the USAAF dropped the Atomic Bomb on Japan. Japan finally surrendered. The night of the surrender was like the Fourth of July. There were fireworks and tracers shooting all over the place. I felt a certain poetic justice, being in the place where the Japs had started the War and hearing that it was all over.

We sailed into Buckner Bay, Okinawa, about the time the Nips were signing the surrender in Tokyo Bay. The following week we sailed to Nagoya and then to Wakayama to take aboard one-thousand Allied prisoners of war. They included Dutch, English and Americans from various camps. They were an emaciated and sad looking group, much like the prisoners of the concentration camps in Poland and Germany.

They gave us liberty in Japan. Being on the Japanese mainland was an odd experience for us. There were defeated Japanese soldiers all over the place, and they were wary of American sailors and soldiers being on their turf.

After we completed our duty in Japan, we went back to Okinawa. Enroute we were struck by a devastating typhoon that flattened the place.[255] The storm destroyed a number of vessels. A few destroyers capsized because their fuel tanks were empty, and they were riding high, unable to maintain their integrity in the high seas. We were well out at sea though, and we weathered the storm well enough.

After that storm we ran a series of cruises from Honolulu to San Francisco, as part of Operation MAGIC CARPET that ferried service personnel and dependents home.

Eventually my points, which had been extended, came to the necessary total and allowed for my discharge. I returned with the Consolation to Norfolk via the Panama

Canal and went to Bainbridge, Massachusetts where I was discharged on 29 March 1946. From there I took a train back to Pittsburgh and another on to Farrell.

Once I got home, I signed up for the 52/20 club. I utilized that for about twenty weeks. One day, while I was walking down the street in Farrell, and I ran into a young man whom I knew through the Sokol Gymnastic organization. He was a freshman at Thiel College.

He said, "Why don't you come to Thiel?"

Well, I wasn't sold on the idea because I was enjoying the summer and my well-deserved break. I told him to get me an application though, and I filled it out. They contacted me and asked me if I'd want to go to summer school. I told them no. Well, this fellow that had encouraged me to apply happened to be friends with the dean. He pulled some strings and got me admitted during the regular semester.

I commuted to Thiel my first two years there because it was only about sixteen miles from my home. In my third year I became a Lambda Chi Alpha, and I lived at the fraternity house. I graduated on Memorial Day 1949. I only attended Thiel three years because I had taken two summer sessions, and that wiped out my last year.

I had no plans for my life after that. I had applied for a teaching position outside of New Castle, but I wasn't really interested in that job. The dean of Thiel was the advisor to our fraternity so I talked to him about my future, and he urged me to go on to grad school. I still had some time left on the GI Bill so I applied to Pitt. In the meantime, he urged me to go to Penn so I applied there and was admitted. I graduated from Penn with my Master's in one year. Two weeks after my graduation my number came up again.

On 25 June 1950 the North Korea invaded South Korea, and my inactive status in the Naval Reserve was reactivated. I was assigned to the destroyer USS *Lyman K. Swenson* (DD–729) that I was to board in Sasebo, Japan.

I took a troop train across the United States to San Francisco and boarded a transport there that took me to Japan. In Japan, a troop train took me south from Tokyo, through Hiroshima and Nagasaki to Sasebo on the sea of Japan. There I boarded the *Lyman K. Swenson.* The ship was fresh from the battle of Inchon where one of its officers had been killed on the bridge. It also had the dubious honor of almost destroying the craft in which General MacArthur was riding to shore during that battle.

From Sasebo, we embarked on screening duty along North Korean waters for one month. From there we headed to Okinawa and on to Pearl Harbor en route to San Diego. We then sailed up the Pacific coast and docked at Bremerton Naval Shipyard in Washington state for repairs. Once the repairs were made, we returned to San Diego in preparation for a return to Korean waters.

During this time, a lieutenant onboard had encouraged me to apply for a commission, but it hanged fire. Even if it had come through, I'd have had to commit myself to two more years of active duty and three years of reserve duty. Anyway, I was about ready to come back to civilian life. My enlistment only had six months left to go, and I was lucky to get transferred to the USS *Dixie* (AD–14) docked in San Diego where I finished out most of my tour.

My last port of call was San Francisco. It was there that I spent my last month of active duty at Treasure Island. On 27 December 1951 I was returned to my inactive status until my official discharge came through.

I had a job waiting for me when I returned with the Pennsylvania Highway Planning Division in Harrisburg. I had worked with them for a short time before going to Korea, and they invited me to come back. It was on one of my projects with them, in 1953, that I found out about an open teaching position in Greensburg. My training was in education so I interviewed for it and was hired. I stayed there until my retirement, thirty-five years later.

In between all of that I traveled many parts of the world with my wife, Nancy. My brother worked for the State Department in different countries, and we'd travel to see him. They say, "Join the Navy and See the World." In a sense that is true. I think that is what put the desire to travel in my bones.

I returned safely from two wars, went to school, raised a family, had a good job and stayed very active. I have had a good life. I made it through some dangerous times without a scratch. I was one of the lucky ones.

USS Julian Jordan commissioning day, December 1943. *Courtesy of Elmer Slezak.*

Elmer Slezak (right) with shipmate Anderson enjoying a day of liberty on Bizerte, Tunisia, North Africa. It was Slezak's birthday, 5 June, 1944, one day before the invaion of Normandy.

USS *Julian B.Jordan*, Destroyer escort (DE) 204. The photo was released by the United States Public Relations Office to Elmer Slezak and the rest of the ship's crew.

“The Higher We Were, the Safer We Were.”

Howard F. Struble

Fifteenth Air Force
2nd Bomb Group, 20th Bomb Squadron
Born in Wilkinsburg, Pennsylvania, 21 November 1923
Evans City, Pennsylvania

“The higher we were, the safer we were, and I was glad we went high and stayed in a tight formation. When they talk about ‘tight,’ they’re tight. The idea was to put our wing between the other guy’s tail and wing.”

During the Depression work was kind of hard to find so my family moved to Florida. We lived down there for five years then we came back to Wilkinsburg, where my uncle had an extra house that we stayed in over the winter. Then there was a family farm about twenty miles from town, and it was a really old house. It had never been painted. It was just like a log cabin. They put electric in for us, and the rent was about ten dollars a month. We had to pump the water and carry that all in by hand. Of course, we had an outhouse. My mother was a city girl, she wanted to look out and see cars and streetlights and all that sort of thing. So, the way my father got her to stay out there was by telling her it was just for the summer. I lived there for about twenty years. We kids enjoyed it out there. I’d hear my mother saying to my dad, “Oh, this is terrible that these kids have to be brought up with no bathtub, no telephone, no anything.”

He said, “They’re having the time of their life!”

And we were.

I was drafted out of college into the Air Force in February 1943. They sent me to gunnery school in Colorado. In addition to being a gunner, I was also an armorer. That gave me added responsibility, and I had to learn about all the different ammunition and the bombing mechanisms and all the elements involved with that. It was a quickie course, because they wanted us overseas.

Denver is where I got sick for the first time. I got a high fever and asked the sergeant if I could sit down until night sick call. You had to be really sick to go, or else. They took me and another guy over, and he went in first to see the doctor. I heard that doctor cursing him out right and left.

He said “You better not come on this again, or you better be really sick.”

He sent the guy back to duty, and I sat there thinking, *‘Oh, gee, what’s he going to say to me?’*

I went in, and after he examined me he said, “You have a temperature of 104 degrees. You’re going to the hospital!”

The hospital was just one floor with wards and wings going off of it. I was so sick from that fever, I didn't know where to go. I was on my own. I did finally find the right place where they tested me for everything. I woke up in the night and about six guys and a couple nurses were packing me in ice. Patients were supposed to mop around their beds and then give the mop to another guy. I was so sick I couldn't get out of bed, so the other guys mopped for me.

That was the first time in my life I had that fever. I got it a couple times after that. One time was when I'd flown half my missions, I was afraid I was going to get separated from my crew. They put me in the infirmary in Foggia, Italy, and kept me about a day. My temperature was sky-high.

There was a captain in charge there. We could always tell how good the doctors were in civilian life from their rank. A specialist would probably have been a colonel.

Anyway, the captain called in a colonel, and one said to the other "Typical pneumonia."

I had no signs of pneumonia; I had no cold, no cough, I had one symptom and one symptom only, a high temperature, which could've been a lot of things.

They put me in the ambulance and took me into a civilian hospital about twenty miles from camp that the Army had taken over. Everything in there was made of marble. When I got in there, I sat down in the hall; eventually they put me in a bed in a ward. The doctor came around, examined me and said, "Not a sign of pneumonia."

An hour before, the guy just said typical pneumonia. I went from typical pneumonia to not a sign of pneumonia! And he was right! I was in there for about a week and got rid of the temperature again and went back to flying.

After training in Denver we went down south to Tampa, Florida. I felt sorry for some of those guys that were older; they just couldn't take that heat marching several miles up the beach in hot sun. Behind us they had a "meat wagon" [ambulance] that came along right behind the formation to pick up the guys that fell out.

To get our shots we had to march up the beach. We got a lot of shots. The only one that ever gave me any trouble was the yellow fever shot. As soon as that guy stuck that needle in there, it was like something hit me. I buckled at the knees. I never had a shot affect me like that before. It wasn't because I was afraid of it or anything like that. I don't know what it was. I had to sit down for a while.

Florida was where we did crew training and we did it round the clock. We had to be in the air six hours from wheels up to wheels down. Sometimes we flew at night, sometimes we flew during the day. I think we lost about as many planes in training as we did in combat because the pilots were still green. There were a lot of errors and there was a lot of bad weather.

One time our copilot's brother was an instructor, and somehow he got permission to take him to North Carolina. We were just to take him up there and drop him off. Well we landed at this little runway. It was all right coming in, but going out? That was a different matter. I was standing in the waist looking out my window and all of a sudden the runway ended and we're still on the ground! Well, I guess we just barely got up and out of there. It was in bad weather too but we made it.

When they gave us our new plane for overseas we had to take it up and try it out. With the first plane we had smoke in the cockpit, so we came down right away. The next day they gave us another plane and we took it up and hit into a thunder head. It was just black all over. The pilot flew straight into it. He shouldn't have done because it could've just doubled the plane up. Planes came back with bent wings and everything else from that kind of weather.

I couldn't see what was happening in the front. All I knew was that we were suddenly in a dive. I was told later that the pilot and the copilot were pulling the stick back as far as they could and we were still dropping like a rock. We got caught inside a downdraft. When we popped out of the clouds, we weren't a long way off the ground. A couple-thousand feet at most.

It was like we had dropped down an elevator and when we popped out we were lost because the navigator wasn't charting where we were. We were just supposed to be flying above the field. Finally we saw a Naval base. We landed there and all these sailors came running out to see the B–17. They'd never seen such a big plane. They treated us well; they gave us supper and everything. After supper we found out that we were only a stone's throw from where we should have been. So we just hopped up and over and landed back at the base where we took of from.

We checked out two or three planes before we got one that didn't have something wrong.

We got assigned to the Fifteenth Air Force in Foggia, Italy. The day before we got to our squadron, seven planes from the squadron had gone down so they were glad to see us.

The base was in an olive grove with a lot of stone fences around. It was flat and there were hardly any trees. There was a shortage of wood over there and they had used them for firewood. There was a limestone cave there, and we used that for a chapel.

The Italians would come into the camp and wash our clothes for us. We'd give them a candy bar or something to do it. Boy, they got them clean and ironed nice and everything. But they must have used straight lye or something in them; it just bleached the heck out of those uniforms!

There was a barter system over there. The Italians were running around with eggs and we'd trade them a can of beer or something. I didn't drink or smoke so I used my beer and cigarette ration to trade with.

Everyone thinks Italy is always warm, but it was cold at times and it would snow just like here. We made stoves out of fifty-five-gallon drums. We mixed high-octane aviation gas with fuel oil. The mixture burned better and it didn't smoke as much. Once the driver who brought the fuel just brought gasoline. It burned clean, but it also burned down lots of tents.

Whenever the refrigerator ship put in at Naples, we'd eat just like back home. We'd get butter and everything. Once that was all gone, we went back to the dried stuff. Some of that dried stuff was terrible. When the olive trees fruited, we put tarps under them and shook the olives onto it. We ate well then.

There were six groups in the Fifteenth Air Force. That was small compared to the Eighth Air Force, and the Eighth Air Force got credit for some of the stuff that we did. In fact the one time there was a great big full-page picture of a wrecked plane that had just broken in two when it landed because the whole middle of the plane had been blown apart. I knew the guys that were killed in that crash. It came out in *LIFE* Magazine and they said it was the Eighth Air Force. Well it wasn't, it was one of ours!

To come home at that time we had to fly thirty missions. When I was about halfway through my missions they changed it from thirty to thirty-five sorties which meant five more than I expected to fly. That was the policy when the Eighth Air Force started flying out of England.

My mother's half-brother was a gunner as well. He was one of the first ones over, and when he was flying nobody got as far as twenty-five missions. He got shot down after a mission or two and spent the rest of the War as a prisoner.

By the time I got in there it was a different story. They had developed tight formations with each plane having thirteen guns. Take that and add it up. That's a lot of protection. Then they came out with the P–51s. That gave us even better chances.

On the day of a mission we'd get up early in the morning around four or five. The guy would come around with a flashlight and a clipboard, calling out the names. We knew the night before who was going, but he made sure we got up. Then we'd go to eat. I never ate anything because my stomach would get a little woozy.

Then there was a briefing and they had all the targets listed on this big map and how many anti-aircraft guns each place had. Vienna was one of the worst. I think they had about a thousand anti-aircraft guns there. At thirty-thousand feet it takes a big gun to get a shell up high, so they used 88s or bigger! The shells would come up, then they'd explode and throw shrapnel around and it looked just like a puff of smoke. From the bigger guns it was always a white puff of smoke, and from the smaller guns it was black.

After briefing we were taken by trucks out to the field which was three miles from where we were camped in the olive grove. At a certain time we'd take off and from that time until we got to the target they could call it off depending on the weather and so forth. We might be just taxiing out to take off, when they'd send up a flare. That meant scratch the mission.

We never knew when they were going to scrub a mission. We'd be loaded with bombs and fuel, and we had to get rid of one or the other before we could land. Sometimes we'd go out in the Adriatic and drop our bombs, or other times we'd just fly around for a few hours to get rid of enough gasoline.

There were many accidents that happened right on the ground before takeoff. It's just a solid line of B–17s on the runway, one behind the other, taking off. One time a pilot didn't stop, and ran right into the plane in front, and the propellers chopped right through.

Another time a plane took off and we heard an explosion and all we could see was the black smoke coming up. Some planes never got up enough power to lift the weight of the fuel and bombs, so they just ran off the runway and blew up. Sometimes the load would be so heavy that the engines would blow cylinders. That happened to us but we were still on the ground, and we had enough time to stop.

Pilots were usually at least second lieutenants, but ours was a flight officer, one step down. He had been busted down in rank for hot-rodding. He was nineteen and he flew that bomber like it was a fighter plane. One time he found a valley between two mountains, a wide valley, and he was flying so low that all the Italians were running around down there shaking their fists at us, and the animals were all stampeding. We had more faith in him than we did some of the other pilots because we knew he could handle it.

We'd fly at thirty-thousand feet and it seemed like we could almost get out and walk on the Alps. They were rugged mountains, snow-covered, and I always wondered what would've happened if I'd had to bail out there. I'd have frozen to death.

When we were at altitude, it got very cold. We had electric suits, but they didn't always work too good, and it's cold up there. Seventy-five below was the coldest I saw it. We wore big fleece-lined boots and I always wired mine on because I'd heard cases of guys parachuting out, and off went their boots and they landed in the Alps. I didn't want that to happen.

In the air, weight is everything. When we first got to the base we took all the deicers off because they slowed us down. At first they had camouflaged ships, but by the time I was there they didn't paint them at all. Paint slowed the planes down too much. Every little thing like that helped. It all added up to survival.

The higher we were, the safer we were, and I was glad we went high and stayed in a tight formation. When they talk about "tight," they're tight. The idea was to put our wing in between the other guy's tail and wing. That formation flying must have been awful tough on the pilots.

The guys that planned these missions would plan it so we barely had enough gas to get back to base. A lot didn't; they'd ditch in the Adriatic, or they'd land in Yugoslavia. There was a landing strip there that was controlled by the underground. We could land there and come back the next day.

We could tell where you were going pretty much by what kind of a bomb load we had. The ground crew loaded the bombs at night and we'd hear from them what kind of a bomb load they put on. Then we'd know if we were going a long distance or a short distance.

There was kind of a friendly rivalry between the B–24 and the B–17 crews. They couldn't go as high as we could and I was glad I was in the B–17 because those B–24s had a reputation of "now you see them, now you don't." We'd see them up there, then they'd explode. They had problems with their hydraulic system that would set off an explosion. The B–24s were actually bigger and they had a bigger bomb load, but they were boxy-looking, and they just didn't look like they were made to fly.

Up until the target area we had fighter escorts, P–38s and P–51s. We had to take off a lot earlier than they did because they were so fast and they couldn't stay in the air as long as we could so, at a certain time, a certain point, they'd meet us. We'd look for their vapor trails and usually they were right on the money. Many times it was the black fighter outfit that escorted us. They had the P–51s with the red noses. They were so fast that they couldn't fly parallel with us. They had to keep weaving around.

We had good protection on the plane itself. They kept adding guns to the B–17. The first ones didn't have any chin turret under the nose for frontal protection. The Germans got wise to that on the early planes and that's where they'd attack from. So they had to put this nose-gun on. At my position there was armor plate about a quarter-inch thick right below my gun. The ball turret, though, that was the worst. It was glass, about two or three inches thick, with no protection really. The gunner would curl up in the turret. I flew one mission in the ball turret. For me, the ball turret was fun, because I got a great view. The only problem was getting back out of it in an emergency.

One time we had an engine shot out. The whole time back to base the plane just shook because the wind kept turning the prop faster and faster, what we called "windmilling." When we landed, the prop just hung there. It could have broken off and cut into the fuselage. We got it down just as it was ready to do just that.

When we flew, we checked in with each other every so often to make sure nobody had passed out. One time we didn't hear anything out of the tail gunner. I was right there in the waist so, I had to go back in there and he was sitting there with his head hanging down and he was black and blue around his eyes and had ice under his mouth. I thought he might be dead. His oxygen mask was off and just hanging there. I reached behind him and I put that oxygen mask up against his face and he started coming to. It was hard to do because there was no room back there. As soon as he started to come to, he started fighting to get the mask off and I'm fighting him to get him to keep it on. I couldn't do it so finally we just dragged him out of there and got him out in the waist. He thanked me for that afterwards. Anybody would've done the same thing, I just happened to be the guy that was the closest to him.

The approach to the bomb run was the worst part of the missions. It started at the IP (Initial Point) and from the time we'd start, the bombardier was in command of the plane. He put all his calculations into the bombsight, and then, theoretically, if he got everything right like the wind drift, speed, elevation, types of bombs, then the bombs would hit dead on. What he had to do was get the cross-hairs in the bomb sight on target, then move the knobs on the bomb sight. The plane would move along with his adjustments. When the bombardier in the lead plane released his bombs, everyone else would do the same.

RESTRICTED MARCH, 1945 BIF 6-1-1

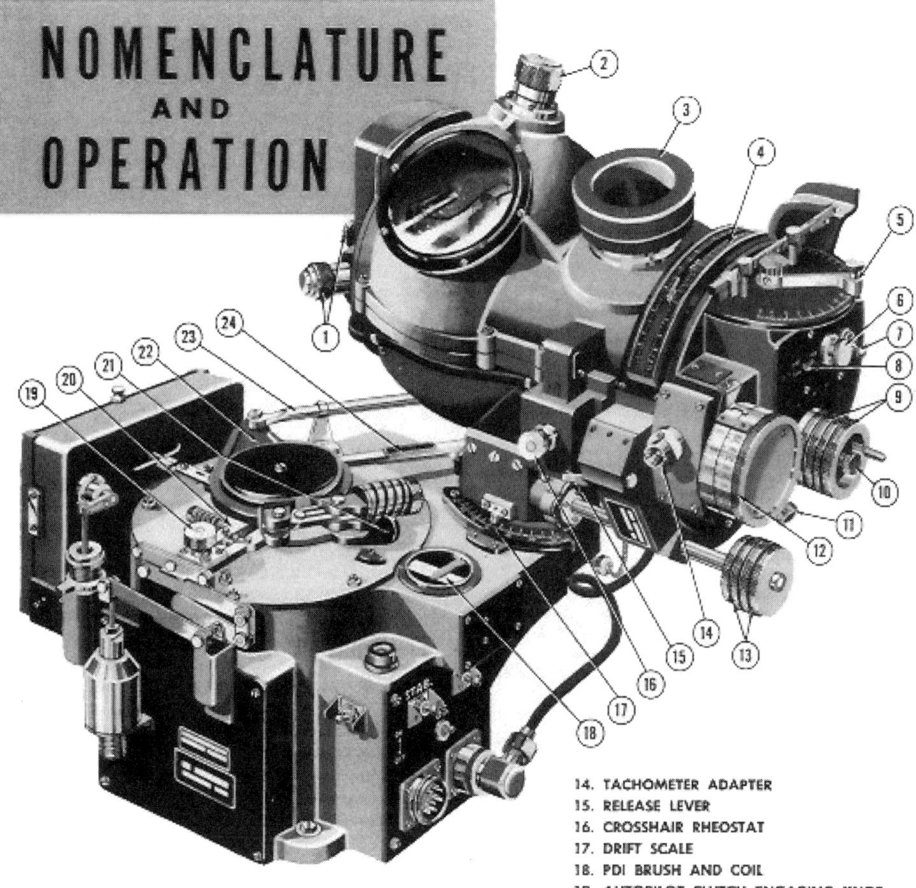

NOMENCLATURE AND OPERATION

1. LEVELING KNOBS
2. CAGING KNOB
3. EYEPIECE
4. INDEX WINDOW
5. TRAIL ARM AND TRAIL PLATE
6. EXTENDED VISION KNOB
7. RATE MOTOR SWITCH
8. DISC SPEED GEAR SHIFT
9. RATE AND DISPLACEMENT KNOBS
10. MIRROR DRIVE CLUTCH
11. SEARCH KNOB
12. DISC SPEED DRUM
13. TURN AND DRIFT KNOBS
14. TACHOMETER ADAPTER
15. RELEASE LEVER
16. CROSSHAIR RHEOSTAT
17. DRIFT SCALE
18. PDI BRUSH AND COIL
19. AUTOPILOT CLUTCH ENGAGING KNOB
20. AUTOPILOT CLUTCH
21. BOMBSIGHT CLUTCH ENGAGING LEVER
22. BOMBSIGHT CLUTCH
23. BOMBSIGHT CONNECTING ROD
24. AUTOPILOT CONNECTING ROD

The bombsight has 2 main parts, **sighthead** and **stabilizer.** The sighthead pivots on the stabilizer and is locked to it by the dovetail locking pin. The sighthead is connected to the directional gyro in the stabilizer through the **bombsight connecting rod** and the **bombsight clutch.**

RESTRICTED

Norden bomb sight.

We also had what we called "Mickey Ships," by the time I got there. Those were planes where they'd take out the lower ball and replace it with an English-developed radar dome in its place. Any plane that had the dome flew in the lead, the safest place to be, because the guys in the tail end ["Tail-End Charlies"] always got the worst of it.

It was "round the clock" bombing by the British and us. The poor Germans, they didn't know when it was coming. I was glad I wasn't on the ground when those bombs were dropping. There was a little hole in the floor of the plane that I'd open up and watch the bombs falling and exploding. Sometimes I used the hole to take pictures. I'd sit in the waist and the bombardier would tell me when to pull the trigger on the camera.

When I'd get back from a mission, I was so cold that I'd head right for my bunk to get warmed up. I just crawled in and put everything I could get on me and it would take me a while to get thawed out. It spite of my heated suit, there was something about the cold up there. It just got to me.

Between missions we listened to Axis Sally. She didn't build up our confidence. She knew everything. She'd tell us over the radio that the clock in the 2nd Bomb Group's orderly room was ten minutes slow and it would be. There were informers everywhere.

After so many missions we could go to a rest camp on the Isle of Capri or Rome. I picked Rome, where I spent a Christmas Day. We could go into any restaurant in downtown Rome, show them our passes and get a Thanksgiving or Christmas meal for free.

Once our required number of missions were over, guys would lose fifty-percent flying pay. In order to keep it, we had to spend four hours each month flying. That's what we did. We didn't have much to spend the money on. I sent mine home and bought war bonds and stuff. In fact, I bought my first car with that money.

When it was time to come home, we flew to Naples where we had a choice of waiting for an airplane or waiting for a ship. I decided to take the ship because, since we weren't flying missions anymore, they had taken our parachutes away, I was used to having that parachute. I came back on the USS *Wakefield*, which had been a passenger liner. It took us ten days to cross. The ship was like a casino. My buddies rounded up a lot of money, including some of mine so they could gamble. I never got a penny of it back.

Once we were back in the States they couldn't send us over for another tour, so they sent us to Santa Ana, California. It wasn't like being in the Army anymore. We could eat what we wanted any time of the day and then get treats at night.

After a while, I went to Texas and worked on B–29s. I had some experience with sheet metal work, and they put me to good use. I was there a few months and then they sent us up to Fort Lewis, Washington, to train us to fight forest fires. We learned how to run the water pumps and how to blow up the trails with TNT. We ended up in Boise, Idaho, fighting fires.

Then they came out with the point system for discharge. I had enough points right from the start to be discharged, but we couldn't get our points because we were attached to the engineers, even though we were still in the Air Force. When I finally got out, I got traveling pay. I went home on a train. I had been in the Army two years and seven months.

I went to school on the GI Bill at Carnegie Tech in the Oakland area of Pittsburgh. The school was close to my parents' home in Wilkinsburg. The tests were tough because of all the calculus. After such a long time, it was stale in my head. I figured I didn't do very well on the tests, but, by gosh, I got a letter saying I was accepted.

There I was, living at home in Wilkinsburg, going to Carnegie Tech. I didn't know anybody at school, so I would come back home to study because I had trouble studying at the college. There were just too many other things going on there.

I was getting passing grades but I didn't like it there. I went to my advisor and he said, "Well, you can get through this, probably, and get your degree, but if you don't like it, I'd advise you to go do something else."

That sounded good to me so I just transferred up to Penn State and took up poultry husbandry. Poultry science, they call it now. That's what I finished in.

As far as the War, I was glad for the experience, glad I lived through it. I always thought I was going to return, it never entered my mind that I wasn't. I was nineteen and I had nobody to worry about.

I read something here recently that said the most dangerous place to be in World War II was in a B–17 flying over Germany. I don't doubt it.

The War is something I don't like to dwell on, but I can't help thinking about it. As I get older, I think about it more. We were young men doing this, remember. Just kids really and scared. War is funny. It made us act strange sometimes. One time my buddy, the lower ball man, got to drinking a little bit. We were in the plane, sitting there, and he comes up to me with his .45, and he held that thing right up to my stomach. I didn't know what he was doing, he didn't even know what he was doing, you know? I still don't know what he was doing. Boy, that scared me, until I got him under control. All he had to do was pull the trigger.

"There Was No Such Thing As a Gentleman."

Howard Symonds

United States Sixth and Eighth Armies, X Corps,
(Attached to the 24th and 31st Infantry Divisions)
655th Field Artillery Battalion, Battery A, Number-Two Gun
Born in Parsippany, New Jersey, 20 February 1925
Glen Gardner, New Jersey

"We had a couple of night attacks by the Japs. They'd get all Sakied up and come at us, but they'd trip the flares, which would light up the place like daylight, and they'd all be standing out there right in the line of fire of our .30-caliber machine guns. We'd mow them right down. One or two might get in. One got in on this one attack and ran down by our tents. He threw a grenade in my tent but it didn't go off. They used a lot of old ammunition. That's probably why it didn't go off. Then he kept on running and he tripped over a tent rope. One of our guys came out and killed him with a machete! Chopped him up! I try to forget a lot of this stuff now."

I am one of seven children. I was the only one born in New Jersey. My father, Goldie Irl Symonds, came from Ohio. Once I got into the Army, you can imagine the kidding I got when the guys found out my father's name! GI Symonds! The whole family had names that rhymed. My mother was Mamie Bair. My sister, Wilma, died in the Asian flu epidemic in 1919. My sister Doris and I are the only ones left. She's out in California.

I was born in an old farmhouse in Parsippany. There was no electricity, and we had dirt roads. Then my father built a house on Route 46, and he traded it to a man for an eighty-acre farm in Lebanon Township. It had three houses, a big barn and a 170-foot chicken house. We raised poultry and hogs, and we had Jersey cows. Farm work was a lot of labor, and we all pitched in milking cows, like everyone else did who had a farm. That's all gone now.

I was raised with a gun. My next-door neighbor was Gottfried Pletzer.[256] We hunted small game; squirrels, ground hogs, rabbits and pheasants, when there were pheasants. We spent a lot of time together. He came to our farm every night to swim in our pond.

When the War came along, a lot of the guys left for the service. I got a farm deferment for the first six months but then I went, too. We didn't have a radio, so I didn't learn about Pearl Harbor until I got to school on the Monday morning after it happened.

All the kids were talking about it saying, "That's something."

I said, "What's that?"

They said, "The Japs attacked Pearl Harbor."

Finally, they needed all the troops they could get, so my deferment ran out and I was drafted in early 1944. I left from High Bridge and went to Fort Dix. From Fort Dix I went to Fort Bragg where I got basic training on 105mm howitzers and infantry weapons. The infantry training was a good thing, because they used us as infantry as well.

Then I had a delayed in-route and got to go home for a while. After that, I went to North Camp Hood, Texas, where I joined the 655th Field Artillery and trained on 8-inch guns. We laid the whole battalion out in an area and aimed the guns with what was called an aiming circle. We also worked with Piper Cub liaison planes and forward observers to direct our fire, and we fired by grid maps. The 655th was an independent battalion, but at different times throughout the War we were attached to both the 24th and 31st Infantry Divisions.

I became the light-heavyweight champion while I was in the States. I boxed an exhibition with a professional named Tom Fend, a heavyweight, from Butler, Pennsylvania. He was the Green Belt heavyweight champion of Nebraska, South Dakota and North Dakota. He told me afterwards it was the hardest fight he ever had.

From Texas I went to Camp Stoneman, California, our point of embarkation. We loaded up on a freighter made in Kearney, New Jersey, the SS *Hawaiian Shipper* and sailed out under the Golden Gate Bridge. We wondered if we'd ever see the bridge again. They had us stacked in these bunks eight-high and some guys got sick in the top bunks and threw up on the guys below. We had to eat chow standing up in the mess. We got two meals a day and guys were puking in their trays. They gave us the saltwater showers. We didn't get clean taking those. They'd turn on the freshwater fountain once a day and we'd fill up our canteens and that would be all the water we'd have until the next day. I was forty-eight days on that ship!

We went to Guadalcanal first and a submarine got after us there, and then we ran to Finchaven, New Guinea. After Finchaven, we made a run to Hollandia where we got together with a convoy. That sub chased us the whole way! He fired torpedoes at us while we were in the convoy, but never hit a ship.

We heard an explosion near shore and I said, "That must have been a mine that washed ashore."

The sailor next to me said, "Naw, that was a torpedo!"

The blast did crack the hull of a Liberty Ship, but it went into dry dock in Hollandia.

In a submarine attack we always got on deck, but with an air attack we were ordered below decks. I hated air attacks because we were confined below decks and couldn't see what was going on, especially if the lights went out. That was scary.

We stayed in the convoy at Hollandia, and then we went to Leyte. On the way into Leyte we saw this destroyer in front of us. Its horn started whooping, and then it dropped some ash cans in the water. Soon after, a Jap sub popped straight up out of the water in front of us and then sank back down. The destroyer sank it right there!

First we went to Leyte for the invasion of the Philippine Islands in October 1944. Then the battalion went to Cebu[257] on a pioneer party. We had to blow down a whole bunch of trees so we could place the big guns. The Cebu campaign only lasted about twenty-eight days, and we never had to bring our guns in. Then we went back to Leyte and from there to Mindanao in the Philippines.[258] I spent about nine months there.

We had the biggest field guns in the South Pacific. The 8-inch fired a 205-pound projectile. I was on the number-two gun, or the base piece for the whole battalion. The number-two gun did all the zeroing-in. The name of our gun was "Angel Puss." Throughout the War we painted Jap flags on our guns to show how many of their guns we knocked out. While we were getting ready for the invasion of Japan, we changed the name of our gun to "Arsenic."

Aside from being a gunner, I also lifted those 205-pound projectiles. We shoved them into the gun with a rammer staff, and then we threw a powder charge in behind. Screwed in behind the charge was what looked like a .30–06 blank shell. That's what fired it. The concussion sometimes was terrible. It would bring me to my knees, it was so bad. It would turn us over in our cots at night! Sometimes we put cotton in our ears, and we kept our mouths open to equalize the pressure. One time, a high-ranking Navy guy was with us. He came up wanting to fire one of our guns. He fired one and the concussion exploded his sinuses. He had snot all over his face. It was the funniest thing. Of course, he didn't think it was so funny.

In combat on Leyte, we'd set up perimeters around our positions with .30-caliber machine guns, barbed wire out in front, "Bouncing Betty" mines and parachute flares on trip wires. We'd take up a large area for the whole battalion. We had a couple of night attacks by the Japs. The Japs would get all Sakied up and come at us, but they'd trip the flares and light up the place like daylight. They'd be standing out there, right in the line of fire from our .30-caliber machine guns. We mowed them right down. Sometimes a couple of them would break through. One night, one of them ran down past our tents. He threw a grenade into mine, but it was a dud. They used a lot of old ammunition, and that's probably why it didn't go off. He kept on running, and he tripped over a tent rope. One of our guys came out and killed him with a machete! Chopped him up!

I try to forget a lot of this stuff, now. I look at the wars we have fought since where a lot of civilians died. I know we killed civilians, too. We didn't know what the hell we were shooting at sometimes, firing ten, twelve-miles away. We'd fire concentrations at what we thought were Japs in a town, but they were Filipinos. We'd fired timed firings, air bursts, and we just devastated them. There was no media there to show any of this stuff. It was just part of the War.

The war in the Pacific was brutal and barbaric. There was no such thing as a gentleman. We didn't collect many of the Jap bodies. They laid and rotted on the roads, and I saw tractors and trucks run over them. We were trying to take care of ourselves, just to survive. We took good care of our dead, but we didn't bother much with the Japs.

I ran into some cannibalism in the Philippines. On Leyte, in the Ormoc Valley, we had them trapped. We were moving forward and there were some of our paratroopers from the 11th Airborne Division coming at them from the other side of the valley. After the battle we moved through this area where the Japs had been and I saw a leg bone roasting on a spit over a camp fire. I don't know if it was from a native Filipino or from one of their own soldiers, but there it was. How could they do something like that? That was barbaric!

I threw up the first time I killed a man. I was on a trail and a Jap came out of the jungle. We were face to face, and I shot him with my carbine. Even as barbaric as they were, they were still human beings. I went on to kill several in one-on-one confrontations. But after that first time, I dealt with it okay. Some of our guys used to really try and hunt them out, but I never did that. I usually just ran into them. But our big guns killed most of them. We fired hundreds and hundreds of rounds. Devastating! At different times we fired our guns for General MacArthur, General "Vinegar" Joe Stillwell and General Eichelberger. They had never seen these guns fired before. MacArthur was duly impressed.

We ran into the enemy quite a bit when they used us as infantry. No soldier was so specialized that he couldn't be an infantryman! The 31st or 24th Divisions bypassed Jap positions in an attack, and we'd go in and clean up those pockets. It was very dangerous work because they'd be in front of us, in back of us, we never knew where they might be. They were desperate. They shot and ran. It was a nasty kind of fighting. The Japs would sometimes go into a Filipino's house, chase the people out and hole up.

Another dangerous situation was when we used forward observers. I was with a forward observer one time and we were cut off, trapped in a little hamlet of mostly thatched huts. We got down underneath these huts with the hogs. The Japs were all around. We still had radio contact with the rear, and the next day we called in a fire mission and were able to escape.

One time we had a forward observer out and he said, "I just saw a whole bunch of Japs go into this building. Fire one over."

I fired one over, and then I fired one short to bracket the target.

He said, "Fire one now."

Our gun had a range of about fourteen miles. That building was at least twelve miles away, and we put a round right in the middle of it. We killed seventy-seven Japanese officers with that round.

The worst time for me was on Mindanao. I made it through Leyte and Cebu, but Mindanao lasted for months. It was a hell of a fight, though I never heard much about it after the War. By the time we got there, our equipment was starting to get worn out, but it was still far superior to the enemy's, and so were our people.

I felt I had made it through two invasions, so I had a good chance of making it through this next one because I had gained some experience. We had replacements in Mindanao, though, that didn't last a week. We'd be on a trail and the Japs would fire a machine gun down the trail and the new guys would jump off onto the sides of the path where the Japs had put mines. We learned that if we were shot at on a trail to run backwards and not to go off to the sides. On the beachhead, they let us pass, then shoot at our backs from holes that they had covered with debris.

We spent the nights in three-man foxholes. One night, they shot one of the guys, and he called to us, and the Japs mimicked him. We couldn't go out and get him. They ended up killing him before daylight. That was hard, and it made us hate them even more.

In one attack on Mindanao, we went across the Davao River, and the Japs drove us back. We brought some Navy ships up off the coast and they pounded the hell out of them with the rocket ships. Then we went across again. The Japs were drunk on Saki, and they came charging at us. I ended up with one of them hanging on the end of my bayonet. They were committing suicide, really. That wasn't a nice feeling either, bayoneting someone to death.

We got to Davao City, in the north of Mindanao. That's where a big prisoner of war camp was. We went into this camp, and most of the guys were dead. There were skeletons lying on the bunks. Every time I saw something like that I hated the Japs more. They hated us, too. There was no remorse on either side.

One time Captain Buffington asked a sergeant to take us back to our camp down the road. We got into these six-by-six trucks, the captain got into a Jeep with the sergeant, and they led the way down this road. We took a fork in the road and pretty soon passed a bunch of infantry burning Japs out of a cave with a flamethrower. They looked at us like we were crazy. We couldn't figure out why they looked at us that way. We went a little farther down the road. There's more of our guys, and we could hear small arms fire. We looked down the road and saw what looked like a company of Japs coming toward us. The sergeant whipped the Jeep around, and we followed in the truck. The sergeant had us on the wrong road! When we got back to camp, where we were supposed to be, Captain Buffington took both feet and pushed the sergeant out of the Jeep, he was so damned mad at him!

I was wounded twice, three times really. I got one wound when I and another guy went out looking for souvenirs. We came across a crashed Jap plane and started poking around. The Japs had the thing booby-trapped. It exploded, and I got shrapnel in my shoulder. Doctors were still picking it out of my body years afterward.

Another time, I was in a foxhole, and a mortar round came in. I think it came from one of those knee mortars the Japs used. The shrapnel shredded my boot, and I could see blood. I cut off what was left of my boot. There was a deep cut across the bottom of my foot. They gave me the Purple Heart for that. I also got the Good Conduct Medal, but it took me the last six months of the War to get that.

I lost a lot of weight overseas. That jungle atmosphere was terrible to live in. The humidity was awful. We all got some kind of fungus on our bodies. I got malaria at Mindanao, and I still suffered it after the War. In Leyte it always seemed to be raining.

Another thing about that environment was the bats. They were enormous. They called them flying foxes and there were thousands and thousands of them. The Filipinos ate them. I took an M1 and me and another guy took a case of ammunition down to the beach. A really big bat flew overhead, and I shot it.

At the time they said, "That's the world's largest bat that's ever been shot; that's ever been recorded."

I don't know how they knew that at the time and I don't know if that was true or not.

Mail was a big thing for us, and I got mail regularly from home. My parents wrote to me, and so did my neighbors. I got a few letters from Gottfried. We were all homesick. Just imagine, I had never been farther than Ohio, and there I was out in the middle of the Pacific! That's what guys worried about most; that they were going to be forgotten. No one knew really where we were or what we were doing because we couldn't write about that stuff in the letters; they were censored. We faced death a lot and it made us think, *'would we be forgotten?'*

When they dropped the Atomic Bomb on Japan, I thanked God for Harry Truman a thousand times. He saved thousands and thousands of lives, not only our own, but the Japanese as well. They were fanatics. They thought we were going to kill all of them and rape them, but we never did that. Japanese people committed suicide when they lost the War and they knew we were coming.

After the War was over, they sent us back up to Leyte. They tried to make us stand formations but I wouldn't do it and I got in trouble for that. They gave me Charge-of-Quarters (CQ) as a punishment, but they're not supposed to do that because Charge-of-Quarters was supposed to be an honor.

It's strange, but I think one of the times I was most frightened was after the War. The 24th Division went home, but I was still in the 655th Field Artillery and they made us into military police. We were in charge of the American stockade and the Japanese stockade.

They said, "There's only five-thousand Japs left in the hills. Go up and see if you can take some prisoners."

We took a six-by-six and drove up past the old front lines and we came to this great big field where cooking fires were still burning, but everyone was gone. It was scary! I had this Jap interpreter with me and I told him to call out and have them surrender, that the War was over and that we'll have trucks here the next day to take them back. They were nowhere to be seen, but we knew they were watching us. We left and the next day we came back with a half-dozen six-by-six trucks and they were out there by the thousands! We couldn't even come close to getting them all back at the same time. They said there were five-thousand Japs left while we were there, but five-hundred of us took thirty-thousand prisoners out of those hills! We could only take about a hundred out at a time. We had to go back and forth for days taking these Japs back to the stockade.

I stood there with this other driver looking at all these Jap prisoners and he said, "Don't show your weapon."

I had a carbine with me in the truck. The last thing we wanted to do was spook the prisoners and have them rush us.

I got in some trouble when I shot one of the Japanese after the War ended. We were going to do a stage show and we needed something for a back drop. I knew about this hemp mill way out near the front line where I thought we could find something to use. A cook, a truck driver and I went to see if the mill was still there. In so doing we ran into this one Japanese with a bayonet. I took him prisoner and told him to get in the back of the truck. We stopped on the road by this little hill, and when the cook and I went over the crest to check things out, we ran into three more of them. One of them grabbed a hand grenade and I shot him. I shot him in self defense. It was just as simple as that. They put me in Charge-of-Quarters after that, which meant I just had to stay in camp. One of the other prisoners turned me in when we returned.

I told my story to the Major and he said, "I agree with you."

There was nothing more said about it after that.

Before coming home we were assigned to work at the harbor sorting through and warehousing eight big piles of ship cargo that were just dumped there. We had fifty Japs helping us and they'd find these gallon jugs of GI alcohol. The Japs would sneak off with those and drink it. One of the jugs had sulfuric acid in it. This Jap took that, drank it and it killed him right on the spot! The acid ate a hole right through him!

I missed the first ship home. It went down to Hollandia to pick up some more troops. It lost a propeller there and was stranded. So, I was lucky there, too. I went home on a big ship, the *General Callan* in April 1946. We hit this ninety-foot tidal wave! We had to go below decks. That five-hundred-foot ship twisted and sheets of paint on the side cracked off.

I thought, *'I went through the whole war, and now I'm gonna die coming home on a damn boat.'*

What happened was there was an earthquake under the ocean up in Alaska and this tidal wave traveled across the Pacific and it even killed some people on Hawaii.

It was a grand experience coming home. We came home into the same place we left from, Stoneman, California. We went under the Golden Gate Bridge. The fire boats were out shooting water in the air. People were out on these cruise boats with banners that said, "Welcome Home." God, it felt wonderful!

I took a train home. Then I came down with malaria and they put me in a hospital in Jefferson Barracks, St. Louis. My duffle bag went on without me and ended up in Fort Dix. I never got that back. I lost a .45 pistol in that bag.

When I got to Fort Dix there were thousands of bags and I thought, *'The hell with it.'*

Then I took a Royal Blue Coach in Trenton, and I got off in New Hampton. While I was walking home, a neighbor picked me up and drove me the rest of the way. It was a good feeling being home, but it was kind of an empty feeling too because my best friend, my brother-in-law Bill, wasn't there. He had been with the 1st Marine Division and was killed by shrapnel from an exploding shell at the end of the Okinawa campaign. I didn't know he had been killed until after the War. No one told me. I guess they were afraid of what I might do. Bill wanted me to be in the Marines. He said I'd have really gone places in the Marines. His death changed our lives. I never thought much about my Purple Heart after he died. Bill also got the Purple Heart, but he was killed for it. That's all he got for that whole thing.

After the War I did well in life. I was an enterprising young man. I sent all my pay home and the money I made selling cigarettes and stuff to the Filipinos and the money I made selling two Samurai swords to some Navy guys. I had twelve-hundred dollars saved up, and I bought a brand-new 1947 Chevrolet. It was a beautiful, black coupe, and it was loaded for those days. It had seat covers, a radio and a heater! That car helped me get my wife, Genevieve. I was going in and out of the hospital with malaria and to have shrapnel picked out of my shoulder. I met Genevieve at a soda fountain in Washington, New Jersey one day when I was on my way to the hospital. She was seventeen and still in high school. She had just gotten her learner's permit, and I taught her to drive using my Chevy. We fell madly in love, and we've been together fifty-six years.

After I came home, I went back to work at the Washington County Drug Store. Then I got in the newspaper business. It was different from farm work. I told Dad that I couldn't believe they paid people to do what I was doing. I started out in the advertising section of The *Washington Star* in Washington, New Jersey. Then it became the Star Printing and Publishing Company, and we printed about seventy-five different newspapers; everything from *Father Divine's New Day* to *The Jewish War Veterans.* Then I got hired to work in the press room for *The Journal of Commerce* in Phillipsburg, New Jersey. I moved up through the ranks to become the vice-president in charge of operations. I was with them for twenty-eight years.

I was also mayor of Lebanon Township for sixteen years. I was the building inspector, zoning officer and secretary of the Board of Health. I did everything for the town for years and years. Now they have ten people to do the same jobs!

We all damaged our hearing from firing those big guns. Today, I get a pension from the government because I'm classified as a disabled veteran for losing my hearing.

After four or five years out of the service I had a good job so I said to them, "Give the money to someone who needs it."

About five months ago, I went back to the VA about my hearing and to be fitted for hearing aids.

They looked up my number and they said, "Where the hell have you been? You have a hearing disability. You should have come in sooner!"

I explained why I hadn't been there in a while!

Looking back on the war years, patriotism was a great thing. We believed in what we were doing. I'll never feel any different about that. I wanted to survive it all. Everyone wanted to survive. I never thought about what it would be like to be terribly wounded and still be alive. I wanted to come back home. I saw others who died and it didn't seem like it was a place I wanted to be.

"I Guess We're Going to See the World."

Michael R. Tandaric

Landing Ship, Tank USS *LST–643*
Born in Mammoth, Pennsylvania, 13 September 1925

"I wrote a letter when we got around Okinawa saying that we'd hit the beach Easter Sunday, 1 April, 1945 and they cut that out. We only hit the beach for Okinawa, we didn't use boats this time. The amphibious landing tore a hole in the bottom of the boat, and we took on water. While we were stuck on the beach, there was a Code Red and we had to shoot down anything in the sky."

When I was sixteen and in school, I never thought I'd have to go into the service. But after the attack on Pearl Harbor, I was angry, and I knew we were going to get into a war. I felt we had to defeat the Japanese, and I wanted to fight. I didn't even know where Pearl Harbor was! When I turned seventeen, I tried to enlist. I had two brothers in the Army, but I didn't like the thought of the Army, so I tried for the Navy. I didn't pass the Navy physical because of a heart murmur. I had to wait until they drafted me. I felt like this was my duty, and that the draft was necessary. It didn't bother me to be drafted; even if it did, there was no way out of it. Before I received my draft notice, I dropped out of Latrobe High School after two years and got a job working construction on the first wing of the Latrobe Area Hospital. That was in 1943.

When I got my draft notice, I went to Greensburg to the armory where draftees had a chance to choose a branch of service. As it turned out, I was officially in the Navy on 24 November 1943. I only owned one dog in my life, a little white one. The day before I left for the service, the dog ran away. My family told me he never came back. I thought that was pretty ironic. I said goodbye to everybody. We corresponded by mail a few times after I left, but I only got a few letters because they were writing to my other brothers as well, and I didn't write much back anyhow.

My basic training took place in Great Lakes, Illinois. I came home for a couple of weeks and when I went back, I applied for Diesel Mechanic school because I wanted to learn a trade for after the War. I got assigned to the *LST–643*[259] that the Navy used to transport supplies, troops and equipment. We picked up our boat in Seneca, Illinois, and then floated down the Mississippi River to New Orleans. Our boat was commissioned there on 23 September 1944. From there we picked up supplies in Panama City, Florida, went back to New Orleans, and then to Gulfport, Mississippi. From there it was through the Panama Canal to San Diego. We crossed the Pacific to Pearl Harbor where we launched for our first destinations— Eniwetok[260] in the Marshall Islands and Saipan in the Marianas.[261]

It was warm in the Pacific, so we went without shirts for most of the time. There were one-hundred men and nine officers aboard. Our officers treated us well, and we had no problems with any of them. The enlisted men were the real leaders; the officers didn't have to do anything. They were topside on the deck usually and would come down to check on us, that's all. For entertainment, we usually played poker.

A typical day for us would start at five o'clock in the morning on the top deck. We'd eat breakfast and then we'd be on watch for eight hours. I worked in the engine room, making sure the engines were full of oil and were running smoothly. Then we'd be off for sixteen hours. I was also assigned to the 20mm onboard during off duty hours in case it was needed. There were a lot of healthy guys in our unit and I don't remember any guy getting sick. My pay got sent home to the bank, and what little I had, I spent on alcohol! We did good. We had no problems; it was smooth sailing.

In February 1945, we landed in Guam for supplies. We took on fresh water and 180 tons of ammunition on the tank deck. We also picked up a deck full of Marines from the 4th and 5th Divisions and headed for Iwo Jima. When we were on the boat, the officers would tell us where we were heading so we could get prepared. For Iwo Jima, we anchored out and the Marines went in on "Ducks" (DUKW).

Before they left, the Marines cried with us and gave away their clothing, money, everything they had. A lot of them knew they weren't coming back. We felt sorry for them. I watched the battle through binoculars and saw them raising the flag on 23 February. They had to do it twice because they got shot at the first time. I was glad to see it was our flag being raised, and I was also glad it wasn't me fighting on shore.

After Iwo Jima, we headed back to Guam and Leyte for supplies and refueling. Our next mission was the Battle of Okinawa.

I wrote a letter when we got around Okinawa saying that we'd hit the beach Easter Sunday, 1 April 1945, but the censors cut that out. We didn't use DUKWs at Okinawa. We just hit the beach with the LST. While we were stuck on the beach, there was a Code Red and we had to shoot down anything in the sky. I had no idea how to use any weapon, but I had been assigned 20mm! Anyway, I accidentally shot down an American plane. I heard the pilot got out safe.

Then a Japanese plane was in the air. I was hoping we'd shoot that plane down because a lot of them were Kamikazes. I fired on it with one magazine. It was pretty close to us. I hit it and it crashed inland. At the same time, the gun barrel blew up and a piece of Flak hit a guy beside me in the elbow and hit me in the upper lip. The medic took care of me right away, but they flew the other guy to Pearl Harbor.

After that, we backed off the beach and started to take on water. We had torn a hole in the bottom when we ran the LST onto the beach. We had to use a bilge pump to get the water out.

After Okinawa, we went back to Saipan and then to Guam to dry-dock and fix the hole. While we were there, we went swimming. I couldn't swim, so I always wore floats and life preservers. I had a bunch of them on me. The captain saw me from the boat and called down to me, "What's the matter? Can't you swim, Woody?"

He was making fun of me! Well no sooner had he said that than he fell overboard and into the ocean! He came to the surface and he was yelling "Help, help I can't swim!"

Everyone looked at me and told me to give him one of my floats, but I said he wasn't getting any of mine because he made fun of me. I laughed the whole time some of the guys were saving the captain.

After the War, we were busy transporting prisoners and hauling soldiers from one island to another. We had one-thousand Japanese prisoners on our boat that we took back to Kure, Japan. We were not allowed to speak to them while they were on the tank deck. We had guys guarding them with guns, but the Japanese didn't harass them or give them any trouble. They never gave us any trouble on the boat either; they made their own food and everything, and it was always rice!

Before the War, I thought Japanese were weird, but after I saw them, I didn't think they were that strange. They looked pretty friendly to me, and I didn't hate them. As far as I know, they didn't hate us neither. They were all told what to do and they did it, just like us. I think they were glad it was all over, just like we were.

Morale was high, and we were anxious to go home. They offered me a bigger rating if I stayed on for another year, but I told them I wanted to go home. In January 1946, we traveled to Tokyo and gave our ship over to the Japanese. They came on board with interpreters, and I had to show some of them how to run the engine. On 18 January 1946, the *LST–643* was decommissioned in Yokohama, Japan. We were in Japan for a while after that, and some of the men visited whorehouses. Actually, we all did; we were young, and this was after the War, and they were okay with Americans there.

I reported aboard the *LST–658* on 9 February 1946. We left Japan for home and made a lot of stops along the way. We stopped in Shanghai first, and we visited whorehouses there, too. The Chinese treated us well! Before we left, a friend and I hired a rickshaw to take us back from a downtown bar. When we got to the pier, we got out of the cart and the driver asked us for money. We didn't have any, and we were drunk, so we beat the hell out of him, and set him on the side of the pier!

After Shanghai, we stopped in Hong Kong, Chinwantao, and back and forth again to Shanghai before going to Haiphong, Hulatao and finally to Hong Kong again—more than 9,276 miles. Our boat was being used for other tasks during this time, so we had to wait until it completed missions before we got home.

We transferred from the *LST–658* to the *APL–11*, a Non-Self-Propelled-Barracks ship on 3 May 1946. From the APL–11, we boarded the *AV–12,* a seaplane tender, on 7 May. Between 8 May and 24 May, we traveled from Hong Kong to Singapore, Colombo, Ceylon and Alexandria, Egypt. We got into Egypt on 4 June. We were afraid of the civilians in Egypt; they didn't like us. They yelled at us and intimidated us, so we left after a few hours of being on land and went back to the boat where we stayed until we left.

We departed Alexandria on 7 June for Naples, Italy, by way of the Suez Canal. From Naples, we stopped in Algiers, Algeria, and then on to Bahia Praia, Azores.

Finally, we left for Norfolk, Virginia, on 21 June. From there, we arrived in Bainbridge, Maryland, where I was honorably discharged 1 July 1946. I rode a train home from Bainbridge to Pittsburgh, and when I got off the train, I bought a new wristwatch with my one-hundred-dollar mustering-out check. It was a twenty-one-jewel Bulova.

I ended my stay in Pittsburgh by getting drunk with a couple of my friends! I rode a train from Pittsburgh to Latrobe and went home where my family welcomed me back.

I liked going overseas. It was a good experience. More than I ever thought I'd see in my life.

After I got home, I tried to get a job as a Diesel Mechanic, but I couldn't find one in Pennsylvania. I moved to Detroit, Michigan in October 1946, and went to work for Chrysler on the assembly line. I hated that job, so I quit after two weeks I moved back to Pennsylvania. The steel mills were hiring, so about five of my buddies and I went down to U.S. Steel in Braddock. We all got hired.

On 3 July 1947 I got married and we had our only daughter, Deborah, on 25 June 1952.

In 1966, I was promoted to yard master at the mill. As Yard Master, I had thirteen men working under me, and my job was to make sure the buggies which held the steel molds were working on the tracks. I was in charge of six engines; the first brought scrap metal from the stock house, the second charged the furnaces, while the third took an empty buggy to the stock house and then the fourth engine conditioned the mold, readying it for molten steel. The fifth engine put the buggies on a platform where the steel was poured, and the sixth took the molds off the steel and moved the steel to where it was to be rolled.

I retired in February 1977 after thirty years at U.S. Steel.

Michael Tandaric's ship LST-643 and approaching dock at Guam, 29 May 1945. *Courtesy: US National Archives photo # 80-G-379466 (Nancy Reed to honor her father-in-law Dallas Dwain Reed CM2/c USNR SV-6 USS LST-643)*

Michael Tandaric

Japanese prisoners of war aboard Michael Tandaric's LST. *Courtesy: Michael Tandaric.*

Michael Tandaric and buddies on board the APA 59, 24 January 1946. Left to Right: Peterson, D.H. Vaillancourt, Franzovich, Jackson, Tandaric, R. P. Vaillancourt.

"King Neptune and his court" (usually including his first assistant Davy Jones and her Highness Amphitrite and often various dignitaries, who are all represented by the highest ranking seamen) officiate at the ceremony, during which the Pollywogs undergo a number of increasingly disgusting ordeals, largely for the entertainment of the Shellbacks. Once the ceremony is complete, a Pollywog receives a certificate declaring his new status. Another common status is the Golden shellback, a person who has crossed the equator at the 180th meridian (International Date Line).

"In My Mind I Was Always Fighting!"

Gino Trombetti

United States Sixth Army
6th Ranger Battalion
Company E
[98th Field Artillery Battalion]
Born in New York City, 25 July 1919
Clinton, New Jersey

> ***"On one night patrol we came across a dead Filipino decomposing in the jungle. Half of the body was bone and the other half still had some flesh. We had to step over the body on the trail and keep going. We put that stuff out of our minds and focused on what we had to do. On night patrols, I felt we may as well be fighting because the tension was so great. We were always fighting in our minds, fighting to stay calm and to stay alert. We may as well have been fighting the enemy."***

MY FATHER SERVED in the Italian Army during World War I. He was in a unit called the *Bersaglieri.*[262] They rode around on bicycles and they wore these hats with feathered plumes in them. He never liked to talk about it, but he was very upset when I went into the Army, maybe because he knew what war was like.

My father was born in Parma, Italy. It's a little mountain town in the northern part of Italy. That's also where my mother was from. They got married in Italy. They had two children over there but they passed away at six-months old. Then my father and mother came to America and they had three boys, me and my two brothers. My father was one of the first ones from my family to come over, then he brought over my grandfather and grandmother and they stayed in the Bronx maybe two or three years, but then they wanted to go back to Italy and die in their home in Parma.

When my father got to America, he opened up a grocery store on 45th Street in New York City. Then he left that job and became a chef. Then he was a maintenance man in one of the buildings on Wall Street. He was there until he retired, and he died when he was ninety-one. My mother passed away ten years prior to that. My oldest brother died and my other brother died, so I'm the only surviving Trombetti. I was born in New York City between 45th Street and 2nd Avenue.

I have a lot of early memories of the Italian immigrants along 45th Street. Around the corner, for some reason, were most of the Irish people. The candy stores were owned by the Jewish people. There were a lot of fist fights! No killings, or knives or guns, though. After the fight was over, they'd shake hands and that was it. As a kid I really don't remember there being "You're Italian, or you're Irish." I only recall it as I got older. In fact, I fought with some of my friends who were Italian more than anything else. Kid fights. I lost one fight and won two fights. But the fighting against different ethnic groups got more so as I got older.

We also had a theater that was across the street from where we lived. We had to go under the Second Avenue El (elevated train) to get to it and they had Tom Mix and Rin-Tin-Tin movies. I went to public school in that neighborhood as well. Just kindergarten. On hot summer days we'd open up the fire hydrant; we called it the "Johnny Pump." The policeman would come by, shut it off, and as soon as he was gone, we'd put it on again. We went to Yankee games, too. I saw Babe Ruth play. Before some games, he threw baseballs up to kids in the stands.

We moved out of there and into a house in the Bronx when I was six. At that time the Bronx was in the country! It's not like it is today. We lived there for twenty-two years. The neighborhood in the Bronx had a mixture of Germans and Italians, but our street was mostly Italian. I think people had a tendency to buy homes where they felt more comfortable, and that meant being with people of their own ethnic background, I guess.

We had a nice house with property in the back. My father used to grow lettuce and tomatoes. I had a pigeon coop and I'd fly pigeons. I was a regular young man, used to go on dates, went to beer parties and played football for St. Mary's Catholic School. We won the New York City Championship. It was a normal teenage life. I met my wife when she was fifteen, but we went around with a whole group. We didn't become serious until I went into the service. In the service, we started to exchange mail. From there we made a commitment to get married when I came home from the War.

During the Depression we always had food. I got hand-me-downs from my two older brothers. At Easter time we dressed up for church, because Easter was a big day. My mother bought me a suit that was a little big so that it would fit me the following year. I didn't feel we had any real hardship. My father always provided for us.

I remember Pearl Harbor like it was yesterday. My father and I were out with our beagles hunting rabbits. My brother Al and my Uncle Andrew were along.

When we got back, my older brother, who didn't come with us, said, "Pearl Harbor was bombed."

And I said, "Who is she?"

I thought Pearl Harbor was a woman! How did I know what Pearl Harbor was? And then he explained to me what happened.

He said, "Mr. Roosevelt said we are going to be at war and that so many Navy ships were bombed."

I said, "There's going to be a war?"

"Yes."

"Well, I'm gonna be in it."

A little more than a month later, on 22 January 1942, I was in the Army.

I was sort of a homebound individual. I had a lot of ties with the people around me and with my family. I realized I'd be leaving home. I felt a loneliness and a sense that I was going into the unknown. I felt that way for about two or three months. But I adapted.

My family had a send-off for me. My future sisters-in-law came over, my father cooked a meal, and we all said goodbye, and my brother and sister-in-law drove me down to Grand Central Station, and I left from there. There was a sergeant who directed us onto the train. There was a bunch of us leaving. We went to Fort Dix. The hardest thing about Fort Dix was I couldn't get used to the toilet facilities. I was used to going to my own bathroom, but they had these bathrooms where guys sat right next to me doing their business! I didn't go to the bathroom for two or three days because I was ashamed.

From Fort Dix I went to Oklahoma, and from Oklahoma we went to North Carolina and then Colorado. I was going to become a ski trooper with the 10th Mountain Division[263], but then they pulled me out of the 10th Mountain and into the 98th Field Artillery at Fort Bragg, which was a new outfit. I had to leave all of my buddies and start all over again.

In the 98th Field Artillery we trained on short-barreled 75mm howitzers. We'd fire the guns and we'd have a spotter who would tell us if our rounds were on target. They didn't give us any ear plugs and our ears would be ringing for days. We also trained on how to break the gun down and load it up onto our pack mules. The mules were going to go to New Guinea with us. New Guinea had this mountain range and they figured the best way to transport artillery up steep ridges was to use pack mules.

After training we got ready to go overseas. We left from San Francisco in December 1942. We had eight-hundred mules and we had the whole 98th Field Artillery on board this big freighter. We didn't go over with an escort. We had two PT boats tied to the freighter as an escort. Our first stop was Hawaii, but we didn't get off the boat. We were there for three days. They had a couple of Hawaiian girls come aboard and do a hula dance for us. From Hawaii we went to New Zealand, but we didn't get off the boat there either. Then we went to the tip of Australia, and we still didn't get off the boat![264] Then we landed in New Guinea. It was at least forty days to cross that sea. In crossing, a lot of the mules in the hold died because of the heat. So that gasses wouldn't build up inside them and make them rise to the surface after we threw them overboard, we gutted them. We didn't want to leave a trail for Japanese subs to follow. That was a dirty job, cleaning up all those guts! That was the worst part about the crossing.

During the journey across the Pacific there was a lot of time to think. At night I liked to go out on deck and sleep because it was hot down below. There were no lights up top, just the stars and they were so bright and there were so many it felt like I could reach up and touch them. I'd lie on my back and look up at them. And the ship would leave this iridescent wake behind. It all seemed so beautiful. It was hard to imagine that a war was going on.

We arrived in New Guinea in Port Moresby.[265] Soon after landing, the Japanese sent about one-hundred planes over and bombed us. We all ran into the jungle. I hid behind a tree. They were blowing up the ships. When I saw these planes come over I realized I was at war. That was really the only incident we had in New Guinea with the Japanese Air Force. In fact, by the time we got to New Guinea, most of the battle was already over, but we were always on alert for Japanese holdouts, especially at night, but a lot of the fight in New Guinea for us was just the fight against nature.

Guys had dysentery, malaria, which I came down with, and jungle rot. The heat was horrible! There were huge centipedes, there were rats running around at night, and we'd be waving flies away from our food constantly. At night, the flies would swirl around the tents and collect in big clumps. The fact that we had the mules along meant we had more flies. I had a terrible fear of rats. At night, I'd stomp my feet as I walked to try and scare away any rats that might be in my path. I used to sleep with my shoes on for fear my feet would get bitten by rats. New Guinea had huge bats, too. They'd be up in the jungle canopy looking down at me with these big eyes. There were some places we went through that still had cannibals, or so we were told. In some ways, just living there was the worst part of the War. I sympathize with the Vietnam vets, because they were in the jungle too. A jungle war is the worst. I look at myself now and I wonder if I could do it again.

One time five of us were taking some training near this swamp and I went to lie down because they were giving us a rest period. I sensed something behind me and I saw this Komodo Dragon-type lizard looking at me out of the undergrowth! I ran one way and he ran the other. I dropped my rifle and everything! That's the kind of place that was.

Our original task of carrying the artillery up into the mountains was no longer needed. Here we had all these mules, plus the Army wasn't sure what to do with us. Then they asked for volunteers for Merrill's Marauders.[266] I volunteered for that, but then I came down with malaria so badly they put me in the hospital. They gave me quinine and they gave me Atabrine, which turned my skin orange. But the malaria came back for years. All my buddies who volunteered for the Marauders went to Burma where they pretty much got massacred. One could call it fortunate that I got malaria.

After that, Colonel Mucci came along and asked for volunteers for the 6th Ranger Battalion, the one that would eventually free the Bataan prisoners at the Cabanatuan Prison Camp. I didn't go on that raid, however. Anyway, I guess a soldier always wants to prove to himself that he's not afraid. I was pushing myself to do this. I felt if I didn't volunteer I'd be ashamed and that ever after I'd doubt myself and I also wanted to do something that was more productive than just sitting around with a bunch of mules.

We trained for the 6th Ranger Battalion while in New Guinea. It was tough training. We learned Jujitsu. It was all dirty work on how to take a man down with our bare hands, kick him in the testicles, hit somebody in the throat, hit them in the nose in such a way that the bone went into the brain. At the time I was 205-pounds, and they'd pick another guy who was about my size and they'd make us wrestle. They wanted to see who could get the other man down.

We learned more about small arms. We broke down guns and put them back together. They put up targets in the jungle and we'd walk through the jungle and try to find these targets hidden in the trees. We trained on crawling through tall grass, all the while trying not to be seen. We went running in the morning and got back before breakfast. Colonel Mucci oversaw our training as did some of his lieutenants. But he'd run with us every day. He was an excellent leader.

The training was so hard that some didn't make it. Some guys cracked. One guy pulled the pin on a hand grenade and he was just holding the live grenade in his hand with the safety held down. He wanted to blow himself and everyone else up. I talked him out of it.

I said, "Why you wanna do that? Come on, give me the grenade."

I looked in his eyes and they just stared back at me. He was gone. But he finally gave me the grenade. He just gave up.

Another guy got boxes of cigars from home. One day we found him out in the jungle with one of the boxes. He had put rubber bands around it, and he was strumming them like they were strings on a guitar. One look in his eyes and we knew he was gone.

Really, it was a miracle we all didn't crack being in that place. At least in the Philippines it was livable. We saw people and houses, but in New Guinea all we had was jungle, a few banana plantations and some natives, but that was it, period.

For those of us who made it through the training, we felt good about ourselves. For me personally, I wanted to see if I was mad enough to do it! I guess I was and I was made sergeant in charge of a .30-caliber machine gun squad just before we went on the invasion of the Philippines in October 1944.

We didn't know we were going to be invading the Philippines until three days before the landings. We were on board ship when they told us. The 6th Ranger Battalion's job on the invasion was to secure these three islands in the southern part of Leyte Gulf so when MacArthur's main army landed three days later, these islands would be secure and the Japanese wouldn't be able to fire on the landing force. So what we were doing was a pre-invasion. Company E, my company, was assigned to secure the island of Dinagat by destroying Japanese communications and knocking out any shore defenses.

We got ready the night before. The Japanese were coming over with planes, but no one attacked our ship. It was near dawn when we climbed ropes on the side of the ship and into the landing craft. The tension was great as we headed toward shore. To relieve it, I goosed the guy in front of me. He turned around an gave me a look, and I immediately knew we were in a war. The look on his face said it all. I'll never forget that look.

We didn't have any resistance on the way in. After landing we chased out some Japanese snipers and pockets of resistance. We were lucky. It was a fairly quick mission for us.

One incident that did happen on Dinagat is an example of how your mind can play tricks on you. We dug our fox holes and I set up my .30-caliber machine gun in this hole. It was a pitch-black night. I was sitting behind the gun and it started to drizzle. I must have fallen asleep and when I woke up I felt for the machine gun and I couldn't feel it. I must have turned in my sleep.

In my mind I thought, *'Some Japanese must have sneaked up and got my machine gun!'*

I felt myself, and I felt fine. Then I started feeling around and hit the cold steel of the machine gun. I just hung onto it until morning. That morning I got orders to lay down fire on this whole hill side in front of me with my machine gun. So I opened up and after that black night and the silence, the noise actually felt good. I don't know if

"Come on, give me the grenade."

I was actually hitting anything on that hill, but we shot it up pretty good.

After securing Dinagat, we landed on Leyte. We did some light patrolling in the mountains on Leyte and then we landed on Luzon.

Sometimes we hunted wild pigs to supplement our rations. There was still a possibility of night attacks, or infiltration by enemy looking for food and supplies, so our perimeters would have trip wires that shot off flares to warn us. One night, a flare went up. and I was in my pit with my men. We all jumped up and opened fire. We thought it was Japanese infantry but here it was just a pig that tripped the wire. The barrel of my .30-caliber got cherry red. In those situations the adrenalin takes over and I think a soldier becomes a hundred times stronger.

We walked with such tension because we don't know if someone was taking a bead on us. That played on our minds terribly. I was often the first man or the last man on a six or a seven-man squad. It was a mental strain. One thing I did was think about my girlfriend and how we were going to get married. I thought about the future and stuff like that. In my mind I could go back home and that got me through a lot. I'd read one letter from home over and over again.

We always carried light weapons on jungle patrols. I had my .45 as a side arm on my hip and I had an M1 carbine. On night patrols we had noise discipline, making sure all of our gear was secured on us. On one night patrol we came across a dead Filipino decomposing in the jungle. Half of the body was bone and the other half still had some flesh. We had to step over the body on the trail and keep going. We put that stuff out of our minds and focused on what we had to do. On night patrols, I felt we may as well be fighting because the tension was so great. We were always fighting in our minds, fighting to stay calm and to stay alert. We may as well have been fighting the enemy.

We did a lot of work with the Filipino guerillas and the Alamo Scouts searching for Japanese. By the time we got to where we thought the Japanese were supposed to be, they had picked up and moved to another place. It was like that on a lot of our missions. It was cat and mouse. Since we were isolated on these patrols, aside from noise discipline, we had to be careful about not throwing stuff away on the path. We'd put any trash in a bag and find a place away from our location to bury it. And the guerillas helped us a lot. I don't think we could have operated as well as we did without their help. We had a lot of confidence when they were with us because they provided us with excellent intelligence on the Japanese and the territory we had to march through.

We traveled as light as we could. We didn't wear helmets. We wore Ranger caps, which kept us cooler than the steel helmet. We didn't eat much on patrol. We took along D-Bars and nibbled on those. What was more important than food was water. We couldn't carry that much water with us so we had to get it from natural sources. They gave us some pills to drop in our canteens to purify water we'd get from the streams up in the mountains. We couldn't get clean either. We stunk! But when we came across these streams, we washed our feet or our privates, or whatever else we had time for. But everyone smelled the same so it didn't bother anyone. I think the worst part was going to the bathroom in the jungle. That was a challenge sometimes and we really couldn't clean ourselves very well.

After a week of marching around in the jungle with the Alamo Scouts, we hiked back to our base camp. On the way back, I took too many salt tablets. I found out that wasn't the best thing to do. I started to pass out from the heat, and I had to sit down. In hostile territory, if one guy had to stop, the others kept going. I got this panicky feeling as I saw the fellas walking by me, but one did stop, a buddy of mine. He waited until I got myself back together. We caught up with the rest and finished our march.

It always seemed the action took place on the other side of the mountain. That's where my buddy Conners got killed.[267] We could hear the gun shots. Another buddy, he got hit in an ambush, and he played dead. The Japanese came by, poked around at his body and moved on. He just lay there in a puddle of mud. He couldn't move his legs because of his wounds. Flies were landing on him so he packed mud all over his face to keep the flies away. We found him a couple days later. He had survived.

The patrol that stands out in my mind the most was the one where I helped a wounded buddy of mine out of a river.[268] The guerillas already knew there was a whole pocket of Japanese on a hill that was covered with dense trees and thick jungle undergrowth. With the Filipino guerillas as guides, ten of us from Company E followed the river to the location where the Japanese were. We moved up and took up positions around the hill. My lieutenant and I laid down and crawled up close to the Japanese positions. Then we threw hand grenades. After the grenades went off, we got up and ran forward. I took cover behind an embankment of rocks. There was a lot of shooting, but I couldn't tell if it was from the Japanese or our guys.

The Japanese also were firing knee-mortars. My buddy was behind me, about forty-yards away. He came out of the jungle and was exposed by the edge of the river below the hill. I had a clear view of him and saw him go down. I thought he was dead. Immediately after that, I saw Japanese running across the river below the hill. A couple guerillas and I opened up and killed them all. I couldn't leave my friend lying in the river there, so I ran over to him. All of this happened in the course of maybe a minute or two. I ran over to my friend, I picked him up and dragged him out of the river and into a sheltered area.

He said, "I'm hit here!"

I looked and saw the bullet hole in his abdomen and I saw another hole in his back. The bullet went clean through.

Then he said, "I gotta pee! I gotta pee!"

I opened up his fly and all this blood started coming out as he was peeing and that frightened me. By this time the medic was there. He patched him up and gave him a shot of morphine. Some trucks came up behind us. We put him on one of those trucks and they rushed him back to the hospital. Last I heard he was hit in the liver. I don't know if he ended up making it. We lost touch with him. They gave me the Bronze Star for that. That was a surprise because I was just doing what had to be done. I wasn't gonna leave my buddy out there. After all the training I went through, how could I sit back and do nothing? I was afraid, but I was still going do it. My mind kept telling me I was going to get shot in the back, but my body kept moving.

After they evacuated him, we continued with the operation. We continued up this thickly-wooded hill, and we ran into some Japanese holdouts left from the group we fought earlier. We grenaded the hell out of those positions, and no one came out afterwards.

After we secured the Philippines, they started preparing us for the invasion of Japan. But then they dropped the Bomb and the War was over, but they were still going to send us to Japan for occupation duty. But I had enough points to go home. New recruits came to replace us. One of them called me by my name.

He said, "Gino! How are you?"

I said, "Who are you?"

"I'm Bruno, your cousin."

That was one in a million, let me tell you! I didn't recognize him, because the last time I saw him he was just a kid. But he remembered me. He was my father's sister's son. He went into Japan as one of our replacements!

I came home on a ship that was full of liberated American prisoners of war. I volunteered to work in the kitchen cooking for them. They had large heads and skinny bodies from not getting enough to eat. Some of them died on the way home and we had a military burial at sea.

We ended up in Seattle. We stayed there two days and then I went to Fort Dix. At Fort Dix I paid someone to take me into New York, and from New York I took a train to the Bronx. I had called ahead to tell the family I was coming home. My father, mother, my future wife, one of my brothers were waiting for me at the house. My other brother was still in the Navy. I took my time walking to the house after getting off the train. I was taking in the scenery of the old neighborhood. It had been a long time, but everything looked the same. It was a great feeling.

First thing I did when I got home was grab my girlfriend, and give her a big hug and kiss. The family had a lot of questions, but we really didn't do too much talking about the War. My girlfriend and I started preparing for our wedding right away, and we got married about two months later, and then about nine months after that my oldest daughter was born.

I went on the 52/20 club, but within a month I got a job working in Manhattan in the dress industry. After a short time, I went to work for Howard Johnson's as a supervisor. I spent twenty-five years in the food industry.

My wife and I stayed in the Bronx for a while with her parents and then we bought a house on Long Island. We stayed there quite a while. Then, when I retired, we moved to Pennsylvania for fourteen years, just north of Allentown. Then my daughters and family wanted us closer, so my son-in-law bought a condo in Clinton, New Jersey, where we live today.

I don't remember it being a tough transition from the military life back to a civilian one. When I first put on my civilian clothes, I thought they were too big because my uniforms were fitted tight. My body was used to military food, but it didn't take me long to adapt to steaks and other food. Mentally and emotionally I was okay. Sometimes I get choked up when I remember things like my buddy getting hit by that river. We didn't talk about the War, but today, in our old age, we talk about it more.

During the War, it always seemed that I was in the right place while some of my buddies were in the wrong place, like that time my buddy Conners got killed. Call it luck or fate, I don't know, but whatever it was, I wonder if I had been in his place would I have gotten killed? Maybe, and it would be Conners who would be telling you this story now and not me.

Gino Trombetti

"Ma'am, I Don't Have Any Legs."

Gladys Waugaman

United States Army Nurse Corps
Born in Greensburg, Pennsylvania, 3 September 1924

"Once, I walked into a room where a black man lay in the bed. I said to him, 'I'll give you a basin. You take care of your face and arms, and I'll wash your body and legs.' He looked at me and said, 'Ma'am, I don't have any legs.'"

Amos Clyde, my father, was a farmer, and he worked different farms around the area. The last farm that he owned was the Kuntz farm, adjoining coal-mining area called Twin Lakes. A spring that went back to prehistoric times fed the lake. They found arrowheads and other Indian artifacts there. Dad died in 1990, when he was ninety, and he lived there alone after Mother died in 1968. After he died, we sold the farm.

I was the first one in the family to get married. Harvey[269] was in the 87th Infantry Division in Europe. After Germany surrendered, Harvey was supposed to go to the Pacific. I was stationed at a hospital in Memphis, Tennessee, when Harvey called from Boston and said, "I'm going to be on my way to Japan, so if you want to get married you'd better come home now."

And so I did.

When I went to Greensburg High School, I took mostly general science subjects because I intended to go into nurse's training. The only place that had a program was the local hospital, so I took training there. After a little more than a year, the hospital joined the government Cadet Nursing Program. That meant that I'd have to go into the military after graduation.

We walked every morning to the hospital in our uniforms, and we worked from seven until ten. We worked six days a week. We were trained in different areas, such as maternity care, general floor duty and operating room procedures. We also had to take classes, and we had to learn how to massage. To learn treatment for mental health, we went to Torrance State Hospital, and I got involved in that while I was at the military hospital.

In 1945, two of us went to Memphis, Tennessee, where we joined a group of twenty-five girls from all over Pennsylvania. The hospital was huge; we had to ride a bus just to get back from the mess hall. We had officers' qualifications, and we weren't allowed to associate with non-coms. Even when Harvey's brothers came to visit we had to sit in the captain's office because they were non-coms.

At the military hospital, the mental health ward sometimes had eighty to one-hundred people on them, though forty or fifty was the norm. Some of the boys were still having strange problems. One very gentle southerner used to go around with a toothbrush and brush all the shelves and ledges. Every now and then there would be a sort of a riot, and the fellows would take me and lock me in the office for safety. I was the only woman there. Then they'd quell the riot, or take whoever was responsible and get him treatment. Basically, I was there to give insulin. That was used at the time to treat shock. It wasn't anything like the treatment we have today.

I also worked in the paraplegic ward. Each of us was assigned four patients that would be in a new type of bed. It was lower and had separations on the bottom to allow for bedpan use. The bed could also be flipped over to allow the patient to take pressure off his body.

We also did "convoy duty." Toward the end of the War, if we were short of work, they'd take us down to the incoming area where patients were being transferred for treatment. They had been flown across the ocean, and medical personnel determined where to send them for treatment. Many hadn't had their wounds treated. Sometimes we'd be there at mealtime, so we served them dinner and take care of any of their problems. The next morning, we'd clean them up. Once, I walked into a room where a black man lay in the bed.

I said to him, "I'll give you a basin. You take care of your face and arms, and I'll wash your body and legs."

He looked at me and said, "Ma'am, I don't have any legs."

The day Harvey called about getting married, I had to get permission for everything. I had to "clear the post," meaning I had to take care of any indebtedness and sign off all the places that had my name on it, and then I had to be off the base that evening. The captain helped me with it. She was very gracious. She called me and said that she had a ticket for me as far as Columbus, Ohio. I was hoping Steubenville, only an hour or so out of Pittsburgh, but it was Columbus, much farther away. In Columbus, I got a train to Steubenville, but there were no seats for me. I stood outside on the front platform to cool off. When we were about to pull into Steubenville, I thought I'd get out of my cadet uniform, clean up and put on a fresh uniform. After I came back out of the washroom, people looked at me in amazement.

"We thought you were a black girl," they said. I had gotten so dirty out on the platform, plus I had a tan from living in Memphis.

Harvey wanted to get married on 7 August, because that would have made our anniversaries 8/7, for the 87th Division. But the minister wasn't available, and the church was closed. We changed the date to 13 August. At seven o'clock that morning, we saw a newspaper with the big headline, "PEACE!" On the back of the page was our wedding announcement. Main Street was so crowded with people celebrating, that nobody could get to the church unless they took a very roundabout way. Our wedding was set for 7:30, but we got there late. In the meantime, all the people from the hospital that were supposed to come to the wedding wouldn't come into the church because they were going to rabble-rouse all night, and they weren't dressed for the occasion. We could hardly hear the minister because of all the noise outside. Well, we assumed we were married. Friends put gas ration stamps on our wedding gifts so we could get enough gas to go on a honeymoon.

It wasn't long before it was time for me to go back to Tennessee. I had to stay until the first of October to fill out the time that I had lost with me coming home.

I didn't do much full-time nursing after the War. When they established Mutual Aid at the Greensburg Hospital (Westmoreland Regional Hospital), I helped out there and at the blood banks. I did work for a while at the hospital relieving nurses, but when I got pregnant, I wasn't able to stay on my feet.

Harvey and I have gone overseas twice with the Battle of the Bulge veterans. We toured the battlefields. In 2004, the Belgian government arranged to have the veterans come and commemorate the 60th anniversary of the Bulge. It was a wonderful trip. The people there will never forget what men like Harvey did for the people of Europe, and the veterans will never forget their time there.

Gladys and Harvey Waugaman at the 60th Anniversary of the Battle of the Bulge in Belgium, 2004. Harvey passed away in Wnter 2007. He was a participant in the Saint Vincent College Faces of Battle class for ten years.

BE A
Cadet Nurse
THE GIRL WITH A FUTURE
For information
go to your local hospital or write
U. S. CADET NURSE CORPS
Box 88, New York 8, N.Y.
A Lifetime Education FREE
FOR HIGH SCHOOL GRADUATES WHO QUALIFY
U. S. PUBLIC HEALTH SERVICE · FEDERAL SECURITY AGENCY

"You Don't Ever Question the Lord, Son."

Harry J. Wilker

6th Marine Division (Okinawa)[270]
10th Marine Regiment (Artillery)[271]
2nd Marine Division
4th Marine Division
Born in Pittsburgh, Pennsylvania, 24 June 1921

"I used to lay there at night in my foxhole thinking and wondering. Those bullets seemed like they would come at me, then go around and hit the guy right behind me, maybe a good friend. I never could figure it out. I talked to priests, preachers, and all they ever told me was, 'You don't ever question the Lord son.' And so, that was that. I didn't question God."

SO HERE'S THE STORY. During the Depression we didn't have any money, so I went to work. First, I worked at a butcher shop, and then for Spear Furniture on Penn Avenue in Pittsburgh. That was in 1936. They needed help carrying stuff up steps. I brown-bagged my lunch. One day I was sitting there eating and Roosevelt came on the radio. He said a few words about us going to war, and I said, "This is for me!"

I went up to the old post office on Smithfield Street and enlisted. It almost killed my mother when I got home and told her that in two weeks, I was leaving for I don't know how long. In 1942, four months after the War started, I got on a train with sixteen guys and we went to Horseshoe Bend in Altoona where we picked up twelve others. We finally ended up having enough for a company of men, and we stayed together.

I got down to Parris Island where I spent three months. That place was torture; the greatest boot camp! Today, you can't say "poop" to a recruit and he's crying. But the DIs there stuffed our heads in bags or put them down in the mud and did whatever they wanted to us, but they made men out of us. I came out of there and they thought I had some knowledge of telephones, so they sent me to telephone school in Quantico, Virginia. That didn't appeal to me. We went to school at seven in the morning and quit at seven o'clock at night. I did Morse code. I'd fall asleep halfway through the day!

So I said to them, "That ain't for me, I wouldn't be no good unless I was out in the field."

So they took me out of there and sent me to Camp LeJeune and put me in service supply department. I was there close to six months before I got orders to ship out with the 10th Regiment.

We were at Guadalcanal,[272] the first push.[273] There was an incident that happened to me on the ship before we landed there. They taught us to open our mouths when our ship's guns fired to sort of let the concussion go through. One day, I was standing around bullshitting and I didn't open my mouth. Just like that, I lost the hearing in my left ear. When it came time to hit the beach, I went over the side, down the rope ladder into the landing barge, and when we got to the beach I couldn't hear anything on my left side.

My Captain said to me, "We've to send you to somebody. I know an old guy down here in the Navy Medical Corps."

He sent me down to see him.

This doctor says to me, "Anybody in your outfit smoke Prince Albert in a can or Union Leader in a can?"

"Yeah, a couple of guys smoke a pipe."

"Get one of those empty cans, pinch it on the end, and piss in it, and when you're through, pour it in that ear."

This guy was a Navy doctor, and I couldn't believe what he was telling me to do! So I went and got a can of tobacco and did what he said. That ear roared like a volcano for about ten minutes. I woke up the next morning and I could hear! There was something to say about old-fashioned home remedies.

Whenever I had chapped hands, my grandfather used to tell me, "Pee on 'em, Boy!"

My hands would burn like hell, but they got cured.

Anyway, we went to the "Canal." I was probably there for four months. I took a prisoner one day and took him before the captain.

I said, "What do I do with him?"

The captain said, "Well, he's yours. He gets half of your food and half of everything you've got."

They didn't have prison camps at the start of the War. You took a prisoner and he was yours. It was a hell of a life. I was twenty-one years old and ready for the prime of my life, and I didn't want that prisoner hanging on me for the rest of it. I walked him in front of me out into the jungle. I just shot him in back of the head. He didn't know it was coming. I shot him three times with a carbine. Now, my mother didn't raise me be a killer, but I got through it. Our blood was up. The battles were gruesome; they were pitiful. I'd be right next to a friend and, boom, down he'd go.

We had an ammunition dump on Guadalcanal from our company on the side of the road up a hill a little bit. Flame-thrower guys would go in to get all of their equipment. One guy went in, and he came back out with his flame-thrower on and grenades hooked on his belt. On the way out, he bumped something and just went up in smithereens. We went around picking up toes, fingers, whatever was left of him. That gave us all a funny feeling when we went around gathering up body parts of the Graves Registration people.

We moved over to Tarawa[274] after that.[275] The "Nips" got wise somehow; they were maniacs, but very smart people. They buried iron on an angle far out from the beach. Usually, the Navy foreman heard a "clap" under the boat that told him we were hitting solid sand in low water. When we hit those iron bars, we got dumped in ten-feet of water and half of the men drowned! He was so used to dropping the gate after he heard that sound! Those guys had sixty pounds on their backs, and that was that.

They sank with all they had. They just went down and never came back up.

We got dumped off in the ocean and there was no other place to go. We couldn't retreat, or anything. We had to fight our way to the beach. The Japs were like animals, dug in like ants. That was pretty much the same wherever we landed. Some of the islands we hit had fifteen to twenty-thousand Japs tunneled in them. Some were all coral: hard stuff to dig in. We'd attack these islands, and when we got a beachhead, we'd crawl. Maybe we'd crawl for weeks, and do only one-hundred yards a day, or not even that much.

Iwo Jima was gruesome.[276] I was there about two months. On Iwo Jima, I was about thirty yards from where that Indian boy[277] helped raise the flag. The Japanese dug holes in the ground, camouflaged them, and we didn't know they were right in under us, under trapdoors, like trap-door spiders. As soon as we went by, they'd flip up that trap-door and shoot one of us in the back. It's amazing how smart they could be, but also stupid enough to lose the War. We got a foothold on every island. Every island was a new adventure, something different.

I used to lay there at night in my foxhole thinking and wondering. Those bullets seemed like they would come at me, then go around and hit the guy right behind me, maybe a good friend. I never could figure it out. I talked to priests, preachers, and all they ever told me was, 'You don't ever question the Lord son."

And so that was that. I didn't question God.

After Iwo Jima, they pulled me out of there and put me into the 6th Division which was the only Division to be created in the Pacific during the War. After we had a division, we were ready for Okinawa.[278]

I was at Okinawa for four months getting the airfields set up. I lived in a tent in Naha, the capital. It was a beautiful city, but we blew it up. We set up machine guns in crossfire position on roadways. One night, we heard some movement and our captain hollered, "Halt!"

He did that three times, and there was no answer. The guys opened up with both guns. In the morning all we found were dead children and grandmothers. Those Jap bastards had pushed them out in front, and that's who we shot.

We didn't know any different. Besides, we were in a war. It was shoot, shoot, shoot. The Japs came at us at night in droves down over hillsides. We'd just sit there and pick them off. When we came to a cave, a flamethrower stood at the entrance and one of the Marines who spoke Japanese yelled for anyone in there to come out. Even the women who came out tried to get close to us. When they did, they'd raise their arms. They'd have grenades taped to their bodies just under their armpits. They'd have the pins tied on their arm, and when they raised their arms, they'd pull out the pins. They'd try to take three or four of us with them. Elderly women did this too!

In six weeks we finished taking Okinawa. The Japanese kept running, right to the end of the island where there were steep cliffs, hundreds of feet above the ocean. The Japanese ran right off of those cliffs and killed themselves.

After Okinawa, I came back to Guam, the headquarters of Admiral Nimitz, commander of all the operations in that part of the Pacific. When the war ended, I got word to get on one of seven delivery ships and go to China.

We went to Tsing Tao, China and set up a base. From there we collected all the Japanese, and trucked them to ships for transfer back to Japan. The Chinese didn't want them there.

A guy I loafed around with was Sergeant Gibbett out of Ohio. He was a bookkeeper in civilian life. One Sunday, some of the Japanese guys took three of us to their home for an eight-course dinner. There was a fish with a big eye laying there on the table dead. As guest of honor Gibbett had to pluck out the eye and eat it. Only then could the feast begin! They took some eggs that they'd and boiled them. They were coal black after they were peeled, except for the yoke.

One night a buddy named Sergeant Stone and I thought the MPs were after me, so we ran into a doorway. A panel opened, and there stood a little Japanese woman about four-feet tall. She invited us in. Her husband and son were there. She sat us down and said, "Eat! Eat!"

She made a delicious meal. Every night after that, we'd take candy bars or something and go to that house and eat. We had five weeks to get the Japanese out of the area, but we saved that family for last. They loved us, and they didn't have any hate. They were a different kind of Japanese in China. On the day we had to get them out, my truck was assigned to go down there where they lived. They were only allowed to take thirty pounds with them; thirty pounds of clothing or anything. I had three jeweled sabers I sent home, and a few guns that were family heirlooms they had given me.

I spent five good years of my life in the Marines. I'm glad I did.

Before I left for the service, I met this girl. She was a Marine too. We were pretty thick for about five weeks, until she said, "Let's get married."

I said, "I don't want to get married now, and then come home with an arm or leg or something else missing."

Anyway, I got home in March 1946. I figured to take a month or so and just raise hell. It was one o'clock in the morning when I got in. My girl was waiting at the Pennsylvania & Lake Erie Station for me. I came home on 15 March, and we got married on the twenty-fourth. We were married fifty some years. She died ten years ago.

I finally went to work managing a store on Liberty Avenue for a guy who nicknamed me "Hirsh," which is Jewish for "Harry." I never lost a day of work. Then we became partners in the Liberty Sales Company at 919 Liberty Avenue in Pittsburgh. You could buy anything there. We made out!

I raised a boy and a girl. My son graduated college and he was a school teacher. He retired three years ago at fifty years old. My daughter had two boys.

The B–17 of La Goulafriere

Earl Edward Woodard
United States Eighth Air Force
1st Air Division
457th Bomb Group "The Fireball Outfit"[279]
750th Bomb Squadron
Captain, USAF Reserve
Born in Naylor, Missouri, 12 April 1920
St. Louis, Missouri

"At a modest hotel near the Austerlitz Station, we were turned over to three agents of the Paris underground. The hotel was a German billet, and we passed Wehrmacht Officers on the staircase on the way up. A distant view of the Eiffel tower reminded us that we were really in Paris! Outside, German troops were having a party, but we dared not leave our rooms."

I LEFT COLLEGE IN my senior year and enlisted in the United States Army at Jefferson Barracks, Missouri, shortly after the Japanese attacked Pearl Harbor. The enlisting officer suggested that my major in Business and Accounting might qualify me for Aviation Cadet training. I chose instead the United States Army Quartermaster Corps and was sent to Fort Warren, Wyoming, for basic training.

The Wyoming winter convinced me that my true military calling was the Sky! I passed all the required tests and was accepted for cadet training. Our sudden entry into the War had caught the country unprepared. As a result, facilities and personnel were at a premium, and I was assigned to Lowry Field near Denver, Colorado, to wait until my name came up for assignment.

In June 1942, my group of cadets took a World War I troop train recently taken out of "mothballs" to Kelly Field in Texas, the "Cradle of the Army Air Force." Though Kelly was a permanent base, we lived in a tent city while we took the physical and mental exams that would determine whether we'd become pilots, bombardiers or navigators. As it turned out, I became a Navigation Cadet and was transferred to Navigation Preflight School at Ellington Field, Texas, located in a swampy area southeast of Houston and close to the Gulf of Mexico. Our barracks there were surrounded by mud and water, and the heat and humidity were oppressive. Each night, we draped our damp GI issue, heavy-twill garments at the foot of our bunks to dry. We put them back on the next morning still damp. On top of that, we were required to wear neckties! Imagine what it was like to do close-order drill that way. Each Friday, as well, we marched in parade.

Before the War, Pan American Airways set up the first navigation school and had trained the few navigators in the Air Corps. Our courses consisted of the sort of mathematics appropriate to navigational theory, and the in-depth math reviews were grueling. We studied Morse code, aircraft identification and meteorology.

After Ellington, we went to the Advanced Navigation School at Hondo, Texas, a tiny Mexican-American community about seventy-five miles north of San Antonio where we put into practice what we had learned. Flight training supplemented our studies in navigation by pilotage, dead reckoning and celestial observation.[280] We became Second Lieutenants when we graduated.

My first assignment was to Ephrata in the desert area of Washington State. There appeared to be nothing on the horizon that resembled a town. I was assigned to a six-bunk Quonset hut. I was alone there until the next morning when Lieutenant John G. Winant,[281] a pilot and the son of our ambassador to Great Britain, joined me. John was so eager to get to England that he flew double duty whenever he could. He was soon on his way overseas. A few weeks after his arrival, his plane was shot down by the Germans who thought that they had nabbed President Roosevelt's son, Elliot!

My group, the 457th, was activated in July 1943 at Spokane, Washington, where our crew assembled with Mac Dickinson[282] as pilot. We were the first crew in the 457th. We were issued an ancient B–17 named *Lucy* and reported to Rapid City Army Air Base at Rapid City on 27 July. They called us a "model crew." We liked to think that the title was based on merit, but it meant only that our composition was to be a model for those that followed.

Training flights distracted us from the oppressive summer heat and the incessant wind of that part of South Dakota. Mac saw to it that the cities we visited had more to recommend them than just their training value. Mac flew us to Seattle, Colorado Springs, Daytona Beach and Nashville, Mac's hometown and that of his girl friend! Our engineer Jim Free got more training than he bargained for trying to keep *Lucy* alive. In Oklahoma City the flight line declared her un-airworthy, and Jim had to scramble to get the okay to take off!

Our next assignment was another outpost of discomfort, Brooksville Field, Florida, where we spent six steamy weeks getting used to flying over water. After Brooksville, they sent us back to Ephrata for simulated combat flying, or "phase training." During phase training we were constantly reminded of our own mortality. At Ephrata, six men died in a crash landing. Phase Training III at Wendover Field, Utah, was the scene of another sobering loss; two planes went down after a midair collision.

At Wendover, Ed Bender replaced Mac as pilot. Finally, we completed our state-side training for combat. In January 1944, the 457th got orders to go to Grand Island, Nebraska. On 17 January we headed overseas via the North Atlantic Ferry Route.[283] We were weathered in at Gander, Newf oundland for three days. Finally, our Group Commander, Lieutenant Colonel James Luper,[284] announced a midnight departure, saying, "I don't want any excuses for failing to head for the British Isles tonight!"

That night, as I climbed aboard our plane, my sextant bumped against the escape hatch door and dropped seven feet to the ground. The sextant was something I needed for celestial navigation.[285] It was a delicate instrument, and any damage it might have suffered would lead to incorrect readings, and there was no way I could determine the damage, if any. Radio navigation was out of the question because we had been ordered to maintain radio silence. Besides, Colonel Luper was an uncompromising West Pointer and had already announced his position on "excuses." I got Bender on the intercom and explained my dilemma. If I'd be able to "shoot" the stars it would give us a good equilateral triangle and I could continue bisecting it to reduce its size. I could plot a correct course to Prestwick, Scotland, but I could make no mistakes!

Thank God, the procedure worked. We arrived over Prestwick on course and on time. The tower, however, told us we couldn't land because of foul weather! With fuel running low, we landed at Nutt's Corner Air Base in Northern Ireland. Later, Charlie Blackwell complained that his flight lunch had disappeared. The Irish were inordinately fond of white bread!

The entire group eventually assembled at United States Army Air Force Station 130 at Glatton, England, between 21 January and 01 February 1944.[286] After we arrived, we put up an eighteen-ship formation for a practice flight. Colonel Luper flew in a separate B–17 to observe us, and we were his crew! On previous practice missions, three navigators had gotten Luper lost. I was the next victim!

The formation took off on schedule. We were to proceed to a designated checkpoint where Luper could observe, but when we got there the formation was nowhere to be seen! Luper was seething.

He got on the intercom, "Lieutenant, where is that group? Are we lost?"

"No, Sir."

I gave him our position.

"Colonel, if you look through the hole in the overcast, you will see Ipswich and the coast."

Luper hadn't had much opportunity to do pilotage over England. All he had was my word, and I wasn't about to lie to him.

The intercom went silent, and I knew the Colonel was grinding his teeth. He was sure I had gotten him lost before we let down through the overcast to the beacon or that the formation itself had gotten lost. He was furious. When we landed, he called a briefing of all flying officers who had participated in the exercise. Before we got to the briefing room, someone had informed Luper that the formation had indeed been off course, and that our observer plane had been at the right place at the right time.

Colonel Luper and General Lacy, CO of the 94th Bombardment Wing, entered the briefing room. The general listened passively as Luper launched into a diatribe about everyone's incompetence, but especially the navigators'. Luper paused in his vilification, and then asked for suggestions. There was dead silence. No one dared respond, except me. I couldn't keep my mouth shut at the injustice of his brutal criticism.

"Colonel, all the groups have similar problems. It's different here from the States. The whole countryside has towns and installations that look the same from the air. It can be confusing to gather around a beacon at the same time, climb through overcast, and then give a mission heading to the pilot."

"Lieutenant, you had better sit down!" Luper snapped back.

Later, Rod Francis told me that at a meeting following the briefing, General Lacy said to Luper, "You had a good crew on that mission. That navigator had the guts to tell you his impressions, knowing that you were angry. Isn't that the spirit you're looking for?"

Two days later, I flew in our first combat mission.[287] We led the 457th over Oschersleben,[288] deep inside Germany. Colonel Luper came along in the copilot seat, replacing Major Rod Francis, and we didn't relish that fact. Some planes never left the ground. Others had problems assembling. Experience would teach us that confusion was normal. Our ship was named *Rene III*,after the colonel's wife.[289]

Colonel Luper, though his methods were often unsuited to the "citizen" army under him, did sometimes drop his aloofness. He was a dedicated leader, a real "soldier's soldier." He seemed to come to respect my moment of courage during the briefing, and he even called me by name. Sometimes he used me as an example when he was castigating bombardiers for lack of precision.

"When the navigators were having trouble, they had the guts to speak up and tell me what was wrong!" he'd say.

I don't think the remark improved a bombardier's aim, but Luper really was shaping us into a close knit and seasoned group.

At one o'clock in the morning of 25 April 1944 I awoke to Mac Dickinson's, "Woody! Come alive. The 457th is leading the 94th Wing today. You're lead navigator!"

Mac had been our pilot until he got promoted to Squadron Operations Officer. It was his practice to personally wake up squadron officers when a mission was scheduled.

Knowing that I dreaded navigating for Colonel Luper, Mac added, "Rod Francis is the command pilot."

Navigating lead was a big responsibility and it took a while for Mac's words to sink in. I was too busy trying to get awake and moving in the chilly English night. A good breakfast helped. Contrary to popular military opinion, I really enjoyed the scrambled powdered eggs and Spam.

While I ate, I heard one of the other navigators say, "I heard we're going to Nancy today."

The briefing for the mission started around three o'clock in the morning.

When we were sure of the target, Ed Bender said, "Woody! We've got it made! It's Nancy, a milk run! We won't know how to handle it!"

I agreed. After Oschersleben, Schweinfurt[290] and Berlin[291], this—my seventeenth mission—promised to be an easy one. After the briefing we rode a Jeep to our plane. The plane was 42–97070. It didn't have a name because we never had a plane long enough to give it a name. Major Francis, as command pilot of the 94th Wing, took Charlie Blackwell's place, and there were a couple other substitutions. We were disappointed with the changes because the regular crew had become a close-knit group. Charlie Webber hadn't missed a single mission, and he was replaced with Lieutenant Munroe ("Jack") Hotaling as tail-gunner.[292] Hotaling was the unofficial aide-de-camp to Colonel Luper. In old Army terms, Jack was known as a "dog robber," someone who saw personal gain in being attached to a superior officer. Anyway, we were relieved that Luper wouldn't be sitting in the copilot's seat.

Lieutenant William Soules, a pilot, took Tom Leahy's place as waist gunner. Soules had just arrived from the States and was anxious to experience some combat before he got his own plane. A B–17 crew usually consisted of ten men, but this time Captain Arthur Cavanaugh, from Idaho, was the eleventh, flying with us as an observer.

We took off with a full load—twenty-five-hundred gallons of fuel and twelve five-hundred-pound bombs. Our plane shuddered as it taxied down the runway, gathering as much power as Ed Bender could coax from the engines. We had to clear Holme Wood at the end of the tarmac. As usual, we were mesmerized by the view as the runway disappeared and the tops of the trees blew in the wind as we cleared them. This was mission number thirty-two of the 457th Bombardment Group, and we were leading two-hundred Flying Fortresses of the 1st Air Division, United States Army Air Force. Our target was a German air installation at Nancy, France.[293]

Assembly of the formation was always dangerous, and took intense concentration on the part of the pilot and copilot. Over England, the skies were frequently overcast and visibility was limited. This was when the danger of midair collision was greatest. Our planes rose in a single file, in a spiral pattern, and assembled in a tight "vee" formation around a radio beacon. Our formations had to be tight to make maximum use of combined firepower.

Once we got above the overcast, I gave the pilots a heading. The other navigators "followed the lead" and, at the same time, plotted their own course in case they had to leave the formation for one reason or another, usually for engine trouble. Number-two plane, and so on, would have to take over lead in the lead plane had to drop out. We leveled at twenty-five-thousand feet and headed for France. Inside, our plane was cold and noisy. We maintained radio silence.

On our approach to the Nancy-Essey Airdrome, we started to take heavy Flak. The target was completely overcast, and dropping bombs was out of the question. We turned back. The plane's intercom was silent except for me giving course alterations to the pilot, or if someone warned of approaching German fighters. We turned westward. As usual, we faced one-hundred-mile-per-hour headwinds.

Suddenly the intercom came alive. "Number-four engine on fire!"

And shortly after that, "Number-three engine on fire!"

Between the announcements we had dropped out of the lead. Number-two plane took our place. Sergeant Free disarmed the bombs, and then Bender jettisoned them. They fell harmlessly on the French countryside.[294] From my position in the plane's nose, I watched the engine fires. A ten-foot wall of flame blocked the escape hatch on the opposite side of the aircraft.

Then we heard, "Abandon ship!"

Ed Bender hit the bell, reinforcing the order.

Sergeant Mahan bailed out through the open bomb-bay in the front of his radio room. He jumped without a specific order to do so. Major Francis left his copilot's seat, brushed past Bender, and jumped out of the left escape hatch. In the rear of the plane, Sergeant Sarico headed for the right-rear escape hatch. He spotted Hotaling standing motionless in shock. Sarico grabbed Hotaling's chest pack, snapped it onto the harness and, tucking his fingers around the pull-ring, pushed him head down through the wall of flame at the exit and then followed him.

Woyurka didn't see Mahan bail out, and he hurried forward to the radio room where he thought Mahan was still trapped. When he realized Mahan had gone, he returned to the rear hatch and jumped. He was severely burned.

Free spotted what he thought was the cause of the fires. Fuel from a broken line was snaking along the flight deck. He quickly jumped through the bomb bay.

When I heard the alarm, I took off my Flak jacket and helmet and unhooked my oxygen line. I was at the escape hatch in no time, Keith Fuller right behind me. I made sure that my harness was secure. Keith tapped me on the shoulder, signaling me to hurry. We stepped out of the burning plane into the sudden silence. We were at twenty-five-thousand feet when we jumped, and I was surprised that I could think clearly without oxygen. I focused on when to pull the ripcord. An opened parachute in a strong wind would descend slowly over a wide area and be an easy target. Bender, true to the captain's tradition, was the last to jump.

In free fall I remembered that Mac Dickinson had invited me to accompany him to Buckingham Palace where he had been invited to a reception for the future queen.

"Now I'll never get to meet Princess Elizabeth," I thought.

I fell rapidly. The ground got closer. I pulled the cord at about five-thousand The parachute opened with a jolt. I watched as fields and orchards passed beneath. I drifted toward a high-tension wire and pulled the lines to avoid it. The chute spilled a bit, and I landed in an apple tree, unhurt except for a wrenched knee. I climbed out of the tree and gathered in my chute. Mahan, who had landed nearby, joined me. Convinced that Germans were close by, we moved off in opposite directions.

Soon after I left Mahan, a couple Frenchmen appeared and directed me to a hollow tree. I found out later that they were connected to the Resistance movement.[295] I was barely hidden inside when a German patrol swept through the woods. Had they looked back, I know they would've seen me.

After the patrol passed, a Frenchman came to my hiding place. His name was Henri Demarguay, and he took me to his home at Sap-André near the village of Heugon. I spent the afternoon in a shed-like room at the rear of his rather manorial-looking house. I had limited college French, but it was good enough to understand Henri when he told me the Germans would be back that night to search the village. After dark, Henri took me in a horse-drawn carriage to a farm some distance away. That same evening I found myself in a brick outbuilding occupied by a middle-aged man who was described to me as a "poacher." Later that evening, I met my host, Lucien Legenvre, a prosperous farmer and owner of a popular *charcuterie*[296] in Paris. Lucien's farm was at Trinite-des-Latiers near Gacé, Normandy, the breadbasket of occupied France. Norman farmers didn't take kindly to furnishing meat, fruit and cheese to the Germans. Lucien and others like him risked their lives and the lives of their families by sheltering downed Allied airmen.

"We must have a coffee *avec Calvados*[297] and to hell with the Nazis!" Lucien said with typical French bravado. After three cups of strong coffee laced with Normandy's lethal apple distillment, I was in a state of supreme confidence about making it safely back to England.

The following evening "Luie" and I were continuing our talks when we heard vehicles approaching. There was a mad scramble to get me to the attic, but in a few minutes I was called out of hiding. At the front door stood Jack Hotaling none the worse for wear, and he was a little drunk. With him were the mayors of two neighboring villages.

"Woody, I want you to meet mon bon amis."

Jack didn't smoke, but his pockets were full of French cigarettes, a precious commodity to the locals. We all had another round of coffee *avec Calvados.*

Jack told me what happened to him since he jumped from the plane. He landed on a horse-breeding farm. A Frenchman had been tracking Jack's descent, and when he landed the Frenchman led Jack to a hayloft. In minutes, two Germans on motorcycles zoomed up the drive and began searching for the American whose parachute they had also spotted. Jack attacked the first German and broke his neck. The owner of the farm, Marguet, made certain of the other German. Jack and Marguet then disposed of the bodies in an abandoned well behind the house, and threw the motorcycles into a pond. Jack then went to sleep in the farmhouse. The next morning a beautiful French girl brought him breakfast.

After Jack finished his story, one that I thought was a little astonishing, I thought, '*What a vivid imagination this guy has.*'

The next to arrive were Art Cavanaugh and Rod Francis.[298] A woodcutter in the forest at Saint-Evroult rescued Art and put him in touch with a resistant named Gerome who drove him to the Legenvre farm.

Rod was "rescued" by Madame Gentay, a young farm wife at Lucien Legenvre's. This was on 26 April 1944. The day before our plane crashed in a field on the Piérre Lapresty farm near La Goulafriére. The French watched as eleven parachutes floated to the ground. So did the SS troops in the area. The Germans immediately began a search on motorcycles, various vehicles and foot. The French, accustomed to airmen dropping in unannounced conducted their own search.

Madame Gentay saw a man making his furtive way through the stubble of a field toward a small building in an adjacent field. She awakened her husband and Maurice Allais, a young student who was working on the farm. Maurice was also in hiding trying to avoid being sent to a German labor camp. Together, the two men approached the building where they found Rod. They hid him in a second floor bedroom of the Gentay home. Rod immediately fell asleep. German troops searched in widening circles, and the family, now uneasy, moved Rod to less comfortable quarters in a loft above a rabbit hutch. Two days later they brought him to the Legenvre farm.

After Mahan left me in the orchard, he made his way to the road, hiding as much as possible. He tried to make contact with "friendlies," and approached an elderly farm couple who became terrified and chased him away. Mahan wandered for three days and nights, not trusting anyone. Finally, some found him and brought him also to the Legenvre's. Mahan was the fifth and final arrival. The Germans had captured the remaining six presumably near the crash site and took them to a place called Château Tremblay, and then to prison camps in Austria and Germany.

The five of us exchanged stories. We all, including our rescuers, found Hotaling's adventure a bit incredible. Several days later, M. Desiree Marguet arrived from the horse farm, Haras Minerais, with his beautiful daughter, Yvette! Marguet and Yvette absolutely corroborated Hotaling's story. We were amazed.

Jack Hotaling was a classic soldier of fortune. He had been a Doughboy in World War I. He served for two years in the Army of Occupation and learned to speak fairly good German. After his military service he became a fireman in Hollywood. His great claim to fame was a "loving" relationship with starlet Paulette Goddard, before she became a "protégée" of Charlie Chaplin. Jack also bragged about being a hunting buddy of Clark Gable's. As it happened, Major Gable was on duty at our Wing headquarters and did some public relations combat flying. As far as we knew, Jack wasn't contacted by Gable to join a British hunt! It was little wonder that we had problems believing Jack until Marguet confirmed their mutual adventure.

Marguet wasn't especially pleased with Hotaling's attentions toward Yvette. He judged him to be a "skirt chaser" and a braggart, and he found Jack's promises to make Yvette a star in Hollywood somewhat hollow and distasteful. Anyway, this was just the beginning of "Jacotaling" saga. Even today, Jack remains a part of the narrative tradition of a special part of Normandy.

As he was with Colonel Luper, Jack was also a bit of a sycophant to Rod Francis. We stayed in a crude, brick shelter on the farm, but it did have a fireplace. Hotaling insisted that his "commandant" should have more suitable quarters. He managed to get Rod a room in the main house.

Cavanaugh, Layman, Mahan and I established a simple routine, but Hotaling, used to living on the edge, would become uncivil over anything or nothing. He claimed to outrank us, but his age was his only claim to seniority.

"Knock it off, Jack," we'd tell him.

Those words finally gave him the excuse he needed. He left one day, grandly announcing that he would see us in England. Our peace would be short-lived.

At fifty-three, Jack was the stereotype of a French veteran. He wasn't a big man, and he had dark hair, a mustache to match, and a ruddy complexion. He managed to borrow a bicycle and rode it about the countryside, a rake or hoe over his shoulder, looking like any other aging farm worker.

Two days after his dramatic departure, Jack came back, a little sheepish but still full of bravado. He regaled us with another "impossible-to-believe" story. While we were at Legenvre's house, we met an attractive woman who spoke English. Her name was Mademoiselle Noelle Guillou, and she ran a dance hall and bar in Eschaufflour.

Anyway, during his wanderings on the bicycle, he was visiting her one evening and it was past curfew when he left.

As he walked down the village street, he heard, *Halt!*

Someone had given Jack identity papers indicating that he was a wounded French soldier, discharged because of deafness! Jack was faced with a dilemma. He couldn't acknowledge the order because he was "deaf." The German soldier who had shouted the order to stop caught up with Jack and demanded his papers. Jack gave him his documents. The German took a look, then signed to Jack, making him understand that he'd better not be out again after curfew. Jack hurried out of town and back to us! Well, a few days later, two Frenchmen from the village confirmed Jack's story!

Funny as it might have been at the time, Hotaling's careless behavior was risky for all of us. Our airmen were issued escape kits that contained forged identification papers, some French money, and water purification tablets. For some reason, the Resistance had given Jack a new card along with more "appropriate" clothing that they gave all of us. Jack was carrying *both* ID cards when the German stopped him in the village.[299]

Our confined quarters continued to be more than Jack could bear. We were never quite sure where or with whom he stayed, but the local people were amused by his attention to Mlle. Noelle. She was a lesbian! For the remainder of our stay in Normandy, Jack's time with us remained sporadic, but each time he returned he regaled us with another oddball adventure.

We were bored. A refreshing walk in the forest was out of the question because Germans from a nearby garrison hunted there. In fact, there were a few times when they came within a few yards of our hiding place. Much to our surprise and relief, they never showed the slightest interest in the building. Sometimes our isolation was relieved by visits from members of the Underground who usually brought us a gift of wine. We were always thirsty, but one day Legenvre expressed considerable concern for my health when I asked for water!

After several days in our "cozy nest," two men arrived with different sorts of gifts—a box of hand grenades and several Bren guns. We tried to explain that if we were captured unarmed and wearing civilian clothes, we'd be considered prisoners of war. If we carried weapons, we'd most likely be shot as spies. With our language limitations, we couldn't fully convey the concept. After all, they carried weapons and thought we should be prepared as well. We ended up accepting the weapons as gracefully as our concern would allow.

As soon as our "guests" left Cavanaugh and I, who were the only ones "at home" at the time, discussed how we might respond if German hunters decided to investigate our hideout. We decided that since they usually traveled in pairs, we could shoot our way out. In preparation for the possibility, we cleaned the guns. They had been dropped by parachute from a British plane, and they were covered in Cosmoline.

As we wiped the grease off the guns, Art and I philosophized a bit. Art, at thirty-four, was ten years my senior, was happily married, had no children, and had left a good law practice behind in Wayne, Nebraska. He was much more concerned about flying combat than most of the younger, basically unattached men, who didn't have the life experience to develop the kind of fatalism Art had. It was in that frame of mind that Art forgot to bring his escape kit on the mission.

When he apologized for his pessimistic outlook, I said, "Forget it, Art. We're going to get back to England!"

As we talked and cleaned the guns, Art seemed to be catching a bit of my optimism. I was so caught up in my pep talk that I absent-mindedly armed the gun and pulled the trigger! I shot four holes in the roof! Art turned white with fear, and then crimson with rage. He wasn't sure if I had shot him, or if we had been surrounded by the enemy. All my talk about a rosy future was wasted. Art calmed down, but we limited further conversation to all the things that had happened at Glatton Air Base, to the missions, and to people we knew, people like Colonel Luper. We agreed that Luper played a pretty decent piano at the Officers' Club on occasion, but that he had little understanding of the young volunteers he commanded. I told Art about my navigational "feuds" with the Colonel.

After two weeks on the Legenvre's farm four men from the Resistance came to see us. I asked the leader about the arms supply we had shared.

"We are well-supplied for an invasion that everyone has been anticipating. Actually, we get another shipment tomorrow. If you like, I will have someone bring you along."

I was pleased to accept his invitation. They picked me up the next day after dark, and around midnight we arrived at a field where we formed a perimeter of sentries. It was chilly, and my hand-me-down French clothing barely kept me warm. We heard a vehicle approaching. Then we heard three shots, and then silence.

My companion shrugged and said with a chuckle, "Probably some *Boche* officer on his way to his billet after a party. No doubt he was disposed of and thrown into a pond."

Apparently, ponds in the area were very useful!

A plane flew in at treetop level about one-thirty in the morning and dropped several large canisters. Then it flew off into the night. We loaded the hundred-pound canisters in farm wagons and covered them with hay. We set off down a road with loud creaks from the wheels. We passed within a hundred yards of a German billet.

I whispered to the Frenchman nearest me, "How can we be getting away with this?"

"Oh," he answered, "Those *Boche* think we're a bunch of crazy "Frogs" who don't have enough sense to go to bed."

The attitude of these Frenchmen was cavalier, to say the least.[300]

The day after the drop, a French-Canadian fighter pilot called Clauterre joined us. He gave us a somewhat vague story of being shot down by the Germans and becoming an "evader," just like us. He'd return from frequent bicycling expeditions and tell us stories of sabotage. We were curious about Clauterre's exploits and questioned the Underground people about him. Their response was guarded, and they told us that Clauterre was probably under surveillance by the Germans. We learned later that

Clauterre was really a Frenchman posing as a Royal Canadian Air Force pilot. The French shot him! Apparently Clauterre might have been a little "loose in the lip" and had he been captured by the Germans, the Underground people felt he would've put too many lives at risk.

I was surprised when an Englishman, John Vallely, and his French girlfriend, Marie-Therése, visited us. John had elected to remain in France rather than join the evacuation at Dunkirk. He became a member of the Resistance. We finally had a chance to talk about our situation in English, and with someone who understood the sense of isolation we felt and how discouraging our prospects of escaping from France had become.

We really had very little with which to occupy our time. We ate regularly, but there were no books, newspapers or radio.

Five weeks after we parachuted into the French countryside, the morning of our departure finally dawned. We gathered at the Legenvre home to wait for transportation. One of the Resistants demanded that Hotaling return his pearl-handled revolver. Earlier that morning, Jack bragged about this "gift from a friend." Jack handed over the pistol, and the Frenchman shoved him to the ground. That wasn't the end of Jack's ignominy. He had also borrowed a sport coat from one of the Frenchmen. When the man asked for it back, Hotaling refused. Major Francis intervened and ordered Jack to return the garment. Jack took it off and flung it aside, at the same time uttering a string of obscenities.

A man named Bernard Neuville drove up in his "milk float," a charcoal-burning, flatbed truck. Bernard was the driver for the Languetot Dairy in Orbec; we were to accompany him on his route. We started off, dressed like farm workers. Our disguise worked. When we passed a small group of Germans, they ignored us. Around noon, we stopped off at Bernard's home where his wife served us a fine meal of hoarded meat and produce from Norman farms.

After the meal, Bernard loaded us into a different vehicle that had a canvas cover, and we took off again. Bernard drove up to the gate of a German garrison where he must have been a familiar figure. The guards waved him through. He parked and conducted some sort of business, while we sat under the canvas biting our nails!

Safely back on the road and out of sight of the garrison, Bernard told us that we were approaching Gacé, the location of the German regional headquarters. We heard many soldiers coming and going, and we cowered under the canvas hoping that Hotaling's frequent observation, *'The closer to danger, the safer we are!'* was correct.'

It was midafternoon when we reached the railway station in the village of Ste. Gauberge where we were met by three Resistants– Henri Beaudet, M. Buffet, and the Englishman, John Vallely. John was there to make sure that we understood our guides' instructions, and that we knew to follow them to the letter. We were to take the Paris-Granville train to Paris, the first real stop on our escape route across the Pyrenees into Spain. We got our tickets and boarded the train without being challenged.

We arrived at the Montparnasse Station in Paris in the early evening. Apparently, the Germans usually paid little attention to ordinary-looking Frenchmen, another tribute to our disguises. We cleared several gates unnoticed. Once out of the station we got into a waiting automobile and were on our way!

At a modest hotel near the Austerlitz Station, we were turned over to three agents of the Paris underground network. We had no time to thank our Norman friends, and our new friends quickly took us to our lodgings. The hotel was a German billet, and we passed Wehrmacht officers on the staircase on the way up. A view of the distant Eiffel Tower reminded us that we were really in Paris! Outside, German troops were having some sort of party, but we dared not leave our rooms.

The next morning we boarded a streetcar for the Gare Austerlitz, our departure point to the South. Rod Francis looked dapper in a shirt, tie, sweater, jacket and felt hat. Mahan and I, as suited our "station," went tie-less, but we did have on jaunty berets.

We were following our guide, *Le Colonel*, when someone said, "Hotaling's missing!"

Someone else said, "How lucky can we get?"

Our luck didn't hold. Jack arrived under the care of another guide who looked very irritated. Hotaling wanted to get lost and spend the duration of the War in Paris, but that wasn't to be. His dream of another astonishing wartime adventure was shattered. By this time, the Resistants were on to his tricks, and they didn't let him out of their sight.

Once on the train, we got instructions on what to do if there were identity checks along the route. We were supposed to get off when the military police entered, then get back on after they passed through the car. The procedure wasn't as bad as it seemed. Frenchmen frequently left the train at stops to relieve themselves along the track. We put the routine to successful use at our first stop.

Back on the train, Mahan, Hotaling and I found seats in an empty compartment. To our horror, a German officer joined us! Further to our horror, Jack engaged him in conversation using the German he had learned when he was in the Army of Occupation after World War I. The officer was delighted. Hotaling's exchange with him continued until the officer reached his stop. He never suspected a thing. I wondered what would've happened if the German decided to try out his French! Jack the Nemesis had struck again. 'The closer we were to danger, the safer we were!'

In Toulouse, we followed our guide at a discreet distance. Something went wrong because the guide's contact didn't show up. We finally arrived at a safe house where a handsome, dark-haired boy greeted us. The house, especially the kitchen, was in a state of disorder. Apparently, someone had left in a hurry. Our guide left to find out what was what.

While we waited, the nine-year-old youngster showed us a tablet containing sketches of airplanes. He explained that his family helped many Allied airman evade capture by the Germans. He proudly showed us the sketches they had drawn for him. One pilot had even given the boy a watch. Before we had time to add to his "art" collection, the guide returned with news that our young friend's father had been killed on a train that had been strafed by Allied fighters. The guide arranged for the boy to be moved to another location, and we moved on to a warehouse in the industrial section of the city.

Toulouse was the "Gateway to the Pyrenees," and the warehouse was the regional headquarters of the Resistance. Ordinarily, for security's sake, we wouldn't have been taken there, but plans had gone awry. We watched as Francoise, the "Queen of the Pyrenees," a woman about sixty-five, bargained with the mercenaries who would lead us through the mountains. She was completely in charge, and used the money delivered to her through Allied Intelligence to pay the mercenaries. They risked their lives for fees significantly higher than the profits from their regular occupation–smuggling!

Later that day, we left Toulouse for a village to the south where me met some *Maquis*. They cared for us until after dark, when our mercenaries arrived. A British flyer joined us, and we six and the guides headed into the mountains.

It was cloudy and cold. We marched in pitch darkness, single-file, each holding on to the man in front. We couldn't see where we were putting our feet, and a step forward often meant a tooth-rattling step down as the ground abruptly fell away.

Hotaling, as usual, complained, but in an ingratiating way.

"This is really difficult for the Major. You know, Major Francis is exhausted and can't take another step."

We had some sympathy for Rod, who wasn't as hardy as the rest of us. The guides, however, had little sympathy.

The leader said, "If the Major can go no farther, then we will have to shoot him and leave him where he falls."

It started snowing, and the clothes we were wearing suddenly became inadequate against the cold. We wished for overcoats, gloves and boots. It snowed through the night, but we continued at a steady pace, determined to get through the mountains to freedom.

At the first light of dawn, we suddenly stopped. The snow had stopped, and it was raining.

One of the guides pointed and said, "Spain is just there, over the next mountain. There is a German patrol in the vicinity. From now on, you are on your own."

At the foot of the "last" mountain, we encountered a wide stream, swift and swollen with rain and melting snow. Our British companion had a badly injured knee, and was having trouble keeping up. He insisted that we move on without him. Major Francis, Captain Cavanaugh, and Lieutenant Hotaling began crossing the stream, but Mahan and I didn't think twice. We helped the Englishman wade the chest deep stream to the other side and staggered up the wooded hillside. We heard the patrol somewhere behind, and they heard us. They took a few pot shots, but missed. That was it. They were probably unwilling to ford the stream and capture us.

It was day when we cleared the border in the valley of the Aran River and stumbled into Spain. Without ceremony, the local gendarmes led us to jail where we collapsed exhausted, oblivious to the stark surroundings.

Spain was a neutral country, but Franco's Fascist government had strong ties to Nazi Germany. The Spaniards were known to return fleeing airmen to France. We knew no Spanish, and our guards knew no English. We were encouraged that we had come so far, but we were not completely at ease.

The village we were in, Pontau, wasn't prosperous after years of civil war[301] and economic crisis, so we weren't surprised that breakfast the next morning consisted of bread and water. After our meal, the guards, brandishing ancient rifles, marched us down a path that led to the main road. Would it be north to France, or south, to freedom?

As we got closer to the road, Major Francis said, "Fellows, we've come a long way together. I just want to say this. When we come to the main road, and if these characters order us to turn left, I'm inclined to make a grab for their guns, tie 'em up, and hightail it south."

To a man, we agreed. We held our breaths. At the intersection, the guards turned us to the south!

At the next village, our jailers turned us over to unarmed civil authorities who actually showed concern for our welfare. They registered us in a small hotel that was more like a boarding house, a kind of a half-star place. The standard meal was rice pilaf with additions of something of indeterminate origin held together with rancid olive oil. The smell permeated the entire building. We were given to understand that the United States Consulate in Lerida was informed of our arrival.

There was little activity in the town and, of course, no books, newspapers or magazines. In the absence of those, each noon the town crier appeared, blew a few blasts on something that looked like a goat's horn. When a small crowd gathered, he broadcast the day's news. After that, he proceeded down the street to gather another crowd. It had to have been a centuries-old custom.

All that stretched before us were days of sheer boredom. Then we discovered a small bar. There was no beer and no fancy spirits, but the Muscatel made up in price what it lacked in character, and the conviviality it generated boosted our morale.

On the third day of our stay, a local official arrived in a stake truck named *The Journey to Lerida.* It was a charcoal-burner, and not as romantic as its name. The stakes on the truck swayed even when the truck was standing still. We boarded and took off like a New York taxi, the driver negotiating mountain turns with careless abandon, oblivious of danger. The six of us lay flat, hanging on to the stakes and one another in terror as we swung out over one precipice after another.

Someone later said, "If we had had parachutes, we could have bailed out over one of the ravines."

Once out of the mountains, we started to pass small farms. Men sat comfortably by doors smoking their pipes, while their women labored in the hot sun. Apparently another custom spanning generations!

In Lerida, our accommodations were more substantial than earlier ones. Someone from the United States consul's visited, and it was cheering to hear "American" spoken. We also got part of our back pay. They put us in a small hotel that had a nice view of the old town and an ancient Moorish castle on a hill. We enjoyed a couple more rounds of Muscatel after a sightseeing tour. In two days, we boarded a bus for Madrid.

Madrid wasn't the romantic city we had seen in our geography books. It had been wracked by civil strife since the late 1930s, and there were few signs of prosperity. People were friendly, but cautious, and they responded to the questions we asked in our newly-learned rudimentary Spanish with the preface, "Franco says...."

We had crossed the border into Spain on 4 June 1944, two days before D-Day. By now our French wardrobe was pretty grubby. Francis Marx, one of the men who joined us in Madrid, remembered being taken to a department store of sorts for new clothes. Our embassy representative took a picture of Mahan, Marx, another new arrival, Serafin, and me. We were pretty conspicuous and sure that the many Germans and Japanese in the city and in the restaurants knew we were Americans. We certainly didn't want to be identified as Allied agents, but unknown to us at the time was the fact that Major Francis and I had been transferred to the Office of Strategic Services. We had been given sensitive information by the Resistance in Normandy concerning the mining of Le Havre harbor. There was nothing on paper, but we had committed the information to memory. We supposed that was fairly close to being spies.

An Army sergeant from the Embassy was our liaison. He was delighted with his assignment in Spain. The bull-fighting season was over, but there was dog-racing. The sergeant and a friend each owned a greyhound, and had worked out a winning "system." Their system, of course, had nothing to do with the fact that there were only six dogs to a race, and they owned two of them. The arrangement seemed to be a profitable one.

After a couple days in Madrid, we went to a small British military base in Gibralter that was surrounded by a high, barbed-wire fence. The many Spanish employees there didn't live on the base. In twenty-four hours we flew to London on a British military transport. The plane wasn't armed, and we were a bit uneasy about German fighter planes, but none appeared.

As we came in for landing, I turned to Rod Francis and said, "Why don't we shoot one more practice landing?"

Rod cracked up.

We arrived in London at the height of the German rocket attacks. The damage was horrendous. At least a half-million people slept on the subway platforms every night. Families set up small cubicles alongside the tracks.

A representative from the Office of Strategic Services[302] met Rod and me at the plane, and we were OSS "guests" for a few days. They interrogated us about the material we had memorized. Before we got orders to return to the 457th, we had to be positively identified by someone from the base who knew us personally. The OSS took no chances.

Before returning to Glatton, I spent ten days in Ireland briefing incoming crews on life behind enemy lines. The value of my information seemed questionable. The D-Day invasion had canceled the necessity for evasion.

Back at Glatton, I listened to grim news about many friends who had been killed or were missing in action. Cavanaugh and Mahan were back home. Mac Dickinson made note of the positive effect my return had on the squadron and threw a party in the Officer's Club.

Soon, Rod Francis sent for me. He showed me a letter requesting a recommendation of an experienced navigator to lead the 1st Air Division. Unless an evadee/escapee requested reassignment or return to combat duty or an administrative job, he was routinely sent home. I chose reassignment back to the States.

Major Francis, looking forward to a career in the Army Air Force, accepted assignment as Group Operations Officer. He was immediately promoted to Lieutenant Colonel.

"I won't fly combat again," he told me, "until my turn comes up to lead the 1st Air Division."

His turn came, and he bailed out once again, this time on Hermann Goering's estate. Allied forces freed him three days later.

On 1 July 1944, I was on a military transport bound for Washington, D.C. The weather was bad, and we were diverted to Mitchel Field, New York. The day after my arrival in New York, I took a train down to DC where I was to report to the Pentagon for de-briefing.

On 12 August, I was on the Pennsylvania Railroad's *Spirit of St. Louis*[303] to its namesake city. Ahead of me were two weeks of leave with my family in Missouri before the obligatory two weeks R&R in Santa Monica, California. The line in the dining car was long. I waited with an attractive brunette who was wearing an unfamiliar uniform. She explained that she was in the Cadet Nurse Corps, a government sponsored program designed to keep the armed services supplied with nurses. She was on her way back to the Washington University School of Nursing after two-weeks leave with her family in DC. Her name was Nancy.

"Two?" said the steward.

"Yes," I answered.

And we had dinner together. When I told her that our plane had gone down on a mission to Nancy, France, she became very interested. Her grandfather had been born there!

I spent the first part of my leave in Farmington, Missouri, where I told my sister I had just met the girl I was going to marry. I spent the second part in Saint Louis proposing to Nancy. We were married three months later on 25 November 1944, at the Canal Presbyterian Church, New Orleans, Louisiana. We left the following day for my next assignment at Alexandria Army Air Base, Alexandria, Louisiana.

In September 1982, nearly forty years after the War, I returned to Glatton with Nancy and two of our friends. As we drove along a divided highway, the flat, foggy farmland began to look familiar. We turned right onto an access road and stopped at the village post office. The postmistress offered us an ancient twelve-inch, cast-iron key and pointed us to All Saints Church in Conington, built by the Norman conquerors in the 11th century.

"You can't miss it," she said, as we drove off.

In a few minutes we were there. Mac Dickinson and I worshiped at All Saints, and the Anglican priest used to bicycle to the base for a visit and a brew. There were ruins of a castle nearby then, but now they were gone, but it was clear that someone was

The crew of the "General's" plane, *Lucy*, the "ancient" B-17 (according to Earl Woodard) issued to the model crew of the 457th. Photo taken in Rapid City. The first crew is: Front row: (lr) Leahy, Mahan, Sarico, Woyurka, Webber, Free. Back Roq (lr) Namar, Woodard, Blackwell, Dickinson (pilot).

Photo taken at Ephrata/Wendover while Earl Woodard trained. Top row (lr): Captain Clark, Squadron Commander, Mac Dickinson, Blackwell. Bottom left: Woodard, Naiman.

22 February 1944. Earl Woodard's crew on the day of its first combat mission over Oscherschleben, Germany. Front row, left to right: Major Haggard (457th Bomb Group surgeon); Lieutenant Bender, pilot; Colonel Luper (group commander). Rear, left to right: Leahy, Munroe "Jack" Hotaling (Group Gunnery officer); English (second navigator); Fuller, Woodard, Hammersly (copilot); Sarico. Not pictured, Sergeant Free. The three B-17 "Rene's" were named after Colonel Luper's wife. Earl Woodard collection.

The lead crew of the mission over Sorau, Germany (11 April 1944). Front row: Webber, Cavanaugh, Bender, Free. Rear: Francis, Leahy, Earl Woodard, Mahan.

(GPR-10-1-457)(8-3-44)(CAPT J. M. DICKINSON)

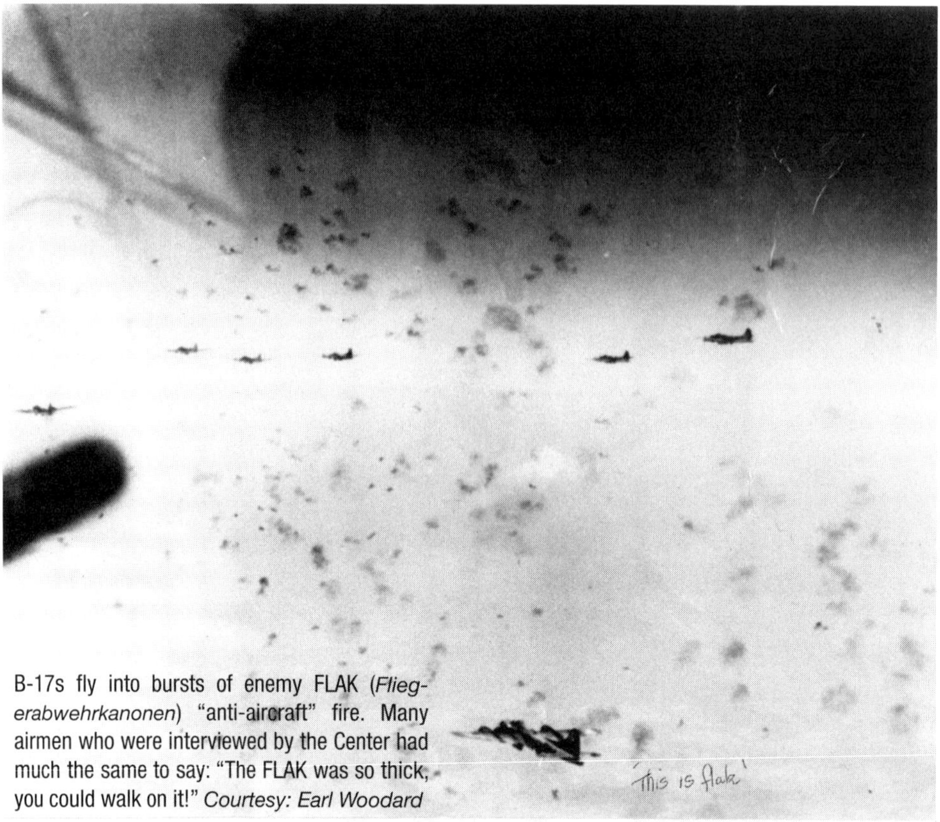

B-17s fly into bursts of enemy FLAK (*Flieg-erabwehrkanonen*) "anti-aircraft" fire. Many airmen who were interviewed by the Center had much the same to say: "The FLAK was so thick, you could walk on it!" *Courtesy: Earl Woodard*

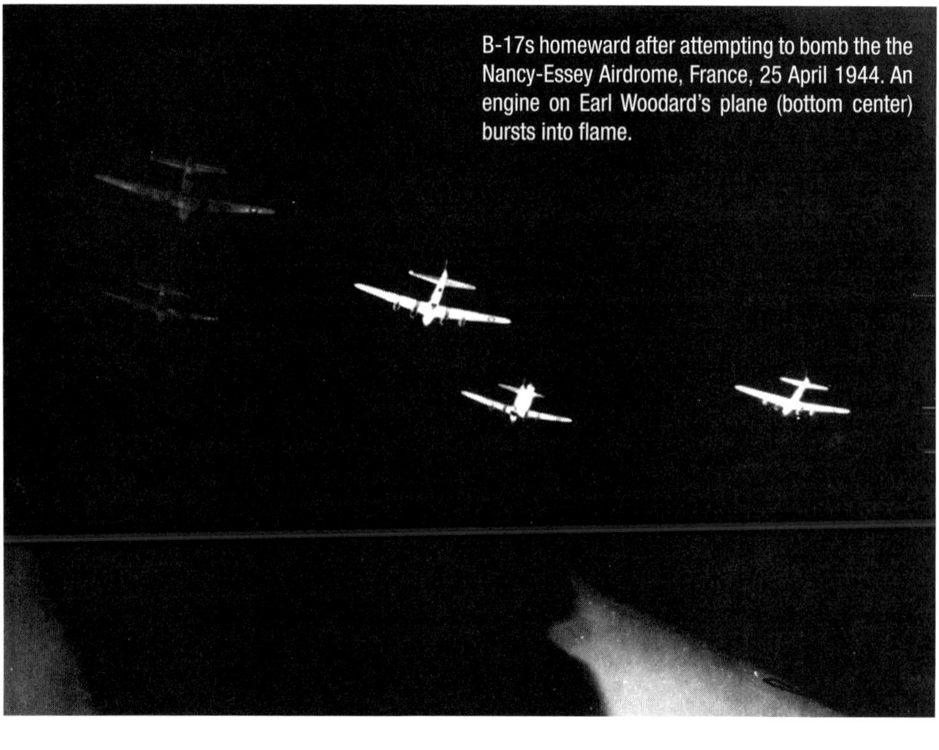

B-17s homeward after attempting to bomb the the Nancy-Essey Airdrome, France, 25 April 1944. An engine on Earl Woodard's plane (bottom center) bursts into flame.

A parachute (lower center) opens from Earl Woodard's stricken bomber 42-97070 as it drops out of formation. All of the crew made it safely out of the plane. Five evaded capture and returned to England. The rest became POWs. *Courtesy: Earl Woodard.*

What the well-dressed evadees were wearing in Madrid, Spain, 1944. Dressed in hand-me-downs from the French Resistance (lr) Layman Mahan, Francis Marx, Earl Woodard, Raymond Serafin. June 1944. *Courtesy: Earl Woodard.*

taking great care preserving the church. The huge key the postmistress gave us easily opened the door. The sanctuary was lined with the same stone figures that reclined atop tombs. The marble memorial plaques still on the walls. Touches of care were everywhere—shining wood, swept floors, fresh flowers.

We found the memorial to the lost men of the 457th. Bright white and still new, it stood in the churchyard among tilted, algae-covered tombstones. On the stone's top was the bust of a young airman, the chin strap of his helmet unfastened. He faced west, toward home.

Just below, framed in laurel, were the words, *Fait Accompli*, 'It is done.'

And beneath that, "Lest we forget. In perpetual memory of those valiant American airman of the 457th Bombardment Group (H) who during World War II gave their lives that freedom might prevail."

As I read the inscription, the song we used to sing came back to me: "There'll be blue birds over the white cliffs of Dover, when the world is free."

There wasn't a sign of Glatton Air Base. We drove a bit farther down the road. On the left, between a misty row of trees where cattle were grazing, I spotted a long strip of concrete. Somewhere in the recess of memory I heard the whine then roar of engines coming alive. It was only a memory.[304]

The monument to the American fliers who flew out of Glatton Air Force Base. *Courtesy of Earl Woodard.*

All Saints Church in Conington

Remains of War:

from the collection of Gottfried Pletzer

A line of heavy caliber artillery-shells. Though these are live shells, many duds still lay buried in the earth and still pose a danger more than sixty years later.

A GI sits atop a German railway gun. The German Army had several types of varying large caliber. Some of them became known to the Allies as "Karl." "Dora," and "Anzio Annie."

Junkers Ju.88, the mainstay of the Luftwaffe. It served in multiple roles: bomber, night-fighter, reconnaissance plane, torpedo plane. German industry turned out 16,000 during the war in dozens of models.

Heinkel He.111. One of the Luftwaffe bombers designed first as a civil aircraft, but German industry produced 7,000 bomber versions during the war. When unchallenged, as at Guernica during the Spanish Civil War, and early in the war over Poland and France, they were a formidable weapon. During the Battle of Britain, against Hurricanes and Spitfires of the RAF, they required substantial fighter escorts.

Junkers Ju87 "Stuka," acronym for Sturzkampfflugzeug "dive bomber." German industry built 5,700 of these feared weapons during the war. It was designed by Hermann Pohlmann, and was in part inspired by the early versions of the American Hell Diver after Ernst Udet, later General, saw a demonstration during a visit to the United States in the early 1930s. Effective at first, it was slow and no match for Allied fighter planes. It was, however, when mounted with two, 37mm cannon under the wings, a very effective on the Eastern Front as a tank-destroyer.

Messerschmitt Me 262. Fortunately for the Allies, Hitler insisted in using it as a bomber. Germany built more than 1,400 during the war, but lack of fuel kept them from playing a decisive part.

Messerschmitt Bf 110. Luftwaffe Chief Hermann Goering's disappointing Zerstorer 'Destroyer,' pictured here as a radar-carrying night fighter, a role in which it had some success. Germany produced over 6,000 in several models.

Messerschmitt Me 410, successor of the Bf 110, and Me 210. It was a fighter-bomber of less than outstanding quality.

Junkers Ju.52 Tri-motor. Designed as a civil transport, the Junkers served as Germany's main transport aircraft throughout the war, carrying ground and airborne troops, supplies, and it served as Hitler's personal aircraft. They were vulnerable targets, and many were lost over the Mediterranean Sea hoping to supply Rommel's Afrika Korps.

A miscellaneous collection of Luftawaffe aircraft at a collection point.

A twin-boomed, Focke Wulf FW 189-1, a ground-support reconnaissance plane nicknamed "The Flying Eye."

One of twenty-four variants of the SdKfz leichter Zugkraftwagen, a half-track. This one is the SdKfz 251/21 with three machine-guns to be used agains low-flying aircraft.

Self-propelled howitzer.

Draw!. Gottfried Pletzer sits astride a German large-caliber howitzer.

Panzer Mainstay. A knocked-out German "Panther" tank, a mainstay of German armored forces.

The grave of a German soldier.

Epilogue

Not Even Half the Story

Major John C. Wilmes
United States Marine Corps
Post Office, Fleet Marine Force
I Amphibious Corps
III Amphibious Corps
Born in Jeannette, Pennsylvania, 24 April 1905
†1983

— *David Wilmes*
Fellow, SVC-CNAS
Hackettstown, New Jersey 18 December 2006

I know very little about what my grandfather did in World War II. I have spoken with and interviewed hundreds of veterans over the years. Their stories I know very well, but my own grandfather's story will remain largely untold. He was much older than most who served. He was already thirty-six-years old when the United States entered the War. He had four daughters at home and a son who would be born in 1942. He had an established career in the US Postal Service as a Postal Inspector for the Philadelphia Division. He had a home and a place in the community of Greensburg, Pennsylvania. Perhaps he didn't have to go to war. However, the conflict that became World War II was all-encompassing. Everyone became involved in some manner. My grandfather, despite all the mitigating factors that could have kept him out of the military, heard the call to serve.

His work as a Postal Inspector in civilian life carried over into the military. He joined the Marine Corps in September 1942 and was commissioned a captain in the Marine Corps Reserve. Later, rising to the rank of major, my grandfather became a Postal Officer with the Fleet Marine Force. At first he was stationed in San Diego at the Headquarters of the Marine Corps Base. Then he went to the South Pacific as a Postal Officer attached to the I Marine Amphibious Corps and later the III Amphibious Corps. His primary job was to make sure the Marines and naval personnel got their mail from home and also made sure that their mail was routed stateside. He carried out his job efficiently and received several commendations from the Marine Corps brass. Most notably, the Commanding General of the 5th Marine Division, Lieutenant General Keller E. Rockey, singled out my grandfather for his "valued assistance" and "efficient distribution of mail for this Division and proved an important factor in connection with the excellent postal service during the recently completed operation."

These sentiments were reiterated in an endorsement by General Holland "Howling Mad" Smith, the Fleet Marine Force Commanding General. The dates on these correspondences are 1 and 9 April 1945, respectively, and the "recently completed operation" General Rockey mentions was the Battle of Iwo Jima.

Among my grandfather's papers is a newspaper clipping of the flag raising on Iwo Jima. Yellowed and musty with age, this iconic symbol tucked away for more than fifty years in a box along with nearly everything else I have gathered of my grandfather's, pays silent testimony to a service I wish I knew more about.

There are other artifacts which intrigue me even more. A single strand of palm taped to a manila folder with "Palm Sunday 1944, Guadalcanal" written beneath it makes me wonder about the places my grandfather went to in the Pacific, and what he saw there. I know he came down with malaria at one point (along with nearly everyone else I spoke with who served in the South Pacific in World War II). He had bouts of malaria thereafter for most of his life. I also know he was aboard a transport vessel, the USS *George Clymer* in March of 1944, perhaps on his way to Guadalcanal. I still have among his papers the radio news broadcasts that were printed out onboard the *Clymer*. Among the news items are pieces on Mickey Rooney passing his physical examination for the military and, on a more somber note, the total number of United States casualties up to that time.

These are all interesting glimpses into the history of the War, but they do not tell me much about my grandfather. He did keep very good records. Many of the photographs are labeled with names of the officers and men in them together with the dates and places the photographs were taken. But the photographs lack intimate details. I do not know what it was truly like for him. The oral and written accounts that appear in this book are real, personal experiences. I can't have that with my grandfather's service. The closest thing I have is a newspaper article by Marine Corporal James W. Thacker, Jr., when my grandfather was on Guam.

It reads:

> *Guam: While rummaging through the ruins of a building in the town of Agat here several days after the invasion, Marine Captain John C. Wilmes, 39 of Greensburg, Pa. uncovered what he termed the "best war souvenir a man in my business could hope to find."*
>
> *It is a regulation United States postal scale like those used in third class post offices in the States and in excellent working order.*
>
> *Captain Wilmes, postal officer for the Third Amphibious Corps, said he was rummaging through the ruins of a building looking for lumber and furniture with which to build and furnish a post office. Kicking aside a piece of old wood he espied a very familiar metal piece sticking out of the refuse.*
>
> *"Right off I knew what it was," said Captain Wilmes, "and, forgetting my original intentions, I immediately began clearing away the rubbish to get at it."*

"The rest of them can have their Japanese paraphernalia. This postal scale is just what I want, but I would like to run across a canceling stamp," said the postal officer whose post office was the first to function on Guam.

Captain Wilmes, whose postal experience dates back to 1924, enlisted in the Marine Corps in September 1942 as a postal specialist. Following an indoctrination course at Quantico, Va., he was assigned to the Leathernecks' postal department and has held his present post for the last year.

He graduated from Jeannette High School in 1923 and following one semester at Duquesne University took a position as a post office clerk. For nine years prior to enlisting in the Marine Corps Captain Wilmes was a postal inspector working out of the Philadelphia Division.

His parents, Mr. and Mrs. Charles A. Wilmes, reside at 423 North 5th Street, Jeannette. His wife, Margaret, and five children, Mary Kate, 9; Jane, 7; Peggy, 5; Pat, 4 and Jimmy, 2 live in Greensburg.

This simple article is all that remains of my grandfather's personal experience in the War. Before he died, I was too young to even think of asking him about his service. Not that I didn't know about World War II, but it seemed remote and unknowable to me. It never occurred to me that people I knew, even in my own family, served in that conflict. The grainy documentary footage of *Victory at Sea* that I watched regularly with my father seemed an ancient, half-forgotten spectacle. Now, that time is closer than ever to me. Having interviewed men like Gino Trombetti, Howard Symonds, and many others over the years who served in the Pacific, I have a feel for what my grandfather must have experienced. I know that as a Postal Officer, he wasn't in harm's way like some of the front line Marines, but his service, too, was vital. One of the questions I always ask a veteran during an interview is how they felt when they got mail from home. Mail was the number one morale booster next to coming off the front line for a rest. Morale, like any other mechanism of a fighting force, is an important element in keeping troops ready to do their jobs. Perhaps it is the most important element.

My grandfather's service, like all the other veterans who appear in this book, served a function in the War. Whether that veteran was a sailor on a battleship, a rifleman in an infantry division, an airman on a B–17, or a nurse comforting the wounded, their parts fulfilled a need. My grandfather saw a role to play as well and his service helped bring a measure of home to thousands of Marines in the form of letters from sweethearts, parents and friends. For that service, I feel honored to have his story here among so many others who felt honored to serve their country. His story may remain untold in his own words, but I will remember him and all the other veterans with whom I had spoken. They imparted to me a legacy of their service and for that, I am honored.

Captain John C. Wilmes on Guam, 1944.

A Japanese midget submarine off Tassafaronga Point on Guadalcanal. The Japanese transport *Yamazuki Maru* is in the background. The Japanese sub was scuttled by its crew in November 1942 around the same time the *Yamazuki Maru* was beached during a re-supply mission. Salvaged in early 1944, the sub's hull was a favorite spot for American troops posing for photographs. *Courtesy David Wilmes.*

Mail call on Guam, 13 August 1944. Left to Right: Private Kuntz, Private First Class Conway, Staff Sergeant Mahoney, Captain John Wilmes, Private First Class McCafferty, and Tech Sergeant Morse.

Works Consulted

"Battle of the Bulge: The Ardennes Offensive." <http://www.ww2-airborne.us/units/508>.

Bellafaire, Judith A. *The Army Nurse Corps in World War II.* Washington, DC: U.S. Army Center of Military History, CMH Publication 72–14, undated.

Berndt, Thomas. *American Tanks of World War II.* Osceola, WI: Motorbooks International, 1994.

Caidin, Martin. *Black Thursday.* New York: Ballantine Books, 1960.

Coffey, Thomas M. *Decision Over Schweinfurt: The U.S. 8 th Air Force Battle for Daylight Bombing.* New York: Charter Books, 1977.

Cole, Hugh M. *United States Army in World War II, The European Theater of Operations, The Ardennes: Battle of the Bulge.* Old Saybrook, CT: Konecky & Konecky, 1965.

"Colin Powell Biography." *Academy of Achievement 2006* <http://www.achievement.org>.

Forman, Wallace R. *B–17 Nose Art Name Directory.* North Branch, MN: Phalanx Publishing, 1996.

Freeman, Joshua B. *Working Class New York: Life and Labor Since World War II.* New York: The New Press, 2001.

Gilbert, Martin. *The Second World War.* New York: Henry Holt & Company, 1989.

Greisinger, Eric B. *A World Away but Close to Home.* Somerset, PA: The Historical and Genealogical Society of Somerset County, 2003.

"Gusen Sub-camp of Mauthausen Concentration Camp." scrapbookpages. 8 Aug 2006 <http://www.scrapbookpages.com/mauthausen/KZMauthausen/Subcamps/Gusen01>.

Harrison, Gordon A. *United States Army in World War II, The European Theater of Operations, Cross Channel Attack.* Old Saybrook, CT: Konecky & Konecky, 1950.

Heidicker, Roy. "History Epitomizes Wingman Concept." *Wright Times* 4 th Fighter Wing newsletter, Volume 50, Number 39. Goldsboro, NC: Seymour Johnson AFB, 30 September 2005.

Huettel, Steve. "Final Report: The Scrap Heap for Passenger Liner SS *Monterey.*" *Saint Petersburg (FL) Times,* 1 July 2000.

Infield, Glenn. *Big Week.* New York: Pinnacle Books, 1974.

Inoguchi, Rikihei, Tadashi Nakajima and Roger Pineau. *The Divine Wind: Japan's Kamikaze Force in World War II.* Annapolis, MD: Naval Institute Press, 1958 (Ballantine Edition, New York, 1968).

Keegan, John. *The Second World War.* New York: Penguin Books, 1990.

Kocher, Leo, Ed.. "Rosebud, Texas Man Directs Sensational Raid to Free 2147 Prisoners." unattributed 15 Aug 2006 <http://www.groups.msn.com/G511thAirborne/gibbs672ndamtrac.msnw>.

Layton, Edwin T. *And I Was There: Pearl Harbor and Midway – Breaking the Secrets.* New York, NY: William Morrow, 1985.

LeFebvre, Hank. "508th Parachute Infantry Regiment 50th Anniversary Speech." 24 Oct 1992 <http://www.508PIR.org>.

MacDonald, Charles B. *United States Army in World War II, The European Theater of Operations, The Siegfried Line Campaign.* Washington, DC: The United States Army Center of Military History, 1993 (cd-rom version).

Matloff, Maurice. *Strategic Planning for Coalition Warfare 1943–1944.* Washington, DC: The United States Army Center of Military History, 1990.

Mayo,Lida. *Bloody Buna.* New York: Doubleday, 1974.

Ness, William N., Frederick A. Johnsen and Chester Marshall. *Big Bombers of WWII.* Ann Arbor, MI: Lowe & B. Hould Publishers, 1998.

"New Guinea 1943–1944." *The U.S. Army Campaigns of World War II.* Washington, DC: U.S. Government Printing Office, 1991.

"Operation MARKET-GARDEN." <http://www.ww2-airborne.us/units/508>

Papuan Campaign: The Buna-Sanananda Operation 16 November 1942 - 23 January 1943 Washington, DC: The United States Army Center of Military History, 1945.

Parks, Robert J. "Nurse Basic Training," excerpted from *Medical Training in WWII.* Washington, DC: Office of the Surgeon General, 1974.

Prange, Gordon W. *At Dawn We Slept: The Untold Story of Pearl Harbor.* New York: McGraw-Hill, 1981.

"Report of Naval Combat Demolition Units in Operation NEPTUNE." Naval Historical Center. Department of the Navy, Washington Navy Yard, Washington, D.C. 15 October 2006 <http://www.history.navy.mil>.

"Report of Sunk and Damaged Ships and Craft." Naval Historical Center. Department of the Navy, Washington Navy Yard, Washington, D.C. 14 October 2006 <http://www.history.navy.mil>.

Ringler, John M. "The Los Baños Raid." *Winds Aloft, 511th PIR Association newsletter.*

Rottman, Gordon L. *U.S. Marine Corps World War II Order of Battle: Ground and Air Units in the Pacific War, 1939–1945.* Westport, CT: Greenwood Press, 2002.

Ryan, Cornelius. *A Bridge Too Far.* New York: Popular Library, 1974.

Santos, Terry R. "Recon Platoon at Los Baños." *Winds Aloft, 511 th PIR Association newsletter.*

Silverstone, Paul H. *U.S. Warships of World War II.* Garden City, NJ: Doubleday, 1965.

Sixteenth Census of the United States. Statistical abstract. Washington, DC: National Archives and Records Administration, 1940.

Shultz, John. "The Military Career of S/Sgt. John Shultz." ts., private memoir, unpublished, 2002.

Smith, Myron J., Jr. *Keystone Battlewagon: U.S.S. Pennsylvania (BB–38).* Charleston, WV: Pictorial Histories Publishing Company, 1983.

Stanton, Shelby L. *World War II Order of Battle.* New York: Galahad Books, 1984.

Toland, John. *The Rising Sun: The Decline and Fall of the Japanese Empire 1936–1945.* New York: Random House, 1970.

Vader, John. *New Guinea: The Tide is Stemmed.* Campaign Book Number 13. New York: Ballantine Books, 1971.

Walkowiak, Thomas F., et al. *Destroyer Escorts of World War Two.* The Floating Drydock. Missoula, MT: Pictorial Histories Publishing Company, 1987.

Wilmes, David. "Forgotten Courage: The Tragedy of the S.S. Leopoldville." ts., private paper, Latrobe, PA, 2003.

"World War II Aerial Victory Credits." *Air Force Historical Research Agency* <http://www.afhra.maxwell.af.mil>.

<http://www.af.mil/bios>

<http://www.aupress.maxwell.af.mil/saas_theses> (discussion of active and passive radar countermeasures)

<http://www.chinfo.navy.mil>

<http://www.hazegray.org/danfs/escorts/de222.txt>

<http://www.94thbombgroup.com>

<http://www.32nd-division.org/history/32hist>

<http://www.usaaf.net/ww2>

<http://www.vectorsite.net/ttwiz7> (discussion of development of German radar)

<http://www.wartimememories.co.uk/airfields/rougham>

Zaloga, Steven J. *US Airborne Divisions in the ETO 1944-45.* Westminster, MD: Osprey Publishing, 2007.

_____. *Armor of the Pacific War.* Westminster, MD: Osprey Publishing, 1983.

Acknowledgements

The Saint Vincent College Center for Northern Appalachian Studies extends thanks to the following for their role in helping the Center in its work;

Special thanks to the Hon. Joseph Petrarca, Commonwealth of Pennsylvania Legislature, for his assistance in securing financial support for this volume and for the Center's *The Long Road: From Oran to Pilsen* (1999-2001).

Special thanks to Joe Reilly of the Saint Vincent College Summer Theatre for his generosity. He provided the means for the Center to obtain the equipment that has enabled Center staff to produce the fine quality photographs that appear in its publications.

Special thanks to Fr. Rene Kollar, O.S.B., Dean of the School of Humanities, for his continuing encouragement and enthusiastic support of the Center.

Special thanks to Archabbot Douglas Nowicki, O.S.B.

Special thanks to Eric Swain, researcher in London, England, for his special assistance.

As always, special thanks to Patti Dellinger, Gina Nalevanko and the staff of the College business office for their efficiency and patience in handling Center's accounts; to Don Orlando and the staff of the Public Relations office for arranging timely publicity; to Shirley Skander, Faculty Secretary and Ms. Lee Ann Ross of the Mailing and Duplicating for their gracious and prompt assistance in important matters; Mr. Joe Strazzera of Facilities Management and Donna Werner of the College Post Office; Father Anthony Grossi, O.S.B. of the College Bookstore; Patty Babusci, Missy Ellis, Lori Rebosky, Roger Wilson, Jeff Klocek, Cindy Hoffmann, Ian Dunlap, Bogdan Ochieno, and all the people in Information Services who keep the Center's equipment up and running; Dave Safin and Fred Findley of the Communications Department; the staff of the Latimer Library; Dennis McDaniel, Bill Snyder and Fr. Wulfstan Clough, O.S.B., of the English Department who "have that within which passes show;" to everyone in the College Food Service who each year make welcome with their service and hospitality the veterans who each year participate in the Faces of Battle class; to Steve Brown and all of the people in Campus Security.

Endnotes

1. Camp Laguna at Yuma, Arizona, was established in January 1943 as a satellite camp of the expansive California-Arizona Maneuver Area. Over one million troops received desert warfare training in this area that ranged from Pomona, California to Phoenix, Arizona and from Yuma to Searchlight, Nevada. See the Yuma Proving Ground Heritage Center website.

2. OMAHA Beach resulted in heavy American casualties. The official record of the 1st Infantry Division states: *"within ten minutes of the ramps being lowered, [the first company in] had become inert, leaderless and almost incapable of action. Every officer and sergeant had been killed or wounded ... It had become a struggle for survival and rescue."* The approximately forty-thousand men of V Corps incurred over three-thousand casualties, most in the first few hours.

3. Casualty evacuation began with the combat medic rearward through the battalion aid station to the division collecting and clearing stations and finally to the field hospital, usually located within ten miles of the front line. At the mobile units, medical personnel stabilized patients, sorted them according to the nature of injuries, treating some and sending the rest on to the rear for specialized care. Mobile field hospitals moved with the divisions they supported. During the Korean War these mobile field hospitals became Mobile Army Surgical Hospitals or MASH units. MASH units became embedded in American popular culture through the novel and TV series *M.A.S.H*

4. Gusen is situated three miles west of *Konzentrationslager (Kz)* 'concentration camp' Mauthausen. Initially, prisoners from Mauthausen were marched daily from the main camp to the granite quarry at Gusen. When too many prisoners died as a result of the march to or from the main camp, it was decided that a sub-camp would be built at the quarry site. *Kz* Gusen became operational in March 1940. Between 1940 and its liberation in 1945, nearly forty-thousand prisoners died at Gusen. Two additional camps were established in the area, *Kz* Gusen II and *Kz* Gusen III. As prisoners quarried, machine shops were placed in the tunnels. The first of these tunnels was used to produce small arms. In March 1944, *Projeckt Bergkristall* or B-8 was initiated. B-8 was to be one of the largest underground manufacturing plants in the Third Reich. (A similar underground factory for V-2 rocket construction was built by slave labor near *Kz* Nordhausen, Germany.) In the tunnels adjacent to *Kz* Gusen, Me–262 jet fighters were to be mass-produced. By the War's end, some one-thousand Me–262 fuselages had been assembled by slave laborers from Gusen. The three camps were liberated on 5 May 1945 by the 41st Cavalry Reconnaissance Squadron, Mechanized, 11th Armored Division. The area fell under the Soviet sphere after the War and the Russians dynamited the tunnel complexes. The crematorium at *Kz* Gusen I is now a public memorial. See *www.scrapbookpages.com/mauthausen/kzmauthausen/subcamps/Gusen01*

5. In late September 1945, fifteen-thousand New York City elevator operators, doormen, porters, firemen and maintenance workers went on strike. In a city of skyscrapers the loss of elevator service was critical. They struck in protest of the building managers' refusal to implement the wage recommendations set by the War Labor Board. On 1 October 1945 the stevedores and longshoremen in the Port of New York struck. Initially, the strikers were disorganized, but eventually gained the support of the City's large Communist contingent; naturally, this antagonized the local organized crime syndicate. New York Harbor tugboat operators and garment district workers struck. This meant thousands of other blue-collar workers such as postmen, delivery men, etc., refused to carry out their work in respect of the picket lines. Between September 1945 and September 1946 some 8.1 million workers nationwide had been on strike at some point. See *Joshua B. Freeman, Working-Class New York: Life and Labor Since World War II,* The New Press, 2001. John DiBattista also refers to this strike in his submission that appears below.

6. The WAVES (Women Accepted for Voluntary Emergency Service) part of the United States Navy. When the War ended the women were not allowed to continue Navy careers. In August 1942, two months after Eleanor Roosevelt convinced Congress to create the WACS (Women's Army Corps), Mildred H. McAfee became director of the WAVES as a Naval Reserve Lieutenant Commander, the first commissioned female officer in United States Navy history. By 1943, there were 27,000 women serving in the WAVES. Most were clerical workers, but some served in legal services, intelligence, aviation, communication and technology. The World War II military was generally segregated. The WAVES did not accept African-American women until late 1944, at a ratio of one African-American for every thirty-six whites.

7. Navy enlisted women were trained at Hunter College, in the Bronx, New York City. Female officer candidates were trained at Smith College and Mount Holyoke.

8. Ben Byrer served with distinction in the 3rd Marine Division. He saw heavy fighting in a number of Pacific island campaigns, including Guadalcanal, Bougainville and Guam. His complete story was published in CNAS' most recent book *They Say There Was a War.* Ben's brother, Clark, was lost aboard the submarine USS *Lagarto,* probably sunk in

May 1945 by a Japanese Minesweeper in the Gulf of Thailand. It wasn't until June 2006, that the Navy confirmed that a sunken submarine located by divers in 2005 was the missing *Lagarto.*

9. The United States Navy calls non-judicial punishment "captain's mast" or "admiral's mast." This allows personnel to be punished for infractions without court martial.

10. The government awarded the "Jeep" contract to Willys Overland Corporation of Toledo, Ohio, in 1941 after a competition with Ford and American Bantam Motors, of Butler, PA, both of whom offered very similar designs. Ford produced the greatest volume of vehicles designated by the military as "GP" vehicles. Other producers besides Willys and Ford included American Bantam, Checker Cab and Chevrolet. Folklore has it that the GP designation stood for "General Purpose," which was pronounced "Jeep" by GIs. Other sources claim that the name derives from Ford's internal designation of GP for the vehicle, which was adopted by the Army as the military designation. According to Ford's service manual for the vehicle, the letter "G" identified the vehicle as produced for the government, and the letter "P" was code for the 80–inch wheelbase. However the name evolved, the Jeep nameplate survives to this day in the form of a vehicle produced by Daimler-Chrysler Corporation. Armored troops called their Jeeps, "Peeps."

11. The United States Merchant Marine is made up of ships that are used to transport both imports and exports during peace time. In World War II, the Merchant Marine served as an auxiliary to the United States Navy and delivered troops and supplies to the military. Merchant Marine ships usually traveled in convoys and the Merchant Mariners, as the civilian crews were called, faced hazards equal or beyond the sort that many combat troops faced. Their wartime casualty record was among the highest of any group in the front lines. Merchant Mariners, often sailing on unarmed ships with little protection against attack by submarine, died at a rate of one in twenty-four. 8,651 out of 215,000 who served died at sea. Though civilians, Merchant Mariners in wartime are considered military personnel according to the provisions of the Merchant Marine Act of 1936. Despite this, they were denied military benefits after the War. Benefits were restored by Act of Congress in 1988 when only 125,000 of those who served still survived.

12. Davey Jones or Davey Jones' Locker is a sailor's idiom denoting the bottom of the sea, or the resting place of drowned sailors.

13. The Oro Bay area was a staging area for Allied ships, with a wharf at the southern end of the bay, many installations along the shore and gun batteries in the surrounding hills. These were the target of Japanese air raids.

14. The cause is an virus spread by the *Aedes aegypti* species of mosquitoes that usually bite in the daytime. It is a form of malaria and is widespread in the Pacific area.

15. The invasion of Morotai occurred on 15 September 1944. The island was a Japanese airbase during World War II. It was taken by American forces in September 1944 and used as a staging point for the Allied invasion of the Philippines in early 1945, and on eastern Borneo in May and June of that year. It was the base for a planned October 1945 invasion of Java that was canceled after the Japanese surrendered in August.

16. 15–17 September 1944.

17. 23 June to the last week in August 1943.

18. 25 August 1943.

19.13 February–5 March 1944.

20. The 80th Division arrived for a short stay at Fort Dix, New Jersey, 5 April 1944. It sailed from Camp Kilmer in late June, first an advance party in that month and the Division proper early in July. Its training area in England was Northwich in Cheshire.

21. 3 August 1944, D+58.

22. UTAH Beach was the codename for one of the Allied landing beaches during Operation OVERLORD, D-Day, 6 June 1944. It was added to the plan near the end of the planning stages, after more landing craft were available. The 4th Infantry Division had landed off course and met with little resistance compared to OMAHA Beach.

23. See Robert Davis' story in this volume.

24. Ste. Mère-Église was the first town in Normandy liberated by American soldiers on 6 June 1944.

25. The 319th was detached from the division 10–28 August 1944 while it did outpost duty at Le Mans, Angers and Orleans.

26. Elements of the 319th reached the Moselle on 4 September 1944. German paratroopers had prepared defenses on the opposite bank.

27. Mr. Chapman's guards were *Feldgendarmerie*, German military police who wore gorgets.

28. Shortly after the beginning of World War II in September 1939, a POW camp called *Kriegesgefangenen-Mannschafts-Stammlager* (*Stalag*) *VII-A* was established north of Moosburg, Germany. Originally it was planned for ten-thousand prisoners, but at the end of the War some eighty-thousand Allied soldiers, many of them French and Soviet citizens, lived in it. See Alexander Robert Nelson's "The Flag is Passing By," in *They Say There Was a War*, Publications of the Saint Vincent College Center for Northern Appalachian Studies, 2005, pp. 231ff

29. See Harold Dougherty's story in this volume.

30. The 106th Infantry Division was a "green" division newly arrived on the Continent when the Germans attacked on 16 December 1944 to begin Hitler's Ardennes Offensive and the Battle of the Bulge. For an account by a veteran of the 106th see Joseph "Sam" Seanor's story in the Center's *They Say There Was a War*, 331 ff.

31. A specialty manufacturing plant located at the intersection of Harrison and 4th Avenues on Jeannette's north side, during WWII the Elliot Company produced ship lighting units under contract for the Navy. See Hubert "Butch" Gower in *They Say There Was A War*, Publications of the Saint Vincent College Center for Northern Appalachian Studies, 2005, p. 125.

32. The 4th Infantry Division's first assault wave at UTAH landed approximately one-thousand yards south of their assigned beach. They encountered significantly weaker German resistance at this "accidental" beach than what had awaited them at their intended target. Many men owe their lives to the underwater cable that delayed the *LCC–80* on 6 June 1944. Gordon Harrison's account of this incident as it appears in the US Army history *Cross Channel Attack* is incomplete. When he notes on p. 304: "*The thirty-two DD tanks that were supposed to land in the first wave (at UTAH) were delayed by the loss of a control vessel that struck a mine,*" he fails to account for the southward drift of the first assault wave. During the editing process for this volume, when asked about the possibility of his ship having struck a mine or a mine anchor cable on 6 June 1944, Davis emphatically stated that his ship's propellers had been fouled by a horizontal underwater cable; *LCC–80* sustained no damage from an exploding mine. *LCC-80* was Red Sector Secondary Control Vessel. Red Sector's Primary Control Vessel, *PC-1261*, became a casualty some eight-thousand yards from the beach when she struck a mine and sank **after** *LCC-80* fouled her screws. Thus, the first wave at UTAH made their way to the beach basically unassisted. The loss of both Red Sector control craft for between 35- and 45-minutes, along with smoke from offshore bombardment that obscured many landmarks, caused the assault troops to drift southward and land in relative safety. See "Report of Naval Combat Demolition Units" and "Report of Sunk and Damaged Ships and Craft," *Naval Historical Center*, Department of the Navy. Other accounts corroborate Davis'. '*The ships in the transport area were completely free of interference from enemy batteries. The LCVPs and LCAs, of the first waves, were loaded from the transports and marshaled without difficulty. All except DD tanks started on their journey to the line of departure on time. The journey toward the shore was almost completely free of enemy interference. The assault landing craft were to have been guided and shepherded to the line of departure by two control vessels in each sector. Unfortunately, Red Secondary Control vessel (LCC–80) was disabled by fouling her screw before the assault waves left the transport area. Red Primary Control Vessel (PC–1261) none the less took the assault waves in.*" Historical Section, COMNAVEU. *Administrative History of U.S. Naval Forces in Europe, 1940–1946.* vol. 5. (London, 1946) [This manuscript, identified as *U.S. Naval Administrative History of World War II #147,* is located in the Navy Department Library's Rare Book Room.] Indexed at the U.S. Naval War College, Newport, R.I., in connection with the preparation of S.E. Morrison's *History of U.S. Naval Operations in World War II,* Volume XI, by Roger F. Schofield, YN1, USN, 9 December 1954.

33. For detailed accounts of these events and other events involving elements of the division see the following Publications of the Saint Vincent College Center for Northern Appalachian Studies: Richard R. "Doc" Buchanan, *Men of the 704: The Pictorial and Spoken History of the 704th Tank Destroyer Battalion,* 1998; John DiBattista, "Cowboys and Germans," Richard R. "Doc" Buchanan, "To Hell with the Germans. Drive on Garrison," and James Herrington, "Wings Like Eagles," in *The Long Road* (1998–2001). Thomas J. Evans, "Reluctant Valor," Harold "Hal" Mayforth, "The Rest of the Story," in *They Say There Was A War* (2005). The present volume contains additions by John J. DiBattista and excerpts from *Men of the 704.*

34. Chemnitz fell into the Russian Zone of Occupation and was renamed *Karl Marx Stadt* (Karl Marx City). It reverted to its original name in 1990 after the collapse of the Soviet Union. The city's aircraft production facilities were heavily bombed by the Allies.

35. Simón José Antonio de la Santísima Trinidad Bolívar y Ponte Palacios y Blanco (24 July 1783–17 December 1830) independence movements throughout South America, collectively known as Bolivar's War.

36. Giuseppe Garibaldi (5 July 1807–2 June 1882) was an Italian patriot and soldier of the *Risorgimento* 'resurgence,' or the reunification of Italy. He was called the "Hero of the Two Worlds," in tribute to his military expeditions in South America and Europe.

37. Sergeant Mayforth's story appears in *They Say There Was a War*, pp. 205 ff.

38. Otto Skorzeny (12 June 1908–5 July 1975). *Obersturmbannführer*, Waffen–SS, who rescued Mussolini in a daring raid on a hilltop where he had been imprisoned. At the beginning of the German Ardennes offensive of December 1944 during which the Battle of the Bulge occurred, Skorzeny created a commando plan using captured American equipment, uniforms and English-speaking German troops who infiltrated American lines causing great confusion. The GIs learned to ask certain questions the answers to which only true Americans were likely to know, e.g., "Who was Mickey Mouse's girlfriend?" "Who is L'il Abner?"

39. 36th Infantry Division landed in North Africa, 13 April 1943, at Arzew and Rabat, Morocco.

40. Operation AVALANCHE, following Operation HUSKY (the invasion of Sicily).

41. Most Japanese Americans who fought in WWII were Nisei, or second-generation Japanese-Americans whose families were victims of one of the most horrendous violations of civil rights in America. The 100th Infantry Battalion and 442nd Regimental Combat Team fought exclusively in the European Theatre and became the most decorated unit in United States military history relative to its size and length of service. It's nickname was "Purple Heart Battalion." Mr. Dougherty's comment about them staying on the line longer than they had to is indicative of their desire to prove themselves worthy and loyal American soldiers. The six-thousand Nisei serving with the Military Intelligence Service as linguists contributed significantly to the Japanese defeat in the Pacific, so much so that General Charles Willoughby, Douglas MacArthur's intelligence officer was prompted to say, "The Nisei saved countless Allied lives and shortened the War by two years."

42. 26–31 October 1944. 1st Battalion, 141st Infantry Regiment, 36th Texas Division that was surrounded by German troops in eastern France in the Vosges. The Nisei 442nd rescued 211 soldiers the "Lost Battalion," but suffered more than eight-hundred casualties itself.

43. The Battle of Monte Cassino (12 January–18 May 1944) fought at a cost of fifty-four-thousand Allied soldiers and twenty-thousand German. The Allied intent was to break through the German Gustav Line. The Germans held the Rapido, Liri and Garigliano valleys and their peaks and ridges. They ***were not*** on the peak of Cassino, but did have defensive positions on the slopes. On the peak was the Benedictine Abbey founded in 524 by St. Benedict. On 15 February the abbey was destroyed by B–17 and B–26 bombers. The rubble the bombing created provided ideal defensive positions for the Germans and two days after the attack, German paratroops poured in to the ruins.

44. 15 August 1944, as part of the American 6th Army Group, the 36th Division made another assault landing against light opposition in the Saint-Raphaël-Fréjus area of southern France in Operation DRAGOON.

45. 23–25 August 1944

46. Joseph Ernest King, Commander-in-Chief United States Fleet and Chief of Naval Operations. He was the first and only individual to hold that combined position. Promoted to the newly- created rank of Fleet Admiral in 1944, he retired in 1945.

47. The Pepsi-Cola Canteen was one of many such places of entertainment for servicemen created during World War II. The most famous was the Hollywood Canteen where entertainment celebrities mingled and danced with those in uniform.

48. Jonathan Mayhew Wainwright IV, Allied commander in the Philippines after Douglas MacArthur was ordered to evacuate in the face of Japanese attack. He became a prisoner of the Japanese and was liberated after the War. He was awarded the Medal of Honor and was present at the signing of the Japanese surrender.

49. On 6 September 1880, the United States War Department established the Dover Powder Depot, and within four days changed its name to the Picatinny Powder Depot. World War II caused the arsenal to curtail research and concentrate on the manufacture of munitions. During the War, the arsenal employed eighteen-thousand people, ran three shifts and turned out bombs and artillery shells. By 1944, it had developed a delay fuse for skip-bombing and special bombs for dams and oil fields.

50. The USS *California* was damaged at Pearl Harbor and repaired. The ship's newsletter comments: *"The seventh of December, forty one, was a day of humiliation and of resolution. After many months of repairs, reconstruction and modernization in the Navy Yards of Pearl Harbor and Bremerton, the resolution was fulfilled. The new California, more efficient and powerful than ever before, took to sea. Off Long Beach, California, she felt the sun and the spray again; she shook down her modern equipment, tested her new armament, trained her new officers and men and headed for the showdown. At Pearl Harbor she tied up again at "Fox-3," the very spot of her humiliation. The fleet at anchor and forces ashore gave her a grand welcome. Admiral Nimitz greeted the now potent 'Ghost Ship,' and soon sent us orders for our first operation. The showdown was nearer."*

51. 6 January 1945. From the ship's newsletter *The Cub: "Lingayen Gulf was by far the scene of our toughest fight. Because of the imminence of renewed enemy attack, we buried our dead shipmates in the gulf and returned before daylight to continue the fight. Three weeks later the Kamikazes had quit, and we headed for Ulithi where, on the 28th of January, we celebrated a Requiem Mass and memorial service topside for our honored dead. Thence to Pearl Harbor and then to Puget Sound Navy Yard for much needed repairs."*

52. Mitchel Field got its name on 16 July 1918, when it was named for Maj. John Purroy Mitchel, a former mayor of New York who was killed ten days earlier in a training flight in Louisiana. It has been mistakenly assumed that the field was named after General Billy Mitchell.

53. The 672nd Tank Destroyer Battalion (Self-Propelled) was redesignated the 672nd Amphibian Tractor Battalion (Separate) on 15 April 1944. Army TO&E specified each amphibian tractor battalion to have twenty officers, two warrant officers, five-hundred enlisted men, 119 Landing Vehicle, Tracked (Combat) and twelve 2-1/2 ton trucks. See Shelby L. Stanton's *World War Two Order of Battle,* Galahad Books, New York, 1984.

54. Lieutenant Colonel Joseph Weldon Gibbs of Rosebud, TX, graduated Texas A&M University 1932, entered active Army service in 1941 as a first lieutenant. Retired as a full colonel and died in Texas on 8 January 1965. From undated Associated Press news article found on Internet web site: groups.msn.com/G511thAirborne/gibbs672ndamtrac.msnw, maintained by a 511th PIR-affiliated archivist, Leo Kocher.

55. The 672nd was equipped with the LVT–4. First deployed in 1943, the –4 variant was known alternately as an "alligator" or a "water buffalo." More than 8,300 LVT–4s were built by the Food Machinery Corporation (FMC) from a total production run of 18,600 tracs. LVTs had drive trains from M3 Lee/Grant medium tanks and 7-cylinder, 4-cycle radial gasoline engines supplied by Continental.

56. The SS *Monterey* was a civilian cruise liner built by Bethlehem Steel of Quincy, MA in 1931. First used to ply the South Pacific passenger route from San Francisco to Australia, in 1941 the *Monterey* was chartered by the Marines to rescue American citizens stranded in the Far East. She was then employed throughout the War on both oceans as a troop transport. Sold and renamed numerous times following the War, the *Monterey* was finally scheduled to be scrapped in 2000. News article from the Saint Petersburg (FL) *Times,* 1 July 2000.

57. The 3rd Marine Division assaulted Bougainville on 1 November 1943 and were reinforced by the Army's 37th Infantry Division one week later, on 8 November. Organized resistance ended after a failed March 1944 Japanese attack, but isolated pockets of stragglers held out until after the War.

58. The 37th Infantry Division began training for their portion of the invasion of the Philippines on 11 October 1944. They broke camp and departed Bougainville for Lingayen Gulf on 14 December 1944. See Stanton's *World War Two Order of Battle.*

59. 3 March 1945.**60.** The raid at Los Baños in the Philippines took place on 23 February 1945. A combined United States Army Airborne and Filipino guerrilla task force liberated 2,147 Allied civilian and military internees from the

Japanese internment camp there. The raid followed the Raid at Cabanatuan, Luzon (30 January), when 513 Allied POWs had been rescued.

61. Laguna de bay. Los Baños itself is situated along the south shore of the lake. Los Baños was a branch campus of the University of the Philippines and the campus buildings were used by the Japanese to house mostly civilian prisoners.

62. The raid was timed to begin at 0700, which was when the Japanese guards began their morning calisthenics. Company B of the 511th Parachute Infantry Regiment, 11th Airborne Division, reinforced with the battalion's machine gun platoon, jumped into a drop zone near the camp from low-flying C–47 transports. The 11th Airborne Division's recon platoon, along with local Filipino guerillas and recently-escaped prisoners as guides, were waiting on the ground outside the camp. The raid actually started three minutes early when a Japanese guard hunting for small game fired at an animal in the brush outside the camp; the recon troopers ringing the camp took this as the "go" signal and began the assault just before the C–47s arrived overhead. The two Filipino Scouts killed were Sergeant Atonacio Castillo and Corporal Anselmo Soler. See various articles from "Winds Aloft," *the 511th PIR Association Newsletter.*

63. Integral to the overall rescue plan was a blocking force made up of the 188th Glider Infantry Regiment reinforced by artillery and Company C/637th Tank Destroyer Battalion, which was detailed to screen the southwest approaches to Los Baños to deny access to the nearby Japanese 8th "Tiger" Division." This blocking force was heavily engaged by the Japanese during the raid, but suffered only two additional fatalities. *See the 511th PIR Association Newsletter.*

64. 2,147 prisoners were liberated in the raid: over fifteen-hundred American civilians, eleven Navy nurses, 329 Britons, fifty-six Canadians, eighty-nine Dutch, twenty-two Poles, ten Norwegians, sixteen Italians, one Frenchman and a lone Nicaraguan were rescued. See undated Associated Press news report cited above. In a tragic postscript to the rescue, several days after the raid the Japanese returned to the town of Los Baños and executed over one-thousand civilians as a reprisal. The Japanese officer responsible for this atrocity, Sadaaki Konishi, was captured after the War, tried, found guilty of war crimes and hanged.

65. Colin Luther Powell, b.1937, City College of New York Class of 1958. Ranger and Airborne qualified, served in Vietnam, earned a Combat Infantry Badge, Bronze Star Medal with combat "v,"Purple Heart and Soldier's Medal. Served in staff billets under Nixon, Carter and Reagan administrations. Chairman of Joint Chiefs of Staff during the First Gulf War. Secretary of State during first term of President George W. Bush. Actual quote referenced by Mr Gazza: *"I doubt that any airborne unit in the world will ever be able to rival the Los Baños prison raid. It is the textbook airborne operation for all ages and all armies."*

66. These "para frags" were the brainchild of General George Kenney. The Japanese considered them to be "terror" weapons.

67. This event occurred on 18 October 1942. Darnton was the first of two New York Times reporters to be killed in the War. Mr. Hiatt explains: *"Darnton's son called me maybe a year ago and wanted my version of the story. We talked quite a bit and corresponded. His dad was eventually buried at Port Moresby. During the War, they recovered the body and brought him back home. He was from Wisconsin. He served with the 32nd Division during World War I, and that's why he asked to be sent to the Pacific, to be a war correspondent with the 32nd Division."*

68. "Knee mortar" was the term applied to the weapon by the American troops. It had a distinctive U-shaped ground plate that the GIs mistakenly thought was supposed to rest on the thigh just above the knee. Those who tested the theory, however, ended up with broken bones or nasty bruises.

69. The Bren Gun Carrier, or Universal Carrier, succeeded the Carden-Loyd Mk.IV tankette developed during the late 1920s. The first production was by Vickers in 1936. There were several different types of Carrier that varied slightly in design according to their function, designated: Medium Machine Gun Carrier, Bren Gun Carrier, Scout Carrier and Cavalry Carrier. They were lightly armored vehicles.

70. Though "Tokyo Rose" (Tokio Rose) was a generic name given by Allied forces in the South Pacific during World War II to at least twenty English-speaking Japanese women who broadcast Japanese propaganda, the name is mostly associated with Iva Toguri D'Aquino (Ikuko Toguri, born 4 July 1916 in Los Angeles, died 26 September 2006 in Chicago). Toguri was born a United States citizen. She was visiting relatives in Japan when the Japanese attacked Pearl Harbor and was unable to leave Japan. She was treated as an enemy and denied a ration card. Refusing to denounce her citizenship, she took a job with the Japanese radio show *Zero Hour* as a transcriber and later as an announcer. She hosted 340 broadcasts.

71. Robert Lawrence Eichelberger (9 March 1886 – 26 September 1961) was a general in the United States Army, who commanded the US Eighth Army in the South West Pacific Area during World War II. General Douglas MacArthur ordered him to "take Buna, or don't come back alive As Commanding General of the U.S. Eighth Army, Eichelberger led the invasion of the Philippines, and by July 1945 his troops defeated Japanese forces on Mindanao.In 1945 the Eighth Army occupied Japan.

72. The Light Tank M3 The name General Stuart or Stuart given by the British comes from the American Civil War General J.E.B. Stuart and was used for both the M3 and M5 Light Tank, in British service it also had the unofficial nickname of "Honey."

73. Nurses throughout the British Commonwealth were called "sisters."

74. Mr. Hiatt speaks here of Gunnery Sergeant John Basilone, killed in 1945 during the assault on Iwo Jima. Basilone's Medal of Honor was actually the third to be won at Guadalcanal, but the first by an infantryman. The first MH was awarded to Coastguardsman Douglas Munro, and the second to "Cactus Air Force" ace Captain John Smith.

75. Basilone Road.

76. The Markham Valley is located in northeast New Guinea. Sheer cliff walls flank each side of the valley and dense, steaming jungle predominates throughout its length. The Australian 7th Division launched an offensive as a part of their campaign to knock the Japanese out of Lae-Salamau in northeast New Guinea. The Japanese were pushed up through the Markham Valley towards American forces in position after the landings at Saidor farther up the northern coast of New Guinea. The instance described in Mr. Hiatt's history took place around in the first part of January 1944.

77. The two incidents that Mr. Hiatt describes are the Port Chicago disaster and the Freeman Field Mutiny. The Port Chicago mutiny came about as a result of a devastating harbor explosion on 17 July 1944 that killed 320 sailors, stevedores and dock workers, 202 of whom were black. The explosion is the worst state-side naval disaster in American history. The black sailors were being used as ammunition loaders who had little or no training at all in the handling and storage of ammunition on board ships. Protests of unsafe conditions by many of the service men and workers, both white and black, went unheeded. After the explosion, many of the sailors refused to continue working under the same conditions that caused the explosion. This refusal led to the arrest of 250 of the mutineers. Two hundred reluctantly went back to work while the fifty who held out were eventually court-martialed. The Freeman Field Mutiny occurred on an air base in Seymour, Indiana in 1945. Black airmen from the 477th Bomb Group attempted to integrate an all-white officers club. This breech of the rules resulted in 162 arrests and three court-martials.

78. Japanese paratroopers in Leyte: This occurred on 6 December 1944. The Japanese dropped seven-hundred paratroopers from the 3rd Parachute Regiment on the night of 6 December in an attempt to aid the Japanese 16th Division in capturing an airstrip above Burauen in Leyte. In the uncoordinated attack, the Japanese were able to create some initial panic among the American soldiers near the air strip which explains Mr. Hiatt's unexpected guest at the front line. See John Toland's *The Rising Sun*, 741–742.

79. General Tomoyuki Yamashita (1885–1946). Yamashita conquered the British colonies of Malaya and Singapore. He was known as the "Tiger of Malaya." In 1945 he was sentenced to death by an American military commission for what was called the "Manila Massacre." Out of his trial grew the "Yamashita Standard," a precedent pertaining to chain-of-command responsibility for war crimes. The legal aspects of Yamashita's trial is still debated for several reasons: 1) he was nit aware if any atrocities; 2) he could not control his soldiers because U.S. forces had disrupted communications; 3) the massacre was carried out by forces not under his command; 4) one unit under his command disobeyed his orders to retreat.

80. First used from 1936, anti-bacterial Sulfanilamide reduced death from infection during World War II. Every soldier was issued a first aid pouch that was designed to be attached to s waist belt.

81. The name derives from monkeys whose pudendas swelled and turn red in estros.

82. Water purification tablets. Thirst made for desperate measures as this account from a Marine on Peleliu attests: *"Near day's end I, along with Moll, Lundberg and another Marine from Lundberg's squad lost contact with the rest of A-1-7. We broke into a clearing and stopped to wait for the platoon, sweating out the night in a shell hole. By dawn, we were out of water and thirst was overtaking us. Lundberg found a swine hole nearby full of a slimy, green liquid that we believed to be wild hog urine. He filled a canteen, poured in Halezon tablets and drank. He looked so relieved that the rest of us partook.*

Not long afterward, the company found us."
<http://www.milmag.com/newsite/features/articles/moll/index.html>

83. Allegheny was a city in its own right from 1840 to 1907 when it was incorporated into the City of Pittsburgh.

84. Ridge Runner was a localism for those who lived near or in the foothills of the Allegheny Mountains. For residents of Derry and Blairsville, Pennsylvania, their "personal" ridge was Chestnut Ridge. For many, the appellation was disparaging.

85. Built by Bethlehem Steel Company of Quincy, Massachusetts, the USS *Massachusetts* (BB–59) was one of four South Dakota-class battleships. She was launched on 23 September 1941 and commissioned on 12 May 1942, with Captain Francis Whiting in command. See *www.chinfo.navy.mil* and also Silverstone, *US Warships of World War II*, Doubleday, New York, 1965. The Massachusetts is currently a floating museum at Fall River, Massachusetts. Her only surviving sister-ship, USS *Alabama (*BB–60) is a floating museum at Mobile, Alabama. The other two ships in the class survived the War but were eventually scrapped in the early 1960s. The South Dakota-class actually had 18-inch armor plate, rather than the 16-inch Mr. Humphreys remembers.

86. USS *Massachusetts* sailed from Casco Bay, Maine on 24 October 1942 and was off Casablanca, French Morocco, as flagship of the Western Naval Task Force supporting Operation TORCH on 8 November 1942.

87. The *Massachusetts* had a shoot-out with French battleship *Jean Bart* and numerous French destroyers at 0740 hours on 8 November 1942. She crippled the *Jean Bart* and sank two of the destroyers, in addition to providing bombardment support to the Allied landing force. *Massachusetts* departed French West Africa on 12 November 1942, enroute to the United States. See *www.chinfo.navy.mil.*

88. The *Massachusetts* arrived at Noumea on 4 March 1943. See *www.chinfo.navy.mil.*

89. William Frederick "Bull" Halsey, Jr. (30 October 1882–20 August 1959) was the United States Navy Fleet Admiral who commanded the United States Third Fleet during much of the Pacific War against Japan, and Raymond Ames "Electric Brain" Spruance (3 July 1886–13 December 1969) who commanded United States naval forces at the turning point of the Pacific War, the Battle of Midway.

90. This would have been a mid-to-late-May time frame, as the *Pennsylvania* was in Bremerton, Washington, Navy Yard for repairs by 2 June 1943. See Myron Smith, *Keystone Battlewagon:* USS *Pennsylvania* (BB–38), Pictorial Histories Publishing Company, Charleston, WV, 1983. USS *Pennsylvania*, moderately damaged during the Pearl Harbor attack, survived the War only to be expended as a target ship during Operation CROSSROADS, the Bikini Atoll atomic bomb tests, in July 1946.

91. "Plank owner" denotes a member of the original crew.

92. Named after Lieutenant, j.g. Robert L. Fowler, USNR, killed in action fighting the destroyer USS *Duncan* against the Japanese in the Battle of Cape Esperance, 11–12 October 1942. Fowler, a native of New York City, was posthumously awarded the Navy Cross for his actions leading to the sinking of the IJN *Furutaka*, a heavy cruiser. *Dictionary of American Naval Fighting Ships*, 1969. Post-battle analysis of Cape Esperance suggests that the shells which struck USS *Duncan* and killed Fowler were probably fired by American ships; such was the confusion during the tense night battle, in which two American rear admirals were also killed in action.

93. Built by the Philadelphia Navy Yard, USS *Fowler* was launched 3 July 1943 and commissioned 15 March 1944 with Lieutenant Commander G.S. Forde, USNR, in command. She was a Buckley-class destroyer escort. In addition to the weapons mentioned by Mr. Humphreys, Buckley-class ships were originally built with three 21-inch torpedo tubes. Later in the War, some Buckley's had their torpedo tubes replaced with 40-mm anti-aircraft guns. Bauer and Roberts, *Register of Ships of the US Navy 1775–1990*. Also, *Destroyer Escorts of World War Two*, Floating Drydock Series, Pictorial Histories Publishing Company, Missoula, MT, 1987. The film *The Enemy Below* (Robert Mitchum and Curt Jurgens) featured a Buckley-class ship.

94. The USS Fowler's first convoy set sail on 22 May 1944.

95. 28 February 1945, two days out of Oran, on a return voyage to the States. *Fowler* made one attack which brought debris to the surface. A second attack, made with the assistance of a French escort ship, sank the U–869. This was USS *Fowler's* fifth round-trip convoy; it began on 1 February and was completed on 16 March 1945.

96. This occurred 17 February 1945.

97. USS *Fowler's* final convoy arrived on the East Coast on 15 May 1945.

98. The *Fowler* was decommissioned and placed in fleet reserve on 28 June 1946. She was stricken from the Navy Register on 1 July 1965 and sold for scrap on 29 December 1966.

99. The government placed restrictions on strategic commodities such as autos, tires, gasoline, meat, sugar, etc., and issued ration stamps to individuals and/or families. Exceptions for gasoline and tires were allowed for doctors, clergymen, military personnel on leave, and other essential professions. Production of personal automobiles ended. Across the nation, individual families and even whole neighborhoods joined to plant Victory Gardens in any space available. Children collected tinfoil, rubber, metal, cooking fat and anything that could be used for the production of war materiel for delivery to central collection points. As more and more men entered military service, women left the kitchen to work in factories. The government instituted Daylight Savings Time to conserve electricity. Men too old for service became air raid wardens and patrolled streets at night to ensure that "blackout" orders were followed. Propaganda posters appeared wherever there was a place for them. The heroes of popular radio serials and movie serials joined the war effort.

100. Ironically, Mersch had been the temporary headquarters of the 89th Division at the end of World War I.

101. "Burp gun" was the name given to the Schmeisser Machine Pistol (MP–40) that had such a rapid rate of fire that one couldn't distinguish the sound of the individual rounds as they were fired.

102. In Germanic myth, Lorelei, a beautiful maiden, threw herself into the Rhine after she discovered the faithlessness of her lover. After she drowned, she became transformed into a siren. From the time of her death and transformation, Lorelei sang from a rock along the Rhine River. Like the siren song of Greek myth, Lorelei's song lured sailors to their deaths. The myth of Lorelei is based on an "echo" rock with the name "Lorelei" near Sankt Goarshausen, Germany

103. General Charles Lawrence Bolte (1895–1989) was a World War I veteran. As a major general he commanded the 69th Division in 1943 and took over command ot the 34th Infantry Division in 1944 in Italy.

104. On 3 November, the *Brazil* docked at Swansea, Wales, were the troops debarked and traveled by rail and truck to the town of Porthcawl, Wales. Around 9 December units of the 75th departed for Southampton, England. Units traveling by rail crossed the English Channel on the *Monrovia*, a liner and the *Invicta*, a civil channel boat. Troops landed at various ports in France. Those crossing on LSTs landed in Rouen on 13 December. The Division assembled near Yvetot, France.

105. Mr. Jones had the same hopes as did most of the men, including the "brass." They thought the War would be over by Christmas. The German attack through the Ardennes changed everything.

106. This was the 2nd SS Panzer Division, *Das Reich*. At the start of the Battle of the Bulge, the Division came within twenty-three miles of the Meuse River, but then was stopped and slowly decimated by Allied counter-attacks. At war's end, most of the Division managed to escape from Eastern Europe and surrender to American troops.

107. Meaning "coward." Though trenchfoot and frostbite were common problems during the Battle of the Bulge, some soldiers tried to evade combat by claiming one or the other of those maladies. The doctor's diagnosis suggests this.

108. Even soldiers who drew blood from the most minor scratch were eligible for the Purple Heart insofar as the scratch was incurred during action with the enemy, even if "friendly" fire was involved. Most soldiers knew this, and many did not report minor wounds out of respect for those who suffered more grievously. Some examples of enemy-related injuries that justified the award of the Purple Heart were injuries caused by enemy bullet, shrapnel, or other projectile created by enemy action; by enemy-placed land mines or booby traps; by enemy-released chemical, biological or nuclear agent; by concussion from enemy-generated explosions. The award was denied for service-related disability, such as post-traumatic stress disorder; environment-related injuries in a combat zone, e.g., frostbite, trench-foot, sunburn, etc.; combat-related injuries not in direct contact with the enemy, e.g., broken limb, contusions, or laceration while traveling through combat zones; physical disabilities acquired years after combat; injuries acquired in the process of retreat; injury delivered by a comrade; deliberately self-inflicted wounds.

109. Replacement depot, sometimes called "repple-depple."

110. See Glossary.

111. See Harvey Waugaman's "We Never Forgot Those People," in *They Say There Was A War*, Publications of the Saint Vincent College Center for Northern Appalachian Studies, 2005, pp. 471, ff.

112. 22 October 1944

113. 1–5 December 1944.

114. The town was Metz.

115. Walsheim, Germany, in the Saar region. Around 17–20 December 1944.

116. Immediately south of Bastogne in the Haies de Tillet Woods, 2–7 January 1945.

117. Bastogne was a crossroads town and important to the German offensive. The Germans hoped to drive to the Port of Antwerp thus cutting off supplies to the Allies.

118. The "Malmédy Massacre" occurred 17 December 1944, one day after the start of the Battle of the Bulge, near Baugnez between Malmédy and Ligneuville in Belgium. The lead unit of 1st Waffen-SS Panzer Division Leibstandarte Adolf Hitler (named Waffen-SS Kampfgruppe Peiper after its leader SS-Standartenführer Joachim Peiper) came upon the American 285th Field Artillery Observation Battalion. Having no antitank weapons, the Americans surrendered. One-hundred-fifty prisoners were made to stand in a snow-covered field near a crossroads, while Peiper, behind in his schedule, continued his advance. Immediately SS troops arrived in a tank and truck. Witnesses to subsequent events said that a SS soldier pulled a pistol and shot two men standing in the front row. Other Germans joined in firing machine guns. There was no direct order to kill the POWs, and no one knows why the massacre occurred. Other surviving witnesses, however, say they heard the order *Macht alle kaput* 'Kill them all' as Peiper's column pulled away. Other evidence is contradictory. Some say that the massacre was prompted after someone accidently fired a pistol. Others say that the Germans started firing after some prisoners tried to escape. What is incontrovertible is the fact that Germans did shoot the critically wounded, a common practice even when dealing with their own troops.

119. There were less than one-thousand nurses in the Army the day Japan attacked Pearl Harbor. By May 1942 there were some twelve-thousand. By the War's end, over 27,300 nurses had undergone formal Army training. During the War 201 Army nurses paid the ultimate price. See Judith A. Bellafaire, *The Army Nurse Corps in World War II*, US Army Center for Military History, CMH Publication 72–14.

120. John Godfrey belonged to the Royal Canadian Air Force before Pearl Harbor. Flying from Debden, England, with the 336th Squadron, 4th Fighter Group, USAAF, Godfrey destroyed 16.33 enemy aircraft. He was accidentally shot down by his wingman, Melvin Dickey, while on a penetration mission on 24 August 1944. Captured by the Germans, Godfrey escaped near the war's end. Reichsmarshall Herman Goering dubbed him and his wingman, Dominic Gentile, the "Debden Gangsters" and said that he would have gladly traded two squadrons for their capture. The two wingmen were further described by Winston Churchill as the "Damon and Pythias of the Twentieth Century." Godfrey's decorations include two Silver Stars, the Distinguished Flying Cross, a Purple Heart, and five Air Medals, among others. Godfrey died of Lou Gehrig's Disease (ALS) in 1958. See *Wright Times*, 4 th Fighter Wing newsletter, Seymour Johnson AFB, Goldsboro, North Carolina, 30 September 2005, vol. 50, no. 39.

121. Prior to the United States' entry into the War, Dominic Salvatore "Don" Gentile was a member of No. 133 Eagle Squadron, a RAF unit made up of American pilots. Gentile destroyed 19.83 enemy aircraft. Gentile and Godfrey would routinely switch during battle between lead and cover-man and so became a more effective dog-fighting team. Their tactics were later borrowed by fighter pilots during the Vietnam War. Gentile became a test pilot after the War and was killed in a flying accident 12 June 1951. His decorations include the Distinguished Service Cross, the Silver Star, the Distinguished Flying Cross, the Air Medal, a Presidential Unit Citation, the British Distinguished Flying Cross, the British Star and other foreign medals. See *Wright Times*, 4 th Fighter Wing newsletter, Seymour Johnson AFB, Goldsboro, North Carolina, 30 September 2005, vol. 50, no. 39. The reader will note that Gentile's and Godfrey's kill totals have decimals. This is a result of post-war re-tabulation of all victory claims. The decimals represent kills shared among multiple pilots. Not all USAAF commands recognized ground-kills as official victories. See "World War II Aerial Victory Credits," US Air Force Historical Research Agency, Maxwell AFB Alabama, *afhra.maxwell.af.mil*

122. For a detailed account of the sinking of the *Leopoldville* see Ross Saunders, "I Figured I Had Bought the Farm," in *They Say There Was A War*, Publications of the Saint Vincent College Center for Northern Appalachian Studies, 2005, pp. 301 ff. Official accounts of the sinking are only now being released.

123. The Women's Overseas League was created in 1921 for women who served overseas in World War I in various capacities. Their numbers approached ninety-thousand. The League aimed to maintain friendships among those who served and to offer various forms of aid. In 1946, 350,000 women served the U.S. military overseas. Members lobbied Congress to grant veteran status to civilian women who served as Women's Air Force Service Pilots (WASP). Today, some of their projects include Hospitalized Veterans Writers Program, the Freedom Foundation Youth Leadership Seminars, scholarships for women pursuing studies emphasizing public service, and grants to members with special needs. <http://www.wosl.org/history.htm>

124. Though such collections included tinfoil and scrap metal, it was not unusual for some mothers to find their favorite pots and pans missing from their kitchens.

125. Each family who had a son or daughter in the service were permitted to display a small banner in their windows that contained a blue or gold star. Banners with gold stars signified that a son or daughter had been killed. Mothers formed support groups called "Gold Star Mothers" that remain in existence today. The organization is absolutely against using their group or the Gold Star for political purposes. See: *http://www.goldstarmoms.com/agsm/Home/index.htm*

126. General Douglas MacArthur's headquarters during the Philippines campaign of 1941–42 was on the island fortress of Corregidor. He had made a single trip to the fortifications there during the campaign, but perhaps made no other because Philippine president Manuel Quezon cautioned him "not to subject himself to danger." In March 1942, President Roosevelt ordered MacArthur to Melbourne, Australia. With his wife and son and selected advisors, MacArthur left on PT Boat 41 (Patrol Torpedo) commanded by Lieutenant John Bulkeley. His words "I came out of Bataan and I shall return" became famous throughout the United States. "I Shall Return," was printed on matchbook covers and other PR materials and distributed to GIs, many of who were not as impressed with MacArthur as others might have been. His single trip to the fortifications in Corregidor and his subsequent escape produced the GI song, "Dugout Doug," sung to the tune of "The Battle Hymn of the Republic": *Dugout Doug MacArthur lies ashakin' on the Rock /Safe from all the bombers and from any sudden shock / Dugout Doug is eating of the best food on Bataan / And his troops go starving on. / Dugout Doug, come out from hiding /Dugout Doug, come out from hiding/Send to Franklin the glad tidings / That his troops go starving on!* Harry S. Truman privately called MacArthur a coward for leaving Corregidor, especially since the general expected General Wainwright to fight to the death. Vainglorious and imperious as he might have been, MacArthur was not a coward.
See *http://www.usafa.af.mil/jscope/JSCOPE97/Lutz97.htm The Exercise of Military Judgment: A Philosophical Investigation of the Virtues and Vices of General Douglas MacArthur* by David W. Lutz.

127. *Kristallnacht* (or *Reichskristallnacht, Pogromnacht)* 'Crystal Night' or 'Night of Broken Glass,' 9–10 November 1938. SA Stormtroopers (*Sturmabteilung*) attacked and destroyed property owned by Jews. The streets were covered in broken glass, hence "Night of Broken Glass." Many Jews were beaten to death and thirty-thousand were deported to concentration camps. 1,668 synagogues were vandalized, 267 of them set on fire.

128. Julius Streicher (1865–1946) whose job it was to propagandize against the Jews. He was hanged in 1946 after the Nuremburg trials, having been found guilty of crimes against humanity.

129. American soldiers in fact did kill surrendered enemy in the War, and various episodes of such are well-documented. Accounts within this book verify that fact, as do accounts in the Center's *Long Road* and *They Say There Was A War.* Aside from a number of incidents occurring in Europe and the Pacific, one now well-known incident took place at Dachau and is known as the "Dachau Massacre." Soldiers of the 45th Infantry Division of the United States Seventh Army machine-gunned at least thirty-five surrendered SS Death's Head Guards (*Totenkopfverbände*). This occurred on 29 April 1945.

130. The Sullivan brothers were five siblings who all died during the same incident in World War II, the sinking of the light cruiser USS *Juneau* (CL–52), the vessel on which they all served. The Sullivans were natives of Waterloo, Iowa. They were: George Thomas Sullivan, 27, Gunner's Mate Second Class Francis "Frank" Henry Sullivan, 25, Coxswain Joseph "Joe" Eugene Sullivan, 23, Seaman Second Class Madison "Matt" Abel Sullivan, 22, Seaman Second Class Albert "Al" Leo Sullivan, 19, Seaman Second Class

131. In early 1942, Camp Roberts, California, instituted what was called a Branch Immaterial Replacement Training Center. Soldiers got basic infantry training regardless of what unit they would go into. Many of these soldiers were used as replacements to fill up the ranks of other units. Prior to going overseas, the 32nd Division needed several thousand replacements to bring the division up to strength. At least three-thousand were added to the 32nd just before embarking in San Francisco.

132. As the fight for Buna took place, the 120th Field Artillery trained in Camp Cable, Australia. All of the field artillery units of the 32nd Division did not go over to New Guinea for this first engagement. The 120th Field Artillery fired in support mostly for the 126th Infantry Regiment throughout the War.

133. Saidor Campaign 2 January 1944 to 14 April 1944. Aitape and the Driniumor River Campaign 22 April 1944 to 25August 1944. Morotai Campaign 15 September 1944 to November 1944.

134. Part of Operation DEXTERITY, itself part of Operation CARTWHEEL designed to neutralize the Japanese base at Rabaul. General Douglas MacArthur's forces advanced along the northeast coast of New Guinea and occupied nearby islands, while the Pacific Ocean Command under Admiral Chester W. Nimitz, advanced through the Solomon Islands towards Bougainville.

135. American troops probably called most of the natives on the islands "Fuzzy-Wuzzies," but if they were the "Fuzzy Wuzzy" Angels they had nothing to fear. The Fuzzy Wuzzy Angels was the name given by Australian troops to a group of Papua New Guinean people who, during World War II, assisted and escorted injured Australian troops down the Kokoda trail. "Fuzzy Wuzzy" was coined by British imperial troops in nineteenth-century Sudan to denote the frizzy-haired soldiers of the insurrectionist Islamic Mahdi in the 19th century. At one point, the Fuzzy Wuzzy broke the "invincible" British square, and were so honored by Rudyard Kipling in his poem "Fuzzy Wuzzy."

136. The 32nd Infantry Division was put in the Sixth Army Reserve for the invasion of the Philippines on 27 September 1944. The Leyte invasion went in on 20 October 1944. The 32nd Division, minus the 121st Field Artillery at Biak on New Guinea went into the battle for Leyte on 14 November 1944. They fought on Leyte until 1 January 1945, when they prepared to move to Luzon.

137. On 27 January 1945, the 32nd Division landed on Luzon eighteen days after the initial landings. The 126th Infantry Regiment along with the 120th Field Artillery remained in Sixth Army Reserve. On 15 February 1945 the 126th Regiment and the 120th Field Artillery were committed. This explains the strange circumstances of Mr. Lesico getting to Luzon before his unit arrived. The 32nd Division was committed to the fight on the Villa Verde Trail in the Caraballo Mountains of northeast Luzon until 28 May 1945. Some time in the months prior to this final day of action on the Villa Verde Trail, Mr. Lesico had enough points to go home and was allowed to leave the front line.

138. The first USS *Santee* was launched in 1855 and fought during the Civil War. Its namesake, *CVE–29*, was one of four escort carriers built upon preexisting oilers and placed in the *Sangamon* Class.

139. At the time of the Leyte landings Seventh Fleet contained 738 vessels. Most of these were amphibious warfare vessels not listed in detail here. The landing vessels were divided into two forces, the Northern Attack Force (Task Force 78) under Rear Admiral Daniel Barbey, and the Southern Attack Force (Task Force 79) under Vice Admiral T.S. Wilkinson. Task Forces 78 and 79 each included a Fire Support Unit containing battleships and cruisers, and each unit of these forces had its destroyer screen. In addition Seventh Fleet (Task Force 77) contained a Close Covering Group (TG77.3) of cruisers and destroyers, most of them being vessels of the Royal Australian Navy, and the Escort Carrier Group (TG77.4) under Rear Admiral Thomas L. Sprague. This last—the Escort Carrier Group—was to play an unexpected and decisive role in the battle. Mr. Lukowsky's complement of escort carriers was attached to Task Unit 77.4.2 ("Taffy Two") under Rear Admiral Felix B. Stump.

140. The pilot attacked with the sun behind him, strafing with machine guns. American sailors sensed the attacking planes seemed to deliberately crash their planes into ships.

141. This action occurred 23 October 1944. The "sister" ship that Mr. Lukowsky witnessed being hit by the Kamikaze was the USS *Suwannee* (CVE–27). The *Suwannee's* medical officer, Lieutenant Walter B. Burwell, MC, USNR, describes what happened: *"Shortly thereafter, we were hit by the first Kamikaze. Our sister ship, the* Santee (CVE–29), *was actually hit first, but nineteen minutes later another Kamikaze managed to get through all the antiaircraft fire and crash into our flight deck about amidships and penetrate to the main deck. This attack did not do nearly as much damage as the second attack the next day."*
http://www.history.navy.mil/faqs/faq87-3h.htm

142. Captain R.E. Blick.

143. Jerry Colonna (17 September 1904–21 November 1986) and Frances Langford (4 April 1913–11 July 2005) were part of Bob Hope's early USO tours during the War. Colonna was an Italian-American comedian, singer, and songwriter, remembered best as the zaniest Bob Hope sidekick on the latter comedian's popular radio shows and films of the 1940s and 1950s. Langford was a successful singer and entertainer during the Golden Age of Radio, who also made occasional film appearances. She continued doing USO shows with Hope into the late 1980s.

144. Company D was formed on 17 February 1942, Captain Edgar W. Meiser, M.C., Commanding Officer. On 28 November, Captain Angelo A. Petraglia, M.C., became Commanding Officer.

145. Clearing Combat Diary, Paul Triano: *"The sea was very rough, causing quite a few to get sick. Haddad, Provence, Kost, Bunker and Cancilla were about the worst. Haddad didn't eat much for ten days, and Bunker made a stab for his steel helmet practically every time the chow whistle blew. . . . We were sliding from one end of the mess hall to the other, and a couple of fellows ended up with their rear ends in the garbage cans with their feet dangling in the air. Kearse watched Lanzy vomit in the can and did likewise on the food in his own mess gear."*

146. Auxiliary Territorial Service.

147. *Clearing Company Diary*, James Puchany: *"The following day, the twenty-fourth, we staggered into a line and marched nine miles to Bricqueville, our bivouac area . . . . St. John was christened here with Zucco's urine while laying in a foxhole. Schubert wore Conrad's trousers, while Art dived into a foxhole for the night when a JU88 flew over the apple orchard."*

148. This would have been Operation COBRA (25 July 1944) when more than fifteen-hundred aircraft carpet-bombed German positions. The bombing was supplemented with 125,000 rounds of artillery. Last-minute changes in planning and obscured target markers unfortunately caused nearly one-thousand American casualties including General Lesley J. McNair, the highest-ranking American general to be killed in the War.

149. GIs called these nocturnal visitors "Bed-Check Charlie." This attack occurred the night of 30 July 1944.

150. *Clearing Company Diary*, Paul Triano: *"We were on the road for no more than fifteen or twenty minutes when we heard the Kraut planes. There were three of the bastards! They dropped flare after flare until the whole sky was lit, and they circled our convoy of fifteen vehicles. There wasn't a thing we could do about it, and we were just hoping and praying that they wouldn't drop anything. From the bright sky we heard a screaming sound, and seconds later we saw a big flash and heard an explosion about fifty feet off the road in a field. They dropped a few more. How we escaped being hit is not explainable."*

151. The location of the hospital was one mile north of La Hurliere, France (Le Mesnil Herman).

152. The potent drink was discovered by Sergeant Frantz of Company C.

153. Before this date Mr. Luther's unit moved to the following locations: 4 August, La Cavee, near Percy; 7 August, Courson.

154. General Wharton was killed at the command post of the 28th Division's 110th Infantry Regiment that was from Greensburg, Pennsylvania.

155. See Gottfried Pletzer's story in this volume.

156. Before 20 August Mr. Luther's unit moved to the following locations: 14 August, Sourdeval; 15 August, Les Haies Martinet. From 21 August through 23 August the unit moved to: La Caucella and Verneiul.

157. The area of Sedan has great historical importance. During the Franco-Prussian War, on 2 September 1870 the French emperor Napoleon III was taken prisoner with one-hundred-thousand of his soldiers at the Battle of Sedan. The victory made Germany's Second Reich possible, and 2 September *Sedantag*, a national German holiday in 1871. At the onset of World War II, German troops invaded neutral Belgium after crossing the Meuse River in Sedan, a maneuver that enabled them to bypass the French Maginot Line.

158. The nurse's name was Lieutenant Frances Sanger.

159. The 28th was strung out twenty-five miles along the Our River, which separates Belgium and Luxembourg from

Germany. In some places along the river men had broken across into Germany and held some of the pillboxes that were dug into the hills of the western bank. The men called the place "Siegfried Boulevard" because from many points on the hills they could look across into the teeth of the Siegfried Line. It was the thinnest stretch in the American lines. The term, "Thin Line," is contemporary to the event and appeared as title of a Yank Magazine article by staff correspondent Sergeant Saul Levitt.

160. *Clearing Company Diary*, Abraham and Gene Fasig: *"Many of our civilian friends crowded around the station, and many begged to be taken along because they feared the German Army. Needless to say, this was an impossibility, so with a promise to return one day, we boarded the trucks and pulled away from the aid station. One of the last things we saw as we pulled away was our Christmas tree, still lit, and one of the last things we said to an Ettelbruck friend was, "Take good care of our tree because we Yanks will return to enjoy with you the day it stands for—Christmas."*

161. During Operation LUMBERJACK (7 March 1945), troops of the United States 9th Armored Division reached the Ludendorff Bridge (Remagen). The bridge was only one of two remaining that spanned the Rhine River. The Germans failed to demolish it. Eisenhower called the bridge "worth its weight in gold." The Army called it "the miracle of Remagen." Eight thousand American troops crossed the Rhine in the first twenty-four hours. Eventually, weakened by German shelling and bombing the bridge collapsed but not before Army engineers had constructed pontoon bridges. Al Kormas (*Long Road*, Publications of the Saint Vincent College Center for Northern Appalachian Studies, 1999, pp. 290) tells of the 69th Infantry Division's experience: *"We went up to defend the bridge from German attacks. At night the skies were red with tracer rounds being fired at German jets [Arado Ar2345 Blitz B2 twin-engine bombers of III Kampfgeschwader 76]. The Germans tried underwater men, but were unsuccessful. We then crossed the treadway bridge. This had a sign on it saying that it was the longest bridge in the world. Vehicles were supposed to cross it thirty-five yards apart, but it was bumper-to-bumper. The thing really sagged! When we got to the east bank, we found a couple of our engineers shooting craps!" The Bridge at Remagen* [1969] is a film produced in 1969.

162. The Landstuhl Regional Medical Center, a United States Army Medical Command (MEDCOM) post is, in 2006, often the first stop for American casualties leaving the ongoing operations in Iraq and Afghanistan.

163. *The Clearing Combat Diary*, Major Angelo A. Petraglia, editor, covers the period 29 July 1944 to 9 May 1945.

164. 15 January; 8, 14, 15 February; 12 March 1945. Targets were East Station, Southeast Communications Area, Foridsdorf Oil Refinery and the Obertraubling Airdrome, respectively.

165. On 9 January and 19, 30 March 1945.

166. Admiral Halsey received warning of the typhoon 17 December, after the fleet had just finished supporting MacArthur's upcoming invasion of the island of Luzon. Halsey's ships were refueling in typhoon territory, but that fact was ignored because the area was closest to Luzon and out of range of Japanese fighters. After receiving warning of the typhoon and experiencing winds and swells that made refueling difficult, Halsey moved the fleet to safer waters, only to change course several times as the typhoon changed direction. The weather became so violent that Halsey, on board the fifty-seven-thousand-ton battleship *New Jersey* later commented that the huge ship was as vulnerable as a canoe. The destroyers *Monaghan, Spence and Hull* sank with a combined loss of nearly one-thousand men. The future United States President Gerald Ford's carrier, *Monterey*, was seriously threatened as it wallowed about helplessly in the water. A Naval court at Ulithi blamed Halsey. It also noted that "errors in judgment" were made under the "stress of war operations and a commendable desire to meet military requirements." Halsey blamed incompetent meteorologists. For more information on the carrier *Monterey*, see John Priolette's "What Did I Need a Gun For?" in *They Say There Was a War*, Publications of the Saint Vincent College Center for Northern Appalachian Studies, 2005, 287ff.

167. Serial Number 337804, so new that it wasn't as yet given a nickname.

168. On this day, the 390th lost six crews and nine aircraft.

169. Claude "Art" Carnahan replaced Sergeant Stonecipher who was removed from flight status because of constant air sickness and was becoming unreliable as a gunner.

170. Virgil Gordon made a safe bailout. He landed on the roof of a house, broke a leg and cut the back of his head. Despite his leg injury, Gordon had to climb down a ladder from the roof and into the custody of the Germans. A German woman helped Gordon. He asked her, "Lady, where am I?" She replied, "Germany." He responded, "Oh, God, Germany." Gordon related this conversation when he received a belated Purple Heart (sixty years after the event). Gordon also served in the Korean War.

171. Leonard J. Jarzynka from Illinois.

172. The word (as related to those jumping from airplanes with parachutes) was inspired by the 1939 Hollywood western about the famed Apache chief. In 1940, Private Aubrey Eberhardt, from Georgia, and a few buddies went to see the film at Fort Bennings' post theater. Bar-hopping that night, his buddies asked Eberhardt whether he'd be fearful of the next day's jump. Eberhardt promised that he'd yell something that everyone could hear as he jumped out of the plane, proving to them that he jumped without fear. "Geronimo" was the word he chose, and he yelled it as he left the plane. The sky soon became filled with parachutes and cries of "GERONIMO," and it has been so ever since.

173. Ironically, it was Italian propaganda that characterized American airmen as "gangsters," picturing them in posters in the likeness of Al Capone, and wearing striped suits and holding "Tommy" guns.

174. Lieutenant S.P. Zieff, of New York, who replaced Sergeant Cecil F. Smith. Smith was assigned to another crew and was also shot down. Mr. McCracken would meet him later.

175. 10 September 1944.

176. Royal Air Force and Royal Canadian Air Force.

177. Blockbusters were also know as "cookies." These were eight to twelve-thousand-pound bombs with thin casings that carried three-quarters of their weight in explosive. They were designed for maximum damage, literally to destroy a "block of buildings," or block houses.

178. 16 September 1944.

179. The camp was between Grosschau, Pomerania and the railroad station of Kiefheide, about sixteen miles southeast of Bergard.

180. "Big Stoop" was also a popular name for American bombers, all types.

181. See John Slaney's (RAF), "My Dear Boy! Are You All Right?" in *They Say There Was a War*, Publications of the Saint Vincent College Center for Northern Appalachian Studies, 2005, pp. 342ff. Barth, Germany was a small on the Baltic Sea. It was opened in October 1942. By January 1944, 507 American Air Force officers had arrived. At the time of liberation the camp held 7,717 Americans and 1,427 British.

182. Francis Gabreski, who was born in Oil City, Pennsylvania, in 1919, flew 266 combat missions in two wars, destroying 37.5 enemy aircraft in World War II flying the P–47 Republic "Thunderbolt," and 6.5 in the Korean War, flying the F–86 Sabre Jet. He crash landed near Koblenz, Germany, July 1944, on what was to be his last mission, was taken captive and spent ten months as a prisoner of war. He died in 2002 of a heart attack.

183. From the German word *Kriegesgefangener* 'prisoner of war.'

184. Colonel Hubert "Hub" Zemke was one of the pre-eminent World War II fighter commanders in the European theater. His 56th Fighter Group, the "Wolfpack," was credited with 665 air-to-air victories, leading all fighter groups in the European Theater of Operations. Zemke alone had 17.75 confirmed victories in 154 combat missions, putting him in the top twenty-five of all Army Air Forces World War II fighter pilots. He died in 1994.

185. The Army Air Force replaced the Army Air Corps on 20 June 1941.

186. Lieutenant General Claire Lee Chennault (6 September, 1893 – 27 July 1958), was a United States military aviator famous for commanding the "Flying Tigers" before and during World War II. He was a favorite of the Chinese leadership. After the outbreak of the War, he and his units were absorbed into the regular Army Air Force.

187. The 410th BS radio call sign was "Total," and their aircraft fuselage recognition code was "GL," or "George Love." The 94th Bomb Group's tail code was a white "A" superimposed on a black square. During the period covered in Mr. Muse's story, the 410th was commanded by Rodger A. Stevenson (November 1943 to July 1944), William O. Hauck (July 1944 to February 1945), and Frank W. Bexfield (February 1945 to May 1945). Between April 1944 and March 1945, the 94th Bomb Group was commanded by Colonel Charles B. Dougher (b. 1907, d. 1978), of Wilkes Barre, Pa, West Point Class of 1931. From March 1945 until after the end of the War, the 94th was commanded by

Colonel Nicholas T. Perkins. See 94th Bomb Group Association web site *www.94thbombgroup.com* and *www.af.mil/bios*

188. Rougham Airfield, Station 468 (ID Code "BU"), is located approximately two miles east of Bury St. Edmunds, Suffolk. See *www.wartimememories.co.uk/airfields/rougham.*

189. There were two types of anti-radar devices in use at this time. Passive jamming devices called "chaff," code named "WINDOW," were thin aluminum strips which, when ejected from the aircraft, blossomed into large clouds which tended to drift, confusing the German radar units. An active jamming device, code named "CARPET," was the equipment described by Mr. Muse. It's full Air Force nomenclature was: "AN/APT–2, Transmitter set, Jamming, 400–700 MHz, AM, "Carpet," "White noise." Chaff was actually the later invention, first used in combat in December 1943. The CARPET jammer was first used on 8 October 1943 on an Eighth AF mission to Bremen, Germany. *www.aupress.maxwell.af.mil*

190. The CARPET transmitters operated on the AM band between 400 and 700 MHz, while the most numerous German radar sets operated in the same band between 430 and 780 MHz. So there were instances when the German sets could overwhelm or circumvent the Allied systems. *www.vectorsite.net*

191. Aircraft equipped with radar jammers had tell-tale antennas extending outside of the fuselage. They were placed in a cluster, one six-inch-long fish hook-like antenna for each transmitter. They were often covered with an opaque plexiglass dome, but in some instances were not covered at all.

192. 21 March 1945.

193. This aircraft was Serial Number 44–8509, a B–17G–VE, built at the Vega plant in California. The crew had nicknamed her *Wagon Wheels. www.94thbombgroup.com* and William Hess, Frederick Johnsen and Chester Marshall, *Big Bombers of WWII*, Lowe & B. Hould Publishers, 1998.

194. Supplemental material concerning Mr. Muse's final mission obtained from an article he wrote for the 94th Bomb Group *Newsletter* in 1991.

195. The plane force landed at Kobylin, Poland. *See www.94thbombgroup.com*

196. According to an agreement between the USAAF and Russia, bombers leaving England to bomb German, rather that having to make the long trip back to home base and risk running out of fuel, could continue to bases in Russia or Russian-held territory where they would refuel, rearm, then hit targets in Southern Germany, and then refuel and rearm in Italy, after which they would bomb a target in Germany and return to England. Shuttle bombing was less successful in practice than envisioned. There were three airfields in the Ukraine that were authorized by Stalin for shuttle missions: Poltava, Mirgorod and Piryatin. There were only seven official shuttle missions during the summer of 1944. On one mission German fighters followed the American bombers to Poltava and the *Luftwaffe* followed up with a full-scale raid on the facilities there, which caused much finger-pointing between the USAAF and Soviet Air Force over protection of the shuttle bases. By October 1944, only Poltava remained in operation, and the shuttle bombing program, Code named FRANTIC, was discontinued. By the time of Mr. Muse's doomed flight, the program had long since been abandoned, but Poltava was still used as a refuge base for stricken bombers over eastern Germany. See *The Center for Military History*, "Strategic Planning for Coalition Warfare 1943–1944," online edition at *www.army.mil/cmh*

197. Peter's twin brother Patrick Muse flew his last mission aboard *The Uninvited* a B–17G-BO, Serial Number 43–37773, piloted by Lt. Walter Ullery of the 410th Bomb Squadron. See Hess, Johnsen and Marshall, *Big Bombers of WWII* and Wallace R. Forman, *B–17 Nose Art Name Directory*, Phalanx Publishing, Ltd., 1996.

198. Rougham Airfield was turned over to the RAF in 1946 and shuttered in 1948. The concrete runways and hard stands were removed and the outlying lands reverted to farming. A local citizen's group, the Rougham Tower Association, has recently restored the control tower to it's wartime configuration. See *www.wartimememories.co.uk/airfields/rougham*

199. The planned invasion of Japan. Operation DOWNFALL was the overall Allied plan for the invasion It was scheduled to occur in two parts: Operation OLYMPIC the invasion of Kyushu, set to begin in November 1945; and later Operation CORONET the invasion of Honshu near Tokyo, scheduled for the spring of 1946. Following the atomic bombing of Hiroshima and Nagasaki, and the Soviet declaration of war against Japan, Japan surrendered and the operation was canceled.

200. Commander Charles McKenna Lynch's estate in Greensburg, Pennsylvania, eventually became an integral part of the University of Pittsburgh at Greensburg.

201. James Vincent Forrestal (15 February 1892–22 May 1949) Secretary of the Navy and the first Secretary of Defense. Forrestal was a strong advocate of naval battle groups centered on aircraft carriers. He was opposed by the new Department of the Air Force, whose principals believed that ground-based aircraft could achieve more effective results. It was assumed the conflict with the Air Force together with attacks by the media for his opposition to the creation of the state of Israel contributed to his mental breakdown and ultimate suicide. Forrestal was vindicated by the prophetic events of the Korean War. The Navy named its first super carrier in his honor.

202. Though initially designed as a destroyer escort, this ship was commissioned as a high-speed transport (APD). See Silverstone, *US Warships of World War II*, Doubleday, 1965.

203. Nakagusuku Bay is a bay off the southern coast of Okinawa. It was given the nickname Buckner Bay by the GIs to honor Major General Simon Bolivar Buckner, Jr., who was ordered to the Pacific Theater in August 1943 to prepare the Tenth Army for the invasion of the island. He was killed toward the end of the campaign by a ricocheting shell fragment, making him the highest ranking American to have been killed during the Second World War, outranking General Lesley J. McNair who was killed by "friendly" bombs during Operation COBRA and the breakout at Normandy, 15 July 1944. Buckner was posthumously appointed to general on 19 July 1954 by special Act of Congress (Public Law 83–508).

204. Typhoon Louise, 9 October 1945.

205. Agnes Sligh Turnbull (New Alexandria, Pennsylvania, 1888–1982). Her first novel *The Rolling Years*, was published in 1936. She wrote fourteen more novels over the next forty years. Her favorite subjects were the Scots who settled in rural Westmoreland County.

206. The *Yamato* was a Japanese battleship of sixty-five-thousand tons (72,800 tons fully loaded) built at Kure, Japan. She and her sister ship *Musashi* were the largest battleships ever built. On a suicide mission to disrupt the invasion of Okinawa (7 April 1945), the *Yamato* was intercepted and sunk by US Navy carrier aircraft. She went down two-hundred miles from Okinawa in one-thousand feet of water, but only after being struck numerous times with bombs and torpedoes.

207. Landing Craft Tank *1224* (Mark 6). Laid down, 21 August 1944, Bison Ship Building, Buffalo, N.Y. Launched, 30 August 1944. Assigned to Pacific Theater of Operations LCT Flotilla 34 in the Okinawa Gunto operation, May 1945. Reclassified Harbor Utility Craft *YFU–34*, 18 May 1958. Final disposition unknown. Earned one battle star for World War II service.

208. This type of LCT was known as an LCG(L) Mk 3. This stood for Landing Craft Gun, Large. It is on this type that Mr. Mickley served on 6 June 1944 on D-Day. Other types of LCTs in the this class included the LCG(R) Mk. 3, for Landing Craft Rocket.

209. The original date for troop landings was 5 June 1944 with supportive Airborne operations to begin on 4 June 1944.

210.UTAH Beach was the second of the two beaches designated for landings by American troops. The other was code-name OMAHA. Three other beaches, SWORD, GOLD and JUNO were invaded by British and Canadian troops. See Robert Davis' story in this volume.

211. Operation DRAGOON, 15 August 1944, between Toulon and Cannes. Churchill called the area the "soft underbelly of Europe."

212. Churchill would be attending the Second Quebec Conference (code named OCTAGON) in Quebec City, 12–16 September 1944 where he would join Franklin D. Roosevelt for talks concerning the Allied zones of occupation in Germany, United States aid to Britain, and British naval participation in the Pacific Theater of Operations. The ship on which Mr. and Mrs. Churchill and returning Canadian and American troops sailed was the Cunard luxury liner, HMS *Queen Mary*. William Terry of Little Rock, Arkansas, writes in the Fall 1990 issue of the Arkansas News, p. 5: *"After flying a B–17 to England via Gander, Newfoundland, we returned to the United States on the Queen Mary. The* *ship was carrying a variety of people of several nationalities, including a few returning air crews and many German prisoners of war. The ship sailed from Glasgow Harbor on September 5, 1944 amid rumors that British Prime Minister Winston Churchill and Mrs. Churchill were on board, which turned out to be true. The Queen Mary let them off at Halifax, Nova Scotia. We arrived in New York harbor the following day. We all got a good look at Mr. and Mrs. Churchill from high on the ship decks. He gave us the "V for Victory" sign before boarding a train on his way to the Quebec Conference."*

213. See E.K. Myers' story in this volume.

214. Ernest Taylor Pyle, known to everyone as Ernie, was a famed journalist during World War II. He was loved by the troops and revered by those on the home front for his honest, descriptive stories that described honestly what the War was like. His book *Here Is Your War* garnered him accolades and he was awarded the Pulitzer Prize in 1944 for his efforts. He was killed by gunfire on Ie Shima on 18 April 1945 and was laid to rest in the National Memorial Cemetery of the Pacific.

215. The "Grinder" was a name the Marine recruits gave to the main drill field.

216. The German-American *Bund* or German American Federation was an American Nazi organization established in the 1930s. Formed from the merger of two 1920s organizations, the National Socialist German Workers Party (NSDAP) and the Free Society of Teutonia. As The Friends of New Germany, the main goal of the organization was to promote friendship between the United States and the "New Germany." After a boycott of German goods in the Upper East Side of New York City, the Friends came under investigation by Jewish Congressman Samuel Dickstein, a Democrat, who later determined that the Friends supported a branch of the Nazi Party in the United States. After some internal discord, the name Friends changed to the German-American *Bund.* Though there were many respectable German organizations in the United States, the *Bund* was one of the few that expressed Nazi ideals. Fighting erupted at many *Bund* meetings across the United States as loyal Americans, German or otherwise, protested the meetings. The Bund maintained its equivalent of the Nazi *Sturmabteilung* (SA), complete with brown uniforms and Swastika armbands. See Warren Grover, *Nazis in Newark*, Transaction Publishers, New Brunswick, New Jersey, 2003.

217. Army Specialized Training Program.

218. The 100th Division was supplemented with thousands of replacements from a variety of sources such as Air Force personnel, anti-aircraft units and service support units. The largest source of replacements came from the Officer Candidate School. As Mr. Pletzer suggests, their presence was a bonus for the division because of their education and intelligence.

219. The 100th crossed the Atlantic in three ships: *George Washington, George Gordon and Mooremac Moon.*

220. December 1914, the Ypres Salient. Combatants from both sides left their trenches and met in No-Man's-Land to exchange gifts, food and good will.

221. In late Autumn 1944, the 100th Division decimated the 708th *Volksgrenadier* when it assaulted the Vosges Mountains. The 100th pursued units of the German First Army through the Lower Vosges, overcame resistance by the 361st *Volksgrenadier* at Mouterhouse and Lemberg and then advanced to the Maginot Line, the formidable but ineffective row of French fortresses built after World War I that faced the German border. Attacking into the Maginot, elements of the 100th took Fort Schiesseck (December 1944), one of the Maginot forts attacked in 1940 by the Germans. The fortress, typical of others on the Maginot Line, was fourteen-stories deep and had disappearing gun turrets and twelve-foot-thick walls.

222. In the 1700s, the town of Bitche was home to a large citadel. Over the centuries, it had been fortified with concentric rings of breastworks, concrete pillboxes, barbed wire, formidable mine fields and Maginot Line installations. It had been besieged several times, notably in the Franco-Prussian War (1870s) and in the German invasion of France in 1940, but it was never taken until the 100th incursion in March 1945. 3rd Battalion, 398th Infantry won the Presidential Unit Citation, a collective equivalent to the Distinguished Service Cross, and the entire division became known as "The Sons of Bitche."

223. The farm was about one mile from Legare near Schiessick, on the road to Bitche. The Bitche area was called "Bitch" by the GIs because of over three-thousand mines sown there by the Germans.

224. The town is in Bavaria, Southern Germany. The Baronial family was the Wiedersperger von Wiedersperg.

225. Carentan and the area around it had a number of nicknames granted to it by the Allies during the invasion of Normandy in 1944. Among them were: "Purple Heart Corner," "Dead Man's Corner," and "Purple Heart Lane."

226. The *New Mexico* was a lead ship of a class of three thirty-two-thousand-ton battleships, and was built at the New York Navy Yard. Commissioned in May 1918, she spent the rest of the First World War operating near the United States, but steamed to Europe early in 1919 to escort President Woodrow Wilson home from the Versailles Peace Conference. Later in the year she became flagship of the Pacific Fleet. A regular participant in Battle Fleet exercises in the Pacific and Caribbean in the 1920s and 1930s, she visited Australia and New Zealand in 1925, also calling on South American ports during the 1920s. She was extensively modernized at the Philadelphia Navy Yard from March 1931 to January 1933. In 1940, her base was relocated to Pearl Harbor as a deterrent to Japan, but the *New Mexico* was sent to the Atlantic in May 1941 to meet the menace presented by German successes in Europe. She returned to the Pacific in early 1942 to help reinforce a Pacific Fleet that had been badly crippled by the Japanese attack on Pearl Harbor. During most of 1942 she operated off the West Coast and in Hawaiian waters, then went to the southwest Pacific until May 1943, when she arrived in the Aleutians to take part in operations to recapture Attu and Kiska.

227. The escort carrier of which Mr. Schaffer speaks was either the USS *Manila Bay* or the *USS Savo Island.*

228. On 5 April, the *New Mexico* again became a flagship. Admiral Raymond A. Spruance, Commander of the Fifth Fleet, came aboard with his staff officers. The next day, suicide planes attacked in great numbers.. The ship's gunners destroyed four in sixteen minutes, and twenty-one more on 7 April. Six battleships, including *New Mexico* sortied to meet a Japanese fleet moving toward them. Task Force 58 attacked them with three-hundred aircraft. In the sixty-four days spent at Okinawa, the *New Mexico* went to general quarters eighty-two times and air defense eighty-six.

229. See E.K. Myers story in this volume.

230. The 28th Infantry Division, Pennsylvania National Guard ("Keystone Division") was federalized in mid-February 1941 by Presidential decree. They were to have spent one year under federal control for training and national defense duties. Ten and a half months into their tour, their "one year" stint became "for the duration," when the Japanese attacked the Pacific Fleet at Pearl Harbor. The fierceness of the Division's attacks led the Germans to give them the nickname "Bloody Bucket." The Division and its 110th Infantry suffered a staggering fifteen-thousand casualties in the Hurtgen Forest and the Battle of the Bulge. See Leroy "Whitey" Schaller's "Today Is Our Day, Tomorrow May Be Yours," in *They Say There Was a War,* and Paul Luther's story in this volume.

231. The Louis/Schmeling championship bout (22 June 1938) was one of the major sporting events of the 20th century, largely because Schmeling was a German and the world was beginning to note the possible effects of Nazi aggression and racial theory. After Schmeling defeated Louis two years earlier, Hitler preached about the racial superiority of Aryans and portrayed Schmeling as a symbol of that superiority. The New York Times, after Louis had visited the White House, quoted President Roosevelt saying to him, "Joe, we need muscles like yours to beat Germany." Louis himself, many years later in his biography, said, "I knew I had to get Schmeling good. I had my own personal reasons and the whole damned country was depending on me." When Schmeling arrived in the United States for the 1938 fight, protestors lined the street outside his hotel chanting, "Nazi, Nazi." A Nazi public relations representative did little to dispel the notion that no black man could defeat Schmeling, and that the German fighter's purse would finance more tanks for the German Army. Louis concluded the fight in short order on a technical knockout. Schmeling regretted allowing himself to be used as a Nazi propaganda tool, but he was not a Nazi, nor was he a racist. His American manager was a Jew, and he once hid two Jewish teenagers in his Berlin hotel room. He was exonerated of any complicity with Nazi war crimes by a British court in 1946.

232. Today the airport is the Arnold Palmer Regional Airport. The regular parachutist was Ott Hoover. The airport was founded in 1924 by aviation pioneer Charles B. Carroll. In 1939, it was the location of the world's first air mail pickup by All American Aviation using the system invented by Lytle Adams. A full account of the history of the airport may be found in Richard Wissolik's, *A Place in the Sky.*

233. Of the 2,056 men who jumped into Normandy with the 508th, 995 returned to England in July following a month of hard fighting as line infantry. See *www.ww2-airborne.us/units/508.*

234. Captain Jonathan E. Adams, Jr., holder of the Silver Star, the Bronze Star and a Purple Heart, which he had earned during Normandy. The 1st Battalion was commanded by Lt. Col. Shields Warren, Jr., holder of a Silver Star and two Purple Hearts. The 508th Regiment was commanded by Colonel Roy E. Lindquist, a Silver Star winner.

235. The 508th PIR had jumped into Drop Zone "N," slightly south of due west of Ste. Mère-Église, France on the night of 5–6 June 1944. Most of the Regiment landed within a mile or two of their assigned drop zone, but there were notable exceptions. Four C–47s deposited 508th men 15 miles north of the drop zone. One stick of 507th PIR troopers were dropped 25 miles south of their intended DZ; most of the remainder of the 507th overshot Drop Zone "T" and were dropped into the inundated Merderet River flood plain west of Ste. Mère-Église. According to Harrison in *Cross Channel Attack*, three 508th sticks and two 101st Airborne sticks amounting to some one-hundred men landed within the town limits of Ste. Mère-Église; they were overwhelmed by the German garrison.

236. There is a great deal of dispute among both veterans and researchers as to the precise lift-off time for the MARKET-GARDEN aircraft. Author Cornelius Ryan, who studied the airfield tower logs, states that the Pathfinders took off at 1025 hours, and the remainder of the armada was in the air by 1155 hours. He further states that the first paratroopers began jumping out over Holland at 1315 hours. German sources cite the jump time as 1330 hours, as does the web site *www.ww2-airborne.us/units/508*, although they give no specific source for that notation. See Cornelius Ryan, *A Bridge Too Far*, Popular Library, New York, 1974.

237. This was deliberate. Drop Zone "T," the 508th Regiment drop zone, was selected due to its distance from the anti-aircraft batteries sited in the town of Nijmegen. It was located on the high ground to the southeast of Nijmegen, on Groesbeek Heights. Other 82nd Airborne Drop Zones were "E," "N," and "O." The 101st Airborne Drop Zones farther south, around Eindhoven, Son and Veghel, were "A," "A-1," "B," "C," and "W." British 1st Airborne Drop Zones around Arnhem were "S," "X," "Y" (Polish 1st Para Bde), and "Z." See Roel Kerkhoff's, <http://www.remembERseptember44.com.>.

238. Company A Commander Capt. Adams led a platoon-sized patrol directly to the Nijmegen post office, where the bridge demolition controls were located. Adams' patrol was able to overpower the German guard force and disable the mechanism, but then he and his men were cut off and surrounded. They held out against numerically-superior German units for three days before being relieved. See McDonald, *The Siegfried Line Campaign*, Center for Military History, p.164.

239. Mr. Shultz is likely referring to "Devil's Hill," named in honor of the 508th's Regimental nickname, the "Red Devils."

240. During this period, the men of the 508th were fighting against the 9th SS Panzer Division's Reconnaissance Battalion as well as elements of the 10th SS Panzer Division. See McDonald, *The Siegfried Line Campaign.*

241. Private Paul B. Singer.

242. During MARKET-GARDEN 139 508th men were killed in action. 479 were wounded. 178 were missing in action. None were taken prisoner. See <http://www.ww2-airborne.us/units/508>.

243. 18 December 1944, although some sources cite the date as the "early morning hours of 19 December." See *www.508pir.org.* The 508th was first positioned just south of the town of Werbomont where, on 19 December, they repulsed an armored attack by Kampfgruppe Peiper. See Cole, *The Ardennes: The Battle of the Bulge.*

244. The 82nd Airborne was tasked with strengthening the north shoulder of the Bulge by initially forming a defensive line along the west bank of the Salm River. On 24 December 1944, the 508th Regiment's portion of this line fell between the towns of Grand-Halleux, Vielsalm and Salmchâteau, a front approximately five-miles long. Opposing them from across the river were their old adversaries from Holland, the 9th SS Panzer Division. See Cole, *The Ardennes: The Battle of the Bulge.*

245. Corporal Duane A. Dennison, holder of the Bronze Star Medal, Army Good Conduct Medal and a Purple Heart, which he earned in Normandy. The Silver Star award cannot be verified through the available records. See *www.508pir.org.* The repositioning action described by Mr. Shultz may have been the 27 December withdrawal to a secondary main line of resistance that tied the 82nd Airborne into the 30th Infantry on their left and the 7th Armored Division on their right. This repositioning, which placed the 508th Regiment on an southwest-to-northeast line roughly between the towns of Villettes and Trois Ponts, further consolidated the north shoulder of the Bulge. Between 25 and 27 December, the 508th withstood two attacks by the 19th Panzer Grenadier Regiment, an elite element of the 9th SS Panzer Division. See Cole, *The Ardennes: The Battle of the Bulge.*

246. Adolf Hitler's autobiography dictated to his deputy, Rudolph Hess, while they were a political prisoners in Landsberg-am-Lech Prison. The book became a "best seller," especially among SS troops. The book also included spurious comments on history and political theory together with rampant racial diatribes, especially against the Jews.

247. Charles Lindbergh made the first solo, non-stop flight across the Atlantic to Paris in 1927 in specially-built Ryan monoplane.

248. The National Prohibition Act of 1919 more popularly known as the Volstead Act (Chapter 85, 41 Section 305) enforced the Eighteenth Amendment to the United States Constitution, dealing with the prohibition of alcohol. The Act was named for its sponsor, Representative Andrew Volstead, (R) Minnesota. In doing so, it defined the term "beer, wine, or other intoxicating malt or vinous liquors" to mean any beverage with greater than 0.5% alcohol by volume. The Act, virtually unenforceable, paved the way for an era of violence, smuggling and gang warfare that brought such names as Alphonse Capone and Elliott Ness into national prominence.

249. "The New Deal" was the name President Franklin D. Roosevelt gave to the series of programs between 1933–37 aimed at the recovery of the nation's economy. FDR created dozens of what would become known as "alphabet agencies." The opponents of the New Deal, complaining of the cost and the shift of power to Washington, stopped its expansion after 1937 and abolished many of its programs by 1943. The National Recovery Administration was ruled unconstitutional by the Supreme Court. The main programs still important today are Social Security and the Securities and Exchange Commission (SEC).

250. Hitler came to power in 1933 and to full-power in 1934. Benito Mussolini, the dictator of Italy, had been in power from 1923. The Second Sino-Japanese War (7 July 1937–9 September 1945) occurred between China and Japan actually from 1931, when Japanese propaganda created a series of "China Incidents." The first of these was the "Mukden Incident" that provoked the 1931 invasion by the Japanese of Manchuria and the last was the "Marco Polo Bridge Incident" of 1937 that began a full-scale war, one that merged with the wider conflict of World War II. The Russo-Finnish War, or "Winter War," began on 30 November 1939 when the Soviet Union attacked Finland three months after Germany attacked Poland (1 September 1939). Despite great superiority in personnel and materiel, the Soviets had a difficult time defeating the valiant Finns who held out until March 1940.

251. Mussolini's armies invaded Ethiopia in 1936 in accordance with the Italian dictator's dream to reconstruct the Roman Empire. The Emperor Haile Selassie was forced into exile, but the Italian hegemony lasted only a short time and ended in 1941.

252. The Spanish Civil War (17 July 1936–1 April 1939) was a microcosm of World War II. It was fought between the Nationalists of General Francisco Franco (a Fascist sympathizer) and the Republicans or Loyalists of the Second Spanish Republic (Communist sympathizers). Franco's forces were aided by Italy, Germany and Portugal, while the Republicans received aid from the Soviet Union, Mexico and the international Communist movement. The powers that would later confront each other in World War II used the Spanish Civil War to test newly developed weapons, notably aerial weapons. The Spanish Civil War saw the first effective terror bombing when the German Luftwaffe's Condor Legion bombed the town of Guernica on 26 April 1937.

253. See Gottfried Pletzer's story in this volume.

254. A PT ("Patrol Torpedo") was a small, fast vessel used by the United States Navy in World War II to attack larger surface ships, and it was one of the more "romantic" craft of the War. The most famous was *PT–109* commanded by John F. Kennedy. Less famous was *PT–41* that rescued General Douglas MacArthur from Corregidor Island early in the war in the Pacific. The Hollywood film *They Were Expendable* remains the most definitive depiction of such boats in action.

255. See E.K. Meyers story in this volume.

256. See Gottfried Pletzer's story in this volume.

257. Cebu (containing Cebu City), a province of the Philippines, lies to the east of Leyte. Cebu became a strategically vital Japanese base after they occupied it in April 1942. American forces re-occupied the city Cebu in March 1945.

258. Mindanao is the second largest and easternmost island in the Philippines. It is also one of the three island groups in the country, with Luzon and Visayas being the other two. On 10 March 1945, MacArthur ordered the US Eighth Army under Lieutenant General Robert L. Eichelberger to finally clear Mindanao in Operation VICTOR V, expecting a four-month operation. Eichelberger assigned ground operations to the 24th and 31st Infantry Divisions. The Battle of Mindanao lasted until 15 August 1945 the day of the official Japanese surrender.

259. *LST–643* was laid down on 10 June 1944 at Seneca, III., by the Chicago Bridge & Iron Co.; launched on 12

September 1944; sponsored by Lt. Cornelia W. Mattert, USNR; and commissioned on 2 October 1944. *LST–643* was transferred to the Military Sea Transportation Service on 31 March 1952 where she operated as USNS *LST–643* until struck from the Navy list on 15 June 1973. On 17 September 1973, the ship was sold to S. S. Zee, Taipei, Taiwan, for scrap. *LST–643* earned two battle stars for World War II service.

260. In November 1942, the Japanese built an airfield on Engebi Island that was used for staging planes to the Carolines and the rest of the Marshalls. When the Gilberts fell to the United States Marines, the Japanese Army's 1st Amphibious Brigade came in to defend the Eniwetok atoll on 4 January 1944. They were unable to finish fortifying the place before the February invasion by the US, which captured all the islets in a week. Eniwetok's real significance came after the War, when the residents were evacuated (voluntarily or involuntarily), and became part of the United States Pacific Proving Grounds nuclear test locations.

261. From 15 June 1944 to 9 July the Marines, under General Holland "Howlin' Mad" Smith, fought a bloody battle for the island of Saipan, defeating the 43rd Division under command of Lieutenant General Yoshitsugu Saito. See Lewis Jacob Steck's account "It Was All Luck," *They Say There Was a War*, Publications of the Saint Vincent College Center for Northern Appalachian Studies, 2005, pp. 407 ff.

262. The *Bersaglieri* 'sharpshooters' were created by General Alessandro Lamarmora in 1836 for the Army of the Piedmontese, later the Royal Italian Army. They still exist and can be recognized by wide-brimmed hats decorated with *capercaillie* 'wood grouse' feathers. During World War I they rode to battle on bicycles in support of the cavalry forming what were called *celeri* 'fast' divisions. Their tactics, it was hoped, would be one way to break stalemates in the trench warfare of 1915–1918.

263. For a detailed story about the 10th Mountain Division see Ralph Sperber's, "The Days Didn't Matter Any More," in *They Say There Was A War*, Publications of the Saint Vincent College Center for Northern Appalachian Studies, 2005, pp. 385 ff.

264. The mules would have been in violation of the Australian government's animal importation laws.

265. 17 February 1943.

266. Merrill's Marauders (5307th Composite Unit, Provisional, code name Galahad) was a commando unit in Burma in the Chine-Burma-India Theatre (CBI) under the command of Brigadier General Frank Merrill. In Burma they were outnumbered by the men of the Japanese 18th division but caused heavy casualties. They were in five major engagements: Walawbum, Shaduzup, Inkangahtawng, Nhpum Ga, and Myitkyina and 32 skirmishes with the Japanese Army. The Marauders have the extremely rare distinction of having every member of the unit receive the Bronze Star Medal and in June 1944 the unit was awarded the Distinguished Unit Citation. The Marauders were consolidated with the 475th Infantry on 10 August 1944. On 21 June 1954, the 475th became the 75th Infantry Regiment. Today's 75th Ranger Regiment traces its lineage to the 75th Infantry.

267. Sergeant Thomas H. Conners, of Minot, North Dakota. Conners' death is described in the 6th Ranger newsletter *In Review*, "Ambush Country": *"On another occasion...the Japs laid an elaborate ambush (Editors' note: south of the village of Cabaruan in the Cabaruan Hills, inland from the landing beaches at Lingayen Gulf) for the second platoon. . . . T/Sgt Conners was killed trying to rescue Troedel. . . . Troedel was found in a carabao wallow. He had been hit by grenade fragments in the neck and had received bulled wounds in the arm, chest and leg. After the platoon had fallen back, the Nips had advanced to where Conners and Troedel had fallen. Although wounded, Troedel had the presence of mind to 'play possum.' The Nip soldiers had rolled him over several times, kicked him and as he made no sign of life, left him for dead. When they had gone, he managed to walk and crawl yards to a carabao wallow and hid there until the following morning of the fourth day when he was found by our patrols who heard him holler, 'Don't shoot, I'm a Yank!"*

268. Sergeant Trombetti received the Bronze Star award for this action.

269. See Harvey Waugaman's "We Never Forgot Those People," in *They Say There Was a War*, Publications of the Saint Vincent College Center for Northern Appalachian Studies, 2005, pp. 471 ff.

270. The 6th Marine Division of the United States Marine Corps was a unit specifically created on 7 September 1944 on Guadalcanal, for the invasions of Okinawa and Japan. It was the only Marine division to never have seen the United States. It was created and disbanded overseas. The division was expanded from the 1st Provisional Marine Brigade (containing 2nd Battalion, 10th Marines) and comprised the new 4th Marines and the 22nd Marines. The new 29th Marines were added to the division, as were artillery components of existing Marine artillery regiments (

10th, 12th , 13th) reorganized as the 15th Marines. It fought in the Battle of Guam in July an d August. The new 2 9th Marine regiment was added to the division, and the artillery components of the three regiments were reorganized as the 15th Marines. See Rottman, "Works Consulted" for data on Marine units.

271. The genealogy and disposition of battalions and other units of Marine artillery units are extraordinarily difficult to trace largely because of their detachments to other units during various campaigns, predesignation and other types of changes. The 10th Marine regiment was the only Marine regiment to serve as an artillery unit for the length of its career. Prior to World War II, the 10th was reactivated on 27 December 1940. Its 3rd Battalion was activated on 1 January 1941. The battalions of the 10th were assigned to the 2nd Marine Division on 1 February in Puerto Rico. The 2nd Battalion was detached to the 1st Marine Provisional Brigade from June 1941 to March 1942, while the 1st Battalion served with the 2nd Marine Reinforced Brigade from December 1941 to October 1942. The 10th Marines' 4th Battalion was activated in April 1941. The 5th Battalion was activated in February 1942. In August 1942, the 5th Battalion was re-designated 1st Battalion, 12th Marines (Artillery). A new 5th Battalion was then created in June 1943. The 3rd and 5th Battalions exchanged their designations in March 1944. On 16 April 1944, the 5th Battalion provided its assets to 2nd 155mm Artillery (Howitzer) Battalion. In July 1945, the 2nd and 4th Battalions exchanged their designations. In 1940, the 1st Battalion, 10th Marines provided assets to the 1st Battalion, 11th Marines, where they remained through 1947. See Rottman, "Works Consulted" for data on Marine units.

272. Guadalcanal-Tulagi was the first American offensive (7 August 1942–8 February 1943) in the drive to reduce the islands and outposts of the Japanese Empire. The primary objective of the campaign was to deny the Japanese bases from which they could threaten supply routes to Australia and New Zealand and isolate the Japanese air base at Rabaul on New Britain.

273. On D+1 3rd Battalion, Battery H established defenses on Tulagi. 3rd Battalion, Battery I were on Gavutu-Tanambogo. 3rd Battalion, 10th Marines were withdrawn on 9 August and redeployed to Tulagi on 21 August 1942.

274. Tarawa in the Gilbert Islands was the second island offensive action (20–23 November 1943) by the United States during the War (the first being Guadalcanal), and the first in the Central Pacific. The landing at Tarawa was the first time American forces experienced serious opposition to an amphibious landing. The Japanese fought to nearly the last man, and the Marines suffered high casualties. Photos of Marines who died on Tarawa were the first such photos to be published in the United States (*Life Magazine*). The objective in the Central Pacific campaign was to set up forward air bases that would support air operations across the Pacific, to the Philippines, and to Japan. In order to set up forward air bases capable of supporting operations across the mid-Pacific, the Philippines, and into Japan itself, the US needed to take and occupy the Marianas that were heavily defended. Before any invasion, it was necessary to "soften-up" Japanese defenses with land-based aircraft. The closest islands capable of harboring bombers were the Marshalls, to the northeast of Guadalcanal. Cutting off direct communications between Hawaii and the Marshalls, however, was the Japanese garrison on Betio, on the western side of the Tarawa Atoll in the Gilberts. The United States, in order to invade the Marianas, needed to begin the campaign from the east, at Tarawa.

275. The 2nd Marine Division (Reinforced Southern Landing Force) led the main assault at Tarawa. Part of Combat Team 2's initial landing force consisted of: Landing Team 2/8 minus Battery H, 3rd Battalion, 10th Marines; 1st Battalion, 10th Marines (Artillery), Battery O; 5th Battalion, 10th Marines. Combat Team 6 consisted of part of 2nd Battalion, 10th Marines (Artillery); 5th Battalion minus Battery O, 10th Marines (Artillery) and a detachment of 3rd Battalion, 10th Marines (2x75mm pack howitzers). Combat team 6 (initially in reserve) was released to the 2nd Marine Division and then detached to secure the outlying islands on 21–28 November. See Rottman, "Works Consulted" for data on Marine units.

276. 5th Battalion, 10th Marines at Iwo Jima was the 2nd 155mm Howitzer Battalion. Other units of the 10th Marines were variously attached. See Rottman, "Works Consulted" for data on Marine units.

277. Ira Hamilton Hayes, a Pima Indian from the Gila River Indian Community, Arizona. Hayes was one of the Americans in the famous second photo "Raising the Flag on Iwo Jima." The flag raising was the subject of the recent film by Clint Eastwood *Flags of our Fathers.* After his tragic death by drowning, Hayes became the subject of a still popular folk/protest song "The Ballad of Ira Hayes."

278. The 6th Marine Division led the landing at Okinawa. Mr. Wilker said to the interviewer that only his company was placed in the 6th Division. 2nd Battalion, 10th Marines remained in floating reserve. Mr. Wilker's unit would have been part of the HQ Battery, 2nd Provisional Field Artillery Group (in general support of the 6th Marine Division) or part of the 15th Marines.

279. The 457th Bomb Group (Heavy) was created on 18 May 1943 and disbanded on 28 August 1945. It flew 236 combat missions for a loss of eighty-six planes and 729 men (KIA, WIA, POW, or interned). There were seventy-eight successful evadees. The 457th participated in six campaigns in the European Theater of Operations: Normandy, France, Rhineland, Ardennes-Alsace, Central Europe and Air Offensive Europe.

280. Celestial navigation was similar to the nautical variety but the greater speed of aircraft necessitated much more rapid calculation. Dead reckoning involved correcting a preset course by noting air speed, calculating wind drift, velocity and direction, and then factoring in the magnetic deviation of the compass. Pilotage involved "navigation" by visual recognition of landmarks.

281. That was First Lieutenant John Winant, Jr. Flying B–17 # 30262, *Tech Supply*, in the last element of the low squadron. They received a direct hit by an air-to-air rocket after bombing the primary target and their aircraft exploded. Six parachutes emerged in rapid intervals before the bomber crashed at Ladbergen, ten miles northwest of Münster. John Winant became a prisoner of war in the camp at Sagan.

282. Captain Jacob McGavock Dickinson had been Mr. Woodard's pilot until his promotion to Squadron Operations Officer. On one mission, flying as an observer with another group, Dickinson was in position behind the pilot. On approach to target the pilot was killed, and the copilot froze at the controls. Mac was hit in the heel and buttocks, but he managed to move the co-pilot and take over the controls. Though knowing that it was impossible to reach base, Mac refused to abandon the plane. To do so would also mean abandoning the wounded. He kept the plane in the air over the English Channel and managed to land on the beach at Dover. Within two weeks, Mac was back on duty, getting along "fine walking on the toes of that foot."

283. Operation BOLERO was the codename for the American troop buildup in England in preparation for the first cross-channel invasion called Operation ROUNDUP, "Bolero" standing for England. The North Atlantic Ferry Route became known as the Bolero Plan. To avoid the threat of Nazi U-Boats, Major General Henry "Hap" Arnold, chief of the Army Air Force, developed the route to ferry bombers and fighters to England from the United States via Canada, Greenland and Iceland.

284. Colonel Luper's plane, 44–8046, was shot down 7 October 1944 over Politz, Poland. Luper led the lead box of thirty-six planes. Luper survived as a POW, but five of his crew died, including passenger Major Gordon H. Haggard, the group surgeon, who often flew on missions with the 457th in Luper's plane. Luper died in a crash several years after the War. A distinguished airman, Luper enlisted as a buck private in Hawaii (1933) and graduated from West Point in 1938. At West Point he was the light-heavyweight boxing champion. Luper also participated in air cadet training programs and wrote a *Military Handbook for Aviation Cadets.*

285. By measuring the attitude of the stars and planets, navigators arrived at lines of position on aeronautical charts. The lines created a triangle, or "fix." The fix allowed the navigators to plot courses. Damage to a sextant could cause major errors in every line of position.

286. The 457th base included the village of Conington. Since there were bases at Honington and Coningsby, the field was named after Glatton in order to avoid confusion. Glatton was a small village four miles to the west. The base call sign was "Nuttree," and the air-call sign was "Woodcraft Baker."

287. The 457th entered combat during "Big Week," the third week of February 1944, when the Eighth Air Force launched massive attacks against the German aircraft industry and ball-bearing plants, in Leipzig, Augsburg, Regensburg, Schweinfurt, Stuttgart, and other cities. The German aircraft industry suffered, but recovered enough to continue production at high levels, especially ball-bearings. Out of one-thousand aircraft, the Eighth lost 244 bombers and thirty-three fighters. The *Luftwaffe* suffered irreparable losses as well, losing many highly skilled fighter pilots. The *Luftwaffe* never recovered from the losses. See *http://www.457thbombgroup.org/*for detailed information and extraordinary collections of photographs.

288. 22 February 1944. The 457th flew the high position and suffered no losses. Results of the bombing are listed as poor in Mr. Woodard's mission board (log). The crew of *Rene III* was Bender, Luper, Leahy, Hotaling, English, Fuller, Woodard, Hammersly, Sarico, Free. Passenger was Haggard, Group Surgeon.

289. *Rene III* SN 42–38113, piloted by Lieutenant Craig Greason, was shot down 21 March 1945 over Hopsten,

Germany while supporting Allied troops preparing to cross the Rhine River. There were dense contrails over the target area and the 457th chose to make a second pass. The 457th dropped to two-thousand feet in squadron formation and bombed under the contrails. *Rene III*, flying deputy lead, was hit by Flak and left the formation. The crew bailed out. All evaded capture except the engineer, Sergeant Wagner, who was taken prisoner.

290. The USAAF and the RAF bombed Schweinfurt twenty-two times with a total of 2,285 aircraft. Two of the early raids resulted in heavy losses to the American forces, largely because they adhered to the American policy of daylight precision bombing as opposed the British practice of area bombing at night. In addition, American bombers reached deep into Germany without long-range fighter escort and were mauled by enemy fighters. On 17 August 1943, 230 B–17s of Eighth Air Force came under terrific anti-aircraft fire and attacks by three-hudred fighters. Eighty-six bombers did not return. On 14 October 1943, "Black Thursday," sixty of 229 bombers were lost. Raids resumed February 1944 during "Big Week." The Germans quickly dispersed their factories and eventually achieved eighty-five percent of pre-raid output. Much of the industrial and residential areas of the city were destroyed, killing more than one-thousand civilians, the factories were restored to production and the industry dispersed, with many placed in bomb-proof factories built underground. The 457th flew missions on 24 February and 19 March in the high position, losing one plane in the first mission and none on the second. Results for 24 February were listed as "FAIR" in the group's mission log, and "UNOBSERVED," respectively.

291. According to his mission board, Mr. Woodard flew one mission over Berlin on 4 March 1944, the seventh mission for the 457th. The 22 April 1944 mission over the Nancy-Essey airdrome was Mr. Woodard's 750th Squadron's seventeenth mission, but the thirty-second for the 457th Group. Mr. Woodard's plane flew low position and dropped no bombs over the target

292. The description for mission #2 (22 February 1944) gives Hotaling the rank of captain. Hotaling was the Group's gunnery officer and was credited with destroying one FW–190.

293. The Eighth Air Force dispatched 229 B–17s on 25 April 1944. Forty-two of these went to the Nancy/Essey Airfield.

294. Before the alarm Ed Bender discussed alternative targets with Major Francis.

295. Resistance groups existed in practically every German occupied country in Europe. Though "underground,' "resistance," "partisan," "guerrilla" and *maquis* are and were often used interchangeably and sometimes erroneously. The French Resistance was an umbrella term for all such groups that fought the German occupation and the collaborationist government of Vichy France. Charles de Gaulle (1 January 1942) and his exiled Government in London, called on Jean Moulin to organize the Conseil National de la Résistance, which Moulin succeeded in doing on 27 May 1943 in residence of one René Corbin, 48 Rue du Four, Paris. The groups were many and varied, consisting of communists, liberals, social-democrats, newspaper editors, militias (*maquis*, named after their thick, wooded hideouts), etc. After the War, some of the various groups fought each other for control of the government. Mr. Woodard encountered several of the types, but his evasion was conducted by those members of the Resistance dedicated to assisting downed Allied airmen to return to England. There were two major "lines" of evasion; The O'Leary Line, starting in France from the areas of Lille, Amiens, Rouen and Rheims, and the Comet Line, originating in Brussels and Belgium. Both converged in Paris. The O'Leary Line moved evadees south, through France and across the Pyrenees into Spain. The Comet Line moved evadees west through Bayonne, and then across the Pyrenees. Both lines ended in Gibralter. Another "line," The Shelburne Line, went north from Paris and Rennes, and transported evadees across the English Channel. Any Resistance worker (in any occupied country, for that matter) caught by the Nazis were dealt with summarily with torture and execution. British records show that more than five-hundred Resistance workers died at the hands of the Gestapo, one for each evadee who made it home. Moulin was one of those tortured and executed. See Charles Fisher, *Mission Number Three: Missing in Action.*

296. From the Middle French, French deli or prepared meat shop.

297. A powerful liquor made from apples.

298. Mr. Woodard's crew mates and rescuers supplied him with additional written and/or oral accounts that he includes at various points in his own narrative.

299. Escape kits contained silk maps, compasses, and other useful items. Members of the French Resistance knew it was imperative that American airmen be issued new ID cards and clothing as soon as possible, and this for good reason. When the Army prepared forged ID documents for airmen who could become prisoners of war, it photographed a large number of them wearing the same sort of jacket. It didn't take German Intelligence nor the Resistance long to discover this. See Charles Fisher, *Mission Number Three: Missing in Action*, Publications of the Saint Vincent College Center for Northern Appalachian Studies, 1997, 28: *"He* [Raoul, a member of the Resistance] demanded all identification we might have on us . . . we showed him the escape pictures they supplied us with back in England. Each of us had passport-sized pictures taken in civilian clothes that we could use for phoney ID papers. Raoul informed us they were of no use because of the difference in the paper. Besides, the Air Force seemed to have used the same jacket for every flier to be photographed in, something that did not escape the attention of German Intelligence."

300. Charles Fisher in *Mission Number Three: Missing in Action* (p.23) describes a number of instances that manifested this "cavalier" attitude. As he was taken by van from one safe-house to another Fisher writes: *"As we drove through towns, passing people the driver seemed to know, he would give the did-dit-dit-dat signal on the horn, and then laugh. It was a big joke to him, but it made us very uneasy. The beeps were Morse code for the letter "V"—for "Victory."*

301. The Spanish Civil War (17 July 1936 to 1 April 1939) was fought between the Francoists or Nationalists (Facists) led by General Francisco Franco, and the Republicans or Loyalists of the Second Spanish Republic (supported by the USSR). Franco's Nationalists, supported by Italy and Nazi Germany, triumphed. The Spanish Civil War was also a proving ground for tactics and weapons that would be used during World War II. The sort of terror-bombing that developed in full during the War was presaged by the attack by Heinkel 111s of the German Luftwaffe's Condor Legion on the Basque town of Guernica (26 April 1937). The attack on the town inspired the painting *Guernica*, by Pablo Picasso. The Spanish Civil War was the setting for Ernest Hemingway's novel *For Whom the Bell Tolls.*

302. The Office of Strategic Services (OSS), the United States intelligence agency formed during World War II that was the precursor to the Central Intelligence Agency (CIA). The recent Hollywood production *The Good Shepherd* (Robert DiNiro, director) portrays the development of both agencies.

303. The train was named after the Ryan monoplane Charles Lindbergh flew nonstop across the Atlantic in 1927.

304. Mr. Woodard did not visit the continent during his 1984 visit to his old airfield. In 1995 he returned to Normandy to visit his Resistance friends, where M. Masson had many decades earlier found pieces of Mr. Woodard's plane. Using a metal detector, M. Thierry discovered more pieces of the plane in the Valee de la Mont Joie. Among others with whom he was reunited were: Bernard Neuville, the driver of the milk truck; Henri Beaudet, one of his escorts to Paris; Raymond Legenvre, son of Mr. Woodard' first host; Mme. Gentay who first spotted Rod Francis creeping through the field near her home; eighty-nine-year old Mms. Therese Taupin who observed the descending parachutes; Henri Demarguay who hid Mr. Woodard in the hollow tree; and the descendants of those Resistants who had died.

Index

Other publications of the Center:

A Place in the Sky: A Pictorial and Spoken History of the Arnold Palmer Regional Airport and Aviation in Western Pennsylvania - ISBN: 1-885851-17-0

They Say There Was a War (World War II Oral Histories) - ISBN: 1-885851-51-0

http://www.stvincent.edu/napp17

Notes

Notes

Notes

Notes

Notes

combat 45 [illegible] 74 ETO, 80+ A-T 81-2 misfires, 98 Nav, 108 air, 125, 131 [illegible] 33+
171 ETO, 179+, 192, 207 ETO 211, 231+ PI 246 ETO, 254 PI, 259 CVE, 325 air
POW 54 5 84, 134, 140, 151, 178, 192, 519, 306, 290 & 302, 442, 466
Mat [illegible] 459
prewar life 264, 362, 408, 425
R&L 42
Ger [illegible] 48
Gers in US army 48, [illegible]
Ger POWs [illegible] 56
Training 62
strikes 31 68
female FO 61
leaders 75, 78-9, 81, 86, 130+, 192, 204, 244, 46-7, 270, 454, 472
sniper 83, 193, 23[illegible], 154, 386
Stress 84, 233, 235
[illegible]
[illegible] 130, 36, 141, 43, 439+, 4[illegible], 468
[illegible] 11[illegible]
[illegible] 119, 186, 235, 249, 389, 442
aussies 123, 29, 395
AF [illegible] 126
uniforms & shoes 130
Basilone 133
hunting 159, 164, 302, 364, 374, 437
age 19 law 157-8, 243
brothers 177-8, 334
[illegible] 196
AD 206, 308, 478
chaplain 208, 12, 365
Theft 214
VJ Day 216, 255, 423
VE 223, 291
Bazooka 232
Flame 237
Raised in ger. 239
Jews like sheep 248
[illegible] 250
Russians 318-19
atheists 278
medics (KIA 276) 364
Mules 278
Trng deaths 285
332nd 290

Spirits 296
Chennault 322-3
GCM 335
Truce 377
ger. opponent 385
Germans 388
USv. Fr. 389
BB fend 396
hotshot B17 431
Flamethr. 441, 466, 67
Record [illegible] 441
Pearl H. 29, 95, 115, 122, 155, 177, 220, 243, 267, 363, 437

[illegible]
[illegible]
376 ETO
397 [illegible]
412
432 [illegible]
439 PI
440
458 PI
467 ok
473 air